Comparative Approaches to Old and New Institutional Economics

Ilkben Akansel
Bartin University, Turkey

A volume in the Advances in Finance, Accounting, and Economics (AFAE) Book Series

IGI Global
DISSEMINATOR OF KNOWLEDGE

Published in the United States of America by
IGI Global
Business Science Reference (an imprint of IGI Global)
701 E. Chocolate Avenue
Hershey PA, USA 17033
Tel: 717-533-8845
Fax: 717-533-8661
E-mail: cust@igi-global.com
Web site: http://www.igi-global.com

Copyright © 2020 by IGI Global. All rights reserved. No part of this publication may be reproduced, stored or distributed in any form or by any means, electronic or mechanical, including photocopying, without written permission from the publisher. Product or company names used in this set are for identification purposes only. Inclusion of the names of the products or companies does not indicate a claim of ownership by IGI Global of the trademark or registered trademark.

Library of Congress Cataloging-in-Publication Data

Names: Akansel, Ilkben, 1978- editor.
Title: Comparative approaches to old and new institutional economics / Ilkben Akansel, editor.
Description: Hershey, PA : Business Science Reference, [2020] | Summary: "This book examines the differences between the old and new institutional economics"-- Provided by publisher.
Identifiers: LCCN 2019021333 | ISBN 9781799803331 (hardcover) | ISBN 9781799803348 (paperback) | ISBN 9781799803355 (ebook)
Subjects: LCSH: Institutional economics. | Institutional economics--History.
Classification: LCC HB99.5 .C66 2020 | DDC 330--dc23
LC record available at https://lccn.loc.gov/2019021333

This book is published in the IGI Global book series Advances in Finance, Accounting, and Economics (AFAE) (ISSN: 2327-5677; eISSN: 2327-5685)

British Cataloguing in Publication Data
A Cataloguing in Publication record for this book is available from the British Library.

All work contributed to this book is new, previously-unpublished material. The views expressed in this book are those of the authors, but not necessarily of the publisher.

For electronic access to this publication, please contact: eresources@igi-global.com.

Advances in Finance, Accounting, and Economics (AFAE) Book Series

Ahmed Driouchi
Al Akhawayn University, Morocco

ISSN:2327-5677
EISSN:2327-5685

Mission

In our changing economic and business environment, it is important to consider the financial changes occurring internationally as well as within individual organizations and business environments. Understanding these changes as well as the factors that influence them is crucial in preparing for our financial future and ensuring economic sustainability and growth.

The **Advances in Finance, Accounting, and Economics (AFAE)** book series aims to publish comprehensive and informative titles in all areas of economics and economic theory, finance, and accounting to assist in advancing the available knowledge and providing for further research development in these dynamic fields.

Coverage

- Internet Banking
- Economics Geography
- Economics of Natural and Environmental Resources
- Corporate Finance
- Public Finance
- Risk Analysis and Management
- Auditing
- Statistical Analysis
- Behavioral Economics
- Evidence-Based Studies

IGI Global is currently accepting manuscripts for publication within this series. To submit a proposal for a volume in this series, please contact our Acquisition Editors at Acquisitions@igi-global.com or visit: http://www.igi-global.com/publish/.

The Advances in Finance, Accounting, and Economics (AFAE) Book Series (ISSN 2327-5677) is published by IGI Global, 701 E. Chocolate Avenue, Hershey, PA 17033-1240, USA, www.igi-global.com. This series is composed of titles available for purchase individually; each title is edited to be contextually exclusive from any other title within the series. For pricing and ordering information please visit http://www.igi-global.com/book-series/advances-finance-accounting-economics/73685. Postmaster: Send all address changes to above address. Copyright © 2020 IGI Global. All rights, including translation in other languages reserved by the publisher. No part of this series may be reproduced or used in any form or by any means – graphics, electronic, or mechanical, including photocopying, recording, taping, or information and retrieval systems – without written permission from the publisher, except for non commercial, educational use, including classroom teaching purposes. The views expressed in this series are those of the authors, but not necessarily of IGI Global.

Titles in this Series

For a list of additional titles in this series, please visit: www.igi-global.com/book-series

Migration and Urbanization Local Solutions for Global Economic Challenges
Denis Ushakov (Suan Sunandha Rajabhat University, Thailand)
Business Science Reference • copyright 2020 • 365pp • H/C (ISBN: 9781799801115) • US $245.00 (our price)

Financial Technology and Disruptive Innovation in ASEAN
Muhammad Anshari (Universiti Brunei Darussalam, Brunei) Mohammad Nabil Almunawar (Universiti Brunei Darussalam, Brunei) and Masairol Masri (Universiti Brunei Darussalam, Brunei)
Business Science Reference • copyright 2020 • 331pp • H/C (ISBN: 9781522591832) • US $195.00 (our price)

International Trade Policies in the Era of Globalization
Ahu Coşkun Özer (Marmara University, Turkey)
Business Science Reference • copyright 2020 • 363pp • H/C (ISBN: 9781522595663) • US $205.00 (our price)

Management Accounting Standards for Sustainable Business Practices
Ionica Oncioiu (Titu Maiorescu University, Romania) Gary Cokins (Analytics-Based Performance Management LLC, USA) Sorinel Căpuşneanu (Titu Maiorescu University, Romania) and Dan Ioan Topor (1 Decembrie 1918 University, Romania)
Business Science Reference • copyright 2020 • 360pp • H/C (ISBN: 9781799801788) • US $215.00 (our price)

Handbook of Research on Economic and Political Implications of Green Trading and Energy Use
Ramesh Chandra Das (Vidyasagar University, India)
Business Science Reference • copyright 2019 • 421pp • H/C (ISBN: 9781522585473) • US $225.00 (our price)

Emerging Research on Monetary Policy, Banking, and Financial Markets
Cristi Spulbar (University of Craiova, Romania) and Ramona Birau (Constantin Brâncui University of Targu Jiu, Romania)
Business Science Reference • copyright 2019 • 322pp • H/C (ISBN: 9781522592693) • US $195.00 (our price)

Modernization and Accountability in the Social Economy Sector
Augusta Ferreira (University of Aveiro, Portugal) Rui Marques (University of Aveiro, Portugal) Graça Azevedo (University of Aveiro, Portugal) Helena Inácio (University of Aveiro, Portugal) and Carlos Santos (University of Aveiro, Portugal)
Business Science Reference • copyright 2019 • 351pp • H/C (ISBN: 9781522584827) • US $215.00 (our price)

IGI Global
DISSEMINATOR OF KNOWLEDGE

701 East Chocolate Avenue, Hershey, PA 17033, USA
Tel: 717-533-8845 x100 • Fax: 717-533-8661
E-Mail: cust@igi-global.com • www.igi-global.com

Editorial Advisory Board

Tugba Aydin-Halisoglu, *University of Artvin Coruh, Turkey*
Hakan Cermikli, *University of Haci Bayram Veli, Turkey*
Zehra Dogan-Caliskan, *University of Abant Izzet Baysal, Turkey*
Cagri Eryilmaz, *University of Izmir Bakircay, Turkey*
Aygul Kilinc, *University of Gaziantep, Turkey*
Ufuk Serdaroglu, *University of Haci Bayram Veli, Turkey*

List of Reviewers

Eray Acar, *University of Dumlupınar, Turkey*
U. Altunoz, *University of Sinop, Turkey*
Huseyin Kutay Aytug, *University of Celal Bayar, Turkey*
Ayhan Bilgin, *University of Artvin Coruh, Turkey*
Mehmet Celik, *University of Kastamonu, Turkey*
Memduh Alper Demir, *Independent Researcher, Turkey*
Dilek Erdogan, *University of Kastamonu, Turkey*
Zekeriya Eray Eser, *University of Artvin Coruh, Turkey*
Cahide Gogusdere, *The Ministry of Finance, Turkey*
Gonul Muratoglu-Dincer, *University of Hacı Bayram Veli, Turkey*
Svetlana Nestrova-Coskun, *University of Ankara, Turkey*
Ibrahim Oral, *University of Ardahan, Turkey*
Orhan Simsek, *University of Artvin Coruh, Turkey*
Emek Yildirim, *University of Artvin Coruh, Turkey*

Table of Contents

Preface xiv

Chapter 1
From Old Institutional Economics to New Institutional Economics: A Short History 1
Ilkben Akansel, Bartin University, Turkey

Chapter 2
Re-Thinking the Role of Institutions in Neoliberalism From New Institutional Economics Perspective 25
Ilke Civelekoglu, Istanbul Ticaret University, Turkey
Basak Ozoral, Istanbul Ticaret University, Turkey

Chapter 3
Reconstruction of the Old Institutions: Crisis, Governance, and the G20 41
Ugur Yasin Asal, Istanbul Commerce University, Turkey
Nazım Ekren, Istanbul Commerce University, Turkey

Chapter 4
The Political Economy of the Market 57
Itir Ozer-Imer, Hacettepe University, Turkey
Derya Guler Aydin, Hacettepe University, Turkey

Chapter 5
Institutional Overview of Technology: Schumpeter and Veblen 70
Fatma Kethudaoğlu, Tübitak Sage, Turkey
Yusuf Bayraktutan, Kocaeli University, Turkey

Chapter 6
Analysing of Erzurum Winter Tourism in the European Perspective 88
Mahshid Mikaeili, Atatürk University, Turkey
H. Kutay Aytuğ, Manisa Celal Bayar University, Turkey

Chapter 7
Social and Economic Transformation With the Institutional Economic Perspective 108
Mehmet Yunus Çelik, Kastamonu University, Turkey

Chapter 8
New Public Administration Understanding and Reform Effects as Products of Neolibal Management Concept 133
Eray Acar, Kutahya Dumlupinar University, Turkey

Chapter 9
Is Turkey a Favorable Environment for FDIs? Institutional Outlook to EU-Turkey FDI Flow 157
Memduh Alper Demir, University of Kastamonu, Turkey

Chapter 10
The Effect of Democratization and Economic Freedom on Economic Growth 171
Ibrahim Orkun Oral, Ardahan University, Turkey

Chapter 11
Institutional Economics: The Historical Foundations of Institutional Economics 185
Zehra Doğan Çalışkan, Bolu Abant İzzet Baysal University, Turkey

Chapter 12
Transaction Cost Approach to the Outsourcing Decision Problem 201
Dilek Erdogan, Gaziantep University, Turkey

Chapter 13
IMF, World Bank, and the European Union With the Perspective of New Institutional Economics 217
Havanur Ergün Tatar, Bartın University, Turkey

Chapter 14
Transformation of the State and Political Economy of the Governance: A Critical Assessment of the New Institutional Economics in the Public Administration 239
Emek Yıldırım, Artvin Çoruh University, Turkey

Chapter 15
Structural Shifts and Patterns in Turkey's Foreign Trade 258
Gönül Dinçer Muratoğlu, Ankara Hacı Bayram Veli University, Turkey

Chapter 16
Classes and Development 282
Zekeriya Eray Eser, Artvin Çoruh University, Turkey

Compilation of References 297

About the Contributors 332

Index 337

Detailed Table of Contents

Preface xiv

Chapter 1
From Old Institutional Economics to New Institutional Economics: A Short History 1
Ilkben Akansel, Bartin University, Turkey

Since different kinds of economics thoughts have been explored, few have been as peculiar as Old Institutional Economics (OIE) and New Institutional Economics (NIE). It is curious that almost every stream criticizing mainstream economics has a left wing. OIE, not a big fan of this, criticizes neoclassical economics/mainstream economics, given it arose in the US. OIE had no sense to left wing, on the contrary, it created an effect criticizing neoclassical economics in its core. Unlike OIE, NIE has many common points with neoclassical economics. NIE has several new aspects different from neoclassical economics, as it has chosen a completely different path than OIE. In this chapter, authors scrutinize circumstances that led to OIE, and what separated OIE and NIE. A brief, successively historical aspect is also provided.

Chapter 2
Re-Thinking the Role of Institutions in Neoliberalism From New Institutional Economics Perspective 25
Ilke Civelekoglu, Istanbul Ticaret University, Turkey
Basak Ozoral, Istanbul Ticaret University, Turkey

In an attempt to discuss neoliberalism with a reference to new institutional economics, this chapter problematizes the role of formal institutions in the neoliberal age by focusing on a specific type of formal institution, namely property rights in developing countries. New institutional economics (NIE) argues that secure property rights are important as they guarantee investments and thus, promote economic growth. This chapter discusses why the protection of property rights is weak and ineffective in certain developing countries despite their endorsement of neoliberalism by shedding light on the link between the institutional structure of the state and neoliberalism in the developing world. With the political economy perspective, the chapter aims to build a bridge between NIE and political economy, and thereby providing fertile ground for the advancement of NIE.

Chapter 3
Reconstruction of the Old Institutions: Crisis, Governance, and the G20 41
Ugur Yasin Asal, Istanbul Commerce University, Turkey
Nazım Ekren, Istanbul Commerce University, Turkey

The recent global economic and financial crisis has fundamentally questioned the crisis management mechanisms of the international institutions. Despite the development of the skills of these institutions, financial vulnerability, economic imbalances, and the instability of the macroeconomic performance indicators are still rising cyclically. The G20 represents roughly 85% percent of global GDP and two-thirds of the world population. It emerged as a leading body for international economic performance. The lack of permanent secretariat of the G20 is decreasing the effectiveness, legitimacy, and the economic viability of the club. Regarding this philosophical background, the role of G20s' institutional structure is examined according to institutional capacity and the macroeconomic performance of the club.

Chapter 4
The Political Economy of the Market 57
Itir Ozer-Imer, Hacettepe University, Turkey
Derya Guler Aydin, Hacettepe University, Turkey

In the modern period, there are two concerns regarding the nature of the market. One is associated with market structures that involve solely the economic sphere and exclude all other factors including historical, social, and institutional ones. Hence, it conducts a static analysis, while the other relates the market process with all the aforementioned factors in addition to the economic ones, and therefore, combines economic and non-economic spheres, and the analysis becomes dynamic. This chapter scrutinizes the conceptualization of the market; that is whether the market is considered as a "structure" or a "process". With this consideration, authors relate the conceptualization of the market with the type of competition. When the market is regarded as a "process", it is possible to claim that market becomes an "institution". Thus, by taking the market as an institution and considering competition within a dynamic framework, the emergent economic theoretical structure provides an in-depth, comprehensive, analytical, and novel approach to real economic and social concerns.

Chapter 5
Institutional Overview of Technology: Schumpeter and Veblen 70
Fatma Kethudaoğlu, Tübitak Sage, Turkey
Yusuf Bayraktutan, Kocaeli University, Turkey

There has been an intense debate on the reasons of variations in economic performances of different countries. Institutions and technological structure are among the leading determiners. Institutions are formal and informal constraints affecting investments in physical/human capital, and technology. Factors like economies of scale, technology, education, or accumulation of physical and human capital are not all for economic growth, which itself represents political and economic institutions as the basis for the fundamental differences in economic development. At the end of the 20th century, economic thought oriented towards analysis of the institutional environment. In the 1990s, significant steps were taken with Heterodox approaches to provide more consistent alternatives to the mainstream economy. The institutional economy shows an alternative approach that adds more depth to the discussions in this area. The main objective of this chapter is to point out the contributions of Schumpeter and Veblen.

Chapter 6
Analysing of Erzurum Winter Tourism in the European Perspective.. 88
Mahshid Mikaeili, Atatürk University, Turkey
H. Kutay Aytuğ, Manisa Celal Bayar University, Turkey

Erzurum is the biggest city in the Eastern Anatolian Region of Turkey. The city has gained great importance in winter tourism during recent years. Accessing to the sustainable winter city requires an innovative approach to these cities' problems in order to enhance the advantages, opportunities, and beauty of the winter season. Winter tourism is one of the good examples that provides benefits to the residents and reinforces the community's ability to attract new business. In this chapter, the conceptual framework of the topic is drawn by putting forth the concept of winter city tourism. Subsequently, EU tourism policy, its political framework, and priorities are summarised. In the next chapter, Erzurum is examined to demonstrate its potential for winter city tourism. Finally, the winter city tourism potential of Erzurum is evaluated by SWOT analysis and brought some suggestions compatible with EU Tourism Policies at five categories such as preserving solar access, designing streets, planting, parks and open spaces, colour, materials and lighting.

Chapter 7
Social and Economic Transformation With the Institutional Economic Perspective 108
Mehmet Yunus Çelik, Kastamonu University, Turkey

The events and phenomena in the period of the industrial society were explained within the context of the Newtonian paradigm. In today's information society and its economic structure, they are explained within the context of the Quantum paradigm. Nevertheless, the assumption of neoclassics claims that consumers decide independently from each other, which is controversial. Consumers decide in real terms, not independently but under the influence of psychological situation, social environment, and cultural infrastructure. The basic mutual point between the two paradigms is to maximize the benefit from the goods to be consumed when making consumption decisions. To this end, the process of social and economic transformation will first be discussed in the light of paradigm shift and technological improvements. Then, with the institutional economic perspective, the change in consumption understanding will be taken into consideration in the social and economic structure of today.

Chapter 8
New Public Administration Understanding and Reform Effects as Products of Neolibal Management Concept 133
Eray Acar, Kutahya Dumlupinar University, Turkey

Globalization has been a process that has deeply and continuously influenced societies and states in the late period of historical development. With neoliberalism, the ideological thought system of the process, all social organizations, especially state apparatus and public administrations, are affected by this process and continue to be affected. This transformation process, supported by its international organizations, has led to the preparation and implementation of reforms in order to adopt a new approach to public administration. This change in public administration has affected both public service understanding and public service delivery. It is a process that aims to provide the citizens/customers satisfaction by offering a faster, more efficient, and high-quality public service along with the new public management understanding. Current practices are questioned and improvements are tried.

Chapter 9
Is Turkey a Favorable Environment for FDIs? Institutional Outlook to EU-Turkey FDI Flow 157
Memduh Alper Demir, University of Kastamonu, Turkey

The aim of this chapter is to measure the impact of institutional variables such as economic freedom and democracy on foreign direct investment from the European Union to Turkey. In this framework, the author models institutional factors affecting foreign direct investments. The model includes economic freedom index, political rights, civil liberties of Turkey, and Gross Domestic Products of selected European countries. In theoretical part, the perspective of institutional economics on economic freedoms and democracy is discussed. A brief literature about the relationship between foreign direct investments and economic freedoms and democracy is revealed. Stochastic frontier analysis was used in the implementation to show the relationship between variables and efficiency of European countries' foreign direct investments to Turkey. Proposals for policy implication have been made in the conclusion part. This chapter shows civil liberties and economic freedom index have positive effect on foreign direct investments that supports institutionalists.

Chapter 10
The Effect of Democratization and Economic Freedom on Economic Growth 171
Ibrahim Orkun Oral, Ardahan University, Turkey

This chapter examines the impact of democratization and economic freedom on economic growth. For this purpose, according to the classification issued by the World Bank, three groups of countries, developed, developing, and underdeveloped, were included in the study. The impact of democratization and economic freedom on economic growth was tested by panel data analysis in the period of 1995-2012. As a result of the analysis, the relationship between democracy-economic freedom and economic growth has been different according to country groups. While there was a positive relationship between economic growth and democracy-economic freedom in developed and underdeveloped countries, a negative relationship was found in the developing country group.

Chapter 11
Institutional Economics: The Historical Foundations of Institutional Economics 185
Zehra Doğan Çalışkan, Bolu Abant İzzet Baysal Unıversity, Turkey

Since the mid-19th century, the thinkers of historical school challenged the deductive, abstractive, and decisive methods of neo-classical economics. According to historical school, social terms have been changed within space and time. Therefore, they defended that the economic theories could not be universal but could only be relative. Instead of professing laws with universal validity, it is more important to reveal the changing structure of society with the extensive studies of economic history. The inductive method of German historical school brought a new perspective into economic theory with theorems such as to consider society as an organism beyond the individuals who would only seek their benefits and the necessity of historical followings in the economic events. From this point of view, it is possible to observe the traces of historical school in the old institutional economics literature.

Chapter 12
Transaction Cost Approach to the Outsourcing Decision Problem 201
Dilek Erdogan, Gaziantep University, Turkey

Outsourcing has become a management tool that is increasingly involved in the manager's agenda, but the decision to outsource is a problematic issue for decision makers in organizations. Outsourcing provides many benefits but also includes many risks, so every outsourcing agreement does not result in success. This chapter aims to provide a better understanding of the outsourcing problem in light of transaction cost economics. For this purpose, the concept of outsourcing is first explained. The transaction characteristics and the behavioral assumptions of the theory, which play a role in increasing or decreasing transaction costs, are clarified. Finally, governance decision (outsource or not) and some critical issues (safeguarding mechanism against opportunistic behavior by supplier, adaptation, and performance evaluation problem) that will arise after the outsourcing decisions are discussed.

Chapter 13
IMF, World Bank, and the European Union With the Perspective of New Institutional Economics.. 217
Havanur Ergün Tatar, Bartın University, Turkey

According to New Institutional Economics, the GDP per capita has significantly improved in the countries where the institutional quality has been improved. In addition to this information, the increase in the quality of institutional determinants has positive effect on economic performance. In this chapter, after the structures of IMF, World Bank, and European Union have been discussed, the governance debate will be made on the aforementioned institutional. Concepts about new institutional economics are discussed, as are the improvement of institutional quality and the relationship of economic development within the frame of IMF, World Bank, and European Union.

Chapter 14
Transformation of the State and Political Economy of the Governance: A Critical Assessment of the New Institutional Economics in the Public Administration.. 239
Emek Yıldırım, Artvin Çoruh University, Turkey

By the 1980s and 1990s, neoliberal policies such as privatizations and deregulations transforming the minimal state model to regulative state model from the Keynesian social welfare state system made some structural and functional changes in the state mechanism, and the public administration has been in the first place due to the changing relationship between the state and the market. In fact, within this context, the new institutional economics (NIE) had a remarkable influence upon the debates upon the altering role of the state. Hence, the transformation of the state in this regard also revealed the argumentations on the governance paradigm along with the doctrinaire contributions of the new institutional economics. Therefore, this chapter will discuss the transformation of the state and the political economy of the governance together with a critical assessment of the new institutional economics in the public administration.

Chapter 15
Structural Shifts and Patterns in Turkey's Foreign Trade 258
Gönül Dinçer Muratoğlu, Ankara Hacı Bayram Veli University, Turkey

Foreign trade has been a principal tool of the economic policies implemented in Turkey since the foundation of the Republic in 1923. In parallel with the significant developments in the national and global economies, several structural transformations occurred in foreign trade patterns and policies of Turkey. Political approaches varied from strictly protectionist trade regimes to semi-open models and free trade regimes. Previously implemented protectionist trade policies were abandoned in the 1980s for the current open economic policy based on export-led growth model. All these facts led to drastic changes in the composition of goods subject to both Turkey's exports and imports. This chapter examines the fundamental shifts and changes in Turkey's foreign trade by reviewing historical developments, and specifies the existing structural problems in Turkey's foreign trade by analyzing detailed trade data.

Chapter 16
Classes and Development 282
Zekeriya Eray Eser, Artvin Çoruh University, Turkey

Classes forming the social division of labor have changed with the capitalist mode of production. The inheritance from the feudal system is not suitable for the capitalist system. For this reason, the class structure which is suitable for capitalism over time has taken place in many societies. This transformation has become more difficult, especially in the late capitalist countries. This chapter examines class structures of some late-capitalist countries outside Europe and North America. Latin America, Japan, South Korea, and Turkey have historically been studied before and after periods of capitalism. While some countries have successfully completed and managed to develop their class transformations under difficult conditions, some countries have failed. Along with an unsuccessful transformation, new classes have emerged which have preventive effects on the development target. It is difficult for the countries that cannot make their class structure compatible with the capitalist system and the development target.

Compilation of References 297

About the Contributors 332

Index 337

Preface

Neoclassical economics which is also called as mainstream/orthodox economics has been a debate for a long time. A collection of economics progress under illusory assumptions recognized by neoclassical economics finds its meaning from both academy and the non-financial sector mutually. The main statement of rationality – the optimization of individual/firm, that is also one of the fundamental assumptions of neoclassical economics, does not only suggest a common idea but also imposes a superficial thought to economics world. This brings an imperial point of view by neoclassical economics.

This viewpoint of economics "is widely recognized that while the mainstream neoclassical economists preach the importance of submitting theories to empirical tests, they themselves rarely live up to their declared methodological canons" (Yalman, 2007, p. 389).

The structure of economics based on only empirical tests and assumptions, thus proving all these theories mathematically, made some economists to forget that economics is a social science mainly studies human behaviors and preferences after all. This caused questioning neoclassical economics since solely mathematics cannot suffice to outwit all challenges to understand all economics actions. Thus, neoclassical economics has been broadened to include other fields of science. Such questioning is however unique per se for a long time including the division of heterodox-orthodox economics.

Although the division of heterodox-orthodox is essentially transitive, there is a reality that everyone agrees at a certain point. Neoclassical economics is recognized as orthodox economics/mainstream economics. This point stems from disputes on the field. Because, there is no consensus on what neoclassical economics exactly covers. Nonetheless, there are some points of neoclassical economics that set off from 1870s and influenced today.

Rationality and presenting benefit maximization and balance regarding this rationality are the certain points of "the neglect of strong kinds of uncertainty and particularly of fundamental uncertainty" (Dequech, 2007, p. 280).

The definitional complexity of neoclassical economics distorted the notions such as neoclassical, mainstream, orthodox, heterodox in many economists' mind. In this sense, although neoclassical economics is called mainstream economics, it is used in the dominant economics education that is referred in the top academic periodicals. In other words, there is an emphasis on the dominance of it in all fields of economics. Assuming as if there is no economics literature aside neoclassical economics, defines neoclassical economics as mainstream and gives an imperial supremacy to it.

When neoclassical economics is called as the orthodox economics, it pertains more intellectual emphasis. Of course, this intellectual emphasis is not caused by neoclassical economics' contextual structure which is extremely solid and reliable. When emphasizing the orthodox way, it is accepted as the school of thought. Put it differently, the school of thought unfolds the field dominance which has been continuing for a long time.

Science is a perpetual process. In the realm of science, articulating a new piece of knowledge every day, gives an imperial power to neoclassical economics – either it is called mainstream or orthodox – as if it does not contribute a new data per se. Thus, there is another thought lying beneath by opposing to mainstream/orthodox economics. It is called heterodox economics.

Heterodox economics has in common a set of principles that reflect the judgement that formalism is not the best way to proceed, while orthodox economists adopt formalist principles. Within heterodox economics, different paths are taken by different schools of thought which reflect different guiding principles for choosing theories and methods. I would argue that these different paths reflect different understandings of the nature of reality, which is an inevitable outcome of a starting position that reality is an open system and thus incapable of being understood categorically in terms of one modelling system. Each then have their own criteria for assessing progress in the sense of progress internal to the school of thought. (Dow, 2000, p. 7)

In this context, generally heterodox economics includes all economics movements opposing to neoclassical economics. These economics thoughts define their oppositions under different names. Naturally, they do not only oppose to neoclassical economics, but also suggest their unique theories as required.

When Alan Gruchy, who is the second generation of institutional economics, has first used "heterodox economic" term in 1987 as the objection to neoclassical economics speaks up. Albeit opposition to institutional economics started since 1930s till 1980s, the real objection starts in 1987 (Lee, 2008).

Heterodox economics generally includes Marxist economics, Austrian economics, feminist economics, Sraffian economics, Institutional-evolutionary economics, etc. The main theme of this book is Institutional Economics, which is one of the most important entities in heterodox economics.

Institutional economics is the dominating economics theory since the late 19th century to 20th century till 1930s in the USA. It has been initially developed by Thorstein Veblen who was the creator of the term "neoclassical economics" even we use today. Now that, if the institutional economics is a heterodox economics, what does "the institution" mean in the first place?

Semantically, the word 'institution' has several meanings depending on the context including: an established organization; the building in which an organization is housed; or a custom, practice, or rule." (Groenewegend, Spithoven, & van den Berg, 2010, p. 24)

It is possible to define many formations or organizations as institution. It is generally used in daily language. For instance, central banks are institutions. Whereas the term "institution", as in institutional economics, formed the core of this study. It has a total integrity in meaning. In other words, the movement called institutional economics has versatile emphasis.

As the name "institutional economics" implies, the term institution is central for this research tradition. Going a little beyond the view of institutions as patterned behaviour, we might specify them as social rules that structure social interaction (Hodgson, 2001, p. 294). These rules enable meaningful social action by giving people a template of how to make sense of other people's behaviour in a certain setting, in this way empowering individuals to undertake problem-solving and reasonable innovation. Only shared understandings of learned social rules allow, for instance, stock (or horse) traders to conclude contracts by hand signs, and only shared social rules allow for the teaching in a classroom to work as the teacher and the students act according to their roles. As a consequence, apart from enabling social action, institutions also restrict certain forms of behaviour. (Dimmelmeier & Heusser, 2016)

On account of not uttering erroneous institutional economics, it links the individual's economics behavior and sociological structure. Every society has a unique economics structure that supports a sociological structure. These are inseparable entities per se. The first genius idea questioning the relationship between a society's economics actions and behaviors has initially arisen in the USA. These circumstances include another peculiarity: made by an immigrant family's child observing how it would be possible to re-live the capitalist recovery process rapidly like the USA.

Whichever country undergoes the capitalist recovery, it does not pass through it easily, because capital accumulation also brings the difference and separation between classes. Existence of unfair income distribution and various social issues pushed Thorstein Veblen, (1857-1929) who is accepted as the founder of institutional economics – the relationship between economics behavior and sociological structure, to suggest that everyone is equal and everyone has rights. The economics constituted by Veblen can be called as the Marxist economics in the USA (Özveren, 2007).

Having said that, we see a Veblen, who tried to exhibit how the gap between classes and economics habits, affecting society's economics structure without an emphasis on a Marxist revolutionary approach. Veblen, who is the child of a Norwegian immigrant family, was educated in Carleton College (1877-1880) after his family moved to Minnesota. Veblen worked for several universities. Moving from one university to another like a nomad deeply affected Veblen's thoughts. When Veblen was developing the institutional economics, for which he prefers to use the term evolutionary economics, he was critically affected by "leading figures such as John Dewey in Philosophy and Psychology, W. I. Thomas and Frederick Starr in Sociology and Anthropology and Jacques Loeb in Physiology – with all of whose work Veblen become deeply engaged" (Hodgson, 2006, p. 16).

This interdisciplinary approach lies down under the calling of economics as evolutionary economics which is founded by Veblen. The point why Veblen may be so unique to suggest that the economics events, can be understood by him being affected from various disciplines in the USA focusing on only mainstream maximization. Of course, one other point why he described his evocations as evolutionary is his great sympathy to Darwin.

With all these respects, the most special feature of Veblen's, "greatest contribution, however, was in neither the time ideological nor the political area" (Hodgson, 2006, p. 18). He didn't try to develop a political choice to understand the economics events. He tried to constitute a relationship between economics habits and economics institutions. So, he rather used some notions. These notions are "conspicuous consumption", "leisure class", "conspicuous idleness" that may even seem dominant ones in economics (Önder, 2016), they are guides to understand why societies exhibit different kinds of economics positions from each other today. Veblen is a great scientist about whom the books have been written. The institutional economics can mostly be understood with the assistance of Veblen; however, similar incidents has been transpired for institutional economics as seen in all economics thoughts: division of schools. It is a reality that Old (Original) Economics developed by Veblen has declined since 1930s.

Of course, as being the leader of OIE, Veblen was however not alone. There were two other important followers: Wesley Clair Mitchell (1874-1948) and John Rogers Commons (1862-1945).

Wesley C. Mitchell was from the first generation of OIE. He was the student of Veblen. The most important point what makes Mitchell prominent is his aim to define the instabilities of capitalism with the notion "money economy" as described by him. He tried to create a theory of business cycles by examining the business cycles in England, Germany and France. Although he adopted the Veblen's evolutionary technique, the biggest criticism to Mitchell is the statistical method when he suggested the business cycles.

In this respect, he referred to use complex statistical methods in OIE, while he played a great role constituting National Bureau of Economic Research (NBER). He proposes to add complex mathematics and statistical methods which would be more effective to analyze economics process rather than constituting abstract, assumptive, and imaginary world as used by neoclassical economics.

He is an evolutionary economist focusing on incessantly changing institutional structures. Mitchell believed that quantitative explanations would accelerate the power of economics. The most important contribution given by Mitchell is he drew a theory with available quantitative data which, as claimed by neoclassical economics, determines economics procedures consistently and hence suggested that theories of economics varies.

"For Mitchell, solving problems for the kind of evolution we live in, has happened in available institutional structure" (Baş-Dinar, 2014, p. 65). Mitchell, who believed in evolution in economics, imitated physics and chemistry that is rather different than neoclassical economics. For Mitchell, questioning continuously many variables in economics makes to determine orderliness (p. 66).

The third contributor of OIE was John R. Commons (1862-1945). The contribution of Commons has come from an interesting however important point to OIE. Making a correlation between economics and law. As Karl Marx suggested the link between the model of capitalism and law, Commons tried to understand the modern USA capitalism between 19th and early 20th century in the similar respect (Chavance, 2012, p. 28).

Thorstein Veblen defined an institution as a widely prevalent habit of thought; Commons defined it as collective action in control of individual action. (http://www.cengage.com/resource_uploads/downloads/0324321457_65788.pdf)

The approach of Commons to individuals and institutions generated a criticism, that it is getting close to neoclassical economics, it must not be really understood in that way. Because:

Commons' institutional economics is a complement to neoclassical economics in that it fleshes-out the institutional infrastructure within which markets and demand and supply work. In other respects, however, Commons' theory of institutional economics is a substitute for neoclassical economics and provides the basis for an alternative heterodox paradigm. In particular, Commons' theory is built on a heterodox methodology (historical, realist, multidisciplinary), replaces or modifies key orthodox theoretical constructs (rationality, autonomous and competitive markets), and denies the validity of the 'Invisible Hand' theorem and other core neoclassical propositions. Importantly, Commons' institutional economics also provides a theoretical framework for an integration of the economic and social dimensions of human behaviour. (Kaufman, 2007, pp. 5-6)

It is known that OIE has started to decline in 1930s. Nonetheless, a new peculiar economics thought was born from the fundamental thought of Mitchell and Commons: New Institutional Economics (NIE).

There is no common point between OIE and NIE aside the term "institution." It is known that NIE is more convergent to neoclassical economics. A study by Richter has shown that after the NIE term first used by Williamson in 1975, it has become more widespread 1980s. From that point, the criteria, that are endeavored by the editors whether a publication is accepted as NIE, are:

Property rights approach, transaction cost approach, evolutionary economics, constitutional choice, collective action theory, public choice theory, economic contract theory, new institutional approach to economic history, modern Austrian economics. (Richter, 2005, p. 4)

In this sense, the main themes of NIE are property rights (Coase & Alcian) and transaction costs (Coase & Williamson). The other important contributors of NIE are Ronald Coase (1910-2013) and Douglas North (1920-2015). There are some conflicts in NIE just as OIE does not contain in a holistic way.

The difference between the "Williamsonian" and the "Northian" approach is described by Ensminger (1992, 21 f.). . . . The Williamsonian approach to the NIE is mainly applied in microeconomic fields like the theory of firm, of industrial organization, antitrust, the economics of organization. The Northian approach is used to tackle with macroeconomic issues as those of the history of national economies, of development economics or transformation economics. (Richter, 2005, pp. 10-11)

The lively escapade from OIE to NIE has been continuing by submitting a brief history. The most prominent criticism to OIE is that it has not constituted a holistic theory. It has not a surprise if one can remember that OIE is a heterodox economics, because the same criticism is made for almost all heterodox schools. This is not lessened for none of the heterodox school.

Historical process and assumed constant rules of capitalism have made school of thoughts popular. The attributed role to institutions in economics and their importance by OIE has been pursued by under "the institutionalization" discourse. The importance of institutions in economics of a country – either a developing country or a developed country – has gradually increased. For that reason, firstly Veblen and then the other philosophers who developed OIE have become important to be re-explored. On the other side, criticizing NIE to resemble neoclassical economics, suggests an interaction between the level of development and institutionalism on macroeconomics variables for both firms' own institutionalism and firm/individual institutionalism by the mediation of property rights and transaction costs. Briefly, the institutionalism effects all economics actors looking at either OIE or NIE. It sometimes handles on micro level as individual/firm, sometimes handles the institutions playing effective roles of developing a county's economics institutions. It sometimes forges how rules, traditions and economics habits contribute to a country's economics. In this respect, the institutionalism is the trend topic of today's World. When first writing the idea of this book, the aim was to become different than other works in the field, including all social sciences not only economics. The aim of doing this, the emphasis of "institutionalism" is not only influential in economics, but it becomes appreciable in other fields as well. For this reason, an approach coming from other disciplines makes it reachable both in institutional field and widespread regions with its interdisciplinary way. This book will give a convenience to initially the colleagues from social sciences in academy and students in social sciences as well, because not only an economist colleague/student needs to know how institutionalism works, for instance, a colleague/student from business administration will see how institutionalism effects the field.

The thought of writing this book goes past. When I have first wished to write this book, I was preparing in a densely tempo to become an Assoc. Prof. Dr. It was a very scary idea writing a comprehensive book aside the other publications. The luck I have this year will not only bring prosperity to the social sciences field, but also it is the first step of an adventure. There must be some lacking words even if several pages are written in institutional economics which is a very dep field. The other words hope to say will be the continuous works. May all readers read it with pleasure, getting knowledge and utility.

ORGANIZATION OF THE BOOK

The book is organized into 15 chapters. A brief description of each of the chapters follows:

Chapter 1 identifies how OIE to NIE emerged. A brief history must be added according to the spirit of the book. Of course, both OIE and NIE separated into different parts per se. There would have been added a widespread approach, however the main aim of this chapter is to unroll how both Ecole started by exactly focusing on the main developers.

Chapter 2 establishes a relationship between neoliberalism and identities. Because, no matter what is said about neoliberalism, it affects people's lives deeply. Neoliberalism is a notion which is not only about affecting peoples' lives economically, but also sociologically, culturally etc. For what, neoliberalism is a widespread mental project. So, the authors of the chapter try to suggest how neoliberalism has a relationship with identity of consumers', interestingly with a non-Western World example.

Chapter 3 takes the importance of the global effect of crisis and institutions. No matter what happened in any economy's conditions, it will directly show adverse indicators for the World economics. As one of the most important institutions of World economics G20 affected the unbalanced situations in the World crisis. Thus, the authors try to show how important one country's institutionalism when articulating the World economics by the mediation of institutionalism.

Chapter 4 reviews the importance of the market. As it is well-known the market is an institution. On the other hand, market is not seen as an institution by neoclassical economics. Of course, not seeing it as an institution raises some issues in competition which is very important for capitalism. The authors will argue if the market is regarded as "process" that it can be possibly claimed as an institution.

Chapter 5 reviews how important heterodox economics is. While doing this, the authors follow the path by comparing two great scientists: Schumpeter and Veblen. As the founder of OIE, Veblen must be accepted as one of the most important heterodox economist, on the other hand, although he isn't accepted as an institutionalist, one of the most elegant contributors and critics of orthodox economics will give the readers a chance to compare their ideas about orthodox economics.

Chapter 6 presents the appropriate spirit of the book how institutionalism is important for economic development of a country by the relationship between tourism as an institution and its offerings. According to the tourism rules of EU, it will be inquired whether it is possible by the mediation of Erzurum city/Turkey example.

Chapter 7 addresses the importance of the relationship between technological improvements and institutionalism, because, technology makes the social and economic transformation available to change. The author tries to suggest a link in terms of technology.

Chapter 8 analyses as a mental Project of how neoliberalism revolves the mind of public administration. Neoliberalism creates a dilemma between citizen/customer satisfaction. So, the author tries to define how this dilemma changes the public administration as an institution.

Chapter 9 reviews foreign direct investments as an institution. One of the most important points of institutionalism is to handle almost all notions as institution in the economics. By that way, all the political, economic and social connections will be understood better. Thus, the author explains foreign direct investments as an institution that influence economics freedom and democracy.

Chapter 10 discusses the importance of the impact of democratization and economic freedom on economic growth. Here, one of the leading institutions of the World economics World Bank is considered. The impact of democratization and economic freedom on economic growth are tested by panel data analysis in the period of 1995-2012.

Chapter 11 presents how Old (Original) Institutional Economics has a relationship between German Historical School, because, it is well-known that German Historical School has a great effect on American economics history. So, the author tries to show this relationship.

Chapter 12 addresses how the transaction costs presented by Oliver Williamson affect managerial tool. The author tries to reveal whether outsourcing problem can be solved by the mediation of transaction costs or a solution can be delivered to governance decision.

Chapter 13 concludes how organizations such as IMF, World Bank are important in terms of NIE. As a continuous school of orthodox economics, NIE gets along with all world economics organizations. So, the author suggests a contribution to the link between NIE and those institutions.

Chapter 14 handles how neoliberal politics gets the privatizations and the deregulations changes the public administration. After the Keynesian economics model left, NIE substitutes it in public administration. For that reason, the author handles the transformation of the state, specifically NIE.

Chapter 15 presents foreign trade policies and Turkey's example. After the declaration of Turkish Republic (T.R.) till 1980 semi-open models were implemented. After 1980s Turkey slides hastily to open economic regimes. So, this is very important in terms of institutional changing that the author will elaborate.

Chapter 16 establishes classes as an institution. It is largely known that institutional economics has never attempted to establish classes like a leftist approach did. Their contributions are in very different ways. So, the author tries to understand how classes are forming into different regions as an institution.

Ilkben Akansel

Artvin Çoruh University, Turkey

REFERENCES

Baş-Dinar, G. (2014). Wesley Mitchell'ın İktisat Bilimine Katkısı Üzerine Bir Değerlendirme [An Assessment of Wesley Mitchell contribution to economic science]. *İktisat ve Toplum, 46*, 60-68.

Chavance, B. (2012). John Commons's organizationol theory of institutions: A discussion. *Journal of Institutional Economics*, *8*(1), 27–47.

Colander, D., Holt, R., & Rosser, B. Jr. (2004). The changing face of mainstream economics. *Review of Political Economy*, *16*(4), 485–499. doi:10.1080/0953825042000256702

Dequech, D. (2007). Neoclassical, mainstream, orthodox, and heterodox economics. *Journal of Post Keynesian Economics*, *30*(2), 279–302. doi:10.2753/PKE0160-3477300207

Dimmelmeier, A. & Heussner, F. (2016). *Institutional Economics*. Retrieved from https://www.exploring-economics.org/en/orientation/institutionalist-economics/

Dows, S. C. (2000). Prospects for the progress of Heterodox Economics. *Journal of the History of Economic Thought*, *22*(2), 157–170. doi:10.1080/10427710050025367

Groenewegen, J., Spithoven, A., & van der Berg, A. (2010). *Institutional economics: An introduction*. Basingstoke, UK: Palgrave Macmillan.

Hodgson, G. M. (2006). What Are Institutions? *Journal of Economic Issues*, *40*(1), 1–25.

Kaufmann, B. E. (2007). The institutional economics od John R. Commons: Complement and substitute for neoclassical economic theory. *Socio-economic Review*, *5*(1), 3–45. doi:10.1093er/mwl016

Lee, F. S. (2008). Heterodox Economics. In S. N. Durlauf & L. E. Blume (Eds.), *From the New Palgrave Dictionary of Economics*. Academic Press. Retrieved from https://hetecon.net/?page=about&side=heterodox_economics

Özveren, E. (Ed.). (2007). *Kurumsal İktisat* [Institutional Economics]. Ankara, Turkey: İmge Yayınları.

Richter, R. (2005). The new institutional economics: Its start, its meaning, its prospects. *European Business Organization Law Review*, *6*(2), 161–200. doi:10.1017/S1566752905001618

Yalman, G. (2007). Economic theories of state or 'economics imperialism': Rent-seeking analysis as an exemplar. *ODTÜ Gelisme Dergisi*, *34*, 387–412.

Chapter 1
From Old Institutional Economics to New Institutional Economics:
A Short History

Ilkben Akansel
https://orcid.org/0000-0001-8167-7416
Bartin University, Turkey

ABSTRACT

Since different kinds of economics thoughts have been explored, few have been as peculiar as Old Institutional Economics (OIE) and New Institutional Economics (NIE). It is curious that almost every stream criticizing mainstream economics has a left wing. OIE, not a big fan of this, criticizes neoclassical economics/mainstream economics, given it arose in the US. OIE had no sense to left wing, on the contrary, it created an effect criticizing neoclassical economics in its core. Unlike OIE, NIE has many common points with neoclassical economics. NIE has several new aspects different from neoclassical economics, as it has chosen a completely different path than OIE. In this chapter, authors scrutinize circumstances that led to OIE, and what separated OIE and NIE. A brief, successively historical aspect is also provided.

INTRODUCTION

Institutionalism is very important for an economy. It covers every shape of our lives. It is in economic institutions, organizations, labor and monetary institutions, property rights, legal institutions, economic actors etc. Institutionalism had affected great economists such as Marshall, Smith, and Mill. But none of them gave such significant focus like USA's institutionalism and like the great philosopher Veblen. This study aims to submit a brief history about the origins of institutionalism.

DOI: 10.4018/978-1-7998-0333-1.ch001

Copyright © 2020, IGI Global. Copying or distributing in print or electronic forms without written permission of IGI Global is prohibited.

Naturally, many of the scholars know that institutionalism has a broad history, but may one elaborate its historical path, it shall be called as Old Institutional Economics (OIE) and New Institutional Economics (NIE). By giving a historical background of the transformation from OIE to NIE, the origins of OIE and its path from today to future will be illuminated. This chapter will cover several aspects of OIE. Firstly, the author will discuss the origins of Institutional Economics in the US which was commenced with Veblen. The chapter proceeds by mentioning the other great contributors of OIE like Mitchell and Commons. Secondly, the author will scrutinize NIE whilst mentioning the three important contributors to NIE, Ronald Coase, Oliver Williamson and Douglas North.

The reason why these great economists and their contributions are being discussed is that the institutional economics history has a wide range. Mentioning the great contributors of each school of institutional economics will provide the readers a thorough history of these two different schools.

BACKGROUND

Since neoclassical economics became an imperial feature, OIE has started by criticizing it. Because, neoclassical economics – frequently called as mainstream economics – is a phenomenon to explain all economics events. Mainstream economics moreover claims that it can explain all other events, all not necessarily in economics. Economic thought sometimes takes a fresh breath, in which case, some new thoughts emerge when it cultivates the pressure of a dominant ideology. So is Old Institutional Economics (OIE). The main ideology of OIE is naturally institution then. So, what is institution?

Institutions are the kinds of structures that matter most in the social realm, they make up the stuff of social life. The increasing acknowledgement of the role of institutions in social life involves there cognition that much of human interaction and activity is structured in terms of overt or implicit rules. Without doing much violence to the relevant literature, we may define institutions as systems of established and prevalent social rules that structure social interactions. Language, money, law, systems of weights and measures, table manners, and firms (and other organizations) are thus all institutions. (Hodgson, 2000, p. 2).

Institutions are embedded in human life. Since the beginning of known history of the human settlements, all cultures have created many institutions. All of them are related with both social and economic life. No matter how social life seems to be separated from economics, in fact, it is very much embedded in economics. As Hodgson clearly states that language, money, law, etc. are related with the market. If one needs and wishes, all institutions can be addressed by economics. So, either OIE or NIE is focused on how these institutions affect our lives. Of course, their approach to scrutinize the institutions are different from each other.

A HISTORICAL PATH OF BOTH INSTITUTIONALIST SCHOOLS

The titles like 'the role of institutions in economics process' are just the tools to make an easy expression. This reminds that more econometrics studies are seen in economics. They presume there is no institution in economics, and then they consider institution as if there would be 'pure economics', namely economics without institution (Özveren, 2007, p. 17). The key point of OIE is to see that the origins of institutionalism and economics are same. This allows OIE to be different than the market.

We have institutions everywhere. We face institutions every time. In other words, institutions are embedded in our daily lives. So, is economics. It means that institutions are in the natural pattern of our lives. Economics cannot be therefore degraded to the market. Mainstream economics tend to recognize economics as the market – to its very definition the place making the action buying and selling. Every saleable and purchasable thing (goods and services, bonds etc.) has a market and so economics is a social science to understand of this buying-selling process. Mainstream economists thusly tend to see the economics as a market. It is however not entirely true. Economics is beyond the market. It has been keeping a history since 'the wannabe science' saw as *economics*. If institutions start to be seen a natural process of economics, it will turn to its own *political economics*. OIE must be *institutional political economics* in that case (Özveren, 2007, p. 18).

The actual turnout of economics and political economics started at the time when economics have set up its political feature. Of course, this has been a long history. However, it doesn't mean that it hasn't been torn off from its historical merits. Tearing a notion of its history is also means that it will lose some part of it. Although, being an economics hasn't had an early date back, it doesn't understand its history. Yet, many economists agree that history of economics is a tool to whom don't handle the hard topics like 'statistics' or 'econometrics' (Chang, 2016, p. 53).

Besides, many institutions have been a part of it. Slaves, child employment, government offices etc. were just the one part of economics mind, or developed capitalist countries have the highest growth rates when they had the highest tax rates etc. (Chang, 2016, p. 54). So, economy is more beyond economics. Every economic action has an institutional way. All institutions have already been embedded in economy; economics needs to deserve *political institutional economy*.

Today, we accept scientist Thorstein B. Veblen (1857-1929), John R. Commons (1862-1945) and Wesley C. Mitchell (1874-1948) as the representatives of OIE that we know. Although, Veblen who is accepted as the leader of OIE has never put into words 'institutional economics; he'd rather to say *evolutionary economics*.

The term "institutional economics" was announced by Walter Hamilton at a meeting of the American Economic Association in 1918. Institutionalism dominated American economics, at least until the 1940s. [...] institutional economics alone could unify economic science by showing parts of the economic system related to the whole. [...] According to Hamilton, institutional economists recognized that, The proper subject matter of economic theory is institutions. Economic theory must be based upon an acceptable theory of human behavior." (Hodgson, 2008, p. 399).

Institutionalism emerged because of a movement in 1918. Especially end of the World War I has a great effect of emerging of a new quest in economics. There was also a quest not only in economics, but in politics as well. Institutionalism was an answer to this quest. Because the available economics theory – classical/neoclassical – this period's reconstruction needed to be reshaped in economics research, education etc. In institutionalism, psychology has a direct effect on "business cycles, the pricing behavior of firms, ownership and control of corporations, monopoly and competition, unions and regulation, and law and economics." (Rutherford, 2001, p. 180).

In that case, every economist takes economy as an institutional process (Özveren, 2007, p. 19). This may be an apprehensive perusal to understand the differences between institutional economics and mainstream economics. Even today mainstream economics is understood as a flow beginning at the turn of nineteenth century. It is well-known that the pioneer intellectuals of classical economics are Adam Smith than David Ricardo, John Stuart Mill, Alfred Marshall. It is no surprise that all these intellectuals were in Britain which is accepted as the first capitalist country in modern sense.

Since twentieth century mainstream economics is called as "neoclassical economics". We owe this term initially to Veblen. Veblen has used this term in order to indicate what Marshall's economics has no difference between classical political economics. Veblen criticizes that it has never give up the obsession of *homo-economicus* methodological breaking off and *the assumption of balance anaysis.* (Özveren, 2007, p. 21). At that point, one of the main hypotheses of institutional economics asserts to neoclassical economics can be found in two terms, *Homo economicus* and *the assumption of balance*. These two notions exclude two important factors which are highly important for the economics, Human and history. Human and history are embedded to each other. One cannot be thought without the other. These two notions also resemble the institutions. Humans have existed and they created the history. Historically, humans have endured under different economic conditions which are very important both economics and history of economics itself. So, institutionalism cannot be as if it was new. On the contrary, institutional economics had emerged as old as neoclassical economics, because every human action is involved in economics, *vice versa*. This makes them institutional. The worst part of neoclassical economics is to exclude institutional actions. In that case, rejecting institutionalism is also a rejection of its history in terms of neoclassical economics '*laisser faire*' – which is the exact gadget of institutionalism. One individual has full right to tenure her/his own property at his/her own disposal. It also means that there must be a right to protect her/his savings. This is an institution per se. Neoclassical economics has however turned another path to explain itself.

Neoclassical economists regularly accept economics as the market. In that way, they make the market spontaneous. The market strays from its institutional roots. In any way of doing this, only one institution remains, the firm (Özveren, 2007, p. 22). Veblen called it 'the enterprise'. Historically, the firms are existed by being different entities than individuals. Firms initially are responsible for the production. They undertake different responsibilities than any individual undertakes. They are institutions per se, thus and so they are also a part of economics institutionalism.

According to Veblen, all institutions are determined by culture. [...] (Özveren, 2007, p. 24). Also, Veblen sees the government is a tool of interest groups and the unions is a tool of prominent employers who imitate these groups. [...] (Özveren, 2007, p. 24).

One of the distinguished terms that Veblen asserts is the dilemma of the industry – the enterprise. For Veblen, the industry is a physical term like production engineering. The enterprise subdues *the industry* in order to make its profit higher. Veblen calls this position as 'sabotage', because it would rather increase the prices rather than increase the capacity utilization. The important point here technology has full capacity of speed, but the enterprise naturally make it slow down (Özveren, 2007, p. 26).

As it is known, OIE starts with Veblen's masterpiece "Why is Economics not an Evolutionary Science?" This question asked by Veblen indicates that economics must tend to an evolution in all senses that seem to be easily solvable issue. In those pieces he debates why capitalist class is accepted as leisure class and their consumption habits are being emulated by working class. Put it differently, unlike Marx's view, Veblen tries to understand how the differences between classes arose and affected each other sociologically. However, this approach cannot be accepted not only sociologically, but also economically. Additionally, it is socioeconomics. Because all sociological habits suggested by Veblen are also embedded in economics. All may be accepted as habits of economics rather than economic exploitation.

In this sense, it can be said that Veblen's view was rather negative unlike Commons' ideas to revitalize the economics. OIE is accepted to start with Veblen and his famous piece "Why Economics is not an Evolutionary Science?" In that legend article he argued that economics should be referred "as a branch of the natural sciences inasmuch as it studied on particular living organism, namely man." (Zingler, 2012, p. 322). For Veblen, economics must rely on biology rather than physics. In that way, economics' methodology can be altered by evolutionary methodology. As an alive organism like a human, economics use generalizations and these use empirical results. Also, economics "must have a sense of cultural perspective." (Zingler, 2012, p. 323). So, Veblen's view has a vast anthropological approach. Economic systems change because there is a dynamic evolutionary change in the economic system.

Put it differently, institutions are the economics or economics are the institutions for Veblen. In any case these two are embedded into each other. The reason is people's preferences and values determine the institutions or economics. These preferences and values have a direct relationship between 'conspicuous consumption.' Rich people do not feel to consume cheap products. They have money and they need to show themselves to public by the mediation of the products which have already bought for big amount of money. For poor people, 'conspicuous consumption' is the way of emulation to wealthy people. Veblen believes in there is an 'invisible hand' in the conditions of small-scale manufacturing, but it cannot be seen in large-scale production, corporate finance, salesmanship (Rutherford, 2001, 175). In a small-scale manufacturing there is rival among competitors. Everyone tries to produce better and to have more customers than the others. As a consequence of mind of perfect competition, (of course in the real world there is no such market completely appropriate for the perfect competition, but here at least converging to perfect competition) it is no puzzling situation for no one is able to determine the price, but 'invisible hand.' However, in a large-scale production, there are a few producers. Everyone is watching to each other's step.

It is no surprise that institutionalism would have affected the developments in 'modern psychology.' There has been a new thought about behaviorism which abandoned the instinct/habit approach. "Institutionalism probably played a part in ridding economics of explicitly hedonistic language, but it did not develop the alternative basis to convince the profession as a whole to abandon its rationalistic foundations." (Lewin, 1996; Rutherford, 2001, p. 183).

An interesting example of today may be social media. People use social media not only for ordinary occasions like having information, dating, to be preferred amongst others, even getting money etc. Thus, social media for instance can be accepted as today's *conspicuous consumption*.

According to Veblen, the environment and the context are important on human behavior into each other. The logic is the last sequence in human's decision making. Believing lies down under the formation on logic; under the formation of believing lies down instinctive behavior. The instinctive behavior cannot only be taken from the past over, but also the institutions can be shaped by human behaviors (Hodgson, 2004, 141-2; Önder, 2015, p. 63).

Persistently, to remind that social media is very important in terms of selling goods and services today. Beyond selling something via technology becomes a habit. The culture of a society has turned to imply themselves in social media. It proceeds sometimes as some tweets, sometimes some photos, sometimes some stories etc. However, no matter what people upload to their social media accounts, they wish to assume that they would belong to one higher class to emulate what others can do. In that way, they can show whatever goods and services consume to others. It's kind like a *potlatch* like in old times. But of course, this time it may happen more explicitly, fresher and sometimes more impolite than it used to be.

Indians fire a special festival called *potlatch*. In this festival chief destroys his worthy belongings in special days like weddings, birthdays etc. (Perelman, 2015, 30). So, in social media many people behave like this *potlatch*. They can use it how they are beautiful, how they are rich, how they are different than anyone else etc. No one should forget that social media today is an institution as an instinctive behavior shaped by our logic. The social media being using today can be a good example for shaping the instinctive behaviors and institutions. Many people use social platforms not only getting information, showing themselves as *conspicuous consumption* but has belonged to wealthy people, today technology allows many people make themselves *idle class consumption*, *conspicuous leisure*, *conspicuous waste* and *pecuniary emulation*. What Veblen said about modern robber barons can be likened to what people do on social media.

Veblenian cultural theory of consumption is not only be seen in advertising business world, but also interestingly seen in the social media too. Explicitly, the social media is the best platform of emulation. This happens mainly into two ways, (1) people use social media to prove themselves economically, preferences, etc. aims. (2) One other important reason why people tend to use social media is emulating. Because the leisure class, no matter what Veblen explains us or today's modern leisure class people like modern businessman, social media usage is a phenomenon. Working class tries to emulate these leisure class in order to show themselves, their ideas, their bodies, their lives in social media.

What neoclassical allocation analysis problem asserted with adequate knowledge, expectations and virtually unbounded rationality. All these assertations will be concluded by only one set of decisions (Hutchison, 1984, p. 27). In other words, human psychology and the institutions created by psychology are excluded. In terms of Veblenian mind this is the exclusion of evolutionary methodology. Because, if economics is an alive process creating mankind, it will conclude with the allocation to certain classes. Of course, this class will be businessman.

Peculiar about Veblen's thought, his methodology is far different than neoclassical economics. Methodologically, Veblen mainly rejects the marginal utility theory. As the founder of the term 'neoclassical economics', whereas many people do not aware that we owe this term to Veblen, he revolves the main rejection to neoclassical economics. Veblen's objection to marginal utility theory is all about his institutionalism. For him, this theory is a passive, adaptive man. Because this kind of a man is stable. (S)he has no intention to change her/his economics benefit. Nevertheless, as a conclusion of an evolutionary economics. Human must change.

"There are markets without capitalist, but there is no capitalism without markets." (Pereira & Lopes, 2018, 452). That's the main reason why OIE has especially focused on capitalism. More explicitly, this is the reason why Veblen has focused on market. Because, every economics action is being done in the market. The truth is where you stand and which ideological way you look, it will be available to understand this basic event. The market is also an institution, it is embedded into the society and its economics event. For OIE, markets are institutions. Because they are not perfect as neoclassical theory claimed. Since neoclassical economics first arose and became predominant, there are no markets whether perfect or imperfect. According to OIE, market is not efficient, their failures are not seen sporadic. *Veblen's 'method' is evolutionary, because its central goal is to understand transformative action ...] Veblen (1914, 1992) sees evolution, from the viewpoint of human action, as a transformative process, in which habits of thoughts are molded by instinct and institutions. (Pereira & Lopes, 2018, pp. 452, 455).*

One particular feature why Veblen is so important in terms of economics history is he has conceived original terms. One of the major terms he created is the dilemma of industry-enterprise. According to Veblen, industry is a term which has been approaching to industrial engineering. Unlike industry, enterprise pursue directly to make profit and it is a capitalist organization. The enterprise subdues the physical production power of the industry directly in order to steer its own profit maximization. The enterprise makes 'a sabotage' what Veblen called, would rather keep the prices high than decrease the capacity utilization.

For Veblen both technology and enterprise are institutions. Technology can be changed rapidly, but enterprise tries to make it slow down. In the second generation of OIE, Clarence E. Ayres, tries to make this dilemma in the focus of economics. They conceptualized as if technology and institutions have a discrepancy (Özveren, 2007, p. 26). How NIE has started to be remembered as Institutional and Organizational Economics after establishing of Organizational Academy, *neo-institutional economics* started by Allan Gruchy has tried to remove institutional economics from Veblen's idea.

More clearly, when technology is to be respected as an institution, it becomes to determine human actions. Technology starts to determine human life ever-increasing. Technology started by being used as a tool targeting economics actions rather than by using technology as a benefit of economics actions. Explicitly, technology started to imply as a tool of economics planning. Using social media technologies is the way of creating new economics actions, for instance, not applying an economic action combined with technology as an institution.

It must be deliberately stated that business cycles are highly related with habits. Because, habits affect demand and supply. Thus, this is directly adjusting the production. Of course, this adjustment can be accelerated from simple goods and services to very complex ones. The habits of societies are related with their economics life or the habits of people are determined by the economics life of them. So, what Veblen is primarily focused on is the kinds of economics actions that determine the people's mind rather than the kinds of people's actions that determine the whole society's economic life. Because, people's instincts and habits totally affect the economics actions.

Because *[…] embodying various instincts that enable them to become active beings. The positive instincts include workmanship, idle curiosity and parenting, and the negative ones are the pecuniary, emulative and predatory traits, although they cross and fuse with each other in a complex interactive pattern. (O'hara, 2002, p. 93).* Veblen's main concern with these habits is how they affect human actions and the economics process. People do act under these instincts. All these actions allow them to plan and transmit them to macrosocial institutions. For instance, emulating to upper class, the administers of trade unions transmit their emulations to working class as a whole macrosocial institution.

Veblen, too, attacked capitalists for believing that the problem was 'overproduction' or 'excessive' competition rather than underconsumption. As he put it, 'The supply of consumable goods is, practically, never greater than the community's capacity for consuming them. (Tilman, 1985, p. 884).

No matter what consumers want, the only attention of capitalists to make their profits the highest amount. This is on the one hand related with industry-enterprise dilemma, on the other hand related with conspicuous consumption. Over production is the unique way to make their profit maximization. The enterprise never thinks that whether consumers do need this production; the only concern is all about to sell them by the mediation of created *conspicuous consumption*.

Naturally, Veblen creates his theory with a different methodology. This methodology is different than neo-classical methods'. There is no doubt that Veblen's mind relies on pragmatism. Also, the deep relationship between Clarence Ayres who was the secondary representative of OIE and John Dewey's literature must be emphasized. Because, pragmatism is very important for OIE given pragmatism affects the habits and routines of economics. Over pragmatism, Ayres tries to make a collaboration between Veblen and Dewey.

It was Ayres who first articulated the close parallel between purposes instrumental to practical activity in Dewey and technological values in Veblen. It was Ayres, too, who first understood the convergence between Dewey's repudiation of the quest for certainty and Veblen's attacks on the ceremonial. (Tilman, 1990, p. 965).

Instead of depicting human activity as a sequence of separate instantaneous 'actions', pragmatism understands it as a unified ongoing process, even so that the acting subject's intentionality are to be found inside rather than outside that process." Methodological individualism maintains that if we want to treat action as rational choice. According to pragmatism it is not so; rational choice is a some-what truncated and pedestrian description of rationality, because human rationality in its essence is long-term affair. (Kilpinen, 2003, pp. 292, 293).

Thus, instincts and habits are so important for human actions. Those human actions determined by economic motivations cannot be pop-outed involuntary. On the contrary, rational mind and rational choices, all preferences are created by outside process. At that point, emulating upper classes is so important. Economic actions fundamentally like buying/selling (at any kind of goods/services/financial liabilities) are pushed by the strain of instincts and habits. All those instincts and habits are very important to be formed by economics rather than being rational. So, pragmatism is the way to use or to find the best solution to describe the society's economic action.

... 'scientific method' was, of course, not the production of course, not the production of more verbal solutions to hypothetical problems but the instrumental philosophy of science which Ayres shared with his friend, John Dewey. (Liebhafsky & Gordon & Redford, 1997, p. 478).

This point is a supporting assumption that Özveren (2007) tells about Veblen's ideas about technology. For Veblen, technology is an institution whereas Ayres fell into the trap of technological determinism. Their pragmatism restraining oligopolistic sabotage with the help of economics planning. What Veblen tries to use *institutional methodology* rather than *methodological individualism* is to find out how institutions make importance in humans' economics actions. These actions seldom seem economical, but sometimes are arose by sociological, ritual, psychological etc. Institutionalism and its methodology are embedded into each other. Intuitionalism is everywhere, people use institutions to realize their economics and these economics actions are sourced by, *methodologically*, in their institutional nature. This is also the reason why Veblen sees some activities as ceremonial and ritualistic.

Ayres's vision of economic organization 'beyond capitalism' is not entirely clear. But what seems to be clear is that he does not call for the abolition of the market system in the sense of replacing commodity production with a centralized or hierarchical organization of the whole of society. Such a vision is inconsistent with his thought. To Ayres, the life process ad human well-being are enhanced by technological progress. Behind that progress is the development of science, and he believed that the republic of science can be developed only under conditions of freedom of inquiry. Attempts at centrally directed scientific inquiry would jeopardize scientific and consequently technological progress. (Pham, 2001, pp. 689, 690).

Starting with Ayres, the second-generation institutionalists approach the dilemma between technology-institutions. This kind of institutional economics is quite different than the original one created by Veblen. Neo-institutional economics has these features which altered OIE view, (1) Emphasizing reality in assumptions and theory. The aim of economics to get goods and services that are vulnerable pursuing of living (Gruchy, 1987, 31). (2) Emphasizing *holism*. Economics is located in social-cultural system. In that position, individuals are not capable to decide their own decision under the *homo institutalis,* way not *in homo economicus*. (3) It is unable to have an economics without values. In that context, the question asked by scientists is to keep away '*what ought to be*' (Gruchy, 1972, 292; Özveren, 2007, pp. 27, 28).

Institutional economics is an approach that recognizes the importance of culture. [...] The situation becomes no better if culture is simply incorporated into the preferences of the individual. In effect, this subordinates rational choice as nothing but the mechanism implementing a culture. The logical problem is that if the preferences are opened up as one of the selections to be made, and selections are always made by applying preferences to available alternatives, we have created an infinite regress. (McFarling, 2004, pp. 339, 341).

Of course, not everyone in a society has a property. As a conclusion of being a citizen protecting property rights is however an obligation for a state. It has many different tools to protect its people or keep them away to digress impairing the property rights. John Dewey had a great impact on Veblen. Veblen developed '*response to action*.' In that Veblen left the psychological behaviorism and he developed *instinct-habit* approach (Önder, 2105, p. 56). Veblen has signed many notions. Even today, these notions haven't lost their importance like *conspicuous consumption*, *idle class consumption*, *conspicuous leisure, conspicuous waste, pecuniary emulation* etc.

A broad network of OIE-scholars formed an influential movement in American economics in the period 1918-1947. Their approach is characterized by, 1) underlining the role of institutions as constraining and enabling behavior, and highlighting the institutional role in shaping values, belief and preferences; 2) incorporating a social psychology which is consistent with recognizing that institutions influence values, beliefs and preferences, and a related rejection of the idea of utility maximizing; 3) an open empirical and critical investigation of social phenomena; 4) critically examining the functioning of prevailing institutions, and; 5) adhering a pragmatic and humanistic approach to social value (Rutherford 2013, 347; Spithoven, 2019, p. 441).

One other important representative of OIE was John R. Commons (1862-1945). This intellectual philosopher of OIE suggests a third way to the idea of OIE. Interestingly, all representatives of OIE school members have proclaimed their ideas in very different ways of institutionalism. Once Veblen has given his ideas connecting a great contribution to economics and sociology; Mitchell has proclaimed his ideas quantitatively and evoked a link to NIE; then Commons has proclaimed his ideas as making a great contribution to political economy and to social science. His major publications are *Legal Foundatios of Capitalism* (1924), *Institutional Economics* (1934), *The Economics of Collective Action* (posthumously published in 1950).

In a manner of speaking, it can be alleged that he was the father of *Constitutional Economics*. He tried to suggest a link between working rules and economics actions. He proposes how law is related to economics rules and is very much important. One should not forget that economics is based upon property rights. And these property rights are directly deriving their power by law. Having an economic value also brings having economics rights with it. This is historical. They are caused by the rigid relationship between law and economics historically.

John R. Commons (1909) holds that free competition, especially in the labor market, is in reality a destructive competition that eventually pulls all down to the least costly set of practices- [...] Therefore, it was Commons's position that, to the extent that free labor market competition facilities destructive competition, it should be prevented by means of substituting labor market outcomes for 'reasonable level outcomes' (Ramstad, 1987, 19, Marangos, 2018, p. 328).

What Commons were trying to do is, if the working rules and laws can be designed to proceed well, it will help the economics. Because, all economics actions must be based upon a legal level. Once an economic action breaks a legal level, there will certain be deteriorations in economics indicators. One other important point must be scrutinized here. As it will be a debate in the NIE section, property rights, transaction costs etc. are the most important terms. Interestingly, either voluntarily or involuntarily, but presumably involuntarily, both Commons and Mitchell were the academic parents of NIE. Of course, they may have not thought that they would cause to create another economics flow, but their notions had great influence for others. Nevertheless, this situation cannot be seen on Veblen. Veblen had a position to underline the capitalisms rules in a way of economics sociology.

Wesley Clair Mitchell (1874-1949) is the other prominent philosopher of OIE. Another importance of Mitchell is that he was the student of Thorstein Veblen. As a matter of fact, he was impressed by his teacher at most. Nevertheless, it is obviously impossible to say that he had the very same ideas with Veblen. His approach suggests different manners to the OIE. His main argument is all about 'monetary economics'. He focused on how capitalism works with this term.

The OIE's mission is to clarify monopole firms, trade union formation; uncertainty on causes of the state in the economy while capitalism has been in a structural transformation (Özveren, 2007, p. 23). At that point, Mitchell's differentiation of Veblen can be seen. Mitchell is very well-known with his statistical works and featuring empiricism. He applied those within business cycles (Baş Dinar, 2014, p. 60). Unlike Mitchell, Veblen has a very cold pose using statistics. Mitchell was one of the most prominent philosophers using statistical and quantitative works in economics and also, he was the founder of National Bureau of Economics Research (NBER).

The main aim of the OIE is to oppose to neoclassical economics assumptions. That's the reason why Veblen is not a great supporter of statistics being applied on neoclassical economics, even today, using statistics to prove its abstract theories with some unrealistic empirical data. Mitchell's distinctive usage of statistics shows a very different way of orthodox economics. Mitchell applies empirical data in order to understand the orderliness of life and the general tendency of economics changing. So, Mitchell's model is a dynamic model.

The very well-known contributions of Mitchell's are *Business Cycles* (1913), *Business Cycles, The Problem and Its Setting* (1927), *Measuring Business Cycles* (1946-with Arthur Burns). The main purpose of Mitchell is to create a wide range of theoretical framework explaining how modern capitalism works.

"The business cycle became a fad with the business community; forecasting became a national sport, for a time even more interesting than the game of national politics." (Hansen, 1949, 245). Undoubtedly, Mitchell does not use the business cycle as a fad. Namely, his great effort in order to understand how business cycles flows, especially in USA, can help all economies to use for them giving efficacy to economics process. "For him, business cycles were essentially *oscillations* or *fluctuations*." (Hansen, 1949, 246). The period Mitchell lived, was the peak and the down of the USA's economy. Many economists were trying to understand how these *oscillations* and *fluctuations* become true. The distinguishing respect how Mitchell is separated by among other economists is that he focused on business cycles as his glance about the topic. Mitchell really believed that the endogenous explanations of business cycle can be proved by statistics. This is the main core idea of his theory.

Endogenous explanations of business cycles came into mainstream with a focus on the flow of goods, capital and loanable funds. The first decades of the 20th century saw split between 'real' theorists and 'monetary' theorists. Both camps saw the periods of slump but attributed them to different causes. What Veblen's and Mitchell's common point in terms of business cycles theory is about the expected profit rate. Thus, both have the same idea that imbalances of supply and demand, assumed fluctuating profitability to be a byproduct of physical disequilibria. (Hlasny, 2008, p. 4, 6). Of course, for Veblen fluctuating profitability is highly related with the dilemma of industry-enterprise. The more enterprises capture the industry, the more fluctuations can be seen in that economy. According to this theory, industry is more flexible, it is like a productional engineering. It moves fast and changes are flexible. On the other hand, the enterprise focuses on raising profits. No matter how business cycles moves depresses or grows, the enterprise will seek to raise profit. This cause for more unemployment or expected fast growth, the enterprise's main concern would be how it would throw these cycles losing less money.

Mitchell is accepted by many neoclassical theorists as if he had no theory about business cycles. Nevertheless, this acquisition is not fair even by the neoclassical mind. In neoclassical theory, there are eternal true laws, but Mitchell's theory states an evolutionary approach, which is no surprise. His close employment period with Veblen must have affected his way of thinking.

Whereas, all neoclassical business cycle theories are exogenous, relying on external shocks to the economy, Mitchell stated an endogenous theory, based on the internal dynamics of capitalism. (Sherman, 2001, p. 85).

One other point what Mitchell focuses on both camps, either neoclassical economics or institutional economics; his great contribution is the statistical approach. Naturally, his seemingly too much interest in statistical methods has been criticized. However, his focus on statistical methods was different from the neoclassical economics. Using statistical methods may have seemed to move *the institutional mind* of *institutional economics*. On the other hand, his way of using statistical methods helps him to understand why capitalism – or another saying neoclassical economics – has been in trouble to explain the real world. His particular mind to explain those business cycles arose by crisis in order to understand its sprits.

Thorstein Veblen, who was at the University of Chicago during Mitchell's period there, doubtless had much to do with stimulating Mitchell's interest in process and dynamic change. One of Veblen's chief criticism of 'orthodox' economics was that it was not an 'evolutionary science', that it did not deal with the problem of 'cumulative' change. (Friedman, 1950, p. 467).

At that point the dichotomy of industry-enterprise comes to the scene. The tendency of economics life is to push the business cycles in favor of enterprise. Because all habits of enterprise owners' aim to raise their profits. The time he lived was the primary era of rise of capitalism. It is no surprise that the instincts of industry would allow to realize its tendencies. Ruling of all economic life enterprises were playing great roles even causing 'sabotage' what Veblen suggests. This is the most exclusive part of Mitchell to separate from neoclassical statistical mind. The orthodox theory namely, neoclassical theory tries to adjust its hypothesis to the reality, on the contrary Mitchell's view finds the reality with the great help of statistics.

The post-World War II interpretation of Burns and Mitchell's program at the National Bureau of Economic Research (NBER) emphasized the dynamics of "aggregate economic activity," rather than "many economic activities." Consequently, the representation of a 'general' business cycle by a single set of dates marking its peaks and troughs-the 'refence cycle' -is accepted by economists and government agencies everywhere in the world. [...] Mitchell's 'grand design' was for a comprehensive institutional explanation of economics behavior, derived from a critical, quantitatively based examination of all existing theory. It was the latter that implied Mitchell's investigations of business cycles as an 'unintended consequence' of the institutional conditioning of the thoughts and actions of individuals into common patterns. (Rutherford, 1987, 64-66; Epstein, 1999, p. 525, 527).

The main purpose of why NBER was founded in order to understand how economics, specifically USA economy, makes the picks and downs work. If the business cycles can be understood well, there would be a chance for an institute to urge for institutional change. Unless, institutional economics could have made a steady theory, Mitchell's great design was a rational theory that would have been accepted in order to understand how economics' picks and downs affect all economics design. Mitchell, also states endogenous effects cause this business cycles. Mitchell's or generally institutionalists interested in how this business cycle can go up and down by the mediation of external shocks sourced by the institutions of capitalism.

A Journey From OIE to NIE

NIE cannot be seen as a continuation of OIE. It has many different points than OIE, mostly epistemological and political. After World War II mainstream economics is seen as neoclassical economics. Here, econometric techniques are utilized to measure theoretical models. The measuring models are divided into two empirical parts, microeconomics and macroeconomics. Microeconomics mostly deals with competitive market equilibrium, with and without uncertainty, market imperfections, on firms' behavior and market performance. Macroeconomics uses econometric models to follow economic activity, income, consumption, investment, inflation, unemployment and economic growth (Joskow, 2008, 1). NIE is a flow that meets with mainstream economics but separating its criticized points. NIE is not mainstream economics, but it is not a continuation of OIE as well. The most common notion it shares with OIE is the term 'institution'. Aside from this common term, NIE is an opposition to OIE which has not played a pioneer role in the Great Depression. Of course, there has been years between OIE and NIE. So, when can NIE be started? B How OIE can be described by its original names in this study; NIE is a large-scale glance, so NIE will be scrutinized by Oliver Williamson (1932-), Ronald Coase (1910-2013), Douglass North (1920-2015).

The first use of the term NIE dates back 1975 when Oliver Williamson first described it. There are several contributors of NIE. Ronald Coase, Fredrich von Hayek, Alfred D. Chandler, Herbert A. Simon, Kenneth Arrow, Douglas C. North, Alchian and Demzets. But, the most important contributors of NIE are Commons, Williamson and North. So, if there will be a summary of what certain minds they have submitted to NIE, it can be aggregated at certain points, methodological individualism, bounded rationality, transaction costs etc.

NIE has started with the definition of Williamson, the first point to look must be his analytical framework. Williamson identifies four interrelated levels of institutional economics. The first level is *embeddedness, social* or *cultural foundations*. It includes informal institutions, customs, traditions, ethics, social norms, religion and some aspect of language and cognition (Joskow, 2008, p. 7). This level can be determined the common aspect of OIE, especially as Veblen's thought. Because all this cultural embeddedness is the key point of OIE. All customs and traditions, social forms etc. are the part of the society.

The second is *basic institutional environment*. Williamson calls this level as 'the formal rules of the game.' This second level covers constitutions, political systems, basic human rights, property rights, laws, courts, human rights, money, basic financial institutions etc. (Joskow, 2008, p. 7). It is no doubt that economics is also a game. Albeit, the simple definition of economics is to meet demand and supply, these events have different kinds of stages embedded into each other. Economics needs formal rules. In any case, the formal rules help to proceed the economics more equal to parties. Today, calling economics reminds everyone as capitalism. Capitalism's the first and the most important rule is property rights. So, this basic institutional environment helps economics property to proceed its basic necessity. The third level what Williamson said is institutions of governance.

Basic institutional environment, like competitive markets are proceeded by institutional (governance) arrangements. These arrangements can cover individual trade goods, services, the vertical and horizontal structure of business firms. The country's basic economic conditions are very important to govern the basic institutional environment (Joskow, 2008, p. 8).

The governance of county determines of its economics environment. The more democratic a country is, the more it has an extensive relationship with the administration of that country. The governance of a country becomes more democratic where arrangements are confident, rapport and extensive to economy. It means that economics circulation flows more easily.

The last level of Williamson is *short-term resource allocation (neoclassical market economy). This level refers to the day to day operation of the economy given the institutions defined at the other three level. Prices, wages, costs and quantities bought and sold are determined here as are the consequences of monopoly, oligopoly, and other neoclassical market imperfections.* (Joskow, 2008, p. 8).

From this aspect, discussions of institutionalization extend to social psychology, sociology and liberal theory. O. Williamson classifies the level of institutionalization similar to the stages of liberal society foreseen by Commons. As for Commons contract making, the regulation of evaluation operations of administrative structures and economic activities, institutional constraints regulating power relations are called as the building process of the positive political theory and the governance structure in Williamson's transaction cost approach (1975). Both Williamson's and Commons' institutions are similar in terms of the function of shaping individual behavior. (Orhan, 2016, p. 194).

Williamson's and Commons' similarity can be understood by the nature of capitalism. The nature of capitalism is based on free property rights and confidence on the property. Williamson's transaction cost is a guarantee to sustainable production. Confidential resource allocation and its assurance of parliamentary system are the necessities of property rights and nature of capitalism. According to Commons, confirming legal rules and its supporter of free constitutional rights are the nature of capitalism. So, Commons can be alleged by the trigger of the main notions initially of NIE.

The question 'What is a firm' may be one of the hardest question that NIE is seeking to answer. One who follows the answer must firstly seek for three different steps, what is going on with a firm? *First, the question of the nature and boundaries of the firm. Why are some transactions internalized and externalized at the same time? Second, the question of the internal structure of the firm. How is the firm organized? How is production organized? What incentives, controls, internal hierarchies exist? Third, the question of the relations between firms and the market. Are firms a substitute for the market? What are the limits of the firms?" All these questions about what is going on with a firm has been initially asked by Ronald Coase (1937) and since the beginning of the 1970s, numerous attention has been noticed increasingly. Coase's (1937) seminal article "points out of contractual decisions.* (Garrouste & Saussier, 2008, pp. 23, 24). Coase's firm idea was not based upon precise definition of what kind of duty a firm undertakes in the market. So, there are four different features to be counted to define the duty of the firm. These are *bounded rationality, uncertainty, institutional environment, different characteristics between markets' and firms'.*

Each transaction yields costs (called 'transaction costs') because the parties need to obtain information, negotiate the terms of the exchange, and enforce agreements. Consequently, the contractors' main objective is to organize the transactions in such a way as to economize on transaction costs. (Gonzales-Diaz & Vazques, 2008, p. 256).

New Institutional Economics (NIE) studies institutions and how institutions interact with organizational arrangements. Institutions are the written and unwritten rules, norms and constraints that human devise to reduce uncertainty and control their environment. (Menard & Shirley, 2005, p. 1).

Although, there is a conflict on whether NIE stands close to neoclassical economics at some certain points, there are lots of differences from neoclassical economics. NIE has an opponent, the assumption of perfect information, rational choices and transactions are costless. NIE has beaten the obsession about perfect information that is to accept people have lack of full information. This incomplete information is supported by unbounded rationality. It means people have unbounded rationality that allows them to make decisions with incomplete information. All institutions are created, or any other formal and informal institutions are created by mankind in order to reduce the risk and transaction costs. In other words, with every institution that any society either written or unwritten make, the society tends to an appropriate path.

Choices are embedded in institutions. This case is underestimated by neoclassical economics. Prices and outcomes are more welcome to deal with in NIE than neoclassical economics. NIE meets to investigate sociology, anthropology, political scientists etc. The reason of this is, many scholars all around the world in different kinds of fields are doing research in NIE. The wide range of assumptions can be found in different fields. According to Ronald Coase, mainstream economics which is called by him "microeconomics" has been going its path without any change. Economists have still been going investigating how demand and supply affect the prices. The issue here, they are doing it by which goods and services are being traded in the market and doing without the factors' priced. The simplest condition of economics is exchange. At that point, according to Adam Smith, the productivity of an economics is related to division of labor. The less transaction costs are available the more exchange is done. The transaction costs are depended on the institutions of that economics like law system, political system, human system, education system, culture system etc. The fact is what controls economics performance is the institutions and the reason why NIE is so important in terms of economists (Coase, 2016, 7-9).

According to North, beliefs are the first process of economics change. Because, it is an institution. Also, beliefs are separated either broadly held within the society or reflecting fundamental divisions in perception about society. After the marginalist revolution, neoclassical economics has put of the institution, institutions have been started to investigate by Veblen, Commons, Mitchell. Nonetheless, this situation has been altered by Coase, North and Williamson, because, one of the analysis tools of neoclassical economics is the firm described as an institution. The one important aim of the firm is not unlike neoclassical economics claims, minimization of the cost, but transaction costs minimization (Çetin, 2016, 11).

What North tries to understand is the long-term performance of formal and informal institutions have a long-term effect of economic growth. Using both formal and informal institutions must have added by NIE in order to seek for neoclassical economics that sees as a closed box. Here, the most important difference between OIE and NIE, the latter tries to understand economics by developing a methodology barely on what neoclassical economics lacks. While neoclassical economics is focused on how a market proceeds rather than how it develops, NIE is focused on how the relationship is developed as designed by institutions (Çetin, 2016, p. 12). NIE is popular both in institutionalism and in orthodoxy. Because, NIE rejects instrumental rationality so they are institutionalist; accepts orthodox scarcity and competition so they are blamed not to deviate neoclassical economics. Even today, NIE has been changing. Started since 1930s till 2015 NIE has been mentioned as NIE. However, the great contribution of transaction costs by Coase has started to use organizational theory by Williamson pushed the rename of NIE. After changing its name as IOEA-Institutional and Organizational Economics Academic of ESNIE-European School of New Institutional Economics, NIE is now Institutional Organizational Economics-IOE.

What an author must understand from 'institution?' Generally, institution is the rule of the game. In economy, there are not only institutions, but also organizations exist too. Organizations are the players of the game. How a sport game cannot be played without rules, economics must be played by its rules as such. In other words, institutions help the quality of the game or economic performance (Çetin, 2016, p. 13). Institutions guide to describe certain decisions on certain actors and help them to use the instincts which maximize the prosperity. Although, organizations are the players, not individuals' purpose per se. All structures like economical, political, legal or bureaucratic constructions constituted by the individuals through a mutual aim. For instance, constitution is an institution, constitution court is an organization (North, 200; Çetin, 2016, p.14).

NIE has both common points with neoclassical economics and different points with it. NIE is essentially using three assumptions. These assumptions are the key points of whether it is NIE or not. Those are 'bounded rationality', 'transaction costs', 'methodological individualism.' One important difference between OIE and NIE is the methodology of investigating economics events. OIE looks all economics events in a holistic methodology. It means while institutions are put in the center of investigation, whole economy is seen to surpass the system. Institutions are the drivers of the economy. It determines all actions and decisions made by the players of the economy. On the contrast of this holistic manner, NIE is firstly focused on 'individuals.' Then it turns to the institutions. It means that the first determiner of any economics is an individual. So, this is 'methodological individualism.'

A middle way alternative exists (Institutional Individualism) and is being used by well- known institutionalists, both in the new and the old-or-original style traditions. [...] All models and theories in the social sciences are, of course, theory-laden to some extent due to the analytical categories, assumptions, rules and criteria adopted by the re searchers in order to build their neoclassical, marxian, new institutional, old institutional, etc. analyses (or even so hybrid ones). (Toboso, 2013, pp. 103, 104).

Naturally, NIE closes to theory-laden analysis, it is claimed that its methodological pose is very close to neoclassical economics, but of course not the very same glance. Because all its assumptions 'methodological individualism' can be felt less or more.

As readers of this journal are undoubtedly aware, OIE adherents believe that NIE accords individual agents far too much scope as regards the creation, maintenance, and modification of institutions, and that herein NIE adherents downplay the fundamental roles of culture and power. OIE does not take individuals as "given." Individuals do not simply create institutions in an institution-free, supracultural "state of nature." Rather, through "reconstitutive downward causation," institutions profoundly affect individuals (Hodgson 2000, 2004; Mayhew 1989; Staden & Bruce, 2015, pp. 112).

The unwieldly adjective, 'methodological' is needed to distinguish the concerns of constructing positive theory from the normative and policy implications wrapped up in the term, 'individualism.' The distinction is not easy to keep clear, and the temptation to join methodology and ideology is strong. (Arrow, 2001, p. 1).

Certainly, methodological individualism of NIE allows it to describe new notions presented to economics literature. Also, these notions make the NIE methodology different than the neoclassical economics. In neoclassical economics, as it is known well that human's actions are rational, humans are the core of the economics action. Surely, humans' actions are very important in NIE too. Nevertheless, in NIE people are accepted not as rational as it ought to be. People's preferences, people's choices become a part of economics activity. At that point, people are expected to act not fully rational, but with bounded rationality.

Bounded Rationality

Neoclassical economics is based perfectly rational upon people to maximize their benefits. Every individual can observe the world, knows perfect knowledge about choices, make costless decisions about the consequences they have chosen (Kreps, 1990, 745). Knight separates the uncertainty and risk from each other. Under the circumstances' uncertainty, decisions can be related by finite events. Under the circumstances' risk, expected values can be calculated and applied for the traditional decisions and choice making. So, Herbert Simon put a new term forward given there are some issues in theory. The new term is aroused by 'bounded rationality.' Simon suggest that using *satisfaction* rather than *maximizing the benefit*. Because all individuals try to get maximizing satisfaction. This is all about our minds not only bound to our budget.

While bounded rationality is discussed within the relationship of property rights and transaction costs in both Coase and Williamson's approaches, economy requires institutional changes due to bounded rationality in North's approach. Transaction costs will be reduced. In this way, development performance of an economy will increase. (Orhan, 2016, p. 203).

One other important notion declared by NIE is transaction costs. Since this notion has first arose, it helped to understand better why firms are in the market. Their only source of existence become more popular than the price mechanism. With this great contribution of firms in economics, firms have realized their importance greater. Ronald Coase explains this circular with these words,

The economic system "works itself." This does not mean that there is no planning by individuals. These exercise foresight and choose between alternatives. This is necessarily so if there is to be order in the system. But this theory assumes that the direction of resources is dependent directly on the price mechanism. Indeed, it is often considered to be an objection to economic planning that it merely tries to do what is already done by the price mechanism. (Coase, 1937, p. 387).

Transaction Costs

Transaction costs have been won by Ronald Coase (1937). He asks if market conditions proceed under the perfect competition and there are no costs to produce, why would anyone else undertake the production rather than a firm? If all markets were efficient and costless, there would be no firm exist. For Hodgson, institutions are embedded and frame the functioning markets. Because, he doesn't ask "how do price equilibration market process produce efficient economic outcomes." He asks "how does learning, habits and routines, technological change, and economic development define economic outcomes, and determine the very nature of efficiency and well-being?" (Davis, 2012, p. 264).

The comprehensive difference between America and Europe shows itself how it is practice and how professional academic economists behave (Frey & Eichenberger, 1993, p. 185). As a conclusion of this formation, especially OIE has come into leaf in USA. Additionally, the understanding of NIE has some differences in both continents in some ways. USA, as the most capitalist country, is the birthplace of institutionalism.

Coase made a revolution especially in microeconomics. Because the first question he asked about the price mechanism have made to understand the relation between production and market *reflected in transactions which would eventually determine the behavior of economic agents, especially companies (Coase, 1937). Transaction costs are in the center of the organization both regarding intra and inter-company costs. [...] the use of the market by productive organization is inevitable, as pointed by Coase (1937); otherwise, the company would be able to solve all its productive problems internally (full vertical integration); nonetheless, transaction costs would not be completely eliminated. (Pereira & Lopes, 2018, p. 460).*

Determining the norms of the economics is very important. Because, as North, the other prominent representative of NIE norms is the rules of the game. Apparently, every game has players. Playing with the good team members or bad team members will determine the end of the game. So do economics players.

Norms are everywhere and we come across with them every day. Because, whether a person switch the TV on, he/she may encounter with a politician who discuss about the next elections or tax regimes applied by the government etc. Norms on the other hand govern our political and social lives. In politics, they appear as informal norms to protect civil rights and civil liberties (Axelrood, 1986, p. 1095). Of course, in economics norms are tougher to describe because economics seems more complicated than norms. Graphs, models, equations etc. are seen in every textbook. The truth is, economics is beyond these mathematical formulations. It is all about human. Human doesn't exist in formulations. As appropriate as to the soul of human, it developed different kinds of norms which are coherent with her/his nature. All these norms are also determined the rules of economics.

Especially, if we talk about capitalism norms have gained to attribute more attention to norms. All these naturally are seen as expectations or values of a behavior. *Definitions based upon expectations or values are favored by those who study norms as they exist in a given social setting. Such definitions are convenient because interviews can elicit the beliefs and values of the participants, whereas systematically observing their actual behavior is more difficult. (Axelord, 1986, p. 1097).*

The relationship between economics and law set by Coase brings different constraint, which has not previously been in mainstream approach, into economic behavior in all economic systems, models and economic politics. [...] On the other hand, based on North's method and NIE approach institutions are the rules of the game which increase the developmental performance of economy. Formal and informal rules provide the institutional change process in market games and improve the performance of economy. According to North's approach institutions are the actors and rules of the game. Institutionalization process is provided by formal and informal rules consisting of culture affecting individual's market behavior, ideology, mental models and social representations, value systems, norms and laws. In this respect North stands at the crossroads between economics and social psychology, anthropology and political science. (Orhan, 2016, p. 197).

One of the main differences between OIE and NIE is about psychology. Psychology has a key role for the individual's behavior. *Conspicuous consumption* is, for instance, a good example of psychology. Because, especially poor people try to emulate the wealthy people. The wealthy people try to show their wealth to other people. Nevertheless, NIE disputes psychology directly. This situation is being discussed by formal and informal rules and norms.

North, particularly states that institutions are not people, but also institutions are aroused and evolved the conclusion of the interaction of individuals. Also, institutions are customs and rules for individuals (North, 1986, p. 231). Institutions are hand-made. All institutions are the reflection of human necessities. Norms and customs shape these necessities. People economically try to maximize their utility. Such as how an organization is available to transaction costs to find the right information in the market, individuals use these norms and customs like transaction costs in order to make their utility to be maximized.

Albeit NIE sometimes is blamed by resembling neoclassical economics, but the truth is NIE is differentiated at certain points than neoclassical economics. Firstly, neoclassical economics uses scarcity and competition. Secondly, neoclassical economics uses rationality and full-information assumption. NIE differs from neoclassical economics at that point. Because NIE uses bounded rationality and rejects full-information assumption. Instead of these assumptions of neoclassical economics would rather use bounded rationality, transaction costs, missing contract, property rights, opportunism etc. However, it must be remembered that accepting these assumptions makes NIE totally different than OIE. NIE tries to find explanations about institutional and economic change. Also, organizational structure allows NIE to use game theory to sociology which is ignored by neoclassical theory. Thus, NIE has a wide-range aspect including anthropology to politics; sociology to law.

One important point between OIE and NIE in terms of institutions declares in informal and formal institutions. Although, it is no doubt that one common point cannot be rejected sharing between NIE and OIE is 'institution' term, OIE has used the informal rules in its analysis. However, this informal rule cannot be proved empirically and individuals' behavior is accepted as irrational.

Essentially, the behavior of individuals must not be accepted irrational to some degree. It has rationality in its integrity. Because, OIE is at the time of the highest peak of the capitalism in USA. In that case, people tend to make their profit/benefit to be maximized. They have found to emulate to one step higher class to make their behavior rational. Though, most of them were unable to maximize their profit/benefit high.

Briefly, from the early beginning of the 20th Century to 21th Century two different economics trends occupied an eminent place in history of economics. Many economics trends follow the path of criticizing capitalism with different aspects. Interestingly, OIE has started this criticizing in the core of the capitalism, USA. While doing this criticism, OIE has used a very clever one. Combing with economics and sociology, socio-economics. Naturally, the era when OIE has first started give an opportunity to make this criticism in a way that not includes a left-side glance. While OIE was being developed, OIE allowed creating a new approach, NIE. Aside sharing 'institutional' term, neither OIE nor NIE shares common points. Nevertheless, OIE helped to generate NIE for some extent by the mediation of OIE's great philosophers.

SOLUTIONS AND RECOMMENDATIONS

Economic thought has revolutionary history in its own. Every economic flow allege its own solutions to make the economy better. Naturally, each of them has different arguments on how economics works and proceeds. All of them have different ideas to solve the problem occurred in economics. However, few of them made very different solutions than institutional economics. The main reason why institutional economics achieved this goal is that being a heterodox school. Nevertheless, NIE is far different than OIE. NIE creates very new notions make available to be seen the adverse effects of neoclassical economics. By creating new notions and to be seen many terms more effective than it used to be (like transaction costs etc.), NIE subrogate the neoclassical economics. Unlike NIE, OIE has begun criticizing from the very beginning. The distinctive point of OIE is to display that "individuals are the product of the society they live in; even they change the rules of society this so." (Chang, 2016, p. 141).

The author's point here, the current economics understanding can be changed to be involved in different voices of economics. Involving individuals' economics more will make the society's structure become better. Consequently, if a powerful economics is desired, strong institutions must be founded to have a strong economics.

FUTURE RESEARCH DIRECTIONS

Since neoliberalism arose, the world of economics became a very formidable area. The unbalance of economics ruined always as disadvantageous for developing countries. Nevertheless, it does not mean that developed countries could not have affected by this ruin. Every country all around the world receives a share less or more of the deterioration. So, how every heterodox approach criticizes neoclassical economics, which is the main idea of neoliberalism, should be heard more. Different kinds of thoughts of schools must be added to economics management. Although, it seems that some economics schools lose its validity, it is not entirely true. Because, every economics thought has followed successively one another and suggest a different solution to solve the economics issues. Some of them are embedded in each other. OIE was one of them, which achieved a criticism of capitalism and its relationship between people in the main country, the USA and the very rising era.

Besides, NIE achieved criticizing neoclassical economics with new notions that is seen problematic in mainstream economics. Consequently, if either developing countries economics management or developed countries management would like to give better condition of life, they must have added different voices thoughts of economics in their economics management. Because, one solution which could have found by one economic approach, will be found by another.

CONCULUSION

In this study, the author tries to display where and how institutionalism is born and developed. As a heterodox approach institutional economics divides into two sections, OIE and NIE. This scrutinizes how these schools emerged. Obviously, both OIE and NIE are required to be analyzed more deeply, but the aim of this study do not cover to examination of the topic deeply. Because, these two schools were emerged by other heterodox schools in themselves. It is impossible to scrutinize all of them. Thus, institutional economics tries to scrutinize firstly OIE by the mediation of Veblen, Mitchell, Commons. Veblen stressfully emphasized that instinct, habit, belief are profoundly embedded in economics action. All of them create human actions and these actions will conclude with institutions. Naturally, these institutions like firm's rules, traditions etc. are shaped by social environment. Mitchell focuses on statistical approach, however rather different way of neoclassical economics. What he tries to do is to make a combination between business cycles and institutions. Commons gives importance to laws. He makes a relationship between the power of laws on economics actions. After the fall of OIE, in the beginning of 1980's, NIE has emerged by North, Coase and Williamson. NIE focuses on institutions different from OIE; NIE believes that institutions arose by the individuals conscious preferences. The most important notions declared by NIE are transaction costs, property rights and bounded rationality.

Briefly, institutionalism is important for any economics. Institutions must be merged into economics management. Either OIE or NIE institutions have vital role for economics.

REFERENCES

Arrow, K. J. (1994). *Methodological Individualism and Social Knowledge. The American Economic Review*, *84*(2), 1–9.

Avio, K. L. (2004). A modest proposal for institutional economics. *Journal of Economic Issues*, *38*(3), 715–745. doi:10.1080/00213624.2004.11506726

Axelrod, R. (1986). An evolutionary approach to norms. *The American Political Science Review*, *80*(4), 1095–1111. doi:10.1017/S0003055400185016

Ayres, C. E. (1977). In memoriam Clarence Ayres. *Journal of Economic Issues, 11*(3), 475–483. doi:10.1080/00213624.1977.11503458

Baş-Dinar, G. (2014). Wesley Mitchell'ın İktisat Bilimine Katkısı Üzerine Bir Değerlendirme [An Evolution on Wesley Mitchell to Economics Science]. *İktisat ve Toplum. Economics and Society, 46*, 59–68.

Çetin, T. (2016). Kurumsal ve Organizasyonel İktisat Üzerine [On Institutional and Organizational Economics]. *İktisat ve Toplum. Economics and Society, 64*, 10–19.

Chang, H. J. (2016). *Ekonomi Rehberi* [Economy Guide]. Ankara, Turkey: Say Yayınları. [Say Publishing]

Coase, R. H. (1991). The institutional structure of production. *The American Economic Review, 82*(4), 713–719.

Coase, R. H. (2005). The Institutional Structure of Production. In C. Ménard & M. M. Shirley (Eds.), Handbook of New Institutional Economics (31-40). Springer, The Netherlands. doi:10.1007/0-387-25092-1_3

Davis, J. B. (2012). The 2012 Veblen-Commons award recipient, Geoffrey M. Hodgson. *Journal of Economic Issues, 46*(2), 263–264. doi:10.2753/JEI0021-3624460201

Epstein, P. (1999). Wesley Mitchell's grand design and its critics, the theory and measurement of business cycles. *Journal of Economic Issues, 33*(3), 525–553. doi:10.1080/00213624.1999.11506185

Friedman, M. (1950). Wesley C. Mitchell as an Economic Theorist. *Journal of Political Economy, 58*(6), 465–493. doi:10.1086/257011

Furubotn, E. G., & Pejovich, S. (1972). Property rights and economic theory, a survey of recent literature. *Journal of Economic Literature, 10*(4), 1137–1162.

Garroste, P., & Saussier, S. (2008). The theories of the firm. In *E. Brousseau & J. M. Glachant* (Eds.), N. I. Economics A Guidebook (pp. 23–36). Cambridge, UK: Cambridge University Press.

Ginzbergz, E. (1997). Wesley Mitchell. *History of Political Economy, 29*(3), 371–390. doi:10.1215/00182702-29-3-371

Hansen, A. H. (1949). Wesley Mitchell, social scientist and social counselor. *The Review of Economics and Statistics, 31*(4), 245–255. doi:10.2307/1928646

Hlasny, V. (2008). Veblen's and Mitchell's profit theory of business cycles. *Ewha Journal of Social Sciences, 20*(2), 1–28.

Hodgson, G. M. (1998). On the evolution of Thorstein Veblen's evolutionary economics. *Cambridge Journal of Economics, 22*(4), 415–431. doi:10.1093/oxfordjournals.cje.a013726

Hodgson, G. M. (2006). What are institutions? *Journal of Economic Issues, 40*(1), 1–25. doi:10.1080/00213624.2006.11506879

Hodgson, G. M. (2008). How Veblen generalized Darwinism. *Journal of Economic Issues, 42*(2), 399–405. doi:10.1080/00213624.2008.11507148

Joskow, P. L. (2008). Introduction to New Institutional Economics, A Report Card. In E. Brousseau & J. M. Glachant (Eds.), New Institutional Economics A Guidebook (1-20). Cambridge, UK: Cambridge University Press.

Kilpinen, E. (2003). Clarence Ayres memorial lecture Does pragmatism imply institutionalism? *Journal of Economic Issues*, *37*(2), 291–304. doi:10.1080/00213624.2003.11506576

Marangos, J. (2018). The 2018 Clarence Ayres scholar An institutional riposte to the "After the Washington consensus". *Journal of Economic Issues*, *52*(2), 323–335. doi:10.1080/00213624.2018.1469856

McFarling, B. R. (2004). The Clarence Ayres memorial lecture, An institutionalist reconstruction of culture. *Journal of Economic Issues*, *38*(2), 339–352. doi:10.1080/00213624.2004.11506693

Ménard, C. & Shirley, M. M. (2005). Introduction. In C. Ménard & M. M. Shirley (Eds.), Handbook of New Institutional Economics (1-20). Springer, The Netherlands.

North, D. (2005). Institutions and the performance of economies over time. In C. Ménard & M. M. Shirley (Eds.), Handbook of New Institutional Economics (21-30). Springer, The Netherlands. doi:10.1007/0-387-25092-1_2

O'Hara, P. A. (2002). The contemporary relevance of Thorstein Veblen's institutional-evolutionary political economy. *History of Economics Review*, *35*(1), 78–103. doi:10.1080/10370196.2002.11733370

Önder, İ. (2015). Thorstein Veblen, Çok Yönlü Bir İktisatçı. [Thorstein Veblen, a well-rounded economist] In A. Öncü (Ed.), *Thorstein Veblen Kullanım Kılavuzu* [User's Guide for Thorstein Veblen]. (pp. 55–80). İstanbul, Turkey: Habitus.

Orhan, S. S. (2016). In the new institutional economics approach R. Coase and Law, D. North and social psychology context, pluralist approach opportunities in economics. *Sosyoekonomi*, *24*(28), 189–208. doi:10.17233e.88088

Özveren, E. (2007). Kurumsal İktisat, Aralanan Karakutu. [Institutional Economics, Spacing Blackbox] In E. Özveren (Ed.), *Kurumsal İktisat* [Institutional Economics]. (pp. 15–44). Ankara, Turkey: İmge Yayınevi. [İmage Publishing]

Pereira, A. D., & Lopes, H. C. (2018). The market for the "old" and the "new" institutional economics. *Brazilian Journal of Political Economy*, *38*(3), 450–468. doi:10.1590/0101-35172018-2774

Perelman, M. (2015). Thorstein Veblen, Bir Amerikalı İktisat Perspektifi. [Thorstein Veblen, An American Economics Perspective] In A. Öncü (Ed.), *Thorstein Veblen Kullanım Kılavuzu* [User's Guide for Thorstein Veblen]. (pp. 27–54). İstanbul, Turkey: Habitus.

Pham, C. (1976). Clarence E. Ayres on the "Market System", A Note. *Journal of Economic Issues*, *10*(3), 688–694. doi:10.1080/00213624.1976.11503371

Pirgan-Matur, E. (2007). Kurumsal İktisat Açısından Firma Kuramı. [Firm theory in terms of institutional economics] In E. Özveren (Ed.), *Kurumsal İktisat* [Institutional Economics]. (pp. 283–308). Ankara, Turkey: İmge Yayınevi. [İmge Publishing]

Rutherford, M. (1998). Veblen's evolutionary programme, a promise unfulfilled. *Cambridge Journal of Economics*, *22*(4), 463–477. doi:10.1093/oxfordjournals.cje.a013729

Rutherford, M. (2000). Intuitionalism between the wars. *Journal of Economic Issues*, *34*(2), 291–303. doi:10.1080/00213624.2000.11506267

Rutherford, M. (2001). Institutional economics, then and now. *The Journal of Economic Perspectives*, *15*(3), 173–194. doi:10.1257/jep.15.3.173

Şenalp, M. G. (2007). Dünden Bugüne Kurumsal İktisat. [Institutional Economics from yesterday till today] In E. Özveren (Ed.), *Kurumsal İktisat* [Institutional Economics]. (pp. 45–92). Ankara, Turkey: İmge Yayınevi. [İmge Publishing]

Sherman, H. (2001). The business cycle theory of Wesley Mitchell. *Journal of Economic Issues*, *35*(1), 85–97. doi:10.1080/00213624.2001.11506341

Spithoven, A. (2019). Similarities and dissimilarities between original and institutional economic and new institutional economics. *Journal of Economic Issues*, *53*(2), 440–447. doi:10.1080/00213624.2019.1594532

Tilman, R. (1985). The Utopian vision of Edward Bellamy and Thorstein Veblen. *Journal of Economic Issues*, *19*(4), 879–898. doi:10.1080/00213624.1985.11504441

Tilman, R. (1990). New light on John Dewey, Clarence Ayres, and the development of Evolutionary Economics. *Journal of Economic Issues*, *24*(4), 963–979. doi:10.1080/00213624.1990.11505096

Toboso, F. (2013). Methodological developments in the Old and the new institutional economics. *History of Economic Ideas*, *21*(1), 77–115.

Williamson, O. E. (2005). Transaction cost economics. In C. Ménard & M. M. Shirley (Eds.), Handbook of New Institutional Economics (41-68). Springer, The Netherlands.

Zingler, E. K. (1974). Veblen vs. Commons, A comparative evaluation. *Kyklos*, *27*(2), 322–344. doi:10.1111/j.1467-6435.1974.tb01909.x

KEY TERMS AND DEFINITIONS

Bounded Rationality: Unlike neoclassical mind, NIE believes that people act restricted knowledge in their economics action.

New Institutional Economics (NIE): An economics approach analyzing how human's conscious preferences emerged.

North, Coase, Williamson: The first important philosophers of NIE.

Old Institutional Economics (OIE): An economics approach criticizing capitalism in terms of economics and sociology in the early beginning of the 20th Century.

Property Rights: The owner of a property can be done by this. Economically, what kind of economics model, technology of production can be done.

Transaction Costs: Although, there is only cost in neoclassical economics. However, NIE sees this cost as a matter of fact that organizing our economics actions.

Veblen, Commons, Mitchell: The first important philosophers of OIE.

Chapter 2
Re-Thinking the Role of Institutions in Neoliberalism From New Institutional Economics Perspective

Ilke Civelekoglu
https://orcid.org/0000-0001-8892-0802
Istanbul Ticaret University, Turkey

Basak Ozoral
https://orcid.org/0000-0003-3075-6362
Istanbul Ticaret University, Turkey

ABSTRACT

In an attempt to discuss neoliberalism with a reference to new institutional economics, this chapter problematizes the role of formal institutions in the neoliberal age by focusing on a specific type of formal institution, namely property rights in developing countries. New institutional economics (NIE) argues that secure property rights are important as they guarantee investments and thus, promote economic growth. This chapter discusses why the protection of property rights is weak and ineffective in certain developing countries despite their endorsement of neoliberalism by shedding light on the link between the institutional structure of the state and neoliberalism in the developing world. With the political economy perspective, the chapter aims to build a bridge between NIE and political economy, and thereby providing fertile ground for the advancement of NIE.

INTRODUCTION

In this chapter, we address the decay of formal institutions in neoliberalism, with a focus on property rights; and discuss why protection of property rights is weak and ineffective in certain developing countries that have embraced neoliberalism. In contrast to the existing literature that associates economic development

DOI: 10.4018/978-1-7998-0333-1.ch002

Copyright © 2020, IGI Global. Copying or distributing in print or electronic forms without written permission of IGI Global is prohibited.

with democracy (Przeworski et al., 2000; Acemoğlu & Robinson, 2012), we argue that neoliberalism can coexist with autocratic regimes. This coexistence, however, substantially transforms the role of formal institutions in authoritarian neoliberal countries in the developing world as these institutions become political tools to control the society and defend the economic interests of the ruling elites. We claim that "property rights" -one of the most essential concepts of New Institutional Economics (NIE)- will not be an exception to the rule and thus, they will be severely eroded in authoritarian neoliberal states (1). Since capitalism lies on property rights, and competition and pursuit of individual interest, this chapter highlights the inherent contradiction between the core features of capitalism and policies of authoritarian neoliberal states in the developing world.

It should be noted that this chapter limits itself to the analysis of a specific type of formal institution, namely property rights. It aims to demonstrate why property rights are violated by power holders in developing countries that are authoritarian and neoliberal at the expense of generating undesirable outcomes, such as corruption, low efficiency and capital flight. With its political economy perspective, the chapter provides a new insight into the role and functioning of formal institutions. Thus, it intends to build a bridge between NIE and political economy, thereby providing a fertile ground for the advancement of NIE. Moreover, by focusing on the institutional structure of developing countries as opposed to a few selected developed countries as in most of the existing NIE research, the chapter contributes empirically to the existing NIE literature.

In pursuit of its goals, this chapter is divided into four sections. The following section briefly reviews the role of institutions and their impact on economic growth and development in NIE literature. It also discusses why secure property rights are important for robust economic performance and it sheds light on the critical role of the state in enforcement of property rights, from the new institutionalist perspective. The second section unpacks the link between neoliberalism and political regimes in the developing world by discussing the rise of a certain type of state, known as the authoritarian neoliberal states. The third section provides a discussion on a specific type of formal institution, namely property rights, to problematize the role of formal institutions in the neoliberal age in the light of NIE thinking. The section discusses the current status of property rights with reference to several authoritarian neoliberal country cases, ranging from Russia to China, and to Indonesia. Basically, it demonstrates why secure property rights are lacking in these countries. The fourth section suggests future research directions in the NIE with regard to the protection of property rights under neoliberal authoritarian states in the forthcoming period. Finally, the chapter concludes by reminding that developing countries, which combine authoritarianism with neoliberalism can achieve economic growth. These countries, however, will be prone to economic stagnation in the medium and long run.

BACKGROUND: INSTITUTIONS IN NEW INSTITUTIONAL ECONOMICS

In simple terms, NIE aims to explain what institutions are, how they arise, what purposes they serve, how they change and how they can be reformed (Klein, 1998). It diverges from neoclassical assumptions by arguing that individuals have incomplete information and bound by rationality. Thus, for new institutionalists, individuals create institutions to reduce the risk stemming from uncertainty about unforeseen events and outcomes, and to lower the transaction costs induced by efforts to acquire information (Menard & Shirley, 2005). While NIE borrows from various social science disciplines, such as law, sociology, anthropology and political science, its primary language is economics.

Following North (1990, p. 3), most NIE scholars define institutions as the effective "rules of the game" in a society. Individuals and their organizations, on the other hand, are the "players of the game". The rules of the game and their enforcement mechanisms create constraints and incentives that shape the behavior of decision makers. Hence, they serve as reference points for human interaction. NIE studies not only formal institutions (rules, regulations, laws etc.) but also informal institutions (corresponding to social norms, beliefs and conventions). After all, for new institutionalists, the performance of a market economy depends on both the formal and informal institutions given their role in facilitating private transactions and cooperative behavior (Menard & Shirley, 2005).

If institutions are so critical for a healthy functioning market economy, then how do we ensure that we have the 'right' set of institutions for economic prosperity in a country? After all, North (2005, p. 67) tells us that variations in performance of economies can be linked to institutional structures existing in these countries. Acemoğlu and Robinson (2012) highlight what sort of political and economic institutions matter for prosperity. Accordingly, political institutions that distribute power broadly in the society, and subject it to constraints, coupled with economic institutions that allow and encourage participation by a great mass of people in economic activities and the best use of their talents and skills are the key to economic prosperity in a society (Acemoğlu and Robinson, 2012, pp. 74, 81). For North, developed countries, with their democratic settings and decentralized market economies, have historically built a well-defined institutional framework. Developing countries, on the other hand, tend to lack such institutional framework as formal institutions could favor personal relations over impersonality (North, 1994: 360).

Once you have a particular set of institutions in a given country, NIE holds that institutional transformations or changes are not necessarily for the better as "it would be naive to assume that any evolutionary process will always lead to better outcomes" (Ostrom and Basurto, 2011, p. 335). The "imbecile institutions", as Veblen (1992) calls them, may be as long-lasting as the others. Similarly, North (1994, p. 360) argues that existence of institutions is not synonymous with institutional efficiency. Furthermore, the "institutional transplant" of formal institutions that have yielded positive outcomes in one setting is not likely to succeed as "you get a different answer for every country and every historical situation" (Coase, 1999, p. 5), due to potential contradiction between imported institutions and preexisting norms in that particular setting. Under these circumstances, for institutional change to take place, individuals cease to uphold existing beliefs and promote new ones for equilibrium (Aoki, 2001; Greif and Latin, 2004). This, however, is likely to take a long time as informal institutions evolve quite slowly in societies, even more slowly than formal ones (Williamson, 2000). Hence, NIE tells us that we should not keep our hopes high about institutional change. Furthermore, NIE might need to collaborate with other disciplines for a proper answer to the question of institutional change. As North (1995) argues, some interdisciplinary research combining economics and political science might be necessary to understand the evolution of institutions in domestic settings.

According to NIE, among the formal institutions that are the most important for economic performance are those involving the definition and enforcement of property rights between the government and private parties as well as between the individuals within a society (2). In a world of incomplete information, enforcement in voluntary interactions is costly, and this is what creates transaction costs. Some argue that transaction costs and property rights are actually two sides of the same coin as the act of acquiring, protecting and transferring property rights creates transaction costs (Eggertsson, 2013, p. 2). Well-specified and secure property rights to safeguard economic transactions are generally regarded as crucial preconditions for economic performance.

As stated previously, this chapter limits itself to the analysis of a specific type of formal institution, namely property rights, given their critical role in economic growth. In the literature, property rights affect economic growth through four major causal mechanisms. First, secure property rights help reduce insecurity, and thereby, increase domestic investments as well as foreign investment activities in an economy (North, 1990; North & Weingast, 1989; Barzel, 1997; Acemoğlu et al., 2001; Greif 2005; Haggard et al., 2008). Several empirical studies have demonstrated that strong property rights protection enhances capital investment, productivity and economic growth (Acemoğlu et. al., 2001), whereas weak property rights protection adds uncertainty to economic activities and lowers expected profits (North, 1990). Secondly, property rights affect advancement of technology and human capital by encouraging high value-added investments (that are technology intensive) in comparison to short-term labor-intensive investments (Keefer and Knack, 1997). Third, they reduce transaction costs as private ordering becomes useless within a secure institutional framework. And finally, insecure property rights might lead to misallocation of resources in case personal ties with the ruling elite are established as substitutes for impartial formal rules. Personal ties and corruption have a downward impact on economic efficiency (Opper, 2008, p. 392).

The need to enforce property rights suggests that the threat of coercion is integral to all property rights regimes (Hall et al., 2011). As state holds the 'legitimate use of power' in a given society, it enjoys better capabilities for the enforcement of formal property rights than any other private actor. This, however, poses a serious dilemma. Investments tend to increase when property rights are protected, but a state strong enough to protect property rights can also be strong enough to expropriate them (Weingast, 1993). As Alston and Muller (2005, p. 586) rightfully ask, if the state can protect citizens from stealing from one another, what prevents the state from stealing from its citizens? Studies in NIE literature underline the need to strike a balance between a state powerful enough to act decisively, yet limited enough to prevent abuse of authority (North and Weingast, 1989; Shirley, 2005).

Coase (1960) reminds us that an effective and efficient legal system helps alter people's incentives to behave opportunistically (3) (Hadfield, 2005; Arrunada and Andonova, 2005). Thus, rule of law enables enforcement of contractual obligations and protection of private property from state predation by restraining the political rulers. Unfortunately, as we will demonstrate in the following sections, states in the developing world can be ineffective at protecting property rights, or, worse, states themselves can become an important threat to the security of property rights. As these countries lack formal institutions to enforce contracts and economic interactions, they are more likely to experience undesirable outcomes, including but not limited to clientelism, low efficiency, and stagnation.

Since the link between protection of property rights and state power is critical for property rights, it becomes crucial to analyze the rise of a specific type of state in the developing world with the onset of neoliberalism. The next section aims to understand the institutional structure of this particular state by unpacking the link between neoliberalism and authoritarianism.

NEOLIBERALISM AND THE RISE OF AUTHORITARIAN NEOLIBERAL STATES IN THE DEVELOPING WORLD

As Rodgers (2012) argues, the term "neoliberalism" represents the refreshment of laissez-faire ideas over the last thirty years and the "conservative" economic thought with its anti-tax, anti-government, and anti-labor union agenda. Neoliberalism simply follows the basic principles of neoclassical economics by proposing that governments must eliminate subsidies, make reforms to expand the tax base, decrease deficit spending, limit protectionism and open up markets to trade. Neoliberalism also seeks to abolish fixed exchange rates and privatize enterprises run by the state. Given these characteristics, Harvey argues that neoliberalism should be seen as a 'political project to re-establish the conditions for capital accumulation and to restore the power of economic elites (Harvey, 2005, p. 19).

With the 1980s, neoliberalism has already become a global phenomenon with its spread from major European countries and the United States to developing countries. According to Buckley (2012), the aim and the process of neoliberalism should be seen as:

a project aimed at freeing capital from the constraints imposed by these "embedded liberalisms", and more directly as a process ultimately focused on restoring the class power of economic elites (Buckley, 2012).

Neoliberal policies and developments have generally been explained as a shifting set of understanding to market-led governance that is distinctly "post-Fordist", "after-Keynesian", or "post-industrial", which in many cases have been concerned with how collective social contracts for labor or democratic and civic rights of residents could be dismantled (Buckley, 2012). Although neoliberalism aims to reduce the role of the state in the economy, neoliberalism in practice has produced not only a very strong state, but also an authoritarian one. Indeed, the sustenance of neoliberalism requires a market society obtained through a change in civil society. For this reason, neoliberalism has nothing to do with markets as usually expected, but rather it is related to the arrangement of social relations in the name of markets through retrenchment of welfare states via cutback strategies, privatization of public properties and the provision of public goods by private enterprise so as to hand over the profitable sectors of the economy to the market (in health care, education, social security, etc.) (Azar, 2015).

In fact, neoliberalism cannot be defined as minimal government intervention and regulation without making a distinction between the types of state intervention. As Bob Jessop claims, neoliberalism aims to roll back forms of state intervention which are related to developmental state while targeting to boost state intervention in order to create new forms of governance that are more suitable for a globalized free market economy (Jessop, 2002, p. 454). According to Jessop, the neoliberal project generally includes high intervention via economic, social and political actions: while provision of social services by the state is reduced, state intervention takes place to implement neoliberal economic policies and suppress possible resistance against these policies, for instance, through policing of demonstrations, raising racist political rhetoric and so on.

There are also clear attempts of the governing elites at maintaining a peculiar form of regime which can be referred to as authoritarian neoliberalism – that is, a neoliberal economy embedded in an authoritarian setting. It basically refers to a strong state operating under a specific type of neoliberalism that expands the economy in a changing global context while enriching the local elites (Juego, 2015, pp. 54-55). Contrary to what Fukuyama (1992) argues, the 'end of history' wouldn't come by the victory of liberal democracy but by authoritarian neoliberalism. As Bruff argued, the rise of authoritarian neoliberalism in contemporary times is a reply to the obvious crisis of current democratic capitalism, as it led to

the reconfiguring of the state into a less democratic entity through constitutional and legal changes that seek to insulate it from social and political conflict (Bruff, 2014).

Since authoritarian neoliberalism is an evolving notion, it is strongly helpful to understand the present conjuncture. As Coulhon claims, the term authoritarian here has a meaning different from its usage in traditional political science since:

government is distinguished by a high degree of state power and discretion and, most often, the absence of procedures for popular consent or for guarding individual rights. (Coulhon, 2002).

According to Poulantzas (1978, p. 203), authoritarian statism refers to a 'strengthened state control over every scope of socio-economic life combined with drastic (weakening) of the institutions of political democracy'. Authoritarian neoliberalism stands for a theoretical outline that tries to explain the present crises of democracy and capitalism as inside-connected, and generative of a marked hinge in the way the state achieves the constant reproduction of capitalist social relations (Tansel, 2017).

Authoritarianism can also be perceived in the reconfiguring of state in an effort to isolate certain policies and institutional practices from social and political opposition. In many developing countries, the neoliberal project was introduced in an environment already characterized by a state structure that was authoritarian and weaker than their equivalents in North America or Europe. Therefore, neoliberalism in practice meant non-democratic and unequal reorganization of societies along the intensification of the differences, inequalities, hierarchies and divisions due to authoritarian states and global corporations. Liberalization, performed from top to down and via undemocratic governance led to a delicate growth and instability in some developing countries (4).

Recent sociopolitical developments in Russia, Hungary, Turkey, Egypt, the United Arab Emirates, Malaysia, Brazil, Greece, and the Philippines (and in various other places) can be taken as examples of the dual process of neoliberalization and rising authoritarianism. The common trait across these countries is that they all have a strong state and a relatively open market economy. These developing countries have integrated themselves into the global world market by obeying the rules of trademark neoliberal policies of privatization and liberalization, but some features of authoritarianism are evident in the political life of these countries as these countries lack procedural requirements of fair elections, equality before law for all citizens, and freedom of expression, and protection of human rights (Zakaria, 1989). The current regime in Turkey, Egypt and Morocco after the Arab Spring, Greece after its recent economic crisis, and the authoritarian neoliberalism regarding China's marketization can be cited as examples. Russia also suffers from serious economic challenges, stemming from a lack of protection of property rights. These countries all fall under the banner of authoritarian neoliberal states. Furthermore, in all these countries, the implementation of neoliberal policies took place under authoritarian governments that suppressed the opposition raised to the high social costs of neoliberal project, particularly for the working class.

While assessing the neoliberal state, it is necessary to make a distinction between different roles the state upholds in these settings. As for the role related to the provision of social services and welfare, we can witness a decrease in the state intervention. Conversely, when it comes to repressing the opposition, enabling the capitalist economic elite to benefit from the process of globalization, and socializing the costs of transformation of the economy, neoliberal state is and should be strong, even by becoming authoritarian in these countries. The United Arab Emirates, especially, the Emirate of Dubai is an excellent example to demonstrate authoritarian states honed to neoliberal perfection. The Emirate supported the free flow of capital, skilled labor, and technology to the country. The UAE sponsored industries best suited to neoliberalism, like tourism, transport, and shipping. Over the last three decades, neoliberalism in Dubai has often been criticized because of its hyper-exploitation of migrant workers in the city.

Migrant workers have faced serious problems such as lack of job safety and unionization and they have been subject to very low salaries, language barrier, long working hours, bad living conditions and so on. in Dubai as well as across the Gulf region. The neoliberal urbanism in a non-democratic country like the UAE stemmed from the exploitation of the working subjects there. The UAE case also provides a clear picture of how the autocratic state and neoliberalism can exist together.

In another country, Malaysia, neoliberalism has been on the rise since 1991. Malaysia's governing elites and their allies back then were driven by their self-interest, rather than pure ideology, in pursuing benefits from neoliberal discourses and policies. Mahathir's 22 years-long administration laid out the "Wawasan 2020 Development Framework", which was constructed by a hegemonic network that cut across classes and ethnicities; operated by a political-business alliance; characterized by conventional neoliberal policies; and implemented by an authoritarian state (Juego, 2018). After the 2008 crisis, massive corruption scandals and crime allegations broke out in Malaysia. The Najib regime then saw authoritarianism as the most feasible political system to strengthen capital accumulation. The enduring institutions of authoritarian neoliberalism in Malaysia have unfortunately resulted in the rise of a culture of impunity, corruption and other institutional malaises.

As the above discussion demonstrates, the concept of authoritarian neoliberalism is useful to understand state practices in many developing countries, and the concept has been used widely to recognize increasingly undemocratic forms of state in these countries. Having examined the link between authoritarianism and neoliberalism in developing countries, the next section aims to discuss the final point that this chapter raises, i.e. the current status of property rights in authoritarian neoliberal states in developing countries.

Discussion: The Status of Property Rights In Authoritarian Neoliberal States In The Developing World

As argued by Sachs (1992), the ethical worth of capitalism stems from its notion that it rewards those who engage in profitable, and therefore useful economies governed by fair competition. Pavlovskaya (2013: 1299) reminds us that neoliberalism holds unrestrained capitalism as morally superior. It follows from these two assertions that private property, as constitutive of capitalism, is essential to achieve ethically justified productivity in neoliberal thinking. Thus, it is important to analyze how protection of property rights is affected by neoliberal yet authoritarian states in developing countries. As we will argue below, when formal institutions, such as fair and transparent rules to govern, and legal infrastructure to enforce contracts are lacking or weak, property rights fail to be protected, as in the case of majority of authoritarian neoliberal states in the developing world.

To re-state, in NIE, secure property rights are important as they help boost private investment, and thus economic prosperity. Goldfinch claims that the proper functioning of property rights requires elementary rule of law and an effective legal/rational bureaucratic structure to found and protect property assets; an independent judiciary and a well-functioning incorrupt court system that is not favorable to the rich; and finally, a state that is not really predatory or has not been taken by corrupt elites so that it rules by some degree of agreement and legitimacy (DeRouen and Goldfinch, 2012).

These conditions, however, are uncommon in non-democratic settings, and many states in the developing world, unfortunately, lack democracy. Empirical studies have found that democracies generally have stronger property rights protection than non-democracies (Leplang, 1996; Knutsen, 2011). One critical explanation for this variation suggests that, in democracies, there is more dispersion of power and stronger institutional constraints on rulers that help reduce the opportunities for leaders to expropriate property for their own benefit (North, 1990). Legalized restraint in the form of rule of law is not strongly associated with protections for investment in developing countries (Haggard and Tiede, 2011).

The robust economic growth in China characterized by weak property rights seem to cast doubt on the necessity or the embeddedness of strong formal institutions, such as rule of law or an independent judiciary system to guarantee unbiased prosecution and secure property rights for growth. From the point view of standard institutional thought, Chinese economy was deemed to fail. It should be noted that in China expropriation of foreign investment due to lack of property rights protection remains a problem for foreign investors. The problem, however, does not stem from a lack of property rights laws as China has passed many laws in the past two decades to reduce the ambiguity of property rights (Li, 2004, p. 101). Li claims that the new challenge common to the emerging markets in the developing world is not the outright confiscation by the state but rather the lack of protection of property rights due to a different institutional structure in these countries. In the absence of formal institutions, such as an impartial and efficient legal system, people are forced to rely on personal relationships to protect their transactions and property rights in China, which leads to business transactions primarily governed by personal connections and informal networks, known as "guanxi" (Lee, 2004, pp. 107-108).

When fair and transparent rules are lacking, and the state is unable to enforce contracts impartially, personal relationships trump over in the protection of investments, at the expense of, what Shuhe Li calls, "rule-based governance." Needless to say, firms that have a better relationship with the government are stronger in reducing the risk of expropriation (5). According to Li (2004, p. 111), without full legal protection of property rights, investors will be less willing to invest in authoritarian states; thus, capital flight will be immense. Consequently, these countries will be more prone to economic instability and economic stagnation in the medium and long run. As the use of guanxi in China suggests, when the formal legal system is opaque and particularistic, personal connections are used to circumvent the legal and regulatory system to protect one's private property.

What happens in China is a typical example of what happens in other authoritarian states in the developing world that ascribe to neoliberal policies without checks and balances in the political system: the legal system in these settings are subject to domination by the ruling elites; thus, they will not be independent or impartial. Faced with unreliable formal institutional protections, investors acquire informal relational ties to secure a particularistic protection in opaque investment areas (Peng & Luo, 2000; Peng, 2003). Clientelistic relational ties ranging from bribery to particular favors and assurances, involving interdependence between power holders (political elites) and investors (domestic and transnational economic elites) through the exchange of resources provide durable solutions in the absence of proper protection of property rights. Often clientelistic relationships can be unstable due to time-inconsistency and a credible commitment problem as well argued in the scholarly literature (6). This is why co-investment relational ties, in which power holders become investors or investors become power holders in order to reduce risks in situations of legal uncertainty, happen to increase the survival rate of foreign investment ventures (Vermon, 1983; Jiang et al., 2015). Moreover, co-investment relational ties reduce the need for legal and binding restraints on the ruler (Hamilton-Hart & Palmer, 2017, p. 435).

In the Indonesian palm oil industry, for instance, Hamilton-Hart and Palmer (2017) explain how co-investment relationships manifest themselves between power holders at the local level (village functionaries, district level politicians and local government officials), and companies in the areas of Riau and West Kalimantan. Accordingly, the expansion of palm industry in Indonesia, which is characterized by an insecure property regime, based on expropriation and illegality can only be explained with co-investment relational ties since political elites providing privileged access to the land often could not make credible long-term commitments and investors wanted to reduce the risks arising from political and legal uncertainty (Hamilton-Hart & Palmer, 2017, p. 435).

In Russia, Pavlovskaya (2013) shows how lingering of non-capitalist property practices from the Soviet era, combined with neoliberal discourse on the efficiency of private property, may result in diverse practices of property, uncommon for a properly functioning neoliberal economy that upholds private property and profit-maximizing enterprises. According to Pavlovskaya, in the post-Soviet era, in Moscow in particular, although socialist property regime was abolished, the new rules for ownership were still vague and small independent entrepreneurs lacked space and logistical support while facing high start-up costs, high rents and corrupt bureaucrats.

To sum up, all the cases discussed above point at the problematic protection of property rights in authoritarian settings, where fair and transparent rules to govern are lacking or weak, no matter how strongly these states endorse neoliberal practices.

FUTURE RESEARCH DIRECTIONS

This chapter aims to build a bridge between NIE and political economy to help contribute to the advancement of NIE. With its focus on the institutional structure of developing countries as opposed to developed countries, the chapter fills an empirical gap in the existing NIE literature. As the chapter problematizes the status of property rights in developing countries that combine neoliberalism with authoritarianism, it will be interesting to examine whether the status of property rights in these settings will continue to be severely eroded as this chapter suggests in these countries in the near future. Also, it will be academically rewarding to study the economic performance of authoritarian neoliberal states in the medium run to see whether they continue to be as successful as they have been in a capitalist world economic order that prioritizes protection of property rights for investors above all. Finally, it will be interesting to study how formal institutions in these countries will change and transform as authoritarian neoliberal states in the developing world undergo regime transition to become fully functioning democracies or dictatorships.

CONCLUSION

This chapter addressed the link between formal institutions and neoliberalism from NIE perspective by focusing on a specific formal institution, namely property rights. As protection of property rights requires a powerful state, on the one hand, and formal institutions, such as rule of law, independent judiciary, so as to prevent the risk of expropriation by power holders on the other (Kiddie, 2010), this chapter addressed why such a legal infrastructure is lacking in many developing countries by shedding light on the rise of authoritarian neoliberal states in developing countries as of the 1980s.

NIE argues that secure property rights are important as they guarantee investment and promote market exchanges for economic prosperity. In the absence of formal institutions, such as fair and transparent rules to govern, and a legal infrastructure to enforce contracts, however, property rights will not be protected. The situation becomes dire as autocratic rulers do not undertake reforms given their fear of losing their hold on power (Daron and Acemoğlu, 2012, p. 92). As Li argued in her discussion on China (2004), without full legal protection of property rights, investors will be less willing to invest in authoritarian states, and capital flight will be immense. This is why this chapter argues that developing countries that combine authoritarianism with neoliberalism can achieve economic growth, but they are more likely to suffer economic stagnation in the medium and long run.

REFERENCES

Acemoğlu, D., Simon, J., & Robinson, J. (2001). The Colonial Origins of Comparative Development: An Empirical Investigation. *American Economic Literature*, *91*(5), 1369–1401.

Alston, L. J., & Bernardo, M. (2005). Property Rights and the State. In C. Menard & M. Shirley (Eds.), *Handbook of New Institutional Economics* (pp. 573–590). Netherlands: Springer.

Aoki, M. (2001). *Toward A Comparative Institutional Analysis*. Massachusetts: MIT Press. doi:10.7551/mitpress/6867.001.0001

Arrunada, B., & Veneta, A. (2005). Market Institutions and Judicial Rulemaking. In C. Menard & M. Shirley (Eds.), Handbook of New Institutional Economics (pp. 229-251). Netherlands: Springer. doi:10.1007/0-387-25092-1_11

Azar, R. (2015). Neoliberalism, Austerity and Authoritarianism. Retrieved from newpol.org/issue_post/neoliberalism-austerity-and-authoritarianism/

Barzel, Y. (1997). *Economic Analysis of Property Rights*. Cambridge: Cambridge University Press. doi:10.1017/CBO9780511609398

Bruff, I. (2013, October 23). The Rise of Authoritarian Neoliberalism. A Journal of Economics. *Cultura e Scuola*, *26*, 113–129.

Buckey, M. (2013). Locating Neoliberalism in Dubai: Migrant Workers and Class Struggle in the Autocratic City. *Antipode*, *45*(2), 256–274. doi:10.1111/j.1467-8330.2012.01002.x

Calhoun, C. (2002). *Authoritarianism, Dictionary of the Social Sciences*. Oxford: Oxford University Press.

Case, W. (1993). Semi-Democracy in Malaysia: Withstanding The Pressures for Regime Change. *Pacific Affairs*, 66(2), 183-205.

Clague, C., Keefer, P., Knack, S., & Olson, M. (1996, June). Property and Contract Rights in Autocracies and Democracies. *Journal of Economic Growth*, *1*(2), 243–276. doi:10.1007/BF00138864

Coase, R. (1960). The Problem of Social Cost. *The Journal of Law & Economics*, *3*, 1–44. doi:10.1086/466560

Coase, R. (1999, September 17). The Task of the Society. *International Society for New Institutional Economics Newsletter*, *2*(2), 3–6.

Eggertsson, T. (2013). Quick Guide to New Institutional Economics. *Journal of Comparative Economics*, *41*(1), 1–5. doi:10.1016/j.jce.2013.01.002

Fukuyama, F. (1992). *The End of History and the Last Man*. New York: Macmillan Press Ltd.

Goldfinch, S. (2015). Property Rights and The Mystery of Capital: A Review of the Soto's Simplistic Solution to Development. *Progress in Development Studies*, *15*(I), 87–96. doi:10.1177/1464993414546971

Gramsci, A. (1971). *Selections From the Prison Notebooks*. London: Lawrence and Wishart.

Greif, A. (2006). *Institutions and the Path to the Modern Economy: Lessons from Medieval Trade*. Cambridge: Cambridge University Press. doi:10.1017/CBO9780511791307

Greif, A., & David, L. (2004, November). A Theory of Endogenous Institutional Change. *The American Political Science Review*, *98*(4), 633–652. doi:10.1017/S0003055404041395

Grief, A. (2005). Commitment, Coercion and Markets: the Nature and Dynamics of Institutions Supporting Exchange. In C. Menard & M. Shirley (Eds.), Handbook of New Institutional Economics (pp. 727-786). Netherlands: Springer. doi:10.1007/0-387-25092-1_29

Hadfield, G. K. (2005). The Many Legal Institutions that Support Contractual Commitments. In C. Menard & M. Shirley (Eds.), Handbook of New Institutional Economics (pp. 175-205). Netherlands: Springer. doi:10.1007/0-387-25092-1_9

Haggard, S., Mac Intyre, A., & Tiede, L. (2008). The Rule of Law and Economic Development. *Annual Review of Political Science*, *11*(1), 205–234. doi:10.1146/annurev.polisci.10.081205.100244

Haggard, S., & Tiede, L. (2011). The Rule of Law and Economic Growth: Where Are We? *World Development*, *39*(5), 673–685. doi:10.1016/j.worlddev.2010.10.007

Hall, D., Hirsch, P., & Li, T. M. (2011). *Powers of Exclusion: Land Dilemmas in Southeast Asia*. Singapore: NUS Press.

Hall, S. (1985). Authoritarian Populism: A Reply to Jessop et al. *New Left Review*, *151*(May-June), 115–124.

Hamilton, H., & Palmer, N. (2017). Co-Investment and Clientelism as Informal Institutions: Beyond 'Good Enough' Property Rights Protection. *Studies in Comparative International Development*, *52*(4), 416–435. doi:10.100712116-017-9250-1

Harvey, D. (2005). *A Brief History of Neoliberalism*. Oxford: Oxford University Press.

Jessop, B. (2002). Liberalism, Neoliberalism, and Urban Governance: A State Theoretical Perspective. In *Antipode* (pp. 452–472). Oxford: Blackwell Publishers. doi:10.1002/9781444397499.ch5

Juego, B. (2015). Elite Capture and Elite Conflicts in Southeast Asian Neoliberalization Processes. In South South Tricontinental Collaborative Programme (Ed.), Inequality, Democracy and Development under Neoliberalism and Beyond (pp. 68-93). Buenos Aires: CLACSO – Latin American Council of Social Sciences.

Juego, B. (2018). The Institutions of Authoritarian Neoliberalism in Malaysia: A Critical Review of the Development Agendas under the Regimes of Mahathir, Abdullah, and Najib. *Austrian Journal of South-East Asian Studies*, *11*(1), 53–79.

Keane, D., & Mc Geehan, N. (2008). Enforcing Migrant Workers' Rights in the United Arab Emirates. *International Journal on Minority and Group Rights*, *15*(1), 81–115.

Keefer, P., & Knack, S. (1997). Why Don't Poor Countries Catch Up? A Cross-National Test of An Institutional Environment. *Economic Inquiry*, *35*(3), 590–602. doi:10.1111/j.1465-7295.1997.tb02035.x

Kiddie, G.L. (2010). Perceived Security of Tenure and Housing Consolidation in Informal Settlements: Case Studies from Urban Fiji. *Pacific Economic Bulletin*, *25*, 193–214.

Klein, P. G. (1998). New Institutional Economics. Department of Economics, University of Georgia.

Knutsen, C. H. (2011). Democracy, Dictatorship and Protection of Property Rights. *The Journal of Development Studies*, *47*(1), 164–182. doi:10.1080/00220388.2010.506919

Knutsen, C. H., & Hanne, F. (2013). Property Rights in Dictatorships: Kings Protect Property Better Than Generals or Party Bosses. *Contemporary Politics*, *19*(1), 94–114. doi:10.1080/13569775.2013.773205

Leblang, D. (1996). Property Rights, Democracy and Economic Growth. *Political Research Quarterly*, *49*(1), 5–26. doi:10.1177/106591299604900102

Li, S. (1999). The Benefits and Costs of Relation-Based Governance: An Explanation of the East Asian Miracle and Crisis. *Paper presented at the American Economic Association Annual Meeting*, New York. Academic Press.

Li, S. (2004). Why is Property Right Protection Lacking in China? An Institutional Explanation. *California Management Review*, *46*(3), 100–115. doi:10.2307/41166223

Linz, S., & Lipset, S. M. (Eds.). (1999). *Democracy in Developing Countries*. Boulder: Lynne Rienner.

Menard, C., & Shirley, M. M. (2005). Introduction. In C. Menard & M. M. Shirley (Eds.), *Handbook of New Institutional Economics*. Netherlands: Springer.

Milne, R. S., & Mauzy, D. K. (1999). *Malaysian Politics under Mahathir*. London: Routledge; doi:10.1007/0-387-25092-1_1.

Milne, S. (2013). *The Revenge of History: The Battle For the 21st Century*. London: Verso.

North, D. C. (1981). Structure and Change in Economic History. New York: Norton.

North, D. (1990). *Institutions, Institutional Change and Economic Performance*. Cambridge: Cambridge University Press. doi:10.1017/CBO9780511808678

North, D. (1993). Institutions and Credible Commitment. *Journal of Institutional and Theoretical Economics*, *149*(1), 11–23.

North, D. (1994). Economic Performance Through Time. *The American Economic Review*, *84*(3), 359–368.

North, D. (1995). The New Institutional Economics and Third World Development. In J. Harris & J. Hunter (Eds.), *The New Institutional Economics and Third World Development* (pp. 17–26). London: Routledge. doi:10.4324/9780203444290.pt1

North, D. (2005). *Understanding the Process of Institutional Change*. New Jersey: Princeton University Press. doi:10.1515/9781400829484

North, D. C., & Barry, R. W. (1989). Constitutions and Commitment: The Evolution of Institutions Governing Public Choice in Seventeenth-Century England. *The Journal of Economic History*, *49*(4), 803–832. doi:10.1017/S0022050700009451

Olson, M. (1993). Democracy, Dictatorship and Development. *The American Political Science Review*, *87*(3), 567–576. doi:10.2307/2938736

Opper, S. (2008). New Institutional Economics and Its Application on Transition and Developing Countries. In E. Brousseau & J.-M. Glachant (Eds.), New Institutional Economics: A Guidebook (pp. 389-407). Cambridge: Cambridge University Press.

Ostrom, E., & Basurto, X. (2011). Crafting analytical tools to study institutional change. *Journal of Institutional Economics*, *7*(3), 317–343. doi:10.1017/S1744137410000305

Pavlovskaya, M. (2013). Between neoliberalism and difference: Multiple Practices of Property in Post-Soviet Russia. *Europe-Asia Studies*, *65*(7), 1295–1323. doi:10.1080/09668136.2013.822708

Peck, J., & Tickell, A. (2002). Neoliberalizing Space. *Antipode*, *34*(3), 380–404. doi:10.1111/1467-8330.00247

Peng, M. (2003). Institutional Transactions and Strategic Choices. *Academy of Management Review*, *28*(2), 275–296. doi:10.5465/amr.2003.9416341

Peng, M., & Luo, Y. (2000). Managerial ties and firm performance in a transition economy: The nature of a micro-macro link. *Academy of Management Journal*, *43*(3), 486–501.

Poulantzas, N. (1978). *State, Power, Socialism*. London: Verso.

Przeworski, A., Alvarez, M., Chaibub, J. A., & Limongi, F. (2000). *Democracy & Development: Political Institutions and Well-Being in the World, 1950-1990*. Cambridge: Cambridge University Press. doi:10.1017/CBO9780511804946

Sachs, J. (1992). Privatization in Russia: Some Lessons from Eastern Europe. *The American Economic Review*, *82*(2), 43–48.

Shirley, M. M. (2005). Institutions and Development. In C. Menard & M.M. Shirley (Eds.), Handbook of New Institutional Economics (pp. 611-638). Netherlands: Springer. doi:10.1007/0-387-25092-1_25

Tansel, C. B. (2017). *States of Discipline: Authoritarian Neoliberalism and the Contested Reproduction of Capitalist Order*. London: Rowman & Littlefield International.

Vernon, R. (1983). Organizational and Institutional Responses to Political Risk. In R. Herring (Ed.), *Managing International Risk* (pp. 191–216). Cambridge: Cambridge University Press. doi:10.1017/CBO9780511664601.011

Weingast, B. R. (1993). Constitutions as Governance Structures: The Political Foundations of Secure Markets. *Journal of Institutional and Theoretical Economics*, *149*(1), 286–311.

Acemoglu, D., & Robinson, J. A.(2012). Why Nations Fail? The Origins of Power, Prosperity and Poverty. New York: Crown Business. doi:10.1355/ae29-2j

Williamson, O. E. (2000). The New Institutional Economics: Taking Stock, Looking Ahead. *Journal of Economic Literature*, *38*(3), 595–613. doi:10.1257/jel.38.3.595

Yi, J., Peng, M., Yang, X., & Mutlu, C. (2015). Privatization, Governance and Survival: MNE Investments in Private Participation Projects in Emerging Economies. *Journal of World Business*, *50*(2), 294–301. doi:10.1016/j.jwb.2014.10.006

Zakaria, H. A. (1989). Malaysia: Quasi-democracy in a Divided Society. In Democracy in Developing Countries (pp. 347-381). Boulder: Rienner.

ADDITIONAL READING

Aligica, P. D. (2014). *Institutional Diversity and Political Economy: the Ostroms and Beyond*. Oxford University Press.

Caballero, G., & Soto-Oñate, D. (2015, December). The diversity and Rapprochement of Theories of Institutional Change: Original Institutionalism and New Institutional Economics. *Journal of Economic Issues*, *XLIX*(4), 947–977. doi:10.1080/00213624.2015.1105021

Clague, C., Keefer, P., Knack, S., & Olson, M. (1996, June). Property and Contract Rights in Autocracies and Democracies. *Journal of Economic Growth*, *1*(2), 243–276. doi:10.1007/BF00138864

Greif, A. (2006). *Institutions and the Path to the Modern Economy: Lessons from Medieval Trade*. Cambridge: Cambridge University Press. doi:10.1017/CBO9780511791307

Knutsen, C. H., & Fjelde, H. (2013). Property Rights in Dictatorships: Kings Protect Property Better Than Generals or Party Bosses. *Contemporary Politics*, *19*(1), 94–114. doi:10.1080/13569775.2013.773205

Weingast, B. R. (1993). Constitutions as Governance Structures: The Political Foundations of Secure Markets. *Journal of Institutional and Theoretical Economics*, *149*(1), 286–311.

Wu, F. (2008). China's Great Transformation: Neoliberalization as Establishing A Market Society. *Geoforum*, *39*(3), 1093–1096. doi:10.1016/j.geoforum.2008.01.007

Wu, F. (2010). How Neoliberal is China's Reform? The Origins of Change During Transition. *Eurasian Geography and Economics*, *51*(5), 619–631. doi:10.2747/1539-7216.51.5.619

KEY TERMS AND DEFINITIONS

Authoritarian State: It is a political system in which the political power is condensed into one authority figure. Authoritarian state is characterized by strong central power and limited individual freedoms. In authoritarian states, the emphasis is on the provision of private goods for the elites rather than providing public goods. Moreover, property rights of non-elites tend to be disregarded in such states.

Developing Countries: The countries that have low levels of industrialization, income per capita and standards of living are known as Developing Countries.

Economic Elite: Economic elite refers to a minority group who enjoys certain privileges and holds economic power in a society, independent of democratic elections.

Institutional Change: It refers to changes in an institutional context that make new bargaining and compromises between the players possible.

Institutions: According to most NIE authors, institutions refer to the effective rules of a social game in which individuals and their organizations are the players. They help create constraints and incentives to shape the behavior of decision makers.

Neoliberalism: Neoliberalism is a comprehensive policy that seeks to transfer control of economic factors to the private sector from the public sector. It favors freedom of markets, deregulation, low levels of government spending, and low taxes.

ENDNOTES

1 In line with the scholarly literature, in this chapter we do not contest the notion that time horizon of autocratic leaders influences incentives to protect property. Leaders, who are uncertain about their hold on power, have fewer incentives to refrain from expropriation or to invest in legal regimes that enforce contract rights, since in the short-run the associated increase in income is lower than pay-offs from forceful confiscation of property (Olson, 1993). Hence, stronger protection of property is likely when political elite enjoys greater certainty about its prospects to rule in the future, even in the absence of constraints on rulers. Having mentioned this particular notion that different types of autocracies vary in terms of their attitude towards property protection, in this chapter, we limit our analysis to durable authoritarian leaders who operate under neoliberal premises, enjoy long time horizons.

2 In NIE property rights are key to the economy. North (1981) claims that sound property rights and incentive schemes made possible by its distinctive institutions were key to Britain industrializing first.

3 It should be noted here that while some scholars underline the role of formal institutions, such as an independent judiciary or a constitutional court as the mechanisms to protect property rights, others focus on informal institutions by arguing that the backbone of the rule of law is the belief that the individuals and political elite will abide by the judgment of an independent third party arbitrator. According to Alston and Mueller (2005:580), a set of universally shared beliefs in a system of checks and balances is what separates populist democracies from democracies with respect for the rule of law.

4 In order to understand the current situation we need to look at Thatcherism between the late 1970s and the 1980s. Since then, we have been witnessing crises of neoliberalism and the rise of un-democratic governance in many countries. During that time a deep crisis for the Left appeared in the UK and elsewhere; but, just like the present days, the Left could not take advantage despite a deep recession, a weak recovery, mass unemployment and spreading inequality in distribution of wealth (Hall, S. 1985). Current circumstances may be described, as Antonio Gramsci states, "the crisis consists precisely in the fact that the old is dying and the new cannot be born; in this inter-regnum a great variety of morbid symptoms appear" (Gramsci, 1971).

5 Shaomin Li suggests that in the Chinese context, the foreign investors in China use their relation-ship with the upper-level government members or local government officials to expropriate other foreign investor's assets, as in the case of eviction of Mc Donald's in Beijing by the Hong Kong

businessman Li Ka-shing, who had close relationship with the Chinese leadership. For details and other examples, see Li's article (2004).

6 A patron with a short time horizon may find it optimal to maximize short term extraction, and thus may consider the client superfluous. Where rulers fear losing power and regime insiders are uncertain about their own political survival beyond the autocrat, expropriation of property for personal gain is much likely to occur. Also, an insecure patron is less able to make credible commitments to protect clients. See North (1993) for details on time-inconsistency and credible commitment and Olson(1993) for further discussion.

Chapter 3
Reconstruction of the Old Institutions:
Crisis, Governance, and the G20

Ugur Yasin Asal
https://orcid.org/0000-0003-1567-9186
Istanbul Commerce University, Turkey

Nazım Ekren
Istanbul Commerce University, Turkey

ABSTRACT

The recent global economic and financial crisis has fundamentally questioned the crisis management mechanisms of the international institutions. Despite the development of the skills of these institutions, financial vulnerability, economic imbalances, and the instability of the macroeconomic performance indicators are still rising cyclically. The G20 represents roughly 85% percent of global GDP and two-thirds of the world population. It emerged as a leading body for international economic performance. The lack of permanent secretariat of the G20 is decreasing the effectiveness, legitimacy, and the economic viability of the club. Regarding this philosophical background, the role of G20s' institutional structure is examined according to institutional capacity and the macroeconomic performance of the club.

INTRODUCTION

International economy is experiencing systemic fractures at regular intervals. The political consequences of these systemic fractures often involve radical changes in the structure and institutions of the global system. These fractures, which can be described as the failure of capitalism, reprise state, society and market relations (Kaletsky, 2017, p. 1). In contrast to this view, it is the fact that all reliable findings of capitalism exceed more than the costs incurred.

DOI: 10.4018/978-1-7998-0333-1.ch003

Copyright © 2020, IGI Global. Copying or distributing in print or electronic forms without written permission of IGI Global is prohibited.

An open international economic system becomes stronger against the crises if a nation is to maintain its hegemonic power in a stable manner and systematically carry out the distribution of economic power. The reflection of the 1997 financial crisis to Russia and Brazil was also minimized by the policies implemented in these years mainly by the US (Pelagidis & Papasotiriou, 2002, p. 521). According to this acceptance, in the process of G20 formation, US recognizing the stability of the global system and realizing that the recipes that strengthen this stability are in the emerging economies is one of the fundamental factors (Cooper, 2010, p. 745).

The level reached by the end of the 20th century and the first quarter of the 21st century is the increasing political economy activities of emerging economies. These emerging powers in continents of Southeast Asia, South Africa and the South America have begun to find a place in the decision-making processes of international institutions. These changes and transformations have brought along the process of redefining the structural requirements of international institutions. According to this view, international institutions are directly affected by the mutual interstate relationship form and political economy orientations of the world (Nelson, 2016, p. 525).

The formation process of G20 is directly related to the key parameters of the global financial crisis. The problems raised by mono-centered financial management were intended to overcome by mutual relationship form and inclusion. Studies specific to this fact have been conducted in the G20 Leaders' Summit held periodically since 2008. G20's expertise in preventing economic crises needs to deepen the existing international institutional mechanism and policy developing system.

While this relationship level is revealed, it is seen that again an institution the Organization for Economic Cooperation and Development (OECD) plays a leading role in the organization of international regulation and taxation issues. Together with this structural integration, one of the main consequences of the 2008 global financial crisis is the increase in the co-efficiency of inclusion of states in financial regulations. Financial intermediaries and institutions failing to provide adequate security and guarantee in the struggle against systemic risks has coordinated the post-crisis institutionalization stages with the state (Germain, 2009, p. 678). State guarantee in risk management and loan funds has become the most fundamental output of the process. Additionally, the argument that the solution of the global crises is not included in the economies of developed countries was directly in line with the development of the G20 process. The fact that emerging economies gained importance since the 2009 G20 summit reveals that the balance of power theory has also evolved.

Regarding to this philosophical background, the role of G20s' institutional structure will be examined in accordance with the new institutional economics mannerism. Thus, institutional capacity and the macroeconomic performance of the G20 will be measured with current severe crises management skills and the role of the club in global income distribution. In addition to qualitative research methodology, numeric data's and statistics predominantly used as part of new institutional economics mannerisms in this study.

THE POLITICAL ECONOMY OF 2008 GLOBAL FINANCIAL CRISIS AND THE ECONOMIC GOVERNANCE

On the basis of the 2008 global financial crisis lies the large real estate and credit bubble that has emerged in the US and spread all over the world in waves. The Mortgage market in the US has become the largest market in the world with as size close to $ 10 trillion. First of all, 'prime mortgage' loans given to customers with secure reimbursement were a problem. Nevertheless, in a short while, it has been observed that 'subprime mortgage' loans were started to be defined to lower quality consumers. The amount of these loans reached to USD 1.5 trillion (Eğilmez, 2008, p. 66).

The expansion of capitalism in the 2008 financial crisis was indexed only to residential trade. Consumers rushing in an effort to expand this welfare by purchasing new real estate started to be unable to pay the loans they received. Banks attempting to procure their loans at risk under *hedge* funds could not provide the guarantees they expected from hedge funds. The 2008 crisis was the result of the diversification of the derivative products which were developed in order to provide the reimbursement of the loans and receding of these derivative products from functionality. In addition to this loan crisis, the US, whose current account deficit was increasing constantly, has begun to shift its capital and technologies predominantly to China. While such balloon was formed on one hand; on the other hand, oil, food and metal prices had started to increase rapidly. When problems started to happen in the countries where the source of hot started, panic and capital outflows was experienced in the developing countries to where aforementioned money was flowing. When decline in growth in developed countries caused demand to decline too, imports from developing countries had started to decrease. Aforesaid situation led to a decrease in foreign trade-based revenues of developing countries and a recession in their economies (Eğilmez, 2008, p. 69). It was inevitable for international regulatory bodies to realize structural changes in this direction. The 2008 global financial crisis also revealed the fact that these changes are inevitable for the stability of the global trade and financial system.

While the share G20 members Argentine, China, India, Russia, Saudi Arabia, South Africa and Turkey received from world incomes was at 8,5% level between 1965-75, it is seen that this ratio has reached to 25% in 2000-2007 and 55% in 2008-2011 (Agarwal & Samantha, 2014, p. 47). It is visible that the destructive effects of the global crisis are less in developing countries than in developed countries. Although the GDP growth of China and India declined, there was no decline in exports of goods and services of these countries (Agarwal, 2010, p. 78).

After the 2008 global financial crisis, the need for reform of the structure of regulatory and supervisory authority has increased (Agarwal, 2010, p. 86). Particularly, at the G20 summit in London in 2009, the roles falling to G20 on macroeconomic policy coordination and prevention of systematic risks related to crisis formation were identified. In this respect, decisions such as the development of access to IMF's resources and the development of multilateral development banks' comprehensiveness and the discontinuation of conservative practices were formed as a result of these initiatives of the G20 (Callaghan, Carmignani, Makin & Strube, 2014, p. 158).

Another reason for the emergence of the 2008 global financial crisis was the financial collapses in the real estate market. Problems of failures in loan reimbursements and inability to balance investments were encountered in this sector, which initially formed a welfare area in the US and UK real estate market (Vines, 2010, p. 163). The coordination of this process was tried to be solved with the changes to be made in the structures of international financial institutions. At the helm of the references that these institutions indicated on resolving the crisis were export policy improvement recommendations (Vines, 2010, p. 160). It is seen that these proposals also overlap with the political economy of international relations and the realities of the real sector. In the entire post crisis restructuring, forward-looking steps have importance rather than past practices (Curran, 2009, p. 267). The structure of international trade actually began to change in 1989 with the fall of the Berlin wall. Not only did the wall that divided the world into two separate blocks have disappeared, but the center line of similar economic models has expanded with the newly opened markets, and trade exchanges on technical issues, particularly information and experience sharing, have strengthened (Escaith, 2009, p. 269).

In this respect, while it was seen that developing countries were trying to raise taxes during the global crisis, developed countries prepared rescue and emergency action plans for banks. It was visible that both country groups took the notion of increasing trade and controlling the public supply chain (Evenett, 2009, p. 284). As a matter of fact, the crisis approaches of developing and developing countries were reviewed in the G20 Summit in Pittsburgh in 2009 and while the reform proposal of financial institutions was expressed, the following points were emphasized (Angeloni, 2009, p. 262).:

1. Enhancing market transparency,
2. Increasing the structural quality in accounting standards, market infrastructure and credit rating,
3. Strengthening capital standards and other risk control instruments such as capital ratios, liquidity and internal risk management.

It was connoted that the G20 was the best mechanism to implement these structural reforms. Inclusive word economy model that was emerged as a result of 2008 global financial crisis stated that the mechanisms to resolve the crisis should be developed in the context of this inclusion. Despite the short-term, urgent measures taken in the Eurozone, reference for the right and long-termed address to solve the public/sovereign debt crisis and carry out structural reforms was started to be shown as G20. The Group of 20, which accounts for 90% of the world GDP and 2/3 of the world population with the 80% of the international trade, had been fictionalized as the leading actor in the global crisis and the structural transformation of international institutions. The fact that G20 member countries are composed of BRICS countries consisting of Brazil, Russia, India, China and South Africa and other countries that are rapidly emerging, not only the countries with the highest indebtment as US, Japan and the EU, strengthens the initiative of G20 to solve the 2008 financial crisis.

Strong actors in the regional economy such as China and Turkey, Mexico, Indonesia taking part in this process with the role played in the recovery of world economy is vital in accelerating mid-termed outcomes and reaching permanent outputs (Dolls, Peichi & Zimmermann, 2012, p. 32). After a while, the role of the G20 in reducing the economic and financial impacts of the global crisis revived the reform calls for the structures of pre-crisis institutions. Especially criticisms directed at IMF has strengthened and reached up to today. The claim that the IMF should only be considered as a policy instrument of industrialized countries has strengthened the quality of the new mechanism to be formed in the G20. The IMF's key words for this process were "representation, justice and ownership". This decision was taken at the second G20 summit held in 2009 (Menkhoff & Meyer, 2010, p. 171). IMF's need for restructuring in such a way, met the criticisms that emerged in the occurrence of the global crisis. IMF structure built after World War II was formed within the framework of hierarchical hegemony of the winning state(s). It is possible to see this systematic even in the operation of loan mechanism, approval and in the selection of countries that apply for loan. The G20 structure has developed the following recommendations against this structure of the IMF (Menkhoff & Meyer, 2010, p. 172).:

1. Shifting 5% of votes from developing countries,
2. Accelerating the next general quota review,
3. Delinking the election of the IMF's managing director from regional origin,
4. Putting forward the Singapore quota and voice reform.

(1) It was considered that by increasing the share of developing countries in the voting process more inclusive decisions could be taken and taking advantage of the initiatives of emerging actors in the solution of global problems was highlighted. It has been stated that justice in representation cannot be observed in the implementation of the quota system until now and that this causes problems. (2) The founding treaty of the IMF states that quota applications should be reviewed every five years. With the decision taken in 2009, it was suggested that the quota review process, which should have been carried out in 2013 under normal conditions, should be carried out in 2011 by taking 2 years forward due to changing conditions and the course of the world economy.

(3) It was emphasized that the IMF directors elected based on the US and EU consensus needed to move away from this mono-centralism. Stating that the hegemonic perspective is not only made in the IMF but also in other international institutions, the need for justice in representation and transparency in management was emphasized. In addition to all these, it was stated that the increasing role of developing countries will be a part of the new selection process in these institutions. (4) It includes reforms adopted in 2006 in the IMF Boards of Governors in Singapore. These reforms include the implementation of increasing the quotas of China, Korea, Mexico and Turkey, the new transparent and simple new quota system in which the current economic weights of the IMF member countries are taken into account and the inclusion of two new African representatives in the main voting process (Menkhoff & Meyer, 2010, p. 173).

As it can be seen clearly, the global hegemony relations and the structures in which they are allocated are questioned by the world's developing countries. In particular, the conjecture that neoliberal policies have their leadership in the occurrence of the crisis maintains its validity on the Eurozone and the Atlantic economy which are the regions where the crisis was most influential (Pardo, 2012, p. 72). The fact that East Asia was affected by this crisis made the crisis resolution mechanisms of global political economy clearly questionable.

Reconstruction Mannerism of the International Institutions and G20

The G20 has been a priority institution in terms of its involvement in the resolution of the 2008 global crisis and being a model for the new global political economy governance. With China, Indonesia and South Korea becoming members of G20, their roles in the global economy became in line with their emerging structures (Pardo, 2012, p. 74). The long-standing discussions of the emerging powers on the structure of the institutions that provide the management of the global financial system have started to fall into place, the global balance of power was observed to follow the changes in the beginning of the 21st century. The decline in American hegemony coincided with the political economy of Europe and the strengthening of the debates within itself.

The process of separation of the UK from the European Union, which aims at absolute integration of the political economy, including the Single Market and the Customs Union, has once again raised the question of the form and sustainability of these structures. When it is read in the axis of balance of power theory, it is possible to express this general process as Asian countries targeting the power transition against the Atlantic pact. This institutional competition systematic, which can be expressed as the different instrumentation of the US – China competition, has started to rise after the global crisis and has reached to today's axis. The question of what will be the persistence of the post-crisis practices began to be expressed frequently by international political economy circles. Continuous supply of structural reforms is the messenger of the new period after the crisis (Eichengreen, 2010, p. 50). Together with these structural components, the need for reform emerged in international institutions is emphasized at intervals (Lane & Maeland, 2011, p. 29). The reason on the basis of the criticisms in question is that institutions governing the global economy do not act in an equitable manner in the organization management, and are more likely to vote for actors who meet the expectations of the international regime. It is often seen as impossible to give a place to an alternative opinion among the dominant actors in these institutions. This voting regime, which is seen in the structure of the IMF and World Bank, reveals the conclusion that the body of rules that was built about 50 years ago is no longer valid (Lane & Maeland, 2011, p. 33).

The mechanism that mediates giving a voice to these calls for reform exists within the structure of the G20. Especially this relationship dynamics, developed within the framework of China's initiatives, are encouraging the restructuring of G20 and related international institutions by developing a close systematic working system with developing countries such as India, Brazil and G8 member Russia. The reflection of this cooperation strategy of China is also felt in BRICS implementations (Wuthnow, Li & Qi, 2012, p. 283). Clearly, the balance of global power is changing by different instruments and the search for new balance of power of states is getting stronger.

It can be said that this balance of power is shaped by the phenomenon of globalization until this stage (Stark, 2010, p. 147). 1990's fact of liberal openness in international trade, the realization of the sanctions that are expected to be observed in economic reciprocity with a single dimension in the pillar of the states reveals the dimension of global capitalism and the platform of inequalities resulting due to the crisis. After the 2008 global crisis, it is possible to state the basic international regulations which are among the expectations from the G20 which became the primary actor of inter-state cooperation as below (Stark, 2010, p. 150).:

1. A mid and long-termed economic orientation,
2. Refraining from calls for macroeconomic sub arrangements,
3. Commitment to stability-oriented macroeconomic policies,
4. Achieving a more balanced pattern of global growth.

Problematic areas of pre-crisis political economy are highlighted on the basis of these demands. In particular, the slowdown in global economic growth has made the structure of international organizations steering this growth critical. The path to be taken in the post-crisis restructuring and its duration will play an important role in global economy reaching to multi-polarity (Soence & Zagha, 2011, p. 335). One of the main actors of multi-polarity is undoubtedly China. With its macroeconomic growth, financial investments and foreign direct investments it attracted to its country in recent years, China has become the main actor of the global balance of power. It is possible to see this rise of China in the positive perception directed at it within the G20. At the same time, BRICS countries, consisting of Brazil, Russia, India and South Africa, see China as a closer partner than the US (Patrick, 2017, p. 56). The current global balance of power and political economy competition between the US and China is expected to deepen as Donald Trump takes the office as the US president. It is a matter of question what kind of sanctions Trump, who holds China responsible for the decline in employment in the United States, is going to impose by the year 2018, which is the second year of his term. The US-China competition in the South China Sea is an example of the regional implementations of balance of power (Gordon, 2017, p. 6).

Together with China, one of the determinants of power balance within the G20, success in development and the change in shape and direction of global development dynamics, it is stated that an alternative model of the Washington Consensus is developed, and this model can be expressed as the Beijing

Consensus. This rise of China, shown as a leader and role model for developing countries, has made the US-based neoliberal hegemony relations between the IMF and the World Bank questionable (Yağcı, 2016, p. 30). The crisis management at the beginning of 2008, the countries that could be called the G5, were involved in liquidity, the provision of Central Banks and the continuation of financial programs and improvements in banks' balance sheets under the coordination of France, the United Kingdom, the United States, Germany and Japan (Nachane, 2014, p. 104).

On the other hand, following the 2008 global crisis, the main focus of the G20 has become the reformation of the international monetary system. The G20 focuses on issues such as the management of foreign direct investment, coordination in macroeconomic policies, the elimination of inequality in global governance and the establishment of justice (Callaghan, Ghate, Pickford & Rathinam, 2014, p. 213). The origin of inequalities emerged in the global sphere goes back to World War I. The pre-war global sharing competition brought a mass war, this competition continued at the level of conflict until the beginning and end of World War II. With the mid-1990s, the global crisis stemming from the emerging Asian countries has caused high budget deficits in these countries (Callaghan, 2014, p. 84). It was envisaged that this inequality difference within the countries could be solved by IMF policy instruments and credits, however, it was seen that the IMF did not play a role in eliminating the plane of global inequality among these countries (Callaghan, 2014, p. 87). In this respect, the international monetary system needs well-functioning and effective institutions (Rahman, Orzechowska-Fischer & Syed, 2014, p. 162). It is possible to express the international monetary system as rules and institutions that monitor, supervise and change the international payments and foreign currency changes. The international monetary system, which has formed its structure with strong economic growth and increasing integration calls, since 1970's, also the builder of many problems (Stavrev, 2014, p. 179).

This phenomenon, which can be expressed as a part of international institutionalization, plays an important role in the solution of global problems and undertaking new economic policy initiatives. This role, which is expected to develop on the basis of mutual trust and cooperation, can be assumed by G20 is a view accepted by the global authorities (Sheel, 2014, p. 277). It is possible to say that this mission that was attributed to the G20 emerged as a result of the change in the global political economy. In this respect, it is seen that the 2008 global crisis allowed the paradigm shift in hegemony.

It has been analyzed that this paradigm shift is based on the classical elements of hegemony, i.e. on military power, economic, political and social impact area, the interconnection of financial structures, and the direction of dependence of this interconnectedness. The center of global relations has ceased to be the Atlantic axis; the initiatives undertaken by Asian and Far Eastern countries together with developing countries have become the key determinants of the post-crisis period. These changes in the parameters of the national power and phenomena of the structure of the global system, suggests that hegemony is intended to be constructed in a structure that pursues stability. In the following section, the explanation of the new hegemony paradigms of the post-crisis period will make it easier to address the arguments of the hegemony theory with a holistic reading.

POST-CRISIS NEW INSTITUTIONAL HEGEMONY: ECONOMY, FINANCE, POLITICS AND SECURITY

At the beginning of the criteria that determine the post-crisis new hegemony paradigms are the changes in the actor structure of the international system (İpek, 2013, p. 29). The new era of hegemony, where international organizations have come to the forefront in addition to the global system whose classic actor is the state, discusses the relations between states and their relations with international organizations. The stability of the modern international system after the global crisis has become one of the most fundamental research topics. As part of the neoliberal hegemony paradigm, not only the structure of the global financial markets that operate irregularly, but the fragilities of this system have also become clear (İpek, 2013, p. 38).

The post-crisis period, which can be defined by the new Gramsci hegemony term, assumes social changes and transformations as the main actor of hegemony (İpek, 2013, p. 39). In the 21st century, the basic parameters that determined the hegemony relations over Gramsci's social structures have become economics and finance. The role of financial markets and credit instruments in the modern economy, the fact that these credits and capital instruments constitute the basis of economic mobility are at the center of the hegemony relations in the new period (Gökay, 2009, p. 2). In addition to raising economic and financial power, the new hegemony paradigms have a direct connection to the social elements of Gramsci. The new hegemon actor also has a number of behaviors and implementations that are also accepted by the international community (Hurrel, 2006, p. 4).

These behaviors and implementations also overlap with market realities, the theoretical background of transitions between state, society and market is being built. If this ground cannot be constructed by associating with each other, the stability of hegemonic power will not be possible and an economic political ground suitable for power transitions will be built. Structural indicators show that this political economy is based within the central and environmental relations. With the increasing share emerging economies take from the center, the issues of welfare, hegemony, and sharing of global goods has reconstructed and the construction of new hegemony paradigms has focused on the capacity and performance of the relationship with emerging economies (Subacchi, 2008, p. 488). These transitions between developed countries and emerging powers are important for understanding the formation of the global financial crisis and for analyzing the direction in which the post-crisis new period has evolved.

One of the determining parameters of the post-crisis period is emphasizing the sovereignty of the individual as a part of the neoliberal hegemony perspective. Neoliberal doctrines, where the preference and rational choices of the individual are at the forefront in state-based power maximization, are brought to the agenda (Prior, 2017, p. 28). The main parameter that determines the platform of the post-crisis hegemony relations has become international financial institutions. It is seen that these organizations instrumentalize the doctrines of neoliberalism in decision-making and implementation processes. On that matter, it is seen that the new hegemony paradigm evolves over three basic pillars. It is possible to list these basic pillars as institutional power (IMF et al.), structural power (dominance of money systems such as Dollar etc.), and ideological power (political economy ideology) (Venhaus, 2013, p. 3).

The main tool for the continuation of the international system and the sustainability of hegemonic stability is the construction of these institutional mechanisms. It is possible to verbalize this international coordination by two basic conceptualizations. These are hegemonic cooperation and collective cooperation (Beeson & Bell, 2009, p. 68). While it is possible to define what is expressed by the hegemonic cooperation as a form of relationship with the directives and directions of hegemonic power, it is possible to define what is expressed by collective co-operation as a holistic cooperation centering on the common interest of states. The role and functions of the market in these hegemony relations have a unique meaning. Hegemonic actors often form cooperation for the formation of a strong market structure.

The key determinant of the market is finance. Both the size of the instruments of finance and the question of by whom these financial instruments are directed are at the center of the hegemony relations after the 2008 global crisis. In this respect, a real political economy mechanism can be seen in the structure of existing liquidity and credit instruments (Jessop, 2010, p. 43). In this new system of international relations formed following the 2008 global crisis, regional competition and the players in global competition directly related to this have been diversified. This diversification presented the changing concepts of institutionalization and rules in the political economy of the 21st century.

INSTITUTIONALIZATION AND RULES IN THE POLITICAL ECONOMY OF THE 21ST CENTURY

In the basis of long-term performance of economies lies their being based on institutional platform (North, 2002, p. 107). According to this argument, which partakes in the rational choice theory, the fact that economic actors have correct, institutional information in the decision-making process reinforces the role and function of economic choices (North, 2002, p. 108). Market economies consisting of institutionalized structures reach a qualified function. After a while, this approach, which unifies the relationship between economics and institutions, recognizes that economics is institutional, such as its natural evolution in the traditional field. In other saying, the market and firms, which traditional economics does not describe as institutions, are institutional economic actors (Özveren, 2007, p. 17).

As the institutional economics approach sees the market as an institution of economics, opposes the reduction of economics to the market. If the market is not constituted as a result of a natural process, and the economy has a larger area than the market, the definition of economics will expand as a natural result of this process. This change in the definition of economics will become a political economy beyond the boundaries of traditional economics (Özveren, 2007, p. 18). The construction of this political interaction has deepened the institutional axis of economics; all the different schools of economics pointing to the importance of rules and institutions have been given the name of the new institutional economics (Aktan & Vural, 2006, p. 19).

At the beginning of the variables that determine the framework of institutional economics and have the volume to affect its capacity and performance come rules. The rules that will be determined for the establishment of the market economy in an effective structure are important within the framework of the law and norms that improve the economy (Aktan & Vural, 2006, p. 25). In addition, questions such as when, where, how and by whom the goods and services produced in the market will be used raise the need for coordination in the economy. There are rules, norms and institutions that these actors must comply with in order to be able to coordinate the activities of the actors involved in the market within the framework of certain principles and the system (Aktan & Vural, 2006, p. 61).

When considered in the axis of this relationship, the relationship between the performance of the economy and the institutions that make up that economy becomes very important. On the other hand, in the endogenous growth models, the institutions of the countries in addition to economic policies are among the key determinants of economic growth. Institutions and political economy within the country are the key determinants of long-term economic growth (Aktan & Vural, 2006, p. 67). In order to ensure sustainability in economic growth and the effectiveness of public investment and financial resources, the implementation of financial and monetary rules is in question. It is possible to sort the justifications for the application of financial and monetary rules as follows:

1. "Ensuring financial discipline: By creating financial and monetary rules, a balance between budget expenditures and budget revenues can be achieved.
2. Ensuring macro-economic stability: The main source of inflationary pressures can be eliminated by limiting the creation of money by the restrictions and prohibitions imposed on the borrowing of the government from all domestic sources, especially from the central bank and thus, ensuring stability can be facilitated.
3. Financial sustainability: Financial and monetary rules may help to ensure a reasonable real interest rate level in financial markets and eliminate the crowding-out effect on private investments.
4. Increasing the creditworthiness of the government: In establishing long-term trust in financial markets, it may be beneficial for governments to subject themselves to permanent restrictions on budget deficits, borrowing or debt stock data.
5. Prevention of political populism: Financial rules can help eliminate or at least reduce public deficits resulting from short-term political concerns, especially as a result of expenditures that are in contrast to the provision of fiscal discipline in pre-election periods." (Hürcan, 1999; Aktan & Vural, 2006, p. 122).

These rules undertake function as a strong policy choice in eliminating the negative aspects of individual capacity and performance based monetary and fiscal policies developed apart from the institutions, ensuring fiscal discipline and sustainability, fulfilling the economic discipline and increasing the efficiency of the political decision-making mechanism (Aktan & Vural, 2006, p. 131). In addressing the political economy of the 21st century, which can be expressed as the age of uncertainties and developing national policies in relation to this, the importance of the rules based on new economic theory emerges once again.

The global governance of the 21st century requires the redefinition of the roles and functions of the existing institutions and the close follow-up of their capacities and performances with quantitative and qualitative indicator sets. It is possible to list this indicator sets as the coordination of effective institutional experience, monitoring and evaluation of the performance of different institutions in social mechanisms, institutions monitoring and evaluating their ongoing performance (Knight & Johnson 2011; Aligica, 2014, p. 35). These indicator sets have a direct relationship with the development of the democratic system in which the relevant institutions are involved. It is envisaged that the improvement in the institutional level in the indicator sets will strengthen the economic and political modernization process. In order to manage the complex dynamics of the 21st century and to create the sharing welfare, it is inevitable that institutions and rules carry an interdisciplinary line (Menard & Shirley, 2005, p. 2).

This hierarchical model commonly constructs a complex relationship. This complex structure, which develops as a natural consequence of the interdependence relationship, originates from the structural integration of the elements of diplomacy and global balance of power (Onuf, 2002, p. 223). These complex rules of global balance of power coincide with the post-modern neo-liberal structure of the 21st century, the global political system built by these institutions with complex rules brings about economic inequality and political instability. In order to minimize the negative impacts of this unstable structure on social mechanisms, the performance indicators of the institutions should be closely monitored. With the performance-based financing model to be established, strengthening the effectiveness and efficiency of the institutions in the short, medium and long term is aimed (Gartner, 2013, p. 266).

As a result of the abolition of the factors that led to Minsky's financial instability approach along with this performance increase economy will build stable, appropriate models and overcome the problems arising from financial borrowing (Minsky, 1980, p. 29). In this respect, institutional change, as the key to understanding historical change, shows what kind of development line societies construct (Güler, 2012, p. 58). This development line, which constitutes the political economy environment relations, emerges in the axis of institutional economics with its economics pillar, and with its political pillar, it emerges in the axis of international institutionalization. Relationship between real sector, public and financial institutions used when considering the environment analysis of political economy refers to the concentric ring approach in the 21st century post-modern neoliberal relationship form.

The development of rules and institutions of this century in which interdependence relationship develops as a collective need after a while, is only shaped by the axis of democracy, transparency and accountability. The construction of this paradigm change will be possible through the new approaches to be introduced in the theoretical field, the new empirical researches, and the analytical perspective to be brought about in the state, society and economic relations in the economic crises and the transformations that will be made in the structure of international regulatory agencies (Helleiner & Pagliari, 2011, p. 170). Reforms executed in the structure of institutions built in the current global political system must take these paradigms into account.

It is possible to list the axes in which the reforms will take place as re-conceptualization of power relations within the state, the changing domestic political structure in states capable of influencing and changing the global system, new constraints in international politics (Helleiner & Pagliari, 2011, p. 181). It can be stated that the key factor involved in the development of this new relationship form is the 2008 global economic and financial crisis. The facts uncovered by the crisis have made clear the economic and political capacities of the institutions that were established to prevent and manage the crisis (Helleiner & Pagliari, 2011, p. 185).

The search for the structural elements that build fragility and efforts to compensate these structural elements within the same system makes fragility and instability continuous. This problematic whole needs to be overcome, reforms, especially the United Nations, IMF, World Bank and World Trade Organization, which are the dominant institutions and organizations of global political economy, are required. The fact that the elimination of these institutions and the construction of alternative mechanisms does not coincide with the real politics makes the reform initiatives within the current global balance of power a priority.

With the international political and security pillars, the United Nations Security Council and NATO and with the finance and economy pillars, the G20 needs to take an actionable dimension and needs to rapidly transition from the hegemony of hierarchy to the principles of collective governance. In the contrary case, it is foreseen that fragility, imbalance and instability will increase in both global macroeconomic and financial data and political risk and threat parameters.

CONCLUSION

The gradual increase in the structural problems of the institutions increased the capacity of economic and financial fragility and gradually decreased the contribution of the international economy to the construction of collective welfare (Beeson & Bell, 2009). The 21st century carried a new breaking process with it by constructing a completely different paradigm from the 20th century. The first global economic and financial crisis of the 21st century emerged in 2008, brought comprehensive discussions with it. It has been observed that the existing governance mechanisms of the western-based international institutions were no longer sufficient to solve the problems. The increasing role and function of G20 in the field of global governance serves as an example (Şenses, Öniş & Bakır, 2013, p. 7).

In order to achieve a high level of harmony between the structure of the institutions and the economy, the structural development of institutions should be pursued by the state (Karakayalı & Yanıkkaya, 2006, p. 137). In this respect, the construction of a collective process is inevitable. This perspective, which is also at the basis of the doctrine developed by Karl Polanyi with reference to historical sociology, supports the vision that economic development and modernization can be made with the state support (Polonyi, 2003). Each country should build institutions that are relevant to its structure taking into account other examples in the world, instead of a single institutional sample (Karakayalı & Yanıkkaya, 2006, p. 137).

These institutions build two types of rules. These rules are called formal and informal. It is possible to express formal rules as the norms built within the political economy structure in which the institutions operate. Informal institutions can be defined as practices and behaviors developed without any legal basis compared to formal institutions (North, 2002, p. 10). When evaluated with its current structure, it can be stated that G20 has an informal appearance. Difficulties experienced in the construction of the institutional mechanism have pulled the G20's stable governance and economic/political performance indicators down. It can be expressed that this informal structure formed in the hierarchy of hegemony is especially protected by hegemonic actors.

This is why the political structure is one of the main instruments for analyzing the share and economic performance of the ever-growing and changing regulations of the modern world system in the Gross National Product (GNP) (North, 2002, p. 145). The interaction of the political structure with the dynamics of the era in which it is current reveals the typologies of the institutional structure built according to that era. The argument of the hegemony of the hierarchy that dominates this study takes the development of the economic, political and military institutions of the 21st century as a natural consequence of economic policy evolution in the international system as a reference (North, 2002, p. 153).

It is clearly seen that the basic institution should be the political leadership mechanism in solving the dilemmas of the political economy of the 21st century; identifying the unforeseen financial risks, decreasing the political uncertainty and economic vulnerability. Thus, fulfilling the sustainable development tasks are initially on the global agenda. These tasks should be periodically assessed regarding to determinant macroeconomic and social indicators. The then, results of the qualitative indicators should be executed in the mannerism of influential political governance. It is part of the critical approach that prevails in this work that the political leadership in question remains dysfunctional in global mechanisms.

REFERENCES

Agarwal, M. (2010). Developing countries: Impact of the crisis and the response-implications for an approach to the G20 by Russia, India and China. *China Report, 46,* 1, pp. 71-87.

Agarwal, M. & Samantha, S. (2014). Financial crisis of 2008 and shifting economic power: Is the convergence?. *China Report, 50,* 1, pp. 45-67.

Aktan, C. C., & Vural, T. (2006). Ekonomi Politikası Yönetiminde Mali ve Parasal Kurallar. *Kurumsal İktisat Kurallar, Kurumlar ve Ekonomik Gelişme*. In C. C. Aktan (Ed.), *Sermaye Piyasası Kurulu Kurumsal Araştırmalar Serisi. No: 2. Yayın No. 194* (pp. 119–135). Ankara, Turkey: SPK.

Aktan, C. C., & Vural, T. (2006). Yeni Kurumsal İktisat. *Kurumsal İktisat Kurallar, Kurumlar ve Ekonomik Gelişme*. In C. C. Aktan (Ed.), *Sermaye Piyasası Kurulu Kurumsal Araştırmalar Serisi No: 2, Yayın No. 194* (pp. 19–43). Ankara, Turkey: SPK.

Aligica, P. D. (2014). *Institutional diversity and political economy: the Ostroms and beyond*. USA: Oxford University Press.

Angeloni, I. (2009). The Pittsburgh G20 Summit. *Inter Economics*, *44*(September/October), 262–263. doi:10.100710272-009-0304-0

Beeson, M., & Bell, S. (2009). The G-20 and international economic governance: Hegemony, collectivism, or both? *Global Governance*, *15*(1), 67–86. doi:10.1163/19426720-01501005

Callaghan, M. (2014). The G20, IMF and global imbalances: The policymakers' perspective. In M. Callaghan, C. Ghate, S. Pickford, & F. Rathinam (Eds.), Global cooperation among G20 countries (pp. 83–94). India: Springer India. doi:10.1007/978-81-322-1659-9_7

Callaghan, M., Carmignani, F., Makin, A. J., & Strube, D. (2014). G20 and development. *South Asian Journal of Macroeconomics and Public Finance*, *3*(2), 155–173. doi:10.1177/2277978714548627

Callaghan, M., Ghate, C., Pickford, S., & Rathinam, F. (2014). Global cooperation among G20 countries: Responding to the crisis and restoring growth. In Global Cooperation Among G20 Countries. pp. 1-21.

Cooper, A. F. (2010). The G20 as an improvised crisis committee and/or a contested 'steering committee' for the world. *International Affairs*, *86*(3), pp. 741-757.

Curran, L. (2009). The impact of the financial and economic crisis on world trade and trade policy. *Inter Economics*, (September/October): 264–273.

Dolls, M., Peichi, A., & Zimmermann, K. Z. (2012). *A challenge for the G20: Global debt brakes and transnational fiscal supervisory councils* (pp. 31–38). Debt Brakes-Intereconomics.

Eğilmez, M. (2008). *Küresel Finans Krizi Piyasa Sisteminin Eleştirisi*. İstanbul, Turkey: Remzi Kitabevi.

Eichengreen, B. (2010). Lessons of the crisis for emerging markets. *International Economics and Economic Policy*, *7*(1), 49–62. doi:10.100710368-010-0149-9

Escaith, H. (2009). Global supply chains in times of international crisis. *Inter Economics*, (September/October): 268–273.

Evenett, S. J. (2009). Systemic consequences of crisis era protectionism. *Inter Economics*, (September/October): 282–286.

Gartner, D. (2013). 21st century international institutions. *Proceedings of the Annual Meeting, (American Society of International Law)*, 107. International Law in a Multipolar World. pp. 264-267. 10.5305/procannmeetasil.107.0264

Germain, R. (2009). Financial order and world politics: Crisis, change and continuity. *International Affairs, 85*(4), pp. 669-687.Gökay, B. (2009). The 2008 world economic crisis: Global shifts and fault lines. *Global Research.* Retrieved from http://www.globalresearch.ca/the-2008-world-economic-crisis-global-shifts-and-faultlines/12283

Gordon, P. A. (2017). Vision of Trump at war: How the president could stumble into conflict. *Foreign Affairs.* Retrieved from https://www.foreignaffairs.com/articles/2017-03-22/vision-trump-war

Güler, E. (2012). Geçiş Ekonomileri ve Yeni Kurumsal İktisat'ın Yeniden Yükselişi. *Doğuş Üniversitesi Dergisi, 13*(1), 52–68. doi:10.31671/dogus.2018.115

Helleiner, E., & Pagliari, S. (2011). The end of an era in international financial regulation? A postcrisis research agenda. *International Organization, 65*(1), 169–200. doi:10.1017/S0020818310000305

Hürcan, Y. G. (1999). *Mali Disiplin Sağlanmasında Yasal Düzenlemelerin Yeri, Önemi, Dünya uygulamaları ve Türkiye Örneğinin İncelenmesi. T.C. Başbakanlık Hazine Müsteşarlığı Yayınları. Araştırma ve İnceleme Dizisi; 23.* Ankara, Turkey: T.C. Başbakanlık Hazine Müsteşarlığı.

İpek, P. (2013, Winter). Hegemony and crisis in global political economy: The importance of legitimacy. *Perceptions, 18*(4), 29–45.

Jessop, B. (2010). The 'return' of the national state in the current crisis of the world market. *Capital and Class, 34*(1), 38–43. doi:10.1177/0309816809353480

Kaletsky, A. (2017). The role of capitalism in the rise of populism. *World Economic Forum,* Retrieved from https://www.weforum.org/agenda/2017/01/the-role-of-capitalism-in-the-rise-of-populism?utm_content=buffer569c7&utm_medium=social&utm_source=twitter.com&utm_campaign=buffer

Karakayalı, H., & Yanıkkaya, H. (2006). Kurumsal Faktörlerin Ekonomik Büyüme Etkileri. *Kurumsal İktisat Kurallar, Kurumlar ve Ekonomik Gelişme.* In C. C. Aktan (Ed.), *Sermaye Piyasası Kurulu Kurumsal Araştırmalar Serisi. No: 2. Yayın No. 194* (pp. 135–170). Ankara, Turkey: SPK.

Knight, J. & Johnson, J. (2011). *The priority of democracy: Political consequences*

Lane, J. E., & Maeland, R. (2011). Global financial crisis and international institutions: Challenges, opportunities and change. *Public Organization Review, 11*(1), 29–43. doi:10.100711115-010-0145-0

Menard, C., & Shirley, M. M. (Eds.). (2005). *Handbook of New Institutional Economics.* The Netherlands: Springer. doi:10.1007/b106770

Menkhoff, L., & Meyer, R. (2010). *The G20 proposal on IMF governance: Has any progress been made?* (pp. 171–179). IMF Reform-Intereconomics.

Minsky, H. P. (1980). Money, financial markets, and the coherence of a market economy. *Journal of Post Keynesian Economics, 3*(1), 21–31. doi:10.1080/01603477.1980.11489192

Nachane, D. M. (2014). Global crisis, financial institutions and reforms: An Indian perspective. In A. N. Ghosh & A. K. Karmakar (Eds.), *Analytical issues in trade, development and finance* (pp. 97–124). India: India Studies in Business and Economics Springer. doi:10.1007/978-81-322-1650-6_7

Nelson, S. C. (2016). *Ayşe Kaya, 2015, Power and Global Economic Institutions* (pp. 523–527). Springer Review of International Organization.

North, D. C. (2002). *Institutions, institutional change and economic performance.* Cambridge, UK: Cambridge University Press.

Onuf, N. (2002). Institutions, intentions and international relations. *Review of International Studies, 28*(2), 211–228. doi:10.1017/S0260210502002115

Özveren, E. (2007). Kurumsal İktisat: Aralanan Karakutu. In E. Özveren (Ed.), *Kurumsal İktisat* (pp. 15–45). Ankara, Turkey: İmge.

Pardo, R. P. (2012). Leadership, decision-making and governance in the European Union and East Asia: Crisis and post-crisis. *Asia Europe Journal, 9*(2-4), 73–76. doi:10.100710308-012-0316-4

Patrick, S. M. (2017). Trump and world order. *Foreign Affairs*, (March/April): 52–57.

Pelagidis, T., & Papasotiriou, H. (2002). Globalisation or regionalism? States, markets and the structure of international trade. *Review of International Studies, 28*(3), 519–535. doi:10.1017/S0260210502005193

Polonyi, K. (2003). *Büyük Dönüşüm: Çağımızın Siyasal ve Ekonomik Kökenleri, Çev. Ayşe Buğra.* İstanbul, Turkey: İletişim.

Prior, M. (2017). Hegemony and all that stuff. *Think (London, England), 72*, 26–29.

Rahman, J., Orzechowska-Fischer, E., & Syed, R. (2014). Reforming the international monetary system: An institutional perspective. In M. Callaghan, C. Ghate, S. Pickford, & F. Rathinam (Eds.), Global cooperation among G20 countries (pp. 161–177). India: Springer India. doi:10.1007/978-81-322-1659-9_15

Şenses, F. Öniş, Z. & Bakır, C. (Eds.). (2013). Ülke Deneyimleri Işığında Küresel Kriz ve Yeni Ekonomik Düzen. İstanbul: İletişim.

Sheel, A. (2014). The macroeconomic policy response to the international financial and economic crisis and the G20. In M. Callaghan, C. Ghate, S. Pickford, & F. Rathinam (Eds.), Global cooperation among G20 Countries (pp. 241–280). India: Springer India. doi:10.1007/978-81-322-1659-9_21

Soence, M., & Zagha, R. (2011). Restoring inclusive growth in advanced economies: A conversation with economists and policy makers from the G20. *Comparative Economic Studies, 53*(3), 333–347. doi:10.1057/ces.2011.25

Stark, J. (2010). Is the global economy headed for a lost decade? A European perspective. *Business Economics (Cleveland, Ohio), 45*(3), 147–151. doi:10.1057/be.2010.12

Stavrev, E. (2014). Strengthening the international monetary system. In M. Callaghan, C. Ghate, S. Pickford, & F. Rathinam (Eds.), Global cooperation among G20 countries (pp. 179–184). India: Springer India. doi:10.1007/978-81-322-1659-9_16

Subacchi, P. (2008). New power centres and new power brokers: Are they shaping a new economic order?. *International Affairs,* 84(3), pp. 485-498.

Venhaus, M. (2013). *Power shift to the East? American hegemony and China's ascent in times of global financial & monetary crises. Freie Universitat Berlin* (pp. 1–26). Graduate School of Global Politics.

Vines, D. (2010). The global macroeconomic crisis and G20 macroeconomic policy coordination. *The Journal of Applied Economic Research, 4*(2), pp. 157-175.

Wuthnow, J., Li, X., & Qi, L. (2012). Diverse multilateralism: Four strategies in China's multilateral diplomacy. *Journal of China Political Science., 17*(3), 269–290. doi:10.100711366-012-9202-6

Yağcı, M. (2016). A Beijing consensus in the making: The rise of Chinese initiatives in the international political economy and implications for developing countries. *Perceptions Journal of International Affairs,* Summer, 21(2). pp. 29-56.

Chapter 4
The Political Economy of the Market

Itir Ozer-Imer
Hacettepe University, Turkey

Derya Guler Aydin
Hacettepe University, Turkey

ABSTRACT

In the modern period, there are two concerns regarding the nature of the market. One is associated with market structures that involve solely the economic sphere and exclude all other factors including historical, social, and institutional ones. Hence, it conducts a static analysis, while the other relates the market process with all the aforementioned factors in addition to the economic ones, and therefore, combines economic and non-economic spheres, and the analysis becomes dynamic. This chapter scrutinizes the conceptualization of the market; that is whether the market is considered as a "structure" or a "process". With this consideration, authors relate the conceptualization of the market with the type of competition. When the market is regarded as a "process", it is possible to claim that market becomes an "institution". Thus, by taking the market as an institution and considering competition within a dynamic framework, the emergent economic theoretical structure provides an in-depth, comprehensive, analytical, and novel approach to real economic and social concerns.

INTRODUCTION

The notion that market has sociological concerns has been supported by both historical evidences and various economic analyses. Different schools of thought advocated different market conceptualizations, and based their analysis on different types of competition. It is necessary to distinguish the two basic dimensions of competition in economic analysis. First of these is the synchronous aspect of competition, while the second one is its diachronous character. In the case of simultaneous competition theories, competition is examined within a certain time period and various economic decisions are taken as a result of determination of price, production and accumulation in a given time period and these decisions

DOI: 10.4018/978-1-7998-0333-1.ch004

Copyright © 2020, IGI Global. Copying or distributing in print or electronic forms without written permission of IGI Global is prohibited.

are influenced directly by the given competitive structure. Within this framework, it is possible to set forth the general structure of simultaneous competition theories with the help of cost-price analysis and equilibrium approaches (Fortman, 1966: 40). Such an analysis excludes social dynamics and is concerned with a single point in time.

Intertemporal competition, on the other hand, analyzes processes. In such a framework, the analysis does not take place in a given time period but rather, structural changes such as technological development, growth of some firms and introduction of new products into the market are given place. Theories within this understanding of competition have a framework that influence and are influenced by not only some firms or industries but also the social structure, which includes the whole economy. In other words, it can be argued that intertemporal competition provides a framework that brings together economics and social dynamics in the existing economic problems. Besides, it is crucial to take into consideration dynamic factors, and accordingly, technological change and its coevolutionary patterns in comprehending the subsequent changes in the economic and social structure.

Within this context, the emergence and functioning of the markets, which is considered as the main economic institution, is the subject theme of economic sociology. It is possible to define economic sociology as an attempt of enlightening economic phenomena by employing sociological approaches to these phenomena. Both economics and economic sociology share similar objectives and concerns. Yet, economic sociology has severely different characteristics than the conventional economics; it attaches great importance to social relations and the role of social institutions.

The subject of competition and the type of competition are directly related to the market, which can be considered as an institution, in the economics literature. It is possible to classify the market either as a "structure" or a "process" in different schools of thought in economics. Whether the market is accepted a structure or a process determines the type of competition. In the approaches that regard and define the market as a structure, competition is static[1], where technology is taken as given, whereas in the approaches that show that the market is a process, competition is dynamic[2] and causes technological changes. In dynamic competition theories that take the market as a process, technological change leads to economic and social changes. Although technological change is seen as diffusion of innovations to the economic sphere, it is inevitable that it will also be reflected in the social sphere. As an economic concept, technology cannot be considered as independent of the process of social knowledge accumulation when viewed from the accumulation of technological knowledge process. Within this context, the market as a process causes dynamic competition, dynamic competition leads to technological change and technological change results in economic and social change, and this analytical relationship falls within the subject theme of economic sociology. This study aims to scrutinize the conceptualization of the market; that is whether the market is considered as a "structure" or a "process". With this consideration, the study relates the conceptualization of the market with the type of competition. When the market is regarded as a "process", it is possible to claim that market becomes an "institution". Such an approach allows for a wider analytical perspective that does not distinguish social reality from the economic reality.

SETTING THE STAGE

This study establishes the crucial relationship between economic sociology and competition within the framework of the concept of sociology of market. The understanding of the market determines the nature of competition. Since competition is not only a "structure" but is also a "process" including technology, rivalry between firms, and institutions, it can be claimed that competition should be regarded not solely as purely economic but it should also comprise sociological aspects and problems, without which the analysis would be incomplete.

When the emergence of the market from the ancient Greek to the present day is considered, it can be argued that the structure and function of the market have changed depending on the historical and sociological factors of the period. The market is not only analyzed by economists but by also sociologists including Max Weber, Harrison White, Neil Fligstein, and Pierre Bourdieu. The market indeed is also a sociological concept, and it results from complex social, political and legal needs (Swedberg, 2007: 233). The historical evolution of the market is also parallel to the changes in these needs. Undoubtedly, the industry revolution has been very effective in the evolution and formation of the modern market structures.

Karl Polanyi states in *The Great Transformation* that the industrial revolution evolved the traditional economy into a new type of economy. The modern market structure is such a concern that markets alone control, regulate, and direct the whole economic and social structure. Accordingly, self-regulating mechanism ensures order in different segments of the economy, i.e. production, exchange, and distribution. Hence, all production, distribution relations are reduced to market relations, while economic domain is embedded in the social sphere, market becomes a mechanism that dominates all institutional, political and historical factors (Polanyi, 1944: 68-69).

Weber also sets forth that during the primitive times of civilization, the sociological structure was very different, and hence the type of market was included in social concerns. "In the beginning commerce is an affair between ethnic groups; it does not take place between members of the same tribe or of the same community but is in the oldest social communities an external phenomenon, being directed only toward foreign tribes" (Weber, 1927: 195). For example, the exchange relations in any primitive social structure depend entirely on the sociological dynamics rather than economic dynamics. In other words, it is not possible that a member of any tribe can behave freely and in accordance with his/her own will (Weber, 1927: 312-13).

Weber believes that in the modern societies, the price on the market is determined as a result of economic struggle. There are two characteristics of the price struggle: i) competition struggle, ii) interest struggle that takes place between two parties, who end in an exchange. Weber also emphasizes that if there is a necessity of determining the "empirical price" in an inquiry rather than the "theoretical price", various factors need to be considered, i.e. there is no such thing as perfect information. Weber bases his analysis of the market on social action. In his work entitled *Economy and Society*, Weber conducts a sociological approach to the market (Swedberg, 2007: 120). A peaceful conflict is inherent in competition....it is such that although opportunities and advantages are desired by everyone, the effort of reaching those prospects is properly peaceful. Weber also gives importance to the interplay between the market and the rest of the society (Swedberg, 2007: 120-121).

It is also possible to show that the market is a sociological concept based on Granovetter's (1974) piece entitled *Getting a Job,* which can be considered as the most outstanding work on the market and its constituents, and as a representative work in economic sociology. *Getting a Job* aims to investigate how people get employed by scrutinizing the social mechanisms and it takes into consideration technical, managerial and professional workers. White (1970) and Baker (1981), in their studies entitled *Chains of Opportunity* and *Markets as Networks*, respectively, set forth a theoretical approach regarding both the empirical study and the sociological theory of markets. In fact, though, it would be more appropriate to view markets not as homogenous but as socially constructed in many ways. It is necessary that the sociology of market focuses not only on the influence of the market on social relations, but also on its dynamic nature, and it regards the market as a tool that can be employed to attain the economic environment.

Whether the market is an institution was also studied by economists. In other words, in the last few decades, the institutional dimension of the market has attracted the interest of economists. Market as an institution is the basic tool of the relationship between economic sociology and competition. For example, in classical political economy, the market is a concrete concept and the basic research topic is the production relations. They regard the market as a place, where economic and social interests meet and reach an agreement. That is, the market theorizes different types of interests. Adam Smith puts forward that natural progression lies behind the evolution of the market in history. Although with the analyses of David Ricardo and J.S. Mill, political economy turned out to be significantly abstract, it was still interested in concrete economic institutions such as the markets. Both Ricardo and Mill adopt the concept of interest and conduct interest analysis. Marx attaches more importance to production than the market when the issue in question is the value of the commodity. In fact, Marx also emphasizes that the market principally comprises social relations.

In the marginalist tradition, market is a hypothetical notion. This tradition analyzes the market only via the theory of exchange. The perfectly competitive market is quite abstract, and perfect competition and perfect information are characterizing it. For example, the perfectly competitive market in Walras is a tool of guaranteeing the general equilibrium of the economy in the spheres of production, distribution and exchange. Here, the market is not considered as an institution.

In the Austrian school, according to Menger, market results from gradual, historical development, which is natural and unintentional. Mises and Hayek conduct an exceptionally comprehensive analysis and involve social theory in addition to economics. At the core of the neo-Austrian analysis lies the theory of market that regards the market as a "process". Mises views market not as a place, a thing or as a collective entity, but instead stresses that market is a "process", which is motivated by the interaction of many individuals, who collaborate under the division of labor.

Under the light of the aforementioned factors, the basic argument raised in this study is that the role of competition in economic theories should be examined within the changing structure of capitalism and the tools of economic sociology should be used by bringing together the conceptualization of the market and the type of competition. Thus, by taking the market as an institution and considering competition within a dynamic framework, the *emergent* economic theoretical structure provides an in-depth, comprehensive, analytical and novel approach to real economic and social concerns.

SIMULTANEOUS COMPETITION APPROACHES AND THE MARKET AS A "STRUCTURE"

The neoclassical perfect competition[3] is one of the main approaches, where the market is considered as a "structure" and the competition is static. Neoclassical economists focuse on exchange relations and the basic role of competition, in this respect, is to ensure equilibrium. Within this framework, it can be argued that competitive capitalism, which is the basic institutional structure of the marginalist tradition, guarantees the formation of market prices and equilibrium within a static structure of analysis. In such an analysis, where production and production relations are given, the prices and quantities determined by competition allow for the most fair distribution conditions for the society, and distribution is no longer considered as a problem (Akyüz, 1977: 104).

It can argued that marginalist tradition has been adopted by all neoclassical economists and that the basic approach has been that equilibrium and social harmony would be guaranteed with the assumption of perfectly competitive market. In the context of this analysis, in which dynamic processes, social factors and hence, sociology of market is excluded, the most crucial analytical tool of equilibrium is, undoubtedly, the assumption of perfect competition, i.e the market is considered as a "structure".

Perfect competition excludes monopoly power, while giving a market structure, in which there are an infinite number of buyers and sellers. It is believed that none of the infinite number of buyers and sellers in the perfectly competitive market can control the market price (Stigler, 1965: 262) and it becomes possible that a competitive industry can reach equilibrium in the long run in the absence of entry and exit barriers into the market. Nevertheless, in an environment where there is risk and uncertainty, it becomes a problem how the decision units will make rational calculations. The assumption of perfect information eliminates this problem and guarantees the equivalence of the returns of resources in the long run under expected return conditions (Stigler, 1965: 264-265). Thus, the problem of resource allocation is solved and the problem of distribution disappears. Through the market, all economic problems are solved, while the problems related to the social field are excluded. Therefore, one of the most important criticisms directed to perfect competition is that the economic sphere is reduced to the sphere of the market.

It can be argued that one of the most important consequences of these criticisms and arguments is the imperfect competition theories[4]. Imperfect competition analyzes monopoly markets that are characterized as an alternative to perfect competition markets, while monopolistic competition markets are an alternative to both market structures. Because markets in the real world are not at the two extremes but are between perfectly competitive and monopoly markets (Bain, 1971: 258).

It should be noted that analytical tools in imperfect competition contain "marginal" concepts, and it can be argued that in fact, it applies marginal concepts to market analysis and prefers marginal revenue and cost concepts (Kaldor, 1960: 54-55). Under the conditions of imperfect competition, factors do not generate as much income as their marginal physical productivity. This leads to a disturbance of resource allocation and a problem of division.

However, while criticizing perfect competition, by defining competition in another market structure, imperfect competition proceeds with the static analysis, which can also be included under the simultaneous approaches. Since the influence of firms over price includes factors, primarily related with demand, the impact of technological innovations and changes in the economic structure are of secondary importance in these markets. It can be argued that the imperfect competition understanding is not a critique of perfect competition but is rather a continuation of this analysis since production and technological change, and hence, time are left out of the analysis and competition is conceptualized as a market structure. Hence, market is not considered as an institution under the imperfectly competitive markets.

Another static approach, based on the criticism of the assumptions of perfect competition, is the contestable markets[5]. These markets analyze the outcomes of perfect competition by starting from a certain number of firms. In contestable markets, while there is free entry into the market, the exit from the market is costless. However, free entry into the market does not mean that this entry is easy and costless.

Profit maximization in perfectly competitive markets depends on the condition that there are many firms in the industry. In contestable markets, there can be two or more firms in the market. When the number of firms are two or more, this does not prevent the equality of prices to marginal cost. The equality of prices to marginal cost is the equilibrium point that guarantees efficient allocation of resources just as in the case of perfectly competitive markets (Baumol, 1982: 4).

As discussed under the different conceptualization of markets, market as a "structure" guarantees harmony in the whole economy by the price mechanism. All social and different types of economic interests are disregarded, and society and social needs are separated from the economic sphere. For this reason, although these analytical frameworks useful in theory, they are insufficient in explaning and understanding the economic and social reality.

INTERTEMPORAL COMPETITION APPROACHES AND THE MARKET AS A "PROCESS"

Classical competition, workable competition and the Austrian school, which are classified under the intertemporal competition approaches in this study, take the market as a "process" and hence, the market is considered as an institution. In such an analysis, there is real rivalry among firms, competition processes and technological change are taken into consideration rather than being excluded from the analysis. For instance, prices, which are set forth with value in the classical school, are production prices or in Smith's words "natural price is a central price, which all goods are continuously attracted to" (Smith, 1993: 56). The most important tool that directs market prices to the center of gravity is "free competition". Different than the perfect competition, free competition is a concept that expresses competition and processes from the viewpoint of firms in obtaining high profit. Natural or production prices are determined under the conditions of given real wages, total output and the technology level, and market prices tend to adjust to natural prices under these given conditions. In classical economics, distribution shares, known as wages and profits, are the main determinants of production prices along with technology. The prices are determined by the profit added to the production cost, which depend on the production technology. This profit is determined by the rate of profit, which is equal in all sectors as a result of free competition. However, in order to determine the profit rate, input prices, which are the output of other sectors, should be known. Market prices are equalized to the production prices through the effect of free competition.[6]

In his book entitled *the Wealth of Nations*, Adam Smith discusses competition and points to two different roles of competition. In Smith, the balancing role of competition is examined in the chapter entitled "On the Natural and Market Prices of Goods", "equilibrium" is defined as the situation, in which the free movement of capital directs natural prices to effective demand and effective demand matches natural prices (Smith, 1993: 56). Nevertheless, according to Smith, free competition increases capital accumulation and leads to developments in the division of labor and technology. Smith explains the increase in labor productivity with the increase in labor skills through the increase in mechanization in production and saving the time wasted when moving from one task to another (Smith 1993: 15-17). Within this framework, the production of goods at lower prices through technological developments and improvements in the division of labor would increase profit as it reduces the costs. In this context, competition not only allows for the transfer of capital from one area to another, but it also leads to the development of production techniques and reorganization of the division of labor in order to produce the goods at lower prices. These improvements in the division of labor increase capital accumulation. The increase in capital accumulation, in turn, increases the productivity of labor by ensuring that new machines are introduced. The increase in the productivity of labor prevents the decrease in the profit caused by the decrease in prices. This refers to a change in the industrial structure, so that technological development and improvements in the division of labor is ensured and the rate of profit can be prevented from falling below the average rate of profit.

Ricardo also regards the production prices as the center of gravity. He summarizes the operation of the mechanism as follows: "When there is an increase or decrease in the price, profits also rise above or fall below the general profit level. Thus, capital either finds an impulse in order to be employed in a certain area, where the price change is present or is stimulated to leave that area. ...the impetuosity of the capital users in moving from a less profitable to a more profitable business creates a tendency of making the rate of profit to be equal for all or being determined at the level, which is not more profitable" (Ricardo, 1955: 48).

In Marx, the concept of the center of gravity is crucial in terms of the interaction of supply and demand, and long-term prices (Semmler, 1984: 22-23). In the theory of Marx, competition, as in Smith, is not a balancing factor but it rather creates instability and disrupts allocation of resources. The starting point of Marx's analysis is the production of surplus and the problem of capital accumulation, and concentration of capital occurs in different sectors because of competition. In Marx's analysis of competition, it is possible to see battles of competition, which starts with the concentration of capital. Marx examines competition as a factor, influencing production, distribution and accumulation of surplus (Eatwell, 1982: 209-210). In terms of production, Marx assumes that the same good can be produced by different techniques and that there is no single technique in the production of goods. In other words, according to Marx, changes in social or effective demand also affect the production technique that determines the production prices, and hence, in the long run, the exchange values of goods can be determined by different techniques in the industries (Dutt, 1987: 57-60). Within this framework, it is possible to claim that in their prioritized analysis of production, classical economists examine the process of capital accumulation, and accordingly, they scrutinize the increase in profit rates. Hence, the aim of making more profit leads capital owners to change their production techniques in the process of competition. Undoubtedly, changes in the technical conditions of production would lead to changes in the initial parameters of the analysis; the level of total output and real wages, and would cause continuous and internal instabilities in the economy. Although Smith and Ricardo provide a framework of analysis that emphasizes the balancing aspect of competition, in the classical competition understanding, it is possible to find the role of the capitalist system that causes technological changes and instabilities due to its nature directed towards profit. Within this context, the classical competition allows for a framework of analysis that examines processes, takes into consideration dynamic instabilities and competition of high profit-making among firms. Such an analysis framework appears to be consistent with the historical holistic approach set forth by the sociology of market.

Similarly, John Maurice Clark, one of the representatives of workable competition theory, aims to show in his study entitled *Competition as a Dynamic Process* in 1961 that competition is a dynamic process. Markham (1950) puts forward that workable competition is more efficient compared to perfect competition. The distinguishing characteristic of workable competition, which is offered as an alternative to perfect competition, is that it is not an abstract theory, and hence, it connects industrial development to dynamic forces through its own competition policy. Clark defines these dynamic forces as a process of innovation, which depends on technological change for the whole economy (Çapoğlu, 1991: 38). In other words, technological innovation and entrepreneur are at the center of competition, which Clark considers to be a dynamic process. With this aspect, workable competition is an element of dynamic processes that express the competition among entrepreneurs as in the case of competition understanding of classical economics. In workable competition, the role of the entrepreneur is to realize technical innovations, while the function of competition is to allow firms to adapt to these innovations (Clark, 1961: 9).

Within this context, Clark (1961) argues that his aim is to investigate the conditions, in which social welfare is optimum in a market structure that takes the realities into account. Clark identifies the innovation of the entrepreneur as temporal delays that are required for the imperfect information and adaptation to the market, and in fact, innovation emerges as a result of the market failure. Although the innovations introduced by the entrepreneurs are regarded as the guarantee of growth and development, this growth may pose a threat to the functioning of the market since it would mean that some firms obtain monopolistic power. In this context, competition, which can be seen both the reason and the result of market failures, are expected to create dynamic and innovative development, while excluding the monopolistic tendencies (Clark, 1961: 178-194).

The static elements of competition are the market share, optimum allocation of resources and supply of goods on the basis of consumer preferences, while dynamic elements are technological development and innovations. From this respect, workable competition is a tool, which refers to the dynamic elements of competition, about which the debates continue regarding the market as a social entity. However, with its emphasis on market failures and innovations, it can be regarded as an analytical framework that carries competition to the real political domain as in the case of classical competition and that is compatible with the sociology of market.

Another approach in dynamic competition at the point of market failure is presented by Friedrich A. Hayek, with the criticism of the perfect information assumption. In spite of the different views of Hayek and other Austrians (Carl Menger, Ludwig von Mises, Joseph Schumpeter), their main starting points are methodological individualism, incompleteness of knowledge, processes and the functioning of the market mechanism.

According to the approach of this school, competition refers to a “process” that includes economic activities, not a market “structure”. The entrepreneur involved in this process is the one, who can evaluate the market environment well for high profit opportunities. While the aim of the entrepreneur in the Austrian tradition is essentially similar, the results of innovation activities differ. For instance, according to Kirzner, when the entrepreneur invests in the high profit areas, this leads the economy to equilibrium at the end of the process, while in Schumpeter, the technological innovations of the entrepreneur lead to instabilities in the economy due to the changing nature of capitalism (Çapoğlu, 1991: 35-36). In the case of Hayek, who sees the economic order as a kind of automatic order, economic activity is regarded as a regular activity at the end of the process (Vaughn, 1999: 129-144). That is, equilibrium occurs based on the decisions of social agents in the process, it does not represent a certain point in time.

Market as a “process” and innovations introduced by the entrepreneur in the market can be defined as the ability of capturing the alternatives, neglected by the other decision-makers. Therefore, according to Hayek, the knowledge of the entrepreneur is not an objective knowledge that everybody knows but it is the practical knowledge, which is predicted to evaluate the profit opportunities (Hayek, 1945: 524). These innovations that emerge as the result of this knowledge, and which affect the structure and operation of the market, are the product of a historical time or process, and at the same time, they change the knowledge that the individuals have and the decisions they take, depending on this knowledge.

With innovations introduced by the entrepreneur, market is not a “structure” but is in a continous process of change, and therefore, it may never reach equilibrium. On the other hand, Hayek argues that the order in economic life is the order, a kind of automatic order, and the decision units can eliminate the disequilibrium through the rules they follow (Hayek, 1948: 95). In other words, innovations that emerge as a result of the aim of obtaining high profit in the market process may lead to instabilities but the belief in the self-regulation of the market in Hayek transforms these instabilities into regular activities. Hayek sees the entrepreneur as a person pursuing the knowledge of a particular time and place, and entrepreneurship is a competitive activity by its nature (Hayek, 1944: 24-25). This is because the profit opportunity is necessarily pushing the entrepreneur to a competitive tendency, and Hayek defines the market as a process of invention. Competition between decision-making units that have to adapt to a process, nourished by technological innovations and inventions, may also be the source of other innovations in the long run. At this point, it is necessary to examine the competition analysis of Schumpeter, which presents another dynamic framework, and that regards the result of innovation as instability.

According to Schumpeter, due to its natural structure, capitalism is in a continuous state of change, and there is no room for stability in the system if there is change. Thus, Schumpeter believes that the role of competition in economic theories should be examined within the changing structure of capitalism. In this context, according to Schumpeter, who defines the basic reality about capitalism as "creative destruction" (Schumpeter, 1981: 144; O'Dennel, 1975: 210-211), the vitality of the capitalist system depends on production of new consumption goods, use of new techniques in production and new industrial organizations. While changing the economic structure, industrial transformation causes the destruction of the old structure and the formation of a new structure (O'Donnell, 1975: 211). The dynamic nature of capitalism stems from the fact that economic life is always a changing social environment. Schumpeter states that the capitalist system is continuously in an "air of revolution" and that this structure destroys old factors and creates new ones (Schumpeter, 1981: 143-144). For this reason, Schumpeter believes that creative destruction is the basis of capitalism.

According to Schumpeter, competition within the capitalist process is not the price competition among firms selling the same goods but is a competition that comprises the production of new goods, new technology and new resources in new organizations (O'Dennel, 1975: 211). This understanding of competition presents a more realistic framework than the static competition approach, which demonstrates a certain point in time (Fortman, 1966: 74), and it is associated with Schumpeter, who does not distinguishing economic sphere from the social sphere. In this context, Schumpeterian competition can be defined as a social process that involves innovations.

Schumpeter states that the emergence of a product, and the effects of a technique, a resource on the emergence of a new form of organization are important rather than the form of competition in the capitalist system. Competition in this conceptualization is not only price competition, but is a pressure, struggle and race, that always exist between businessmen, hence, it is, in fact, a competition of change (Schumpeter, 1981: 148-149).

As can be seen above, the link between market as a "process" and the type of competition can be established by taking into consideration economic and social reality. The entrepreneur, the capitalist, here, is considered as a social entity but is not an abstraction. Competition based on the goal of achieving high profit leads to technological changes and the effect of this change is realized in the social sphere even though it shows itself in the economic sphere.

CONCLUSION

A conflict of economic interests surrounds a market just like various economic incidents. In the case of markets, this conflict is mainly between buyers and sellers (Weber, 1978, 635-40). However, it is not only exchange that takes place in the market, Weber believes that competition also exists. Competition takes place for the sake of being the final seller and the final buyer, this is referred to as the "struggle between competitors". Only after this struggle has been completed, the exchange can start, this means "struggle over the exchange". Simply, rational capitalism revolves around the modern type of market. In the alleged political capitalism, in order to obtain profit, either some are favored by the political authority with the provision of grants or private economic interests are assisted in certain different ways (Weber, 1978).

The market is scrutinized by both economists and sociologists, while sociologists mainly take into account the institutional aspect of the market, some of the economists define the market as a "structure", and accordingly, develop a static competition analysis. Another group of economists regard the fact that competition is a dynamic process that involves both the market processes and the impact of market relations on the social domain. The market is a product of human action, not of human conception. Different than the mainstream economists, there is no center of the market but rather the market comprises a network of various connected economies (Morris & Monning, 2005: 121). If economic and social life are embedded, capitalists, entrepreneurs, even producers and consumers need to be considered as social entities, the market cannot dominate economic life on its own and the economic domain cannot be squeezed in the market. In an environment, where the market is a "process", technological changes and the effects of economic and social life on each other are constantly felt, and hence, the market should be considered as an institution.

Competition is also a tool frequently used in analyses with its changing function depending on what is understood from the economic issue. Considering the economic issue as production or exchange makes competition either static or dynamic, and each school of thought handles its own understanding of competition within this framework. In their analysis of capital accumulation and the division of production between social classes, classical economists deal with the two different aspects of competition, namely, its equilibriating and disequilibriating aspects, while the economic issue for neoclassical economists is defined as the efficient allocation of scarce resources, and their analysis mainly focuses on exchange relations. Perfect competition is used as the main tool for this framework of analysis. Classical economists determine the reason for the movement of capital from one production area to another as the high profit aim of the capital owners, and puts forward that this is the source of capital accumulation and economic development. Since the problem is the accumulation of surplus, it necessitates the problem of distribution, while the problem of distribution necessitates social relations and a dynamic structure. Consequently, with its equilibriating and disequilibriating functions, free competition causes changes in economic and social structure. On the other hand, perfect competition remains only as an analytical tool of the economic sphere, and as an abstract market structure definition, demonstrating how prices and quantities automatically ensure equilibrium.

Dynamic competition changes the environment due to technological change and innovations, and processes are required for technological change and innovation. The aim of high profit creates instabilities as it causes technological changes, without being associated with issues such as the distribution of total production. Capitalism requires social relations and change, and deals with its own understanding of competition. The high profit aim of the capital owner and the entrepreneur, which requires innovations, arises from the same source; the conflict that exists between social classes. Conflicts create mismatches, while mismatches create instabilities, and competition becomes a tool that reproduces these instabilities. This is a natural result since capitalism, which is the main theme of the analyses, requires high profit aim due to its functioning, and this necessitates technological change.

While economic analysis deals with the behavior of people at any time and the economic impacts of their production with this behavior, economic sociology scrutinizes why people behave the way they do. If the definition human behavior comprises social institutions, which are related with economic behavior such as government, property inheritance, contract, in addition to actions, motives and propensities, then this expression is really useful in telling us all we need (Schumpeter, 1954: 21).

Finally, it is not possible to fully comprehend the dynamic behind the different natures of competition, static or dynamic, without understanding that interests and social relations have a very crucial role in their structures. For this reason, market should be considered as an institution in order to grasp the socio-economic reality.

REFERENCES

Akyüz, Y. (1977). *Sermaye bölüşüm büyüme*. Ankara, Turkey: Ankara Üniversitesi Basımevi.

Bain, S. J. (1971). Chamberlin's impact on microeconomic theory. In H. Townsend (Ed.), Price theory (253-287). UK: Penguin Books.

Baumol, J. W. (1982). Contestable markets: An uprising in the theory of industry structure. *The American Economic Review*, *7*(1), 1–15.

Çapoğlu, G. (1991). *Prices, profits and financial structures*. Aldershot, UK: Edward Elgar.

Clark, J. M. (1961). *Competition as a dynamic process*. Washington, DC: Brookings Institution.

Dutt, A. K. (1987). Competition, monopoly power and the uniform rate of profits. *The Review of Radical Political Economics*, *19*(4), 55–72. doi:10.1177/048661348701900405

Eatwell, J. (1982). Competition. In I. Bradley & M. Howard (Eds.), Classical and Marxian Political Economy (203-228). London, UK: Macmillan.

Fortman, B. G. (1966). *The theory of competition policy*. Amsterdam, The Netherlands: North Holland Publishing Company.

Granovetter, M. (1995). *Getting a job: A study of contacts and careers*. Chicago, IL: Chicago University Press. doi:10.7208/chicago/9780226518404.001.0001

Hayek, F. A. (1944). *The road to serfdom*. London, UK: The Institute of Economic Affairs.

Hayek, F. A. (1945). The use of knowledge in society. *The American Economic Review*, *35*, 519–530.

Hayek, F. A. (1948). *Individualism and economic order*. The University of Chicago Press.

Kaldor, N. (1960). *Essays on value and distribution*. Illinois: The Free Press of Glence.

Markham, J. W. (1950). An alternative approach to the concept of workable competition. *The American Economic Review*, *40*(3), 349–361.

O'Dennel, L. A. (1975). Rationalism, capitalism and the entrepreneur: The views of Veblen and Schumpeter. *History of Political Economy*, *5*(1), 199–214. doi:10.1215/00182702-5-1-199

Polanyi, K. (1944). *The great transformation. The political and economic origins of our time*. Beacon Press Books.

Ricardo, D. (1955). *Principles of political economy and taxation*. London, UK: J. M. Dent and Sons Ltd.

Schumpeter, J. A. (1954). *History of economic analysis*. New York, NY: Oxford University Press.

Schumpeter, J. A. (1981). *Kapitalizm, sosyalizm ve demokrasi* (T. Akoğlu, Trans.). İstanbul, Turkey: Kurtiş Matbaası. (Original work published 1974)

Semmler, W. (1984). *Competition, monopoly and differential profit rates*. New York, NY: Columbia Press. doi:10.7312emm90706

Smith, A. (1993). An inquiry into the nature and causes of the wealth of nations. (K. Sutherland, Ed.), Oxford University Press.

Sraffa, P. (1926). The laws of returns under competitive conditions. *Economic Journal (London)*, *36*(144), 535–550. doi:10.2307/2959866

Stigler, G. J. (1965). *Essay in the history of economics*. The University of Chicago Press.

Swedberg, R. (2007). *Principles of economic sociology*. Princeton University Press.

Tanyeri, İ. (2000). Adam Smith'in rekabet analizi üzerine. *Hacettepe Üniversitesi İ.İ.B.F. Dergisi*, *18*(1), 307–320.

Vaughn, K. I. (1999). Hayek's implicit economics: Rules and the problem of order. *The Review of Austrian Economics*, *11*(1/2), 129–144. doi:10.1023/A:1007784225432

Wayne, B. (1981). *Markets as networks: A multimethod study of trading networks in a securities market*. (Doctoral dissertation). Department of Sociology, Northwestern University.

Weber, M. (1927). *General economic history*. Glencoe, IL: The Free Press.

Weber, M. (1978). *Economy and society: An outline of interpretive sociology*. Berkeley, CA: University of California Press.

White, H. C. (1970). *Chains of opportunity: System models of mobility in organizations*. Cambridge, UK: Harvard University Press. doi:10.4159/harvard.9780674437203

ENDNOTES

1 Static competition theories are referred to as simultaneous competition approaches in this study.

2 Dynamic competition theories are classified as intertemporal competition approaches in this study.

3 The main assumptions of the perfectly competitive markets are the existence of a large number of buyers and sellers in the market and their perfect information regarding the supply and demand

conditions, the absence of barriers to entry and exit of the firms, perfect mobility of factors of production from one production area to another and the homogeneity of goods that are produced. However, "it is not possible to say that firms are competing with each other if all assumptions of perfect competition are valid. Perfect competition becomes an analytical tool to explain the ultimate equilibrium condition. Since firms, operating under the perfectly competitive market, have to take the market price as given, they have no competitive behavior other than determining the level of production, which will maximize their profit at the given market price (Tanyeri, 2000: 311-312)."

4 Imperfect competition theories of Robinson and Chamberlin in the 1930s are based on the paper entitled "The Laws of Returns Under Competitive Conditions" written by Sraffa in 1926. As Sraffa states, traditions, personal acquaintances, product quality, spatial proximity of the firm to the individual, characteristic of the good or credit facilities also influence demand (Sraffa, 1926: 542). In imperfect competition, it is assumed that goods are not homogeneous, the number of buyers and sellers are limited, there are barriers to free entry and exit and information is not perfect. Under imperfect competition conditions, demand does not depend only on price. Compared to perfect competition, production is less, while prices are higher in imperfect competition. In perfect competition, firm equates marginal cost to price in order to maximize its profit. However, since price is equal to average and marginal revenue in perfect competition, the firm equates marginal cost to marginal revenue. The same condition is valid for the monopolist, who produces in a monopoly market. Hence, there is no clear distinction between perfect competition and monopoly in profit maximization.

5 Three factors are required for a market to be considered as contestable. The first of these is that potential entrants have the same technology as the incumbents. The second feature is that entries are costless, that is, there are no sunk costs. In the absence of sunk costs, after entering the industry, a firm can leave the industry without incurring any costs. The final feature is that the entry of the potential entrants into the industry does not affect prices. Since the incumbent firms know that potential entrants cannot change prices, they determine the level of the profit based on the prices.

6 The process proceeds as follows. In the event that the quantity demanded of any good is more than the quantity supplied of the good, those who want to buy the good would be willing to pay a higher price for this good. This would increase the market price of the good and increase the market price above the production price. Since the quantity of goods in the market is small, competition would inevitably start among those, who want to sell this good. When free competition conditions exist in the economy, the rise of wage, profit and rent would direct the capital owner, landowner and labor to the production areas, where prices are high, and hence, production would increase in this area. With the increase in the production of the good, the market price would again decrease to the level of production price. The most important factor in the gravitation of the market price towards production prices is that the factors move freely from one production area to another. In this process, production prices are defined as the center of gravity since market prices tend to move towards production prices. The basic factor that creates the center of gravity is free competition.

Chapter 5
Institutional Overview of Technology:
Schumpeter and Veblen

Fatma Kethudaoğlu
Tübitak Sage, Turkey

Yusuf Bayraktutan
Kocaeli University, Turkey

ABSTRACT

There has been an intense debate on the reasons of variations in economic performances of different countries. Institutions and technological structure are among the leading determiners. Institutions are formal and informal constraints affecting investments in physical/human capital, and technology. Factors like economies of scale, technology, education, or accumulation of physical and human capital are not all for economic growth, which itself represents political and economic institutions as the basis for the fundamental differences in economic development. At the end of the 20th century, economic thought oriented towards analysis of the institutional environment. In the 1990s, significant steps were taken with Heterodox approaches to provide more consistent alternatives to the mainstream economy. The institutional economy shows an alternative approach that adds more depth to the discussions in this area. The main objective of this chapter is to point out the contributions of Schumpeter and Veblen.

INTRODUCTION

As a result of increasing attention on the relationship between economic performance and efficient use of resources, and hence advanced technology, the development, adaptation and use of new technologies has become the strategic priority of the countries at different development levels. Research and development (R&D) as a direct source of technological improvements supports growth, increase the competitiveness of countries and their share in international markets. The growth gap between developed and developing

DOI: 10.4018/978-1-7998-0333-1.ch005

Copyright © 2020, IGI Global. Copying or distributing in print or electronic forms without written permission of IGI Global is prohibited.

countries is due to technological capabilities, R&D activities, institutional and structural problems, and macroeconomic instability.

Economic literature closely relates the quantity and quality of labor, capital accumulation, saving rates, innovation, entrepreneurship, learning by doing, public investments, technological development and R&D activities, etc. with economic growth and in this sense, the transformation observed in the world shows a great parallelism with the theoretical developments. Although classical economists suggest that machine use positively affects productivity, they have not exclusively emphasized the phenomenon of technology as a determinant of growth. Keynesians considered capital as the main determinant of growth per capita. According to Neoclassics, income levels of countries converge in the long run. Considering innovation and hence newly organized knowledge express technology, the Neoclassical assumption of external and fixed technological development has become questionable. The efficient use of technology and technological progress itself require appropriate institutional and social structures.

Technology is not only about tools, but also is related to human work style and thinking. Basic changes in technology reflect and change the vision. As a result of the effective use of technology, the time period between scientific discoveries and its implementation has shortened. Transformation of economic structure also changes social structure. Progress in science and technology is connected to culture, where the change is reflected. In a knowledge-based economy, which is also called as information society or new economy, human beings and technology are at the center of economic development.

Studies within the framework of mainstream economics are insufficient in analyzing the complex structure of technological phenomena. Apart from the mechanistic and deterministic assumptions, an institutional economic outlook will provide a more explanatory approach to the causality in economic growth. Technological approaches that have come to the forefront in the evaluation of technological innovation as the driving force of social and economic transformation have an important place in the understanding of the subject and are used predominantly by the evolutionist and institutional economists. In this context, theories of Thorstein Veblen and Joseph A. Schumpeter, can be regarded as representatives of traditional evolutionary economics. In Schumpeter and Veblen's studies, the most important phenomenon that provides the change is technological progress, and technology is one of the main factors in realizing social-institutional transformation, and economic development.

In the literature studying economic performance of countries, it is observed that non-economic factors are considered as important variables, especially after 1990s. Demographic, cultural, institutional structures, government policies and innovation capacity are the variables that should not be ignored in explaining the growth rate differences. When examining the differences in economic performance among countries, institutional structures, technical capacities and human capital need to be primarily taken into consideration.

The role of institutions is of great importance both for Schumpeter and Veblen. This chapter examines Schumpeter's relationship with Veblen through technological change and determinism, individualism and institutions, and evaluates the views of both, who share the view that technology has revolutionized capitalism and has serious implications for the future of the system.

The role of technology in institutional change and economic growth under the views of both Schumpeter and Veblen will be discussed respectively and comparatively in two parts of this chapter. Thus, the evolutionary process of entrepreneurship, and its relationship with technology will be put forward. What Schumpeter and Veblen meant when talking about evolution and the role of technology on the economic system will be explained. This chapter will contribute to a better understanding on the ideas of two leading economists on how economics could become an evolutionary science, and on their contributions to evolutionary economic theory at the context of technology perspective.

TECHNOLOGICAL DEVELOPMENT IN CLASSICAL ECONOMIC THOUGHT

Over the years, traditional economics has gained considerable proficiency in theoretical sense, but it has been subject to many criticisms due to insufficiency in understanding many of the major problems of real economic world. While traditional economists have a lot to say about economic decision making in public and private sectors, they are more relevant to the earlier (Gruchy, 1977: v). Neoclassical economics has been criticized for being insufficient in analysis of institutional structure, with an emphasis on the necessity of a new theoretical paradigm (Hodgson, 1999: 44). These mechanical assumptions in economics were, in fact, the product of a mechanical standpoint, and this view emphasized the constant, lasting characteristics of economy, underestimating the dynamic and changing aspects of it.

One of the most widely accepted principles of neoclassical economics is the rationality of economic agents. Indeed, many economists consider the concept of rational/maximizing behavior as synonymous with economic behavior (Bayraktutan, and Kethudaoğlu, 2018: 680). Thus, economists whose studies are not based on the assumption of rationality appear outside the boundaries of neoclassical economics. Many heterodox schools criticize the concept of homoeconomicus/rational economic behavior of individuals.

Another point is the critique of the neoclassical market equilibrium model. In microeconomic theory, given a large number of producers and consumers, cost minimization by firms and utility maximization of consumers emphasizes the balance of supply and demand. However, the concept of market equilibrium was criticized by those who objected to the application of microeconomic theories to the Austrian School, Post-Keynesian approach, and real-world markets. Heterodox economists have argued that microeconomic models rarely reflect the reality (Shadmehri, Khadem, and Ghadimi, 2014: 27). They emphasize the need to examine real world rather than a concrete, fictional and abstract model.

From the 1930s onwards, the word heterodox has been used in institutional literature to indicate the approaches of economic analysis in the disagreement with neoclassical economics. The term, which began to gain a wider meaning as of the late 1960s, turned to be a common view in the 1990s on how economic analysis should be conducted as an oppositional and consistent alternative to neoclassical economics (Lee, 2006: 497). Heterodox economics relies on explaining, proposing and advocating the change in the historical process, including the flow of goods and services required to meet the recurring needs of the society, and the welfare of those who participate in economic activities. The most general criticisms of heterodox economics, which are trying to express reality with an emphasis on institutions, history and social structure, are in the concept of rational individual and market equilibrium.

The orthodoxy concept, which is shaped essentially from the static point of view, seems to contradict with the evolutionary, dynamic point of view that will help to understand the idea that human nature contains the possibilities of development and the formation of institutions. The expansion of the concept of evolution in heterodox economics, which is prominent with a social and realistic understanding, can provide an enlightenment to better analyze the individual human within the society and the social transformation.

EVOLUTIONARY ECONOMICS

The evolutionist approach has been directed to explore the social, organizational, and institutional ties of technological development dynamics (Fagerberg, 2003: 140). Veblen (1973: 131- 145) emphasizes that human cultures evolve in an unspecified way, pointing to the similarity between the struggle for existence observed in natural life, and the process of natural selection of the social structure and institutions. While who can adapt to the changing conditions survive, who cannot adapt to the changes will disappear in the struggle for existence. Developing theories on instincts, thinking, and habits, Veblen sees the relationship between institutions and changing human nature. Therefore, institutions are a part of the evolutionary process together with individuals.

Following industrial revolution, increasing machine usage, and technological improvements have affected the way of thinking, and changed the production structure accordingly. Because man can learn scientific thinking like the process of technological process. Social change differenciates the habits, and scientific approach. Recognizing the importance of the successive process of change, Veblen (1919: 15-18) suggests that the post-Darwinian science corresponds to the realities of the era. Science should not just try to achieve natural laws with causality, but is also required to process it. He therefore regards modern science as evolutionary, and expresses the importance of the cumulative change in the material life, emphasizing the role of knowledge and technology.

Schumpeter (1939: 80) takes over the importance of technological change in terms of economic development within the framework of evolutionary theory. Like Veblen, he explores the dynamic driving forces of the institutional evolution process, also believes that institutions play a vital role in shaping the behavior of individuals, and that the most important dynamic power is technological development along with other institutional changes.

Schumpeter (1976: 71) was primarily concerned with the evolutionary process when dealing with capitalism. He considers economic development as a process within the system, and evaluates external variables such as population growth and consumer preferences as parts of the process internal to the system. Such dynamic parts are elements of a circular flow, and so, the term "evolutionary" can be read as the dynamics of development. This approach is an attack on orthodox neoclassical theory. Time, which is a theoretical and reversible variable of mechanical theory, is treated differently in a historical and irreversible nature. The importance of innovation, which is taken as an internal parameter, is emphasized on the basis of capitalist system examined in an off-balance evolutionary process. Schumpeter rejects the concept of perfect competition, which emphasizes the role of competition in balance. Capitalism is never a static, stagnant economic system, it is an ever-changing process. Entrepreneurs pursue profit opportunities through innovations that are constantly being realized, and shape the dynamic feature of competition process.

Schumpeter threats economic development and growth differently. Unlike neoclassical economists giving the concept of growth priority, Schumpeter emphasizes internal transformation of economic system and the role of the entrepreneur as the source of economic transformation. When changes in economic growth and adjustment of the economy are in question, the current economic structure is changing as a result of economic development. Technological improvements, and restructuring of the industry accordingly are leading factors that cause change.

In summary, classical thought is attached to the Newtonian concept of change, that is also branched into the entire body of classical doctrine. Human nature, social universe, and development concepts in classical thought reflect the mechanical and repetitive Newtonian change in accordance with the fixed and eternal laws of social mechanics. However, the concept of developmental evolution, not mechanically, is the Darwinian concept that shapes the institutional theory. This concept also characterizes the institutionalist's understanding of development as a model of human nature, social organization, and evolutionary change (Hamilton, 1953: 15). Economic development process includes cumulative and continuous change. This emphasizes the institutional transformation of socio-economic life, and necessitates an institutional perspective on economics. Institutional economics, which considers economics as an institutionalized process rather than merely as a market, assumes an important role in the development of economic thought as a reflection of evolutionary thought, providing comprehensive and more explanatory answers to the questions on economic development.

WHAT IS "TECHNOLOGY"?

Technology is the transfer of scientific knowledge to the production process; information, organization and techniques. Management and coordination systems as the whole related public and private sector activities, including scientific knowledge, engineering, and know-how or management skills; machinery, tools and other equipment and their rules of use, as well as auxiliary activities such as maintenance, repair and training, refer to the technique (Bayraktutan and Bıdırdı, 2016: 3). The concepts of information and technology are often used together, but have different meanings. Scientific knowledge and human expertise are useful in the economic sense, in production and supply of goods, and in invention and design of new products and processes. If the information in the coded or implicit form is identical to the individual, it is called human capital to distinguish it from physical capital; the addition of new qualities or additions to knowledge increases individuals' human capital. Technology is the whole of the techniques used in design, packaging and distribution of goods and services, and the application of selected parts of information stock to production activities.

The technology including all kinds of knowledge, skills and processes that allow the emergence of a new commodity, and its production with low cost and / or high quality, can also be defined as a bundle of systematic information about how something is produced, consumed or used (Bayraktutan and Bıdırdı, 2016: 4). The set of techniques that can be used in the production process, the firm's technology, which includes different methods that combine inputs in a narrow sense; broadly, it is a combination of technology sets at industry or country level, including organizational processes.

Although the concepts of technological change and development are used interchangeably from time to time, they have different meanings. Changing technology or choosing a different technique does not always mean using advanced technology. Technological development, new production methods, organization, marketing and management techniques and changes in the quality of production is expressed by the development of new designs (OECD, 2003: 7; Mansfield, 1968: 10-11). Systematic R&D activities, technical partnerships, publications, observation/learning processes, and staff transfer etc. technological skills and knowledge dissemination, and the creation of technological capabilities through learning and doing, using innovations developed by other industries or countries, or adapting to the production processes of intermediate goods are the factors leading to technological development (Dosi, 1998: 1125).

Technological development refers to a process of invention, innovation and propagation. The use of information resulting from R&D activities for the production of a new goods or for the purpose of providing efficiency in the current production is called "innovation" (Case, Fair, and Oster, 2014: 361). Innovation is to adopt, develop or imitate a new product, method or organizational structure by adopting and commercializing. Propagation refers to the movement of technology from one place to another or from one user to another. Technological spread takes place not only as a result of the conscious efforts of the innovators, but also unintendedly.

International dissemination of technology occurs through trade in goods and services, foreign direct investments, technology purchases or licensing (Bayraktutan and Bıdırdı, 2016: 7). Countries import information and technologies that are embodied in tradable goods which were produced mostly by leading countries in technology (Ranis, 2011: 7; Limam, and Miller, 2004: 7). Imported capital goods and technological inputs make direct contributions to productivity by using them in production processes; export opportunities, incentives for acquiring and developing technologies. Foreign direct investments by multinational corporations facilitate the transfer of technological information to the countries where the subsidiaries are established; they generally increase access to effective technologies in the developing countries. Technology acquisitions allow direct exchange of information between joint ventures or unregistered firms, depending on the degree of protection of intellectual property rights in countries concerned.

There are three different approaches to explain how the technological development emerged, namely evolutionary, progressive and evoked (Ruttan, 2001: 101). According to the evolutionary approach, entrepreneurship is the basis of innovation. The phased approach has increased returns to scale; the stimulated approach emphasizes the relative impact of changes in market demand on knowledge and technology supply.

In terms of its contribution to growth, technological development is divided into "disembodied" and "embodied". Disembodied technological development, regardless of investment and accumulation phenomena, refers to increases in productivity, and the resulting improvements in management and organization. As technological information increases the amount of output generated by the data input, the production possibilities curve extends outward. With the technological development, new investments, machinery and equipment stock needs to be increased; technological development is mostly integrated with capital goods (Hahn, and Matthews, 1964: 838). The increase in capital stock allows more output with the same amount of labor input. An example is using computers, or digitalization in the operation of a machine.

Technology increases labor and capital efficiency; changes workflows and demand structure. The production of a new product and/or the development of production methods allow for more production with the same quantity of production factor; the same amount of product can be obtained by using less input. In this sense, technological development is the source of growth through production increase and resource savings (Dickson, 1992: 55). On the one hand, production costs are falling; the value of the total output and thus the income are increasing. A relationship between inputs and outputs includes new product and/or production methods; thanks to innovation, the profitability of investments increases due to falling unit production costs.

TECHNOLOGY AND GROWTH

Undoubtedly, the first target of economies is to achieve a long-term, sustainable and balanced growth. This issue, which many economists have been discussing for centuries, still does not have a definite formulation. Linking economic growth of countries to the quantitative sum of capital and labor will not only lead to unintelligible results, but will also be far from being explanatory. A widely held belief is that healthy evaluations cannot be reached, unless social, institutional and technological factors are included in the analysis.

A new production process allows an increase in output per unit input, as improved technology leads to higher productivity, and new products create new markets. In fact, the Classical, Neoclassical, Keynesian and Schumpetherian economists recognize the importance of technical change in promoting economic growth. Despite the causal link between technical change and growth, many theoretical and empirical methods have been used to demonstrate the impact of technological innovation in economic performance. At the end of the 1950s, Abramovitz (1956), and Solow (1956) attempted to show that growth could not be achieved only with the increase of productive inputs, such as labor and capital. They placed a larger part of growth on the "relic" to express the share of technical change.

The major difference in growth rates, which is a feature of long-term economic growth, is closely linked to whether there is social capability for institutional change, e.g. innovation systems, which facilitates high rate of technical change. This social capability can be expressed as the capacity to provide institutional change that will make a difference in the growth rate.

Many historians and economists emphasized the importance of technical and institutional change. Even in the early stages of economic theory, List (1841) criticized Smith and other classical economists for ignoring the issue of technology and skills even though they recognized the importance of science and technology (Freeman, 2002: 192). The evolutionary and institutional perspective, which has started to gain popularity, especially as of 1980's, has included technological process in the growth analyzes in response to this insufficiency in economics.

Technology, which can be defined as the sum of human tools and skills, does not simply express the function of human behavior. It is also a function of the vehicles which themselves play an important role in economic development, since the tools can be recombined to develop new vehicles. Since inventions and discoveries are dependent on human skills as well as existing tools and equipment, technology should be considered as a dynamic force. Besides, it should not be ignored that economic development is a function of institutions.

Institutional theory has made various attempts to identify the key issues underlying the complex process of technological innovation (Archibugil, and Michie, 1998: 4). In general, the four aspects of the nature of technology should be considered: Firstly, technology is a private property. Mainstream economics tends to see technology as a public good, a property that is provided free of charge to all economic agents. The institutional approach rejects this assumption and argues that the producers of new knowledge have a variety of legal and economic methods to protect the return of their innovation. Secondly, institutional theory implies that only a part of the information is in codable sources, such as books, projects, scientific papers, and a significant part is implicitly available only through long learning processes. In this context, knowledge is specific to economic units such as individuals, firms, industries, and countries. Some know-how can be transferred from the manufacturer to the user, but this assumption is not generalizable. Thirdly, there are basic variations between different technological areas. While technological innovation in some areas is easily accessible for many units, the expertise required to achieve technological innovation in other areas will be limited to a certain number of users. Technological systems, industry and countries have a more accessible or more specific technology allocation regime. Finally, the evolution of knowledge is path-dependent, meaning that it is already influenced by the knowledge accumulated by economic agents in the past. In this way, technology perception offers important implications for understanding the connections between technical change and growth.

The institution consists of formal rules, such as law and property rights that determine the relations between individuals and informal practices in political, economic and social fields (North, 1991: 97). In this context, culture, social structure, private and public traditions, and the political environment differ from country to country, and their effects can also undergo an evolutionary transformation that has emerged over time. According to Rodrik (2000: 28), the institutional structure fulfills the five main functions that can be listed as establishing property rights, ensuring regulation, ensuring macroeconomic stability, carrying out social security services, and resolving disputes.

In the absence of a properly functioning institutional structure, contract sanctions guaranteeing investments are eliminated (Rodrik, et. all., 2002: 11). For example, borrowing is a transaction based on mutual trust, and includes a promise of repayment in the future. The possibility of not paying the debtor's debt requires the trust relationship to be guaranteed by a debt agreement and guarantee. The agreement requires the existence of a legal sanction mechanism with the institutions that set and implement the rules to which the interlocutors of the transaction in question are to be complied with. Otherwise, transaction costs are increasing. In countries where property rights are not guaranteed, and there are no strong contractual sanctions, physical and human capital investments are decreasing due to uncertainty and risks. Effective institutions reduce entrepreneurial investments by reducing uncertainty and transaction costs. The institutional arrangements for the production of goods and services eliminate the distortions in the resource distribution by equalizing the social marginal product sectors.

Innovations are influenced by the quality of institutions. Corruption and infringement of property rights increases the uncertainty about the cost of investments needed to develop new products and services and the financial returns of innovations (Silve, and Plekhanov, 2015: 2). In this case, entrepreneurs who do not want to allocate resources to new technologies that can easily be copied by others are emerging, and the competition gets harder.

The institutions that govern the type and acquisition of knowledge and abilities of individuals and organizations affect learning and growth through two channels, demand and supply. Institutions that increase knowledge stock as a way of validating values and ideologies through passive education and media are built with administrative arrangements on the basis of current knowledge (North, 1990: 78).

Universities, research centers and patent mechanisms shape information or ideas. In this sense, investments will change the structure of the basic institutions gradually. Infrastructural investments are based on demanding skills, and contributes to basic knowledge, ideas and research stock.

TECHNOLOGY IN ECONOMIC THOUGHT

While economic development level of a country is mainly measured by the amount of goods and services it produces, as well as the structural transformation from agriculture to industry and services in the production and employment structure, technological innovations as an outcome of human mental labor and creative intelligence have come to the fore as the source of long-term growth. At this context, how technology is treated in the literature as an explanatory variable is discussed here. Theoretical and empirical literature indicates that the quantity and quality of labor, capital accumulation, saving rates, entrepreneurship, public investments, technological development, innovation and R&D activities are associated with economic growth, and in this sense, there is a parallelism with the transformation observed in world practice, to a great extent.

Growth theories explain differences between countries and times. Smith (1776: 272-276) considers knowledge and technology as a variable of capital stock, drawing attention to division of labor and specialization as the basis of growth, and emphasizes that openness will decrease income differences between countries. According to Ricardo (1817: 8-28), the total output in the economy is a function of land, labor, machinery and capital, and technical knowledge is embodied in machines.

With the Industrial Revolution, mass production became widespread; wage rates in the cities rapidly increased. The fact that prosperity was not shared fairly between and within countries (e.g. Britain's economic superiority) has revealed socialist thought against classical economics. Marx's views on the growth model are based on Ricardo's labor theory of value but differ in terms of the conclusions reached. According to Marx (2003: 315), the existence of the capitalist system is based on the new product and production processes which are formed by technological development. Accordingly, innovations and technological improvements allow production increase, and the way of growth passes through inventions that can be obtained as a result of R&D activities. The work of human labor is replaced by machines; science contributes to capital in the industry, and invention becomes a new field of work. While capitalism increases labor productivity as a result of the development of new technologies, it accelerates the spread of technology by increasing investment rates. Technology is a function of the rate of profit, capital accumulation and surplus value. The way of increasing this value is to increase the productivity of labor through technological development, change in production methods and education. There is a special exchange between paid labor and capital; the need to create relative surplus value in the production process constitutes the dynamics of the mechanization and transition to large-scale industry. In order to create added value, technological innovations should be used to increase the supervision of the production process, and to expand the market.

In classical growth theories, technological development based on capital accumulation is not accepted as an entirely independent production factor. Savings and investments are emphasized for capital accumulation. It is argued that population growth eliminates the positive effects of technological development. Smith (1776) explained economic growth in the manufacturing industry by focusing on the division of labor, the use of new machinery, and the skills of the users of the machines. Malthus (1815) noted that population increases were faster than agricultural production with a pessimistic view. Ricardo (1817) stated that the technological development which he regarded as an external factor would increase economic growth, but he also warned about decreasing productivity. Marx (1867) pointed out the importance of innovation in capital goods, and productivity based on technology. Due to innovation and technology, the developments in machinery would allow production increase, and the way of growth would evolve trough inventions. In the mid-1800s, GDP per capita increased despite high population growth in Europe. This led to the questioning of the classical theory because of treating technological development as an external factor.

According to Marx (2003: 326), technology is the result of the active relationship between man and nature, social relations and mental designs arising from them. In the capitalist system, technology is used to increase production, and reduce labor costs. The relative increase in productivity in the business lines that produce subsistence goods is generated. While wage rates decrease, surplus value increases, benefiting the capital-owners. Therefore, the introduction of technology to increase productivity in the subsistence goods sector emerges from the capitalists' strategy. Science is a prerequisite for new machines, production methods and technologies; technological innovations emerge as a result of mental skills.

Institutional economists argue that technology creates conditions that require institutional regulation, and it is a key element in the organization, functioning and performance of the economy. In the 1920s, a series of books focused on engineering and technical development. Institutional economist Thorstein Veblen, one of the most important premises of technical change, first, looked at social change in terms of tensions between changes in technological development, and in cultural or organizational models. He developed a kind of anthropological technology perspective by trying to show how cultural values and preconditions affect the way technology develops.

Although classical economists suggest that machine tools positively affects productivity, they have not directly emphasized the concept of technology as a determinant of growth. In classical growth theories, technological development based on capital accumulation is not accepted as an entirely independent production factor. Savings and investments are emphasized for capital accumulation; it is argued that population growth eliminates the positive effects of technological development.

Neoclassical growth models focus on capital accumulation as an internal determinant of growth; unpredictable changes are attributed to the total factor productivity called Solowgil "relic" (Tang, Hu, and Lin, 2005: 3). Accordingly, the income levels of countries converge in the long run, based on the decreasing returns of capital accumulation; technology and population growth rate affect growth externally. According to Solow (1956: 70), productivity is due to increases in capital accumulation. In a stagnant situation where net investments are growing at the same rate as labor and capital, all of the per capita income increases are due to a constant default and labor-saving external technological development. The diminishing returns of capital accumulation do not allow for a growth exceeding the technological progress rate. Although Solowgil approach is now associated with technology factor, it expresses all that are actually overlooked in economic growth. The fact that the growth rates of countries do not converge in time has questioned the validity of the assumption that the technology is external and fixed.

In the neoclassical model, sustainable growth and ever-increasing living standards are explained only by technological development, but technology is treated as fixed and external, as in classical theory. On the other hand, the high saving rate can only allow growth until a new equilibrium is reached. According to this model, in an economy where the capital increases faster than the labor force, it is predicted that interest rates will decrease, and countries with low income will grow faster and converge to higher income countries. It is emphasized that technological development is necessary for growth, but there is no explanation for how technological development can be achieved.

In order to overcome the shortcomings of the neoclassical theory, Endogenous Growth Models emerged. For these models, it is possible to increase the growth rate through macroeconomic policies, and technological development and human capital are main sources of growth. Moreover, monopolistic profits, information, human capital, R&D, financial innovations, public sector, and market structures are presented as alternative explanatories to neoclassical surplus. While technology and innovation are given a leading role in R&D activities, it can be said that technology investments can lead to continuous growth, and therefore convergence assumption is not compulsory. With these theories developed as of the 1980s, it is emphasized that growth rate may be above the steady state level due to the increasing returns. The term "endogenous" is used to point out innovations resulting from conscious activities for profit maximization (Dinopoulos, and Şener, 2007: 14).

Engdogenous growth theories are examined in two main categories: indirect technological development, and models based on competitive markets; the latter is based on direct technological development and non-competitive markets. In this context, Arrow (1962), Romer (1986), Lucas (1988) and Barro (1990), and the first group of pioneering overflow models evaluate that technology is created by special research activities and human capital accumulation by internalizing technology. Romer (1990), Grossman and Helpman (1991), Aghion and Howitt (1992) have developed R&D-based endogenous growth models that take monopolistic competition into account; where technological improvement is a result of profit maximization and R&D efforts.

In the countries which make R&D investments, the variety and efficiency of capital goods required for production increase; directing resources to the R&D sector contributes to the technological capacity, and hence growth. While the experience of growth performance can be explained by technological innovations, this argument cannot be used for developing countries; no definitive conclusions can be drawn about the sources of growth. As a reason of the difficulties faced in adapting technological innovations in developing countries, regional and structural characteristics of countries and stock of human capital, tastes and preferences, and market scale are effective. In general, neither neoclassical models addressing capital accumulation nor endogenous growth models focusing on technical development and human capital accumulation have developed a holistic explanation of the determinants of growth.

INSTITUTIONAL CHANGE AND INNOVATION

The modern evolutionary theory, which began to be effective in economics after the 1980s, aimed to develop a realistic approach to technology based on behavioral interpretations. This new evolutionary theory, which is increasingly gaining weight in the literature, is widely acknowledged to be based on such concepts as innovation, entrepreneur, invention and business cycles. Although the influence of Veblen may be overlooked in the new economic view of technology, the roots of Schumpeter's theory are based on Veblen's approach to social change theory and technology. Therefore, the role of technology in Veblen's theory of social change and technology, and innovation in Schumpeter's theory require the examination of technology and processes from an institutional economic point of view.

VEBLEN'S PERSPECTIVE

Veblen's theory is based on cultural transformation process determined by economic interests. The usual elements of human life change continuously and cumulatively, and cause continuous and rapid development of institutions. There is a constant change in the institutional structure in response to the changing order of living under changing cultural conditions (Veblen, 1914: 18). While human nature remains unchanged, the technical act of society as a whole provides change. The rules of society consist of traditions and culture, the institutions of society, and even shapes the thinking structure. The usual behavior and ways of thinking become permanent, and form habits of thought. In this way, the style of thinking depending on conditions of material environment become institutionalized in time. In other words, a material change in society with a change in economic activities creates new habits of thought, which in turn gains a corporate character. In modern civilization, industry, industrial processes and products, which are the outcome of human creativity, have been the achievements of humanity until finally taking a dominant position in the cultural order. These are main elements shaping the daily life of people. Therefore, man has learned to think in the direction of technological progresses. Institutions change their living habits and determine the speed and direction of technological change and function as a series of exchanges involving institutions that affect technology, and technology affects institutions.

In this sense, technology in Veblen's design is a genuine factor that establishes a causal link between directions (Cordes, 2005: 4).

As can be seen, at the center of Veblen's analysis is the process of technological change. However, it considers technology as a common stock of information. Technology is an ongoing accumulation of knowledge inherited from previous generations rather than a personal enterprise or innovation (Veblen, 1914: 103), based on social action. According to Veblen, the secret behind technological development, the beginning of modern industry and social change, and more generally the evolutionary process, lies in the tendencies of man. Moreover, the process of technological progress resulting from the tendencies of man lies behind the change in institutional change and habits of thought (Milonakis, and Fine, 2009: 165). The process of social action is seen as the interaction of the natural tendencies of man in the form of instincts, and the institutions in the form of habits that represent or prevent the expression of these trends. The basic understanding that instincts are associated with is the "tendency to act". The expression of these instincts is shaped by rational thinking and intelligence. In this way, man is not entirely a product of culture, he is able to take into account the forces of the environment. Human instincts become rationalized and become new institutions. Thus, social institutions are clustered around human instincts, but this does not mean that instincts determine the character of institutions. Therefore, the concept of instinct is the building block of the theories of teleological action and cumulative causality.

Technology is central to Veblen's social and economic theory. He examines technological phenomena, and their far-reaching consequences on social and economic life from a heterodox point of view. To that end, he begins with forming a novel viewpoint. Rejecting the metaphysical assumptions and fixed logical deductions of the orthodox theory, he makes a point of building up a theory of social change in which technology provides an inner dynamics. Around it, a range of social sciences is blended in order to present a realistic economic and social theory. As such, by breaking off the strict boundaries of social sciences, and thereby, opening up a new scientific standpoint, he constitutes a multi-disciplinary approach to technological, economic and social phenomena.

Veblen (1919: 56) defines "the state of the industrial arts", as "the community's joint stock of technological knowledge". Therefore, technology consists of technique that is the common stock of technological knowledge of the community other than mechanical arts. To Veblen, technology is a cultural inheritance of the community deriving from the past social experiences (Lower 1987: 1148). Technology in Veblen's system can be understood best only if it is recognized within its social context. Technology in Veblen's social theory is not an exogenous phenomenon, but an endogenous dynamic factor, as a result of social and collective activities oriented towards realizing their material interests. However, in orthodox view, technology is considered to be a gift of nature. This opinion stems from its passive and hedonistic conceptualization of human nature. Technology appears as the driving force of change in Veblen's social theory. Economic change in a community is a change in the community's methods of turning material things to account. The last part of this statement implies change in the state of the industrial arts, namely, technology (Veblen, 1919: 37).

Veblen (1919) states that institutions are influenced by change and influence change, and that institutions also include certain attitudes, tendencies and abilities, and human relations. These institutions related to economic structure should be clearly identified in terms of social change theory. There are two types of behavior patterns and institutions that are interrelated and even opposed. While the first group refers to the business world, the second group refers to the industry (O'Hara, 2002: 83, 84). This dual situation creates the dichotomy of Veblen, and the institutions undertake two types of behavior as "instrumental-technological" and "static-ceremonial". The pattern of "instrumental-technological behavior" that usually arises from the reflection of constructive instincts, is of an active nature, and is dealt with in the context of meeting human needs. The "ceremonial mold" refers to the purpose of the monetary gain of the business world. It originates from the instincts of exploitation and looting, and slows down the technological process, which is the reflection of constructive instincts. The instincts in the first group, expressed as constructive or peaceful, point to the behavioral tendencies of the individual in the social and economic process, which are prone to technique to improve the conditions of the material life of the society. While the source of the dynamic, technical institutions as the primary element of change, the predatory instincts in the second group constitute the origin of traditional institutions that symbolize the behavioral tendencies of the individual to protect the status quo and the habits of thought that resisted the institutional change process, and prevent the increase of material well-being as a result of the technical action of the society.

Veblen builds up his social theory around the dichotomy of technological and institutional behaviors. While the former is constantly engaged with creating new material conditions by eliminating the outmoded habits of thought, the latter tries to preserve the existent situation. Instrumentalist and ceremonial knowledge are diametrically opposed to each other (Dugger and Waller, 1996: 171). Change in institutional order happens gradually, and with a delay. Veblen's theory of social change should be examined by considering the differences between short run and long run effects of technological change. The process related to "cultural lag" or "the imbecile institutions" stands for only the short run effects of technology. In the long run, change on institutional "base" is inevitable, because of the iconoclastic nature of technology.

SCHUMPETER'S VIEW

Schumpeter (1939: 130) sees technological change as one of the main sources of growth, and argues that without innovations, there will be no economic development. With "creative destruction", which is based on the historical role of technological innovations, new innovations will create dynamism, as well as new firms. The dynamics of change are innovation, entrepreneurs and bank loans. Entrepreneurs implement innovations that ensure constantly changing capitalist system. Creativity depends on learning and monitoring processes of individuals and organizations, and successful innovators obtain monopoly profits.

According to Schumpeter (1934: 84), economic order has a dynamism through technology. Each new technology leads to the collapse of the previous one. Successful innovations in this process constantly destroy the old ones, and lead to industrial change. There is a gradual increase in technological sense. On the other hand, unit costs of producers who cannot adapt innovations will be higher than the ones who can. Thus, in capitalist system, adaptation to technological developments is a necessity.

Growth is based on the presence of an entrepreneurial segment with successive waves of innovation (Schumpeter, 1934: 201-202). Entrepreneurs, who renew their production structure through inventions, form a talented minority. The entrepreneur creates new consumer goods, transportation methods, markets and organizations with the expectation of profit; and fosters the innovation capacity of capitalism by determining the purpose and vision to follow with leadership (Schumpeter, 1934: 228). Entrepreneur's successful implementation of technical innovation in an industry leads other entrepreneurs to move their investments into this area by imitation. Innovation clusters emerge due to the domino effect of the first entrepreneur's innovation efforts.

Types of innovation are production of different qualities of a new commodity or existing ones, introducing new production methods, opening up to different markets, discovering raw material resources, and diversifying organizational forms (Schumpeter, 1934: 66). Schumpeter (1939: 84) described discoveries by making a sharp distinction between invention and innovations. The production of new products with less cost, or the use of new cost-cutting techniques leads to increased profitability. Innovations arising as a result of profit expectation stimulate the economy through new facilities or renewing old ones. Thus, unit costs fall; factor composition and techniques of production vary. Innovations are divided as process and product innovations (Schumpeter, 1934: xx). Process innovation is the application of technical developments to the production process, which reduces the average costs when input prices are fixed. Product innovation is the development of a product, the addition of new ones through improvement or revision of existing product line.

Innovation changes the production function, and increase the quantity and quality of production. The inventor sells his invention if it is innovative, and/or applies it to the production process. Innovative firms operating in competitive markets are leading actors. Inventions are merely prototypes, ie, intellectual production. Innovation, however, is abstract inventions in the mind of the inventor, and turn to be an output of the actual production process (Schumpeter, 1939: 81-83). Therefore, innovation that emphasizes profitability rather than technological dimension is accepted as a commercial activity of entrepreneurs.

Schumpeter views entrepreneurial and technological development as complementary to each other, and explains that technological development, which is co-opted with innovation, is an internal variable in terms of growth (Schumpeter, 1939: 82). Inventions that characterize a thought or model of a newly developed product and production process are transformed into innovation if they are deemed worthy of investing and expanding a practical need. Each invention does not have to be transformed into innovation. In this sense, while inventions are external to economy, innovations arise internally to meet a need. In this context, Schumpeter played a leading role in seeing innovation as the source of growth; on the other hand, he could not develop a growth model in which scientific and technical innovations were considered internally.

RECOMMODATIONS AND FUTURE RESEARCH DIRECTIONS

Labor, human capital, physical capital, and natural sources are considered as factors affecting growth in the literature. The effects of institutional factors and technological development on productivity should be evaluated when researching the basics of growth; the dynamic structure of both factors needs to be emphasized. At this point, the application of the definition and types of technology, and institutional structure to the statistics are of great importance in terms of economic analysis. It is expected that this issue will be taken into consideration by researchers, and studies taking economic impacts of technology into account from different perspectives would increase. As a matter of fact, while technological progress is seen as the key to economic growth and development in the process of transformation from agricultural to knowledge-based economy, countries at different development stages contribute to the competitiveness by supporting innovative capacities, and efforts to improve the national stock of human capital, institutions, and the corporate culture.

CONCLUSION

Besides human capital, infrastructure deficiencies, financial, institutional and structural problems, and factor equipment differences as well as useful information and technological capacity/capability must be addressed among the reasons of the differences in productivity and competitiveness between developed and developing countries. Technological development plays a leading role in the formation of new professions and products by allowing various combinations of products, companies, and industries, and increasing competitiveness. Technological change, the number of scientists and engineers, the stock of human capital, work skills of labor force, the capacity of firms and individuals to learn, the way companies look at technology, the degree of protection of property rights have effects on growth.

Improving technology is an activity that requires a conscious effort and involves cost. In this context, technology is not a public good that can be obtained free of charge. Innovative activities focused on technological development are carried out by a small number of developed countries due to the high cost involved. Technological development is gaining momentum, and a rapid increase in the number of inventions has been observed due to allocation of larger resources to R&D.

Veblen and Schumpeter represent the institutional approach to technology. Their conflicting and congruent arguments present a detailed conceptual framework to evaluate contemporary technological phenomena in economic development from the perspective of entrepreneurs. To Veblen's views, technology manifests itself as a countervailing power against business/finance-oriented capitalist order, and it enables us to develop a modern critical theory of business enterprise. To Schumpeter's origins, technology appears to us a routinized business experiment in the hands of professional managerial teams under the large corporate concerns, which is far from generating the process of "creative destruction", the essence of capitalism.

Technology that provides efficiency in the production process and advanced human resources are important elements that add strength to the institutional structure. Effective institutional structure of a country contributes to the formation of physical, human and intellectual capital through formal and informal rules, enables technical development, and prepares the basis for economic development. Sustainable growth is only possible with technological progress, innovative business climate and high-quality institutional structure. Providing necessary incentives for technological development and creative destruction requires sound and well-functioning institutions.

REFERENCES

Abramovitz, M. (1956). Resource and output trends in the United States since 1870. *The American Economic Review*, *46*(2), 5–23.

Aghion, P., & Howitt, P. (1992). A model of growth through creative destruction. *Econometrica*, *60*(2), 323–352. doi:10.2307/2951599

Archibugil, D., & Michie, J. (1998). Technical change, growth and trade: New departures in institutional economics. *Journal of Economic Surveys*, *12*(3), 1–20.

Arrow, K. J. (1962). The economic implications of learning by doing. *The Review of Economic Studies*, *29*(3), 155–173. doi:10.2307/2295952

Barro, R. J. (1990). Government spending in a simple model of endogenous growth. *Journal of Political Economy, 98*(5), 103–125. doi:10.1086/261726

Bayraktutan, Y. & Hanife Bıdırdı (2016). Teknoloji ve Rekabetçilik: Temel Kavramlar ve Endeksler Bağlamında Bir Değerlendirme [Technology and Competitiveness: An Assessment in Terms of Main Concepts and Indexes], *Akademik Araştırmalar ve Çalışmalar Dergisi*, 8(14), 1-24.

Case, K. E., Fair, R. C., & Oster, S. M. (2014). *Principles of Macroeconomics*. London, UK: Pearson Education Publications.

Cordes, C. (2005). Veblen's 'instinct of workmanship', its cognitive foundations, and some implications for economic theory. *Journal of Economic Issues, 39*(1), 1–20. doi:10.1080/00213624.2005.11506778

Dickson, D. (1992). Alternatif Teknoloji [Alternative Technology], (Çev. Nezih Erdoğan), İstanbul, Turkey: Ayrıntı Yayıncılık.

Dinopoulos, E. & Şener, F. (2007). "New directions in Schumpeterian growth theory". Retrieved from https://ideas.repec.org/h/elg/eechap/2973_42.html

Dosi, G. (1998). Sources, procedures, and microeconomic effects of innovation. *Journal of Economic Literature, 26*, 1120–1171.

Dugger, W. M., & Waller, W. (1996). Radical institutionalism: From technological to democratic instrumentalism. *Review of Social Economy, 2*(2), 169–189. doi:10.1080/00346769600000035

Fagerberg, J. (2003). Schumpeter and the revival of evolutionary economics: An appraisal of the literature. *Journal of Evolutionary Economics, 13*(2), 125–159. doi:10.100700191-003-0144-1

Freeman, C. (2002). Continental, national and sub national innovation systems-complementarity and economic growth. *Research Policy, 31*(2), 191–211. doi:10.1016/S0048-7333(01)00136-6

Grossman, G. M., & Helpman, E. (1991). Quality ladders in the theory of growth. *The Review of Economic Studies, 58*(1), 43–61. doi:10.2307/2298044

Gruchy, A. G. (1977). Institutional economics: Its development and prospects. In R. Steppacher, B. Zogg-Walz, & H. Hatzfeldt (Eds.), *Economics in Institutional Perspective* (pp. 11–29). Toronto, Canada: Lexington Books.

Hahn, F. H., & Matthews, R. C. O. (1964). The Theory of Economic Growth: A Survey. *Economic Journal (London), 74*(296), 779–902. doi:10.2307/2228848

Hamilton, D. (1953). *Newtonian classicism and Darwinian institutionalism*. Albuquerque, NM: University of New Mexico Press.

Hodgson, G. M. (1999). *Evolution and institutions, on evolutionary economics and the evolution of economics*. UK: Edward Elgar Publishing.

Lee, F. S. (2006). Introduction to the special issue. *The Review of Radical Political Economics, 38*(4), 497–498. doi:10.1177/0486613406293216

Limam, Y. R. & Miller, S. M. (2004). Explaining economic growth: Factor accumulation, total factor productivity, and production efficiency improvement, *University of Connecticut Department of Economics Working Paper Series*, No: 2004-20.

Lower, M. D. (1987). The concept of technology within the institutionalist perspective. *Journal of Economic Issues*, *21*(3), 1147–1176. doi:10.1080/00213624.1987.11504699

Lucas, R. E. Jr. (1988). On the mechanics of economic development. *Journal of Monetary Economics*, *22*(1), 3–42. doi:10.1016/0304-3932(88)90168-7

Mansfield, E. (1968). *The economics of technological change*. London, UK: Longmans.

Marx, K. (2003). Kapital I [Capital I], (Çev. Alaattin Bilgi), İstanbul, Turkey: Eriş Yayıncılık.

Milonakis, D. & Fine, B. (2009). *From political economy to economics method, the social and the historical in the evolution of economic theory*. London, UK: Routledge.

North, D. (1990). *Institutions, institutional change and economic performance*. Cambridge, UK: Cambridge University Press. doi:10.1017/CBO9780511808678

North, D. (1991). Institutions. *The Journal of Economic Perspectives*, *5*(1), 97–112. doi:10.1257/jep.5.1.97

O'Hara, P. A. (2002). The contemporary relevance of thorstein veblen's institutional-evolutionary political economy. *History of Economics Review*, *35*(1), 78–103. doi:10.1080/10370196.2002.11733370

OECD. (2003). *Developments in growth literature and their relevance for simulation models*. Paris, France: OECD Publications.

Bayraktutan, Y. & Fatma Kethudaoğlu (2018). Ar-Ge ve İktisadi Büyüme İlişkisi: OECD Örneği [The relationship between R&D and economic growth: The case of OECD], *Uluslararası Sosyal Araştırmalar Dergisi*, 10(53), 679-694.

Ranis, G. (2011). Technology and human development. *Yale University Economic Growth Center Discussion Paper Series*, No: 1004.

Ricardo, D. (1817). *On the principles of political economy and taxation*. Kitchener, Canada: Batoche Books.

Rodrik, D. (2000). Institutions for high-quality growth: What they are and how to acquire them. *Studies in Comparative International Development*, *35*(3), 3–31. doi:10.1007/BF02699764

Rodrik, D., Subramanian, A., & Trebbi, F. (2002). Institutions rule: The primacy of institutions over geography and integration in economic development, *NBER Working Paper Series*, No: 9305.

Romer, P. M. (1986). Increasing returns and long-run growth. *Journal of Political Economy*, *94*(5), 1002–1037. doi:10.1086/261420

Romer, P. M. (1990). Endogenous technological change. *Journal of Political Economy*, *98*(5), 71–102. doi:10.1086/261725

Ruttan, V. W. (2001). *Technology, growth and development: An induced innovation perspective*. New York, NY: Oxford University Press.

Schumpeter, J. A. (1934). *The Theory of Economic Development*. London, UK: Transaction Publisher.

Schumpeter, J. A. (1939). *Business cycles a theoretical, historical and statistical analysis of the capitalist process*. London, UK: McGraw Hill.

Schumpeter, J. A. (1976). *Capitalism, socialism, and democracy* (5th ed.). London, UK: Routledge.

Shadmehri, M. T. A., Khadem, F., & Ghadimi, A. (2014). Economic schools thought: Mainstream, orthodox and heterodox economics. *Kuwait Chapter of Arabian Journal of Business and Management Review*, *3*(12a), 24–30. doi:10.12816/0018843

Silve, F. & Plekhanov, A. (2015). Institutions, innovation and growth: Cross-country evidence, *European Bank Working Paper Series*, No: 177.

Smith, A. (1776). An Inquiry into the Nature and Causes of the Wealth of Nations - An Electronic Classics Series Publication (Ed. Jim Manis, 2005), University Park, PA: The Pennsylvania State University.

Solow, R. M. (1956). A contribution to the theory of economic growth. *The Quarterly Journal of Economics*, *70*(1), 65–94. doi:10.2307/1884513

Tang, S., Hu, Z., & Lin, Y. (2005). Knowledge as production factor: Toward a unified theory of economic growth. *Journal of Evolutionary Economics*, *2005*, 1–68.

Veblen, T. (1914). *The instinct of workmanship and the state of the industrial arts*. New York, NY: The Viking Press.

Veblen, T. (1919). The place of science. In *Modern Civilization and Other Essays*. New York, NY: B. W. Huebsch.

Veblen, T. (1973). *The theory of the leisure class: An economic study of institutions*. Boston, MA: Houghton Mifflin.

Chapter 6
Analysing of Erzurum Winter Tourism in the European Perspective

Mahshid Mikaeili
https://orcid.org/0000-0002-8126-3069
Atatürk University, Turkey

H. Kutay Aytuğ
https://orcid.org/0000-0002-6353-7468
Manisa Celal Bayar University, Turkey

ABSTRACT

Erzurum is the biggest city in the Eastern Anatolian Region of Turkey. The city has gained great importance in winter tourism during recent years. Accessing to the sustainable winter city requires an innovative approach to these cities' problems in order to enhance the advantages, opportunities, and beauty of the winter season. Winter tourism is one of the good examples that provides benefits to the residents and reinforces the community's ability to attract new business. In this chapter, the conceptual framework of the topic is drawn by putting forth the concept of winter city tourism. Subsequently, EU tourism policy, its political framework, and priorities are summarised. In the next chapter, Erzurum is examined to demonstrate its potential for winter city tourism. Finally, the winter city tourism potential of Erzurum is evaluated by SWOT analysis and brought some suggestions compatible with EU Tourism Policies at five categories such as preserving solar access, designing streets, planting, parks and open spaces, colour, materials and lighting.

INTRODUCTION

During history, physical and economic factors influenced people's choices of where to settle. The physical factors include water, topography, vegetation and natural defence system. The economic factors include communication and resources (wood, fuel, iron, etc.). Good locations of favourable places allow

DOI: 10.4018/978-1-7998-0333-1.ch006

Copyright © 2020, IGI Global. Copying or distributing in print or electronic forms without written permission of IGI Global is prohibited.

maximum communication between different settlements and increase trade. On the other hand, besides these factors, there is another important factor which is climatic situation. To a considerable extent, Climatic situation and weather have shaped city form, customs and traditions of them during the time. After starting modernization in the cities, auto-oriented culture in modern urban planning has ignored the pedestrians in wintertime. In this period, the most attention is on the resources devoted to keeping streets and highways clear of snow and ice.

Winter cities are places with the long winter season, snowy, very cold weather, and harsh climatic conditions. Due to the effects of climate conditions on urban life, creating public places for supporting community life and their social relations is one of the most considerable designing issues. A responsive design based on the climate conditions, where negative effects of climate condition are mitigated, is essential for establishing a sustainable environment (Gürer, 2017, p.19).

On the other hand, one of the important attentions in urban planning is the compound of city-form and weather, particularly within the context of sustainable development and walkability (Akkerman, 2014, p.161).

One of the most important aspects in cities with long winter is the cold weather that affects the mobility of pedestrians. Cold, snow and glacial situation influence not only people's ability to walk in the winter, but also their desire to walk during the cold season. So snow, cold weather and the condition of the walking on surface are major factors in human mobility.

In recent years, one of the important attempts to generate climate-responsive in architecture and urban designing is the winter cities movement. The purpose of this movement is to establish the needs of the people who live in the areas with high snowy and cold weather, by improving the comfort of lifestyles and recognizing the human needs in order to plan and design better.

The sustainability of winter cities requires a creative and innovative approach that addresses the problems of these areas while enhancing the advantages, opportunities, and beauty of the winter season. Winter tourism is one of the good examples that provides benefits to the residents and reinforces the community's ability to attract new business.

In this study, conceptual framework of the topic will be drawn by putting forth the concept of winter tourism, winter city and liveability. Subsequently, EU tourism policy, its political framework and priorities will be summarised. In the next chapter, Erzurum will be examined to demonstrate its potential on winter city tourism. Finally, the winter city tourism potential of Erzurum will be evaluated by SWOT analysis and will bring suggestions at the local and national level to set in motion of the potential of Erzurum in the field of winter city tourism in the context of EU Tourism Policies.

CONCEPTUAL FRAMEWORK

In this chapter, to draw a conceptual framework, firstly the concepts of winter tourism will be defined then winter city and liveability concepts will be explained.

Winter Tourism

Today, winter tourism is one of the great economic importance for different regions in the world, such as Alpine regions of Europe or northern cities. In certain regions, winter tourism accounts for 20% of the created economic value and provides thousands of jobs (Yfantidou, Nikou, & Matsouka, 2018, p.

77). Technically, "*Winter Tourism defined as the coldest season of the year, between autumn and spring, astronomically from the December solstice to the March equinox in the N hemisphere and at the opposite time of year in the S hemisphere*" (Journal of Tourism & Hospitality, 2018).

On the one hand, the general public, consumers, and policymakers regard winter tourism and winter sports as synonymous for some countries like Germany. On the other hand, local or national governmental organizations and institutions recommend the development of snow-independent products and services (Bausch & Unseld, 2018, p. 204).

Today, there is an important demand for snow-related tourism activities such as skiing and snowboarding. So, tourists are engaged in winter sports, such as ski, ice-skating, snowboard, curling, etc. They visit the winter tourism destinations to watch national and international sports competitions or they prefer to use entertaining facilities like SPA, sauna or Turkish bath or some services for relaxation and health beside varied snowy landscape (Yfantidou, Nikou, & Matsouka, 2018, p. 74; UNWTO, 2018a).

Furthermore, local or national authorities and policy makers plan some snow-independent products and services year-round or summer related such as wellness (Pechlaner & Fischer, 2006), health (Schalber & Peters, 2012), nature and culture-based experience to support winter tourism and sustainable development in winter tourism centres such as Alps mountainous area (Bausch & Unseld, 2018, p. 204).

In the light of all these definitions, this paper defines the winter tourism as an integrated tourism products and services including winter sports, such as ski, ice-skating, snowboard, curling etc., visiting the winter tourism destinations to watch national and international sport competitions and to use snow-independent products and services such as SPA, sauna or Turkish bath facilities in the coldest season of the year, between autumn and spring.

Winter City and Liveability

The main problem in the communities with heavy snowfall and cold temperature is the effect the climate has on people outdoor life. During the long winter, people's outdoor activities are affected seriously by the heavy snow and frost condition (Hong & Cun-Yan, 2017, p. 28).

During the history, urban public spaces have been designed, based on the climatic necessary, to decrease cold weather influence on urban outdoor environment. On the other hand, in order to turn these city places into a year-round city, it is needed good planning and designing of public outdoor spaces based on the creation more innovative, attractive, sustainable and walk-able. Because, these cities present the visual beauty outdoor sports, carnivals, and festivities in snow-covered urban landscape (Pressman, 1996, p. 521).

Traditionally, northern communities or communities with heavy snowfall have struggled for their existence in a harsh climate. In these areas, winter is the season which dictates the conditions of construction. For example, construction elements are developed to complement the conditions, such as sheltered yards against winds, plants which replace dead winter nature and sheltering roofs against harsh climate. The formation of a city and buildings are protection elements made the whole construction.

In this perspective, the international winter cities movement has established explicit, systematic inquiry which analyses national and local strategic action directed at improving the comfort and lifestyles of northern dwellers. Winter city movement is a concept for cities in northern latitudes in order to recognize people's needs for better planning and designing.

The Winter Cities Institute[1] was organized to identify, promote and share the positive attributes of winter living, new concepts in architecture and urban design, success stories from these places that are thriving in the north. The main aim of the Winter City Institute is to offer resources, contacts, and networking for improving the quality of life in northern places on the wintertime. The members of the institute include cities and towns, architects, planners, engineers, parks and recreation professionals, chambers of commerce and economic developers (Winter City Institute, 2018).

At first appearance, it seems the Winter Cities Institute's aim is about only the Northern countries or cities. But around the world there are many cities with very cold weather, heavy snowfalls and harsh weather. So, the important question in the conceptual framework of the Winter City is: Which cities are recognized as a winter city? According to the World Winter City Association for Mayors[2] (WWCAM), "*A winter city is one that faces harsh winter climatic conditions, including heavy snowfalls and cold temperatures*" (WWCAM, 2018). Moreover, WWCAM (2018) emphasizes that winter city includes two groups of cities:

- A winter city also has an annual snow accumulation of more than 20 cm (8 in.),
- A winter city has an average temperature of 0°C (32°F) or below during the city's coldest month.

On the other hand, according to WWCAM (2018), these factors are just standards. Even if a city does not meet these standards, it may join the association as long as it is a winter city faced with winter-related challenges in city planning (WWCAM, 2016, p.2).

Livable winter city's topic, based on the pamphlet World Winter Cities Association for Mayors (WWCAM, 2016, p.4-5), during 16 conferences the discussed issues are illustrated in table 1. According to the table 1, all issues are about the comprehensive city planning and construction in the northern regions, transportation problems, improving living environments, promotion of the cultural activities in these areas, economic development in winter cities, urban development in winter cities, sustainable development, city quality and quality of life, snow management and transportation in participant cities, creation harmony in the city (promotion of arts, culture, sports, and recreation), and climatic change.

The concept of "Liveability" is the most important concept in the winter tourism. According to The National Research Council (2002, p.23); *"liveability is a broad term with no precise or universally agreed upon definition. The concept embraces cognate notions such as sustainability, quality of life, the character of place, and the health of communities. Liveability is an ensemble concept".*

Liveability is one of the important new concepts in the field of the city planning. Liveability is used in a wide array of contexts within the field of planning: transportation, community development, resilience, and many other sub-disciplines have been incorporated with liveability (SCI, 2017, p.1). Liveable city includes wide ranging of human needs from food, basic security to beauty, cultural expression, and a sense of belonging to a community or a place. Liveability refers to a citizen's satisfaction with residential environments, traffic, employment opportunities, or the amount of open space (National Research Council, 2002, p.23-24).

Partnership for Sustainable Communities (PSC, 2012, p.2) has prepared a set of guiding principles for creation of liveability in cities. Guiding the Partnership's Liveability Principles are:

Table 1. Discussed issues in 16 conferences (WWCAM, 2016, p.4-5)

Conference	Issues discussed
First Conference, Sapporo	- Future direction in city planning in the northern regions - Transportation problems - Improving living environments - Promotion of arts, culture, sports, and recreation
Second Conference, Shenyang	- Planning and construction of the northern city - Utilization and exploitation of energy and economic development in northern cities - Afforestation and cultural activities in northern cities - Exploitation and utilization of water resources, preservation and excavation of cultural relics in northern cities
Third Conference, Edmonton **Main theme: "Business of Winter"**	- Economic Development in Winter Cities - Potentials of Winter Cities - Urban environment in winter cities
Fourth Conference, Tromsø **Main theme: "Warm Winter Cities-Quality of Life and Economic Development"**	- Urban Transportation in Winter - Comprehensive City Planning - Development of Winter Technology - Challenges of Small Cities - Art and Culture of Winter Cities
Fifth Conference, Montréal **Main theme: "Living in Harmony with Winter"**	- Environment - Urban planning - Health and physical strength
Sixth Conference, Anchorage **Main theme: "North to the Future"**	- Communications: "Developments in Communications Technology" - Transportation: "International Air Commerce" - Health: "Changes in the Global Climate" - Business: "Marketing Winter Destinations and Winter Tourism"
Seventh Conference, Winnipeg **Main theme: "Global Living, Working and Playing in the Winter City"**	- Economic development: "Warming the North for Business Development" - Accessibility: "Accessibility in Winter Cities" - Leisure / recreation: "How are the long-term needs of winter-city citizens
Eighth Conference, Harbin **Main theme: "Let Us Unite to Create a Winter World Kaleidoscope!"**	- What Winter Means to Senior Citizens and Children - Develop and Exploit Winter Tourism Resources - Promoting the Culture of Ice and Snow
Ninth Conference, Luleå/Kiruna **Main theme: "Sustainable Development in Winter Cities"**	- Countermeasures against natural disasters, support networks among IAMNC members during natural disasters - Snow removal and civil cooperation
Tenth Conference, Aomori **Main theme: "Sustainable Winter Cities 21"**	- Revitalization of Central Urban Area - Urban System with the Less Negative Impacts on Environment
Eleventh Conference, Anchorage **Main theme: "Challenging Winter Frontiers"**	- Winter City Designs: Satellite Town Centers - The Role of the Sports Community in the Development of Municipal Services and Venues
Twelfth Conference, Changchun **Main theme: "Grow in Winter"**	- Environmental Issues in Winter - Problem Solving in Citizens' Winter Lifestyles
Thirteenth Conference, Nuuk **Main theme: "Climatic Changes in the Arctic"**	- Climatic Changes and Living Conditions among Young People in the Arctic - Measures against Global Warming in Winter Cities
Fourteenth Conference, Maardu **Main theme: "Features of Environmental Protection in Northern Cities"**	- Multicultural Society in Winter Cities - E-state
Fifteenth Conference, Ulaanbaatar **Main theme: "Energy Supply and Efficient Consumption of Heat Supply in Winter Cities"**	- Efficient Uses of Heat Supply - Efficient Uses of Electricity - Air Pollution in Winter Cities and Its Methods to Decrease Air Pollution
Sixteenth Conference, Hwacheon **Main theme: " Conservation of Nature and Natural Resources in a Winter City, and Sustainable Application Methods"**	- Development of tourism and the promotion of tourism industry using natural resources - Enhancing winter cities through environmental protection

- *"**Provide more transportation choices:** Develop safe, reliable, and economical transportation choices to decrease household transportation costs, reduce nation's dependence on oil, improve air quality, reduce greenhouse gas emissions, and promote public health,*
- ***Promote equitable, affordable housing:** Expand location and energy-efficient housing choices for people of all ages, incomes, races and ethnicities to increase mobility and to lower the combined cost of housing and transportation,*
- ***Enhance economic competitiveness:** Improve economic competitiveness through reliable and timely access to employment centres, educational opportunities, services and other basic needs by workers, as well as expanded business access to markets.*
- ***Support existing communities:** Target national or federal funding toward existing communities through strategies like transit-oriented, mixed-use development and land recycling to increase community revitalization and the efficiency of public works investments and safeguard rural landscapes.*
- ***Coordinate and leverage national or federal policies and investment:** Align national or federal policies and funding to remove barriers to collaboration, leverage funding, and increase the accountability and effectiveness of all levels of government to plan for future growth, including making smart energy choices such as locally generated renewable energy.*
- ***Value communities and neighbourhoods:** Enhance the unique characteristics of all communities by investing in healthy, safe, and walkable neighbourhoods, rural, urban, or suburban."*

According to The Sustainability and Liveability Element addresses sustainability and liveability through three components (Move DC, 2014, p.s-1):

- Urban forestry
- Storm-water management
- Public space management

Well-designed public spaces and open access to these spaces are known as the most important indicators amongst the other factors to create a liveable urban space. However, in winter cities where winter dominates, inadequate weather conditions such as wind, frost, ice, snow, declining sunshine and long-term cold restrict the use and access of public open spaces. In particular, urban public open spaces that are not designed for winter season conditions lose accessibility, reduce the quality of life and the liveability of the city. A well-designed public space balances the mobility and access of needs for users and unifies key elements in the public right-of-way including roadways, sidewalks, tree box areas, intersections, plazas, and open spaces.

To access this important aspect, climate-sensitive design can create a more positive winter experience by using climatic design strategies in very cold and snowfall environment. The main aim of the climate-sensitive design is not to create year-round summer conditions, by exploiting these areas opportunities to create safely winter environment, comfortable, and enjoyable. A liveable winter city properties are compact city, mixes land uses and provides connected pedestrian places (Winter City Design Guidelines, 2000, p.1-3).

EUROPEAN UNION TOURISM POLICY AND WINTER TOURISM

Tourism is one of the essential pillars of the economies of many EU countries, and winter tourism is a very important component of some European states tourism. The EU has been one of the most important tourism markets and has very important winter tourism destinations in the world. According to the United Nation World Tourism Organisation (UNWTO), EU area is the most frequently visited region in the world tourism destinations (UNWTO, 2017, p. 5). EU shared 41% of international tourist arrivals market with 537.6 million visitors and gained 388 billion EUR from international tourism in 2017 (UNWTO, 2018bb, pp. 5-7). Albeit EU is the world's first tourist destination and, tourism is an important driver of economic growth in EU (European Commission, 2010, p. 2), tourism was not formulated clearly in treaties until Lisbon Treaty[3]; because EU Countries were reluctant to relinquish part of their domestic powers to the EU (Estol & Font, 2016, p. 231). Nevertheless, there have been several regulation and topics connected directly and indirectly with tourism. Such regulations can be grouped as follows;

Topics and Regulations Affecting Tourism Directly:

- Information Exchange and Dissemination of Information in the Field of Tourism,
- Improvement of Vocational Education and Training,
- Integrated Quality Management,
- Safety of Tourism Enterprises,
- Use of New Technologies in Tourism,
- Tourist Rights and
- Disabled Tourist Rights

Topics and Regulations Affecting Tourism Indirectly:

- Single Market,
- Economic and Monetary Union,
- Tax Policy,
- Competition Policy,
- Business Policy,
- Regional Policy,
- Rural Development Policy,
- Environmental policy,
- Migration Policy,
- Transportation Policy,
- Social Policy and Employment and
- Cultural Policy (Aytuğ, 2011, pp. 69-110).

European Commission established a new strategy and an action plan for EU tourism after Lisbon Treaty and 2008 financial crisis in 2010. Today EU tourism policy intends to preserve leader positions of member states while maximising the industry's contribution to growth and employment and promoting cooperation between EU countries particularly through the exchange of good practice in the global tourism market (European Commission, 2017). EU tourism strategy has been focusing on four priorities for action since 2010. These priorities;

- "To stimulate competitiveness in the European tourism sector,
- To promote the development of sustainable, responsible, and high-quality tourism,
- To consolidate Europe's image as a collection of sustainable, high-quality destinations,
- To maximize the potential of EU financial policies for developing tourism" (European Commission, 2017).

However, there is no specific regulation, directive or strategy paper which target directly winter tourism at EU level. The states and local authorities put into practice their own policies according to EU tourism strategy, its priorities, regulations and topics connected directly and indirectly with tourism mentioned above. In today's Europe, winter tourism is an important economic activity or has a significant economic potential in Central and Eastern European States and Nordic States such as Austria, Bulgaria, Czech Republic, Finland, Poland, Slovakia, Slovenia, Sweden (Jordan, 2006, p.75; Bacharov,2006, p. 251; Aho, 2014; Ivanov & Dimitrova, 2014, pp. 88-89; Egger, Novak, & Taurer, 2014; Indrová & Petru, 2014, pp. 184-185 Kucerová & Makovník, 2014, p. 269).

ERZURUM CASE STUDY

Erzurum is the largest city of the Eastern Anatolian Region. The city is settled in the areas with the hardest continental climate in the country, as it is far away from the sea effect. Generally, the climate of the city is cold temperate. The city is located at the highest altitude in Turkey 39° 57′ 23″ N, and 41° 10′ 12″ E, and at 1.859 m. above sea level. Erzurum city is established at the northern skirts of Palandöken Mountain. This region is identified with three important ski centres. The importance of these ski centres depends on long winter season and snowy time almost 5 months, the long of the ski track, snow thickness and the quality of snow. The runs "Ejder" and "Kapıkaya" are the longest ones in the Olympic-sized. The total lengths of the runs are 28 km (17 mi) and the longest one is 12 km (7.5 mi) long (Tanfer et al., 2015, p. 347). This mountainous area has gained great importance in the field of winter tourism during the recent years in the whole country. Due to the mountainous situation of the city, Erzurum has some of the finest winter sports facilities in Turkey and hosted the "XXV Winter Universiade" in 2011.

Erzurum is one of the world's winter tourism centres due to its geographical features, snow quality, long ski tracks and is convenient for skiing during 5 months in the year. In Erzurum, it starts snowing between October-November, and the skiing season begins at the beginning of November and continues till the end of April (Erzurum Anatolia's Preface, 2018).

Although Turkey is settled in middle latitudes (not northern latitudes), Erzurum is one of the important winter tourism centres in national and international scale due to its special location. In Turkey, there are 5 winter tourism centres: Bursa (Uludağ), Erzurum (Palandöken), Kayseri (Erciyes), Bolu (Kartalkaya), and Kars (Sarıkamış). Erzurum has special importance between them due to its own special character (KUDAKA, 2012, p.36).

On the other hand, due to the tectonic origin of this region, there are thermal water sources in Erzurum and its surrounded areas. These waters have superior properties in terms of flow rate, temperature, physical and chemical properties where these areas are suitable for thermal tourism and health tourism (Toy et al., 2010, p. 7).

Table 2. Erzurum extreme maximum, minimum and average temperatures measured in long period (Turkish State Meteorological Service, 2018)

ERZURUM	Jan.	Feb.	Mar.	Apr.	May	June	July	Aug.	Sep.	Oct.	Nov.	Dec.	Annual
Average Temperature (° C)	-9.2	-7.7	-2.5	5.3	10.7	14.9	19.3	19.5	14.7	8.1	1.0	-6.0	5.7
Average Max. Temp. (° C)	-4.0	-2.4	2.4	10.8	16.8	21.6	26.4	27.1	22.6	15.0	6.7	-1.0	11.8
Average Min. Temp. (° C)	-13.9	-12.6	-7.1	0.0	4.3	7.3	11.1	11.1	6.4	1.7	-3.7	-10.3	-0.5
Average Sunrise Time (hours)	3.1	4.3	5.1	6.2	7.9	10.2	11.1	10.6	9.0	6.7	4.7	3.0	81.9
Average Number of Rainy Days	11.1	11.1	12.3	13.7	16.1	10.8	6.5	5.1	5.0	9.5	9.3	10.6	121.1
Monthly Total Rainfall Average (mm)	22.4	27.0	34.9	53.4	72.9	48.7	26.6	17.5	23.7	48.2	33.3	22.6	431.2
Highest Temp. (° C)	8.0	10.6	21.4	26.5	29.6	32.2	35.6	36.5	33.3	27.0	20.7	14.0	36.5
Lowest Temp. (° C)	-36.0	-37.0	-33.2	-22.4	-7.1	-5.6	-1.8	-1.1	-6.8	-14.1	-34.3	-37.2	-37.2

The measurement period is in 1929 – 2017.

Due to its natural conditions and geographical location of the city, it is one of the most important civilization centres of Anatolia. Owing to this physical situation, it was known as one of the important trade centres on the traditional Silk Road. Erzurum city has been governed by many cultures over the centuries and has owned a lot of cultural landmarks that are settled in the city centre or around the city. Erzurum owns high quality potential for historical tourism, besides the winter and thermal tourism potentials.

According to the General Directorate of Meteorology report (Turkish State Meteorological Service, 2018), the table 2 illustrates annual snowy days and the number of days in Erzurum when the temperature was below 0 °C between 1929 and 2017. The table includes the information about the average temperature, maximum temperature, minimum temperature, average rainy days and the annual amount of rainfall in each month in the Erzurum city.

Based on this table, the average minimum temperature in the three months of winter (December, January, and February) is -7.63° C and annual total rainfall average (mm) is 431.2 mm (43.12 cm). In comparison, due to the WWCAM report (2018) for adding a city to the winter city list these number for temperature and rainfall are 0°C (32°F) or below, and annual snow accumulation of more than 20 cm (8in.) adequate. On the other hand, due to the WWCAM (WWCAM, 2018) definition of winter city, Erzurum owns a harsh winter climatic conditions, including heavy snowfalls, long winter season and cold temperatures.

According to results of the table 2 data's, Erzurum owns a high capability for application as a member of winter city by annual snow and average temperature. The main aim of the Winter City Institute is to provide suitable factors for accessing liveable winter city not only in the winter but also all-round the year. These factors are guidelines for creating Liveable Winter City.

Figure 1a. Some views of open space in Erzurum during winter season (the temperature is between -10, -18) (original, 2018): A view of the Ataturk University Campus (Erzurum).

According to the Winter City Design Guidelines (2000, p.3), the main items in designing a liveable winter city are to create a compact city, to mix land uses and to provide connected pedestrian places. The meaning of the compactness in the city is to use city spaces efficiently, to create the possibility for walking people between places, and to create shelter for public open spaces and streets in front of the wind.

Historical Erzurum city has a compact urban fabric form. But new development areas own sprawled urban fabric form. Creating compactness in Erzurum can be achieved through higher density in new development areas or infill of existing urban areas.

The best way to create mix land uses in Erzurum is to decrease the daily travels by gathering housing, offices, and stores in the same building or on the same street. This will help to sustain street vitality throughout the day whilst commercial downtown streets are often abandoned after working hours during long winter season.

In most of the cities' urban open space create separation between cars and people. In Erzurum, the best way to connect pedestrian spaces is to create a connected network between public open spaces, sidewalks parks and etc. So, people can walk around the city in wintertime. Figures 1 and 2 illustrate some views of Erzurum in winter season.

This study has used SWOT analyse method for evaluating and understanding the strengths and weaknesses points of the city. This analyse method has prepared based on the research on important factors for creating a liveable Winter City in order to develop winter tourism in Erzurum. These factors are recognized in the template of strong, weak direction of city, and related opportunities and threats about the tourism development. Table 3 presents the results of SWOT analyse in Erzurum.

One of the most important factors in strength direction of the city is the nearby location of Palandöken Mountain as a branded ski centre (13 km) from the city centre like a winter tourist attraction. The second important factors in the strength direction are historical past of the Erzurum city and many numbers of the historical buildings have created a high potential for historical and cultural tourism attraction. Besides

Figure 1b. Some views of open space in Erzurum during winter season (the temperature is between -10, -18) (original, 2018): A view from the open place of an apartment.

Figure 1c. Some views of open space in Erzurum during winter season (the temperature is between -10, -18) (original, 2018): A view of the Bilkent School Campus.

these two important tourism attractions, there are the other kinds of tourism like thermal and natural tourism and relative activities like trekking. According to the 2018 census the population is 767.848 people. But in the city there are two universities, one vocational school of higher education and Tourism Department in Vocational School. So there are a lot of young people who study at university during the winter season. As most of the academic year is in the winter season, there is an important potential

Figure 1d. Some views of open space in Erzurum during winter season (the temperature is between -10, -18) (original, 2018): A view of the Ataturk University Campus (Erzurum).

Figure 2a. Some views of Erzurum during the winter season in night with high fog (the temperature is between -10, -18) (original, 2018): A view of the Airport

to improve winter sports in Erzurum. Finally, due to the Turkey's 2023 Winter Tourism Strategy Plan, Erzurum is settled in Tourism Corridor.

Figure 2b. Some views of Erzurum during the winter season in night with high fog (the temperature is between -10, -18) (original, 2018): A view of the Airport

Figure 2c. Some views of Erzurum during the winter season in night with high fog (the temperature is between -10, -18) (original, 2018): A view of the Airport

The weakness of direction of Erzurum city could be ameliorated by correct policies at local and national level in the mid or long term. For example, lack of employee who speaks foreign language in

Figure 2d. Some views of Erzurum during the winter season in night with high fog (the temperature is between -10, -18) (original, 2018): A view of an apartment entrance

Table 3. SWOT analyse for winter city in Erzurum

Strengths	Weaknesses
- Winter tourism attraction (branded ski centre in Palandöken) - Historical tourism attractions - Thermal tourism attractions - Natural tourism attractions and trekking way - Being a university or a student city - Existence of the Faculty of Tourism in the Atatürk University and Tourism Department in Vocational School - Erzurum settlement in Turkey's 2023 Winter Tourism Strategy Plan in order to create a Tourism Corridor, -Increasing winter tourism investment -High quality accommodation alternatives for winter tourism - Long ski track	- Lack of employee who speaks foreign language (English, French, German and etc.), - Lack of good environmental designing - Inadequate suitable factors for creating liveable winter city - Lack of the city infrastructure - Lack of / inadequate open public spaces in city specially in long winter season - Choosing unsuitable constructional material using - Unsocial city - Depressed city during cold months - Self-enclosed city,
Opportunities	**Threats**
- Global trends on creating high quality winter city in national and international scale - Continuous investments for environment projects - Increasing demand for creating liveable city around the year - Creating sustainable city - Continuous demand for winter tourism and winter sports	- Disturbing the urban compact fabric form specially in historical city centre - Forgotten historical city centre as a result of no attention to the place-making -Global warming - Disrupted natural environment

tourism sector during winter season could be solved by employing students of tourism faculty with part-time jobs. To solve the lack of the infrastructure problem in the city, using good methods of designing the streets, pedestrian spaces and open public spaces could be stimulated. Using climatic responsible design for creating suitable open public spaces could be good solution for a more liveable winter city.

To minimise negative environmental effect of tourism, high environmental standards could be implemented by local authorities. Finally, the urban compact fabric form especially in historical city centre could be preserved for integration of winter tourism with other alternative tourism types.

CONCLUSION

On a political level, although Turkey-EU relations and negotiations are in their worst time, as a candidate country, Turkey still has to reorganise and regulate its own policies and development plans for tourism according to the EU tourism policy and its regulation and topics connected directly and indirectly with tourism industry. On the other hand, planning of tourism policies and diversifying tourism investments have a crucial role for adaptation of Turkish policy to the EU's. In this context, winter tourism is an important alternative tourism type for Turkey and Erzurum has an important potential for winter tourism.

Erzurum as a historical city with special natural and geographical situation owns a special capability for development in different kinds of tourism; historical tourism, cultural tourism, winter tourism, thermal tourism and natural tourism. On the other hand, the cold weather conditions and long winter season create a high potential for adding city in the winter city list. Due to this feature, Erzurum can be recognized as a winter city on an international scale. The main aim of tourism development is to create tourism attraction annually, not seasonally, for sustainable economic development. Albeit some kinds of tourism like winter tourism is seasonal. But tourists prefer to enjoy all types of local attraction in seasonal tourism time. The main step in tourism development is to provide the necessary infrastructures for four seasons liveable city.

Furthermore, to improve sustainable winter tourism in Erzurum city, it is important to create high quality liveable winter city. So, it is better to use key climate-sensitive principals in order to reduce the effect of cold temperature on outdoor life of people. Here, there are some suggestions for accessing liveable winter city;

1. **Preserve Solar Access***:* To access a liveable winter city, preserving solar access is an important factor by using:
    a. Pedestrian spaces should remain sunny throughout December, when the sun is at its lowest situation. Locate taller buildings on the north side of the streets to reduce the shaded area in street,
    b. Tall buildings increase wind speed at ground level. Create shelter in front of the winter wind by designing step buildings down instead of tall and isolated buildings.
    c. Design a strategic location as wind barriers with and storage areas of snow to reduce snow removal costs and increase safety,
    d. Create a wind barrier, by screens, buffers, and buildings can reduce wind speed,
    e. Location of pedestrian places in the city like parks and main pathways should be located on the sunny side of streets and buildings,
    f. The buildings should be in similar height. Tall, isolated buildings increase wind speed at ground level.

2. Designing the Streets:
   a. Buildings should not shade on the street.
   b. Use warm colour in building façades for creating visual interest and absorbing the sun light,
   c. Use continuous building façades with awnings,
   d. Create slightly-raised pedestrian way in street in order to be slow traffic eliminate and help to snow melt or ice formation.
   e. Street and pedestrian lighting and furniture increase comfort and safety,
   f. Bicycle pathway allow using bicycles in the summer and snow storage in the winter,
   g. Places sheltered from the wind and exposed to the sun will be felt much warmer and will be usable for a longer part of the year,
   h. Awnings, balconies and other façade projections reduce ground-level winds.
3. Planting
   a. To improve tree health, choose cold and salt-resistant species.
   b. Street trees reduce wind speed and provide separation between pedestrians and cars.
   c. Protect trunks from winter snow removal operations with temporary tree guards,
   d. Evergreen trees to block winter winds,
   e. Evergreen trees create removable fence on street side for safety,
   f. Using deciduous trees allow sun to reach areas of the park used in winter,
   g. Divide the parking lot into smaller ones separated by planted islands for reducing wind speeds,
   h. Provide room for pedestrian pathways and planted islands to serve as wind barriers.
   i. Grouping trees together improves their resistance to wind exposure and reduces surface evaporation,
   j. Use pieces of 2×4 lumber to protect trees against snow and wind,
   k. Small plants are inadequate for winter and they need to be protected from snow and wind
   l. Large plants are adequate hardy species and can be used as street furniture.
4. Parks Open Space
   a. Designing open amphitheatre in parks and using it as sheltered in winter,
   b. Using evergreen trees in green area to block winter winds,
   c. In green spaces grass mounds can be used for sleigh riding by children at festivals,
   d. Create sheltered stop points in parks,
   e. Private parking lots can be shared with public for winter festivals,
   f. Lake can be used as a skating rink. Landscape with temporary evergreens and lighting.
5. Colour, Materials, and Lighting
   a. Use warm colours in winter environments like earth tones (ochre, sand, and terracotta) and pastel hues and keep brilliant colours (reds, oranges, and yellows) for accents,
   b. Special structures, such as bridges, are good opportunity to use colours.
   c. Wood, plastics and certain composite materials stay comfortable for a longer period of the year than metal and concrete.
   d. Using metal may prove a hazard in certain situations, such as children playgrounds,
   e. Salt will corrode metal and porous concrete, brick or stone,
   f. In shorter days, lighting is an essential component; in vehicular street using cobra-head lighting provides safety but does not create a pleasant pedestrian atmosphere.
   g. On important commercial streets and parks, add pedestrian lighting and use the lamppost for attaching banners and speakers.

h. Lighted buildings, infrastructure or sculptures become focal points.

REFERENCES

Aho, -S. K. (2014). Finland tourism policies: From helping to build new state identities to branding a modern specific destination. In C. Costa, E. Panyik, & D. Buhalis, *European Tourism Planning and Organisation Systems The EU Member States* (pp. 44-60). Bristol, UK: Channel View Publications.

Akkerman, A. (2014). Towards a phenomenology of the winter-city: Urbanization and mind through the little ice age and its sequels. University of Saskatchewan. *Studia Phenomenological, 14*, 161–189. doi:10.5840tudphaen2014149

Aytuğ, H. K. (2011). Avrupa Birliği Ülkelerinde Tarımsal Turizm Uygulamaları ve Türkiye'de Gelişme Potansiyeli: Yeşilköy Örneği. İzmir: Dokuz Eylül Üniversitesi, Sosyal Bilimler Enstitüsü Yayımlanmamış Doktora Tezi. -Bachvarov, M. (2006). Tourism in Bulgaria. In D. Hall, M. Smith, & B. Marciszewska (Eds.), *Tourism in the new Europe The challenges and opportunities of EU enlargement* (pp. 241–255). Oxfordshire, UK: CABI.

Bausch, T., & Unseld, C. (2018). Winter tourism in Germany is much more than skiing consumer motives and implications to alpine destination marketing. *Journal of Vacation Marketing, 24*(3), 203–217. doi:10.1177/1356766717691806

City of Sapporo. (2018). Retrieved from https://www.city.sapporo.jp/somu/kokusai/wwcam/history.html

Egger, R., Novak, J., & Taurer, W. (2014). Austria: Where tourism has tradition. In C. Costa, E. Panyik, & D. Buhalis (Eds.), *European tourism planning and organisation systems The EU member states* (pp. 163–182). Bristol, UK: Channel View Publications.

Erzurum Anatolia's Preface. (2018). Retrieved from http://www.goerzurum.net/en/tourism-in-erzurum/winter-tourism-in-erzurum

Estol, J., & Font, X. (2016). European tourism policy: Its evolution and structure. *Tourism Management, 52*, 230–241. doi:10.1016/j.tourman.2015.06.007

European Commission. (2010). *Communication from the commission to the European parliament, the council, the European economic and social committee and the committee of the regions; Europe, the world's No 1 tourist destination a new political framework for tourism in Europe*. Brussels, Belgium: European Commission.

European Commission. (2017). Overview of EU Tourism Policy. Retrieved from https://ec.europa.eu/growth/sectors/tourism/policy-overview_en

Gürer, N. (2017). The role of local governments for creating sustainable urban places in winter cities. Çağdaş Yerel Yönetimler, Cilt 26 Sayı 1 pp. 19-42.

Hong, W. L., & Cun-Yan, J. (2017). A field study on climate comfortable conditions of urban public open spaces in marginal season of winter cities. *Open House International, 42*(2).

Indrová, J., & Petru, Z. (2014). The Czech Republic: A destination in the heart of Europe. In *C. Costa, E. Panyik, & D. Buhalis (Eds.), European tourism planning and organisation systems the EU member states* (pp. 183–197). Bristol, UK: Channel View Publications.

Ivanov, S., & Dimitrova, M. (2014). Managing tourism in Bulgaria: Between 'Mission Impossible' and new hope. In C. Costa, E. Panyik, & D. Buhalis (Eds.), *European tourism planning and organisation systems The EU member states* (pp. 87–125). Bristol, UK: Channel View Publications.

Jordan, P. (2006). Tourism and EU enlargement: A central European perspective. In D. Hall, M. Smith, & B. Marciszewska (Eds.), *Tourism in the New Europe The challenges and opportunities of EU enlargement* (pp. 65–80). Oxfordshire, UK: CABI. doi:10.1079/9781845931179.0065

Journal of Tourism & Hospitality. (2018). Winter tourism. Retrieved from https://www.omicsonline.org/scholarly/winter-tourism-journals-articles-ppts-list.php

Kucerová, J., & Makovník, T. (2014). Tourism in Slovakia: The best-kept secret in Europe. In *C. Costa, E. Panyik, & D. Buhalis (Eds.), European tourism planning and organisation systems The EU member states* (pp. 257–278). Bristol, UK: Channel View Publications.

KUDAKA. (2012). *Kuzeydoğu Anadolu Kalkınma Ajansı*. Erzurum Konaklı Bölgesi'nde Finansal Fizibilite Raporu.

Move DC. (2014). The District of Columbia's multimodal long-range transportation plan.

National Research Council. (2002). Community and quality of life: Data needs for informed decision making. National Academy Press, Washington, D.C. Retrieved from http://nap.edu/10262

Pechlaner, H., & Fischer, E. (2006). Alpine wellness: A resource-based view. *Tourism Recreation Research, 31*(1), 67–77. doi:10.1080/02508281.2006.11081248

Pressman, N. (1996). Sustainable winter cities: Future directions for planning, policy and design. *Atmospheric Environment, 30*(3), 521–529. doi:10.1016/1352-2310(95)00012-7

PSC (The Partnership for Sustainable Communities). (2012). EPA, 560-R-12-001, June.

Schalber, C., & Peters, M. (2012). Determinants of health tourism competitiveness: An Alpine case study. *Tourism Review, 60*(3), 307–323.

SCI (Sustainable Cities Initiative). (2017). *What is Livability?* Eugene, OR: University of Oregon.

Tanfer, N., Çavuş, A., & Zaman, N. (2015). A new winter tourism centre in Turkey's winter tourism corridor: Konaklı. Marmara Geographical Review (Marmara Coğrafya Dergisi). No: 31, January - 2015, S.345-365. İstanbul. Retrieved from http://www.marmaracografya.com

Toy, S., Çatakçi S., EYmirli E., B., Karapinar, M., (2010). Erzurum Termal Turizm Potansiyeli, Turizm Raporları No: 3.

Turkish State Meteorological Service. (2018). Retrieved from https://mgm.gov.tr/veridegerlendirme/il-ve-ilceleristatistik.aspx?k=A&m=ERZURUM&fbclid=IwAR0VScglMspCKDTIoI6FVKZJMLdc_6WbSmqJyeYoV7P9L-GxB3b4yGb5l0

UNWTO. (2018a). UNWTO International Conference on Tourism and Snow Culture Snow Experiences and Winter Traditions as Assets for Tourism Destinations. Retrieved from http://asiapacific.unwto.org/event/unwto-international-conference-tourism-and-snow-culture-snow-experiences-and-winter-traditions

UNWTO. (2018b). *UNWTO Tourism Highlights*. Madrid, Spain: World Tourism Organisation.

Winter City Design Guidelines. (2000). *Urban System*. Fort St. John, The Energetic City.

Winter City Institute. (2018). Retrieved from https://wintercities.com/home/about

WWCAM. (World Winter Cities Association for Mayors Pamphlet). (2016). International Relations Department, City of Sapporo. UNWTO. (2017). UNWTO World Tourism Barometer. UNWTO.

WWCAM. (World Winter City Association for Mayors). (2018). Retrieved from https://www.city.sapporo.jp/somu/kokusai/wwcam/definition.html

Yfantidou, G., Nikou, M., & Matsouka, O. (2018). Wınter tourısm in Greece: An approach to tourısts' behaviour and needs. *Geo Journal of Tourism and Geosites*, *21*(1), 74–87.

KEY TERMS AND DEFINITIONS

Liveability: Is an ensemble concept which includes stainability, quality of life, the character of place, and the health of communities.

Winter City: Is a concept for communities in northern latitudes with the long winter season, snowy, very cold weather, and harsh climatic conditions that encourage them to plan their transportation systems, buildings, and recreation project around the idea of using their infrastructure during all four seasons.

Winter City Movement: The purpose of this movement is to establish the needs of the people who live in the areas with high snowy and cold weather, by improving the comfort of lifestyles and recognizing human needs in order to plan and design better.

Winter Tourism: Could be defined an integrated tourism products and services including winter sports, such as ski, ice-skating, snowboard, curling etc., visiting the winter tourism destinations to watch national and international sport competitions and to use snow-independent products and services such as SPA, sauna or Turkish bath facilities in the coldest season of the year, between autumn and spring.

ENDNOTES

1 The Winter City Institute was founded by Patrick Coleman, AICP (American Institute of Certified Planners), recognized for his work with the Liveable Winter Cities Association (WCA). From 1982-2005, the WCA organized conferences, published books and the quarterly magazine "Winter Cities". The Institute has taken the place of the WCA in carrying out the mission of promoting the liveable winter city.

2 The World Winter Cities Association for Mayors (WWCAM) is a network of winter cities around the world that provides members with opportunities to meet and learn from each other about winter technologies and experiences under the slogan "Winter is a Resource and an Asset." The associa-

tion, originally the Northern Intercity Conference of Mayors, was initiated by the city of Sapporo in 1981, and the following year the first Mayors Conference was held. In 2004 the organization became the World Winter Cities Association for Mayors. (City of Sapporo, 2018). The member cities of World Winter City Association for Mayors include 21 cities from 10 countries: Canada (Edmonton, Winnipeg), China (Changchun, Harbin, Jiamusi, Jilin, Jixi, Qiqihar, Shenyang), Estonia (Viimsi), Finland (Rovaniemi), Japan (Matsumoto, Sapporo), Mongolia (Ulaanbaatar), Norway (Tromsø), Republic of Korea (Hwacheon, Inje, Taebaek), Russia (Magadan, Novosibirsk), U.S.A. (Anchorage). Every two years World Winter Cities has held the conference for Mayors. The first conference has held in 1982 Sapporo (Japan), and the 17th Mayors Conference will be held in Sapporo (Japan) in 2016. During these conferences, all related items to city-planning are introduced. Livable winter city's topic is discussed by participants during these conferences. On the other hand, non-member cities may also participate in the conference as observers (WWCAM, 2016, p.5-7).

3 Tourism merited the attention of legislators for the first time in Maastricht Treaty (1992) with article 3 "*measures in the spheres of energy, civil protection and tourism*" in 1992. Lisbon Treaty (2007) enacts tourism with article 2E "*The Union shall have competence to carry out actions to support, coordinate or supplement the actions of the Member States. The areas of such action shall, at European level, be: ...(d) tourism...*" and Article 176 B "1. *The Union shall complement the action of the Member States in the tourism sector, in particular by promoting the competitiveness of Union undertakings in that sector. To that end, Union action shall be aimed at: (a) encouraging the creation of a favourable environment for the development of undertakings in this sector; (b) promoting cooperation between the Member States, particularly by the exchange of good practice. 2. The European Parliament and the Council, acting in accordance with the ordinary legislative procedure, shall establish specific measures to complement actions within the Member States to achieve the objectives referred to in this Article, excluding any harmonisation of the laws and regulations of the Member States*".

Chapter 7
Social and Economic Transformation With the Institutional Economic Perspective

Mehmet Yunus Çelik
https://orcid.org/0000-0003-4793-8306
Kastamonu University, Turkey

ABSTRACT

The events and phenomena in the period of the industrial society were explained within the context of the Newtonian paradigm. In today's information society and its economic structure, they are explained within the context of the Quantum paradigm. Nevertheless, the assumption of neoclassics claims that consumers decide independently from each other, which is controversial. Consumers decide in real terms, not independently but under the influence of psychological situation, social environment, and cultural infrastructure. The basic mutual point between the two paradigms is to maximize the benefit from the goods to be consumed when making consumption decisions. To this end, the process of social and economic transformation will first be discussed in the light of paradigm shift and technological improvements. Then, with the institutional economic perspective, the change in consumption understanding will be taken into consideration in the social and economic structure of today.

INTRODUCTION

Change and transformation has been generating the essence of presence and history (Hughes, 1995, p. 9). Besides, it has been the constant destiny of social structures (Yazıcı, 2013, p. 1490). The process of change and transformation is an integrated system that includes the technological, economic, socio-cultural and political dimensions, within the historical structure, from being an individual to society. The main technological paradigm, which forms the basis of the social development stage, has moved to a new and higher level each time. This process of change and transformation has sometimes been

DOI: 10.4018/978-1-7998-0333-1.ch007

Copyright © 2020, IGI Global. Copying or distributing in print or electronic forms without written permission of IGI Global is prohibited.

thousands of years according to different periods of social development and structuring and sometimes it is limited to centuries. Today, this process is much shorter than in the past. As humanity reached knowledge, it accelerated the process of change and transformation, but it never prevented change and transformation. It is a fact that the phenomenon of change and transformation will change and it must be accepted that the change and transformation will always remain in existence. The underlying reason for the inability of preventing change is the endless needs of people. Meeting the needs seen infinitely brings the phenomenon of consumption to the fore. The differentiation in the social structure also ensured that the consumption concept differed according to the social structures. In this context, since the early ages, every person who uses innovation and information to dominate nature has shaped his needs and consumption activity accordingly. After that, innovation and knowledge began to dominate people. In order to be able to see this process in a sound framework, it is necessary to explain the change and transformation in societies, the pioneering developments and basic activities, and the reasons for the people's reaction to these developments for years.

In this study, the effects of change and transformation and its impacts on social and institutional structures will be examined in the light of the Veblenist scientific thought, which criticizes the orthodox economic theory and forms the theoretical foundations of institutional economics. Additionally, the effects of social and institutional change and transformation on consumption activities will be analyzed. In this context, it will be explained that traditional understanding is shaped within the framework of Newtonian mechanical thought and modern understanding is shaped within the framework of Quantum thought. As a result, beyond the Newtonian thought, it will be emphasized that Quantum thought should dominate social and institutional life.

BACKGROUND

Demirel and Yeğen (2015) examined the role of the media in the consumption process with the assumption that individuals see consumption as an identity or a means of improving social status. They examined how the media promotes consumption as a consumer promoter. According to Şentürk (2008), every process with economic, social and political content brings its own conditions. The societies that are influenced by the processes they live inform the ideal way of life that differs according to their structural characteristics. This ideal form of life, consisting of a combination of priorities, acceptances and values, has changed from the past to the present. Karakaş (2017), in his study, considers consumption as a form of behavior that provides for a discourse, an institutionalized defense strategy, a form of communication and the integration of the group. It states that the consuming individual has ceased to be a subject at the point of meeting his needs and has changed to the position of the object being dragged into the stream. Halis (2012) discusses the changing meaning of consumption and the means used in consumption from past to present and the social network paradigm that fueled this change. Güleç (2015), based on the opinions of Veblen, which argues that consumption may create waste when it is in the form of conspicuous consumption. In this context, he argued that Veblen stated that conspicuous consumption is a psychological or social status signal. The upper class may use expensive consumptions to show their wealth off. Middle and lower social classes use the symbol products from the upper classes' consumption bundle, to signal the society that they belong to better classes. Yildiz, Kalagan, Yildiz and Cetin (2013) studied the effect of consumption pattern change in the society on consumption behavior of individuals and tried to determine the determinants of irrational consumption. Aydoğan (2009) examined the phenomenon of transformation in the cities as a result of the functioning of the consumption society in Turkish society. Alan (2016) emphasized the transition from the production society to the consumption society, the basic parameters of the consumption society and the value of consumption in the consumer society, and the transformation of value in the society. In his study, Wilk (2002) concludes that factors limiting consumption may be counterbalanced or unbalanced in many interrelated variables with relatively small changes. In his study, Dickson (2000) showed how the major changes that emerged with economic innovation and which changed profoundly the consumer behavior, led to encouraging research on the development of consumer behavior in consumers and across the country. Jannson, Kautsky and Miliander (2006), in their study, stated that the relationship between consumption and production would cause further shifts to contaminated foods. Warde (2009), was examined the critical perspective within the sociological aspect by concluding that consumption is an unprejudiced sociological concept, which is usually considered as a distributive way of social class. Burrows and Marsh (1992) examined the state of consumption habits in this geography by introducing new evidence in the debate on consumer revolution in early modern England. Açıkalın and Gül (2006) focused on the role of consumption in determining social status. Vergragt, Akenji and Dewick (2014) argued that the transition to a sustainable production and consumption system is very difficult to conceptualize and research, so the area of research is not yet very well structured, the boundaries are still in fluid research, and where social practices and policies are generally unclear.

SOCIAL AND ECONOMIC TRANSFORMATION

Throughout history, human beings have never had the chance to live in a social structure that they had information beforehand. All of the emerging social structures were formed and shaped within the framework of the needs and knowledge of the time. For example, activities such as hunting and gathering, which were made by people living in the primitive periods to find food, to feed and to sustain their lives, formed the structure of societies, production and consumption styles at that time. (Canlıoğlu, 2008, p. 28). In this context, in the process of change and transformation based on infinite needs, innovation and knowledge, societies emerged with four different social development and structuring which are expressed as the primitive, agricultural, industrial and information society (Çalık and Çınar, 2009, p. 82).

The primitive society refers to the hunting and gathering society in which the physical power comes to the forefront as the dominant power and the primitive paradigm reigns in which primitive tools and materials such as the simple arrow, spear, sharpened stone are used.

The agricultural society refers to the society in which the traditional nature paradigm, where agricultural production is carried out by means of tools such as wheels, sickles and plows, which are based on the formation of tools and equipment which are free in nature, where water and soil come to the forefront as the dominant power.

The industrial society refers to the society that, as the dominant power, comes to the forefront of capital, as the paradigm, the society that produces capitalist and communal organization based on the Newtonian thought which is the first scientific revolution, in the cause-effect relationship, based on the laws of mechanical processing of the visible nature.

The information society refers to the social structure that produces information and innovation, an output of the human brain. It is emerged by technological improvements in the fields such as nanotechnology, microelectronic, microbiology, etc. that improved within the reciprocal and cumulative cause-effect

Figure 1. Social improvements from the primitive society to the information society
Source:Erkan, 2004

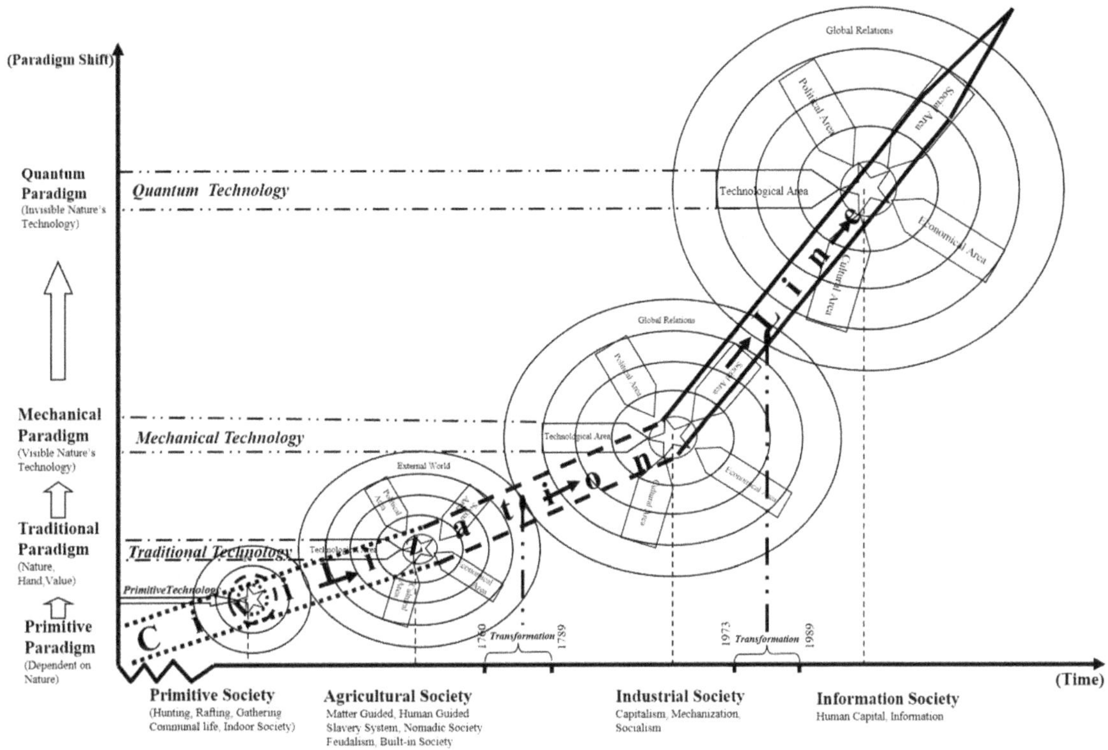

relationships network based on quantum thought, which is considered as a second scientific revolution. Information is the dominant power in this society (Erkan, 2019).

Primitive Society

The primitive social structure was the first social structure in human history. In this process, a structure in which the behavioral pattern was revealed by the people to meet their basic needs has emerged. This social structure consists of clans with a very large family type, which has a nomadic life and is shaped by kinship ties. Protection against in clans, animals and natural events is emphasized (Arklan and Taşdemir, 2008, p. 68). In the light of the concepts, improved about the first period of human communities formed by taking into account the developments in the historical process, it is stated that groups of at least twenty or thirty people constitute the primitive society organizations. It is thought that there is no other social unit above and below the primitive society organizations. In this respect, the primitive community formed did not establish regular relations with any other primitive community, did not become a member of any unity or confederation and was not divided into another group as a family or profession in a narrow sense (Şenel, 1982, p. 44).

In the early stages of the primitive society, individuals have pursued a lifestyle to meet their primary needs just enough for their daily lives. In this early period, because of the fact that human knowledge, skills and equipment had not developed enough to hunt animals yet, everyone in a tribe is obliged to perform gathering. Although people spend almost all of their time for this purpose, aggregation efficiency is very low. Only a variety of herbs, plants, fruits or small insect-like animals that are free in nature had been gathered and consumed enough food to provide life support. There is nothing in social life that makes one person superior to the other. All members of the tribe had struggled for nutrition, which is a common denominator, and everything that had been acquired, shared by all members of the tribe, regardless of who had acquired it. There is a common sense of ownership and the only community stage where the class difference is not clear is the stage of the primitive society (Canlıoğlu, 2008, pp. 28-29).

As a result of the gathering activities that lasted for thousands of years, it has become necessary to experience a change that will enable people to dominate nature and benefit more from nature. This change was realized when people realized that nature was not only limited to a consumption and gathering activity, but also a means of production. As human beings began to use tools (arrow, spear, trap, etc.) by taking advantage of nature, hunting activities started to gain importance as well as gathering activities. Thus, alternative resources have emerged to meet the nutritional needs of the community and work efficiencies have also increased significantly. As one of the first concrete examples of the use of knowledge as an outcome of human activity, the human being began to hunt larger animals in size than himself and was able to obtain more nutritious products for the nutrient source. In this process, people have learned to use nature not only as a source of food but also as a source of production (post, shelter, bowl) which facilitates defense and daily life. The knowledge of hunting and production methods, which is considered as a major transformation, refers to the primitive technology dimension of the primitive period. (Senel, 1982, pp. 52-53).

In the early stages of the primitive society, there was no division of labor. However, with the development of hunting, the first division of labor in human history began to develop. In this context, men with their physical power and endurance, and had no responsibility for maternity, focused on hunting activities to obtain meat for nutrition, and hide for clothing and accommodation. On the other side, women and children had taken care of gathering (fruits, molluscs, edible roots, wild grapes, etc.), fishery, and maternity.

Elderly people have long been engaged in the production of work tools through life experiences. In a way, they have been the transporters of the generations of collaborative work habits developed by knowledge and experience of generations. At the same time, for the elderly, who are the most knowledgeable people of the primitive period, this has provided them with respect in the eyes of other members of their primitive communities. The elders, who gained a status expressed as the chief in all common activities, especially the hunting, have gradually become decision-makers in all the activities of the community. The situation that is based on gender, knowledge and experience is the first natural division of labor (Zubritski, Mitropolski, & Kerov, 2006, p. 31).

The management approach in the primitive society is based on the Chieftaincy. Unless there was an exceptional situation, the chieftaincy was a system that continues from father to son. All daily works of the tribe are planned by the chef. Being a chef and agreeing to it, as well as being old and experienced, are connected to being a warrior, courageous, knowledgeable and respected person. He has also been a manager with basic responsibilities and specialties such as chief, generosity, preacher, diligence and dedication. These features expected from the chief are, in a sense, personalized in the chef, the features that others do not have to own, and that they are reluctant to have even places. Generosity has been the main indicator of the good intentions of the chief to his people. In fact, these characteristics, the chief, if the owner does not have, if he does not have the status was seen as important as a feature (Sönmez, 2018, p. 9).

In the primitive society, the economy is shaped by the abundance of resources and the exchange system, which is called a gift. Production activities consisted of hunting animals and gathering foods; on the other hand, while consumption referred equal share among all members of the society at first, it changed into a system, which powerful members acquire more portion in the following periods.

It is understood that in the primitive society, thought and communication activities do not have the level of influence that will enable the formation of knowledge and thus change the behavior of individuals in society. Therefore, the social and economic structure has no effect on the structure of thought and communication. In such a case, there is no other way for individuals in society to replicate each other's old ways of behaving like an imitation. Therefore, the primitive society has become a traditionalist and stable society with both its behavior and thought activities (Şenel, 1982, p. 47).

In the primitive stage of society, tribes lived thousands of years without being aware of each other. This has prevented any socio-cultural interactions with each other, competing or establishing economic relations. However, in this period, hunting and gathering had taught people to be in social solidarity with each other. In the following periods, the presence of fire has given people the opportunity to create socialization and tradition with some ceremonial rituals such as gathering around the fire and cooking what they hunted and gathered. This situation helped communication to become stronger and formed a visual language, consisting of figures and writings in the later period. By this way, ancient civilizations began to be settled (Ünal, 2009, p. 127).

In primitive societies, some phenomena have changed as people realize that there are communities living outside of themselves. Cultural interaction between tribes has increased with a different language, people with different religious beliefs, and meeting people with different leaders.

Although this cultural interaction provides positive results such as acting together or marriage, results such as rejecting each other leaders or stealing food from another tribe forced them to defend their own tribes. This situation arose wars between tribes, so human beings had to kill their own kind first time in history. The tribes, who had been defeated in wars, were forced to comply with the religious beliefs and leadership rules of the other tribes. This situation revealed the first examples of social conflict (Güneş, 2014, p. 161).

The tendency to make agriculture after the experiences in the primitive society has been the most important determinant in the transition to the model of the agricultural society. Although it is not known exactly when the agriculture started, it is defined as the last of primitive life. It was pointed out that the human communities had to do agricultural activities, to observe the growth of the crop from the seed sown and to use it as food. In addition to the necessities such as irrigation, protecting crops from animals become a more significant obligation.

This situation has been quite difficult for a nomadic community. People, who move to the settled life started to live in a place called a village between the years 12000-10000 BC. In this context, fertile and wetlands, where the nutrition and product resources are high, constitute the first settlements where regular agriculture is made. In this way, human communities have been able to stay in these regions for a very long time and to increase their population. The transition to settled life also referred to as the agricultural revolution, revealed the first human civilization (Canlıoğlu, 2008, p. 32), (Kuper, 1995, p. 15).

Agricultural Society

In order to better understand the cultural diversity that societies have formed over time, it is necessary to look at the diffuse types of society that exist in history and the changes taking place with the transformation of social structures. The history of mankind, which has passed through three important stages in the past timeframes, has undergone the process of transformation by experiencing three important revolutions. The first of these was the transition to the agricultural society. Approximately ten thousand years ago, a team of gatherers and hunting tribes gathered and learned to keep the catches for later consumption. This increased the efficiency of product acquisition of the groups, and the groups of hunters no longer tend to think about daily nutrition but also later. The tradition of storing some of the gathered products under the ground has emerged in this way. The people saw that the product they stored under the ground had been germinated after a while. Therefore, humans acquired the knowledge of reproducing from the product through the soil. People, who objectify this knowledge through trial and error method, took the first steps of transition to settled life. These people later learned to cultivate their domesticated animals and planting their lands. By discovering the growth underground, tribes who were able to reach and consume the nutrients on the ground became the agricultural society, so they started to cultivate seeds and animals with the help of tools such as simple sickles or plows (Kocacık, 2003, p. 1).

In the world dominated by agriculture, which Toffler (1981) expressed as the first wave, societies were divided into primitive and civilized societies. In society, which is expressed as primitive, people have to be living in tribes, hunting and gathering food and they are trying to survive. Therefore, these people are not met with the agricultural revolution. In society, which is expressed as civilized, people are engaged in agriculture in settled order and by making their living by cultivating the land. Soil took part in the economic system, family structure and cultural basis of these societies. Each community, which is basically a decentralized economic structure, has been able to satisfy its own needs (Bensghir, 1996, p. 9).

Agriculture has been an effective factor that creates the first relationship between people and nature. Approximately ten thousand years ago, the transformation from the primitive society to the agricultural society reached its peak in three places, including the valleys of Tigris and Euphrates (Mesopotamia), in the valley of the Indus, in the Nile valley. The beginning of the process of cultivation has been a milestone for human history. Agriculture has brought about the beginning of the establishment of life, as well as the development of vital equipment and the shaping of civilized social life. This inhabited state, which constituted the first civilizations, prepared the ground for many transformations and changes that would emerge in the later periods. (Yurtseven, 2015, pp. 19-20).

The action of resident life has made human life regular. Two production factors in this period; labor and soil have become important. In this way, human beings have been in the process of continuing to live thanks to the traditional agricultural knowledge used in the production from the soil. Developments in the techniques used in agriculture and the discovery of precious metals increased the productivity of agricultural production. Thus, human beings have obtained more products by consuming less labor. All these developments have brought about important changes in economic and social life (Bayraç, 2003, p. 45). In this process called as the agricultural society, it was possible to use energy resources such as human and animal power, sun, water and wind and to shape the means of production according to these sources.

In the agricultural society, all activities have started to intensify almost between people and nature. The basis of culture and economy has always been the soil. In other words, the dominant power in the social structure was soil. Every community in the formation of society has produced enough production and consumption to satisfy its own needs. Hand labor has played an important role in the realization of production. The goods obtained after the production by a small number of merchants were distributed. However, work efficiency remained very low during this period.

In the agricultural society, class consciousness emerged from a sociological point of view and social classes, called nobles, clerics, warriors and slaves, were formed. In this period, more consumption needs to be emerged due to the increasing population and the distribution of goods became important. Over time, traders started to establish commercial companies due to the expansion of their business. The increasing intensity of trade caused the merchant class to come to the fore in society and to increase its profits and capital (Ünal, 2009, p. 128).

Together with the transition to the agricultural society, the development of community consciousness as the material foundations of the hierarchical structure in societies has been one of the most important results of this change and transformation. With the emergence of private property in the following periods, individualism and the created hierarchy have destroyed equality in the agricultural society. The problems related to the society that emerged as a result of the change in social values formed the source of change of thoughts, feelings and attitudes of nature. With this period, the departure from nature has increased with regard to social problems (Yurtseven, 2015, p. 20).

The people in the agricultural society have been the locomotive of sustaining an agricultural economy which is highly dependent on geographical and climatic conditions. However, in a world of perception connected to unity, the technological possibilities of this human being have been less than the present (Meder, 2001, p. 73).

Despite the great empires and major developments, the spread of knowledge and innovations was still very slow during this period. B.C. IV. The Sumerians, who settled in the south of Mesopotamia from the east of the millennium BC, dried the marshes there. After that, they discovered the most important discoveries in the historical process and they succeeded in establishing the big city-states by discovering the writing. The Sumerians, who are still controversial about where they came to Mesopotamia, have made an important breakthrough in the development of humanity by providing the discovery of the cuneiform (Özgül, 2011, p. 402). Social, legal, economic, etc. the scripts were adapted to the order and the empires began to be managed through writing. The writing, which is a tool for trade, agreements and epics, shed light on human beings in the way of transferring past knowledge to the present, much more clearly than the periods in which there was no writing. In this sense, finding the writing accelerated the dissemination of knowledge and at the same time, the social and economic life of that period, systematically put into a systematic, has carried out radical changes and transformations. The periods in which economic and diplomatic regulations were written on stone tablets were replaced by a more innovative system with the first paper (papyrus). Afterwards, with the presence of the printing press, the rate of dissemination of information has increased tremendously, making it easier to access and reproduce information. These developments have been the triggers of the Renaissance, Reform and Enlightenment Age, which will take place in Europe on the following dates.

Because the information is now more accessible in the agricultural society because cultural interactions have begun to occur and human beings have the ability to produce, the intellectual structure of people has changed completely, and the process of social change and transformation has gained momentum. In the areas of education, health, trade and transportation, although modern structures are not mentioned yet, infrastructure has started to form. The internal training of the clans was replaced by agriculture-based on-the-job training in small settlements of the agricultural community. The educational activity has become widespread, but both the religious and the formal education activity has been limited to nobles in most places. In this direction, important developments have been observed in the fields of health and science. Although it is a bit difficult in this period to ensure the trade of the goods and services produced, it has become much better in the coming periods due to the changes in the economic structure and the improvements in transportation.

In particular, some technical inventions that began to be seen from the 16th century have helped to facilitate maritimely. In this way, the discovery of new places and sea routes has become possible. Thanks to these discoveries, the development of trade has been ensured. Many different products from the production points located in each region of the world have been brought to the centers which are easily developed in the advanced agricultural society. Thus, the welfare of these centers increased. The increase in the level of welfare caused the social structure to be affected and the social life changed. This prosperity increase and the growing wealth brought about the dizzying developments in the fields of science and technology, especially in the late 18th century (Ünal, 2009, p. 128).

Due to economic and social developments, it has become mandatory to establish qualified and larger settlements. These new settlements were places where the social division of labor increased, the production forces developed, and new economic and social forms emerged. This change observed in the settlement model brought together people living in more crowded groups. On the other side, there has been a need for established rules for reconciliation and public order between these groups. Therefore, the society model has started to require more powerful forms of organization, which can prevent the resolutions that may occur during the structuring. In the beginning, this authoritarian power was created to eliminate the problems that may be encountered in the society, and it has become a factor that puts pressure on society with the changes taking place in different ways over time. The feudal regime that emerged during the Middle Ages was the largest example of the use of authority as an element of oppression in the hands of certain classes. (Canlıoğlu, 2008, p. 33).

The one-goded religions were the dominant ideology in the agricultural society, the first stage of transformation of humanity. The soiled structure of humanity by the agricultural revolution, the ownership of soil as a means of production, and the soil owner upon soil ownership have shaped the understanding of management. However, the religion that influenced political administrations led to the emergence of different understandings and sects. (Kocacık, 2003, p. 1).

Starting with the periods before Christ, shaping society with agriculture continues its existence partially. However, within the framework of general assumptions, in terms of the concept, the agricultural society ended with the discovery of the industrial society by other societies, especially Europe, shaped by the Industrial Revolution. The feudalism in the Middle Ages Europe, which was shaped especially after the fall of the Roman Empire, was replaced by a new system of capitalism, which was replaced by a wide range of new production systems caused by commercial development and industrialization. From this perspective, the Industrial Revolution, thanks to the shock waves it brought towards the end of the 18th century, has been characterized by a boom, a touchstone that reveals a new civilization that carries out the change and transformation of all aspects of the ancient societies around the world (Canlıoğlu, 2008, p. 40). (Ünal, 2009, p. 128).

Industrial Society

The power from the steam engine, discovered by James Watt in England in 1765, was used as an energy source in production and transportation. The Industrial Revolution, which took place after the discovery of the power of steam, was a fundamental building block that accelerated the transformation process of change initiated by Mercantilism. In other words, the emergence of new formations along with the change and transformation which traditionally appeared in the structure of the agricultural society has gained an even more different and effective dimension with the Industrial Revolution. From this point of view, the integration of the steam engine into the production activities, on the one hand, had an effective role in the history of social and economic transformation through the sociological transformation in the formation of economics on the other (Yalçinkaya, 2001, p. 1). Because the new technologies introduced after the industrial revolution caused the change of sociocultural, technological, economic and political lifestyles of people, the emergence of new social and institutional structures and the differentiation of production-consumption activities. This new social structure is defined as the industrial society (Çalık and Çınar, 2009, p. 82).

The book of the Wealth of Nations, written by Adam Smith in 1776, enabled the industrial revolution to be firmly grounded in the economic aspects and formed the economic leg of the revolution. Thought as the division of labor and the necessity of specialization, the production of industrial goods will provide more productivity than agricultural production, as well as innovations, this book has also emerged as a science of economics. The production, consumption and sharing activities carried out in the previous social structures based on primitive and traditional procedures and principles have been scientifically shaped in this period.

Another development that led to the industrial revolution was the French Revolution in 1789. This political and ideological change and transformation in France constituted the political pillar of the Industrial Revolution. In this respect, the emergence of liberal thought, together with the French Revolution, played a leading role in the development of industrialization. The French revolution has affected political, cultural and social areas. In other words, this way of thinking has been renewed by preserving its essence in the face of economic and technological changes (Canlıoğlu, 2008, p. 55). Thus, the industrial revolution was the common product of the political developments taking place in France with technological and economic developments in England. (Erkan, 1998, p. 4).

Industrial Revolution with a rapid increase in economic activities, it has led to the transformation and transformation of the layers of society as a whole. Thanks to the utilization of the opportunities provided by the new technologies obtained in the production and the increase of the division of labor and specialization, production and productivity have increased rapidly. In the process following the industrial revolution, there have been changes in the institutions, rules, structures and behaviors of the society, and in this context, traditional behavior has been replaced by rational behavior. This change in lifestyle has been one of the most holistic change and transformation processes that humanity has ever experienced. The new technologies introduced in the aftermath of the industrial revolution produced innovations in the production environment and lifestyle. The industrial revolution took place in a process involving the use of innovations in the field of technology in production activities and their reflections on economic, social, cultural and political fields (Selvi, 2012, p. 197).

The new social structure, which emerged after the Industrial Revolution, was shaped very differently from the structure, which was defined as the traditional society, whose main economic activity was agriculture, and that production was carried out with primitive methods and more for self-consumption. Production factors, production forms, production in the range of products and the amount of products in the new process has come to the fore with many different features (Yalçinkaya, 2001, p. 2).

Contrary to what is seen in traditional societies, capital has come to the forefront in terms of the weight of production factors in industrial societies. The labor factor, on the other hand, has partially lost its importance with differentiating production methods. Instead of working with physical labor, machines are now replaced. In fact, capital has been an important factor in increasing the productivity of labor. In this case, although labor is taken into consideration, its place and efficiency in production have been revealed as a result of its connection with capital. (Yalçinkaya, 2001, p. 2).

In the industrial society, the places where factories were established became the center of migration of society. People in the factories within the framework of the facilities within the framework of the factories, where the first occurrences, the city moved to settlements expressed as. Due to this migration movement, the family structure in the industrial society has started to change and a gradual transformation has started in the societal family type formed by parents and children. Due to this transformation, the shrinking of the family and the responsibilities among the family members decreased, the relations began to loosen and the aid gradually decreased. As a result, human beings first began to become an alienated entity with their surroundings and then with themselves (Bayraç, 2003, p. 45).

The emerging needs of the industrial society were rather physiological needs. While production is directed to these needs, the development of the most prominent sectors has been in this direction. Within the framework of the opportunities provided by mechanization in the process of the industrial society, meeting the material needs of people, such as nutrition, clothing and shelter, has been achieved by increasing the amount of production. After mass production, the masses showed a development in the masses, unlike Malthus's Population Theory. In Malthus's thesis, the increase in the supply of food in parallel with the increase in population, and the idea that large masses will disappear after a short period of 70-80 years has been negated in a sense. As a result of the economic activities that show development for basic needs, sectors such as textile and food have become important sectors (Yalçınkaya, 2001, p. 3).

Some social problems emerged in the early stages of the industrial society structure. In addition to the social segments that can benefit from the change and transformation experienced with the industrial revolution, the social segments that have not benefited from this change and transformation have emerged. The beneficiaries of the change and transformation process created the elite and the rich, while those who could not benefit were 16 hours a day and the poor people working in heavy work and having no legal security.

The transformation and change occurring in the market economy have revealed some fundamental changes in the competition understanding of the economic system that determines the success as well as the existence of markets. In the period following the Industrial Revolution, the implementation of the free market economy maintained its free nature in competition, which is a sign of a liberal perspective. While free competition has left a wide range of mobility in the economic units of mobility and work, it also has a wild sense among companies or workforce owners, but in terms of their results. As a matter of fact, this concept of competition has been called wild capitalism by the idea of the economic system of the period. The competition concept that emerged in the companies has created a monopolistic structure that provides a high price and results against labor and consumers despite the low prices. Thus, the applied form of free competition researched at the scientific level was monopolistic competition, but the results were discussed (Yalçinkaya, 2001, p. 8).

In the second period of the industrial social structure (after 1873), when the integration problem between social class segments became unsustainable, policies and practices focused on social integration were put into use. The development of liberalism, the philosophical basis of the industrial society, and the development of the enlightenment era from this period has been ensured with the development shown since the Renaissance.

In this period, individualism and socialism became a new synthesis with the renewal of the way of thinking. As the individual and society were considered as complementary elements, there was differentiation in the structure of society. In this process, the effects of the production process have revealed a two-class social structure. Thus, it led to the formation of two different ideologies and the formation of a world order structure consisting of opposite poles called the eastern bloc and the western bloc. Some underdeveloped countries, which are not included in the industrialization process, have created the so-called a third world block (Çalık and Çınar, 2009, p. 82).

Within the industrial social structure, especially in recent years (1960s), the ideas expressed as Welfare Society and Consumer Society reached the peak points. However, the economic recession and crisis occurred in the USA and Western European countries, which were the most prominent in the welfare society in the late 1960s. This painful process in the industrial society has been observed in both the Western world and the Eastern Bloc countries. As a result, although the reaction movements emerged in the countries that make up the Western bloc, similar reactions in the Eastern Bloc countries have been seen much later since the systems implemented in these countries have limited freedom. The reactions to the painful process in these countries could only be seen after 15-20 years. The consequences of the reactions arisen in the early 1990s as the disintegration of the Soviet Union and Eastern Bloc occurred.

The followings are the major changes and transformations after the industrial revolution in terms of economic, technological, socio-cultural and political:

- The emergence of capital as a dominant power,
- Systematic and broad implementation of scientific knowledge and experience-based knowledge on the production process for emerging markets,
- Providing specialization of economic activities towards production in a way that can be used in national and international markets rather than domestic or local uses.
- Migration from rural areas to cities and the emergence of urbanization through this migration,
- To take political decisions to eliminate class distinction and to ensure social integration,
- Instead of the production of the basic goods of the labor force, the production of finished goods,
- Capital resources should be used more extensively and more intensively in a complementary manner than human effort,
- Expansion of the typical production units from being personal and therefore less effective for families and tribes, and more effective partnership and public enterprises,
- The formation of new professional and social classes defined by the production of new capital and the relationship with these instruments,
- Labor liberation and marketability,
- The emergence of colonialism,
- Start of economic activities in factories other than hand and home looms,
- Ensuring productivity increase in social life and economic life with the invention of electricity and steel,
- Implementation of diversity and resource utilization in production and consumption in parallel with the developments in the petrochemical industry,
- With the discovery of synthetic substances, nature-dependent and environmentally sensitive needs are eliminated in different ways,
- Increasing productivity and efficiency in economic decision-making units by mass production
- With the new inventions in the electronics industry, technology is expressed as a new dimension.

In the industrial society phase which lasted nearly two centuries, it has taken many years for a development to take place and become widespread. Their effects and differentiation were in a slower process than the conditions of the time. However, developments in different fields such as satellite, computer, mobile phone, fax, biotechnology have been the innovations since the 1950s and they have been the basis for further innovations. In other words, the necessity of forming faster, flexible, stronger structures and prioritizing of producing innovation increased with the elements of information and emergence of new perspectives in societies (Yalçinkaya, 2001, p. 7).

Information Society

The post-World War II process is regarded as the beginning of the information age. The development of the first electronic computer in 1946 is of great importance in the scientific field. In 1947, ATT Bell laboratories developed a tool for controlling the electric current called the transistor by scientists. This tool has changed the production technology of computers and enabled the production of less costly, more functional computers (Yurdakul and Çağlayan, 1997, p. 2-3).

In 1956, in the United States, employees in the form of white-collar employees interested in administrative affairs and technical affairs gained superiority compared to blue-collar employees. Thus, the US entered the new process and left behind the industrial revolution, which has created a new society structure (Unal, 2009, p. 131). The World Economic Crisis, which started after the Oil Crisis that emerged in 1973 in the world, marked the end of industrial societies and industrial civilization, on the one hand, and the formation and infrastructure of the information society which was accepted as a new civilization along with the quests that emerged to exit the crisis as soon as possible. to bring the technology to the fore (Erkan and Erkan, 2007, p. 2).

This new type of society, which began to be seen after the 1950s, was distinguished by a number of features that became evident from the industrial society. Firstly, the basic building blocks of the information society is the information, whereas in the industrial society the basic structure is capital. On the other side, values related to certain work such as discipline, loyalty, ambition, competition and aggression in the industrial society have been replaced by values such as individuality, freedom, solidarity and participation in the information society. While the capital, raw material, labor and energy are among the basic elements of the production in the industrial society, the information society has also added information that has exceeded all the other elements (Tekman, 2002, p. 266).

The steam engine, which was accepted as the beginning of development in the industrial society, was at the forefront in the production of goods and services, while computers in the information society replaced the steam engine. While arm strength is the mainstay in the industrial society, brainpower has become the mainstay in the information society. Human capital, which contributed to production in terms of physical power in the industrial society, has been replaced by intellectual qualification in the information society. While industrial goods and services are seen in the industrial society, computer, electronic communication, robots and new advanced material technologies are the products of the information society. The factories in the industrial society have left their places to the information networks and data banks, where information used in the information society comes into prominence. In this way, the information is produced all over the world and is transmitted to all sides instantly by means of information highways. In the industrial sector, agriculture, industry and services, which are seen in the industrial society, have been primary, secondary and tertiary factors. The information sector has been included in these sectors as a quaternary sector in the information society. While the production factors that we face in the industrial society are entrepreneur, capital, nature and labor, technical knowledge has come to the fore as an additional production factor in the information society. While the political system seen in the industrial society was applied as representative democracy, the practice in the information society emerged as a participatory democracy (Ünal, 2009, p. 135-136).

This progress is identified as Post-Modernity Era by Amittai Etzioni, Third Wave by Alvin Toffler, Post-Economics Society by Herman Kahn, Post-Industrial Society by Daniel Bell, Post-Bourgeois Society by George Lichtheim, Civilization Society by Kenneth Boulding, Service Class Society by Ralf Dahrendorf, Individual Service Society by Paul Holmes, Information Society by Peter F. Drucker, Technocratic Period by Zbigniew Brzezinski, and Information Society by Yoneji Masuda. Data, information, and information constitute the distinctive and determinative concepts of this new society model (Hazar, 2006, p. 17).

The new social structure, which is formed within the framework of this change and transformation, has been named as the information society with the most inclusive integrity. In this context, the information society includes a process where information is accepted as a strategic source, learning is perceived as a lifestyle in an organizational and social structure, and the change and transformation resulting from technology has gained considerable speed and global competition is highly concentrated (Ünal, 2009, p 125.

Scientific information and technology are the basis of new solutions produced by the information society against the problems. At the same time, developments in the field of information and communication are based on nanotechnology, microelectronics, microbiology and genetics studies. Therefore, it is accepted that scientific information is at the base of the process that arises in the field of information. As a result, the information society stands out in the place of the knowledge society (Erkan and Erkan, 2007, p. 3).

The most striking feature of the information society is the new improvements that have arisen in the stages of publication of the collected information after reorganization. This feature enabled the marketing of information. In light of these improvements, companies that provide information services at the forefront of information production and management have been established. In this way, the information can be bought and sold for the first time as a value began to be seen (Aydin, 1997, p. 26-27).

The transformation of information into economic value has led to a universal dimension of information. The value of the information varies according to the conditions such as time, space used. In the information society, the most important factor in the process of converting information into an economic value is information systems (Kara, 2003, p. 1).

The production of information uses the synergy economy instead of the exchange economy. The expansion of communication networks in which information production is carried out has resulted in the removal of national borders and the emergence of a new structure called globalization. As a result of this process, the national economy was replaced by the new world economy (Şanlısoy, 1999, p. 171).

Due to the improvements in globalization and information communication technologies, these changes in the social and civilization level of the information society structure are restructuring all other areas.

According to Erkan and Erkan (2007);

- In the area of Science and Technology, Newtonian uses Quantum technology and ideas based on mutual and multiple network interaction of the subatomic world from mechanical technology and thoughts,
- In the social area, from the independent-disconnected individualism to the synergistic social structure in which cooperation comes to the fore,

- In the political area, from the behaviors that keep the individual in the foreground, from the civil society organizations formed by the group interests, from a parliamentary democracy to participatory democracy;
- In the cultural area, from absolute and closed cultural values to a cosmopolitan cultural diversity where differences are seen as wealth and live together in social tolerance;
- In the economic area, from the mechanical and atomic capitalist market economy to the information economy where network interaction works;
- In the global area, the establishment of transnational corporations (global blocks) and companies instead of national relations and companies.

In brief, such structures in the information society have emerged as the main stages of a great change and transformation. The priorities in the information economy, determined by the processes expressed, have led to the diversification and change of the choice of profit maximization in the static conditions of the industrial society. In the structuring of the information society revealed by new technologies; In the economic context, the increase in productivity, quality improvement, speed and competition understanding, resulting in dynamic conditions, uncertainty, confidence and change has become important.

The concepts of time and space are not important within the structure of the primitive, agricultural and industrial society. In the information society, which is based on information and innovation, the difference of time and space in individual and social activities and behaviors is a strategic feature. In this context, information and innovation within the structure of the information society have been a possible, relative and subjective factor that has a high level of background and which can be continuously transformed in the dimension of time and space and has a differentiation within its structure. (Güvel, 2002, p. 69).

In addition to all these improvements, technological developments and the information society based on globalization consider information as a scarce resource and need qualified labor force has created a number of problems on individual, firm and national basis (Tekeli, 1994, p. 270-293).

The problems can be listed as gathering information in one hand, inequality in facilities to access information, theft of information because of easy access, exposing physical and psychological health problems depending on extensive usage of information and communication technology, frequency pollution, contamination of the natural environment, and becoming a technology garbage (Şanlısoy, 1999, p. 170-178).

In general, the structures of societies are shaped by the economic, socio-cultural and political evolutions, and they are changed and transformed in a multidimensional way. In essence, the information and technology used in the model of the primitive society remained limited. In the model of the agricultural society, the functionality of information and technology has not started to increase in the eyes of the people who have started to operate on the basis of soil. In the industrial society model, with the introduction of machines based on Newton-based mechanical thinking, new information and technologies have become easier for human life. In the information society model, information and technology have become the main determinant of all functions of life depending on Quantum based thinking. Thus, information and technology have reached a level that exceeds traditional patterns. (Canlıoğlu, 2008, p. 126).

Table 1, which combines the main determinants in the change and transformation stages of societies in a single scheme, will contribute to understanding the differences experienced in this process.

Table 1. Social transformation and basic determinants

	Primitive Society	Agricultural Society
TECHNOLOGIC		
Energy	Physical power and human energy	Human, animal, air
Materials	Plant, Stone and Animal leather, lambskin	Renewable resources (wood, cotton, wool)
Tools	Minimal cutting and forging (arrow, spear, sharpened stone construction)	Human and animal power (leverage, sail, water mill)
Dominant power	Physical power, Nature	Soil, Nature
ECONOMIC		
Production Method	Hunting and Gathering	Hand and animal labor
Transportation System	Walking	Horse, donkey, wagon, sailboat
Communication System	Speech	Speech, handwriting, visual elements
Economic Tools	Goods Exchange	Goods exchange, metal money
Economic Activity	Gathering, hunting, fishing	Self-sustaining local and decentralized economic activity. The simple division of labor: the restricted authority of the levels (nobles, slaves, serfs, soldiers, priests)
SOCIAL		
Society Life	Clan life, Nomadic lifestyle, Protection from natural events and animals	Earth-based settled life, Soil Wars
Family Life	Very large family structure due to blood ties	Large family structure
Job Life	Business life to satisfy personal needs	Agricultural activities, Agriculture-based business organizations
Education	Learning through trial and error, Clan training	Generally, agriculture based on job training, limited education
POLITICAL		
Management Approach	Management based on physical power and different religious beliefs, tribal as the main political unit on the axis of the elders' and chief's rules	Religious, racial or class-based social qualifications management, feudalism, aristocratic rules The basic political unit is the local community.
PARADIGM	Observation of the world in its natural form (Primitive Paradigm)	Science-based: Astronomy, Mathematics, Science Central thought is that people are controlled by mystical vision (astrology) in which people are controlled by superior powers (God). The value system is based on harmony with nature. (Traditional Paradigm)
	Industrial Society	**Information Society**
TECHNOLOGIC		
Energy	Electricity, Fossil Fuels (Petroleum, coal)	Natural (solar, wind), nuclear energy
Materials	Non-renewable sources (plastic, metal, synthetic, etc.)	Renewable resources (Biotechnology, Nanotechnology) ceramic, recycling
Tools	Steam engine, The Substitution of physical labor	Computer (Memory, Information Network)The substitution of mental labor
Dominant Power	Capital	Information, Human capital
ECONOMIC		
Products	Useful goods and services	Communicative information, technology, scientific information
Production Center	Modern factories (machinery equipment)	Computers, networks, data banks
Market	New World, colonies, consumer buying power	All of the World, New World
Production Method	Fabricated mass production, Install-Assemble and substitutable parts, Material production power	Robots, Information generating power
Transportation System	Steamboat, railway, automobile and airplane	The Spaceship, remote and driverless vehicle
Communication System	Press and television	Unlimited expansion of communication with electronic tools
Economic Structure	Goods economy (a division of labor, production and consumption)	Synergy economy (common production and use)
Economic System	Private ownership of capital, free competition, profit maximization	Network structure, synergy principle, social benefit maximization, effective competition
Economic Tool	Paper money (symbolic money) domination	An Instant transfer based on information (super symb. money, magnetic money, crypto money)

continued on the following page

Table 1. Continued

	Primitive Society	Agricultural Society
Economic Activity	Mass market economy at the national level, standardization in the production of material goods, Complex distribution of labor, limited partial expertise, the standard mode of operation	The integrated global economy, a supply of information services that integrate consumers and producers of basic economic activity
SOCIAL		
Society Life	Fast urbanization, industry-bound worldwars	The Cold War period, Social Networks, İnformation reign
Society Form	A society with Class (central power, class control)	Functional society (multi-center, function, autonomy)
Family Life	The transition from large family structure to core family structure	Core family, individual life
Social Values	It is at the forefront of convenience, exclusivity and class elements.	The role of sexual division of labor, the development of human ability and the role of humanitarian institutions, social values of diversity, equality, individualism
Job Life	The industrial revolution, industrial organizations, large working class	The information revolution, information organizations, decreasing labor need, information workers
Education	Fast schooling, compulsory education at specific ages	Learning by living, learning to learn, self-taught responsibility is always and everywhere training beyond the school walls, lifelong learning
POLITICAL		
Management Approach	Industrial production tools and economic management	Management as a professional profession, information-based management
Government System	The strong central national government in the form of parliamentary democracy, capitalism and Marxism, nationalism, representative government or dictatorship	Participatory democracy, Global cooperation, The institutionalization of supranational organizations for control and ownership of information, The decentralization of management is the basic norm.
PARADIGM	Foundation of Science; Physics, Chemistry Fundamental Thought: It is believed that human fate depends on the coherence of the reward and punishment system and rational social structure in a competitive world. Values: Material values (meeting psychological needs), basic human rights, Renaissance (human emancipation). Newtonian Mechanical Paradigm	Fundamentals of science: Quantum electronics, molecular chemistry and biology, nanotechnology, etc. Central Thought: Continuous increase in human talent and development (thinking of the whole brain) Value System: It is directed towards a decentralized society of free individuals, where the values of women are effective. Values: Time value (meeting target specific success requirements), self-discipline, social participation, globalization. Quantum Paradigm

Source: Crawford (1991, p. 6), Masuda (1990, p. 6-8), Erkan (1998, p. 165-190), Fındıkçı (1996, p. 58), Yurtseven (2015, p. 22) ve Canlıoğlu (2008, p. 61)

When the models of the primitive and agricultural society are examined, it is seen that there is minimal paradigm based social change and transformation. In both societies, a process of technological, economic, sociocultural and political changes and transformations based on nature and manpower emerged. However, the paradigm-based change and transformation in the transition from the agricultural society to the model of the industrial society and from the industrial to the information society model have been more comprehensive and significant. The transition from the agricultural society to the industrial society model has brought the social whole to different dimensions. Manpower is replaced by mechanization, labor is liberated and marketable, mass production becomes feasible through factories, the dominant power phenomenon from the soil to the capital, the transition from rural village to urban life, and the changes and transformations that survive to the human class, completely differentiated. In the context of this differentiation, traditional technology based on nature has been replaced by science-based Newtonian mechanical thought and technology.

The transition from the industrial society to the model of the information society has emerged as the biggest change and transformation of social structures. This process, which started with the discovery of computer technologies, gave the social structure an effective paradigmatic leap in the journey of civilization. Newtonian, which shaped the structure of the industrial society, replaced the mechanistic thoughts and technologies in the information society structure by taking Quantum ideas and technologies.

All perception, phenomenon, understanding, thinking and viewpoints of human and social relations have changed with Quantum thought system. The information age and the information society are shaped as new society, a new human and social relations, a new global relationship and a system of global order.

The industrial society has shaped the organization and operation structure of material goods by the ownership and production relations. The information society is human-centered, highlighting the organization of scientific information, technology and innovation production, which is the product of the brain's use and operation potential.

In contrast to the fact that the industrial society only puts forward the logical intelligence, the information society puts forward the multi-intelligence, the emotional and social intelligence and the intuitive thought together, as the full use of the brain.

In order to produce scientific information, technology and innovation in the information society, education, cognitive learning, intellectual capital and human development are highlighted, university-industry-organized with teamwork, corporate culture, technopark, research and development (R&D) and innovation centers, social capital to improve community relations is prominent.

The information society has developed to create positive synergies in the inter-interactive relationship, as well as the relationship between the neural networks in the brain. For this reason, it was not aimed at conflicts and contradictions, but on cooperation based on positive thinking and relationship.

The information society has shifted to the system and process thinking of the industrial society, as opposed to point-based static thinking, as in the multiple and dynamic interaction of subatomic and neural networks. In the system and process thinking, the complex content of dynamic flow and operation, rather than dots and lines, are considered as a whole. For this reason, it is not the static-point planning but the strategic management of the process with its strategic planning. In the strategic process management of the information society, the future is valid. The concept of science in the industrial society, the finished events, back and review later, the formation of the future in the information society and the end of the future of a walk, formed the basis (Erkan, 2019).

TRANSFORMATION OF CONSUMPTION

Consumption refers to a historical differentiation process in the social structure (Bacock, 2009, p. 59).

In other words, consumption is seen as any kind of social activity that people benefit from determining their qualities or positioning themselves within the social structure (Dikici, 2017, p. 60). Because, the concept of consumption should not be only considered as the utilization of products and services, as Veblenist thought states.

Consumers, considered to be one of the decision mechanisms within the science of economics, do not always take consumption decisions depending on the hierarchy of needs. In that sense, they will be counted as irrational economic agents according to the neoclassical approach. However, in microeconomic and macroeconomic theories related to neoclassical approaches, consumers have always been considered as economic decision-making units with rational behavioral patterns in consumption activities. In the calculation of the benefit of consumption for rational consumers, it is assumed as if the consumers do not have any advantage other than the product's direct and visible benefits. In other words, any indirect benefit arising from psychological or social aspects from consumption will be disregarded.

Consumers and society are considered to be independent from each other when making consumption decisions. However, according to its benefits, the decision-making criteria in consumption activity emerged as utilitarian and hedonic. What is correct is the consideration of the total benefit that will arise from the end of the consumption activity, which is taken into consideration not only separately in these two criteria when making the consumption decision. In particular, hedonist criteria are excluded from the decision-making and analysis process due to their inability to be internalized in the calculations. In their work, Holbrook and Hirschman (1982), "Hedonic Consumption: Emerging Methods and Propositions", integrate objectivity and emotional criteria and subjectivity in meaning. Consumers feelings of being more affluent than they are, and the feeling of belonging to the higher social status, are expressed as one of the qualities of consumption activity that are not according to Newtonian mechanistic thinking. The consumer, who is obliged to live in the social environment, is also benefiting from the goods and services to be consumed according to the subjective criteria, which are rather difficult to calculate, not just objective criteria. In this context, analyzing the social and cultural environment of human being, which is a social and cultural asset, by excluding the social and cultural environment of its consumption constitutes a serious deficiency in calculating the benefit and value of consumption activity to consumers (Açıkalın and Gül, 2006, p. 16). Because, in essence, consumers decide not only economic but also social, cultural, political, technological interactions (Williams, 2002, p. 249).

In the years following World War II, the emergence of the structure of the information society, which was expressed as a new society structure, was an important and effective process for building the real meaning of consumption activity. In light of the improvements in science and technology, Newtonian mechanistic thinking system based on static and point analysis of the industrial society structure has changed. With the formation of the structure of the information society, the Quantum thought system, which is related to the multiple causality relationship, which involves interactions, shaped the social structure and thus the consumption activities.

The perspective of events and phenomena was expanded from the static and point analysis of Newtonian Mechanic thought to dimensions of time and space of Quantum thought system. After this paradigmatic change, approaches such as chaos, complexity and relativity theory emerged. Moreover, the relation between the concepts of Newton and Quantum with the economic concepts has been the subject of mathematical modeling and has enabled the emergence of new disciplines (Ulusoy, 2017, p. 138).

The tendency towards the analysis of the spontaneous balance of Newtonian mechanical thought, the social events and processes, or the dynamic, multidimensional, chaotic, and complex situations in nature has taken place. The interactive interaction of innumerable complex relations in the Quantum thought system is considered as a whole. This is a process of creating a network and systems and the interaction between the system in time and space dimension has formed the process of thinking. The transition from Newtonian mechanics to Quantum thought system has revealed the transformation from static and point analysis to system and process states. Economic and social phenomena are now discussed within the holistic and new interaction scheme, which is expressed as a system and process. In the Newtonian mechanistic thought system, the assumption that the universe is rationally operated by the image of the machine and the mode of operation of society and nature has been valid. In other words, it is assumed that the universe exhibits invariant, definitive, determinist and mechanical interaction. The Quantum thought system has a different perspective on the whole universe. In this context, the probability and quantifiable uncertainty instead of the principle of certainty put forward by Newtonian mechanical thought, instead of the unilateral and definite causality instead of the holistic system and the objective one reality, has brought the virtual reality and network structure that is created by the interaction system. In the process of formation and improvement of Quantum thought system, random participation, indeterminism, uncertainty, chaos, complexity, fuzzy logic, totality, dynamic interaction, multiple and reciprocal linkages, complementarity as well as the concepts of behavior, the whole of the social whole and the nature of a completely different It has moved. (Erkan, 2019)

In other words, the univariate and unidirectional analysis is replaced by a multivariate and multidimensional equilibrium myth, which affects everything and is influenced by everything (butterfly effect) (Vukotic, 2011, p. 274). interactive linkage and relations are left to the structure in which the system and process are formed.

At the end of the nineteenth century, when neoclassical approaches began to make sense, the science of economics was changed and transformed in a way that was dominated by general and precise rules, principles, and behavioral stratification. On the other side, in these approaches, the fact that the science of economics is a science to study the economic behavior of human beings, and that the fields such as anthropology, history, sociology, psychology and politics, which are the building blocks of technological and social change and transformation, shape the economic behavior of people. (Yalçınkaya, 2006, p. 2).

In this context, the concept of consumption, which is one of the key elements of economics, is a dynamic, natural and multidimensional human behavior which emerged with the existence of humanity in the sense of the destruction, the meeting of the needs, the use of the manufactured goods and services. However, with the static and point analysis of the Neoclassical approaches that emerged on the basis of Newtonian mechanics, consumption was seen as a phenomenon whose external effects were ignored.

In this sense, the benefit or consumption value that can be included in the cultural, sociological, institutional and psychological terms which are not directly or in view of the benefits provided by the consumption activity, which cannot participate in the mathematical or statistical models and calculations, are not taken into account according to the Neoclassical approach. In general, however, it is important to examine the perspective of consumption in economic science in general and to analyze the economic behavior of the human, who has cultural, social, institutional and psychological dimensions together with internal and external factors (Açıkalın and Gül, 2006, p. 17). Because people convey the situations that arise with consumption activity to the social and institutional structure through various behaviors and thoughts. From this perspective, the activity of consumption is a multi-dimensional, dynamic, natural, social and institutional expression (Yalçınkaya, 2006, p. 10).

CONCLUSION

The change and transformation forming the foundation of existence provide the social structures to be differentiated with the economic, socio-cultural and political foundations. The change and transformation of social structures throughout the process have always improved and differentiated the paradigms that shape the structure and the technological background of the structure. While primitive paradigm was valid in the primitive society, the traditional nature paradigm in the agricultural society, Newtonian mechanical paradigm in the industrial society, and Quantum paradigm in the information society were valid.

In the emergence of the economy as a science, the paradigm that dominated the social whole was Newtonian mechanical paradigm. Therefore, the economic structure of the period was shaped on the basis of this paradigm, especially production and consumption. The Newtonian paradigm has been the point of view of the consumer and its consumption activities, one of the economic decision-making units, by static and point analysis. Consumption activities are analyzed as a behavior independent of social and institutional structure and external effects. This approach puts consumption activities directly, only into a utilitarian behavior pattern. However, in today's world, it is necessary to think that consumption activities are multi-dimensional external, social and institutional determinants. Especially institutional economics thoughts where it is accepted as Veblen's ideas are the base and indirect utility from consumption, such as reaching status, conspicuous and other psychological and social benefits, supply strong backup for these ideas. Because it is revealed that the benefit that consumers get from consumption activity is underestimated. Transition to the information society and the Quantum paradigm dominated by the social structure, consumption activities, multidimensional externality, technological, economic, socio-cultural and political determinants and influencers, interconnected with the social and institutional structure, a printout of the system and process in the dimension of time and space it was determined to be a behavior. For this reason, analyzes performed independently from the interactive interaction in the dimension of the social whole, externality, time and space have been incomplete in explaining the consumer behavior in today's world at an adequate level. In this context, it is necessary to revise the traditional perspective which is directed to consumption activities and the economies in general. The idea of analyzing the economic behaviors of human beings with technological, economic, sociocultural, political, institutional and psychological dimensions together with internal and external factors is important for future contributions and studies.

REFERENCES

Açıkalın, S., & Gül, E. (2006). Sosyal Sınıflarda Tüketimin Sınıf Belirleyicilik Rolü. *Sosyal Ekonomik Araştırmalar Dergisi*, *6*(12), 15–28.

Alan, S. (2016). *Üretim Toplumundan Tüketim Toplumuna Geçiş ve Değer Dönüşümü*. İstanbul, Turkey: Toplumsal Değişim Sempozyumu.

Arklan, Ü., & Taşdemir, E. (2008). Bilgi Toplumu ve İletişim: Bilginin Yayılması Sürecinde Kitle İletişim Araçları ve İnternet. *Selçuk Üniversitesi İletişim Fakültesi Akademik Dergisi*, *5*(3), 67–80.

Aydın, T. (1997). *Bilgi Toplumu ve Demokrasi*. Trabzon, Turkey: Efor Masaüstü Yayıncılık.

Aydoğan, F. (2009). Tüketim Kültürünün Gölgesinde Kentler. *Marmara Üniversitesi İktisadi ve İdari Bilimler Dergisi*, *27*(2), 203–215.

Bayraç, H. N. (2003). Yeni Ekonomi'nin Toplumsal, Ekonomik ve Teknolojik Boyutları. *Osmangazi Üniversitesi Sosyal Bilimler Dergisi*, *4*(1), 41–62.

Bensghir, T. K. (1996). *Bilgi Teknolojileri ve Örgütsel Değişim*. Ankara, Turkey: TODAİE.

Bocock, R. (2009). *Tüketim, çev. Kutluk, İ.* Ankara, Turkey: Dost Yayınları.

Burrows, R., & Marsh, C. (1992). Consumption, class and contemporary sociology. In *Consumption and Class* (pp. 1–14). London, UK: Palgrave Macmillan. doi:10.1007/978-1-349-21725-0_1

Çalık, D., & Çınar, Ö. P. (2009). *Geçmişten Günümüze Bilgi Yaklaşımları, Bilgi Toplumu ve İnternet. XIV*. İstanbul, Turkey: Türkiye'de İnternet Konferansı.

Canlıoğlu, G. (2008). *Değişen Toplum Yapılarında Bilginin Değişen Konumu (Basılmamış yüksek lisans tezi)*. İstanbul, Turkey: Marmara Üniversitesi Türkiyat Araştırmaları Enstitüsü.

Crawford, R. (1991). *The era of human capital*. USA: Harper Business.

Demirel, S., & Yeğen, C. (2015). Tüketim, Postmodernizm ve Kapitalizm Örgüsü. *Ankara Üniversitesi İLEF Dergisi*, *2*(1), 115–138.

Dickson, P. R. (2000). Understanding the trade winds: The global evolution of production, consumption, and the internet. *The Journal of Consumer Research*, *27*(1), 115–122. doi:10.1086/314313

Dikici, E. (2017). Tüketim Algısındaki Değişim; Kitle İletişim Araçları ve Tüketim İlişkisi. *Sosyal ve Beşeri Bilimler Dergisi*, *1*(1), 58–85.

Erkan, H. (1998). *Bilgi Toplumu ve Ekonomik Gelişme*. Türkiye İş Bankası Kültür Yayınları.

Erkan, H. (2004). *Ekonomi Sosyolojisi*. İzmir, Turkey: Barış Yayınları.

Erkan, H. (2019). Bilgi Toplumu'na İlişkin. Retrieved from http:/www.deu.edu.tr/userweb/husnu.erkan/BILGI_TOPLUMUNA_ILISKIN_NOT.doc. (Unpublished Scientific Paper).

Erkan, H. & Erkan, C. (2007). Bilgi Toplumu Ve Ekonomik Kalkınma, *UNAK'07 Sayısal Dünyada Yeni Paradigmalar: Sınırsız Kütüphaneler.* Retrieved from http:/www.deu.edu.tr/husnu.erkan

Fındıkçı, İ. (1996). *Bilgi Toplumunda Yöneticilerde Kendini Geliştirme*. İstanbul, Turkey: Kültür Koleji Eğitim Vakfı Yayınları.

Güleç, C. (2015). Thorstein Veblen ve Gösterişçi Tüketim Kavramı. *Erciyes Üniversitesi Sosyal Bilimler Enstitüsü Dergisi*, *1*(38), 62–82.

Güneş, A. (2014). Sosyolojik Olarak Din ve Toplum İlişkileri. *Fırat Üniversitesi Sosyal Bilimler Dergisi*, *24*(1), 153–164.

Güvel, A. G. (2002). Piyasa Ekonomisine Biyolojik Bir Yaklaşım: Biyonomik. *Piyasa Dergisi*, *1*(4), 67–73.

Halis, B. (2012). Tüketimin Değişen Yüzü: Elektronik Ticaret Uygulamaları ve Sosyal Paylaşım Ağlarının Rolü. *Tarih Kültür ve Sanat Araştırmaları Dergisi*, *1*(4), 149–160.

Hazar, Ç. M. (2006). *Bilgi Toplumu*. Ankara, Turkey: Turhan Kitabevi.

Hirschman, E. C., & Holbrook, M. B. (1982). Hedonic consumption: Emerging methods and propositions. *Journal of Marketing*, *46*(3), 92–101. doi:10.1177/002224298204600314

Hughes, H. S. (1995). *Toplum ve Bilinç. çev. Özkan, G.* İstanbul, Turkey: Metis Yayınları.

Jansson, U., Kautsky, U., & Miliander, S. (2006). Rural landscape, production and human consumption: Past, present and future. *Ambio*, *35*(8), 505–513. doi:10.1579/0044-7447(2006)35[505:RLPAHC]2.0.CO;2 PMID:17334058

Kara, O. (2003). Bilgi Ekonomisinin Olası Mikro Ekonomik Etkilerinin Teorik Analizi. Pamukkale Üniversitesi ve Türkiye Ekonomi Kurumu, Ekonomi Yaz Seminerleri-2 Konferansları, Denizli

Karakaş, M. (2017). Bir Zihniyet Olarak Tüketim Kültürü ve İhtiyaçların Yabancılaşması. *International Congress On Political, Economic And Social Studies*, 19-22

Kocacık, F. (2003). Bilgi Toplumu ve Türkiye. *Cumhuriyet Üniversitesi Sosyal Bilimler Dergisi*, *27*(1), 1–10.

Kuper, A. (1995). *İlkel Toplumun İcadı- Bir İllüzyonun Dönüşümleri. çev. Türkmen, İ.* İstanbul, Turkey: İnsan Yayınları.

Masuda, Y. (1990). *Managing in the information society: Releasing synergy Japanese style*. Cambridge, MA: Basil Blackwell.

Meder, M. (2001). Bilgi Toplumu ve Toplumsal Değişim. *Pamukkale Üniversitesi Eğitim Fakültesi Dergisi*, *9*(9), 72–81.

Özgül, O. (2011). Sümer Sosyal Hayatında Eğitimin Yeri ve Önemi. *Erzincan Üniversitesi Sosyal Bilimler Enstitüsü Dergisi*, *4*(2), 401–414.

Şanlısoy, S. (1999). Bilgi Toplumunda Ortaya Çıkabilecek Sorunlar. *Dokuz Eylül Üniversitesi İktisadi ve İdari Bilimler Fakültesi Dergisi*, *14*(2), 169–184.

Selvi, Ö. (2012). Bilgi Toplumu, Bilgi Yönetimi ve Halkla İlişkiler. *Gümüşhane Üniversitesi İletişim Fakültesi Elektronik Dergisi*, *1*(3), 191–214.

Şenel, A. (1982). *İlkel Topluluktan Uygar Topluma Geçiş Aşamasında Ekonomik Toplumsal Düşünsel Yapıların Etkileşimi*. Ankara, Turkey: Ankara Üniversitesi Siyasal Bilgiler Fakültesi Yayınları.

Şentürk, Ü. (2008). Modern Kontrol: Tüketim. *Cumhuriyet Üniversitesi Sosyal Bilimler Dergisi*, *32*(2), 221–240.

Sönmez, F. C. (2018). İlkel Toplumlarda Siyasi Örgütlenme ve Yaygın Ekonomik Model. *Pivolka*, *8*(28), 9–13.

Tekeli, H. (1994). *Bilgi Çağı*. İstanbul, Turkey: Simav Yayınları.

Tekman, E. (2002). *Enformatik Sistemler ve Bilgi Toplumu. Bilgi Toplumuna Geçiş, (Der., İlhan Tekeli ve Diğerleri)*. Ankara, Turkey: Türkiye Bilimler Akademisi Yayınları.

Toffler, A. (1981). *Üçüncü Dalga. Çev. Seden, A.* İstanbul, Turkey: Altın Kitaplar Yayınları.

Ulusoy, T. (2017). Ekonofizik ve Finansal Entropi. Kastamonu Üniversitesi İİBF Dergisi, (Özel Sayı), s. 138-149. Retrieved from http://dergipark.gov.tr/iibfdkastamonu/issue/31886/350620

Ünal, Y. (2009). Bilgi Toplumunu Tarihçesi. *Tarih Okulu Dergisi*, *5*, 123–144.

Vergragt, P., Akenji, L., & Dewick, P. (2014). Sustainable production, consumption, and livelihoods: Global and regional research perspectives. *Journal of Cleaner Production*, *63*, 1–12. doi:10.1016/j.jclepro.2013.09.028

Vukotic, V. (2011). Quantum economics. *Panoeconomicus*, *58*(2), 267–276. doi:10.2298/PAN1102267V

Warde, A. (2009). Production, consumption and social change: Reservations regarding Peter Saunders' sociology of consumption. *International Journal of Urban and Regional Research, 14*(2), 228–248. doi:10.1111/j.1468-2427.1990.tb00670.x

Wilk, R. (2002). Consumption, human needs, and global environmental change. *Global Environmental Change, 12*(1), 5–13. doi:10.1016/S0959-3780(01)00028-0

Williams, T. G. (2002). Social class influences on purchase evaluation criteria. *Journal of Consumer Marketing, 19*(3), 249–276. doi:10.1108/07363760210426067

Yalçınkaya, T. (2001). Sanayi ve Bilgi Toplumlarında Rekabet Ekonomisi. *Rekabet Bülteni Dergisi, 5*

Yalçınkaya, T. (2006). *Sosyo-ekonomik Sınıflaşma Bağlamında Tüketim Etiğine İlişkin Bir Değerlendirme: 'Tüketimci' Tüketiciler Yaratma*, II. Ulusal Uygulamalı Etik Kongresi Bildiriler Kitabı, 695-702.

Yazıcı, M. (2013). Toplumsal Değişim ve Sosyal Değerler. *Electronic Turkish Studies, 8*(8), 1489–1501. doi:10.7827/TurkishStudies.4782

Yıldız, Z., Kalağan, G., Yıldız, S., & Çetin, B. (2013). Toplumsal Dönüşüm ve İrrasyonel Tüketim. *Bartın Üniversitesi İİBF Dergisi, 4*(8), 67–102.

Yurdakul, C., & Çağlayan, M. U. (1997). *Bilgi Teknolojileri Türkiye İçin Nasıl Bir Gelecek Hazırlamakta.* Ankara, Turkey: Türkiye İş Bankası Yayını.

Yurtseven, M. (2015). *Bilgi Toplumu Olma Yolunda Kütüphane ve Sivil Toplum Kuruluşu Etkileşimi: Türk Kütüphaneciler Derneği Örneği (Tkd) (Basılmamış yüksek lisans tezi).* İstanbul, Turkey: Marmara Üniversitesi Türkiyat Araştırmaları Enstitüsü.

Zubritski, Y., Mitropolski, D., & Kerov, V. (2006). *İlkel Köleci ve Feodal Toplum. Çev, Belli, S.* Ankara, Turkey: Eriş Yayınları.

ADDITIONAL READING

Bagwell, L., & Bernheim, B. (1996). Veblen Effects in A Theory of Conspicuous Consumption. *The American Economic Review, 86*(3), 349–373. Retrieved from http://www.jstor.org/stable/2118201

De Bresson, C. (1987). The Evolutionary Paradigm and the Economics of Technological Change. *Journal of Economic Issues, 21*(2), 751–762. doi:10.1080/00213624.1987.11504667

Jacobs, G. (2015). The Need For A New Paradigm in Economics. *Review of Keynesian Economics, 3*(1), 2–8. doi:10.4337/roke.2015.01.01

Karsten, S. G. (1990). Quantum Theory and Social Economics: The Holistic Approach of Modern Physics Serves Better Than Newton's Mechanics in Approaching Realty. *American Journal of Economics and Sociology, 49*(4), 385–399. doi:10.1111/j.1536-7150.1990.tb02461.x

Patsiaouras, G., & Fitchett, J. A. (2012). The evolution of conspicuous consumption. *Journal of Historical Research in Marketing, 4*(1), 154–176. doi:10.1108/17557501211195109

Rengs, B., & Scholz-Wäckerle, M. (2019). Consumption & Class in Evolutionary Macroeconomics. *Journal of Evolutionary Economics, 29*(1), 229–263. doi:10.100700191-018-0592-2

Swaney, J. A., & Premus, R. (1982). Modern Empiricism and Quantum Leap Theorizing in Economics. *Journal of Economic Issues, 16*(3), 713–730. doi:10.1080/00213624.1982.11504029

Turan, Z., Nakiboğlu, A., & Bozkaya, Ş. (2015). Öğretileriyle T.B.VEBLEN, *İşletme ve İktisat Çalışmaları Dergisi,* 3 (4), 161-200. Retrieved from http://dergipark.org.tr/iicder/issue/31650/347043

Veblen, T. (1899). *The Theory of the Leisure Class.* New York: MacMillian Press.

Weisskopf, W. A. (1979). The Method Is the Ideology: From a Newtonian to a Heisenbergian Paradigm in Economics. *Journal of Economic Issues, 13*(4), 869–884. doi:10.1080/00213624.1979.11503709

KEY TERMS AND DEFINITIONS

Consumption Society: It means the organization of societies within the framework of their consumption rather than the production of goods and services, and is the result of capitalism.

Globalization: Globalization is the spread of products, technology, knowledge and business across national borders and cultures. Explain the interdependence of nations in the world supported by free trade economically.

Industrial Revolution: It is a process that started with the use of steam engine in production in 1765. The industrial revolution is defined as changes in manufacturing and transport using machines in larger factories rather than manual production.

Newtonian Paradigm: It is a paradigm, also known as mechanical thinking, which predicts static and Point analysis based on cause and effect relationship.

Paradigm Shift: It is the replacement of the old paradigm by the emerging new paradigm, depending on scientific improvements. Particularly technological, economic, socio-cultural and political field is to experience radical changes.

Quantum Paradigm: It is the paradigm in which everything affects everything and everything is influenced by everything within the multiple, mutual and cumulative causal relationship that emerges on the basis of quantum physics.

Tribe: It is a social structure in the primitive society, consisting of families linked by social, economic, religious, blood ties, with a common culture, dialect and traditionally having a recognized leader.

Chapter 8
New Public Administration Understanding and Reform Effects as Products of Neolibal Management Concept

Eray Acar
https://orcid.org/0000-0002-5375-7555
Kutahya Dumlupinar University, Turkey

ABSTRACT

Globalization has been a process that has deeply and continuously influenced societies and states in the late period of historical development. With neoliberalism, the ideological thought system of the process, all social organizations, especially state apparatus and public administrations, are affected by this process and continue to be affected. This transformation process, supported by its international organizations, has led to the preparation and implementation of reforms in order to adopt a new approach to public administration. This change in public administration has affected both public service understanding and public service delivery. It is a process that aims to provide the citizens/customers satisfaction by offering a faster, more efficient, and high-quality public service along with the new public management understanding. Current practices are questioned and improvements are tried.

INTRODUCTION

The state structure which emerged with the aim of meeting the needs of the individuals forming the societies and providing services to the individuals has undergone structural changes in the historical process. The reasons underlying these developments, which also transform the powers and responsibilities of the state towards society, were mostly economic reasons. This process of change, which has gained momentum with the effect of globalization on the life of societies, can be seen as the process of adapting the change in the production structure to the management structures. The transformation of the state apparatus has become inevitable, as the welfare state, known as the social welfare state and

DOI: 10.4018/978-1-7998-0333-1.ch008

Copyright © 2020, IGI Global. Copying or distributing in print or electronic forms without written permission of IGI Global is prohibited.

associated with the Fordist production process, is replaced by the post-production process. This change, especially in the last quarter of the twentieth century, revealed the need for reform in the structure of Public Administration, which is the state's service to society.

The concept of cumbersome, bureaucratic, efficient and inefficient service provision of the traditional public administration structure of the social welfare state period has been criticized. Globally, underdeveloped and developing countries have been faced with the pressure of reform in the transition to a new understanding of public administration compatible with neoliberal economic understanding. National governments have begun reform initiatives to shift to a more effective, efficient, transparent, accountable, market-compliant and governance public administration approach. In particular, international financial and political organizations have been factors that have contributed to this reform pressure.

In this context aimed to explain the process of change and transformation in roles and functions of state and public administration within the framework of neoliberalism approach at causality level. The ways in which economic changes and actors affect the changes that took place in the administrative and political spheres and the views of the changes have been tried to be conveyed by considering the data obtained through the literature review

BACKROUND

In 1933, Elton Mayo's The Human Problems of Industrial Civilization reform, published by Herbert A. Simon on reform Administrative Behavior, and Dwight Waldo's Administrative The Administrative State published in 1948 is the first scientific source in the field. These works are published by Woodrow Wilson of the USA in 1887 at the end of the 19th century with an article titled Study The Study of Administration G (Güler, 2003, p 533; Ergun, 2004, p 341; Eryılmaz, 2010, p 12). by questioning the classical management theories in which public administration has developed as an academic discipline, they emphasized the instrumental aspect of productivity, pluralism and participation in public administration. In addition, these theorists have been effective in the development of American pragmatism and this effect has re-emerged in the discourse, discussion and application level in public administration discipline after 1980s (Şener, 2005, p 2; Yalçın, 2010, pp 282-284). Therefore, in terms of the development of public administration, these theories emphasized the human (socio-psychological) -behavioral aspect of organizations and highlighted the notion of intra-organizational participation in the development of productivity (Simon et al., 1985, p 17). This notion then had a major impact on the development of theories of public administration by addressing different aspects (productivity, participation, democracy). Subsequently, the foundations of the theories of public administration in terms of social participation and pluralism (Şener, 2005, p 2), and therefore in terms of postmodern philosophy, were published in the 1968 "New School of Public Administration" (Thompson, 1972, p 620; Lamidi, 2015, p 21). It can be said that it was based on different approaches such as Democratic Administration which was analyzed by Vincent Ostrom in the past. In addition, in 1983, American academics, James Perry and Kenneth Kraemer, announced the emergence of the science of public business with their books "Public Management: Public and Private Perspective".

H. George Frederickson et al. (2012, pp 99-100) in his Public The Public Administration Theory Primer and Frederickson (1997, pp. 8-15; 2012, p 251) in his 1970s, He stated that new public administration management has started to strengthen and democratic management, social equality, citizenship, ethics and localization". In the 1990s, the theories developed were based on the rejection of previously problematic areas, and thanks to the so-called "postmodern theories, new mechanisms were sought outside the bureaucracy, and the truths were replaced by temporary or" discursively formed communicative lines Ş (Şener, 2005, p 15). Thus, the positive public administration approach was challenged at a concrete and discursive level (Lalor, 2014, p 197). Because modern public administration, as a partner between citizens' participation activity and the responsibility of citizens as a customer causes a tension (Vigoda, 2002, p 527). Charles J. Fox and Hugh T. Miller, after the 1990s in a way connected to postmodernism, including the thinkers like Habermas aim to establish the basis of a theory of public administration (Şener, 2005, p 15). As a matter of fact, Fox and Miller, in their books titled mod Postmodern Public Administration: Towards Discourse 1995 published in 1995, regard public participation as a necessity as a speech or dialogue in order to make democracy more functional in the solution of public problems and the adoption of public policies. Gruening, 2001, p 9; Fox and Miller, 2007, Fox and Miller, 1993, p 14). It is the area where the public policies are determined (Özcan and Ağca, 2010, p12).

TRANSFORMING STRUCTURE OF PRODUCTION IN GLOBALIZATION PROCESS

From the depths of history up to the present, globalization has taken place in various waves. According to others, the phenomenon of globalization, which brings societies closer to each other, according to others, alienates societies and opens the development and prosperity shear among countries. This process, which renews itself based on capital accumulation, sees that the system is experiencing blockages in itself.

During the period between 1870 and 1914, there was an intense free trade, and this phenomenon was interrupted for a while, and the wave of globalization, which began in the late 1960s, reached a peak in the 2000s against the interventionist state concept of the Keynesian Social State.

Taylor and Flint Economic, political, social, technological, financial, cultural and ecological globalization as a globalization analysis of eight different dimensions of the globalization of political globalization; Free market economy, the reduction of public expenditures, the spread of neo-liberal policies envisaging privatization worldwide; They have defined (Taylor and Flint, 2000, pp 2-4).

The dominant discourse of the recent wave of globalization Neo-liberal policies have marked the last globalization process with the new understanding and perception change brought about in almost all fields, especially in the political field.

Transition From Production Oriented Fordist Conception to Consumption-Oriented Postfordist Understanding

Fordist production and organization model, which is the main foundation of developmental social state in private sector; the weakening of capitalism due to the period of structural crisis and the transition from Keynesian policies to Friedmanist policies in the economic sphere. (Saran, 2001, pp 45-46) After the accumulation crisis of capital, both the production process and the institutional and functional structure of the state in the parallel changes experienced in parallel with this period spread rapidly all over the world.

Taylorism and Fordism

It emerged from the systematic management movement that emerged in the United States in the years 1880-1890. It is a management approach developed by Frederick Winslow Taylor and has a worldwide impact on the organization of capitalist production. In 1911, Taylor developed his approach to the way and organization of the work he developed, both ideologically and experimentally. According to the Taylorist principles organized by the labor process, especially the problems of the worker to adapt to this new process, after him, industrial psychology and sociologists who prepared the foundation of sociology were interested (Ansal, 1999, p 9).

This period, which is the name of H. Ford, means mass production for mass consumption; capital intensive large-scale production, an inflexible production process, a rigid hierarchical and bureaucratic structure, and the preservation of national markets were dominant (Jarry and Jarry, 1991, p. 173).

The new stage of development, which began in the aftermath of the Second World War and lasted until the 1970s, was also called the Fordism era.

Changing Structure of Production

Especially II. After World War II, when the last 50-60 years were taken as base and the developments in different countries and regions of the world were analyzed separately, we are faced with a very contradictory process. World capitalism, which came to balance with the second world war, was based on the economic policy of the state, which is called the 'Keynesian Economic Policies' on the international scale, and which envisaged the active role of the state in the regulatory and economic affairs. The Fordist and Keynesian models were valid in both central and peripheral countries. When Keynes is left to the market itself, it seems that a balance cannot be achieved where full employment of social resources will be achieved. He suggested state intervention in the case of incomplete employment. In order to achieve this goal, the social state refers to the understanding of a total state of conservation, full employment, economic growth and stability. On the basis of this, the concept of Keynesian Social State has been defined as Keynesian Social State as. In order to achieve these objectives, the state needs to intervene more in the economy by using the policies of money and finance (tax, expenditure and transfer of income). In this sense, the social state was widely implemented in many countries, especially in western European countries in the years following the second world war, and this period became the 'golden age' of the social state. In this period, economic stability and welfare-social security and social assistance programs became universal and their institutional foundations were strengthened (Gül, 2004, pp 147 - 148).

It has been suggested that the direction of the social state based on the labor-capital-state reconciliation is in harmony with Fordism and that the Fordist accumulation regime can reproduce itself within the framework of the social state. The function of the social state, which allows the aspirations in the field of democracy and human rights to be expressed more intensely by the organized workers, is not to ensure the continuity of capital accumulation in contrast to the liberal state. Ensuring equitable and fair share of goods and services. The social state has begun to produce goods and services for all segments of the society, and to perform trust-making transactions for the working population. In doing so, the labor sector has been involved in the financing of the system through taxes and social security shares (Şaylan, pp 116-118).

NEOLIBERAL INTERPRETATION OF SOCIAL STATE UNDERSTANDING

Development has been tried to be explained with prosperity in the classical economic sense and this prosperity has been equated with industrialization only (Çelik & Erkan, p.183). Social State, that some of the prices in the sense that some of the prices are not limited to the blind and unconscious laws of the market conditions, which are sensitive to the fulfillment of vital needs and are seeking remedies, and that the national income should be distributed to the more equitable extent (with a certain social security policy) it is the state that tries to reduce the cost to the level. This state also:

1. Eliminating social injustices and eliminating the causes that constitute these injustices;
2. To ensure that a person or such person, in this or that class's egoism, or the luxury of a happy minority, establishes a system of order for every human being to live in humankind, human dignity, and to prioritize the needs of all;
3. To prepare the necessary environment for each person to benefit from equal conditions and thus to have a wide development opportunity; and it is the most important feature that it does not mimic the authoritarian regimes that reject the principles of human rights and freedoms and democratic rule of law (İnsel, pp 15-16).

It protects the social structure, as in the liberal state. However, this structure, not only individuals, individuals formed by various social, economic, professional, etc. organizations. In this structure, the source of the society and the state is the individual, but it is seen that the social structure of the state is not the individual, but also the social institutions. In addition, the social state provides for state intervention while maintaining the economic structure of the liberal state based on private property and entrepreneurial freedom (Göze, 1998, p 98).

After the Second World War, representative democracy took place on the basis of reconciliation between labor, capital and the state. However, the erosion of labor has resulted in the capital pushing for reconciliation (Şaylan, 2002, p 129).

The skepticism about the role of the state emerged in the late 1960s, strengthened in the 1970s, and is now heavily on the agenda. The phenomenon that prepares the necessity of the restructuring of the state is the striking change in the environment in which the states operate, as well as the problems that the social state has come into. Technological changes in the process has created new opportunities that allow services to become widespread and markets play a larger role, while taxes, public expenditures, investments and economic policies have had to adapt to a globalized world economy. Such changes have meant new and different roles for the state, creating the need for the state to be considered not only as providing, but as facilitating and regulating elements.

In the post-1980s world, the period of globalization and neo-liberalism is a period in which transnational capital wants the state to shrink, and that it can only enter into competition with this condition. Transnational corporations whose activities are independent of national borders are evidently seeing the most profitable investment opportunities in the sectors dominated by the state. In case of ruthless competition, lowering the costs was impossible with the state enterprises in which the public interest was considered. This is not just about the sale of 'State Economic Enterprises' (SEE). These groups see each area as a source of profit, and want to turn the future of health, education, social security, laborers, into a property that can be bought and sold. Therefore, the concept of social state is sacrificed in the interests of transnational capital for more competitive conditions in the global economy.

Generally, the prescriptions and principles of a solid marketed approach lead to negative consequences, especially in developing countries (Kızılcık, 2003, p. 181). This approach based on public election policy should be paid attention as it is based on the rejection of the principles of public interest and public service which have an important role in the development of democracy and state administration (Kızılcık, 2003, p. 192).

However, Keynesian policies in Western countries have been adapted to underdeveloped countries by development economists such as Gunnar Myrdal, Executive Secretary of the United Nations Economic Commission for Europe and Raul Prebisch, Secretary General of the Latin American Economic Commission. While planning policies are adopted for economic and social investments, it is envisaged that these policies should be implemented as far as possible within a technocratic network of relations, free from social contradictions and dynamics. For example, while the main causes of 'poverty in underdeveloped countries are identified as governments and international organizations, these solutions are also used in the proposed solutions. Thus, the ideologies of international capital are attributed to them the real gains of underdevelopment and dependency theory rather than to workers and peasants (Leys, 1992, p. 81).

The theorists of the School of Addiction are mainly driven by the contradiction of development and underdevelopment, rather than the contradiction of planning with the market. It focuses on the center-periphery polarization, considering the production and distribution of surplus value on a world scale, not on a scale of countries. In this sense, the theory of addiction acts from an anti-imperialist and non-Marxist perspective (O'Brien, 1992, p 24). Development and underdevelopment are the different outcomes of a single process. Therefore, it is not possible to develop by following the line of developed countries. This criticism, however, refers to capitalist development (Wood, 2003: 35). The development of underdevelopment (Frank, 1975) distinguishes the development of the environment formation from the West's line of development with its distorted (Amin, 1977) and deformed (Alavi, 1975). Thus, the development in the theory of underdevelopment and dependence refers to capitalist development in metropolises (Leys, 1992, p 77). In this case, the capitalist development of Western countries is considered 'ideal' or 'normal and opens the door to a series of theoretical problems in terms of dependency analysis.

After 1980, with the implementation of neo-liberal policies in parallel with the changes in the world economy, economists such as Dani Rodrik, Daron Acemoğlu and Haa-Joon Chang made different views as economists who did not advocate globalization and liberalizing policies. Daron Acemoğlu and James A Robinson, who are in the corporate economic trend, stated that development cannot be achieved through liberalization and globalization and that development will not be possible without inclusive institutions (Acemoğlu and Robinson, 2014, pp 437-438). In addition, it is unclear how economic freedom, free capital movements and globalization will affect political freedoms in countries when the freedoms are taken as a whole. It was also stated by Acemoğlu and Robinson (2016) that contrary to the aforementioned views, economic freedoms may not create political freedom. He argued that globalization may weaken the ability of democracy to improve the welfare of the majority (Acemoğlu and Robinson, 2016, p 382).

Chang opposed the continuous suggestion of liberating policies with reference to developed countries. He stated that developed countries do not develop through emancipatory policies. He stated that Globalization and Neo-Liberal policies are not the only options, but rather a large number of other options, and that Neo-Liberal policies result in disaster and cause misery (Chang and Gabriel, 2016, p 259). Similarly to Chang, Fikret Şenses emphasized that liberalization policies are not the only options, especially for developing countries and post-Soviet transition economies, although they are accepted as such by the neoliberal view (Şenses, 2016, p 382).

INTERNATIONAL ACTORS OF THE REFORM PROCESS

Step-by-step resolution of the central social state has undergone pressures to, privatize the public's social expenditures, to undergo an intense – privatization in public institutions, including those that are strategically and those who profit. All these are presented as postmodern / contemporary / new approaches and continue to be presented. It is possible to consider these two major international organizations, such as the IMF and the World Bank, as the main policy recommendations to these environmental countries (Kazgan, 1997, pp 185-186). In addition to these two organizations, it should not be forgotten that organizations such as WTO, GATS, TRIPS, OECD, MAI, G7, G20, EU which support the process have gained momentum.

There are four main areas: 'budget, personnel reform, central structure, and local government', which are trying to bring public administration into a new identity (which is also expressed in the Neoliberal State Reform). The process is primarily the area of intervention of the World Bank, the OECD, the European Union (EU) and the United Nations (UN). The role of the IMF in this process is embodied in the reduction of public expenditures pressure. The IMF emphasizes that good governance, transparency and cooperation are key elements in the prevention of financial crises (Erdönmez and Tulay, 1999, pp 64-76).

International Monetary Fund (IMF)

The IMF was established in 1944 at the Bretton Woods Conferences with the World Bank. The aim of the IMF is to solve unforeseen and incidental liquidity problems of the member countries and to eliminate the disruptions in international trade and to open loans that will overcome the bottlenecks in the countries experiencing balance of payments bottlenecks.

Another aim of the IMF is to prevent the disruption of payments made by member countries to each other. In practice, this means that underdeveloped countries pay their debts to developed countries on time and with interest (İyibozkurt, 1999, p 25).

IMF stabilization policies implemented in underdeveloped countries in the 1980s led national economies to repay the loans provided by the IMF and to ensure the comfortable circulation of financial capital. Reforms to do this are made mandatory (Ozdek, 1999, p 29).

In the 1970s, developed countries began to lift these restrictions step by step, as the process of seeking profits in the global arena necessitated the abolition of measures restricting international capital movements. Germany, Canada and Switzerland in 1973, USA in 1974, England in 1979 and Japan in 1980 removed all restrictions on international capital movements. In the following years, the transition to convertibility and financial liberalization policies were included in the comprehensive policy package envisaged by the IMF in developing countries. Therefore, the IMF has undertaken the function of generalizing policies appropriate to the requirements of the internationalization of capital to developing countries (Demir, 1999, pp 179-181). After the end of the Bretton Woods fixed exchange rate system, the change in the fundamental nature of the international monetary system through mandatory floating exchange rate regimes led to a significant change in the role of the IMF. The major developed countries themselves regulated their exchange rate policies without confusing the IMF. In this period, in general, the IMF financed the imbalance of payments by developed countries in support of the fixed exchange rate system. Over time, the IMF's interest shifted to developing countries in terms of financing the balance of payments, overseeing economic policies, providing technical assistance and information on member economies and the international economy. The latest IMF-backed programs for developed countries were implemented in England and Italy in 1977 after the transition to floating exchange rate regimes in general (Yoon, 2005, pp 182- 183; Carvalho, 2000, pp 3-17).

Especially after the collapse of the Bretton Woods system in 1973, the IMF has lost its effectiveness in ensuring the stability of the exchange rates with the freeing of the money of the world's leading countries. On the other hand, it is observed that the IMF aims to increase the effectiveness of international liquidity and payments. The IMF undertook the role of the organizer of capitalism in the new world order, which describes the process of capitalism becoming dominant all over the world and its internationalization and which is explained by concepts such as neo-liberalism, globalization and flexibility (Ozturk, 2002, pp 95-96).

The IMF, which links the granting of loans to the implementation of the proposed policies, began to work jointly with the World Bank on stand-by agreements and structural adjustment credits, in particular on financial sector-related programs. It is noteworthy that the programs including structural adjustment credits are aimed at increasing the efficiency of resource use rather than micro-economic demand management (Canpolat, 2004, pp 64-72). Conditionally, it is one of the most important features of IMF programs. In return for its loans, the IMF demands that national economic policies be followed, policies pursued by itself, balance of payments and institutionalization of the free market (Ener and Siverekli, 2004, pp 89-90). In this context, real wages are reduced and the labor market is cheapened by recommending that public expenditures to be increased by cutting public expenditures to pay debts and to keep workers wages independent from price increases. Programs that emphasize privatization with the public sector's downsizing discourse cause many employees to be dismissed. The privatized organization is mostly transferred to multinational companies.

Stand-by Agreements

The most important and well-known concept in the relations with the countries as a political influence of the IMF is the stand-by concept. Stand-by in the dictionary literally means stored, pending, support and assistance for use when needed. The IMF stand-by arrangement is a fund decision that ensures that a member can withdraw from the Fund's General Resources account for a certain period of time and in certain amounts. Stand-by arrangements consist of two basic documents, one of which includes certain legal requirements, stand-by arrangement and letter of intent.

It is stated that, the IMF regularly opens its safes to the member states during the financial crises, but it does so under some conditions. According to this; in the globalizing world, the IMF has become the organizer and the last resort of the rescue packages. However, in the past, because the solutions were actually economic, they often complicated the problem; because as the crisis deepens, it becomes political. The IMF is not equipped to deal with the political consequences of the programs (Kissinger, 2002, p 201).

Under the IMF's decision-making mechanisms, underdeveloped member states are made to be dependent to this institution, not to participate in the decision-making process and to protect their interests, but rather to account for how much debt can be taken (Raffinot, 1998, p 91).

Especially after the 1974 oil crisis and the general economic crisis in the world, this division of labor has disappeared, and the IMF and the World Bank have been carrying out projects together with the so-called 'structural adjustment programs' to ensure the full integration of less developed countries with the system. While the World Bank is planning the structural adjustment programs, the IMF also supervises the implementation of these compliance programs through stand-by agreements (Seyidoglu, 1994, p 684).

World Bank

Economic developments in the 1970s led the World Bank, such as the IMF, to short- and long-term structural adjustment programs, so that the distinction between the two institutions began to be obscured. While the IMF undertakes macroeconomic stability by identifying monetary and fiscal policies, the World Bank undertakes efficient allocation of resources through social-size projects such as structural adjustment programs and poverty reduction.

The World Bank first introduced the concept of good governance in 1989, in a report on the development of Africa, to legitimize the structural programs it proposed. The concept of good governance which the World Bank has filled with democratic management elements such as, International Monetary Fund, Organization for Economic Co-operation and Development, World Trade Organization, United Nations has been adopted by other international organizations and has been used as a global slogan.

In accordance with the globalization - localization - marketization approach, which is the pillar of the global process, according to the Bank, local governments should have their own budget resources and their dependence on the center should be removed. For reasons of weakness in terms of personnel and equipment, it is recommended to make investments by private sector, privatization through localization (Erdogdu, 2004, pp 68-84).

Chossudovsky sees the globalization of poverty as an input for an export economy based on cheap labor on a world scale. The World Bank's aid to alleviate poverty also implies that it is aimed at suppressing the risk of major social change, and that various non-governmental organizations undertake to achieve this aim (Chossudovsky, 1999, pp 78-79). The World Bank has also developed a policy of anti-corruption to reduce poverty. The World Bank considered corruption as a problem of governance and defined public resources as abuse for private interests. According to the World Bank, the cost of corruption in developing countries borrowing is high. Because corruptions push firms into the external economy, by decreasing the direct investments of foreigners, preventing the growth of small entrepreneurs, disrupting macroeconomic stability, causing environmental problems and adversely affecting the poor. The reforms helped to re-establish infectious diseases such as tuberculosis, malaria and cholera in various regions of the developing world.

The World Bank's policies on poverty are criticized, especially in terms of structural balance programs. According to the widespread view, these policies have produced negative effects on the poor because of the deregulation of labor markets and high interest rates (Uzun, 2003, p 163). In other words, it is argued that orthodox economic policies, including the reduction of public expenditures and devaluation, bring heavy burdens on the poor. Some economists argued that structural equilibrium programs did not create growth and that the poor benefited marginally from these programs (Chossudovsky, 1999, p 37).

The inclusion of anti-poverty policies in compliance programs has not changed the basic logic of compliance policies. These measures did not cause deviation from adaptation programs and were designed to support these policies by allowing the poor to participate in the commodity economy. The problems encountered are considered to be problems specific to the transition period. Moreover, these negative impacts are not attributed to direct adaptation programs, but rather to the distortions of the economic structures of the countries in which the programs are implemented and the social resistance to programs. The source of resistance, according to the World Bank, was that these established interests of the groups that had long dominated these countries were threatened within the framework of compliance programs. Therefore, taking temporary and short-term measures in line with the spirit of compliance policies will be sufficient to overcome these problems (Tatar, 1996, pp 41-42).

Although the World Bank's founding regulation included poverty alleviation and environmental protection, its support for large-scale hydroelectric and agro-industrial projects accelerated deforestation and destruction of the natural environment, which led to the displacement and evacuation of millions of people (Chossudovsky, 1999, p 38).

Structural Adjustment Programs

In particular, the adaptation to the globalization process in terms of developing countries is equated with the implementation of IMF Structural Adjustment Policies originating from the IMF and World Bank. The countries that are in a state of collapse due to the globalization process are forced to impose adaptation programs defined by the IMF and the World Bank in the 1980s, and defined the adaptation programs that are defined as relying on more market forces and reducing the role of the state in economic management (Ghai, 1995, p 39). The basic philosophy of these programs is the realization of neo-liberal economic thought

Privatization is the' main goal 'of all IMF policies. In this way, foreign capital can enter into the fields left by the public institutions and high incomes will be obtained from these areas which generally give high profitability. In addition, it is expected to generate revenue in foreign currency by privatization, thus it is considered that it is possible to close the public deficits and pay foreign debts. However, the result is a loss of state control and a significant decrease in tax revenues even in the most strategic sectors.

In the context of these policies, it has been obligatory to go from the concept of state to democratic rights, from health to education, from housing to labor, from privatization to foreign trade and many other structural arrangements. Therefore, not only economic but also political regulations are covered by structural adjustment policies.

In recent years, countries that have followed the standard development prescriptions recommended by leading institutions, such as the IMF and the World Bank, have undermined the hopes of achieving the goals set for the reduction of poverty, even in some regions, where the situation has worsened (Uzun, p.156).

GATT (GATS)

When the World Trade Organization, which is one of the effective international organizations of the globalization process in the reorganization of world capitalism after the Second World War, examines GATS, which is an important place in the liberalization of the sector. It was the money and finance conference held in 1944 by the UN in the town of Bretton Woods. Apart from the establishment of the IMF and the World Bank, an important decision taken at the Bretton Woods Conference is about the General Agreement on Tariffs and Trade (GATT). GATS (General Agreement on Trade in Services), the structure of GATT in 1986-1994, which was signed and signed in Uruguay Interview Round and included in the GATT, then transferred to the World Trade Organization, a deal.

The importance of the Uruguay Round negotiations is an emphasis on the need for countries to be included in the international negotiation process of the services sector they conduct in accordance with their own legislation. On the other hand, in addition to trade in services, banking, telecommunication, construction and related engineering services, consultancy services, transportation, tourism, education, health, environmental services, municipal services and many other sub-service branches (cluster effect), such as many intellectual property rights In the Uruguay Round, where new areas of negotiation are covered by negotiations, commitments to reduce taxes in certain categories of goods and services are decided.

In 1995, with the Marrakesh agreement, developed countries were convinced to reduce their protection in the agricultural and textile sectors, while the same countries made significant concessions to patent and service sector developed countries. In this respect, while there have been changes in favor of developed countries in service sectors such as telecommunications and finance, there has been no progress in the free movement of real persons concerning developing countries (Yağcı, 2001, pp 26-27).

Within the framework of GATS, it is argued that the privatization of public services will increase the tax burden by increasing the costs of services, the amount of service production will be reduced if the social tax burden remains constant, the quality of service will be eroded or the exploitation on the labor factor will increase (Onder, 2002, p 74).

Organization for Economic Cooperation and Development (OECD)

The Organization for Economic Co-operation and Development (OECD) is one of the international organizations that reviews the developments in the world economy and the economic and financial policies of its members, conducts researches and publishes reports on future expectations and traditionally takes on the leadership role of the US. The MAI (Multilateral Agreement on Investment), which was prepared confidentially by OECD countries in 1995, is the constitution of globalization with the aim of harmonizing international law with international capitalism.

The MAI, which aims at spreading globalization on the nation state and providing full liberalization in capital, has not been implemented. However, 15 years against the risks that they will face, they will not take any necessary administrative and legal measures to establish MIGA (Multilateral Investment Guarantee Agency) which is a lower step of MAI contract to be insured (Giray, 2003, pp 154-157).

Multinational Companies

Multinational corporations, Unilever, Deutsche Bank, BP, which can make transnational investment decisions, carry the production chain across the country and operate in different countries. Ericsson are big companies like Nike. Similar discourses and targets of international financial institutions such as IMF, WB, WTO, OECD aim at the globalization of capital serve almost multinational companies.

According to Arıboğan, increasing the world trade volume of these companies, bringing technological innovations and facilitating modernization by distributing them to GOUs as well as positive aspects such as creating employment, monopolizing production, contributing to the creation of cartels that will contribute to inflation, limiting employee wages, increasing the welfare of local elites against the poor There are also negative aspects to expand the gap between the rich and poor nations (Arıboğan, 2001, p 175).

Multinational Corporations demands have led to a step-by-step restriction of governments social rights and the flexibility of the labor market. It is inevitable that large firms will first transfer their jobs to small firms working with non-union workers through the possibility of employing part-time or temporary workers, changing the number of workers according to the conjuncture, and subcontracting according to the conjuncture (Kazgan, 2002, p 211).

THE NEO-LIBERAL APPROACH OF THE PUBLIC ADMINISTRATION

Each stage of capitalism is defined by specific economic policies and accumulation strategies. The general conditions of capital accumulation also determine the functions of the state. The growth process continues as long as a certain accumulation strategy provides high profit rates and is conducive to the expansion and expansion of capital. When the opportunities offered by this accumulation model are consumed, there is a crisis that shows itself in the falling rates of profit. In this case, a new accumulation strategy should be found. The basic tools for transition to the new accumulation model, new regulations that increase labor productivity, technological progress, the opening of new regions of the world to capitalism and the new roles that the state undertakes to support capital accumulation. The changing new conditions of capital accumulation change the functions of the state and require the restructuring of the state (Gülalp, pp. 122-123).

There is no period in the history of capitalism where the state does not actively support capital accumulation. The first thing that comes to mind is the state intervention in every situation where the needs arise. Pure liberalism is no more than an ideology that the leading countries of the world economy export to other countries.

In the world economy, a strap from manufacturing to service, from national to global, from wide-ranging public obligations to limited public obligations is remarkable. While the traditional industries are transforming into industries requiring high technology, international economic relations come to the fore; the economic relations of the regional and local administrations come to the fore, and the demands of the regional and local governments to increase their responsibilities and roles in the economic development process are effective. In the same way, it is interesting that consumers want to have more voice in administration and more to voice their voice as individuals or groups (Tutum, 1994, p 27).

The process of reorganization of the field of public administration is still a continuing process, although it has started to be discussed with the emergence of different opinions after the Second World War (Sayre, 1997, pp 136-138).

In terms of the Social State, the importance of public administration, whose importance and function will be diminished due to the weakening of the centralist bureaucratic administration structure in Postmodern society, is no longer a field of relation taken and controlled by the state organization; In the recent years, the so-called new governance theory has emerged in the context of a relationship between public and private sector organizations, non-governmental organizations, international organizations and political forces. it appears to be linked to the new approach discussed (Jessop, 1994, p. 6).

Contrary to liberal discourses, it is not surprising that the new right-wing policies are not meant to have a function limited to providing law and order. In capitalism, it is only in theory that production and distribution takes place through the market mechanism, and that the state outside the market undertakes a limited function to protect the law and order. Despite the sovereignty of the liberal theory, which excludes the state intervention, capitalism has invited state intervention since the very beginning.

According to Klicksberg, the subject of the rediscovery of faith in the state, as the unique source of the solution of social and economic problems implies that a real epistomological break in has occurred in the management sciences, while on the one hand it will be established between the state-market and the state-society. It represents a paradigm transformation in terms of relationship forms and the redefinition of the role of the state (Klicksberg, 1993, p 52). The views that state that it is necessary to make it, better jobs and spend less besides minimizing the state rather, they focused on the ways in which this intervention could be carried out and on what means.

Therefore, from the point of view of the postmodern intellectual and political approach based on the basic assumption that the state will be largely abolished from the roles and functions undertaken by the state, the public institutions like the private sector enterprises. One enterprise, the public service to see the citizens of these customers as customers, public management approach to the understanding of a world that is increasingly spread all over the world. Pointing to this direction, Frederickson stresses that the basic element of public administration should be integrated into the function of better and more efficient functioning of public services with the logic of economic management (Frederickson, 1971, p 311). In recent years, the main approaches in the field of public administration are quantitative / analytic management, political management, liberalization management and market. Market-driven management approaches are noteworthy (Kettl, 1997, p 148). These approaches are a more comprehensive and complex new type of business that has recently emerged and is called the neo managerialism. The concept of managerial leadership which wants leaders in the public administration to function as leadership public entrepreneurs is also supported by these views and approaches (Terry, 1998, p 194).

According to the interpretation of the critical point of view, the effects of neoliberal policies implemented as a fundamental characteristic of the postfordist period on the economic dimensions of public administration are privatization or private sectorization of public administration, and this change is generally escape from public to private (Güler, 1996, p 100).

Considering the public service as a commodity expressed by trading values, public service providers should be treated in the form of public enterprises, such as private enterprises, which should operate under the principles of profitability and efficiency in a free competition environment as a customer approach has brought with them.

Development of a New Right State Thinking as a Reform Ideology

The origin of the new right thought II. It corresponds to the end of World War II. Hayek's views on this issue are very effective. In fact, the new right is known as a new interpretation of 19th century liberalism. The new right is gaining a new shape with the economic crises (Aksoy, 2003, p 24).

The new right-wing idea shows that countries are preparing an ideological environment for their change in the demands for universalization. Citizens perceive the state authority as a limitation of their freedom and negates the virtues of market conditions. The fact that the concept of social state has widened the understanding of the welfare state to a great extent causes the state to be seen as a major obstacle to personal freedom. In fact, the welfare state is made possible by the workers in peace. The prohibitions of the state impede the harmonious functioning and moderation of the market. Paperwork that is already in place and does not do a job already causes wasteful use of resources. The new right governments argue that these problems will be solved by the idea of (abolishing the state as a direct distributor, producer and locator in economic terms by allowing the state to be withdrawn or reduced to its own shell, which is satisfied with the ongoing tasks (Güler, 2005, p 24).

The names of James Buchanan, Milton Friedman and Friedrich von Hayek are the founders of the new righteous thought. The only difference of this idea, known as the new right (liberalism), from the traditional Liberalism thought system is that it accepts the country's involvement in the economy. In doing so, it should make it as exceptional and limited as possible (Peker, 2008, p 70).

According to Friedrich Von Hayek, this intervention by the state shows that it has negative consequences on the market and the freedom of the person. The economic situation of liberalism is based on this thought flow and the former violence and primitive practices are reintroduced in a more sensitive environment. The new conservatism or the new right is formed by the convergence of two currents that contradict each other. The social base is dominated by conservative thought, while in the economy liberalism is dominant. On the other hand, it is tried to express the importance of right management by merging the idea that social structure is moral. Hayek places the necessity of limiting the country on two ordinary sociological rules without relying on mixed economic and monetary aspects. According to the first, if a personal freedom is ensured, a well-functioning mixed social system is established by itself. According to Hayek, this situation will take a holistic understanding as the intervention of the country in the understanding of social equality will create another intervention. It will not be possible to have a rule of law with a fair rule for all. What is said to be social justice is in fact nothing other than injustice. In order to protect the person from these injustices, a person or group should not have special applications. It is possible to remove the person from the pressure on the person by the state (Peker, 2008, p 71).

According to Friedman, the main west of growth is the distrust of Hayek. It expresses a reaction against the strong countries that cannot fulfill their goals. In 1979, this development brought Thatcher to power in England, and in 1976, it led to the renewal of the long-standing social democratic power in Sweden. In France, state control over wages and prices and other state interventions are reported to be blocked (Baltacı, 2004, p 71).

Elements of New Right State Understanding

According to Friedrich Von Hayek, the intervention of the state on the personal and the market has negative consequences. The economic situation of liberalism is being re-examined with a more flexible approach. The new conservatism or the new right is the result of the merging of two currents which coincide with each other. While the social base maintains its conservative ideology, liberalism is observed in the economy. On the other hand, the importance of the right ideas is explained by the awareness that the social structure is moral. Hayek is based on two simple sociological constructs, without relying on the financial constraints and the complex economy. According to the first of these, in the case of guaranteeing personal freedoms, a regular working order of social order will be established. The country does not need to interfere in socio-economic life. This situation reveals the unreliability of public administrators, while also limiting public power. This is what Hayek calls the order of society itself and this can be nothing more than the essence of the market. The whole of the conscious and non-purposeful behavior of people is defined as a social order and this occurs spontaneously. In order for the order to take place, the goals of the people must conflict. Justice is also a product of an individual assessment and is related to freedom in human life. According to Hayek, the state blockage in social justice understanding would cause a new obstacle, and therefore, there would be no opportunity to establish a state of law with equal rules. What is defined as social justice is nothing more than an injustice. In order for a person to avoid these inequalities, it should not be possible to apply special practices to any society or individual. The pressure of the state on the individual is only possible if he is taken away from his powers (Peker, 2008, pp 70-71).

Principles of New Right State Understanding

The elements of the new right country understanding are listed below (Balkız, 2007, pp 80-81);

1. The new right is ideological in that it offers a new conservative lifestyle.
2. In the new right-wing ideology, the right to property, as in the same liberalism, is indispensable.
3. The conservatism of the new right is sensitive to progress and technological innovation.
4. The state has no market intervention. The new right believes in the indispensability of the free market in economic terms.
5. The new right has many contrasts due to its complex structure. It is opposed by its conservative ideology. The new right thinks that revolutionary ideologies do not do very well in the name of humanity. The new right did not think of removing the regime and re-introducing a new regime, but rather agreed to peace with the system. The important thing here is not the regime but the economic system. Again, the anti-socialist tendency is strong.
6. This idea of thinking, which has managed to integrate the new right-wing conservative ideology and liberalism in an environment, is neither new nor old. The new right accepts practices for the protection of the personal rights and freedoms of the Welfare State. It demands more protection of personal rights and freedoms against the state. At the same time, it is necessary to reduce the prevention of the state in the family, education and moral fields and to fill these environments by the traditional communities. The necessity of privatization of social and educational security by state administration is emphasized. It is seen that the moral values are strongly emphasized. This emphasis shows that contemporary life is in harmony with the new values.

Neo-Liberal Discourses: Governance - Privatization - Total Quality Management

The policies that capitalism has produced to overcome the crisis that has been intensifying since the 1970s; the internationalization of production, trade, financial capital, communication, management and control has been continued through liberalization, irregularization and privatization, which have focused on the liquidation or contraction of the public sector for the last two decades.

Neoliberal approaches based on a market-friendly and supportive state administration, legitimacy, transparency, participation, effective and efficient state services; In practice, they envisage or even mandate the integration of Governance, Privatization and Total Quality Management into state administration and institutions.

Governance

'Governance', a multi-actor, is presented as a global model after the neo-liberal reforms aimed at minimizing the state. The term management and its use as opposed to the concept of management in the last two decades are used to mean governance, a new governance process or a, new management style of society (Rhodes, 1996, p 652).

Governance refers to a multi-actor and mutual, an interactive form of government that takes place with the participation of public sector - private sector - non-governmental organizations. According to Tekeli, governance is the transition from a management concept that collects itself into a single subject, center, hierarchical, resources and management, and to act as a multi-actor, decentralized, decentralized, actor who makes the actors in society rather than doing it himself (Tekeli, 2003, p 627).

It is also seen that the governance, which underlines the responsibility of the Communities to participate in the decision-making process and thus take the services they need, overlaps with the total quality management. (Şaylan, 2003, p 592)

Governance is structured on localization policies that enable the expansion of political and economic power. The decentralization, which supports the downsizing of central government, emerges in the form of independent administrative authorities, strengthening of local administrations and privatization. (Eryilmaz, 2001, p 77).

Decentralization - Internationalization - In accordance with the chain of marketization, the act of governance advocated by governance theorists is no longer limited to the nation-state, but from national to local and international. In this context, governance offers a multi-centered state structure. The subjects of the multi-structure are the non-governmental organizations, which are the public sector, the private sector, non-governmental organizations and organizations of the board type, especially the state with different roles.

In a new structure where the state-market social society is united with a common state, instead of the pyramid state, which is dominated by a single-center hierarchical, bureaucratic organization, and a network state model, the state to distribute in the form of 'joint venture is obliged to support the entrepreneurship.

Guler, the three-seat (bureaucracy-private sector-civil society) in the governance formula does not have a democratic appearance, the private sector in the second chair is included in the structure as the yap locomotive of social development ın thanks to its creative and productive nature, while the private sector cannot be represented and that the social sectors would be represented by non-governmental organizations in the third chair. However, since non-governmental organizations are already capital-based organizations in terms of qualifications and qualifications, in this case the chairs outside the bureaucracy in the governance formula are left to the capital. Criticisms are gathered in such a formula that the governance approach is a model for all power capital s and is a participatory but not a democratic model (Güler, 2005, pp 37-41).

In the new public management paradigm, which is called the public administration or the entrepreneurial state model, the theme proposed for the state is essentially the same the transfer of concepts such as competition, markets, customers, efficiency to the state organization; marketization of the state, such as state organization competing with the private sector, like a market actor. The common point here is that market-based discourse and concepts constitute the essence of this theme.

In the new Public Management approach, five principles are highlighted to achieve an effective state. These; shrinkage, business, decentralization, bureaucracy reduction and privatization. With the implementation of these principles, which are seen to be in line with the principles of governance, it is stated that the targeted quality will be achieved in service provision in public administration.

Privatization as a Deregulation Tool

The second one is the privatization of public-owned production vehicles, factories and similar production units into the private sector. The capital spreading from the central economies to the environment imposes the privatization of the public enterprises, which is the biggest obstacle in front of them. The privatization of public-owned production units means the transfer of public accumulation to the private sector at a certain cost. The realization of the transaction in the actual stock value of the business in question is the instant collection of the current value of the future revenues. At first glance, the process may be thought to mean a simple transfer. However, the impact of the process on the long-term economy and society is very different; it is not wrong to see this process as a kind of change of accumulated assets

In order to create an effective and efficient public administration for customer satisfaction, public administration needs to have a flexible organizational structure to adapt to rapidly changing conditions, and to break the bureaucratic structure of the Fordist period. Therefore, one of the first steps in restructuring is the creation of a flexible organizational structure. Although the implementation of the postfordist flexibility principle applied to the public administration by means of different methods and institutions, it can be summarized at the point of privatization, the contracting of public services to the private sector, the establishment of independent public authorities and localization points. This process, in which the institutional integrity of public administration is disintegrated and public services are presented by organizations of different statuses, in a sense reflects the fragmentation of public administration.

In the restructured state, in particular, the understanding of public administration has shifted to an understanding of intervention to provide capital accumulation. Customization of this conception, the rules and rules that prevent the front of the capital (deregulation) can be shown as an example (Saylan, 2003, p 133).

It is a fact that the deregulation policies, which constitute an important element of globalization, have eroded democratic institutions capacity to direct and control their economic, social and political functions and resources. Globalization, therefore, can be regarded as a structure that penetrates independent nation states and breaks down their economic, political and social order.

Since the 1980s, the state has had a minimal role in the development of national economies, leaving as much space as possible to market forces, and there must be minimal restrictions on trade and private enterprise. The basic mechanisms for this are privatization and liberalization of trade. The impact of privatization and trade liberalization policies is to protect the sovereignty of multinational corporations in developed countries. It does this by removing state intervention support. However, developed economies and companies owe their current position to a similar support. (Joon, 2003, p 26)

Total Quality Management

In the general framework, the difference between the public services and the goods and services produced by private sector organizations in terms of their basic qualities, which are the continuous and regular activities offered by the state or other public legal entities in order to ensure the common needs, peace and security of the society for the public benefit; these services are usually not produced in any competitive environment because they are related to the basic functions of the state such as justice, internal and external security, general education, general health and environmental protection, but the public authority is under the service monopoly (Gözlü, 1996, p 48).

The restructuring in the public sector is not only seen as a simple process of changing the organizational structures of public institutions and organizations in this sector, but rather it is considered as a multifaceted transformation. These include public institutions; In the short or long term, it is necessary to consider the temporary and permanent arrangements of the existing shortcomings and shortcomings in the objectives, duties, division of tasks, organizational structures, personnel systems, resources, methods, legislation, communication and public relations systems (Kalkandelen, 1998, p 99).

NEW PUBLIC ADMINISTRATION AND NEW CONSERVATISM

Social-philosophical human impressions, basic ideas, cultural, socio-scientific theory and theory parts and experimental explanations intensified, a number of political theses are called new conservatism. Contrary to this thought, new conservatism is not accepted as a theory. The concept of theory is a hypothesis that can be replicated from each other. New conservatism does not have rules for the multiplication of such a scientific central assumption. In short, new conservatism is a social science based on the solution of political problems. The similarity of this science is in things that it is not in itself, but in which it is judged. Conservatism is also a reaction formation (Helmut, 1998, p 34).

New conservatism, human rights, individualism and liberal democracy are aimed at protecting the free financial market, but rather as a social profession aimed at the solution of political problems. Neo-conservatism, socio-biology, neo-liberal political economy and human genetics, the critique of conservative culture, the criticism of factual Marxism, and the elitist theory of democracy have mobilized the arguments for liberal rationalism's political defenses in Western societies that it knows are under threat (Philippe, 1991, p 98).

The emergence of neo-liberalism in the late 1970s has caused the emergence of negativity as a result of the economic crisis. Neo-liberalism emerges in a process where the country is a social state, especially in large industrial societies, and thus is predominant in social and economic life. In the light of these considerations, a tendency that does not contradict the qualifications of the country is determined. According to the neo-liberal intellectuals, it emphasizes the pioneering of private enterprises by narrowing the fields of activity of the state (Işıklı, 1997, p 42).

The basis of the New Public Administration (NPA) is based on neoliberalism. With this understanding, NPA needs to limit the duty of the state by means of privatization and addressing the task systems in different areas. In the framework of this understanding, the idea of achieving activity and economy in the context of private sector and state relations emerges from the essence of the reforms realized with the effect of the NPA (Balcı, 2005, p 42).

Liberal economic concept based on two main assumptions depends on the idea of implementing the principles of business management in public administration. The first of these assumptions; the fact that the distribution of resources is more efficient than the social way; the real dimension of productivity is the view of rational business organization. The first of these assumptions affects the rules of public finance which open the way for realization of fair calculations in the budget process by seeing the relationship between market and budget as a contradiction. The other assumption is; pioneers in business orientation science. In the field of public administration in the field of business management, the techniques of management are tried to be accepted. This acceptance remains within the framework of fair measures describing the budgetary process in the welfare state and in the liberal period. In the neo-period, the public administration structure and the budget process are restructured within the framework of market conditions. NPA is the most important tool of this process. With the adoption of this approach in the field of public administration, especially the disruption of the market and production structures of the environmental capitalist countries has been accelerated, thus reducing transaction costs, increasing the production and service life in the market system (Akbulut, 2007, p 42).

CONCLUSION

The phenomenon of globalization has shown its effects in economic, social, political, cultural and technological areas with different discourses in different periods from past to present. As a result of technological developments, the simplified and changing production technique increased the capital and goods mobility as a result of the ease of communication and transportation, and the boundaries between the countries become artificial. This situation allowed the capital accumulation regime to be maintained and profit rates increased.

The liberal economic policies, which started to be questioned after the economic crisis of 1929, which had heavy and devastating effects all over the world, lost power in the face of the Keynesian understanding, which considered the state's effective intervention in economic and social life. During the Second World War, the fordist production adopted by the developmental social welfare state was restructured and became dominant until the 1970s in the provision of capital accumulation regime. In the 1970s, the financial crisis, which began with the oil crisis and the collapse of the Bretton Woods system, led to the fall of capitalism into a new crisis in the field of capital accumulation. Factors such as the decrease in productivity and profitability, inflation and unemployment caused contraction in demand, and a return to demand-oriented structure began to emerge from a supply-oriented structure

Postfordism, a demand-driven production concept as a remedy for the crisis of the accumulation regime; flexible production, flexible employment, product differentiation, shifting to work without stool in line with changing consumption demands, compensation according to the principle of specialization in labor force, prevention of unionization has begun to be adopted globally. The social state, which has an understanding of state compatible with Fordist production, has been an obstacle in the postfordist production process. The active intervention in economic life has lost power in trade unions as a result of the loss of this activity by the social state, which has an important role in labor-capital-state balance. Neoliberalism was the ideological infrastructure of the reconstructed capitalism in this process.

In order for neoliberalism to work in harmony with the state and public administration, it has become a necessity to transform the traditional understanding of public administration. In particular, the problems in the size of the public sector in the economy and the quality of service have been the main reasons for these reforms. When we look at the world, we see that the public sector has a big share in the economy. In the same way, it has a role in the whole economy as a regulatory and supervisor. The need for an effective and minimal structure of such a strong and wide structure has made public administration reform inevitable.

The high expectations of citizens from public administration reform are a factor that reduces the level of success of the reforms. Especially the underdeveloped state of the public administrations cumbersome, late decision makers, the balance of authority and responsibility could not regulate, such as solid bureaucracy, slowed down the reform process. The interventionism of national governments and the resistance of traditional public administrations against this reform have been tried to be broken by the pressure of international institutions.

Concerns about the state interventionism have become more evident since the 1980s. The multinational corporations, which consider the state to be dominant in the most profitable investment areas, have suggested that the free trade will develop and profitability and prosperity will be increased by removing the obstacles to foreign investments by minimizing the state as much as possible, reducing its interventionism and privatization. WTO, GATT, OECD, MAI, G7, G20, UN and the EU have been the main international organizations to accelerate the process.

Neoliberal ideology-based insights expressed as lar Public Administration li and de Management Restructuring; In the public service provision of the state, they put forward the view that the principles of sensitivity to cost, reduction of bureaucracy and customer-oriented service principles should be taken into consideration. Manageralism, which means that the business principles adopted by the private sector can also be applied in the public sector, emerged as a necessity to provide an effective, efficient and economic service to public administration. Neoliberal approaches based on a market-friendly and supportive state administration, legitimacy, transparency, participation, effective and efficient state services. In practice, governance, privatization and Total Quality Management principles and principles of integration into the state administration and institutions, or even mandatory.

Governance, which is a multi-actor and mutual, that is, an interactive form of governance with the participation of the public sector - private sector - non-governmental organizations; In particular, it aims to enable local communities to participate in the decision-making process and thus have the responsibility and decision to take the services they need. On the basis of a multi-centered state structure, we can say that the process of decentralization-privatization and marketization is a key concept in the realization of governance. In particular, private sector participation and cooperation in the provision of public services are among the primary objectives of governance. It is the success criterion of the neoliberal process that public enterprises are transferred to the private sector by the privatization method, and the public and structural arrangements are made in order to benefit from the private sector participation of the public.

These radical changes in the state administration and public administration have also shown themselves in the service conceptions offered by the public. The concepts of authority width, privatization and civilization are various applications of the term modernization.

FUTURE RESEARCH DIRECTIONS

With the rise of neoliberalism, from the model shaped as New Public Management (YKI) inspired reforms, the results of public administration to date radical transformations. Within this scope, the state public service areas that can be opened to the market, services that cannot be "marketed" are transferred to autonomous organizations, agencies, regional and local administrations. However, since the 2000s, the GIQ model and its applications have been subjected to severe criticism. Especially in the fight against the ongoing global financial crisis minimal state ineffective and disasters and social problems affecting whole life institutional structures that are ineffective in the face of the government have been discredited and capable state discourses have come to the forefront.

REFERENCES

Acemoğlu, D., & Robinson, J. A. (2016). *Diktatörlük ve Demokrasinin Ekonomik Kökenleri, 2. Basım*. İstanbul, Turkey: Bağlam Press.

Akbulut, Ö. (2007). Kamu Yönetiminde İşletmecilik Sorunu. *Mülkiye Journal, 254*, 73–86.

Aksoy, Ş. (2003). *Yeni Sağ ve Devletin Değişimi, Türkiye'de Kamu Yönetimi* (B. Aykaç, Ş. Durgun, & H. Yayman, Eds.). Ankara, Turkey: Yargı Press.

Alavi, H., & Khusro, A. (1971). Pakistan The burden of US Aid. In R. I. Rhodes (Ed.), *Imperialism and Underdevelopment*. New York, NY: Monthly Review Press.

Amin, S. (1977). *Accumulation on a world scale, A critique of the theory of underdevelopment*. New York, NY: Monthly Review Press.

Arıboğan, D. Ü. (2001). *Globalleşme Senaryosunun Aktörleri*. İstanbul, Turkey: Der Press.

Balcı, A. (2005). *Kamu Yönetiminde Çağdaş Yaklaşımlar ve Kamu Hizmet Sunumuna Etkileri*. Ankara, Turkey: Hizmet İş Union Press.

Balkız, Ö. (2007). *Sanayi Sonrası Dönüşüm: Ekonomik Analizler*, (Unpublished dissertation), Adnan Menderes University, Social Sciences Institute, Turkey.

Baltacı, C. (2004). Yeni Sağ Üzerine Bir Eleştiri. *Süleyman Demirel University Economic and Administrative Sciences Faculty Journal*, *2*, 359–373.

Canpolat, N. (2004). Merkez Bankası Yüzmekten Korkuyor mu?, *İşletme-Finans Journal,* July, 76–85.

Carvalho, F. J. (2000). The changing role and strategies of the IMF and the perspectives for the emerging countries. *Brazilian Journal of Political Economy*, *20*(1), 3–17.

Çelik, M. Y. (2010). Küreselleşme Kalkınma İlişkisi. *Dumlupınar Üniversitesi Social Sciences Institute Journal*, *26*, 183–196.

Chang, H. J. (2003). *Globalization, economic development and the role of the state*. London, UK: Zed Books Press.

Chang, H. J., & Ve Gabriel, I. (2016). *Kalkınma Yeniden*. Ankara, Turkey: İmage Press.

Chossudovsky, M. (1999). *Yoksulluğun Küreselleşmesi: IMF ve Dünya Bankası Reformlarının İçyüzü* (N. Domaniç, Trans.). İstanbul, Turkey: Çivi Yazıları Press.

Demir, G. (1999). *Asya Krizi ve IMF*. İstanbul, Turkey: Der Press.

Dubiel, H. (1998). *Yeni Muhafazakarlık Nedir?* (E. Özbek, Trans.). İstanbul, Turkey: İletişim Press.

Ener, M. & Demircan, S. E. (2004). *Küreselleşen Dünyada IMF Politikaları ve Türkiye*, Ankara, Turkey: Roma Press.

Erdoğdu, S. (2004). Kamu Personel Rejiminde Uyarlanma, *Kamu Yönetimi Temel Kanunu Symposium*, Ankara, Turkey: TMMOB.

Erdönmez Ataman, P., & Tulay, B. (1999). Küresel Krizlere Yeni Yaklaşımlar. *Bankacılar Journal*, *31*, 64–76.

Frederickson, G. (1971). Toward a new public administration, The Minnowbrook Perspective, Marini Frank (Ed.), San Francisco,CA: Chandler Publishing.

Ghai, D. (1995). *Yapısal Uyum, Küresel Bütünleşme ve Sosyal Demokrasi, Piyasa Güçleri ve Küresel Kalkınma* (R. Prendergast & F. Stewart, Eds.). İstanbul, Turkey: Yapı Kredi Press.

Giray, F. (2003). Çok taraflı Yatırım Anlaşması (MAİ) ve Alternatif Öneriler Üzerine Bir Değerlendirme. *Mülkiye Journal*, *240*, 135–160.

Göze, A. (1998). *Liberal, Marxist, Faşist ve Sosyal Devlet*. İstanbul, Turkey: Beta Press.

Gözlü, S. (1996). Kamu Hizmeti Veren Kuruluşlarda Toplam Kalite Yönetimi, *Kamu Yönetimi Disiplini Symposium*, Ankara, Turkey TODAIE Press.

Gülalp, H. (1993). *Kapitalizm, Sınıflar ve Devlet* (O. Akınhay, Trans.). İstanbul, Turkey: Belge Press.

İnsel, A. (1997). Geçmişten Geleceğe. *Birikim Journal, 104*, 19–29.

Işıklı, A. (1997). Kamu Kesimi ve Siyasal Rejimin Demokratikleşmesi. *Mülkiyeliler Birliği Journal, 200*, 75–79.

İyibozkurt, E. (1999). *Küreselleşme ve Türkiye*. Bursa, Turkey: Ezgi Press.

Jary, D. & Jary, J. (1991). Fordism and Post-Fordism, The Harpercollins Dictionary of Sociology. New York, NY: Harper Perennial Press.

Jessop, B. (1994). The transition to post-Fordism and the Schumpeterian workfare state. In R. Burrows & B. Loader (Eds.), *Towards a post-Fordist welfare state?* London, UK: Oxford Press. doi:10.4324/9780203359846_chapter_2

Jessop, B. (1994). *Post Fordism and the state* (A. Amin, Trans.). London, UK: Black Well Publishers. doi:10.1002/9780470712726.ch8

Kalkandelen, A. H. (1998). Kamu Yönetiminde Yeniden Yapılanma (Süreç ve Aşamalar). *Türk İdare Journal, 420*, 97–109.

Kazgan, G. (1997). *Küreselleşme ve Yeni Ekonomik Düzen*. İstanbul, Turkey: Altın Kitaplar Press.

Kazgan, G. (2002). *Küreselleşme ve Ulus – Devlet: Yeni Ekonomik Düzen*. İstanbul, Turkey: İstanbul Bilgi University Press.

Kettl, D. (1997). The global revolution in public management: Driving themes, missing links. *Journal of PolicyAnalysis and Management, 16*(3), 446–462. doi:10.1002/(SICI)1520-6688(199722)16:3<446::AID-PAM5>3.0.CO;2-H

Kissinger, H. (2002). *Amerika'nın Dış Politikaya İhtiyacı Var mı?* (T. Evyapan, Trans.). Ankara, Turkey: METU Press.

Kızılcık, R. (2003). 21. Yüzyılda Yönetişim ve Kamu Yönetimi, Yeni Eğilimler ve Yeni Teknikler. *Türk İdare Journal, 438*, 181–193.

Klicksberg, B. (1993). *Redesigning the state profile for social and economic development change*. Toluca, Mexico: Clarendon Press.

Leys, C. (1992). Azgelişmişlik ve Bağımlılık: Eleştirel Notlar, Emperyalizm, Gelişme ve Bağımlılık Üzerine, M. Ersoy (Ed.), Ankara, Turkey: Verso Press, pp. 75-92.

O'Brien, P. J. (1992). In M. Ersoy (Ed.), *Latin Amerikan Bağımlılık Kuramlarına Bir Eleştiri, Emperyalizm, Gelişme ve Bağımlılık Üzerine* (pp. 23–40). Ankara, Turkey: Verso Press.

Önder, İ. (2002). GATS ve Kamu Hizmetleri. *Mülkiye Journal, 235*, 65–75.

Özdek, Y. (1999). Globalizmin İdeolojik Hegemonyası: Yanılsamalar. *Amme İdaresi Journal, 32*, 25–47.

Öztürk, N. (2002). IMF'nin Değişen Rolü ve Gelişmekte Olan Ülke Ekonomilerine Etkileri. *Ankara University SBF Journal, 57*(4), 95–125.

Peker, K. (2008). *Yeni Sağ Düşünce Ekseninde Belediye Hizmet Anlayışı* (Unpublished dissertation), Sakarya University Social Sciences İnstitute, Turkey.

Philippe, B. (1991). *Muhafazakârlık* (C. Akalın, Trans.). İstanbul, Turkey: İletişim Press.

Raffınot, M. (1998). *Borç Krizinden Sonra Kalkınmayı Nasıl Finanse Ederiz? Üçüncü Dünya'nın Sonu mu?* (A. İnsel, B. Gürbüz, & A. Akarçay, Trans.). İstanbul, Turkey: İletişim Press.

Rhodes, R. A. W. (1996). The new governance: Governing without government. *Political Studies*, *44*(4), 652–667. doi:10.1111/j.1467-9248.1996.tb01747.x

Sallan Gül, S. (1998). *Kamu Yönetiminde Kalite, Piyasa ve Müşteri Arayışlarının İdeolojik Temelleri.* Ankara, Turkey: TODAİE Press.

Sallan Gül, S. (2004). *Sosyal Devlet Bitti Yaşasın Piyasa.* İstanbul, Turkey: Etik Press.

Saran, U. (2001). Küresel Değişimin Dinamikleri Kamu Yönetimi Alanındaki Etkileri. *Türk İdare Journal*, *4333*, 41–49.

Şaylan, G. (2002a). *Değişim Küreselleşme ve Devletin Yeni İşlevi.* Ankara, Turkey: İmge Press.

Şaylan, G. (2002b). *Postmodernizm.* Ankara, Turkey: İmge Press.

Şaylan, G. (2003). *Kamu Yönetimi Disiplininde Bunalım ve Yeni Açılımlar Üzerine Düşünceler, Türkiye'de Kamu Yönetimi* (B. Aykaç, Ş. Durgun, & H. Yayman, Eds.). Ankara, Turkey: Yargı Press.

Sayre Wallace, S. (1997). Kamu Yönetiminin İlkeleri, Tr.: Erkan Oyal, Amme idaresi Journal, 4, 135–138.

Şenses, F. (2004). Neoliberal Küreselleşme Kalkınma için Bir Fırsat mı, Engel mi? *ERC Working Paper in Economic.*

Seyidoğlu, H. (1994). *Uluslararası İktisat.* İstanbul, Turkey: Beta Press.

Tatar Peker, A. (1996). Dünya Bankası: Büyüme Söyleminden İyi Yönetme Söylemine. *Toplum ve Bilim Journal*, *69*, 5–59.

Taylor, P. J., & Colin, F. (2000). *Political geography: World-economy, nation-state and locality.* London, UK: Prentice Hall.

Tekeli, İ. (2003). *Yönetim Kavramı Yanı sıra Yönetişim Kavramının Gelişmesinin Nedenleri Üzerine, Türkiye'de Kamu Yönetimi* (B. Aykaç, Ş. Durgun, & H. Yayman, Eds.). Ankara, Turkey: Yargı Press.

Tutum, C. (1994). *Kamu Yönetiminde Yeniden Yapılanma.* Ankara, Turkey: TESAV Press.

Ülman, B. (2001). *Uzun Süreçte Küreselleşme: Bir Sihirli Kavramı Tarihteki Yerine Koyma Denemesi, Küreselleşme ve Ulus Devlet.* İstanbul, Turkey: Yıldız Technic University, Strategic Reseraches Center Press.

Wood, E. M. (2003). *Kapitalizmin Kökeni* (A. C. Aşkın, Trans.). Ankara, Turkey: Epos Press.

Yağcı, F. (2001). Dünya Ekonomisi Nasıl Yönetiliyor?, *İktisat Journal*, 416, 24–32.

Yoon, H. (2005). The changing role of the IMF: Evidence from Korea's crisis. *Asian Perspective*, *29*(2), 179–201.

ADDITIONAL READING

Arslan, N. T. (2010). Klasik-neo klasik dönüşüm süreci: Yeni kamu yönetimi. *CÜ Economic and Administrative Sciences Journal*, *11*(2), 21–38.

Dunleavy, P., & Hood, C. (1994). From old public administration to new public management. *Public Money & Management*, *14*(3), 9–16. doi:10.1080/09540969409387823

İnsel, A. (2013). *Neo-liberalizm: Hegemonyanın yeni dili*. İletişim Press.

Lane, J. E. (2002). *New public management: an introduction*. Routledge. doi:10.4324/9780203467329

Rhodes, R. A. W. (1996). The new governance: Governing without government. *Political Studies*, *44*(4), 652–667. doi:10.1111/j.1467-9248.1996.tb01747.x

Saklı, A. R. (2013). Kamu yönetimi disiplininde bunalım ve çıkış yolu arayışları. *Dokuz Eylül University Social Sciences Journal*, *15*(1), 145–171.

Tunçer, P. (2013). Değişim yönetimi. *The International Journal of Social Sciences (Islamabad)*, *6*(2), 891–915.

Vickers, M. H., & Kouzmin, A. (2001). 'Resilience'in organizational actors and rearticulating 'voice': Towards a humanistic critique of new public management. *Public Management Review*, *3*(1), 95–119. doi:10.1080/14616670010009478

KEY TERMS AND DEFINITIONS

Deregulation: The state of reducing or abolishing state restrictions in a particular business or segment.

Fordism: The production system that Henry Ford pioneered, including the introduction of the production line.

Governance: The mutual dialogue of these processes by involving relevant stakeholders in decision-making and implementation processes. and in a pluralistic way.

New Public Management: Privatization and alternative services through the presentation methods, the role of the state conception.

Postfordism: The abandonment of the mass production of very large quantities of similar products, and the introduction of a flexible production line model that is able to adapt to sudden changes in demand with a small number of different types of production.

The New Right Approach: The understanding of liberalism as a synthesis of market economy and limited state principles and conservatism's emphasis on social values.

Welfare State: Providing people a comfortable, healthy and safe life state.

Chapter 9
Is Turkey a Favorable Environment for FDIs?
Institutional Outlook to EU-Turkey FDI Flow

Memduh Alper Demir
https://orcid.org/0000-0002-9926-2611
University of Kastamonu, Turkey

ABSTRACT

The aim of this chapter is to measure the impact of institutional variables such as economic freedom and democracy on foreign direct investment from the European Union to Turkey. In this framework, the author models institutional factors affecting foreign direct investments. The model includes economic freedom index, political rights, civil liberties of Turkey, and Gross Domestic Products of selected European countries. In theoretical part, the perspective of institutional economics on economic freedoms and democracy is discussed. A brief literature about the relationship between foreign direct investments and economic freedoms and democracy is revealed. Stochastic frontier analysis was used in the implementation to show the relationship between variables and efficiency of European countries' foreign direct investments to Turkey. Proposals for policy implication have been made in the conclusion part. This chapter shows civil liberties and economic freedom index have positive effect on foreign direct investments that supports institutionalists.

INTRODUCTION

Institutional economics reveals that the institutional structure that constitutes the political and social environment of the countries should be operated effectively. In this context the factors like the low perception of corruption, strength of property rights, protection of political-economic rights and freedoms, ensuring political stability, the rule of law etc. should be intact. The effective functioning of the institutions will prevent waste of resources in the country, eliminate market failures, decrease the uncertain-

DOI: 10.4018/978-1-7998-0333-1.ch009

Copyright © 2020, IGI Global. Copying or distributing in print or electronic forms without written permission of IGI Global is prohibited.

ties, diminish transaction costs, create positive externalities, create a safe environment for investments. Achieving high level of development of countries will be provided to the extent that economic institutions and institutional structure can promote production-investment decisions. This investment can be foreign investment as well as domestic ones.

The interaction between institutions and Foreign Direct Investment (FDI) has been obtaining increasing attention. One of the reasons is that the number of studies mentioning institutional importance as a determinant of economic growth has increased in the literature on economic growth. Therefore, as FDI is largely linked to economic growth, it has become important to study the link between FDI and institutions. In emerging economies, the role of institutional parameters as indicators of FDI is crucial. With the expanding globalization since 1980, adjustments in trade and investment environment policies of emerging market governments are facilitating FDI in these markets. These economies have become attractive for many multinational corporations due to their growth performance and large market sizes. An emerging market can be described as a country where its national economy is growing rapidly, its industry is changing structurally, its market is tempting but volatile, its regulatory environment promotes economic liberalization and the adoption of a free - market system, and its government is lowering organizational and bureaucratic control over business operations (Dumludağ and Sükrüoğlu, 2007:134-135).

In addition to the geo-political position of Turkey have democratic and secular political system and free market compared to the Middle Eastern neighbors. In other words, Turkey is closer to western standards in comparison to other Middle Eastern countries. The European Union is one of the most capital-exporting regions to the global economy and has also a continuous increase in direct investment to Turkey. Turkey have some causal agents such as low and abundant factor of production, a robust consumer profile and dynamic labor market. Because of these factors European Union does not want to lose Turkey market. So, EU increases investments to Turkey. The Customs Union treaty signed between Turkey and the EU in 1996, it has also accelerated foreign direct investment coming to Turkey from the EU. Also in this process, in particular the European Union including Turkey took against the Copenhagen criteria. Copenhagen Criteria, which is democratic and transparency criteria of the European Union has been active in investment decisions will make foreign investors to Turkey.

Consequently, the purpose of this study is to measure the impact of institutional variables such as economic freedoms and democracy on FDIs between the European Union and Turkey. In this context, the next section reveals the perspective of Institutional Economics on Economic Freedoms and Democracy, in the second chapter literature review of the linkage between FDIs and Economic Freedoms and Democracy is given, the section three and four consist of econometric methodology of the study, data and empirical findings, respectively. Finally, findings are discussed in the last section.

The Perspective of Institutional Economics on Economic Freedoms and Democracy

Economic freedom is a compound that seeks to describe the level to which an economy is a market economy — that is, the level to which it involves the facility of voluntary contracts under a stable and predictable rule of law upholding contracts and preventing private property, with limited interventionism in the form of government ownership, regulations and taxes. It is likely for purely theoretical reasons that economic freedom is an important factor accounting for economic growth. The incentives faced by economic players (entrepreneurs, inventors, financiers, industrialists, and others) are strongly influenced by the institutions in place, which, as Douglass C. North (1990) figures out, may be ineffective or effective. They make a contribution to economic growth to the degree that the institutions revive actions that subscribe to producing more precious output. Institutions able to provide growth-enhancing incentives have the capacity to assure economic freedom for several cases (Berggren, 2003: 194-196).

Murphy et al. (1991) stated that a superior return to productive efforts by low taxes, independent judicial system, and private property conservation; institutions are allocated where they produce the greatest value (Berggren, 2003:197). If the corporate profit tax rate falls. This fall may relate to improving property rights as indicated by North and Thomas (1973), as well as reducing corruption or taxes. This brings high rewards to official institutions that have well - specified property rights over private wealth. Public officials or the army have significant authority and caution, they can expand their operations and collect larger amounts without being hindered by law or custom. In this regard, less defined property rights are responsible not only for entrepreneurs ' large potential markets, but also for entrepreneurs ' ability to perform bigger 'firms' (Murphy et.al, 1991: 506-520). After discussions about property rights and tax burden, it is concluded that the effect of independent judicial system on economic freedoms is inevitable. However, the independent judicial system is sometimes a subject to democracy. The important point is that institutional economists explains the independent judicial system is undeniable for the development of the economy.

Law in its various forms (constitutions, statutes, common law, contract terms, etc.) is the most important and prevalent type of formal institution, so the focus on institutions is often on the law. Legal issues are at the heart of their science for many new institutionalists. The rule of law is the legal embodiment of freedom and the fundamental concept of the freedom law. The concept is open to interpretations of various kinds. The first, most popular understanding of the term, by arbitrary forms of government, separates rule or rule of law from rule. In contrast to powerful persons, it emphasizes the rule of impersonal law. Political power can be exercised only within legal constraints, according to the rule of law, so that government is placed under the law. It limits government functions to those that can be performed through general rules. The second separate but related definition considers the rule of law to be a ' meta - legal ' principle to guide lawmakers. The rule of law is the precondition for the individual's concrete rights, including those economic freedoms that are most prominent to entrepreneurship. ' The rule of law can be likened with a tree that brings forth the fruits of liberty from the unseen deep roots of freedom and grows and shines in magnificence. In the lack of the rule of law, government agencies are inclined to problem a flood of arbitrary and inconsistent decrees that can break the sense of agency of individuals and hence their awareness of opportunities (Harper, 2003:64-65).

As a result, established institutions set the economic incentives in any given period and impact what high and stable economic freedom enables a dynamic economy to function and grow, although an increase in economic freedom from a low exerts a much more different influence on the growth rate over a certain period of time. In addition, sustained high growth rates finally mention big wealth, and long - term economic freedom that increases growth can also increase accumulated wealth (Berggren, 2003:197). Finally, if the resources needed for economic growth cannot be obtained from internal dynamics, they are obtained from foreign sources through foreign direct investments. Therefore, the necessity of economic freedoms for economic growth proposed by institutional economists is indirectly valid for foreign direct investments.

According to many economists, liberal democracy is the most fundamental institution for economic growth. Liberal values such as freedom of expression and association, the existence of multiparty elections, protection of human rights and the existence of separation of powers constitute the institutional framework and process in which economic development will take place. According to this view, democracy facilitates the transfer of economic powers, provides a stable investment environment (Doğan, 2005:4).

One of the first institutionalists to highlight democracy as a "principle of concomitant value" was Marc Tool. Clarence E. Ayres had written, for one reason only, that "democracy is better than other systems: it is more efficient in the long run. The connection between instrumental valuation and democracy depends on the understanding that human beings are able to think and act instrumentally. This means that causally they can reason. Evolving societies are constantly defining and redefining what a reasonable society, a serviceable society, maybe even a "just society" means to them at any time. A fair society — that is, a society that improves human life— goes far beyond a lack of racism based on race, gender, ethnicity, etc. To be sure, it's intolerable. In the service of optimal (maximum) output, the presence of such states of affairs, and such other fact as high unemployment, restricts the "efficient" distribution of resources. Similarly, instrumental valuation leads to a view of the consequences of concentrated economic power - actually, of any kind of concentrated power. In summary, key components of instrumental valuation and instrumental efficiency critical requirements are the universal aspects of free inquiry, dissent tolerance, and empirical verification. Democracy is certainly the best hope of ultimately reconciling belief with proper critical interrelationship assessments. This is how instrumental thinking continually reshapes the condition of person, offering the maximum potential for real progress. This binds together democracy and instrumental valuation symbiotically. (Klein and Miller, 1996:272-275). Bhagwati compared authoritarian regimes with democratic regimes. It states that technical innovations are necessary for continuous development and this leads to an environment that facilitates the development of entrepreneurship. It is not right to consider that democracy is better for development in absolute terms. Even if the country has democratic institutions that facilitate the creation of new ideas and technologies, the possibility of transforming these ideas and technologies into productive production will be limited in the absence of markets. As a result, democracy and markets should be considered as twin pillars in building continuous development (Bhagwati, 2002:158-159).

Linkage Between FDIs and Economic Freedoms and Democracy: Literature Review

Companies evaluate several economic, social and political factors of the host country when they choose the countries, they will invest in. Among the economic determinants occupied broad place in the literature are technology, labor and commodity costs, trade deficit, trade barriers, openness, exchange rate, taxes, inflation, growth rate, infrastructure investments and market size. In addition to economic factors; corruption, political instability, democracy/freedom and weak institutional qualities also influence foreign direct investments (Demir et. al., 2018: 1080). Considering this, there are so many studies that investigate the linkage between FDIs and economic freedoms and democracy. In this section, it is summarized this relationship literature concerning Turkey. There are few studies directly about Turkey. Şahin (2018) examined the relationship between direct foreign capital investments, economic freedoms and economic growth in BRICS-T countries using the data for the period 1995-2014.The causality of economic freedom to foreign direct investment has been only observed for Turkey. Acaravcı et al. (2018) investigated the institutional quality in Turkey's economy, real income and long-term foreign direct investment relationships between 1990- 2015 period with ARDL method. The study emphasizes the importance of institutional factors in the entry of foreign direct investments. For this reason, efforts to increase institutional quality will encourage foreign direct investment inflows. The effects of democracy on foreign direct investment inflows were estimated by Farazmand and Moradi (2015). Using data from 1990 to 2012, Malaysia, Philippines, Singapore, Thailand and Turkey are represented. Democratic systems are shown to increase the flow of FDI to developing countries. Arslan and Okten (2010) investigated the relationship between FDI and democracy in Turkey from 1970 to 2010. The results of the analysis of co-integration show that there is a long - term relationship between FDIs and democracy. In addition, model suggests a causal unidirectional relationship between democracy and FDIs. Apart from these studies, in the literature, there are so many studies describing the relationship between foreign direct investments, economic freedoms and democracy with panel data regressions. Turkey is included in the data sets in most of these studies. But there is no country-specific result for Turkey because of the nature of panel data regressions. However, some studies that include Turkey as an id are explained as below.

Oransay and Mike (2016) modelled socio-political factors which influencing foreign direct investment as ownership rights such as independence of the legal system, fairness and suitability of competition conditions, transparency of applied policies and political stability. According to the estimation results; there is a positive relationship between socio-political factors and direct foreign investments. Kazemi and Saini (2017) investigated the relationship between economic freedoms, foreign direct investment and democracy was analyzed for 87 countries between 1981 and 2010. The results of the analysis showed that economic freedoms positively affected foreign direct investments. The findings of the analysis showed that democracy has no important role in attracting foreign direct investments. Badri and Sheshgelani (2017) analyzed the effect of economic freedoms on foreign direct investment by panel data method between 2001 and 2013 for 10 developing countries. Analysis findings showed that economic freedoms affect the foreign direct investments positively. Moreover, the developed free market and financial development index are factors that have a positive and significant effect on FDI. Beheshtitabar and Irgaliyev (2008) analyzed the effects of economic freedoms on direct foreign capital inflows for 43 developing countries and 12 Middle Eastern countries between 1995-2006. In this study, the effects of corruption, public expenditures, commercial and investment freedom indicators on foreign direct investment are discussed as economic freedoms. As a result, it was seen that only the freedom of trade and freedom of investment had a significant effect on foreign direct investments. Azman - Saini et al. (2013) reviewed the role of economic freedom in attracting FDI inflows from 1981 to 2005 for 75 countries. They showed that the positive impact of economic freedom on local decisions by multinational enterprises to send FDI to a specific country is unquestionable. They illustrated that greater economic freedom leads to a business environment that is more enabling. Azman-Saini *et al.* (2010) investigated the systemic link between economic freedom, foreign direct investment (FDI) and economic growth in a panel of 85 countries. FDI's effect on the level of economic freedom in the host countries is contingent It means that countries benefit significantly from the presence of multinational corporations to promote greater freedom of economic activity. Ghazalian and Amponsem (2019) examined the effects of economic freedoms and its sub-components reflecting the quality of institutions on FDI inflows. The results emphasized positive effects of economic freedoms on FDI inflows. Busse (2003) analyzed the complex relationship between democracy and FDI empirically. They illustrated that multinational investments in democratic countries were significantly higher, thus confuting the hypothesis that FDI is fostered by political repression. Li and Resnick (2003) stated that FDI inflows are reduced by democratic institutions by using data for 53 developing countries from 1982 to 1995. Demir et. al. (2018) determined the influence of economic, social and political indicators on foreign direct investment of selected countries. They stated that foreign direct investments were significantly affected by economic freedoms but not from democracy.

It is shown that literature about subject is not in consensus. Economic freedoms usually effect foreign direct investments, but it cannot be thought for democracy. Democracy variables sometimes do not affect foreign direct investments. It is concluded that this situation occurred for some reasons. These are proxies for democracy variables, time span and/or country selection of the analysis.

Econometric Methodology

In this part of the study, methodology is given used in analysis. In this context, the methodology of panel stochastic frontier analysis technique is discussed. Panel data analysis is the whole of the statistical methods used in the analysis of observations of the same entities like same individuals, companies, firms and countries with observations at multiple time points. In other words, panel data observes the relations of country or company units with multiple time dimensions.

When the performance of economic units is the subject to discussion, the concepts of productivity and efficiency are important. Productivity is the ratio of output to input. But efficiency means the ratio of the potential output (or input) to the observed output (or input) (Fried et.al., 2008:6). Although the concept of efficiency is as old as neoclassical economics, studies on measurement have begun with Koopmans (1951), Debreu (1951) and empirically with Farrell (1957) (Daraio and Simar, 2007:16; Kalirajan and Shand, 1999:150). The measurement of the technical efficiency involves comparing the actual values of the input and output with their potential values. In general, efficiency analysis can be applied in all areas where the potential values and observed values differ. The volume of foreign direct investment and potential foreign direct investment volume may change so it is aimed to make a comparison between the countries and to contribute to the policy formation for the improvement of the efficiency values obtained.

Potential values need to be estimated because there are no observable quantities. Some approaches have been developed to perform this estimation process and to measure technical efficiency. In the literature, nonparametric Data Envelopment Analysis (DEA) and parametric Stochastic Frontier Analysis (SFA) are the most widely accepted ones. Stochastic frontier analysis was independently proposed by Aigner - Lovell et al. (1977) and Meusen - Broeck (1977). Unlike the DEA models, this model consists random error term. Thus, deviations from the maximum output are not entirely attributed to inefficiency, in which the term error is divided into two parts as the term ineffective effects and the term random error. The estimation of the stochastic frontier function can be used as a cross section (data set where each unit is observed once) or panel data (data set where each unit is observed at more than one-time point) (Demir ve Bilik, 2018:32).

The stochastic frontier function using the panel data can be expressed as follows;

$$y_{it} = \beta x_{it} + v_{it} - u_i$$

$$v_{it} \sim i.i.d.N\left(0,\sigma_v^2\right)$$

$$u_i \sim i.i.d.N^+\left(\mu,\sigma_v^2\right) \quad (1)$$

here; x refers to input, y is output. In the frontier function, the term error is divided into two parts. The first one (v_{it}) is a random error term which is not under the control of the unit being examined and ensures that the frontier function is stochastic. The second (u_i) refers to the effects of inefficiency. In the equation, as can be understood from the index of the term u the inefficiency effects in the model does not change according to time. Battese-Coelli (1988), Pitt-Lee (1981) models can be shown as examples of time-invariant inefficiency models. If the time period considered in the estimation of the frontier function is long, the assumption that ineffectiveness does not change over time may lead to misleading results. This rigid assumption has been eliminated with time-varying inefficiency models. Examples of time-varying inefficiency models are Cornwell-Schmidt et al. (1990), Kumbhakar (1990), Battese - Coelli (1992), Lee - Schmidt (1993), Battese-Coelli (1995) models. As mentioned earlier, the measurement of technical effectiveness involves comparing the actual values of the input and output with their potential values. In general, efficiency analysis can be applied in all areas where the potential values and observed values differs (Demir ve Bilik, 2018: 32- 33). So, stochastic frontier analysis was also used in this study.

Jondrow et al. (1982) formula was used to estimate country specific efficiency scores. Jondrow et al. (1982) proposed the following formula;

$$E\left(u_i|\varepsilon_i\right)=\sigma_*\frac{\varnothing\left(\frac{\mu_{*i}}{\sigma_*}\right)}{\varphi\left(\frac{\mu_{*i}}{\sigma_*}\right)}+\mu_{*i} \qquad (2)$$

the parameters μ_{*i} and σ_* contained in the equation are defined as follows;

$$\mu_{*i}=\frac{-\sigma_u^2\epsilon_i}{\sigma^2} \text{ and } \sigma_*^2=\frac{\sigma_v^2\sigma_u^2}{\sigma^2},\ \left(\sigma^2=\sigma_v^2+\sigma_u^2\right) \qquad (3)$$

From the equation 2, the technical efficiency is calculated, and it is $TE=\exp\left(-u_i\right)$ (Demir and Bilik, 2018:39).

Data and Empirical Findings

Data set of this study includes foreign direct investment flows of EU countries through Turkey, political rights (PR) and civil liberties (CL) data of Turkey for democracy proxies, Gross Domestic Products (GDP) of selected European Countries for investment capacity and economic freedom (EF) index of Turkey that averages of property rights, government integrity, tax burden, government spending, business freedom, labor freedom, monetary freedom, trade freedom, investment freedom and financial freedom indices. Democracy proxies obtained from Freedom House, GDPs obtained from World Bank, Economic freedom index is from Heritage foundation and finally foreign direct investments are from Central Bank of Turkey database. GDP and FDI data are in current dollars. Political rights and civil liberties are measured on a scale of one to seven, one of which is the highest degree of freedom and seven the lowest. Time span is

Table 1. The descriptive statistics of variables

Variable	Observations	Mean	Standard Deviation	Minimum	Maximum
Ln FDI	234	21.46	1.85	15.76	24.43
Ln PR	234	1.17	0.15	1.09	1.60
Ln CL	234	1.31	0.22	1,09	1.79
Ln EF	234	4.08	0.07	3.92	4.17
Ln GDP	234	27.09	1.21	23.78	28.98

2000 to 2017. Data set includes 13 countries in European Union because these countries included in the analysis were investing uninterrupted to Turkey in selected years. All variables are in logarithmic form. Table 1 gives descriptive statistics of variables.

The empirical phase of the study includes two stages. Firstly, stochastic frontier analysis is introduced as Battase and Coelli (1995) approach. Table 2 shows stochastic frontier results and then country specific results are shown by using Jondrov et. al (1982) formula in Table 3.

Depends on the estimation results, all variables other than political rights are significant. Depends on the further studies and theoretical expectations; GDP variable is positive and have significant effect on FDI. A %1 increase in GDPs of EU countries increases Turkey's FDI % 0.29. So that means growth in Europe also give chance to Turkey for growth. A significant and positive coefficient on the economic freedom index variable means that an increase in economic freedoms increases FDI. This situation is examined in the context of the other sub-indices constituting the content in the index. Thus, in the host country, labor and business markets, monetary institutions, trade, investment and financial sector have to be more independent. In addition, depending to sub-indices of economic freedom index some applications should be done for increasing economic freedoms. These are government expenditures have to be more transparent, government intervention on economy should be reduced, consumer rights should be increased, and tax burden should be eliminated. It is stated in the section 3 that democracy variables sometimes do not affect foreign direct investments. In this analysis, while political rights are insignificant,

Table 2. Estimation results of the stochastic frontier model

Variables	Coefficient	Z Scores	Prob
Constant	-10.97	-2.20*	0.028
Ln PR	0.11	0.13	0.898
Ln CL	-1.48	-2.28 *	0.022
Ln EF	6.83	6.07*	0.000
Ln GDP	0.29	4.36*	0.000
$\sigma^2(u)$	3.37	2.95*	0.003
$\sigma^2(v)$	0.62	6.33*	0.000
γ	5.39	4.76*	0.000
LOG LIKELIHOOD	-420.33		
* significance at 5%, $\gamma=\sigma^2(u)/\sigma^2(v)$, The variance of the efficiency is $\sigma^2(u)$ and the variance of the random error term is $\sigma^2(v)$			

Table 3. Efficiency scores of countries

	Austria	Belgium	Denmark	Finland	France	Germany	Greece	Italy	Lux.	Neth.	Spain	Sweden	UK
2000	0.1	2.9	0.6	0.6	13.7	16.1	0.2	6.0	7.0	57.5	0.6	0.4	11.4
2001	0.4	11.6	1.7	12.8	26.9	18.0	0.4	5.5	19.6	55.6	1.0	0.3	23.9
2002	0.7	13.6	3.4	10.0	28.9	30.7	1.2	10.8	18.0	60.7	2.0	2.0	31.9
2003	2.1	28.1	10.2	45.3	52.0	53.6	3.9	34.1	38.3	72.2	11.8	4.0	51.3
2004	1.8	18.3	5.3	37.6	36.9	44.9	2.4	19.9	24.7	69.6	8.9	2.7	35.7
2005	4.5	55.3	10.0	71.6	62.0	59.8	7.3	49.1	49.9	78.5	13.9	5.3	56.6
2006	7.0	49.9	5.6	61.8	42.6	37.0	31.2	29.3	40.2	71.5	11.2	2.6	40.0
2007	41.2	56.4	7.0	63.3	55.0	46.9	50.3	22.3	68.7	77.1	24.8	3.3	54.1
2008	18.2	23.9	2.7	38.9	24.3	20.1	32.3	5.8	48.6	63.6	8.8	1.1	24.6
2009	35.6	38.0	3.2	40.0	38.1	39.4	35.2	13.8	59.1	70.1	16.7	2.1	34.7
2010	45.7	33.0	2.6	34.3	28.1	41.8	34.6	14.3	62.0	69.5	18.6	1.8	39.9
2011	47.8	28.1	1.7	24.0	18.0	28.3	24.1	9.2	44.9	60.3	22.4	1.1	25.7
2012	69.9	18.7	5.9	48.4	41.5	54.7	39.4	26.2	66.2	76.4	53.3	3.8	50.4
2013	51.2	20.7	4.3	39.5	33.3	54.7	27.0	21.6	68.5	71.5	45.8	3.0	37.9
2014	52.6	18.9	3.8	38.3	34.5	50.1	26.8	22.4	68.7	70.3	43.8	2.9	34.5
2015	54.4	24.0	3.7	2.4	34.9	49.6	43.5	23.1	66.4	72.1	45.7	25.0	42.3
2016	64.8	33.4	4.7	34.1	37.9	58.7	2.0	32.6	71.2	76.2	54.3	4.9	44.7
2017	44.3	39.5	6.1	30.6	40.3	62.8	2.4	37.6	71.3	79.9	59.9	6.6	47.6

but civil liberties variable is significant. Civil liberties variable is negative, but it depends on nature of this variable. Because it is measured on a scale of one to seven, one is the highest degree of freedom and seven the lowest. So, the proliferation of civil liberties in Turkey is an effective in investment decisions of the European Union countries. More suggestions about variables are shown in conclusion part of study. FDI efficiency scores are supplied using the results of our model. Estimated efficiency scores of countries for the years 2000-2017 are submitted in Table 3. Efficiency is estimated to be 31.1 percent on average, maximum 79.9 percent and minimum 0.1 percent.

The annual distribution of the country's activity scores is uneven. This is because of FDI is not as continuous as trade data. In other words, the country that has a high direct FDI for a year does not show this performance for another year. Even in this case, Luxembourg, Netherlands and United Kingdom have better scores than other countries. After 2012, most of the scores were above the average score of 31.1. Especially, the scores of Germany, France, Austria, the Netherlands and England are remarkable. It is thought that the Turks abroad work well for to give information about the business environment in Turkey.

CONCLUSION

In this study results pointed out that the effect of institutional variables such as civil liberties and economic freedom on foreign direct investment flow from European Union to Turkey is significant and positive. In addition, this study also committed that Gross Domestic Products (GDP) of selected European Countries effect on FDIs is also positive and significant. It means that the size of the economies of the investing countries increases their investments to Turkey. So, this is the win-win situation. It is considered that the European Union countries will give weight to growth policies. Democratic countries have high civil liberties. It is thought that higher civil liberties increase the efficiency of the labor force. If a country has a high labor productivity, it will take more investment from abroad. Through this investment will enable the increase of country's growth. These results show that Turkey should give importance to the civil liberties. In this context, Turkey must be developed freedom of belief and expression, association and organizational rights, rule of law, personal autonomy and individual rights. Depends on the results of economic freedom variable, Turkey should develop some economic instruments to get better FDI from abroad. Subject to the sub-indices of economic freedom, Turkey have to be more liberal labor and business markets, monetary institutions, trade, investment and financial sector, government expenditures have to be more transparent, government intervention on economy should be reduced, consumer rights should be increased and tax burden should be eliminated.

As a result, institutional economists stated that the good functioning of the institutions of a country is effective in the economic growth of the country. The efficiency of institutions is ensured by the accessibility of the institutions and the dynamics of the market economy. In order to provide these two conditions some advances should be done. These are; more transparent government, more independent money and financial markets, elimination of tariff and non-tariff barriers in trade, ensuring fair distribution of taxes, protecting consumers, the decisions taken by governments are constructive in the business world. It is necessary to provide the environment of libertarian ideas on which free market economy is based. In other words, it is necessary in the formation of liberalism politically. This is achieved through the increase of civil liberties. All these conditions necessary for the economic growth process are valid for foreign direct investments. Because the countries provide economic growths by investments.

REFERENCES

Acaravcı, A., Artan, S., Erdoğan, S., & Bostan Göktürk, T. (2018). Türkiye'de kurumsal kalite,reel gelir ve doğrudan yabancı yatırımlar ilişkisi. *Mehmet Akif Ersoy Üniversitesi İktisadi ve İdari Bilimler Fakültesi Dergisi*, *5*(2), 132–145.

Aigner, D., Lovell, C. A. K., & Schmidt, P. (1977). Formulation and estimation of stochastic frontier production function models. *Journal of Econometrics*, *6*(1), 21–37. doi:10.1016/0304-4076(77)90052-5

Arslan, Ü., & Ökten, N. Z. (2010). The relations between FDI and democracy: Evidence from Turkey. *International Research Journal of Finance and Economics*, *56*, 111–123.

Azman-Saini, W. N. W., Baharumshah, A. Z., & Law, S. H. (2010). Foreign direct investment, economic freedom and economic growth: International evidence. *Economic Modelling*, *27*(5), 1079–1089. doi:10.1016/j.econmod.2010.04.001

Azman-Saini, W.N.W, Tun, Y., & Ibrahim, S. (2013). International evidence on the link between foreign direct investment and economic freedom. *Pertanika Journal of Social Sciences and Humanities, 21*(S), 157-170.

Badri, A. K., & Sheshgelanib, A. (2017). Economic freedom and FDI in selected developing countries. *Noble International Journal of Economics and Financial Research*, *2*(5), 82–87.

Battese, G. E., & Coelli, T. J. (1988). Prediction of firm-level technical efficiencies with a generalized frontier production function and panel data. *Journal of Econometrics*, *38*(3), 387–399. doi:10.1016/0304-4076(88)90053-X

Battese, G. E., & Coelli, T. J. (1992). Frontier production functions, technical efficiency and panel data: With application to paddy farmers in India. *Journal of Productivity Analysis*, *3*(1-2), 153–169. doi:10.1007/BF00158774

Battese, G. E., & Coelli, T. J. (1995). A model for technical inefficiency effects in a stochastic frontier production function for panel data. *Empirical Economics*, *20*(2), 325–332. doi:10.1007/BF01205442

Beheshtitabar, E. & Irgaliyev, A. (2008). *The impact of economic freedom on FDI inflows to developing countries: The case of the Middle East* (Unpublished bachelor thesis). Jönköping University, Sweden.

Berggren, N. (2003). The benefits of economic freedom: A survey. *Independent Review*, *8*(2), 193–211.

Bhagwati, J. N. (2002). Democracy and development: Cruel dilemma or symbiotic relationship? *Review of Development Economics*, *6*(2), 151–162. doi:10.1111/1467-9361.00147

Busse, M. (2003). Democracy and FDI. HWWA discussion paper No. 220, Hamburg Institute of International Economics, Germany.

Cornwell, C., Schmidt, P., & Sickles, R. C. (1990). Production frontiers with cross-sectional and time-series variation in efficiency levels. *Journal of Econometrics*, *46*(1-2), 185–200. doi:10.1016/0304-4076(90)90054-W

Daraio, C., & Simar, L. (2007). *Advanced robust and nonparametric methods in efficiency analysis: Methodology and applications*. New York, NY: Springer Science & Business Media.

Debreu, G. (1951). The coefficient of resource utilization. *Econometrica*, *19*(3), 273–292. doi:10.2307/1906814

Demir, M. A. & Bilik, M. (2018). Türkiye'nin ticaret etkinliği: Stokastik sınır çekim modeli yaklaşımı. *Ömer Halisdemir Üniversitesi İktisadi ve İdari Bilimler Fakültesi Dergisi*, *11*(1), 29-48.

Demir, M. A., Bilik, M., & Aydın, Ü. (2018). Effects of political and socio-economic indicators on foreign direct investments: Stochastic frontier analysis. *İnsan ve Toplum Bilimleri Araştırmaları Dergisi*, *7*(2), 1078-1096.

Doğan, A. (2005). Demokrasi ve ekonomik gelişme. *Erciyes Üniversitesi İktisadi ve İdari Bilimler Fakültesi Dergisi*, (25), 1-19.

Dumludağ, D., & Şükrüoğlu, D. (2007). The impact of macroeconomic and institutional variables on foreign direct investment flows in emerging markets. *Marmara Üniversitesi İİBF Dergisi*, *23*(2), 133–136.

Farazmand, H., & Moradi, M. (2015). Determinants of FDI: Does democracy matter? *Strategic Management*, *20*(1), 38–46.

Farrell, M. J. (1957). The measurement of productive efficiency. *Journal of the Royal Statistical Society. Series A (General), 120*(3), 253–290. doi:10.2307/2343100

Fried, H. O., Lovell, C. A. K., & Schmidt, S. S. (2008). Efficiency and productivity. In H. O. Fried, C. A. K. Lovell, & S. S. Schmidt (Eds.), *The Measurement of Productive Efficiency and Productivity Change* (pp. 1–89). Oxford, UK: Oxford Scholarship. doi:10.1093/acprof:oso/9780195183528.003.0001

Ghazalian, P. L., & Amponsem, F. (2019). The effects of economic freedom on FDI inflows: An empirical analysis. *Applied Economics, 51*(11), 1111–1132. doi:10.1080/00036846.2018.1524979

Harper, D. A. (2003). *Foundations of entrepreneurship and economic development.* New York, NY: Routledge. doi:10.4324/9780203380215

Jondrow, J., Knox Lovell, C. A., Materov, I. S., & Schmidt, P. (1982). On the estimation of technical inefficiency in the stochastic frontier production function model. *Journal of Econometrics, 19*(2-3), 233–238. doi:10.1016/0304-4076(82)90004-5

Kalirajan, K. P., & Shand, R. T. (1999). Frontier production functions and technical efficiency measures. *Journal of Economic Surveys, 13*(2), 149–172. doi:10.1111/1467-6419.00080

Kazemi, M., & Azman-Saini, W. N. W. (2017). Foreign direct investment, economic freedom and democracy. *International Journal of Economics & Management, 11*(1), 1–15.

Klein, P. A., & Miller, E. S. (1996). Concepts of value, efficiency, and democracy in institutional economics. *Journal of Economic Issues, 30*(1), 267–277. doi:10.1080/00213624.1996.11505776

Koopmans, T. C. (1951) An analysis of production as an efficient combination of activities. In T. C. Koopmans (Ed.), Activity analysis of production and allocation (pp. 225-287), Cawles Commission for Research in Economics Monograph No: 13, New York, NY: Wiley.

Kumbhakar, S. C. (1990). Production frontiers, panel data, and time-varying technical inefficiency. *Journal of Econometrics, 46*(1-2), 201–211. doi:10.1016/0304-4076(90)90055-X

Lee, Y. H., & Schmidt, P. (1993). A production frontier model with flexible temporal variation in technical inefficiency. In H. Fried & K. Lovell (Eds.), *The measurement of productive efficiency: Techniques and applications* (pp. 237–255). New York, NY: Oxford University Press.

Li, Q., & Resnick, A. (2003). Reversal of fortunes: Democratic institutions and foreign direct investment inflows to developing countries. *International Organization, 57*(1), 175–211. doi:10.1017/S0020818303571077

Meeusen, W., & van Den Broeck, J. (1977). Efficiency estimation from Cobb-Douglas production functions with composed error. *International Economic Review, 18*(2), 435–444. doi:10.2307/2525757

North, D. C. (1990). *Institutions, institutional change, and economic performance*. Cambridge, U.K.: Cambridge University Press. doi:10.1017/CBO9780511808678

North, D. C., & Thomas, R. P. (1973). *The rise of the western world: A new economic history*. Cambridge, UK: Cambridge University Press. doi:10.1017/CBO9780511819438

Oransay, G., & Mike, F. (2016). Doğrudan yabancı yatırımların sosyo-politik belirleyicileri üzerine bir analiz. [AKAD]. *Akademik Araştırmalar ve Çalışmalar Dergisi*, *8*(14), 97–107. doi:10.20990/kilisiibfakademik.264409

Pitt, M. M., & Lee, L. F. (1981). The measurement and sources of technical inefficiency in the Indonesian weaving industry. *Journal of Development Economics*, *9*(1), 43–64. doi:10.1016/0304-3878(81)90004-3

Şahin, D. (2018). BRICS-T ülkelerinde ekonomik özgürlükler ve doğrudan yabancı sermaya yatırımları arasındaki ilişki: Bootstrap panel nedensellik testi. *Bingöl Üniversitesi Sosyal Bilimler Enstitüsü Dergisi*, *8*(16), 285–294.

ADDITIONAL READING

Acemoglu, D., Johnson, S., & Robinson, J. (2005). Institutions as the Fundamental Cause of Long-Run Growth. In P. Aghion & S. N. Durlauf (Eds.), *Handbook of Economic Growth* (pp. 386–464). Amsterdam, Netherlands: North-Holland.

Banerjee, A. V., & Ghatak, M. (2005). Symposium on: Institutions and economic performance. *Economics of Transition*, *13*(3), 421–425. doi:10.1111/j.1468-0351.2005.00232.x

Coase, R. (1992). The institutional structure of production. *The American Economic Review*, *83*(4), 713–719.

Eggertsson, T. (1990). *Economic Behaviour and Institutions*. Cambridge, UK: Cambridge University. doi:10.1017/CBO9780511609404

Kasper, W., & Manfred, S. (1998). *Institutional Economics: Social Order and Public Policy*. Cheltenham, UK: E. Elgar Publishing.

Lipsey, R. E. (2001), "Foreign Direct Investment and the Operations of Multinational Firms: Concepts, History and Data. Working Paper 8665 *National Bureau of Economic Research* 1050 Massachusetts Avenue Cambridge:NBER, MA 02138.

Nunnenkamp, P. (2002). *Determinants of FDI in developing countries: has globalization changed the rules of the game?* (No. 1122). Kiel Working Paper.

KEY TERMS AND DEFINITIONS

Civil Liberties: It is the state of being subject only to laws established for the benefit of the community, particularly with regard to freedom of speech and action.

Democracy: It is a system of government, typically through elected representatives, by the entire population or by all eligible members of a state.

Efficiency: It means a performance level that describes how to use the least amount of input to achieve the highest output level.

European Union (EU): It is a group of countries in Europe continent that works as a connected economic and political block.

Foreign Direct Investments (FDI): It is an investment made by a firm or individual in one country into business interests located in another country.

Institutional Economics: It is an economics school that develops the importance of non - market factors (as social institutions) in influencing economic behaviour, subordinating economic analysis to sociological factors, history, and institutional development.

Chapter 10
The Effect of Democratization and Economic Freedom on Economic Growth

Ibrahim Orkun Oral
https://orcid.org/0000-0002-1949-6355
Ardahan University, Turkey

ABSTRACT

This chapter examines the impact of democratization and economic freedom on economic growth. For this purpose, according to the classification issued by the World Bank, three groups of countries, developed, developing, and underdeveloped, were included in the study. The impact of democratization and economic freedom on economic growth was tested by panel data analysis in the period of 1995-2012. As a result of the analysis, the relationship between democracy-economic freedom and economic growth has been different according to country groups. While there was a positive relationship between economic growth and democracy-economic freedom in developed and underdeveloped countries, a negative relationship was found in the developing country group.

INTRODUCTION

The notion of democracy dating back to the 5thB.C. is one of the concepts that have been discussed and kept important until today. Since the emergence of the concept of democracy, different theories of democracy have emerged and at the same time different definitions of democracy have emerged. Among these definitions, democracy is the most general definition of the basic principles of democracy; it is defined as the form of government that aims to enable people to have a better life standard based on the freedoms of individuals, to give them the right to choose, to be elected, to decide and to control.

The association of democracy with the economy gained momentum in the Second World War after some underdeveloped countries had declared freedom. The first study to link democracy to the economy was conducted in 1959 by Lipset. In this study, Lipset investigated the level of income and the sustainability of democracy. It was concluded that the countries with lower income levels are less democratic

DOI: 10.4018/978-1-7998-0333-1.ch010

Copyright © 2020, IGI Global. Copying or distributing in print or electronic forms without written permission of IGI Global is prohibited.

and the countries with higher income levels are more democratic. Other studies conducted on the subject showed similarity with Lipset's work.

Similarly, another variable associated with the economy is the notion of economic freedom. The economic freedoms that advocate the freedom and individual welfare of individuals in their economic activities were among the defences of the founder of classical economics Adam Smith and have been the subject of many researches until today. As a result of research on economic freedoms, the prevailing opinion is that economic performance will increase with the provision of freedoms in politically transparent societies.

In this context, since democracy and economic freedom have similar characteristics at many points, both concepts will be analysed in the same model and the effects of these concepts on economic growth will be analysed. In this chapter, firstly, after giving information about the concepts of democracy and economic freedom, previous studies on the subject will be included. Then, the findings obtained from the analysis will be included. Finally, results and evaluation will be presented.

THE CONCEPT OF DEMOCRACY

"Democracy is derived from the combination of the words "demos" and "keratin" in Ancient Greek. In this case, the most classical definition of democracy is the self-governance of the people." (Schmidt, 2001) Aristotle, an ancient Greek philosopher, describes democracy as a deviation from politia (Dursun, 2002).

In the definition of democracy based on freedoms, democracy; can be defined as a system where people only listen to the voice of their conscience and the administration is based on the consent of the people and the coercion is eliminated (Yılmaz, 2000). The freedoms contained in democracy by this definition of democracy; guaranteeing the physical and spiritual existence of the person freedom of expression, assembly and association and freedom of the press. Democracy in another study is defined as anything that allows the expression of freedom, and it is stated that freedom here means choosing any political system, lifestyle, religion and work (Stefan & Guimaraes, 2003). Keeping this in mind, Stefan reveals that democracy is a form of government in accordance with the decision of the majority, in accordance with the arrangements made to ensure the protection of individual and social rights of people.

When the historical development process of democracy is examined, it is seen that there are many period points. Magna Carta Libertatum, the Renaissance movements in Italy in the 1350s, the 1776 American Declaration of Independence, the 1789 French Revolution played an important role in the progress of democracy. In addition, it had a significant impact on the development of democracy in the first and second world wars. Samuel Huntington summarizes the development process of democracy as follows: (Huntington,1991)

1. First, long wave of democratization (1828-1926)
2. First reverse wave (1922- 1942)
3. Second, short wave of democratization (1943- 1962)
4. Second reserve wave (1958-1975)
5. Third wave of democratization (1974 -)

It may be stated that there is a need for an institutional structure in order to ensure the freedom in the democracies, to sustain and maintain the continuity. In this respect, Dahl (1971) argues that according to the democracy he advocates, democracies should have the following institutional features:

1. Freedom of expression
2. Right to vote
3. Freedom of organization and participation
4. The existence of different news sources
5. Free and fair elections
6. Right to participate in public duties
7. The right of political leaders to compete in order to win
8. The presence of institutions to base the Government policies on votes and other preference symptoms.

On the other hand democracy can be expressed in three categories according to the way it is implemented.

1. Direct democracy
2. Representative democracy
3. Semi-direct democracy

In the understanding of direct democracy, the decisions that are necessary for the state are taken by the society without intermediaries. On the other hand, in the concept of representative democracy, the sovereign right of the nation is transferred to the representatives elected by the nation. In this sense, the representatives use sovereignty on behalf of the nation. In semi-direct democracy which combines direct and representative democracy in a sense, there is participation in the nation as well as representatives.

Within the framework of the explanations, the indices related to measuring the concept of democracy on a global scale; Freedom House Index, Polity Index, Poe & Tate Index, Vanhanen Index, Bollen Index, Arat Index, Przeworski Democracy Index. Although different measurement tools are used, these indices are classified countries as democratic, semi-democratic and non-democratic. In this study, the Polity Index was preferred due to the fact that it contains more countries and more historical data. The Polity Index classifies countries in the range of -10 to +10.The Polity index shows the countries' democratic tendencies, on the basis of management transparency, political participation, political competition, restrictions on the head of government, competition in the election of the head of the country, administrative governance regulation.

THE CONCEPT OF ECONOMIC FREEDOM

Freedom concept in the philosophy; It is defined as the situation of self-determination, control and regulation of self-regulation or it is defined as the power to act according to the own wishes, not according to the orders and wishes of others (Cevizci, 2002).From this point of view, economic freedoms; it can be defined as the structure that mobilizes the free market system, minimizes state intervention, maximizes individual welfare, stimulates the dynamics of economic growth, directs the economy to natural equilibrium (Patry, 2009).

Adam Smith, the defender of the market economy states economic freedom; defined as free competition and protection of property rights. Similarly, Friedman, who was classical thought advocate, stated that economic freedom defined that has the right to protect property rights, to have special means of production, to be free of market entry and exit and to have the right to trade and to compete (Friedman, 2002).

In another definition of economic freedom, Berggren (2003) stated that free competition, small volume of government and low number of regulations. In another definition, Lawson (2003) emphasized property rights as well as free competition (Tunçsiper, 2014,28).

In this context, it can be stated that the concept of economic freedom is based on the following factors: (Akıncı, 2013)

- Personal preference
- Voluntary exchange
- Protection of private property
- Freedom of contract
- Freedom of competition
- Free market mechanism
- Liberal foreign trade regime

Recently, some institutions published indexes on the concept of economic freedom, which has increased interest in the issue. The publication of the indices allowed the comparison of countries on the one hand, and on the other hand, the empirical studies on the relationship between the concept of freedom and the main macro indicators such as economic growth and prosperity.

Among the organizations that do index work are Heritage Foundation and Fraser Institute. Since 1995, the Heritage Foundation, based in the United States, publishes the concept of economic freedom in 10 sub-indexes. Created sub-indices; level of tariffs, restrictions on capital inflows and foreign investments, black market formation, taxation, weight of public sector in economy, average inflation, independence of the banking sector; wage and price controls; regulations; and property rights. The economic freedom index published by the Fraser Institute annually after 2000 consists of 17 sub-indices. Created sub-indices; international trade, international capital flows, the black market, taxation, the state's position in the economy, monetary policy and inflation, banking, price controls, regulations, freedom of entr freedom of entry and property rights.

LITERATURE REVIEW

In addition to the social effects of democracy, it is very difficult to reach a consensus on the existence or direction of the relationship with the economy. Therefore, previous studies on the subject; it is possible to classify as having no relationship and to argue that the relationship has positive or negative effects.

The first study examining the relationship between democracy and economy belongs to Lipset (1959). In this study, Lipset classified the countries as European and English speaking and Latin American countries. The basic hypothesis of the study; the increase in the level of income of the countries will increase their chances of sustaining democracy. To test hypothesis to compare countries by using industrialization, education, urbanization and wealth variables. As a result of the research; Lipset states that countries with lesser income had less democratic countries and more countries with more income had more democratic countries.

Coleman (1960) in the study; covered 75 developed countries and democratic political performances of countries were examined. As a result of the study, it was concluded that socio-economic development has a positive effect on democracy.

Bollen (1965) analysed the relationship between economic development and democracy. in this study used Bolen democracy index and covered 99 countries. As a result of the study, it is concluded that the level of development is important in deciding whether a country is democratic or not.

Arat (1988) used the Arat Democracy index in the study which included 127 countries in the years 1948-1977. As a result of the study, Arat emphasized the existence of a positive relationship between economic development and democracy in the lower stages of economic development in middle-income countries.

Helliwell (1992) examined the relationship between democracy and economic growth in his study which cover 125 countries, 1960-1985 period and it tested the relationship with the panel data analysis. Gastil and Bollen democracy index used to measure democracy. As a result of his work; found that income has a positive and reliable effect on democracy.

Burkhart (1994) analysed relationship between economic development and democratic performance. in his study covered 131 countries in the period 1972-1989. In their study, Bollen and Gastil index was used as democracy index and energy consumption per capita was used as indicator of economic development. As a result of the analysis; economic development has increased democratic performance and argued that international and domestic economic factors have a decisive role in shaping the democratic future of nations.

In his study of Colaresi (2003), he examined the relationship between economic development and democratization in terms of the effects of external threats and international dependence. It included 112 countries with the panel data covering the period of 1960-1992. As a result of the research; He argued that the relationship between economic development and democracy was not independent from external factors and that economic development supported democratization when external threats and international dependency were controlled.

Gould (2003) used the survey technique to explain the relationship between economic development and democracy. In his study, Gould classified the population as elite, non-elite and soldier, forming a sample size of 325 persons. As a result of the analysis, it was found that economic growth affected the possibility of transformation to democracy in dictatorial regimes and in democratic regimes, that democracy has a decreasing effect on the possibility of falling.

Paresh et al. (2011) examined the relationship between democracy and economic growth in 30 sub-Saharan African countries. In the study covering the period of 1972 - 2001, RGDP and democracy variable were used. The economic data were generated from the World Bank's data set and the data on democracy from the Freedom House data set. As a result of the study, it was concluded that RGDP has a positive effect on democracy which supports Lipet's hypothesis.

In another study on sub-Saharan African countries, Vishal (2013) discussed the 28 countries in the 1980-2005 period. In his analysis, he tested the relationship between democracy and economic growth by using panel data analysis. The variables used in the analysis are the democracy index obtained from the GDP and Freedom House index, respectively. As a result of the analysis, it is emphasized that democracy has a positive effect on economic growth.

Green (2013), in another study on African countries, examined the relationship between democracy and economic growth for 45 African countries in 1963-2001. The panel used the data analysis technique and obtained the Democracy Index from the Polity IV data and the GDP variable from the World Development Indicators. As a result of the analysis, Green concluded that democracy has a significant impact on economic growth.

In a multinational study, Miller (2012) included 167 countries in the study period between 1875-2004. In the study, author defended the hypothesis that the autocracy is important in the relationship between democracy and economic growth. Miller used Democracy, GDP, and dummy variables in his study. as a result of study has emphasized the existence of a positive relationship between economic development and democracy.

Acemoğlu (2005) analysed the effect of income on democratization in 196 countries. In the study, the democracy index was obtained from the Freedom House and Polity IV indices, and the income from the Maddison 2003 data set. It is concluded that there is a positive relationship between income and democracy.

Demirkan and Kaya (2012) analysed that the relationship between democracy and economic growth in Turkey. Author analysed the relationship using the co-integration and Granger causality tests under 1980-2006. Civil rights and freedoms, political freedoms and population growth rate are independent variables; GDP growth rate is used as dependent variable. As a result of the analysis, it has been concluded that there is a long-term relationship between civil rights, population growth rate, political freedoms and economic growth. It is stated that the direction of the relationship is from civil rights and political freedoms to economic growth.

In another study related to Turkey, Uysal (2010) examined the relationship between democracy and economic development in Turkey between the years 1955 to 2006. Democracy index obtain from Polity IV and GDP data from TURKSTAT were used in the study. It was concluded that there is a relationship between economic growth and democracy in long term with using the co-integration test in the analysis.

Bilecen (2012) tested the relationship between economic growth and democracy in Turkey under period 1980-2010. Vector error correction model was applied to the analysis by including Polity IV democracy index and GDP growth rate variables. As a result of the analysis, it was concluded that there is a relationship between economic growth and democracy.

In another study Başar (2009), during the period 1923 to 2003 the impact of economic growth on democracy analysed in Turkey. Başar concluded that the economic growth has a positive effect on democratization by applying the KPSS unit root test by including the variables Polity IV, GDP and inflation.

In his study, Barro (1996) emphasized that the level of democracy will have a positive effect on growth until a certain level of development, but that it will have a negative impact on growth as the level of democracy reaches maturity.

Olk (2003) simulated the relationship between democracy and economy to the S curve. in other words, he stated that in the absence of democracy, political development would be ensured along with economic development.

Another variable of the analysis, the concept of economic freedom, has an important place among the main areas of study recently examined in the context of the liberal thought movement and the effect of the concept of freedom granted to individuals on the economy. In this context, it has been emphasized that the economic freedoms will have positive effects on economic growth.

Spindler et al. (1994) examined the possible effects of economic freedoms on economic growth in the period of 1985-1988. In study using panel data analysis, it emphasized that the use of economic resources for the establishment of freedoms would have an accelerating effect on economic growth.

James Gwartney et al. (1999) examined the effects of economic freedoms on economic growth in the period of 1975-1995. In the study, money, inflation, economic structure, taxes, international trade, human capital and ratio of investments to GNP were used. As a result of the analysis, it was concluded that economic freedoms have a strong effect on economic growth.

Cole (2003) analysed the relationship between economic freedoms and economic growth in two different growth models. The study included growth rate, human development index, ratio of investments to GDP, ratio of government expenditures to GDP, openness, population rate, property rights, political rights index. Using the Solow growth model and Gallup growth model, Cole emphasized that in the analysis obtained the relationship between economic freedoms and economic growth in both economic growth models.

Williamson et al. (2011) analysed the impact of economic freedoms and culture on economic performance. The panel data and OLS tests were used in the study, which included 41 countries during 1970-2004. As a result of the analysis, it was stated that economic freedoms and culture had a positive effect on economic performance. In addition, it was stated that economic freedoms affect economic growth more than culture.

Piatek (2013) examined the relationship between economic freedom and economic growth in transition economies. Having included 25 post-socialist countries during period between 1990 and 2008 in study. Variables obtained the economic indicators from the World Bank database, democracy data from the Polity IV index and economic freedoms from the Heritage Foundation database. As a result of the analysis, it was stated that economic freedoms would have a positive effect on economic growth in transition economies.

Bunda et al. (2012) tested the relationship between economic freedoms and economic growth in terms of new corporate structure. Study covered the 27 European Union and countries analysed using regression model. As a result of the analysis, there is a positive relationship between economic freedoms and economic growth.

Doucouliagos and Ulubasoğlu (2006) analyzed the relationship between economic growth and economic freedom in their studies involving 82 countries. They emphasized that there is a positive and meaningful relationship between economic freedoms and economic growth.

Justesen (2008) used the panel data method to analyze the relationship between economic growth and economic freedom in the 1970-1999 period. He stressed that economic freedom is a fundamental component of economic growth.

In line with the conceptual infrastructure on democracy and economic freedoms and previous studies, it can be stated that these concepts have a common denominator at many points. In other words, both concepts are emphasized freedom, social equality and justice. However, in the literature review, it was seen that these concepts were not dealt with together, although they had common denominators. Therefore, in this study, unlike the other studies in the literature, the effects of democratization and economic freedom on economic growth were analyzed in the same econometric model.

When the empirical studies in the literature are examined, it is seen that the results obtained differ according to country groups. The differences in management, the lack of institutional structure in some countries, and different econometric models used in the studies can be shown as the reasons for achieving different results. In this study, in developed countries, in accordance with the theory, a positive relationship was achieved between the concepts of democracy and economic freedom with economic growth. However, the results obtained in the study differed in developing and underdeveloped countries.

EMPİRİCAL METHODOLOGY

Panel data set can be defined as time series of sections or section data of time series (Greene, 2003: 283-84). In other words, it can be interpreted as the expression of horizontal cross-section observations consisting of units such as countries with time dimension (Baltagi, 2001: 1). In this way, multiple linear correlation problem can be eliminated by adding more variability to the measured relationship with the increase in the number of observations (Hsiao, 2006: 7).

A general panel data model can be expressed as follows:

$$Y_{it}=\pm_{it}+^{2}{}_{it}X_{it}+u_{it}\ i=1,\&\ ..,N;t=1,,,,,,,N$$

Y_{it}-dependent variable, X independent variable, α constant coefficient and β slope parameter in equation shows. It is necessary to determine which unit root test is used to test the variables before proceeding to the unit root test which is the first step in panel data models. Horizontal cross-sectional dependence must be tested to determine the appropriate unit root test at this stage. In this context, the correlation between units can be tested with the CD test developed by Pesaran (2004). The hypotheses of the test can be expressed as follows;

H_0: $p_{ij} = 0$

H_1: $p_{ij} = 1$

p_{ij} is the correlation coefficient. The test statistics calculated to test the hypotheses are calculated as follows.

$$CD=\sqrt{\frac{2T}{N(N-1)}}\left(\sum_{i=1}^{N-1}\sum_{j=i+1}^{N}Æ_{ij}\right)$$

The hypothesis H_0 is rejected if the probability value of the test statistic is lower than the significance value. In other words, horizontal cross-section dependence can be mentioned. If the cross-sectional dependence is obtained in the panel, unit root tests that take into account the cross-sectional dependence should be used. The equations and hypotheses of the CADF unit root test taking into account the cross-sectional dependence are shown below.

$$◆y_{it}=\pm_{i}+^{2}{}_{t}y_{i,t-i}+^{3}{}_{i}f_{t}+\mu_{it}\ i=1,2,\&\ ..,N,t=1,2,,,,,T$$

$H_0{:}^2{}_t=0$

$H_1{:}^2{}_t<0$

In the equation, f_t represents the unobservable common effects of each country, the individual error "ε_{it}". Rejecting the H0 hypothesis means that the series is stationary. There are basically two methods for panel data analysis estimations that provide the opportunity to use horizontal cross-section and time series together. The first of these methods is the "fixed effects" model, which allows different fixed coefficients to be obtained for each horizontal section. The fixed effects model can be shown as follows.

$$y_{it}=\pm_i+\sum_{k=1}^{K}{}^2{}_k X_{kit}+u_{it}\ i{:}1+,,,,,N,t=1,,,,,,T$$

Another model is "random effects" model. The model is used when the units are randomly taken from the population. In other words, units or time-specific effects are added as components of the error term (Balgati, 2005; Gujarati & Porter, 2009). The random effects model can be expressed as follows (Arellano, 2004; Stone ed., 2014).

$$y_{it}=\pm_i+\sum_{k=1}^{K}{}^2{}_k X_{kit}+\left(\pm_i+u_{it}\right)i=1+,,,,,N,t=1,,,,,,T$$

There are many tests to decide which model to use in panel data analysis. The most commonly used test is Hausman Test (1978). The Hausman test uses the H0 hypothesis, which argues that the random-effect model is more effective than the fixed-effect model, and the alternative hypothesis that the fixed-impact model is more effective than the random model.

SOLUTIONS AND RECOMMENDATIONS

In this chapter, 38 developed, 43 developing and 25 underdeveloped countries are included in the analysis according to the income groups published by the World Bank in order to analyse the impact of democracy and economic freedom on economic growth. In the analysis, the democracy variable was obtained from the Polity IV database, the economic freedom variable was from the Heritage Foundation database and the economic growth variable was obtained from the World Bank database. Period of the analysis was determined as 1995-2012.

For this purpose, in the panel data analysis for each country group, the cross-sectional dependence test, unit root test, unit effect-time effect, hausman test, heteroskedacity and robust estimator tests were applied. The results obtained for the developed country group are aggregated in Table 1.

When the results of the table are examined, the existence of horizontal cross-section dependence between the units forming the panel was determined. Accordingly, CADF unit root test was used for unit root test taking into account the cross-sectional dependence. In addition, both unit and time effect were found as a result of the tests carried out to examine the unit, time and the effect of both the unit and the time. According to the results of Hausman test performed in the selection of appropriate estima-

Table 1. Advanced country group results

	Coefficient	Standard error	Prob
Dem	0.217728	0.1302815	0.000
Ef	0.20055324	0.0987131	0.004
C	16.60047	6.63828	0.017
Prob>chi2=0.0003			
Cross-Section Dependency Results Pesaran: 0.000 Friedman: 0.000 Frees: 3.000			
Unit Root Results CADF: -2.656			
Unit effect-time effectTYBESE: 2.730 TYBEEÇO: 0.000 TYZEEÇO: 0.000 IYEÇO: 0.000			
Hausman Results Prob> chi2 = 0.0000			
Heteroskedacity Results Chi2 (38): 3947.03 Prob>chi2: 0.0000			

tor, fixed effects estimator was preferred in the model. Since the Heteroskedasticity is obtained in the model, the values in the table show adjusted value. Results from similar tests for developing countries are shown in Table 2.

When the results of the table are examined, the existence of horizontal cross-section dependence between the units forming the panel was determined. Therefore, CADF unit root test was used for unit root test taking into account the cross-sectional dependence. In addition, both unit and time effect were found as a result of the tests carried out to examine the unit, time and the effect of both the unit and the time. According to the results of Hausman test performed in the selection of appropriate estimator, random effects estimator was preferred in the model. Since the Heteroskedasticity is obtained in the model, the values in the table show adjusted value. Results from similar tests for underdeveloped countries are shown in Table 3.

When the table results are examined, it is determined that there is no cross-sectional dependence between the units forming the panel. LLC and IPS unit root test were used because there is no cross-sectional dependence for unit root test. In addition, unit effect was found. According to the results of the Hausman test performed in the selection of the appropriate estimator, the estimation of the random

Table 2. Developing countries group results

	Coefficient	Standard error	Prob
Dem	-0.255044	0.0135365	0.066
Ef	-0.0098353	0.0888173	0.089
C	4.585389	5.196303	0.383
Cross-Section Dependency Results: Pesaran: 0.0000 Friedman:0.0000 Frees: 1.779			
Unit Root Test Result CADF: -2.51			
Unit effect-time effect TYBESE: 3.764 TYBEEÇO: 0.000 TYZEEÇO: 0.000 IYEÇO: 0.000			
Hausman Test Result: Prob> chi2 = 0.3824			
Heteroskedacity Results : W0: 0.0000 W05: 0.0000 W10: 0.0000			

Table 3. Underdeveloped country group results

	Coefficient	Standard error	Prob
Dem	0.049528	0.0251686	0.049
Ef	-0.0659347	0.0986684	0.504
Sabit	1.330422	5.358912	0.804
Cross-Section Dependency Results: Pesaran: 00876 Friedman: 0.3539 Frees: 0.275			
Unit Root Test Result: LLC: 0.000 IPS: 0.000			
Unit effect-time effect TYBESE: 4.056 TYBEEÇO: 0.000 TYZEEÇO: 1.000 IYEÇO: 0.000			
Hausman Test Results: Prob> chi2 = 0.3491			
Heteroskedacity Results : W0: 0.0000 W05: 0.0001 W10: 0.0000			

effects in the model was preferred. Since the Heteroskedasticity is obtained in the model, the values in the table show adjusted value.

CONCLUSION

The concepts of democracy and economic freedom, which include characteristics such as the freedom of individuals in their economic activities and the right to choose, to be elected and to make decisions, are similar in many points.

The relationship between democracy and economy, which was started to be researched especially during the Second World War, has been one of the topics discussed since the war years. at the same time, in many studies, the more democratic, transparent and freedoms observed in developed countries are shown as examples of developing and underdeveloped countries.

As a result of the academic studies conducted, the strengthening of the democracy concept, which is presented as a key to economic and social development, emphasized the social-political dimension of democracy as well as its relationship with the economy.

As a result of the tests, it was found that there is a positive relationship between GDP and economic freedom in developed countries. In other words, it is concluded that an improvement in democracy and economic freedom has a positive effect on economic growth. The positive directional relationship between GDP and democracy and economic freedoms supported that the advocacy of developed countries as a model for developing and underdeveloped countries. Moreover, the results obtained support the academic studies on the subject.

For the developing country group, the test results differed. There is a negative correlation between economic growth and democracy and economic freedom in developing countries. Considering the problems such as lack of capital in the developing countries classified according to the World Bank data, the fact that there are many emerging industries and the lack of a transparent management approach, the results can be based on an academic basis. In addition, it can be stated that most of the countries that make up the group of developing countries are managed with management approaches other than democracy, is effective in the emergence of this result.

For the underdeveloped countries in the third and last country group in study, obtained the results are supported the theory results. The relationship between economic growth and democracy, which is mainly studied by academic studies, has been achieved positively for underdeveloped countries. When the social, political and economic structures of the underdeveloped countries are analysed as a whole, it can be thought that the provision of freedoms, constitutional guarantees and the adoption of more human-centered administrations will contribute more positively to the economic structures of underdeveloped countries.

REFERENCES

Acemoğlu, D., Johnson, S., Robinson, J. A., & Yared, P. (2005). "Income and Democracy", *NBER Working Paper Series,* No: 11205, 5-12.

Akıncı, M. (2013). *Ekonomik Özgürlükler İle Ekonomik Büyüme Arasındaki İlişki: Gelişmiş, Gelişmekte Olan ve Azgelişmiş Ülkeler Üzerine Bir Uygulama, (Yayımlanmamış Doktora Tezi).* Erzurum, Turkey: Atatürk Üniversitesi Sosyal Bilimler Enstitüsü.

Arat, Z. F. (1988). Democracy and economic development: Modernization theory revisited. *Comparative Politics, 21*(1), 21–36. doi:10.2307/422069

Arrelano, M. (2004). *Panel data econometrics (Advanced tests in econometrics).* New York, NY: Oxford University Press.

Baltagi, B. (2001). *Econometric analysis of panel data* (2nd ed.). UK: John Wiley & Sons.

Barro, R. J. (1996) "Determinants of economic growth: A cross-country empirical study", *NBER Working Paper*, Sayı: 5698, 40-41.

Başar, S., & Yıldız, Ş. (2009). İktisadi Büyümenin Demokratikleşme Üzerindeki Etkileri. *Balıkesir Üniversitesi Sosyal Bilimler Enstitüsü Dergisi, 12*(21), 56–75.

Bilecen, H., & Kibis, E. Y. (2012). Economic growth and democracy in Turkey. *Yönetim Bilimleri Dergisi, 10*(20), 137–155.

<bok>Dahl, R. A. (1971). Polyarchy: Participation and opposition. New Haven, CT: Yale University Press.

Bundă, N. R., Ţiţei, A. M., & Jaliu, D. D. (2012). A new institutional approach of the complex correlation between economic freedom and economic growth. *European Journal of Science and Theology, 8*, 75–84.

Burkhart, R. E. & Lewis-Beck, M. S. (1994) Comparative democracy: The economic development thesis. *American Political Science Review, 88*(4), 903–910.

Cevizci, A. (2002). *Felsefe Sözlüğü.* İstanbul, Turkey: Paradigma Yayınları.

Colaresi, M., & Thompson, W. R. (2003). The economic development–democratization relationship. *Comparative Political Studies, 36*(4), 397–398. doi:10.1177/0010414003251174

Cole, J. H. (2003). The contribution of economic freedom to world economic growth, 1980-99. *The Cato Journal, 23*(2), 189–198.

Demirkan, E., & Kaya, V. (2012). An analysis of relation between economic growth and democratization: An empiric application (a sample of Turkey). *Yönetim ve Ekonomi*, *19*(2), 123–132.

den Aktaran Arat, Z. F. (n.d.). Democracy and development: Modernization theory revisited. Comparative Politics, 21(1), 22.</edb>

Doucouliagos, C., & Ulubaşoğlu, M. A. (2006). Economic freedom and economic growth: Does specification make a difference? *European Journal of Political Economy*, *22*(1), 60–81. doi:10.1016/j.ejpoleco.2005.06.003

Dursun, D. (2002). *Siyaset Bilimi*. İstanbul Beta Basım Yayım Dağıtım A.Ş.

<edb>Coleman, J. S. (1988). Conclusion: The political systems of the developing area. In G. A. Almond & J. S. Coleman (Eds.), The politics of developing areas. Princeton, NJ: Princeton University Press, 1960, 532-581.

Friedman, M. (2002). Economic freedom behind the scenes. In J. Gwartney, R. Lawson, C. Edwards, W. Park, V. Rugy, & S. Wagh (Eds.), Economic freedom of the world: 2002 Annual Report, (pp. 17-21), The Fraser Institute, Vancouver, Canada, p. 18.

Green, A. (2013). Estimating the effects of democratization in African countries: A simultaneous equations approach. *Economic Systems*, *37*(4), 555–571. doi:10.1016/j.ecosys.2013.02.003

Greenee, W. H. (2003). Econometric analysis (5th ed.). New York, NY: Prentice Hall.

Gujarati, D. N., & Porter, D. C. (2009). *Basic econometrics* (5th ed.). New York, NY: McGraw-Hill.

Gwartney, J. D., Lawson, R. A., & Hocombe, R. (1999). Economic freedom and the environment for economic growth. Journal of Institutional and Theoretical Economics (JITE). *Mohr Siebeck, Tübingen*, *155*(4), 643–643.

Huntington, S. (1991). *The third wave: Democratization in the late Twentieth Century*. University of Oklahoma Press.

John, F. H. (1992). Empirical linkages between democracy and economic growth, *NBER Working Paper*, No: 4066.

<jrn>Kenneth, A. B. (1979). Political democracy and the timing of development. American Socialical Review, 44, 572.

Justesen, M. K. (2008). The effect of economic freedom on growth revisited: New evidence on causality from a panel of countries 1970-1999. *European Journal of Political Economy*, *24*(3), 642–660. doi:10.1016/j.ejpoleco.2008.06.003

Lipset, S. M. (1959). Some social requisites of democracy: Economic development and political legitimacy. [</jrn>]. *The American Political Science Review*, *53*, 73–74.

Miller, M. (2012). Economic development, violent leader removal and democratization. *American Journal of Political Science*, *56*(4), 1002–1020. doi:10.1111/j.1540-5907.2012.00595.x

Olk, S. (2003). The relationship between economic development and democracy in africa: a quantitative and qualitative perspective. Retrieved from https://Www.Uni-Trier.De/Fileadmin/Fb3/Pol/Studium/Ausgewaehlte_Abschlussarbeiten/Olk.Pdf

Paresh, K. N., Narayan, S., & Smyth, R. (2011). Does democracy facilitate economic growth or does economic growth facilitate democracy? An empirical study of sub-Saharan Africa. *Economic Modelling, 28,* 900-910.

Patry, W. (2009). *Moral panics and the copyright wars*. New York, NY: Oxford University Press.

Piatek, D., Szarzec, K., & Pilc, M. (2013). Economic freedom, democracy and economic growth: A causal investigation in transition countries. *Post-Communist economies*, *25*(3), 267–288. doi:10.1080/14631377.2013.813137

Safty, A. (2003). Democracy and governance: The global advance of democracy. İstanbul, Turkey: Bahçeşehir University Press.</bok>

Schmidt, M. G. (2001). *Demokrasi Kuramlarına Giriş, (Çev.: Köktaş, M. Emin)*. Ankara, Turkey: Vadi Yayınları.

Stefan B. & Guimarães R. (2003). Do the poor need democracy? Tracing the debate on democracy and pro-poor development. ZEF Bonn, Zentrum für Entwicklungsforschung Center for Development Research, Universität Bonn

Tunçsiper, B., & Bicen, Ö. F. (2014). Ekonomik Özgürlükler ve Ekonomik Büyüme Arasındaki İlişkinin Panel Regresyon Yöntemiyle İncelenmesi. *Eskişehir Osmangazi Üniversitesi İİBF Dergisi*, *9*(2), 25–45.

Uysal D., Özşahin M. C., & Özşahin Ş. (2010). Co-integration analysis of economic development and democracy: The case of Turkey. *Current Research Journal of Economic Theory*, 2/3, 102, 111.

Vanssay, X. D., & Spindler, Z. A. (1994). Freedom and growth: Do constitutions matter? *Public Choice*, *78*(3-4), 359–372. doi:10.1007/BF01047764

Vishal, C. J. (2013). Democracy and economic growth in sub-Saharan Africa: A panel data approach. *Economic Modelling, 45*, 987–1008.

Yılmaz, A. (2000). *Modern Demokrasi Gelişimi ve Sorunları*. Ankara, Turkey: Yeni Türkiye Yayınları.

Chapter 11
Institutional Economics:
The Historical Foundations of Institutional Economics

Zehra Doğan Çalışkan
Bolu Abant İzzet Baysal University, Turkey

ABSTRACT

Since the mid-19th century, the thinkers of historical school challenged the deductive, abstractive, and decisive methods of neo-classical economics. According to historical school, social terms have been changed within space and time. Therefore, they defended that the economic theories could not be universal but could only be relative. Instead of professing laws with universal validity, it is more important to reveal the changing structure of society with the extensive studies of economic history. The inductive method of German historical school brought a new perspective into economic theory with theorems such as to consider society as an organism beyond the individuals who would only seek their benefits and the necessity of historical followings in the economic events. From this point of view, it is possible to observe the traces of historical school in the old institutional economics literature.

INTRODUCTION

Institutional Economics emerged in the 19th century, and the thought of Historical School was influential for this emergence. Historical school is a consensus that is deeply influenced by pragmatism, empiricism and evolutionary philosophy. In this regard, the main theme of institutional economics is that the flow of historical events is different for every society and therefore, suggesting a universal method for economic problems is not possible. Institutional structure and human behaviors should be considered as changing and influencing processes each other with up and down causal relations. In other words, social behaviors and decisions reshape the institutions by influencing them, and in the same manner, institutions affect human behaviors with taken decisions and the policy executions. Within this context, institutional structure and society are the conclusions of processes which are interwoven. Thus, societies

DOI: 10.4018/978-1-7998-0333-1.ch011

Copyright © 2020, IGI Global. Copying or distributing in print or electronic forms without written permission of IGI Global is prohibited.

should be considered with some specific features, and they should be administered with policies that are suitable for these features.

The term 'institutional economics' was first coined by Walton Hamilton at the meeting of the American Economic Association held in 1919. Although the contributions were previously made regarding the importance and place of institutions in the economy, it was this period in which the term was named properly. The pioneers of the movement known as the old institutionalist school were T. Veblen, J.R. Commons and W.C. Mitchell (Hodgson, 2000: 317).

Even though institutional economics does not provide point-time equilibrium solutions as revealed by the Neo-Classical economics, it has different characteristics in terms of human behavior, the changing structure of societies, and a process-time economic understanding based on institutions (Chavance, 2009: 17- 18).

In the institutional economics literature, the criticisms towards the Neo-Classical economy are concentrated in three aspects: Firstly, institutional economics philosophers are opposed to Neo-Classical economics abstractions independent of time-and-space. Secondly, institutional economics thinkers are uncomfortable with the uniforming view of neoclassical economics which isolates people and differentiates them from economic, behavioral patterns.

The third is the opposition of Neo-Classical economics to theories disconnected from deductive history, society and other sciences (Hodgson 1998: 167; Mitchell 1935: 636; Kızılkaya, 2007: 12).

Although institutional economics contains a number of highly complex and alternative ideas, it is mainly concentrated on some common points such as reflecting social action rather than individual action, considering the economy with evolutionary thought, and emphasizing both experimental and historical observations (Ata, 2009: 11). The common sense that comes to mind upon considering institutional economics involves institutions and institutional structure which constitute economic processes that are perceived as the sub-branches of societal and social events. Moreover, it is more noteworthy to refer to an institution-based economic approach rather than a human-based economic approach (Demir, 1996: 65).

In his article entitled "What is the Essence of Institutional Economics?" Hodgson stated that the methodology of institutional economics which is comprised of the five elements should be explained in the following manners:

- Although institutional economists are eager to put forward practical theories, their proposals have not been identified politically.
- In order to develop an extensive analysis of institutional economics, institutions, and human behavior, institutional economics also investigates the works of other fields of science such as psychology, sociology, and anthropology.
- Since institutions are the key elements of every economy, the most important issue of economists should be the monitoring of innovation and change processes of institutions.
- Since the economy is an open and improving system, it is necessary to explain the social, cultural, political changes and strong social relations influenced by technological changes.
- Individual interests and utility maximization are considered to be inadequate or erroneous. Institutionalist thought is not an individual analysis. Therefore, individuals do not deliberately (or accidentally) establish institutions. The institutions influence and shape the individuals through "reconstitutive downward causation" (Hodgson, 2000: 318).

The basic ideas of institutional economics are improved within the framework of five main elements. With this framework, Veblen, Commons, and Mitchell have developed different institution definitions and prepositions. However, institutional action, not individual action, takes place in the core of institutional economics (perhaps the most important point). The process, referred to as 'downward cumulative causality' by Hodgson, is significant enough to indicate why some countries are wealthier, whereas others are poorer.

The perspective of institutional economics is shaped on four pillars. Analysis of the changing institutional structure of capitalism, critical analysis of the neoclassical economics, development of new tools for the solution of social and economic problems, creation of empirical methods against mathematical modeling (Fusfeld, 2000: 257).

From this point of view, institutional economics focuses on different analyses other than the analysis of neo-classical economics. The society has incorporated concepts that are not included in neo-classical economics such as behaviors and habits, cumulative causation, historical conditions into its research area. Institutional economics is a social change and control theory that includes the analysis of corporate activities and institutional cohesion. There are at least three aspects of this theory: Firstly, institutional economics constitutes a collection of information. Accordingly; the main field of study of this thought school is not only the allocation of resources, the distribution of income, the determination of prices, employment and outputs, but also the evolution of the institutions and control of the economy as a whole. As a result, the institutionalists claim that they approach the problems with a wider variable domain than the neo-classical economists and maintain a collection of information. Secondly, institutional economics is a problem-solving approach. Accordingly; the Institutional economists believe that their own approaches create a new approach to solving problems via policy analysis, different apprehension, and analysis techniques. Thirdly, institutional economics is a protest movement. Institutional economists conduct a protest movement against the current structure of the orthodox theory, which they regard as closely associated with the established market economy as well as the existing institutional regulations (Samuels, 1969: 70). Institutional economics does not perform this protest movement by remodeling, theories and abstractions. The method of institutional economics involves human behavior and habits which result in cumulative causation in historical, social, cultural and economic processes. It is meaningless to express economic events and processes without understanding institutions. The study field of institutional economics pertains to how and in which direction social relations can be developed for the satisfaction of people (Kapp, 1976: 212). Institutional economics aims to examine concrete economies without paying much attention to the solution of technical, intellectual problems. The political propositions of institutional economics loom large in the concrete economics (Demir, 1996: 70).

While the propositions of Historical School and the traces of their philosophical basis can be seen clearly in old institutional economics, the philosophical basis of Historical School is become distanced in new institutional economics. In the study, it will be aimed to express the propositions of Historical School and the influence of Historical School on both old and new institutional economics.

GENERAL FRAMEWORK AND LITERATURE

It is widely accepted that German Historical School started with the publication of Roscher's work in 1843, ''The Studies of Political Economy According to Historical Method''. W. Roscher, B. Hildebrand, K. Knies are accepted as old school and first generation. G. F. Knapp, K. Bücher, G. Schmoller, M. Weber and W. Sombart, on the other hand, are called second generation and young school.

Generally, the historical school can be defined as a school that aspires to examine economics through the development of social relations in history (Kazgan, 2004:185). The ideas that the bedrock of social structure is the institutions and the changes of institutions in time have fundamentally evolutionary quality (adaptable to space and time) and their combination formed the foundation of vanguard institutionalism (Yıldırım, 2009: 22).

Historical school objected the deductive, abstractive point of view of neo-classical economics and claimed that historical events differ for every society; therefore, establishing a universal economic theory is not possible. According to this approach, economic prognosis should question what people think, what they expect and feel, and what efforts people make for the realization of these (Tribe 2003: 217). According to W. Roscher (1843), who is accepted as one of the founders of the historical school, economics have some meanings beyond being a science of wealth or being a science for searching the ways of treasuring wealth. How a wealth of nation can be increased best is the main problem, but it is not the main objective of political economics as well (Roscher, 1843:19, as cited in; Ashley: 1894:99).

Historical school is against the mechanical society approach of classical school, and it adopts an organic approach that the individual has associated with social life. Since social life is quite complicated, it cannot be understood with theories and formulas only. In this respect, forming universal theorems for all societies is a meaningless effort. Economics is a social science that includes previous social and cultural changes. The people are not eternal creatures who live only today. In this regard, economics is not a significant field of research without a historical perspective. Within this context, German historical school has determined its perspective to economic events with several objectives. These objectives are conducting historical and statistical researches by avoiding the deductive method, accepting that economics cannot produce ubiquitous policies with constant laws and considering the fact that institutions and theories are interrelated.

The historical school never acknowledges that economics has permanent laws. It advocates that social institutions are bound to space and time. Hence, even if it is logically consequent, the examination of economic history rather than producing laws without universal acknowledgment is more acceptable for historical school as well. Nevertheless, they refused the principle that self-interests and social interests will be harmonized. Furthermore, since this approach rejects natural order conception, it also does not acknowledge the interest union between the countries in international trade as well (Erim, 2011: 110).

Historical school is shaped upon four main principles. These are; evolutionary approach in economics, the positive economic side of the state, inductive/historical approach and conservative reforms. According to the evolutionary approach, a dynamic and evolutionary approach should be adopted for the examination of society. Hence, the processes of development and growth succeed in time, and these processes accumulate their gains by amassing. Since society is a social organism and it always in a state of change, a most compatible economic view for one country cannot be matched with the other. Therefore, the economic policies that are unique to the countries should be produced. According to historical school, the force that vitalizes industrial and economic growth is coming from the state. Thus, the role of the state on the economic process is vitally important. The thinkers that belong to historical school have accepted the branches of social sciences as an integral part of one entirety, which integrated each other. As a consequence, historical researches have a significant place in economics (Bocutoglu, 2012: 146-7).

The historical school of economics has the most significant impact on the old institutional economics. In other words, the economic reflection of the old historical school has been included in the old institutional, economic thought. Veblen, Mitchell, and Commons, who incorporate the historical school into economics, have changed their institutional economics literature irreversibly by following its working principles. In this sense, it would be meaningful to mention the fundamental views of the authors which influence institutional economics.

Veblen's Contribution to the Institutional Economics

Thorstein Veblen is one of the economists who are harshly opposed to the Neo-classical theory. Veblen's ideas were later adopted by heterodox economists who objected to the Neo-classical theory, and he was one of the founders of the economic thought, namely the institutional economics (Savaş, 2000: 648).

One of the basic and most crucial concepts that constitute Veblen's economic analysis is the concept of the institution. Veblen defines the concept of the institution as "thoughts, behaviors, and habits that are widely accepted in a certain period" (Veblen, 2014: 82). In Veblen's analysis, institutions reflect the sum of ideas and habits inherited from the past and are considered as an important factor shaping individual tendencies, preferences, and values (Dinar, 2013: 47). Veblen examined the impacts of the institutional structure on economic activities, the foundations of social institutions and their developmental stages in detail. He conducted research studies on the importance of the institutional structure and its role in the shaping of human behavior and was opposed to the idea that personal interest underlies individual behavior motive (Aktan, 2006: 6). According to Veblen, habits underlies human behaviors whereas instincts underlie habits. Veblen's idea of habits is nothing but institutions. In other words, human behaviors are driven by institutions. Instincts underlie the institutions. The first instinct is workmanship which expresses the feelings of work ethic and production. The second one is parental bent which relates to the tendency of individuals to protect future generations unconditionally. The third instinct is idle curiosity. Idle curiosity in human beings leads to the pursuit of new knowledge in order to create new theories along with the instinct of workmanship (Demir 1996: 95). Neither Veblen nor the Marxist economists embraced economic proposition of the neo-classical economists, and they have found several alternative propositions. Veblen was not concerned with the rational individual in pursuit of pleasure as suggested by the Neo-classical economics (Köse, 2003: 284). According to Veblen, the individual's wishes, objectives, and activities are determined by the highly complex institutional structure. Here, the existing institutional structure both shapes and restricts the activities of individuals. Likewise, the individual has the ability to change the institutional structure by creating new social habits. Throughout this process, as well as tradition or laws, human nature also undergoes significant changes. In other words, changing habits, not only alter human behavior, but also lead to some changes in human nature (Dinara, 2011: 16). Veblen has expressed technology as the answer to the question of how human behavior and thought habits affect institutions. Accordingly, institutions would be transformed through technology within a structure that adapts to people's needs. This process of change should not be expected to occur instantly. The process of technological and institutional change is a slow, but a decisive process. The organic nature of the social structure contains a series of cultural change and cumulative work. For this reason, economists should not give up on creating a basic theory of human behavior and activity. Instead, studies should be conducted to apprehend human behavior and the cumulative structure of society (Veblen, 1898: 14).

Veblen's basic framework involves the fact the path dependence as the most important element of institutional change and cumulative causation processes would lead to institutional change along with technological change. These institutions are nothing but human behaviors and thoughts. Institutional behaviors (for Veblen and other institutional economists) are more important than individual behaviors. Institutional behavior and thought patterns determine the way how individuals think and behave. At this point, Veblen explained the concept of snob effect and emphasized that such consumption pattern would control the financial markets and companies, and influence the financial strategy, advertising and business managers and cause business fluctuations (Rutherford, 2001: 174). Snob effect is an important point made by Veblen. According to Veblen, consumption is a useful and socially productive activity for the livelihood of individuals. Nevertheless, if consumption goes beyond the survival dimension, it should be considered as a social problem. The driving prosperity to waste rather than utilizing it for society's benefit, and the imitation of this behavior by all sections of society, would deprive society of any purpose (Veblen, 1899: 398). Veblen, by emphasizing the intentional and purpose-oriented features of individual behaviors, recognizes that individuals use their intelligence to search for ways to best accomplish their goals. According to Veblen, individuals are not in pursuit of maximization but tend to adjust their habits and routines in a way to create better alternatives over time. According to Veblen, individuals are also conditioned by their social and economic environment within certain thought patterns. Therefore, in the analysis of Veblen, the individual is considered as a rational and social entity (Dinar, 2013: 52). Individual behaviors and motives can be handled differently in every society, and it is possible to obtain different results. Therefore, it may lead to better alternative theories, firms, and policies to examine the thought patterns and institutional change that occur within each society (Hodgson, 1998: 172). Veblen's notion of the concepts that are not included in the neo-classical economics such as institutions, instincts, behaviors, and habits in the late 19th and early 20th century, led the researchers to apprehend these concepts, made additions and produce new ideas in this way. Veblen was opposed to the idea of an economy disconnected from human beings, their habits, behavior, and instincts. According to him, institutions are the sum of human behaviors and habits. In this respect, it would not be significant to implement an economic policy unless the institutional structure for each society is not comprehended and analyzed.

Commons' Contribution to the Institutional Economics

John R. Commons is a researcher who has contributed greatly to the 20th century through social sciences, occupational safety and labor legislation, economic theory, and ideas and has influenced subsequent researchers. In addition to his university studies, Commons is well-known for his works on governments, trade unions, and political parties, particularly for his works on labor economics and labor laws. The fact that Commons is effective and knowledgeable in the field of politics has caused institutional economics to gain a political dimension and importance (Barbash, 2005: 44). According to Commons, the institution can be defined as "social action under the control of individual actions". Veblen brought the concept of Darwinian evolution to institutional economics literature, whereas Commons added the concept of behavioral economics borrowed from behavioral psychology (Hodgson, 1998: 167).

According to Commons, learned abilities in society are inherently embedded in habits. Whenever habits become a part of a social culture or social group, these habits constitute routine and traditions (Commons, 1934: 45). Institutions appear as durable, integrated and complex forms of traditions and routines. Habits and routines and nonverbal information move in time, such as the transfer mechanism of institutions (Hodgson, 1998: 168).

According to Commons; institutions, behavior, thought and behavioral habits affect social cohesion. What this sentence implies is that the behaviors and meanings (such as political, social or economic policies) that will find its expression in society in the social and economic sense affect the behaviors of individuals and the institutions affect human behavior through information. Institutions are the clear and accepted forms of common relations that are transferred from generation to generation and shape each individual (Commons, 1934: 49).

According to Commons, economic transactions allow us to analyze the institutional structure depending on the situation of individuals, laws and private property. This means that there is a contractual relationship between the transaction, the working rules, and the ongoing institutions. All economic processes are shaped through these three structures, and improvements in these structures (improvements in habits and routines) allow for better social action. Innovations observed in these three areas would lead to progress in the recovery of income and redistribution in society (Ollila, 2009: 13).

According to Commons, no consensus could be reached on the definition and scope of the concept of the institution. According to him, the institution is sometimes defined as a framework of laws or natural rights that allow individuals to live in a community or, indeed, the behaviors of these people who live as a community. According to Commons, the expression of the institution is sometimes used to describe any idea that is not included in the neo-classical economics or that criticizes these views. Sometimes dynamic instead of static, the process instead of metamorphosis, activity instead of emotions, group behavior instead of individual behavior, management instead of equilibrium are defined as institutional economics (Commons, 1931: 648).

Commons influenced institutional economics with its thoughts such as behavioral economics, habits, routines and their impact on the social and economic structure. He stated that the necessity of establishing an order in the economy and the things that would establish such order are the institutions which determine human behavior. All issues such as organizing labor, investing in the most appropriate areas, avoiding unemployment and poverty, and income distribution inequality can be solved by supervision and organization. With this point of view, Commons attributed to institutions (and the state) more than the value attributed by the Neo-Classical economics and imposed duties on regulating, organizing and re-distributing economic and social processes.

Mitchell's Contribution to the Institutional Economics

Wesley C. Mitchell studied the monetary field in the economy, and he contributed to the institutional economics with his two-section work entitled "Rationality of Economic Activity" published in 1910. Mitchell rejected the notion of a rational individual in explaining human behavior; instead, he utilized instincts and habits to explain the economy. According to Mitchell, economics is a branch of science that studies human behaviors. He criticized the deductive methodology in his studies the same as institutional economists. Instead, he highlighted statistical analysis as an inductive method. The impact of an experimental approach, as the basis of all his studies, was significant for the establishment of the National Bureau of Economic Research. This establishment aims to collect and improve statistical data on fluctuations in the economy. Although the establishment has eventually expanded its subject of investigation, its research still indicates an experimental approach (Yıldırım 2009: 28). Mitchell described the notion of the institution in the form of well-accepted standardized social habits. Mitchell was closely interested in the statistical analysis of the crisis and economic fluctuations, and he found that each conjuncture period had its own characteristics. Mitchell based his analysis on historical and theoretical findings (Aktan 2006: 11).

According to Mitchell, there are only a few researchers who included human behavior psychology in economics. The inclusion of human nature, behavior, and habits in economic studies is a very consistent approach. Demoting human nature to a few theories, or making it monotonous as a rational individual, leads to the emergence of theories that are completely disconnected from the social phenomenon (Mitchell, 1910: 97). According to Mitchell, the essence of social institutions involves social concepts. The norms according to habits and general acceptance reveal social concepts after a while. Social concepts are definitely above individual ones. This is also the case in monetary economies as in the case of primitive economies. The most powerful institution of society is its culture. The truth is that human nature is about giving similar reactions to similar circumstances and its ideal is about revealing the truth, the good and the beautiful (Hodgson, 2000: 324). Mitchell's empirical works on macroeconomics and money led to an apprehension of national income accounts. Mitchell's works conducted on national income accounts have greatly influenced Keynes. In this respect, there are similarities between institutionalism and Post-Keynesian macroeconomic understanding. Nevertheless, Mitchell concluded that microeconomics has macro-foundations rather than macroeconomics with micro-foundations (Hodgson, 1998: 172).

THE TRACES OF HISTORICAL SCHOOL ON BOTH OLD AND NEW INSTITUTIONAL ECONOMICS

The philosophical basis of institutional philosophy is the evolutionary mentality, empiricism, and pragmatism. The combination of these three mentalities and the views of historical schools paved the way for the emergence of institutional economics. The perspective that is predominant to old institutional economics is the discourses of historical school and the philosophies of evolutionism, empiricism, and pragmatism.

It is possible to see the traces of Newtonian physic and Euclidean mathematics on the basis of economics. After the period that Newton explained the earth scientifically, the economists who were influenced by this movement endeavored to form the economic events and the life within an order concept. "Market organization" have been constituted in this regard, and it is basically accepted as a reflection in the economics from natural world order which Newton explained.

In the operation of the market organization, rational and rationalist individuals with their own free right to choose, make their production and consumption choices through natural prices which emerge in the market, and balanced production and consumption levels for all economic actors have been provided. The established economic theories are suited for this approach, and these theories are independent of space and time, ahistorical and theories that are established for a nonorganic society (Boschma 2009: 8). Yet, every situation and case vary according to space and time. From this point of view, institutional economics has also advocated that economic situations and cases have an evolutionary aspect. According to Veblen, economic theory is determined by human behaviors that are depended on the instinctive habits of historical, economic, political and social events. Therefore, the theory of social evolution presents the most suitable instruments to understand the change while it has interested in social and economic facts (Demir, 1996: 94).

Another philosophical basis of institutional economics is empirical thought. It has influenced institutional economics by forming a basis to pragmatism. According to empirical thought, experience and experiment are the sources of knowledge. All the source of our knowledge is experiments and habits (Locke 2002: 83). This thought objected rationalist argument that knowledge could be obtained with mind and it expressed that the knowledge can be obtained with sensation and experiences. Empirical philosophy does not acknowledge the modelings of rationalism which got these modelings with mind and rationalist worldview because the human mind has changed in everywhere with experiments and sensations. Since institutional economics has grounded on such a thought economically, it has advocated that humans are an entirety of relationships socially and without perceiving these social relationships, it is impossible to seen economic events as well.

The third philosophical basis of institutional economics is the thought of pragmatism. It is a movement of thought that reject metaphysics and knowledge can only be obtained with the examination of the phenomenal world. It is a thought of facts and practical results. Pragmatism is a result-oriented thought; if information were useful in the daily life, then, this information would be correct, but if it were not, then, it would not be true (Commons 1931: 655). Starting from this judgment, science is a process, and for the examination of this process, the data belonging to the past is important. In social sciences, this method can be actualized by following historical ways. Another important matter in pragmatism is that since every individual has their own perception of their social life, a system of common values for everybody can never be established. In this regard, institutional economics has no difficulty to acknowledge pragmatism as a philosophical basis. According to this point of view, economic theories are not intangible and hypothetical, and they should be developed based on the concepts that have equals with real situations.

From the point of historical school view, the philosophical bases of old institutional economics are the evolutionary, empirical and pragmatic thoughts. Old institutional economists have grounded on these ideas, and they opposed the neo-classical intangible approach that is independent of space and time. Moreover, they have felt uncomfortable with another neo-classical thought that isolates people, separate them from economic, behavioral patterns and makes people monotonous, and they are against their deductive theories that are disconnected from history, society, and other sciences. Old institutional economics advocates that society should be bodily studied with its own nature and habits. In order to achieve this, historical deductions should be made, and the society should be analyzed instead of mathematical models or abstractions.

Institutional economics has objected the concepts of neo-classical economics such as rational individual, profit-utility maximization, deduction, and abstraction, and it has pointed out the importance of institutions in the economy as well. New institutional economics, on the other hand, has not fully objected the analyses of neo-classical economics but instead, it has expressed the missing points of it. Furthermore, it has developed a new movement of thought that researches how these missing points can be completed. In this regard, new institutional economics is not completely supportive towards the assumptions and methods of neoclassical economics, but it has a productive side and new institutional economics researches about how this method can be improved as well. Like his old counterpart, new institutional economics supports that institutions have a crucial role in economic behaviors. According to new institutional economics, since neo-classical economics could not comprehend the roles of institutions, the unrealistic assumptions of neo-classical economics (full knowledge, zero transaction costs, and full rationality) should be defined in more comprehensible levels. Although it does not absolutely acknowledge the assumptions of neo-classical economics, it also advocates that these assumptions can be used by flexing them somewhat.

According to Coase (1984), the knowledge and experiences that are in the historical and philosophical background of old institutional economics have demonstrated us how the institutions have vital importance. Because old institutional economics could not achieve to form a positive theory, this paved the way for the failure of institutional economics. The extreme hostility of old institutional economics against the traditional theory (neo-classical economics) exacerbated this failure (Coase, 1984: 230). The approach of new institutional economics has become successful in adding new terminology such as transaction costs, bounded rationality, property rights, incomplete contracts and opportunism on institutions, rules, and organizations. Moreover, it has achieved to present a new methodological perspective, and therefore, it has become a dynamic economics discipline by putting the institutional foundations of economic activities into the center of positive research (Çetin, 2012:43).

According to old institutional economics on the emergence of institutions, individual behaviors appears as a product of institutional structure that the individual is in, and this behavior affects both economic and social structure. According to new institutional economics, habits, thoughts, and traditions have shaped the behaviors of individuals, and these behaviors have shaped the institutional structure (Hodgson 2000: 327). The issue of the emergence of institutions has been approached by old and new institutional economics differently. While old institutional economics claimed that existing institutions shape human behaviors, it is possible to argue that new institutional economics treated the process of the emergence of institutions as individual-based. In this regard, it is probable to state that the traces of historical school have slowly lost in new institutional economics.

SOLUTION AND RECOMMENDATIONS

There is no single economic policy suitable for every society. The propositions of Neoclassical economics such as perfect information, rationality, and zero transaction costs do not correspond to the real world. In this context, understanding of the historical school of economics in which institutions formed by unique characteristics of the societies shape both individuals and establishments, in turn, the economy per se, is a realistic approach. Since institutions and institutional structure, in other words, the lifestyles and production patterns of societies differ in different countries, problems such as poverty and income distribution inequality occur in different magnitudes. In this sense, it would be possible to claim that economic policies should not be disconnected from the historical and institutional structure and that each society should establish policies in accordance with its own institutional structure.

Human and group behaviors constitute the main subject of the economic issue. Human behaviors determine or should determine what the economic issue would be. Since human behaviors are subject to change according to time, place and geography, it is pointless to propose general theories. Change and process are essential factors in the economy. The understanding of a static and point-time equilibrium cannot be mentioned. Instead, dynamic analyses should be implemented for detecting such change. According to institutional economists, economic behavior is strongly dependent upon the institutional environment in which economic activities occur. In addition, economic behaviors also influence the structure of the institutional environment simultaneously. According to institutional economists, the core of economic issues should include the functions and evolution of institutions. Time and place change of institutions should be taken into account (Aktan 2006: 12-13). For institutional economists, the concept of the institution does not merely consist of buildings or government offices. At the same time, the concept of institution reflects the result of a culture and knowledge. Therefore, upon mentioning institutions, concepts such as tradition, habit, thought structure, lifestyle should be connoted. The method of institutional economics suggests that human behaviors and habits lead to a cumulative causality within the social, cultural and economic processes. It is vague to define economic circumstances and processes without the comprehension of institutions (Kapp, 1976: 212). Social, cultural, political changes and strong social relations should be well explicated by technological changes. In this respect, individual interests and benefit maximization are inadequate or inaccurate. Institutional thought is not present in the individual analysis. Thus, individuals do not deliberately (or incidentally) establish institutions. Institutions do affect and shape individuals. In this respect, institutional economics has been an economic understanding that apprehends the strong historical ties correctly.

FUTURE RESEARCH DIRECTIONS

This study, following a brief description of institutional economics, examines the existence of the definitions and concepts of the historical school of economics within the old institutional economics. In this context, the basic principles of the old and new institutional economics and the aspects of the historical school of economics that influence the institutional economy are mentioned. It is possible to assert that a comparative evaluation can be made from a wide perspective in future studies.

CONCLUSION

Historical school is against the mechanical society approach of the classical school, and it adopts an organic approach that the individual has associated with social life. Social life is too complicated to comprehend only with theories and formulas. In this regard, it is meaningless to constitute universal theorems for all societies. Economics is a social science that is involved with previous social and cultural changes. The people are not eternal creatures who live only today. In this sense, economics is distant to become a significant field of research without a historical perspective. The historical school determined its point of view to the economics with conducting historical and statistical researches by avoiding deductive method, accepting that economics cannot produce ubiquitous policies with constant laws and considering the fact that institutions and theories are interrelated.

Historical school examined economic events and institutions with its evolutionary, empirical and pragmatist philosophical bases by considering them from a different angle. By emphasizing institutional structure and the determinant role of institutions on economic events, the necessity of analyzing societies with an evolutionary point of view was surfaced by old institutional economics. In new institutional economics, on the other hand, the importance of institutions have been emphasized and it also has advocated that the assumptions of neo-classical economics (full knowledge, zero transaction costs, full rationality) can be used by flexing the concepts of neo-classical economics (imperfect data, transaction costs, bounded rationality, property rights, incomplete contracts).

The old institutional economics has brought about a very different framework in the field by putting forward alternatives to the views of Neo-classical and Marxist economics, explaining the economics as an interdisciplinary science, and making non-economic definitions such as human nature, behavior, routine, and habits. Moreover, it has stated that the concepts among the fields of interest of institutional economics such as market structure, property rights, and technology are also very crucial for the economy.

The fact that the old institutional economy does not present a general theory about the concept of the institution has rendered the perspective of institutional economics implicit. This implicit perspective is interpreted by the way in which institutional economics suggests solutions to basic economic circumstances such as production, consumption, distribution and economic problems such as income distribution inequality, unemployment, and poverty. By courtesy of these annotations, it can be asserted that economic problems tend to occur in organization, regulation and control mechanisms in terms of institutional economics. Based on the concept of cumulative causation and path dependence, it does not seem possible to solve the economic problems of a country if there are no well-established, strong and efficiently functioning institutions in that country.

The cumulative causation reveals the institutional order brought by the society throughout many years, the extent to which it developed habits and thoughts for the happiness of the people, the social and economic relations, the technological development and innovation processes (Fujita, 2004: 2), in other words, the answer for the question of how to live better. In this respect, cumulative causation is a concept frequently used by Veblen and other institutional economists in explaining the institutions and institutional change. The concept of path dependence is utilized to express the path (historical route) of a society. Accordingly, every society has evolved through its own historical, social and economic path. The path of society is absolutely unlike of any other. Therefore, it is not possible to apply solutions for the general problems of poverty, growth and development problems for every society (Boschma, 2009: 16).

The New Institutional economics, as well as the Old Institutional economics, argues that institutions have a crucial role in economic behaviors. The unrealistic assumptions (such as full information, zero transaction costs, and perfect rationality) of Neoclassical economics which cannot apprehend the role of institutions should be defined at more comprehensible levels. Although it does not fully accept the assumptions of neoclassical economics, it argues that these assumptions can be used with some bending. Institutional economics argues that individuals have limited mental capacity in the presence of unobservable circumstances and uncertainty, and therefore cannot have full information about the course of events. Nonetheless, Neo-classical economics offers an opposite view by recognizing every aspect of life as predictable. In other words, it is possible to estimate the whole structure in the evaluation of the future (Kama, 2011: 186). According to an approach that determines the study field of the new institutional economics, the basic problem of the old institutionalists involves mentioning the importance of institutions without economic theory, whereas the New Institutional economics both presents the economic theory and gives the institutions the value they deserve (Kirsten and Kherallah, 2001: 5). Coase, as one of the founders of the new institutional economics, explains the same situation as follows: the knowledge and experience in the historical and philosophical background of the old institutional economics indicate us how vital the institutions really are. The fact that the old institutional economics did not achieve a positive theory has resulted in the failure of institutional economics (Coase, 1984: 230).

According to the old institutional economy in terms of the emergence of institutions, individual behaviors appear as a product of the institutional structure within which individual dwell and have an impact on the economic and social structures. According to the new institutional economics, habits, thoughts, and traditions shape the behaviors of the individual and, in turn, these behaviors shape the institutional structure (Hodgson, 2007: 327). As can be seen, the issue of the emergence of institutions has been handled differently by both schools. The Old Institutional economics states that existing institutions shape human behaviors, whereas it is possible to claim that the New Institutional economics deals with the emergence of institutions on the basis of individuals. The difference between the Old and New Institutional economists in the process of emergence of institutions involves the response to the question of how institutions change. The key factor in institutional change is technology according to old institutional economists. As technology develops, new forms of social structure would emerge. Within this new social structure, the contradictions between social values and individual values would be solved to the extent to which a conciliatory rule is realized (Demir, 1996: 205).

Essentially, the New Institutional economics expresses that the role of institutions in the economy should not be denied. Since this role requires an interdisciplinary analysis, many new views and areas originating at the New Institutional economics have been identified. One of the most important arguments of the New Institutional economics, by bending some of the assumptions of the Neo-Classical economics such as full information, zero transaction costs, perfect rationality, involves the presence of such concepts as transaction costs in the economy, limited rationality, property rights, incomplete contracts, and opportunism. All of these economic improvements are made through social and economic institutions.

According to the generally accepted view, institutions consist of formal and informal rules. All of the institutions formed through them determine the rules of the game played in society. Formal rules constitute the content of the framework formed by the top authorities such as law, contract, organization, market and political system. Informal rules refer to the values, traditions, religion, habits, sociological tendencies in society. Informal rules make it easier to understand the relationship between individuals or groups in public affairs and management. Institutions render human behaviors more prominent. The institutions are closely associated with economic activity, growth, and development process since they all have impacts on human behaviors (North, 1990: 42). The point that needs to be carefully considered is that there is a macro- and micro-level understanding of the New Institutional economics. Macro understanding is associated with the institutional framework or, in other words, the rules of the game. The institutional framework, i.e., the rules of the game, influences the effectiveness and behaviors of economic actors, in turn, the organizational form and process. In an economy, the political, social and legal framework constitutes the basis of production, trade, and distribution (Williamson, 1985: 19). The micro-level analysis of new institutional economics includes institutional regulations for building governance. Institutional regulations refer to decisions made by economic units in managing more individuals (Williamson, 2000: 42).

New institutional economics has indicated that economics cannot be reduced into one single theory due to the existence of institutional structure. Moreover, it also has expressed the existence of different fields such as New History of Economics (North, Fogel, Rutherford), Public Choice and Constitutional Economics (Buchanan, Tullock, Olson, Bates), New Social Economy (Becker), Social Capital (Putnam, Coleman), Economics of Property Rights (Alchian, Demsetz), Economics of Transaction Costs (Coase, North, Williamson), Knowledge Economy (Akerloff, Stigler, Stiglitz), Collective Action Theory (Ostrom, Olson, Hardin) and Law and Economics (Posner). All the developments of these fields are in a tight connection. The thing that provides this connection is the institutional structure itself. Although new institutional economics has become distant to the evolutionary mentality of historical school and has got close to neo-classical doctrine, it will continue to stay as a dynamic field in terms of shaping the economic policy of our age.

REFERENCES

Aktan, C. C. (2006). Kurumsal İktisat, Kurallar, Kurumlar ve Ekonomik Gelisme. Sermaye Piyasası Kurulu Yayınları, Yayın no: 194, Ankara, Turkey.

Ashley, W. J. (1894). Roscher's Programme of 1843. *The Quarterly Journal of Economics*, *9*(1), 99–105. doi:10.2307/1883638

Ata, A. Y. (2009). *Kurumsal İktisat Çerçevesinde Yolsuzluğun Fırsat Ve Motivasyonları: AB Ülkeleri Üzerine Bir İnceleme*. (Unpublished doctoral dissertation), Çukurova Üniversitesi, Sosyal Bilimler Enstitüsü, Turkey.

Barbash, J. (2005). John. R. Commons: Pioneer of labor economics. *University of California Working Paper,* 42-49. Retrieved from http://www.bls.gov/1989/05/art4full.pdf

Bas, D. G. (2011). *Kapitalizmin Istikrarsızlıgı: Veblen, Keynes ve Minsky*, (Unpublished doctoral dissertation), Hacettepe Üniversitesi, Sosyal Bilimler Enstitüsü, Turkey.

Bas, D. G. (2013). Kurum İçgüdü ve Alıskanlık Kavramları Temelinde Veblen'in Kurumsal Evrim Teorisi. *Amme Dergisi*, *46*(4), 45-65. Retrieved from http://www.todaie.edu.tr/resimler/ekler/

Bocutoglu, E. (2012). *İktisadi Düşünceler Tarihi*. Trabzon, Turkey: Murathan Yayınevi.

Boschma, R. (2009). Evolutionary economic geography and its implications for regional innovation. *Journal of Policy Utrecht University*, *5*(1), 55–63. Retrieved from http://econ.geo.uu.nl/peeg/peeg.html

Çetin, T. (2012). Yeni Kurumsal İktisat. *Sosyoloji Konferansları No: 45*. Retrieved from journals.istanbul.edu.tr/iusoskon/article/viewFile/1023018512/10230177

Chavance, B. (2009). *Institutional economics. (F. Wells, Trans.) Routledge Press*. Taylor & Francis e-Library.

Coase, R. (1984). The new institutional economics. *Journal of Institutional and Theoretical Economics*, *140*(2), 229–231.

Commons, J. R. (1931). Institutional economics. *The Journal of American Economic Review*, *21*(4), 88–102. Retrieved from http://www.jstor.org/stable/495

Demir, Ö. (1996). *Kurumcu İktisat*. Ankara, Turkey: Vadi Yayınları.

<eref>Ollila, P. (2009). Principles of Institutional Economics. University of Helsinki WP, No: 56, 1-73. Retrieved from http://www.helsinki.fi/taloustieconomics.pdf

<eref>Samuels, W. J. (1969). On the future of institutional economics. Journal of Economic Issues, 3(3), 67-72. Retrieved from http://www.jstor.org/stable/422401

Erim, N. (2011). *İktisadi Düşünce Tarihi*. Umuttepe Yayınları, Kocaeli.

Fujita, N. (2004). Gunnar Myrdal's Theory of cumulative causation. *Economic Research Center*, Discussion Paper 147, 72-86. Retrieved from http://www.soec.nagoya/erc/DP/paper147.pdf.

Fusfeld, D. R. (2000). A manifesto or institutional economics remarks upon receiving the Veblen-Commons award. *Journal of Economic Issues*, *34*(2), 257–265. doi:10.1080/00213624.2000.11506265

Hodgson, G, M. (1998). The approach of institutional economics. *Journal of Economic Literature*, *36*(1), 166–192. Retrieved from http://www.geoffreyhodgson.info/user/image/approachinec.pdf

Hodgson, G, M. (2000). What is the essence of institutional economics? *Journal of Economic Issues*, *34*(2), 317–329. doi:10.1080/00213624.2000.11506269

Kama, Ö. (2011). Yeni Kurumsal iktisat Okulunun Temelleri. *Gazi Üniversitesi İktisadi Ve İdari Bilimler Fakültesi Dergisi*, *13*(2), 183–204.

Kapp, W. K. (1976). The nature and significance of institutional economics. *Journal of Kyklos*, *29*(2), 182-196. Retrieved from http:www.kwilliamkapp.de/documents.pdf

Kazgan, G. (2004). *İktisadi Düşünce veya Politik İktisadın Evrimi*. İstanbul, Turkey: Remzi Kitabevi.

Kirsten, J. & Kherallah, M. (2001). The new institutional economics: Applications for agricultural policy research in developing countries. *International Food Policy Research Institute*, Working Paper, No: 41, 1-38.

Kızılkaya, E. İ. (2007). Weber, Veblen ve Kapitalizmin Ruhu. Kurumsal İktisat, (Ed.) Eyüp Özveren, İmge Kitabevi Yayınları, Ankara.

Köse, S. (2003). Institutıonalism of Thorstein Veblen and the theory of business cycles. *Süleyman Demirel Üniversitesi, İİBF Dergisi*, *8*(1), 283-297. Retrieved from http://sablon.sdu.edu.tr/fakulteler/iibf/dergi/files/2003-1-18.pdf

Locke, J. (2002). *Uygar Yönetim Üzerine İkinci İnceleme*. Çeviren: Serdar Tasçı & Hale Akman, Metropol yayınları, İstanbul, Orijinal yazım tarihi 1690.

Mitchell, W. C. (1935). Commons on institutional economics. *The American Economic Review*, *25*(4), 635–652. Retrieved from http://www.jstor.org/stable/1807801

North, D. C. (1990). *Institutions, institutional change and economic performance*. Cambridge, UK: Cambridge University Press. doi:10.1017/CBO9780511808678

Rutherford, M. (2001). Institutional economics: Then and now. *The Journal of Economic Perspectives*, *15*(3), 173–194. Retrieved from http://pubs.aeaweb.org/pdf</eref

Savas, V. F. (2000). İktisadın Tarihi. Siyasal Kitabevi, Ankara.</eref>

Tribe, K. (2003). In W. J. Samuels & J. E. Biddle (Eds.), *A companion to the history of economic thought* (pp. 215–230). Blackwell Publıshing. doi:10.1002/9780470999059.ch14

Veblen, T. B. (1898). Why is economics not an evolutionary science? *The Quarterly Journal of Economics*, *12*(1), 117–182. Retrieved from http://eleganttechnology.com/resource/ECO_SCI.PDF

Veblen, T. B. (1899). The preconceptions of economic science. *The Quarterly Journal of Economics*, *13*(4), 396-426. Retrieved from http://www.jstor.org/stable/1883645.

Veblen, T. B. (2014). *Aylak Sınıfın Teorisi. Çeviren: Enver Günsel*. İstanbul, Turkey: Tutku Yayınevi.

Williamson, O. E. (1985). The reflections of new institutional economics. *Journal of Institutional and Theoretical Economics*, 2nd Symposium pp. 187-195. Retrieved from http://www.jstor.org/stable/40750794

Williamson, O. E. (2000). Transaction cost economics. In C. Menard & M. Shirley (Eds.), *Handbook of New Institutional Economics* (pp. 41–65). Springer.

Yıldırım, S. (2009). *Kurumsal iktisat Bağlamında Ülkeler Arası Büyüme Farklılıklarının Analizi.* (Unpublished doctoral dissertation), Anadolu Üniversitesi, Sosyal Bilimler Enstitüsü, Eskişehir.

KEY TERMS AND DEFINITIONS

Empirical Thought on Institutional Economics: The human mind has changed in everywhere with experiments and sensations.

Historical School: It can be defined as a school that aspires to examine economics through the development of social relations in history.

Institution: Individual behaviors and this behavior affect both economic and social structure.

Neoclassical Economy: The view of neoclassical economics which isolates people and differentiates them from economic, behavioral patterns.

Chapter 12
Transaction Cost Approach to the Outsourcing Decision Problem

Dilek Erdogan
https://orcid.org/0000-0002-2079-777X
Gaziantep University, Turkey

ABSTRACT

Outsourcing has become a management tool that is increasingly involved in the manager's agenda, but the decision to outsource is a problematic issue for decision makers in organizations. Outsourcing provides many benefits but also includes many risks, so every outsourcing agreement does not result in success. This chapter aims to provide a better understanding of the outsourcing problem in light of transaction cost economics. For this purpose, the concept of outsourcing is first explained. The transaction characteristics and the behavioral assumptions of the theory, which play a role in increasing or decreasing transaction costs, are clarified. Finally, governance decision (outsource or not) and some critical issues (safeguarding mechanism against opportunistic behavior by supplier, adaptation, and performance evaluation problem) that will arise after the outsourcing decisions are discussed.

INTRODUCTION

The outsourcing discussion refers to a situation which is traditionally well known in theory and practice as "make or buy" a decision. One of the traditional definitions of outsourcing is "outside resource using" (Quinn & Hilmer, 1994). Outsourcing is the handover of an activity to a supplier; it is an alternative to internal production (Aubert, Patry, & Rivard, 2002). Outsourcing subject, outsourcing object, outsourcing partner, and outsourcing design are four major elements of outsourcing. Outsourcing subject is the economic institution which decides outsourcing decision (or not). Outsourcing objects are transaction or transactions that are outsourced. Transactions can take place at different levels of activity of an organization and activities of an organization are divided mainly into four groups: the core business activities (activities related to the existence of a company), core-close activities (linked directly to core activities),

DOI: 10.4018/978-1-7998-0333-1.ch012

Copyright © 2020, IGI Global. Copying or distributing in print or electronic forms without written permission of IGI Global is prohibited.

core-distinct activities (supporting activities), and disposable activities (activities with general availability). For example, while information technology is a supportive activity, the flight operation is the core activity for an airline company. The decision to outsource support activity or core activity will be at different levels of difficulty because outsourcing of the core activity will be a more strategic decision, while the outsourcing of support activity will be a more operational decision. All potential suppliers who can provide the activities needed by the organization are called outsourcing partners (Arnold, 2000). The outsourcing design is a matter of governance structure and will be explained in more detail in the following sections.

Outsourcing has become a vital source of competitive advantage because it provides several benefits for organizations, such as reducing the cost of ownership of products/services, resolving technical problems without increasing the number of staff, and enabling the company to focus on its core business. However, it is not always easy for to organizations to manage outsourcing deals as it also involves many risks, such as increase of dependency on the supplier, loss of knowledge of how to conduct business, the difficulty of calculating transaction costs, and opportunist behaviors by the supplier. These risks of outsourcing lead to failures in some situations, so it is vital that managers have a good understanding of what makes outsourcing useful. For instance, according to a survey conducted by Deloitte Consulting in 2012, it was found that 48% of companies were not satisfied with the IT outsourcing contract (Qi & Chau, 2015). Given all these risks, it is essential that decision-makers know what increases or decreases transaction costs to achieve the set goals.

The transaction cost economy (TCE) focuses on whether the transactions are more effective through which mechanism (hierarchy or market). This also refers to as make (refers to hierarchy) or buy (refers to market) decision in the transaction cost economics (Williamson, 1998 p. 30). This chapter's objective is to provide a better understanding of economic factors affecting outsourcing decision, and governance of outsourcing transactions in the light of transaction cost economics.

THE CONCEPT OF TRANSACTION COST

The roots of the transaction cost economics are based on Ronald Coase's 1937 article "The nature of the firm". In this article, Coase criticized the simplified view of the economy by asking his famous question, "why are there firms?" Price theory could not answer this question, because according to the theory, there is no cost element other than production and transport costs. However, Coase emphasized that the complexity of the price system by stating how complex a transaction is, it is more costly to negotiate, compose and implement the agreement between the parties concerned (Coase, 1937). He was the first economist arguing that price theory not able to explain about costs that accompany exchange relationship on markets. In his article, he tried to answer the reasons for the existence of the firms and the determinants of the firm size. According to him, the main reason as to why it is profitable to establish a firm, is that there is a more costly way of using the price mechanism (Coase, 1937 p. 389). The price includes costs associated with negotiating and concluding contracts, in addition to production costs. Therefore, it is likely that firms will emerge when contracts become too expensive. According to Coase, firms exist because they can sometimes reduce the costs of transactions relative to market transacting. Coase asked the following questions to explain the determinants of firm size. Why, if by organizing one can eliminate certain costs and in fact reduce the cost of production, are there any market transactions at all? Why is not all production carried by one big firm? According to Coase, if all transactions are completed within a firm, the extra internal cost will arise in addition to production cost and the entrepreneur will lose his capability to making the best use of production factors. A firm will tend to expand in its own hierarchy until the cost of completing an additional transaction is equal as the cost of completing the same transaction in the market (Coase, 1937 p. 393).

Coase's transaction cost approach developed by Williamson. He discussed the sources of transactions, and operationalized Transaction Cost Economics (TCE) by focusing on the behavioral assumptions and transaction attributes (Williamson, 1979; 1981; 1985). According to Williamson (1981 p. 552), transaction is the unit of analysis in transaction cost economics. The transaction is defined as "occur when a good or service is traded across a technologically separable interface" (Williamson, 1996 p. 377). Williamson is described transaction cost as the "equivalent of friction in physical systems".

Transaction cost is classified ex-ante cost and ex-post cost. Ex-ante costs include costs such as potential trading partners and relevant prices, negotiation and writing of contracts while ex-post costs include costs such as maladaptation, renegotiation, monitoring, and breach of contract (Williamson, 1985 p. 388; 1996 p. 379). According to TCE, the problem of economic organization arises from contracts. Determining the transaction costs of a contract-based transaction is an essential determinant in choosing between the market and the hierarchy.

The primary objective of TCE is to explain why the transactions in specific institutional arrangements take place at different levels of efficiency. According to TCE, attributes of transactions and institutional structure lead to high conversion efficiency. Additionally, according to TCE, make or buy decision should be given according to transaction costs, by organizations. Transaction costs that have a significant impact on this decision are affected by the nature of the transaction and environmental uncertainty condition. The following paragraphs provide an overview of the attributes of the transaction.

Transaction Attributes

According to TCE, the transaction has three attributes. One of them is asset specificity; specific assets are defined as an asset that cannot be re-used without sacrificing its productivity value if the contract is interrupted or terminated early (Williamson, 1985 p. 96). As the asset's next best use value is much lower, the investor will lose some of its investment if the transaction is not completed (Aubert, Rivard, & Patry, 1996). In his study Williamson (1981 p. 555), described three types of asset specificity; site specificity, physical asset specificity, human asset specificity. Site specificity is the need for a party (buyer or supplier) to be physically located near the other party to participate in the transaction. Positioning fixed assets (e.g., building, factory) close to production to reduce inventory and transport costs can be a site specificity example. Physical assets specificity consists of the apparatus required for transaction completion. For the specificity of physical assets, the investment in special molds required for a particular production can be given as an example. Human asset specificity represents the learning and the knowledge parties need to acquire in order to participate in the exchange. The specificity of human assets includes the knowledge of staff, the allocation of staff, the training and learning processes of staff, for the only particular transaction (Rindfleisch & Heide, 1997 p. 35; Williamson, 1981 p. 55). In his early work, Williamson argued that asset specificity emerged in three ways, while in his later studies (Williamson, 1985 p. 96; 1996 p. 60) he added that there is three more asset specificity including dedicated assets, intangible assets, and temporal specificity. Dedicated assets for the supplier are all general investments to be made when a particular customer purchases a significant amount of product or service (Joskow, 1987). Due to the limited size of the market for these assets, they cannot be re-used for other buyers.

For example, the ground handling company, which is the supplier of the airline company, invests ground handling equipment (e.g., push-back car) under the type of aircraft owned by the airline. This investment can be called a dedicated asset for the supplier (Erdogan, 2019). The intangible asset is intangible capital such as a brand name. Temporal specificity is the possibility of a delay in production or delivery. This would be a bargaining device for outsourcing partners. For example, newspaper publishers generally own presses whereas book publishers generally do not (Ruester, 2010 p. 9).

The high specificity of transactions is an indication that the transaction has an idiosyncratic nature. Asset specificity arises when significant investments in physical assets or human resources are required in an outsourcing relationship (Poppo & Zenger, 2002 p. 708). In the TCE literature, the concept of relationship-specific investments, which is equivalent to the asset specificity, is also used. Relationship-specific investments are investments that are not suitable for alternative use when the relationship ends, or they depreciate when the relationship ends (Anderson & Weitz, 1992 p. 20). The asset specificity of transactions is an important determinant of the decision to outsource because the asset specificity locks the parties to the relationship. In such a relationship, both the buyer and the supplier will be locked into the relationship, because the supplier will want to win the return on his investment and buyer will have difficulty to find an outsourcing partner who can invest in the relationship.

According to TCE, another transaction characteristic affecting the selection of governance mechanism is uncertainty. Studies based on transaction cost theory do not have a full consensus on the types of uncertainty, but environmental uncertainty, behavioral uncertainty are often discussed. Environmental uncertainty is due to the dynamism of the environment, and it is difficult to predict the possible future situations in the dynamic environment (Cannon, Achrol, & Gundlach, 2000 p.181). Issues such as rapid technological change, rapid price change, product availability and the presence of support services in the market cause environmental uncertainty. The existence of environmental uncertainty in an outsourcing relationship causes adaptation problems. According to Williamson, behavioral uncertainty means that people can be opportunistic with "non-disclosure, disguise or distortion of strategic knowledge" (Williamson, 1985 p. 57). In the context of outsourcing, behavioral uncertainty is related to the difficulty of measuring the performance of the vendor. If the supplier's behavioral uncertainty is high, this will make it difficult for the buyer to assess the vendor's performance.

Another attribute of the transaction is the frequency of the transaction. Transaction frequency refers to the extent to which transactions recur. In other words, the frequency is the number of times a client organization initiates the transaction (Williamson, 1985 p. 62). Higher levels of transaction frequency provide an incentive for firms to choose the hierarchy mechanism because the overhead cost of hierarchical governance will be easier to recover for recurring transactions.

TCE states that depending on the transaction characteristics described above and based on behavioral assumptions, the most appropriate governance structure should be selected. For example, when transactions are in a high environmental uncertainty, and there are few partner alternatives, market governance is ineffective or unsuccessful (Fink, Edelman, Hatten, & James, 2006 p. 501).

Behavioral Assumptions

Transaction costs theory has two underlying behavioral assumptions, bounded rationality and opportunism. According to Williamson (1975), if the information is complete and economic actors are perfectly rational, transaction costs will not be occurred theoretically, because all the unexpected situations are known and economic actors could adapt to these unexpected situations easily. However, people have limited rationality. According to Simon (1957 p. 198), people with bounded rationality do not have enough cognitive capacity to see all problems. Bounded rationality also involves language limits. Individuals are not able to articulate their knowledge clearly to be entirely understood by others. Therefore, even if decision makers intend to make rational decisions, it is not possible to make rational decisions with limited information processing and limited communication capabilities (Williamson, 1985 p. 46). In the context of outsourcing, the impact of limited rationality depends on the knowledge and skills that the buyer can use to identify requirements, select appropriate suppliers, prepare a contract and manage the relationship.

The other assumption of the theory is opportunism. Opportunism is defined as "self-interest seeking with guile" (Williamson,1985 p. 45). Opportunism means that given the opportunity, one or both parties may resort to poor behavior such as: lying, cheating, deceitful concealment of information, or violating agreements to further their own self-interest. Two types of opportunistic behavior are distinguished as active form of opportunism and passive form of opportunism. The form of passive opportunism arises from the lack of dedication to doing the best from one's own competencies. Active form of opportunism refers to "self-interest seeking with guile" (Wathne & Heide, 2000).

In the context of outsourcing, the opportunistic behavior of the supplier may take many forms. For example, opportunistic behavior may arise in such as withholding valuable information, bargaining, shirking, failing to fulfill obligations (Lioliou, Zimmermann, Willcocks, & Gao, 2014). For this reason, the biggest concern regarding outsourcing is what control mechanisms are to be used to protect against the opportunism of the outsourcing partner. The main drivers leading to opportunistic behavior, and the role of the contracts as a control mechanism against opportunism will be explained in detail next.

Transaction cost theory, based on these behavioral assumptions, it is based on the decision of economic actors to choose the governance mechanisms. For example, the market governance would be preferred to the hierarchy governance, which would reduce them despite the problems of unbounded rationality and opportunism. On the other hand, if the established market governance cannot solve these transaction problems, hierarchical governance systems can be chosen, which are more costly.

Governance Structures

Transactions are governed by governance structures (markets, hybrids, hierarchies) (Williamson, 1996 p. 377). According to TCE, firms are a particular form of organization for managing transactions between one party and another (Coase, 1937). In this conception of the firm, the firm itself is characterized as a hierarchy (Williamson, 1975, 1985). Hierarchies are based on the centralization of property rights by management (Arnold, 2000 p. 24). In the form of this governance, the parties to the transaction are dependent, and the transactions are carried out within the organization. The market exchange is generally based on price, competition, and contracts that enable the parties to be aware of their responsibilities (Williamson, 1985 p. 104). In the market exchange, the parties are entirely independent of each other. For example, if a supplier cannot meet the customer's requirements, they will no longer be able to participate in an exchange relationship. There are many governance structures called hybrid governance, which are neither markets nor hierarchies. The hybrid governance structure has the power to effectively reduce the transaction costs associated with market exchange while at the same time reducing the need for vertical ownership (Rindfleisch & Heide, 1997). Hybrid forms generally emerge in long-term contracts, mutual trade and franchising agreements between partners.

Table 1. Theoretical associations between transaction attributes and governance structure

Insourcing	**Internal Outsourcing**			**External Outsourcing**		
Make (own production)	Center approach	Cooperation	Capital investment	Formal co-working	Co-working without formal agreement	Spot transaction
Only Hierarchy	***Hybrid Forms***					***Only Market***

Source: (Arnold, 2000)

There is a strong relationship between outsourcing design and governance structure. This relationship is shown in Table 1. Outsourcing can be designed as insourcing, internal outsourcing, and external outsourcing. The hierarchy is directly related to insourcing. External outsourcing and internal outsourcing are an alternative to internal production (hierarchy mechanism). External outsourcing means long-term relationships with spot transactions or suppliers. It relates to the market element. Internal outsourcing refers to a higher order hierarchical organization by creating independent profit centers instead of hierarchical divisions. The use of internal outsourcing can sometimes be arranged as horizontal cooperation of independent companies or with capital investment by a general service company (joint venture).

According to TCE, the relations between transaction attributes and the governance structure are summarized in Table 2. According to Williamson (1985 p. 56), asset specificity is the most essential attribute of a transaction, "it only takes on importance in conjunction with bounded rationality/opportunism and in the presence of uncertainty." As shown in Table 2, non-specific assets call for market structure, irrespective of the level of frequency and uncertainty. This is because there will be no assets at risk and therefore there will be no need to protect from possible opportunism and in this case, the market structure would be suitable. In the outsourcing context, if the specificity of the asset is low, buyer may use the supplier's standard contracts because assets are not at risk and therefore, the buyer does not need to use a detailed and customized contract against relational hazards.

The concept of mixed assets refers to the integration of standardized and customized elements, and the concept of idiosyncratic asset refers to highly specific assets. If there is a high level of uncertainty for an idiosyncratic asset and mixed assets, hierarchy would be appropriate governance structure regardless of the frequency level of the transaction. The supplier's likelihood of opportunistic behavior will increase when mixed and highly specific assets, so it would be more logical to keep the transaction in the organization (Williamson, 1979 p. 234). Moreover, because of the bounded rationality of individual,

Table 2. The relations between transaction attributes and governance

		Asset Specificity			**Asset Specificity**		
		Non-specific	**Mixed**	**Idiosyncratic**	**Non-specific**	**Mixed**	**Idiosyncratic**
Frequency	**Occasional**	Market (standard contracting)	Market (customized contracting)	Market (customized contracting)	Market (standard contracting)	Hierarchy	Hierarchy
	Recurrent	Market (standard contracting)	Market (customized contracting	Hierarchy	Market (standard contracting)	Hierarchy	Hierarchy
With low or medium uncertainty					**With high uncertainty**		

Source: (adapted Williamson 1979:253 and Aleghanband, 2011:130).

it is impossible to predict all changes in an uncertain environment. If there are highly specific assets and uncertain environment, the hierarchy structure would be the appropriate governance structure. However, if there are mixed assets and low uncertainty environment, the transaction can also be completed through the market structure, irrespective of its frequency level (Table 2). In such a situation, using a detailed and customized contract will protect buyer against opportunism of supplier.

According to TCE, frequency level of transaction is decisive factor for the governance choice when uncertainty is low to medium and assets are idiosyncratic, it is proposed that appropriate governance structure would be market if the transactions occur occasionally. However, for a recurrent transaction with high level of specificity, hierarchy would be appropriate governance structure (Alaghehband, Rivard, Wu, & Goyette, 2011 p. 130).

OPPORTUNISM

The assumption that one of the parties may be opportunistic in an exchange relationship is likely to affect governance selection (make or buy). However, the fact that this behavioral risk becomes an action is a factor that will affect the performance and continuity of the relationship. In this section, the drivers causing the parties to act as opportunistic will be explained first, and the role of the contract, which is a formal control mechanism against opportunism, will be revealed from the TCE framework.

Drivers of Opportunism

Information asymmetry is one of the leading elements of opportunism. Information asymmetry between the parties is due to the fact that one of the exchange parties has relatively more information about some aspects of the exchange than the other party. This will facilitate the opportunistic behavior of the party with more information (Heide, 2003 p. 19). If the buyer believes that the supplier has a much broader knowledge of the issues related to certain transactions, buyer may be concerned that the supplier may mislead.

If the parties with information asymmetry between them hide their real intentions before and after the contract, they can lead to opportunistic behavior in two ways; adverse selection and moral hazard (Gurçaylılar-Yenidogan, 2013a). Adverse selection results from pre-contractual confidential information and provides an incentive for ex-ante opportunism. Especially in the contract negotiation process, the buyer may concern that the supplier may use this situation in his favor because the supplier has more knowledge over the contract. Given the buyer is preparing the contract for the first time for this transaction, the supplier has prepared a similar contract several times for different buyers. In this case, the supplier can foresee future situations and hide information advertently in a manner from the buyer. In the case of information asymmetry, the buyer may take some measures to prevent the supplier's opportunistic behavior. One of the two basic methods that will prevent ex-ante opportunism during the preparation of the contract is to get legal or technical consultancy services from the outside, and the other one is to involve the people who worked in similar outsourcing projects in the company or outside (Barthelemy, 2005 p. 545).

Moral hazard is an asymmetric information problem that occurs as a result of secret actions that take place after the contract is signed, and it leads ex-post opportunism. Moral hazard arises from the fact that it is impossible for a principal to observe the behavior of the agent without extra costs. As the buyer cannot directly observe the level of effort performed by the supplier, the buyer cannot easily understand whether a problem is due to the negligence of the supplier or an unforeseen event. The supplier is aware that the buyer has a lack of information and may claim that poor performance has occurred due to events beyond his control (Aubert et al., 1996). Monitoring compliance with standards developed by the buyer for quality, distribution or other performance objectives can be used to reduce information asymmetry and control opportunistic behavior (Stump & Heide, 1996).

Incomplete contracts under environmental uncertainty are one of the main driving forces of opportunist behavior by enabling the opportunist behavior of the partners. According to TCE, and due to the bounded rationality of individuals, it is not possible to compose complete contracts under environmental uncertainty (Williamson, 1988 pp. 569-570; 1996 p. 47), it is not possible for the contracts prepared by individuals to predict all possible situations, so all contracts are incomplete. Environmental uncertainty may increase the need for adjustments during the execution of the contract. Therefore, outsourcing partners rely on contingent contracts that permit some revisions in the initial agreement. But because of incomplete nature of contracts, they have limited coordinating capacity to promote mutually beneficial behavior under each unforeseeable circumstance. In this case, the stronger partner of the relationship is likely to interpret the contingency clauses of the contract in their own interest (Gurcaylılar-Yenidogan, 2014). For example, when an unforeseen situation occurs during the execution of the contract, the stronger party in the relationship can benefit from this situation in its own interests and may exhibit opportunistic behaviors.

The existence of relationship-specific investments in an outsourcing relationship can encourage the parties to opportunistic behavior. Transaction-specific investments refer to the extent to which assets are specialized to a particular relationship (Williamson, 1985). These assets would be intangible investments as well as tangible or physical investments that cannot be redeployed. As transaction-specific investments have lower value in alternative uses, this situation results in a hold-up problem where the other party (not investing) could extract an advantage from the investor by threatening to withdraw from the transaction. If one of the parties to the relationship invests in specific assets, the other party may wish to gain benefit for his favor from the relationship with the threat of withdrawal from the outsourcing relationship. On the other hand, the investor may expose the risk of opportunistic behavior to the other party (not invest) who wishes to obtain above-normal returns from specific investments and hence to its unilateral gains. As a result, in a relationship in which the relationship-specific investments exist, both parties may exhibit opportunistic behaviors by not fulfilling their promises or trying to bring new provisions in line with their own advantages (Carson, Madhok, & Wu, 2006; Gurcaylılar-Yenidogan, 2013b).

Safeguarding Mechanism Against Opportunism: Contract

The contract is a formal safeguarding mechanism that will be used to prevent the partner's opportunistic behavior in an exchange relationship. As a formal safeguarding mechanism, contracts have many functions in managing the relationship. Traditionally, it is accepted that a formal relationship between the parties has been established with the signing of a written agreement between the buyer and the supplier. Undoubtedly, the outsourcing relationship begins on the basis of a written contract. Otherwise, it may not be possible to engage in commercial relations. One of the most important features of the written contract is that it is an official document that will provide legal protection to the parties. The signatories of the written agreement explicitly agree that legal action will be sought in the case of failure. In this way, the parties may protect themselves by applying the penalties specified in the contract or applying to court (Achrol & Gundlach, 1999 p. 109). Another function of the contract is to constitute a common understanding between the parties about responsibilities and expectations and thus reduce the misinterpretation of expectations. In written contracts, the roles of the parties are clearly determined, and these roles are fixed and unchanged. The parties may monitor whether the counterparties have fulfilled their obligations through these contracts (Lioliou et al., 2014 p. 513).

As well as contracts, Service Level Agreements (SLA) based on contracts are also a critical mechanism for managing the relationship. The contract describes the products and services purchased by the client, how each party has measured its responsibilities, penal sanctions, and the supplier's services. The purpose of the SLA is to provide a clear, concise and measurable definition of what the supplier should do for the buyer. For example, the SLA prepared for an information technology outsourcing may include the following: Network and server responses will be such that 98% of screen queries turn around in 1,500 milliseconds and will be available 99.998% of the time, with scheduled maintenance periods measured on a calendar monthly basis (Simmonds & Gilmour, 2005 p. 9). If the buyer can prepare a detailed SLA for the service, he/she receives, he/she can minimize the performance evaluation problem that will lead to the buyer's opportunistic behavior. However, it should not be forgotten that preparing a detailed contract or SLA is a factor increasing the transaction costs.

The contracts used in an outsourcing relationship can be standard or customized and detailed. The standard contract is usually the same contracts prepared by the supplier and applied to each buyer. The use of a standard contract is appropriate for a relationship where there is no relationship-specific investment for the buyer. However, the use of a standard contract in a relationship where there are a high asset specificity and environmental uncertainty can increase the opportunistic behavior because the contract composed by the supplier may contain clauses in favor of the supplier (Lacity & Hirschheim, 1993 p. 75). In such a case, the buyer may choose to personalize a standard contract prepared by the supplier or to prepare a more complex contract. In such a case, the buyer may propose a new customized contract by adapting some issues in the standard contract such as price, responsibilities and intellectual property rights. Another alternative for the buyer is the preparation of highly detailed and complex contracts under the characteristics of the transaction subject to the exchange. Detailed prepared contracts are considered as complex contracts which are prepared in detail in all matters such as the responsibilities of the parties, penalties, and solutions in case of conflict, considering all possible situations in the future. In a relationship with high relationship-specific investments, the dependence of the party investing more on the relationship will increase to another party (not invest), and the counterparty will be more likely to be opportunistic. For this reason, as the buyer's relationship-specific investments increase, more complex contracts will be needed (Williamson, 1991 p. 282) because complex contracts will minimize the potential opportunistic behavior of the supplier. Thus, a complex contract will provide more effective outsourcing by giving the parties a narrower space for opportunistic behavior in the face of unforeseen events in a relationship.

Although the buyer or supplier intends to make detailed contracts to prevent the risks of the relationship, it is not easy to convince the other party to accept all terms of the contract. During the contract negotiations, the tension between the parties is high, and there is a tight bargain between the buyer and the supplier. Buyers always aim to get the highest quality service at the lowest costs, while the suppliers aim to get maximum profit in return for the service they provide. If the contract is prepared on a one-sided basis only for the benefit of the buyer, this can be detrimental to the buyer in the long term because the supplier will then try to compensate for the loss by trying to apply extra fees. In the contract negotiation process in which the parties engage in mutual conflict of interest, it will not be possible for the agreement to have a long-term partnership relationship if the terms of the agreement, which would only benefit one party, are not abandoned (Gottschalk & Solli-Sæther, 2006 p. 158).

After deciding on the use of outsourcing, it is necessary to determine the duration of the contract by decision makers. This is a critical decision because the contract duration is seen as an optimization process in which the benefits of the increase in service to be purchased in a buyer-seller relation are balanced between the costs that will arise accordingly (Crocker & Masten, 1988). In an exchange relationship, the contract duration can be determined as short, long or indefinite (López-Bayón & González-Díaz, 2010). According to the TCE, contract duration is a control mechanism that will protect the parties against opportunistic behavior of the other party. According to TCE, the optimum contract duration varies depending on the asset specificity of the transaction subject to the exchange, and uncertainty (Crocker & Masten, 1988; Saussier, 1999). In outsourcing relationships with highly dedicated assets which are one of the types of asset specificity, if the contract is terminated prematurely, the supplier will have excess capacity, and the probability of using these assets in other relations will be less (Joskow, 1987). Similarly, the buyer would prefer to make a long-term contract due to the difficulty of finding a supplier to invest in the relationship and high ex-ante transaction costs (e.g. negotiation costs). However, in exchange relations, where environmental uncertainty is high, the parties will have to prepare detailed contracts to anticipate any future situation. This will increase the transaction costs due to difficult information acquisition and negotiation processes in uncertain environments. At the same time, no matter how detailed the contracts are prepared, it is not possible to foresee all possible situations in the future. Therefore, when environmental uncertainty is high, buyers may not prefer to be signed to a long-term contract with the supplier.

There are some limitations to the written contracts used as a formal mechanism in the management of the outsourcing relationship despite the functions mentioned above. For example, the preparation of detailed contracts that try to anticipate every possible situation in order to avoid the risks of the relationship increases the transaction costs (Poppo & Zenger, 2002 p. 708). Due to the fact that the preparation of detailed contracts is a laborious task, parties need to take extra time, do research, and if their expertise is not sufficient, it may be necessary to take external counseling. In addition to this, all contracts are incomplete, and therefore they are insufficient to respond to all situations that occur in the future between the parties, no matter how detailed they are prepared. Another significant limitation of written contracts is that they are not flexible. By the nature of the contracts, it is not easy to adapt the contracts to the new situation when a new request or need arises that is not previously mentioned between the parties (Williamson, 199 p. 283). The parties may need negotiation when an unexpected situation occurs which is not specified in the current contract. As a result, it may be necessary to prepare a new contract or protocol that creates additional processing costs.

Briefly, a contract provides an institutional framework in which legally binding parties are set, rights, duties, and responsibilities are identified, and the objectives, policies, and strategies underlying this relationship are determined. The purpose of a contract is therefore to facilitate exchange and to prevent opportunistic behavior. However, given the nature of contracts that are incomplete, there is always a risk of opportunistic behavior in an outsourcing relationship. Social safeguarding mechanism (e.g., trust) is therefore proposed as a complementary mechanism for managing inter-organizational relations (Poppo & Zenger, 2002 p. 721).

ADAPTATION AND PERFORMANCE EVALUATION PROBLEM

Adaptation and performance evaluation can be two major problems during the execution of the contract after the decision on outsourcing. According to Williamson (1991), adaptation is seen as the main problem of economic organization. The difficulty of modifying contractual agreements against changes in the external environment leads to the problem of adaptation (Rindfleisch & Heide, 1997). Adaptation pressures are evaluated in two categories: (a) demand, supply and changes in the transaction environment due to changes in technology, and (b) the need to adjust the business environment for reasons arising from the mutual dependence of the buyer and the supplier. The transaction environment is composed of commercial conditions (demand, supply, and technology conditions) affecting the content of the transaction and the terms of the contract. The rate and extent of change in demand and technology in a transaction indicate transaction instability (Gulati, Lawrence, & Puranam, 2005). The lack of information on the changes in the transaction environment is the main element that makes it difficult to respond to change.

Environmental uncertainty and task uncertainty are seen as antecedents of the adaptation problem. According to TCA, as the degree of environmental uncertainty increases, the cost of adapting formal contracts to the changing situation will increase. When a firm is faced with the need to adjust to an uncertain environment, it will attempt to decrease transaction costs through vertical integration (Williamson, 1991). According to Masten (1984), manufacturers are more likely to produce a mounting component than to buy from an external supplier, to produce a mounting component when faced with a high degree of environmental uncertainty. The task complexity (product complexity), which is one dimension of transaction uncertainty, also leads to adaptation problems and creates a need for mutual adaptation. Complex products require more monitoring and coordination. Thus, organizations will need more information processing and more detailed contracts to monitor complex task/ complex product.

If an organization has difficulty in assessing the contractual compliance of its outsourcing partner, performance evaluation problem arises. Bounded rationality and behavioral uncertainty are the antecedents of performance evaluation problem. According to TCE, the increase in the degree of behavioral uncertainty increases the cost of evaluating the performance of the exchange partner. Organizations try to reduce performance evaluation costs through the use of different forms of governance. An option for organizations is to minimize the cost of evaluating the performance of the partner through its vertical integration mechanism (Williamson, 1985). In the literature, empirically supported that vertical integration has the power to reduce performance monitoring and measurement costs (Anderson, 1985; Weiss & Anderson, 1992). Another option is the hybrid governance mechanism, which can be used to reduce performance evaluation costs related to behavior uncertainty for firms. For example, Heide and John (1990) provide supportive findings that there is a relationship between the behavioral uncertainty faced by manufacturers and monitoring supplier performance.

SOLUTIONS AND RECOMMENDATIONS

When we evaluate the outsourcing decision from the TCE framework, this decision refers to TCE's choice of governance issue, which is the main topic of discussion. If an organization decides to take some of its activities from the outside rather than self-fulfillment, then in order to complete these transactions, it has chosen the market mechanism by leaving the hierarchy mechanism. Unlike the TCE price theory, TCE emphasizes that outsourcing should be decided not only on production and transportation costs but also on transaction costs. In this context, decision-makers in organizations should take into account all ex-ante and ex-post transaction costs in order to make a more rational outsourcing decision. The biggest challenge for decision makers is the difficulty of measuring transaction costs. For example, the effort spent on finding suppliers is an ex-ante transaction cost element but how it will be measured. According to TCE, all contracts will be incomplete due to the limited rationality of the individuals and the supplier tends to act opportunistically. Therefore, it will create transaction costs in controlling and monitoring the supplier; at the same time, decision-makers should also not ignore these issues.

FUTURE RESEARCH DIRECTIONS

In this study, factors affecting the outsourcing decision and the problems encountered during the execution of outsourcing contracts are discussed conceptually. This discussion was conducted within the framework of the assumptions and recommendations of TCE, which belongs to the neoclassic economics. While TCE has a broad framework for explaining the outsourcing issue, it has some limitations. For example, outsourcing is likely to fail if a correct supplier is not selected, even if the transaction costs are low. Another critical point for outsourcing decision is made whether outsourcing activity is a core business activity or a support activity for the organization. Even if the transaction costs are very low, it may be more appropriate to complete the activity within the organization if the activity is core business for the organization. TCE ignores the impact of relationship norms while a strong emphasis on the impact of contracts as a safeguarding mechanism against opportunism. Together with the TCT, it is possible to look at the outsourcing issue deeply by providing a multi-paradigm by using theories such as theory of social change, resource-based theory.

CONCLUSION

As discussed above, the decision of outsourcing for decision-makers is quite complex. The activities that are outsourced can be called transactions from the TCE framework. TCE calls the outsource decision governance decision and argues that this decision should be made by evaluating the transaction costs. Transaction costs include all costs incurred before and after the outsourcing deal (Williamson, 1985). According to TCE, the characteristics of the transaction will affect transaction costs and, therefore, whether to use outsourcing or not. Asset specificity, uncertainty, and frequency are the attributes of the transaction. TCE recommends which governance mode will be appropriate according to the different combinations in which these features come together. For example, for a transaction with high environmental uncertainty and high transaction-specific investments, the completion of transactions within the organization (hierarchy) will minimize transaction costs because it will be difficult to assess the supplier's performance in an environment where environmental uncertainty is high, and relationship-specific investments will increase the supplier's likelihood of opportunistic behavior. If there are specific assets, market governance will fail by increasing the cost of partner replacement, therefore creating a bilateral monopoly in which partners may engage in opportunism without being replaced. Hence hierarchy or some hybrid forms would be more safeguarding mechanism against opportunistic behaviors (Carson, 2006).

TCE is based on two behavioral assumptions, bounded rationality and opportunism. These assumptions are the source of relational hazards. The bounded rationality assumption is that people have limited cognitive capacity and are not able to predict every situation (Simon, 1957). It is not possible for the contracts prepared by individuals to predict all possible situations, due to the unbounded rationality of individuals, all contracts are incomplete. When an unforeseen situation occurs during the execution of the contract, a powerful partner of relationship may take advantage of this situation in their own interests and show opportunistic behavior. The other assumption of the theory is opportunism. Opportunism means that given the opportunity, one or both parties may resort to acting such as lying, cheating, deceitful concealment of information, or violating formal or informal agreements to further their own self-interest (Wathne & Heide, 2000). Opportunistic behaviors in a buyer-supplier relationship may arise from the existence of information asymmetry between the parties, the existence of investments specific to the relationship, and the incomplete design of contracts. The TCE emphasizes the fact that the parties will not always be opportunistic while advocating the possibility of opportunistic behavior of the parties. However, if the supplier exhibits opportunistic behavior, the transaction costs will increase, and outsourcing will perhaps result in failure. In this case, the buyer should use a safeguarding mechanism against the supplier's likelihood of opportunistic behavior. According to TCE, complex contracts are seen as an effective mechanism for protection from opportunistic behavior. However, the preparation of detailed contracts is also an increase transaction costs, and it is not possible for people to foresee every situation due to their limited rationality, no matter how detailed the contracts are prepared.

REFERENCES

Achrol, R. S., & Gundlach, G. T. (1999). Legal and social safeguards against opportunism in exchange. *Journal of Retailing*, *75*(1), 107–124. doi:10.1016/S0022-4359(99)80006-2

Alaghehband, F. K., Rivard, S., Wu, S., & Goyette, S. (2011). An assessment of the use of transaction cost theory in information technology outsourcing. *The Journal of Strategic Information Systems*, *20*(2), 125–138. doi:10.1016/j.jsis.2011.04.003

Anderson, E. (1985). The salesperson as outside agent or employee: A transaction cost analysis. *Marketing Science*, *4*(3), 234–254. doi:10.1287/mksc.4.3.234

Anderson, E., & Weitz, B. (1992). The use of pledges to build and sustain commitment in distribution channels. *JMR, Journal of Marketing Research*, *70*(2), 18–34. doi:10.1177/002224379202900103

Arnold, U. (2000). New dimensions of outsourcing: A combination of transaction cost economics and the core competencies concept. *European Journal of Purchasing & Supply Management*, *6*(1), 23–29. doi:10.1016/S0969-7012(99)00028-3

Aubert, B. A., Patry, M., & Rivard, S. (Eds.). (2002). *Managing IT outsourcing risk: Lessons learned information systems outsourcing*. Berlin, Germany: Springer.

Aubert, B. A., Rivard, S., & Patry, M. (1996). Development of measures to assess dimensions of IS operation transactions. *Omega*, *24*(6), 661–680. doi:10.1016/S0305-0483(96)00019-9

Bahli, B., & Rivard, S. (2003). The information technology outsourcing risk: A transaction cost and agency theory-based perspective. *Journal of Information Technology*, *18*(3), 211–221. doi:10.1080/0268396032000130214

Barthelemy, J. (2003). The hard and soft sides of IT outsourcing management. *European Management Journal, 21*(5), 539–548. doi:10.1016/S0263-2373(03)00103-8

Cannon, J. P., Achrol, R. S., & Gundlach, G. T. (2000). Contracts, norms, and plural form governance. *Journal of the Academy of Marketing Science, 28*(2), 180–194. doi:10.1177/0092070300282001

Carson, S. J., Madhok, A., & Wu, T. (2006). Uncertainty, opportunism, and governance: The effects of volatility and ambiguity on formal and relational contracting. *Academy of Management Journal, 49*(5), 1058–1077. doi:10.5465/amj.2006.22798187

Coase, R. H. (1937). The nature of the firm. *Economica, 4*(16), 386–405. doi:10.1111/j.1468-0335.1937.tb00002.x

Crocker, K. J., & Masten, S. E. (1988). Mitigating contractual hazards: Unilateral options and contract length. *The Rand Journal of Economics, 19*(3), 327–343. doi:10.2307/2555660

Erdogan, D. (2019). Sözleşme süresinin belirlenmesi: İşlem maliyeti teorisi bakışıyla yer hizmeti sözleşmeleri üzerine ampirik bir araştırma. *Gaziantep University Journal of Social Sciences, 18*(2), 623–637.

Fink, C., Edelman, L. F., Hatten, K. J., & James, W. L. (2006). Transaction cost economics, resource dependence theory, and customer–supplier relationships. *Industrial and Corporate Change, 15*(3), 497–529. doi:10.1093/icc/dtl008

Gottschalk, P., & Solli-Sæther, H. (2006). *Managing successful IT outsourcing relationship*. Hershey, PA: IRM Press. doi:10.4018/978-1-59140-760-7

Gulati, R., Lawrence, P. R., & Puranam, P. (2005). Adaptation in vertical relationships: Beyond incentive conflict. *Strategic Management Journal, 26*(5), 415–440. doi:10.1002mj.458

Gürcaylılar-Yenidogan, T. (2013a). Yeni kurumsal iktisat geleneğinde işlem maliyeti teorisinin rolü ve son gelişmeler. *Business & Economics Research Journal, 4*(2), 109–134.

Gürcaylılar-Yenidogan, T. (2013b). The impact of transaction attributes and trust on ex-post opportunism. *International Journal of Management Sciences and Business Research, 2*(6), 39–44.

Gürcaylılar-Yenidogan, T. (2014). Örgütlerarası ilişkilerde sözleşme tasarımını etkileyen faktörler. *Journal of Yasar University, 9*(34), 6063–6082.

Heide, J. B. (2003). Plural governance in industrial purchasing. *Journal of Marketing, 67*(4), 18–29. doi:10.1509/mkg.67.4.18.18689

Heide, J. B., & John, G. (1990). Alliances in industrial purchasing: The determinants of joint action in buyer-supplier relationships. *JMR, Journal of Marketing Research, 27*(1), 24–36. doi:10.1177/002224379002700103

Joskow, P. L. (1987). Contract duration and relationship-specific investments: Empirical evidence from coal markets. *The American Economic Review*, 168–185.

Lacity, M. C., & Hirschheim, R. (1993). The information systems outsourcing bandwagon. *Sloan Management Review, 35*(1), 73.

Lioliou, E., Zimmermann, A., Willcocks, L., & Gao, L. (2014). Formal and relational governance in IT outsourcing: Substitution, complementarity and the role of the psychological contract. *Information Systems Journal, 24*(6), 503–535. doi:10.1111/isj.12038

López-Bayón, S., & González-Díaz, M. (2010). Indefinite contract duration: Evidence from electronics subcontracting. *International Review of Law and Economics, 30*(2), 145–159. doi:10.1016/j.irle.2010.03.001

Masten, S. E. (1984). The organization of production: Evidence from the aerospace industry. *The Journal of Law & Economics, 27*(2), 403–417. doi:10.1086/467071

Poppo, L., & Zenger, T. (2002). Do formal contracts and relational governance function as substitutes or complements? *Strategic Management Journal, 23*(8), 707–725. doi:10.1002mj.249

Quinn, J. B., & Hilmer, F. G. (1994). Strategic outsourcing. *Sloan Management Review, 35*(4), 43.

Rindfleisch, A., & Heide, J. B. (1997). Transaction cost analysis: Past, present, and future applications. *Journal of Marketing, 61*(4), 30–54. doi:10.1177/002224299706100403

Saussier, S. (1999). Transaction cost economics and contract duration: An empirical analysis of EDF coal contracts. *Recherches Économiques de Louvain/Louvain. Economic Review, 65*(1), 3–21.

Simmonds, A. & Gilmour, D. (2005). Governance of outsourcing from IT governance institute. Retrieved from http://www.isaca.org/Knowledge-Center/Research/Documents/Governance-of-Outsourcing_res_Eng_0105.pdf

Simon, H. A. (1957). *Models of man: Social and rational: Mathematical essays on rational human behavior in a social setting*. New York, NY: Wiley.

Stump, R. L., & Heide, J. B. (1996). Controlling supplier opportunism in industrial relationships. *JMR, Journal of Marketing Research, 33*(4), 431–441. doi:10.1177/002224379603300405

Wathne, K. H., & Heide, J. B. (2000). Opportunism in interfirm relationships: Forms, outcomes, and solutions. *Journal of Marketing, 64*(4), 36–51. doi:10.1509/jmkg.64.4.36.18070

Weiss, A. M., & Anderson, E. (1992). Converting from independent to employee salesforces: The role of perceived switching costs. *JMR, Journal of Marketing Research, 29*(1), 101–115. doi:10.1177/002224379202900109

Williamson, O. E. (1979). Transaction-cost economics: The governance of contractual relations. *The Journal of Law & Economics, 22*(2), 233–261. doi:10.1086/466942

Williamson, O. E. (1981). The economics of organization: The transaction cost approach. *American Journal of Sociology, 87*(3), 548–577. doi:10.1086/227496

Williamson, O. E. (1985). *The economic institutions of capitalism*. New York, NY: Simon & Schuster.

Williamson, O. E. (1991). Comparative economic organization: The analysis of discrete structural alternatives. *Administrative Science Quarterly, 36*(2), 269–296. doi:10.2307/2393356

Williamson, O. E. (1996). *The mechanism of governance*. New York, NY: Oxford University Press.

Williamson, O. E. (1998). Transaction cost economics: How it works; Where it is headed. *De Economist, 146*(1), 23–58. doi:10.1023/A:1003263908567

ADDITIONAL READING

Earl, M. J. (1996). The risks of outsourcing IT. *Sloan Management Review, 37*, 26–32.

Grover, V., & Malhotra, M. K. (2003). Transaction cost framework in operations and supply chain management research: Theory and measurement. *Journal of Operations Management, 21*(4), 457–473. doi:10.1016/S0272-6963(03)00040-8

Holcomb, T. R., & Hitt, M. A. (2007). Toward a model of strategic outsourcing. *Journal of Operations Management, 25*(2), 464–481. doi:10.1016/j.jom.2006.05.003

Milberg, W. (2000). *Outsourcing economics economic representations*. London: Routledge.

North, D. C. (1990). A transaction cost theory of politics. *Journal of Theoretical Politics, 2*(4), 355–367. doi:10.1177/0951692890002004001

Quinn, J. B. (1999). Strategic outsourcing: Leveraging knowledge capabilities. *MIT Sloan Management Review, 40*(4), 9–21.

Robins, J. A. (1987). Organizational economics: Notes on the use of transaction-cost theory in the study of organizations. *Administrative Science Quarterly, 32*(1), 68–86. doi:10.2307/2392743

Williamson, O. E. (1993). Transaction cost economics and organization theory. *Industrial and Corporate Change, 2*(2), 107–156. doi:10.1093/icc/2.2.107

KEY TERMS AND DEFINITIONS

Adaptation: The level of difficulty in adjusting the outsourcing contracts to the situation in the face of changing situations.

Contract: A formal agreement between the buyer and the seller.

Exchange Relationship: A commercial relationship between the buyer and the seller, which may be short or long term.

Moral Hazard: It is an asymmetric information problem that occurs as a result of the secret actions that take place after the contract is signed.

Opportunism: The behavior shown to provide unilateral personal benefit from a relationship.

Outsourcing: The transfer of an activity of organization to an external supplier.

Task Complexity: The degree of difficulty in determining the standards and performance evaluation of a task.

Transaction Cost: Transaction costs are all expenses incurred when purchasing a good or service.

Chapter 13
IMF, World Bank, and the European Union With the Perspective of New Institutional Economics

Havanur Ergün Tatar
Bartın University, Turkey

ABSTRACT

According to New Institutional Economics, the GDP per capita has significantly improved in the countries where the institutional quality has been improved. In addition to this information, the increase in the quality of institutional determinants has positive effect on economic performance. In this chapter, after the structures of IMF, World Bank, and European Union have been discussed, the governance debate will be made on the aforementioned institutional. Concepts about new institutional economics are discussed, as are the improvement of institutional quality and the relationship of economic development within the frame of IMF, World Bank, and European Union.

INTRODUCTION

The improvement of institutional quality determinants has a vital role for the development of institutional environment and economic progress. In other words, the quality of unofficial and official sociopolitical regulations on the development or prevention of economic performance is crucially significant.

New institutional economics and international institutions have been analyzed through various studies in the literature. However, the difference of this study from the other existing studies is to analyze the relationship between the improvement of institutional quality and the economic development with the institutions such as International Monetary Fund (IMF), World Bank (WB) and European Union (EU) which have been approached as an example. Furthermore, the approached institutions (IMF, WB and EU) have been analyzed from the perspective of institutional quality and economic development from the point of the primary concepts of new institutional economics in the study.

DOI: 10.4018/978-1-7998-0333-1.ch013

Copyright © 2020, IGI Global. Copying or distributing in print or electronic forms without written permission of IGI Global is prohibited.

In this study, IMF, WB and EU has been approached on behalf of institutions. The primary purpose of this study is to analyze the economic development which will occur when the institutional quality determinants have been concentrated sufficiently. This study has also asserted how important the institutions and organizations, that have concentrated adequately on the institutional quality determinants, are for providing the macroeconomic stability.

BACKGROUND

In the literature, there are several studies that analyze the relationship between institution and economic development. Those studies have been emphasized that institutional improvements have a positive effect on economic growth.

One of the most significant studies that has remarked the relationship between the improvement of institutions and economic growth is belonging to North. According to North, securing the property rights of individuals and decreasing transaction costs affect economic performance positively (North and Thomas, 1973: 8; North, 1984: 7).

In his study, Rodrik (2003) revealed that geography and international trade have an indirect effect on economy via institutions. In a similar way, Dollar and Kraay (2003) manifested that better institutions and high commercial shares have a positive effect on growth in their studies. In their studies, Acemoglu et al. (2004) approached Korean Peninsula in order to analyze the effect of institutions on economic development. According to Acemoğlu, the reason of the rapid increase of per capita incomes at South Korea vis-à-vis North Korea is that institutional development is more prospering in South Korea. Scilicet, the market structure is more developed, private property is protected and the decisions have been taken in a more democratic manner at South Korea.

The recent studies have approached the relationship between institutions and economic development econometrically. For instance, in their studies, Killick et al. (1992) analyzed the relationship between economic growth and the institutions by approaching a specific institution (IMF). According to the result of their studies, IMF programmes affect economic growth positively. Similarly, in his study, Javed (2015) studied the relationship between developed institutional determinants and the successful execution and completion of IMF programmes. At this point, institutional determinants have a significant role for decreasing the macroeconomic instability. It has been concluded that IMF programmes which have not sufficiently concentrated on the entity of institutional structure cannot provide the essential economic growth.

CAN INTERNATIONAL MONETARY FUND (IMF), WORLD BANK (WB) AND EUROPEAN UNION (EU) BE EXPLAINED BY NEW INSTITUTIONAL ECONOMICS?

IMF Programmes and Their Objectives

In the 1970s, a stagflation crisis that inflation and stagnation occurred together arose. In order to get rid of the crisis, the developed countries began to execute neo-liberal policies in 1980s. In this process, international debt crisis began to threat the economic system of the world. The concept of globalization and its necessity became a debatable topic in this period as well. The stability and structural adjustment programmes via the granted credits through the institutions such as IMF and WB began to be executed in the developing countries (Akdemir, 2001:45).

The credits bound up with structural adjustment programme are determined according to the needs of the countries (WB, 1980:68). The structural adjustment programmes include the below measures:

- Taking measures for the production to adapt the high energy prices,
- Emphasizing the labor-intensive investments that will increase the employment although it will be completed in the long term,
- Encouraging the investments that diversify the nontraditional and export products in the economies where the exports are consisted of few goods,
- Taking a number of measures towards the increase of competitive power in the economies where the export opportunity is decreased due to the breakdown of cost structures and the overprotection of domestic industry,
- Providing the improvements of public investments by providing the reform on the balances of public expenditures and public investments,
- Taking measures for providing the active usage of national resources,
- Providing the essential institutional alteration that will allow the active usage of resources.

The international debt crises after 1980 caused to change the structure of provided funds by IMF. Within this process, IMF has taken an active role for preventing the debt crisis by installing programmes for the countries. The restructuring of debts, providing the essential credits for the countries, providing the harmony between cost and monetary policies and providing credits from developed countries are the opportunities that IMF has provided (Frankel and Roubini, 2001).

The below mentioned objectives are effective on all the decisions and the policies of IMF. The relevant objectives are as below (IMF, 2016:2):

- Encouraging the international monetary cooperation via a permanent institution for counseling and cooperation about international monetary problems,
- Facilitating the expansion of international trade and its balanced growth, and therefore increasing the levels of employment and real income and contributing their sustainability,
- Assuring the stability of foreign exchange rate among the member countries,
- Aiding for an establishment of multilateral payment system among the member countries and abolition of all foreign exchange restrictions that handicap the growth of world trade,
- Making the sources of fund accessible temporarily for the member countries, insuring the member countries, and therefore giving opportunities for them to regulate the disequilibrium of current payments without taking measures which will damage the domestic or international welfare,
- Shortening the periods of member countries on the disequilibrium of current payments and contributing the decrease of disequilibrium level according to the above-mentioned objectives.

The IV. Article of IMF has defined one of the fundamental roles as the facilitator of the member countries for reaching the IMF's target of sustainable economic growth. The IV. Article of the articles of agreement of IMF stipulate a condition that the member countries must make policies in accordance with the objectives of IMF. Each member country should guarantee that the regular foreign exchange regulations will be provided, a stable foreign exchange system will be encouraged and the cooperation will be made with the member countries. In order to collaborate with IMF and the other members, there are four obligations. It is necessary for each member to execute the conditions as below (IMF, 2007:7):

- Working to direct the economic and financial policies in order to support regular economic growth and reasonable price stability,
- Encouraging the stability by empowering economic and financial conditions and monetary system,
- Avoiding to change the foreign exchange rates and international monetary system in order to prevent the regulation of balance of payments or in order to obtain an advantage of unfair competition vis-à-vis other members,
- Following the suitable barter policies according to the stipulations in Article IV, Section 1 of IMF.

Encouraging the stability of rate and facilitating the world trade between the member countries are the paramount reasons for the formation of IMF. However, after the occurred financial crises in following years, the main objective of IMF has changed and instead of supporting the countries that have financial problems and the administration of the system of payments, the objective has become to encourage the countries to make structural reforms (Özkaya, 2009:103).

According to the IV. Article of IMF Article of Agreements; the members countries should fulfill the below stipulations. The related stipulations are as below (IMF, 2007:7):

- The member countries have the right to adjust their own selection of the foreign exchange rate regulations on condition to inform IMF about the regulations and changes.
- IMF has the right to supervise the international monetary system and the convenience of countries on the stipulations of the first section of this article in order this article to work efficiently. For IMF to carry out this mission, a strictly supervision on the foreign exchange policies of the countries is necessary.

The Structure of World Bank (WB) and Its Objective

This institution was formed after World War II in order to rebuild Europe. In this process, WB make credit allocations. The criteria that the credit allocations are based on by WB is as below (Candan, 2007:45):

- Whether the member countries have the opportunities of credit extensions from private markets or not, and whether they can get finance from the resources except banks or not,
- The qualification of the project or program which will use the credit, the role of the project and program in the national economy,
- The institutional status of the loanee which demands the credit,
- Whether the state institution which asks for the credit meet the obligations or not. These stipulations are significant for the credit allocations from WB.

WB includes five development group within itself. These are as below (WB, 2016):

- The International Bank for Reconstruction and Development–IBRD
- The International Development Association–IDA

- The International Finance Corporation–IFC
- The International Centre for Settlement of Investment Disputes–ICSID
- The Multilateral Investment Guarantee Agency–MIGA

The founding objectives of WB are aligned as below (Eğilmez, 1997:65):

- Aiding the member countries after the war, assisting their development, helping them via productive capitals, encouraging the development of national resources on the countries in the wake of development,
- Guaranteeing or supporting private and foreign investments, backing them up with its own resources when the private capital is not sufficient,
- Pursuing the stability of balance of payments and endorsing the investments towards development for contributing the development of international trade,
- Providing the usage of credits from other channels into the primary and urgent projects,
- Managing the international investments in the transition period after the war to peacetime

The provided credits from WB have been used in the building of highway, dam and telecommunication systems and social welfare projects (especially in the health and education sector) However, the bank has created new resource after 1980. Especially this resource has been created towards the countries that have the problem of balance of payments and this resource is called as "Structural Adjustment Programmes". The credits have been given for the realization of social and structural reforms and the support of political and institutional reforms with the provided credits within the scope of this programme. However, there are some stipulations for providing these credits. On the other hand, IMF has provided supports to its members for their balance of payment problems and in return, it stipulates condition that several structural reforms will be made (Usal, 2008:236).

Since it was founded, WB have aim to aid the development of developing countries. The granted credits with this purpose is in the branch of project credit. The chief points of project credits are as below (Kaya & Denetçi, 2003:33):

- The main objective of these credits is the development. Since the development has been aimed, these credits have been given to developing countries rather than developed countries.
- The range of project credits are quite extensive. The primary fields of project credits are the infrastructure investments, industrial investments, and the quality of health services and the increase of quality of education.
- Credits have been used in the investment projects of countries that possessed the repayment capacity of their debts because WB is an international financial institution at the same time.
- The project credits are not provided for every case. The project should be satisfying in terms of economy, technique and finance in order these credits to be issued. Moreover, it is expected that the finance which will be taken should contribute the economic development.
- Finally, these credits have been provided for the governments of the countries or state institutions or organizations under the guarantee of them.

European Union

EU was formed with 1957 Treaty of Rome and was developed with 1993 Treaty of Maastricht. It emphasizes the common policies and the importance of the foundation of a single market. It has been expressed that an economic and political union will be founded among the member countries with the foundation of a single market. In the Treaty of Maastricht, several topics such as unanimity among the member countries for the decision-making, the necessity to adopt joint principles on the topics like politics and security and the necessity to act with collective action have risen into prominence (Kıraç & İlhan, 2010:194).

The free movement of goods, capital and individuals have been aimed among the member countries. The topics such as the foundation of economic and monetary union, the execution of common competition policy, the socio-economic integrity and the consolidation oriented foreign policy are the other aims of the union as well. The points that EU has especially aimed to achieve on its foreign relations have significance. The related points can be summarized as below (Akdemir, 2018:192):

- The protection of EU's independency, integrity and fundamental interests,
- Strengthening and supporting civil rights, international legal maxims, democracy and supremacy of law,
- Keeping the peace, preventing the conflicts and empowering the international security,
- Supporting the sustainable economic, social and environmental developments of developing countries by making the removal of impoverishment as primary goal,
- Encouraging the member countries for the integration with world economy and removing the restraints on international trade gradually,
- Providing the maintenance of environmental quality and national resources sustainably, developing international measures for sustainable development,
- Aiding the countries and the regions that have been damaged due to natural or man-made disasters,
- Supporting an international system based on global good governance and mutual cooperation.

EU necessitates the common policies on various fields among the member countries. The common policies of European Union can be summarized as below (Kıraç & İlhan, 2010:194-198):

The Competition Policies of EU, Budget Policies, Regional Policies, Industry and Technology Policies, Economic and Monetary Policies, Tax Policies, Environmental Policies, Energy Policies, Transportation Policies, Telecommunication and Science-Research Policies, Agricultural Policies, Fishing Policies

The Discussion of "Governance" for International Monetary Fund (IMF), World Bank (WB) and European Union (EU)

The concept of governance is a concept that emphasizes a kind of a complexity relationship or the importance of participation in the management process rather than the governing-governed distinction. This concept is begun to be used in English firstly, and then, it was translated into French as *"gouvernance"* and German as *"steuerung"*. Governance is considered as tool for the democratization of the state and the establishment of civil mobilization via upward organization. The concept also emphasizes the increase on the roles of the economic actors and companies (Şenalp, 2003:64). Governance means the democratization of administration as well. Especially liberal thought has made some developments towards the democratization of both economic and political system. The democratization of political system signifies the pluralist structure of democracy. The democratization of economic system, on the other hand, expresses the removal of in and out restraints on the market and the liberalization of the trade (Eryiğit & Sarıca, 2018:62).

The concept of governance has been defined in the literature diversely. For instance, Rodrik (2000) referred that there are various ways to reach the best governance. He approached the necessary institutions separately for (i) macroeconomic stability (ii) social security and (iii) decreasing the conflicts. Rodrik (2000) classified the ultimate objectives of the institutions separately as well. Therefore, he did not dwell on what the results of governance data will generate or what the category of them will be in his classification. He emphasized the importance of the adopted way for reaching the objectives of governance in the study that he referred the importance of democracy. Kaufmann, Kraay and Mastruzzi (2003) approached the three different aspects of governance. These are:

- The provided process for the election, supervision and change of governments
- The capacity of governments for the execution of sound policies besides the production of sound policies by the governments
- The respect of governments and citizens towards the institutions

The concept of governance and the phenomenon of globalization are related. At this point, it is necessary to divide among the globalization methods. First globalization method is the concept of "globalized localism". According to this method, a phenomenon in a local level can be globalized. Second globalization form is "localized globalism". Third globalization form is "cosmopolitanism". This concept attributes the individuals a universal mission. According to this concept, the local loyalty is replaced with the universal loyalty. All the world is seen as a one single country with the influence of global thought. Finally, the fourth form of globalization refers to the international law with reference to the thought that the earth is intrinsically global (Eryiğit & Sarıca, 2018:67).

The good governance principles are the effective terms for the discourse of both IMF and WB. For example, the discourse of WB took form around three basic concepts. These concepts are: "New Institutional Economics", "New Political Economy" and "Theories of Civil Society" (Hibou, 1998). The development of property rights is enormously crucial for new institutional economics. At this point, new institutional economics call the state for a duty and attributes it some missions. This dilemma is similar to WB which means that there is no clearness on the role of state. On the other hand, the concept of governance has become extremely significant for both IMF and WB. The concept of governance is not only contributing to IMF and WB but also to the international institutions such as OECD and WTO. After the significance of institutional change is discovered, international finance and credit organizations have emphasized the contribution of institutional change in their everlasting research and/or reports after 1990 (Şenalp, 2003:61).

The concept of governance is significant not only for new institutional economics but also to various institutions at the same time. According to the global finance or political organizations, the concept of governance is defined differently. The relevant definitions are as below (Şenalp, 2003:66):

Governance according to WB: WB has defined the concept of governance in three forms: (i) Political regime form; (ii) the process that the social and economic resources of one country is used by political authority in order to ensure the economic development and (iii) the capacity of governments to perform planning, formulation, execution and et cetera functions.

UNDP: The concept of governance has expressed the usage of economic, political and administrative authority to solve every kind of problems of the country. The concept has expressed the process and the institutions that individuals and social groups can clearly express their thoughts, they use their legal rights and they know their liabilities.

Organisation for Economic Co-operation and Development (OECD): The concept of governance means the usage of political authority and the execution of control on the administration of national resources for providing the social and economic development. The limits of this definition are quite extensive. This definition includes the role of public authority on the issues how the environment of functioning governing body of economy can be identified and how the social utility will be distributed between governing and governed.

Institute on Governance: Governance includes the relevant institutions, process and traditions on the issues how the political authority will be used, how the decisions which will affect the social life will be decided and how the harmony will be provided between different interest components.

The subject of good governance is consisting of substructure of several institutions, especially IMF and WB. According to WB, the basis of good governance is as below (WB, 1994; Şenalp, 2003:69):

- Accountability: It is divided as two subjects on micro and macro levels. In macro level: External controller system is significant for effective financial management and expenditures. In micro level: Competition and the extensification of the participation of the non-governmental organizations should be supported, the significance of localization should be emphasized and the pricing of local services should be assisted.
- The Legal Framework of Development: Means of economy and state should be in interaction. At this point, a stable and just legal system for everyone should be. Clear legal rules are extremely important in the market system.
- Informing: Budget, markets and governmental bills should be crystal clear and accessible.
- Transparency: Corruption should be decreased, the extension of clear government and accountability, and the solidarity between public and private sectors should be supported.

The changes on the economy and the countries in time have paved the way for the concept of governance to be in international areas. For example, Asian Crisis and the statements against IMF have caused to turn the debates of institutional economics and governance into a different direction. In the same period, the slogan of "good governance" have a central role for the institutional development and the problems of developments. One of the indicators for this evolution is that the concept of governance has found more places in IMF. As a result, Washington Consensus has reformed and several advices of governance and institution have been included in the New Washington Consensus. The institutions such as IMF and WB have prioritized the issue of governance and institutions and one of the significant reasons for this development is their necessity for renewal their policies (Aysan, 2006:2).

The debates of governance have been mentioned in the study that EU prepared, European Governance: A White Paper. In the mentioned book, "governance" was defined as processes and actions that affect the usage of power and government in Europe. The book is consisted of four chapters and according to the book, the more participation of citizens has been suggested on the issue of modeling of politics in the first chapter. The quality of politics has been emphasized in the second chapter. In the third chapter, the relationship between the significance of EU and the concept of governance has been approached.

In the final chapter, the role of EU institutions has been analyzed. A White Paper analyzed the concept of governance in detail and it emphasized that EU should change itself by considering the concept of governance. According to A White Paper, five principles have significant role for good governance. These principles are as below (Okçu, 2007:300-305):

- Openness: It is expected from the institutions that they should have clear and transparent operational structure in the manner that will provide confidence.
- Participation: The participation of people in all the political processes is expected in terms of the activity of EU.
- Accountability: The roles of every institution should be indicated clearly.
- Activity: It is expected from the policies that will be conducted to be presented actively, in time and in consideration of previous experiences.
- Adaptation: The actions towards the realization of policies should be adaptable and clear.

The effect of nation states have begun to be decreased with the globalization. The cooperation between the countries have increased and the countries have experienced difficulties for the control of their borders. This condition leads the emergence of new social organizations and the popularization of social institutions. "Governance" is spread to the world under the leadership of international finance organizations. Especially after 1990, the institutions that give credits have grounded on the conditionality principle. In other words, the international finance organizations have exported governance in return for the credits that they have given. The acceptance of governance by the countries that have high debts is the example of conditionality transfer. The internalization of governance in underdeveloped and developing countries cannot be possible in return for the credits that they have got from the developed countries. The governance has been transferred to the underdeveloped and developing countries with the aim of guaranteeing the applicability of credits from international finance organizations. At this point, governance has an instrumental value internationally (Eryiğit & Sarıca, 2018:68-69).

The Concept of "Institution" in New Institutional Economics

The institutions are the most significant structures that form social life. The increasing presence of institutions in social life leads the structuring of human activities and interactions by clear or closed rules. For instance, while the language rules enable the communication, traffic rules facilitate the secure and smooth traffic flows and the laws leads the increase of personal security. Therefore, the institutions express both actions and restrictions (Hodgson, 2006:2). North (2002) defined the institutions as the rules of the game created by people and having restrictions. The aforementioned restrictions describe what people can do or cannot do under which conditions. The institutions are found everywhere that people keep in touch (North, 2002: 9-12). Another important representative of new institutional economics, Coase (1937), approached the concept of institution in the axis of firms. He reviewed the structure of institution from the firms. He considered the firms as the important institutions of capitalism and he tried to elucidate the essence of firms.

The institutions are not comprised of not only with statutes but also the informal rules penetrates into the institutions as well. In other words, formal rules, contract, property rights, constitutions, common law and common regulations are included but the behavioral norms with public acceptance such as informal rules, customs, traditions and taboos are included in the institutions as well (North, 2002: 49-65).

There are differences in the emergence of informal and formal rules. The informal rules spontaneously emerge as a result of interaction. By following the rules and norms of the society, the individuals in the society paves the way for the emergence of social order. Thus, informal rules are created by the society and they have become internalized institutions in the society in time. Formal rules, on the other hand, contain the contractual agreements, and economic and political rules (Eroğlu, 2018:165). As well as legal rules, the rules include the behavioral norms and social contracts as well. These types of rules can be codified potentially. The members of society share the clear and net information about these rules. Thanks to "Codability", the violations of the rules can be identified clearly. The social structures that includes the uncodable relationship sets are not considered as an institution (Hodgson, 2006:3).

The development of the economic institutions of capitalism in last 150 years leads to a reassessment in terms of transaction costs (Williamson, 1985:17). The economy of transaction costs according to Williamson (Williamson, 1985:18):

1. It is more micro analytical,
2. It is more deliberate in the behavioral assumptions,
3. It introduces and develops the economic importance of asset specificity
4. It leans on more to comparative institutional analysis
5. It considers a business firm as a structure of governance rather than a production function,
6. It put emphasis more to the institutions after the contract.

The economy of transaction costs is one of the significant parts in the new institutional economics (Williamson, 1985:16). The economy of transaction costs is the modern equal of institutional economics and it is largely based on comparative analyses (Williamson, 1979:361).

Institutional environment, governance and individual are involved in an interaction. Institutional environment is the determinant of the rules of the game. If the property rights, the legislation of contact and customs were changed, the restructuring of economic organization would be necessary (Williamson, 1993).

The entity of institutions that takes the property rights into consideration have encouraged real capital and social capital, and have enabled the active usage of resources. At this point, every institution that encourages novelty, active technology and active distribution of resources paves the way for the increase of welfare in the economy (Acemoğlu et al, 2005: 389).

The Concepts Belong to New Institutional Economics

New institutional economics has contributed the concept of "institution" and the three principal topics in below. The related concepts and their explanations are as below.

Theory of Firm

According to new institutional economics, theory of firm lays the foundation of the transaction costs and the property rights. New institutional economics has evaluated theory of firm with a different perspective. The first view about theory of firm is belong to Coase (1937). In his "The Nature of Firm" article in 1937, Coase (1937) expressed that the disequilibrium in the production and consumption will be extinguished by the markets. He manifested the emergence of firms by correlating with the transaction costs. The related transaction costs can be approached in two separate ways: The first one is the costs that are necessary to obtain prices. This cost can never be extinguished completely. The second one is the costs that have originated from the contracts. In this sort of cost, forming several contracts (forming the contacts in both short and long terms), boosts the costs. In his study, Coase (1937) indicated that the state intervention has a certain cost in the case that there is a possibility of negotiation (bargaining) and this cost is more than the expected returns (Coase, 1937).

The transaction costs are not involved in the neo-classical theory. This assumption does not accord with the real life and it causes that the firms cannot be analyzed in detail. Since the transaction costs can be decreased by the firms, this condition makes "theory of firm" essential. Firms incorporate a part of the contracts between the parties and they lead the decrease of transaction costs (Kama, 2011:194).

New institutional economics has approached the continuity and results of transaction costs. At this point, contracts and commitment problems have become significant in theory of firm. The related commitments are the liability of parties against each other and they are determined with the contracts as well. According to new institutional economics, the people and the firms have problems about receiving their commitments fully due to some restrictions. Unreliable commitment, incomplete contracts and transaction act have constituted problems for the firms. In a similar manner, commitment problems disrupt the market structure in long-term. New institutional economics has analyzed the relationship of firm, contract and institution (Williamson, 1975).

While Williamson (1990) explained his views about the structure of firms and market, he had two principal assumptions. First one is of the reality that the individuals seek their own personal benefits. Second one is the concept of bounded rationality. Williamson (1990) emphasized that the economic units act in accordance with these two principal assumptions (Williamson, 1990).

Theory of Contract

Contracts gain prominence about making the planned variations at a future date. Postponing the exchange at a future date rather than making it today is the sign to the necessity of contracts. The parties make some commitments about a future date. When one or two of the sides have suspected that the promised commitments cannot be received, the variation simultaneously will be realized. This condition, however, will affect the markets to become shallow and therefore, it will be a hindrance towards development (Kama, 2011:197).

According to new institutional economics, the concept of contract has concentrated on the principal institutional structures that regulate the bilateral relations. Contracts have the characteristics of keywords for the comprehension of market structure. The contribution of new institutional economics to the contracts is as below (Çetin, 2012:57):

- The analysis of contracts in the range of economics aids to analyze the economically existing difficulties of coordination.
- The approach of contract in new institutional economics helps to uncover various coordination conditions such as routines, impetuses, principle of authority, tools of coercion and the solutions of conflicts.
- It assists for the comprehension of economic actors, their decision-making structures and how they have conceptualized their rules.
- It lends assistance for the understanding of significant changes in the economic activities.

Contract represents normative ground and the methods for solving the conflict in the market which is one of the organizational forms. It especially consists of the methods for solving the conflict, bargaining and sanctions based on indenture (Powell, 1990).

If the parties faced with the unexpected incidents and bilateral relationship became complicated more, then, this condition would require that the parties should renegotiate. In this process, since the parties have no possibility to encounter again, they act in a selfish and rogue manner. When the society especially has developed, the individuals have made more risky choices. This condition not only obliges the additional security measures to the contracts that have become risky but also causes the increase of costs at the same time. The existence of effective institutions contributes the decrease on the costs (Kama, 2011:198).

Property Rights

Property rights define the responsibilities and freedom of individuals, scilicet, they comprise of the rules of the game. In the economies that property rights are well-defined, the disputes between the individuals decrease as far as possible. Property rights are divided under two forms; economic property rights and legal property rights. Economic property rights express the rights that the individuals make an effort to obtain, while legal property rights express the instruments that are used by the individuals for the rights that they make an effort to attain (Aktan, 2006:32). Theory of property rights reveals the relationship between wealth and property rights. The existence of property rights is essential for the effective functioning of trade. Otherwise, there will be no trade without the existence of property rights. Moreover, property rights assist the development of competition environment by preventing the conflict between individuals. In terms of providing the economic development, providing the competition environment is crucially important (Oğuz, 2003:25).

Property rights and transaction costs are the concepts that have emerged against neo-classical economics' theory of firm. These concepts asserted that the equilibrium of market is provided by an invisible hand by ignoring the firms of neo-classical economics and the corporate identities of them. At this point, by addressing the structure of firm, Coase analyzed the issues of transaction costs and externalities. He advocated that transaction costs and externalities can be prevented in the economies that property rights are effectively protected. Therefore, property rights should be effectively protected for the effective usage of resources and well-placed economy (Kim & Mahoney 2005: 225).

Economy is a branch of science that take the effective usage of scarce resources as a goal. The foundation of economic organization is grounded on who have possessed or used the scarce factors. The other significant and debatable issues are who does own the production factors, what will be made with those factors, how the property rights are protected and how they can be transferred. Thus, economy and law are the disciplines that complete each other. Conducting a research about the effect of law on the economic systems is tremendously important for clarifying the economic problems and concentrating on the issue of property rights (Seçilmiş, 2016:12).

For the emergence of property rights, the assets should both be limited and be desired. New institutional economists have attached great importance to the concept of property. Property-oriented studies have been made due to two reasons. These reasons are as below (Kama, 2011:200):

1. Explaining how a determined control system has been developed, protected and disrupted,
2. Analyzing a determined control structure in terms of both economic results and the organization of economic behaviors.

Property rights have three principal features. In the first one, a tangible asset should be mentioned for the full definition of size. The rights should be defined for making the redistribution possible in the second one. Finally, the rights belong to an asset should be allocated to a certain person or the groups. In other words, property rights is the name given to the rights that are possessed by the people who hold the property. The individual who has the property right has the right for the usage of asset by thyself, leasing it in a profit-making way or sale. In a similar manner, the one who has obtained the property right also has the right to alter the form of asset or to destroy (Çetin, 2012:64).

According to Williamson, institutional analysis is realized in four levels. There are traditions, unofficial institutions, customs and norms in the first level. The most significant common trait of them is their change in a slow manner. The second level is comprised of institutional framework. In comparison with first level, change is more rapidly occurred in this level. According to North, the recognition of property rights and their execution is quite important. Third level is the governance level and it has a micro structure. The last level that Williamson expressed emphasizes the employment and the distribution of resources. The second level from these four levels that Williamson expressed is in the field of property rights economics. (Williamson, 1998b: 28-29).

The Improvement of Institutional Quality and Economic Development

Institutions are defined as the constraints that are developed by the people who defines the social, political and economic relationships for constituting order and decreasing equivocalness. Institutions can be constituted by constitutions, laws and official institutions such as property rights; but they can be created by unofficial institutions such as customs, doctrines and ethics as well (North, 1981).

According to the literature of new institutional economics, substantial increases on GDP per capita occurred in the countries where institutional quality is improved (Acemoğlu & Johnson, 2005; Afonso and Jalles, 2011). At this point, the quality determinants should be improved for the development of institutional framework and economic progress. The decrease of transaction costs, the protection of property rights, the improvement of supremacy of law and the execution of contracts are the principal institutional quality determinants which will be improved (Javed, 2015:38). The literature of new institutional economics revealed that improvement in institutional determinants have positive effect on economic growth (Hall & Jones, 1999). One of the most significant factors that affect economy negatively is the external shocks. For the protection of economy against these external shocks, it is necessary to strengthen the supremacy of law, to consolidate the democratic institutions (or putting in place) and to constitute participant mechanisms. If the essential institutional strengthening was made, macroeconomic stability would be provided relatively (Rodrik, 1999). After the financial crisis of 1997-98 in Asia, the opposite experiences of South Korea and Indonesia have presented quite spectacular results (Rodrik, 2006:10).

In their work, Acemoglu et al. (2004) indicated the reasons of wage gaps as institutions, geography and culture. One of the best examples for especially the effect of institutions on economic development is the South Korea. The Korean Peninsula was under the invasion of Japan for several decades and after the end of invasion, Korea was divided into two parts. GDP per capita was in the same progress in South Korea until 1970s and after 1970s, the levels of GDP per capita have begun to become different in a good way. The GDP per capita of South Korea began to rise rapidly. For instance, the GDP per capita of South Korea was $16,100, while the GDP per capita of North Korea was only $1.000. The principal factor of this difference is the strengthened political and economic institutions. The market structure has been developed, the private property has been protected and the decisions have been made democratically. As a result of these developments, the Korean peninsula is not only divided into two different parts geographically but also culturally (Acemoglu et al., 2004:404-406).

The institutions are related with the quality of official or unofficial sociopolitical regulations on the development or hindrance of economic performance. (Rodrik, 2003). The debates for the effect of economic institutions on growth and economic developments have went back to Adam Smith. According to Smith, one of the most significant duties of the state is to form the public institutions because the public institutions, notably defense and health facilities, are the public-minded services. These related public institutions are different according to the development levels of societies (Weingast, 2017).

According to North, who emphasized the importance of the relationship between the institutions and economic performance, the concepts of property rights and transaction costs have importance. Securing the property rights of individuals and the decrease of transaction costs have positive effect on economic performance (North & Thomas, 1973: 8; North, 1984: 7).The studies in the literature have revealed that the increase of institutional quality has positive effect on trade. In addition to this, there are several studies to demonstrate that trade will affect the income levels indirectly by increasing the institutional quality. For example, in their study, Dollar and Kraay (2003) manifested that better institutions and high shares of trade have a positive effect on growth in the long term.

Economic growth-oriented policies have approached the income that has been generated in the economy. At this point, individuals and institutions have a crucially significant role in the welfare-based distribution. Institutions are not only affecting the relationship among the individuals but also the decisions of economic actors about savings, investment, production and consumption.

Improvements that will generate the institutional quality will lead to decrease the uncertainties of market and provide required resources with lower costs. Thereby affecting "transaction costs", institutional quality will contribute economic performance positively. Nevertheless, thereby protecting property rights, decreasing informality, avoiding corruption, and increasing transparency, the economic performances of countries will be affected positively as well.

The Improvement of Institutional Quality, Economic Development and International Institutions (IMF, World Bank, European Union)

Geography and international trade have indirectly affected the economic growth via institutions (Rodrik, 2003). The common idea about the reasons of underdevelopment in the poor countries is that these related countries have institutions with low quality. In addition to this, the institutions that subsidize and provide consultancy service (International Money Fund, World Bank, World Trade Organizations) and the demanded reforms for the improvements of institutions in return for aid are considered the other reasons of underdevelopment (urija, 2017:4; Chang, 2011).

The pressure of the adoption of better institutions in the developing countries which is called as Global Standard Institutions has been stipulated for the signing of international agreements and subsidies, and relieving the debts in the mid-1990s. Another perspective about the weak institutional structure in the developing countries is the reality that the relevant countries have different priorities rather than this matter. Furthermore, the finance of reliable institutions for underdeveloped countries is not economically sustainable (urija, 2017:4; Chang, 2011).

New Institutional Economics considered asymmetric information and transaction costs as serious problems. At this point, the quality in the institutions have importance on the decreases of costs and effecting growth positively (Hall & Jones, 1999). According to NIE literature, in the countries, there are political and economic institutions that will affect the quality of institutions of each other (Acemoğlu and Robinson, 2008; Acemoğlu and Robinson, 2012). One of these institutions is IMF. In the countries that IMF programmes have been applied, institutional determinants have been affected positively. In the countries that IMF programmes have been applied, real GDP has been affected positively directly or indirectly through macroeconomic stability (Javed, 2015:38). Economic growth has been increased by the existence of strong institutions and macroeconomic stability. Social and political instability, inflation and high public expenditures (location in Sub-Saharan Africa and Latin America) have negatively affected economic growth (Butkiewicz &Yanikkaya, 2005).

By centering on the concept of "governance" which has taken an important place in new institutional approach, EU has aimed peace and economic development, the increase of life standards and the creation of domestic market in Europe. However, despite these mutual purposes for the member countries, several Europeans do not have a sense of belonging to EU and they has the expression that they are abstracted from the union as well. Moreover, food safety, crime fighting and unemployment have induced to the creation of perception that the union has not acted efficiently. The people has not realized the quality increase originated from union and they have expected from the EU that it should be effective like their national states and visible in their lives. Through all these expectations, ıt has been expressed as an importance that the reform process of union should be started on one hand, while the preparations for the institutional changes in the future have been made on the other. Therefore, EU started the institutional reform by centering on governance (Okçu, 2007:301-303).

When the literature of new institutional economics is examined, the recent empiric studies have emphasized the importance of institutional quality. Especially in the countries that improved institutional determinants have been improved have sustainable macroeconomic stability and economic growth For instance, in his study, Javed (2015), examined the relationship between improved institutional determinants and the successful execution and completion of IMF programmes. At this point, institutional determinants have a significant role for decreasing macroeconomic instability. The background of his study is comprised of the reason of searching the insufficient effect of IMF programmes on economic growth. Since IMF programmes have not concentrated on enough the essence of institutional structure, they cannot provide the necessary economic growth. At this point, NIE literature have significant contributions for providing the economic growth. (Javed, 2015:15). IMF programmes that have concentrated on institutional quality determinant sufficiently are both successful and providing macroeconomic stability. The economic institutional quality (Like legal framework and the protection of property rights, the freedom of trading internationally, the access to sound currency) and the political institutional quality (Like political structure, regime change) are important determinants for the countries where IMF programmes are used (Javed, 2015:17).

The approaches that have been called as "structural reforms" by IMF, "good governance" by WB and "regulatory reforms" by OECD represent the same ideals in their essence. Especially the main objective is to change the institutional structures of underdeveloped countries (Şenalp, 2003:84). However, notably IMF and WB has not still been successful for the decrease of impoverishment and providing the economic stability in the countries where their suggested policies have been applied. Even, the economic conditions of some of those countries became worse as well. Hence, IMF and WB have heavily criticized in terms of their applied policies (Eryiğit & Sarıca, 2018:69-70).

IMF and WB give credits to developing countries. Most of the time, these credits are considered responsible for the negative economic results in those developing countries. One of the most significant reasons for this condition is that the provided funds from IMF have been used for solving the crises. Since the structural reforms and sound policies have not been adopted by the debtor nations, taking funds are not productive (Butkiewicz & Yanikkaya, 2005:382).

According to the structure of WB, the liberal economic policies have three ideological grounds. These are: "New Institutional Economics", "New Political Economics", and "Theories of Civil Society" (Hibou, 1998). "The governance structures" of NIE have been used by supranational financial institutions such as IMF, WB, OECD and WTO. Those institutions have presented the concepts of property rights that belong to new institutional rights, transaction costs and governance structures as a part of their policies that are applied by themselves globally. A structure that property rights are protected, the transaction costs are low and the market mechanism is fully operational is needed at global size. The state within this structure should be in a manner that it will not hinder the operation of international markets (Şenalp, 2003:91).

The transition from government to governance in time has caused the change of the role of state as well. As a result of experienced transformations, instead of liberal-oriented state model, "exterior/non-state" model is suggested. In that model, the communication between institutions and organizations has become significant. This condition can be felt intensively in the structure of EU, scilicet, while the hierarchy has pushed into the background, functionality has risen to prominence. This change has been reflected into its administrative system by EU. According to EU which accepted the approach of governance as an operational principle, all of the design of politics and the processes of execution became open to participation due to the activation of communication and information technologies. Another development about the governance in EU is that the participation is considered as "multi-center" rather than "multi-layer" (Okçu, 2007:311).

Governance has been exported and spread to the world thanks to international organizations. The international organizations that grant loans added the governance as a stipulation especially after 1990. The policy transfer that has been made to the underdeveloped and developing countries with high debts is actually expressed as "conditionality transfer". Governance has been transferred by the international finance organizations for providing the applicability of neo-liberal policies in the countries that has granted loans. The core purpose of institutions such as IMF and WB is to provide global economic growth and to integrate the countries with world market. Thanks to the governance transfers of the related institutions (IMF and WB) to the underdeveloped and developing countries, the improvement of administration structures with poor quality can be facilitated (Eryiğit & Sarıca, 2018:69-70).

''Washington Consensus'' was concentrated on the improvement of good institutions, transparency and good governance. The significance of institutions has been comprehended especially in the Second Washington Consensus (Yıldırım, 2011:20).

The most important issue that has become clear in time about Washington Consensus is that policy reforms have no perpetual effect in time. The most significant reason of this is the weakness of institutions on background. The thoughts towards the importance of institutions have concentrated on one of the driving forces of economic performance in empiric literature, the existence of institutions (Rodrik, 2006:10).

Supranational financial institutions have an ideological background in their economic policies and this background is "new-institutional economics". Especially after 1980, United Nations, World Bank, IMF and international non-governmental organizations have been using the concept of "governance" frequently. In the following processes, concept of "good governance" have been developed by World Bank.

The new roles have been assigned to the states by the new-institutional economics in order to provide the operability of market economy. At this point, World Bank has assigned new roles into the states for a better performance of global market as well. In a point that neo-classical economics comes to a deadlock, the approach of new-institutional economics has become effective in the international institutional policies. The perspective of new-institutional economics has a significance in the transition period "from minimal state to active state" after the period of 1970s.

As a part of their policies, supranational financial institutions such as IMF, World Bank, OECD and WTO have been using the concepts belonging to new-institutional economics like transaction costs, property rights and concept of governance. At this point, institutions need the structure of a state that will not constitute an impediment for the operation of international markets.

The perspective of new-institutional economics that has been preferred and adopted by international institutions comes under intense criticism in the literature. Especially the policies that have aimed to alter the institutional structure of underdeveloped countries could not achieve success in terms of decreasing poverty and providing economic stability.

SOLUTIONS AND RECOMMENDATIONS

Institutions have a significant role in terms of shaping social, political and economic relationships for creating the order and decreasing the instability. At this point, the literature of new institutional economics has revealed that the improvement of institutional determinants have a positive effect on economic growth. Empowering supremacy of law with international institutions (IMF, WB, EU etc.), consolidating democratic institutions and strengthening institutional structure by constituting participative mechanisms are necessary. Macroeconomic stability can be provided with only this way.

FUTURE RESEARCH DIRECTIONS

This study has addressed new institutional perspective specific to IMF, WB and EU. For that purpose; those institutions, governance, institutional improvement and economic development have been analyzed with perspective. Supranational institutions are one of the significant topics for examining their acts in accordance with institutional quality in the future.

CONCLUSION

According to new institutional economics, institutional environment is quite important and it is interrelated with individual interaction and governance. Especially the issue of good governance, accountability, legal framework of development, transparency and clearness have comprised of the substructure of institutions (especially in IMF and WB). IMF, WB and EU are the institutions that have been constituted for decreasing the instability and restoring the order. According to the literature of new institutional economics, in the countries, there are political and economic institutions that will affect the institutional qualities of each other. IMF, WB and EU are some of those institutions and organizations.

New social organizations have emerged and the nation state conception have decreased with the globalization process. These emerged organizations have paved the way for the intensification of social institutions and the concept of "governance" to become a widespread concept around the world under the leadership of international finance organizations. The programs that have concentrated on institutional quality determinants sufficiently are both successful and contribute the macroeconomic stability as well. To conclude, the approaches that have been called as "structural reforms" by IMF and "good governance" by WB represent the similar values essentially. Especially they aim the change of institutional structures in underdeveloped countries. The increase of institutional quality has a positive effect on both trade and economic growth.

REFERENCES

urija, M. (2017). *Institutions Quality and Economic Growth in Albania.* Retrieved from https://www.researchgate.net/publication/322677353_Institutions_Quality_and_Economic_Growth_in_Albania/download

Acemoglu, D., & Johnson, S. (2005). Unbundling institutions. *Journal of Political Economy, 113*(5), 949–995. doi:10.1086/432166

Acemoglu, D., Johnson, S., & Robinson, J. (2004). *Institutions as the Fundamental Cause of Long-Run Growth.* Retrieved from http://economics.mit.edu/files/4469

Acemoğlu, D., Johnson, S., & Robinson, J. A. (2005). Institutions as a fundamental cause of long-run growth. In P. Aghion & S. Durlauf (Eds.), *Handbook of Economic Growth* (pp. 386–469). Amsterdam, The Netherlands: Elsevier.

Acemoglu, D. & Robinson, J. (2008). *The Role of Institutions in Growth and Development.* Retrieved from https://siteresources.worldbank.org/EXTPREMNET/Resources/489960-1338997241035/Growth_Commission_Working_Paper_10_Role_Institutions_Growth_Development.pdf

Acemoglu, D., & Robinson, J. (2012). *Why nations fail. The origins of power, prosperity and poverty.* New York, NY: Profile Books. Crown Publishers. doi:10.1355/ae29-2j

Afonso, A. & Jalles, J. T. (2011). *Economic performance and government size.* ECB Working Paper Series No. 1399. ECB. Germany.

Akdemir, E. (2018). Avrupa Birliği'nin Dış İlişkileri ve Politikası: Avrupa Birliği'nin Bütünleş (eme)mesi Üzerine Bir İnceleme. *Ankara Avrupa Çalışmaları Dergisi, 17*(2), 181–218. doi:10.32450/aacd.511238

Akdemir, S. (2001). Yapısal Uyum Programları ve Uygulamalarının Değerlendirilmesi. *Ekonomik Yaklasim Association, 12*(40), 45–72. doi:10.5455/ey.10339

Aktan, C. C. (Ed.). (2006). Kurumsal İktisat, Kurallar, Kurumlar ve Ekonomik Gelişme. Sermaye Piyasası Kurulu Yayınları, (194).

Aysan, A. F. (2006). *Yönetisim ve Kurumlar Terimlerinin Iktisat Literaturundeki Yukselisi.* Retrieved from http://www.econ.boun.edu.tr/content/wp/ISS_EC_06_16.pdf

Butkiewicz, J. L., & Yanikkaya, H. (2005). The effects of IMF and world bank lending on long-run economic growth : An empirical analysis. *World Development, 33*(3), 371–391. doi:10.1016/j.worlddev.2004.09.006

Candan, E. (2007). Dünya Bankası Kredilerine İlişkin Genel Esaslar, Proje Kredilerinin Özellikleri, *Avantaj ve Dezavantajları. Sayıştay Dergisi, 18*(64), 41–65.

Çetin, T. (2012). *Yeni kurumsal iktisat.* Retrieved from http://dergipark.gov.tr/download/article-file/101303

Chang, H. J. (2011). Institutions and economic development: Theory, policy and history. *Journal of Institutional Economics, 7*(4), 473–498. doi:10.1017/S1744137410000378

Coase, R. H. (1937). The nature of the firm. *Economica New Series, 4*(16), 386–405. doi:10.1111/j.1468-0335.1937.tb00002.x

Dollar, D., & Kraay, A. (2003). Institutions, trade and growth. *Journal of Monetary Economics, 50*(1), 133–162. doi:10.1016/S0304-3932(02)00206-4

Eğilmez, A. M. (1997). Dünya Bankası IMF ve Türkiye. İstanbul, Turkey: Creative Yayıncılık. 65.

Eroğlu, M.Y. (2018). Kurumsal İktisatta Açılan Yeni Bir Pencere: Douglass C. North Perspektifinden Kurumların Değerlendirilmesi. *Optimum: Journal of Economics & Management Sciences/Ekonomi ve Yönetim Bilimleri Dergisi, 5*(2), 163-178.

Eryiğit, B. H., & Sarıca, A. (2018). IMF, Dünya Bankası, OECD'nin Yönetişim Yaklaşımı ve Kü-Yerelleşme. *Marmara Üniversitesi Siyasal Bilimler Dergisi, 6*(1), 61–74.

Frankel, J. & Roubini, N. (2001). *The role of industrial country policies in emerging market crises.* NBER Working Paper. No: 8634.

Hall, R. E., & Jones, C. I. (1999). Why do some countries produce so much more output per worker than others? *The Quarterly Journal of Economics, 114*(1), 83–116. doi:10.1162/003355399555954

Hibou, B. (1998). *The political economy of the world bank's discourse.* CERI Working Papers. No: 39.

Hodgson, G. M. (2006). What are institutions. *Journal of Economic Issues, 40*(1), 1–25. doi:10.1080/00213624.2006.11506879

IMF. (2007). *International Monetary Fund handbook: Its functions, policies, and operations.* Retrieved from https://www.imf.org/external/pubs/ft/imfhb/eng/handbook.pdf

IMF. (2016). Retrieved from https://www.imf.org/external/pubs/ft/aa/pdf/aa.pdf

Javed, O. (2015). *Essays on institutional quality, macroeconomic stabilization, and economic growth in International Monetary Fund member countries.* Retrieved from https://www.tdx.cat/bitstream/handle/10803/319439/OMER_JAVED_PhD_THESIS.pdf?sequence=1&isAllowed=y

Kama, Ö. (2011). Yeni Kurumsal İktisat Okulunun Temelleri. *Gazi Üniversitesi İktisadi Ve İdari Bilimler Fakültesi Dergisi, 13*(2), 183–204.

Kaufmann, D., Kraay, A., & Mastruzzi, M. (2003). *Governance matters III, Governance indicators for 1996–2002*. Retrieved from http://siteresources.worldbank.org/INTWBIGOVANTCOR/Resources/govmatters3_wber.pdf

Kaya, S. & Denetçi, U. (2003). Dünya Bankası ve Dünya Bankası Kredilerinin Denetimi. *Sayıştay Dergisi*, 3-42.

Killick, T., Malik, M., & Manuel, M. (1992). What can we know about the effects of IMF programmes? *World Economy*, *15*(5), 575–598. doi:10.1111/j.1467-9701.1992.tb00538.x

Kım, J., & Mahoney, J. T. (2005). Property rights theory, transaction costs theory, and agency theory: An organizational economics approach to strategic management. *Journal of Managerıal and Decısıon Economıcs*, *26*(4), 223–246. doi:10.1002/mde.1218

Kıraç, S., & İlhan, B. (2010). Avrupa Birliği Oluşum Süreci ve Ortak Politikalar. *Milli Eğitim Dergisi*, *40*(188), 191–201.

North, D. C. (1981). *Structure and change in economic history*. New York, NY: Norton.

North, D. C. (1984). Transaction costs, institutions, and economic history. *Journal of Institutional and Theoretical Economics*, *140*(1), 7–17.

North, D. C. (2002). *Kurumlar, Kurumsal Değişim ve Ekonomik Performans, Çev. Gül Çağalı Güven*. İstanbul, Turkey: Sabancı Üniversitesi Yayınları.

North, D. C., & Thomas, R. P. (1973). *The rise of the Western World: A new economic history*. UK: Cambridge University Press. doi:10.1017/CBO9780511819438

Oğuz, F. (2003). *Mülkiyet Hakları*. Ankara, Turkey: Roma Yayınları.

Okçu, M. (2007). Yönetişim Tartışmalarına Katkı: Avrupa Birliği İçin Yönetişim Ne Anlama Geliyor? *Süleyman Demirel Üniversitesi İktisadi ve İdari Bilimler Fakültesi Dergisi*, *12*(3), 299–312.

Özkaya, M. H. (2009). IMF'nin Değişen Rolü: Bretton Woods'tan Günümüze. *Uşak Üniversitesi Sosyal Bilimler Dergisi*, *2*(2), 102–117.

Powell, W. W. (1990). *Neither market nor hierarchy: Network forms of organization*. Retrieved from http://www.uvm.edu/pdodds/files/papers/others/1990/powell1990a.pdf

Rodrik, D. (1999). Where did all the growth go? External shocks, social conflict, and growth collapses. *Journal of Economic Growth*, *4*(4), 385–412. doi:10.1023/A:1009863208706

Rodrik, D. (2000). *Institutions for high-quality growth: What they are and how to acquire them*. Retrieved from https://www.nber.org/papers/w7540.pdf

Rodrik, D. (2003). Institutions, integration and geography: In search of the deep determinants of economic growth. In D. Rodrik (Ed.), *In search of prosperity: Analytic narratives on economic growth*. Princeton, NJ: Princeton University Press. doi:10.1515/9781400845897

Rodrik, D. (2006). *Goodbye Washington consensus, hello Washington confusion*? Retrieved from http://citeseerx.ist.psu.edu/viewdoc/download;jsessionid=5D6EDB435CCB6542BCDF92AE678D3747?doi=10.1.1.90.6133&rep=rep1&type=pdf

Seçilmis, E. (2016). Coase Teoremine Alternatif Bakis/An alternative view of the coase theorem. *Finans Politik & Ekonomik Yorumlar*, *53*(612), 9–20.

Şenalp, M. G. (2003). *Yeni Kurumsal İktisat ve Küresel Yönetişim. (Yayınlanmamış Yüksek Lisans Tezi)*. Ankara, Turkey: Ankara Üniversitesi Sosyal Bilimler Enstitüsü İktisat Anabilim Dalı.

Usal, Z. (2008). Dünya Bankası ve IMF Kapsamında Uluslararası Finans Kuruluşları ve İnsan Hakları. *İ.Ü. Siyasal Bilgiler Fakültesi Dergisi,* (39), 231-246.

Weingast, B. R. (2017). *Adam Smith's Constitutional Theory*. Retrieved from https://www.researchgate.net/publication/323972866_Adam_Smith's_Constitutional_Theory

Williamson, O. (1975). *Markets and hierarchies: Analysis and antitrust implications*. New York, NY: Free Press.

Wılliamson, O. (1990). A comparison of alternative approaches to economic organisation. *Journal of Institutional and Theoretical Economics*, *146*(1), 61–71.

Williamson, O. (1993). *Transaction cost economics and organization theory.* Retrieved from file:///C:/Users/User/Downloads/Cap9_Williamson%20%20The%20Mechanisms%20of%20Governance.pdf

Williamson, O. E. (1979). Transaction-cost economics: The governance of contractual relations. *The Journal of Law & Economics*, *22*(2), 233–261. doi:10.1086/466942

Williamson, O. E. (1985). *The economic institutions of capitalism: Firms, markets, relational contracting. New York, NY: Free Press.*

Williamson, O. E. (1998b). Transaction cost economics: How it works; where it is headed. *De Economist*, *146*(1), 23–58. doi:10.1023/A:1003263908567

World Bank. (1980). Retrieved from http://documents.worldbank.org/curated/en/528401468739276346/pdf/multi-page.pdf

World Bank. (1994). World Development Report: Infrastructure for development. New York.

World Bank. (2016). Retrieved from http://documents.worldbank.org/curated/en/896931468189267370/pdf/99896-PUB-Box393211B-PUBLIC-PUBDATE-9-30-15-DOI-10-1596978-1-4648-0654-4-EPI-210654.pdf

Yıldırım, C. (2011). Birinci ve İkinci Nesil Washington Uzlaşması: Neoliberal İktisat Politikalarının 1980'den Sonraki Evrimi. *International Journal of Economic & Social Research*, *7*(2).

KEY TERMS AND DEFINITIONS

Corruption: The misuse of a position or power.
European Union: Economical and political union that is created.
Governance: It is term which underlines the importance of participation in the process of management.
IMF, World Bank and OECD: Supranational Financial Institutions.
Inflation: The rise in the common level of the prices.
Institution: The institutions are the most significant structures that form social life.
Neoliberalism: It can be called new "liberalism".
Stagflation: The case of having recession and inflation at the same time.

Chapter 14
Transformation of the State and Political Economy of the Governance:
A Critical Assessment of the New Institutional Economics in the Public Administration

Emek Yıldırım
https://orcid.org/0000-0002-9101-8243
Artvin Çoruh University, Turkey

ABSTRACT

By the 1980s and 1990s, neoliberal policies such as privatizations and deregulations transforming the minimal state model to regulative state model from the Keynesian social welfare state system made some structural and functional changes in the state mechanism, and the public administration has been in the first place due to the changing relationship between the state and the market. In fact, within this context, the new institutional economics (NIE) had a remarkable influence upon the debates upon the altering role of the state. Hence, the transformation of the state in this regard also revealed the argumentations on the governance paradigm along with the doctrinaire contributions of the new institutional economics. Therefore, this chapter will discuss the transformation of the state and the political economy of the governance together with a critical assessment of the new institutional economics in the public administration.

INTRODUCTION

Just at this moment, somehow or other, they began to run. Alice never could quite make out, in thinking it over afterwards, how it was that they began: all she remembers is, that they were running hand in hand, and the Queen went so fast that it was all she could do to keep up with her: and still the Queen kept crying "Faster! Faster!" but Alice felt she could not go faster, though she had not breath left to

DOI: 10.4018/978-1-7998-0333-1.ch014

Copyright © 2020, IGI Global. Copying or distributing in print or electronic forms without written permission of IGI Global is prohibited.

say so. The most curious part of the thing was, that the trees and the other things round them never changed their places at all: however fast they went, they never seemed to pass anything. "I wonder if all the things move along with us?" thought poor puzzled Alice. And the Queen seemed to guess her thoughts, for she cried, "Faster! Don't try to talk!" Not that Alice had any idea of doing that. She felt as if she would never be able to talk again, she was getting so much out of breath: and still the Queen cried "Faster! Faster!" and dragged her along. "Are we nearly there?" Alice managed to pant out at last. "Nearly there!" the Queen repeated. "Why, we passed it ten minutes ago! Faster!" And they ran on for a time in silence, with the wind whistling in Alice's ears, and almost blowing her hair off her head, she fancied. "Now! Now!" cried the Queen. "Faster! Faster!" And they went so fast that at last they seemed to skim through the air, hardly touching the ground with their feet, till suddenly, just as Alice was getting quite exhausted, they stopped, and she found herself sitting on the ground, breathless and giddy. The Queen propped her up against a tree, and said kindly, "You may rest a little now." Alice looked round her in great surprise. "Why, I do believe we've been under this tree the whole time! Everything's just as it was!" "Of course it is," said the Queen. "What would you have it?" "Well, in our country," said Alice, still panting a little, "you'd generally get to somewhere else–if you ran very fast for a long time, as we've been doing." "A slow sort of country!" said the Queen. "Now, here, you see, it takes all the running you can do, to keep in the same place. If you want to get somewhere else, you must run at least twice as fast as that!" (L. Carroll, 1998, pp. 141-143).

With the incentive of saving the world markets from the critical economic crisis arisen in the 1970s, a new era of global capitalism has been arisen and named as neoliberalism, which was truly as a product of Washington Consensus debates between international economic institutions, developed countries and some major mainstream economists. By the 1980s, the neoliberal paradigm was first launched by the political attempts of Ronald Reagan in the USA and Margaret Thatcher in the UK, and then it was endeavored to function all around the world, especially in the 1990s in Latin America and in the post-socialist countries. Within this period, for the success of neoliberal policies, it was aimed that the states would withdraw from the economic territory and give its place to the markets for the liberalization. However, by the end of 1990s, Asian Financial Crisis had a significant impact on the markets and it was recognized that the markets could not operate steady without the states' intervention. As a result, it has been needed to re-modify the state's role to become more interventionist by new market-oriented regulation policies due to the interrelation with the markets. As a consequence, it was time to the minimal state model, which replaced with the Keynesian social welfare state model by the 1980s, would be displaced by a new state model as the regulatory state model and a new kind of public administration paradigm as the governance (Majone, 1997). For this reason, firstly post-Washington Consensus debates and then the discussions upon the public administration through the concept of governance have been arisen among the economists, political scientists and other specialists in the international and national bodies, which are interrelated with this issue. In the meantime, the new institutional economics (NIE) has also a significant ground within the debates, as such: "The definition of institutions as rules is central to NIE and places governance at its heart" (Chhotray and Stoker, 2009, p. 53), and, "NIE from the economical aspect is in an appearance of a current furnishing the "governance" institutions required by the neoliberalism" (Akansel, 2016, p. 17). Therefore, in this work, it will be aimed to deliberate the transformation of the state and the political economy of the governance paradigm in conjunction with a critical assessment of the new institutional economics upon these issues.

GLOBAL CAPITALISM AND TRANSFORMATION OF THE STATE

First of all, globalization paradigm, or in other words, global capitalism has been conceptualized as a result of that the capital flux exceeds the national borders through mobilization of the investment, commodity and service, and its spatio-temporal transmission is on the rise internationally. That is to say, this concept can be described as the new facet of the capitalist system runs globally. Furthermore, it is clear that using the term global capitalism could be more appropriate to define the process capitalist system included for mentioning the new kinds of modes and relations of production currently exist (Robinson, 2004; Sklair, 2002). So, the global capitalism stays on course included such significant stages: Becoming more transparent of the national borders; decentralization of the production procedures; becoming easier of the mobilization of the capital and the commodity globally; becoming more integrated of the national economics and becoming more fragile to any crisis or problem, which simultaneously affects the whole world critically; commencing the discrete manufacturing and piecework production instead of the mass production; globalization of not only intensive manufacturing of the technology especially in the fields of communication and information but also the financialization; spatio-temporal permeation of the capitalist production processes; and emerging a transnational capitalist class (Robinson, 2012; W. K. Carroll, 2012; Guzelsari, 2008, pp. 23-26).

By the 1970s, the capitalist order needed to shift its route from the fordist regime of accumulation, which was based on mass production, and the Keynesian social welfare state system, which was based on mass consumption, to new kinds of production and consumption systems after the economic and political crises emerged because of the current systems. Thereby, it has begun to transform to the regime of flexible accumulation, also called as the post-fordism, from the regime of intensive accumulation (Dikmen, 2017, p. 216). Moreover, scientific and technological developments, which were nourished and flourished within the competition conditions arisen by the Cold War, has accelerated this transformation. Today, both production and consumption processes are transformed within the current epoch, which is labeled as "knowledge era", "information society" or "post-industrial period" by emphasizing only upon the technological transition. However, on the one hand, the production process is fractionalizing, partializing, becoming flexible and precarious both in manufacturing and service sector by the means of post-fordist regime of accumulation; and on the other hand, relations of production are introducing new kinds of labor-capital relation extending from transnational to national, to regional and to local by the spatio-temporal permeation of the global capitalism. In fact, the main reason behind this progress is that the capitalist order necessitated to resolve the organic structural crises emerged during the last quarter of 20th century. This is because, "while periodic and cyclical crises appeared at regular intervals within the capitalist production were influential to balance the production and consumption sectors and to recast the market mechanisms, structural crises provided restoration of the sovereignty of the capital over the labor by generating the redefinition of the class compounds, the class praxes, the historical bloc and the role of the state towards the class power" (Ongen, 2004). Or in other words, "[t]he movement of the capitalist economy is determined by the development of productive capital under such conditions and accumulation necessarily proceeds along a path of combined and uneven development punctuated by crises (since crises are necessary to stimulate the restructuring of capital). This pattern of accumulation is a necessary part of the operation of capital and the capitalist state's economic intervention is fundamentally determined by capital's economic requirements" (Fine and Harris, 1976, p. 99).

In principle, within the fordist regime, with the instant and acute falls in the rates of profit, employment security and state expenditures have begun to be burden to the capitalist class. So that, the production model also started to evolve to post-fordist regime from the fordist one because of its inoperative role due to the crises. Correspondingly, it was so important to restructure the system had a severe crisis both in the production-consumption processes and in the field of public finance. Hence, the Washington Consensus introduced in 1978 was became the means deliver the route map of the restructuring. The program submitted to the world by the International Monetary Fund (IMF), World Bank (WB) and the U.S. Treasury prescribed a transformation shaped by neoliberal policies and led by the Anglo-American countries. It was aimed to be dissociated the political and economic fields, to restructure the production process, minimize the public institutions, to shrink the protective and interventionist role of the states, to maximize the liberalization of the markets. This is because, it was required to abandon the fordist regime and Keynesian policies initially, and then to actualize relevant policies within a neoliberal context. Indeed, as J. Williamson (2000, pp. 252-253) described, the Washington Consensus comprised of these main steps:

- *Fiscal discipline*
- *A redirection of public expenditure priorities toward fields offering both high economic returns and the potential to improve income distribution, such as primary health care, primary education, and infrastructure*
- *Tax reform (to lower marginal rates and broaden the tax base)*
- *Interest rate liberalization*
- *A competitive exchange rate*
- *Trade liberalization*
- *Liberalization of inflows of foreign direct investment*
- *Privatization*
- *Deregulation (to abolish barriers to entry and exit)*
- *Secure property rights*

On the other hand, as distinct from the fordist regime, which was the mass production and consumption model, post-fordist regime brings about that production and consumption processes operate in a fragmental and diversified structure within the context of the relations inside and between them. Accordingly, the post-fordist regime, which rules since the last quarter of 20th century, could be conceptualized as the "flexible production and accumulation regime" (Saylan, 2016, p. 148). In fact, it is the current accumulation regime described as on the basis of the flexibility (via flexible production, flexible specialization, flexible organization, flexible management and etc.) and technological developments (such as notably information and communication technologies). "It is a period characterized by the "becoming flexible" of the technology, labor, division of labor, organization structures, and such progress makes the mobilization of the capital to speed up" (Belek, 1999, p. 169). In other words, by the post-fordist regime, it is administered a complete restructuring in both the accumulation regime and the regulation mode, as Belek (1999, pp. 255-256) also states:

In the new accumulation regime:

1. *Transition to post-Taylorist organization of the production and the labor on the basis of new information technologies. This means to minimize the demand a new structuring and labor-force, instead of the disappearance of the mass production*

2. *Industrialization of the service sector progressively on the basis of the new technologies [... and] development of the new urban service sector centers*
3. *Industrialization of the agriculture [... and] losing its significance of the agriculture with regards to its contribution to the national income and the labor-force employed in the agriculture*
4. *Dissolution of the productivity and the income of the masses from each other. Increasing of the disparity of the income and the consumption for that reason. Transition to a accumulation regime with low growth rate.*
5. *Dissolution of the relationship between the wages and the works, realizing of the socialization based on the information, and individualization and pluralization tendencies as the results of differentiation of the consumption tendencies*

In the new regulation mode:

1. *Proliferation of the small business*
2. *Disruption of the social security systems*
3. *Decay of the trade unions, increase in unemployment, disordering of the employment types and increase in heterogeneity within the working class*
4. *Development of the labor/capital relations called as "decentralized corporatism", which means the deterioration of the collective bargaining at the national level*

As a matter of fact, it is possible to put forward that the post-fordist regime is a complete and multi-dimensional paradigm paves the way for some various transformations emerged in the political, social and even cultural fields as well, besides being a fact operating in the economic field fundamentally. In the meanwhile, production, consumption, employment, labor-force and commodity are also internationalized together with the transnationalization of the capital and capitalist class (Robinson, 2011). In the last phase of the global capitalism, there are, on the one hand, multinational corporations (MNC) and transnational capitalist class (TCC) that have investments in cheap labor-force among several regions all around the world (Robinson, 2001; Sklair, 2000, 2001; Embong, 2000), and, on the other hand, the post-fordist production model, which consists of the workshop production model based on flexible and lean manufacturing and the service sector using information and communication technologies along with an advanced specialization, instead of the fordist mass production. Within this context, it has been started to actualize step-by-step via neoliberal policies introduced within the program aspiring to all these changes. In the 1980s, the neoliberal agenda, of which Reagan in the USA and Thatcher in the UK were only counter-display, laid the groundwork for that the transformation fundamentally proposed by the international financial institutions could be carried into action. The most evident instances were Latin America and the post-socialist countries notably Russian Federation. Nevertheless, the main idea establishing the framework of the program is as follows:

The movement toward the neoliberal utopia of a pure and perfect market is made possible by the politics of financial deregulation. And it is achieved through the transformative and, it must be said, destructive action of all of the political measures [...], designed to protect foreign corporations and their investments from national states) that aim to call into question any and all collective structures that could serve as an obstacle to the logic of the pure market: the nation, whose space to manoeuvre continually decreases; work groups, for example through the individualisation of salaries and of careers as a func-

tion of individual competences, with the consequent atomisation of workers; collectives for the defence of the rights of workers, unions, associations, cooperatives; even the family, which loses part of its control over consumption through the constitution of markets by age groups (Bourdieu, 1998).

However, the separation of the economics and the politics entirely excluding each other in the way that institutions were trying to operate isolated from each other unavoidably brought about a loss in the balance between the state and the market. This is because, as Clarke (1991, pp. 3-4) discusses, "the institutional separation of the state from the economy, and so stressed the autonomy of the state as a political institution. This analytical separation of the 'political' from the 'economic' was based theoretically on a radical separation of production from distribution." As a matter of fact, the divergence of the states and the markets in all fields such as production, distribution and consumption as one of the results of the neoliberal program also inevitably caused some certain crises in various sizes and in various areas. For instance, as the consequence of the shifts from the Bretton Woods system to the Washington Consensus system and then from the Washington Consensus system to the post-Washington Consensus system, the accumulation regimes have been transforming from the fordist regime to post-fordist one, as well as the state models have from the Keynesian social welfare state model to the minimal state model and then from the minimal state model to the regulative state model. In the course of such developments, on the one hand, the private sector started to interpenetrate some main areas of the public sector by the help of privatizations and deregulations done within the context of the neoliberal agenda, on the other hand, the role of the state began to change from an omnipotent nation-state project to one of the actors to regulate the order within the national or regional boundaries in accordance with the politically and economically internationalized and transnationalized world system. In this respect, "such facts as small workshops instead of big enterprises, need-based employment and contracted/subcontracted labor instead of job security and full employment, and human resources management instead of trade unions and collective bargaining gained currency and prominence in the new period diversely from the old period" (Firincioglu, 2015, p. 42). By the means of all these transformations, the production process has become much more fragmented and as a result the labor market has been about to be raveled. Hereby, both the trade union struggle and the class struggle organizing upon the masses starts to weaken, loosen and become stunted. By the melting trade union struggle besides the mall-scaled, flexible and insecure employment conditions, the erosion of the security and the rights belonging to both the working conditions and daily-life influences the masses negatively. Post-fordism eventually spreads as a flexible, lean, small-scaled, fragmented, diversified and decentralized management and organization model to the all fields of the life.

By the end of the 1980s and during the years of 1990s, the world completely was under an economic and political winds of change. The capitalist transition process of the post-socialist countries also caused a widespread expansion of the transformation of the global capitalism all around the world. Moreover, no one had any doubt about the accuracy and the necessity of the introduced neoliberal agenda, while the triumph of the capitalism was declared versus the socialism. Consequently, post-fordist regime has provided the consent necessary for shrinking the state and collapsing the public sector. As a matter of fact, it is diffusing throughout the world foremostly from the developed countries to developing and underdeveloped countries by the new rightist or neo-conservative governments, which are economically liberal but politically and socially conservative, supporting and carrying out the neoliberal agenda, from the 1980s and 1990s up to present. At the same time, legitimacy of the nation-state, transparency of the national borders, margins of the sovereignty of the states, efficiency of the states within the economics, and position and importance of the public sector against the private sector respectively become a highly questionable topic at all (Jessop, 2002). As a consequence, an internationalizing, transnationalizing process has been begun to function in general, incidental to the becoming transparent of the national borders, with regard to not only accumulation of the capital but also both the commodity and the labor, alongside the existence of the fact that uneven and combined development of the capitalism processes as always under the sun (Oguz, 2006, p. 156). Furthermore, it is possible that international capital flow could extend spatio-temporally on the global scale by the way of the development of the information and communication technologies.

However, on the other side, by the end of 1990s, after the cyclical depression critically staggering the East Asian, Latin American and Russian economics, it was comprehended that trying to minimize the state was a mistake in regard to maximize the functionality of the market mechanism. Conducting the activities of the state as a night watchman caused that the authority, which not only controlled and restricted the markets but also imposed the necessary sanctions in case of need, has disappeared. Nevertheless, when the state became minimal, the markets spread with its all impunity and cruelty throughout the world within the bounds of spatio-temporal possibility. It has introduced a rapid increase on poverty and crime on the one hand, and some certain economic crises as the results of sudden boom of the financialization (Foster, 2017, pp. 50-51). As a consequence, it needed to arise a reorganization of the state system. Therefore, without abandoning the post-fordist regime, it has been put forward the necessity of the revision of the relationship between the state and the market. Accordingly, it has been proposed to take a promotive position of the state within the economic arena instead of the the minimal state model (Sarisoy, 2010, p. 279). However, the new kind of state model would be neither protectionist and interventionist as much as Keynesian social welfare state model nor the night watchman states giving refine to the markets got out of the hand as the minimal state model did suggest. In fact, the Third Way approach, which was shaped by compounding the convenient sides of the social democracy and the neoliberalism by favor of some European established leftist parties in the mid-1990s, was asserted and attracted a considerable attention as well (Arestis & Sawyer, 2007, pp. 293-294). In this context, in regard to the regulative state model, which is supposed to be the compromise of the two inoperable state model; the state would be responsible for monitoring and controlling the market on the one hand, and providing the required grounds for the construction of the political, administrative and juridical infrastructure in order to the operation of the markets by the book on the other hand (Bayramoglu, 2003, pp. 145-146). From now on, the state again takes the incumbent role as one of the actors operating within the economic arena instead of the minimal state model prescribing an economic space beyond the state's control. In this way, the state, which experiences a second transformation under the post-fordist regime as the last phase of the global capitalism, takes its place among the transnational actors such as market institutions and non-governmental organizations as the regulative establishment. Therefore, in other words, as Sonmez (2016, p. 61) indicates:

The approval of the neoliberal paradigm as the only mechanism providing growth, stability, efficiency and welfare, preventing unemployment and poverty, regulating the society besides the economics should be rejected by considering all kind of intervention of the state as the intervention of the politics in the economics. Within the process of the accumulation of the capital, the role of the state is different from the past; priorities of the neoliberal policies are discharge of the state intervention gradually and being regulatory of the state such as to guard the big business groups, commercialization of the public service and social service fields. Discharge of the state is out of the question; economic and financial activities are regulated through the medium of the state on behalf of global capital, and its judicial and institutional infrastructure and framework are arranged by the political power.

Furthermore, this progress definitely affects the state structure, public administration and local governments, and thus it necessitates "to re-regulate the hierarchy within the interior organization of the state and to create new institutions" (Akcay, 2013, p. 25). Hence, the public administration and the local governments has started to change as a result of that the state proceeds to evolve to a decentralized structure simultaneously withdrawing from the economics not only by the means of privatizations and deregulations but also by the way of international cooperation forums and international concession agreements. As a matter of fact, a spatial expansion and connection line is establishing from local to global and *vice versa*. Furthermore, the *cross-territorial* interconnections set up among global, national, regional and local dynamics are predominantly based on the functionality of the market mechanism (Jessop, 1994, pp. 271-272). At the same time, within the context of the *cross-territorial* interconnections, the national, regional and local allies of the transnational capitalist class are the national or the regional capitalist class, technocrats in the state bureaucracy and non-governmental organizations (NGOs), together with the replacement of the national state institutions with the international governmental institutions (Sklair, 2000, p. 99; W. K. Carroll, 2007). Hereby, by the governance mindset that it is aimed to replace with the administration approach emerged due to the Keynesian social welfare state system, it is proposed a more flexible and decentralized administrative model. According to this model, it is intended that the public sector would be organized, governed and carried out its activities almost as the private sector, and accordingly it is amended in the field of the public administration. Within the public administration area, "while before the 1980s reforms were focused on the implementing power of the executive, it was indicating a reform process, which was economy-centered between 1980-1990s and objectified the state as a whole after 1990s. [...] In particular, the general feature of the steps launched in the 1990s and concretized in the 2000s is to re-establish the operation of the state and to re-actualize its organization within the framework of the market logic" (Ovgun, 2013, pp. 14, 16). However;

The accumulation strategy is not simply imposed on the state by external, economically constituted, forces, but is constrained by the institutional forms of political representation, administrative organization, and economic intervention of the state. Moreover the selection of a particular accumulation strategy is determined politically, according to the need to secure social bases of support for the strategy. Thus the successful adoption and implementation of a particular 'accumulation strategy' depends on its consistency with a viable 'hegemonic project' through which such support is secured (Clarke, 1991, p. 50).

POLITICAL ECONOMY OF THE GOVERNANCE PARADIGM

Initially it was brought the fact of the public administration up for discussion by actualizing of the neoliberal policies based upon the Washington Consensus after 1980s. Neither the state structure nor the public administration could escape from the complete transformation created by the post-fordist paradigm. Moreover, since it was first emerged, "a materialist critique of the discipline of 'Public Administration' might throw considerable light on conflicts within the bourgeoisie and on changing forms of class rule" (Holloway & Picciotto, 1977, p. 100). Within this context, in this period that the capital has been internationalizing and global capitalism has been expanding spatio-temporally throughout the world regardless of the circumstances, the public administration is exposed to the reform programs and even the paradigm shifts (Guzelsari, 2004, p. 1). In this respect, two fundamental stage can be mentioned: The first one is the new public management (NPM) model, which was put forward together with the minimal state model; and the second one is the governance model, which is brought forward in conformity with the regulative state model. The place, location and the responsibilities of the state are re-described through these two models with regard to the purpose of re-identifying the role of the state and the market. As Guler (2003, p. 101) indicates; "within the twenty years it has been faced with the third "paradigm shift": "*public administration*" at the beginning of 1980s, "*new public management*" in the 1980s, and "*public governance*" at the end of 1990s."

First of all, by the years of 1980-1990s, which was the period that the Washington Consensus became influential, the comprehension of "the small state and the powerful market" began to actualize. It has been providing to enable the global liberalization of the commodity, labor and the capital and financialization by means of neoliberal policies such as privatization and deregulations. Hence, a reconstruction has been launching for the public administration area as an important function of the state, which was tried to be minimized. With the reform programs, it has been endeavored to apply the efficient and influential service mentality, which is incidental to the private sector, to the public administration. "By this way, in the public administration, "juridical rationality" replaced with "economic-managemental rationality"" (Guzelsari, 2004, p. 3). So, this also brings the efforts to reduce the political and social sides of the public administration guarding the public benefit and to substitute the technical and mechanical properties, which are profit, competition and productivity driven. Additionally, it brings into the use of the methods such as "professional management, performance measure, management by results, customer orientation, total quality management" within the public administration (Guler, 2003, pp. 99-100). Correspondingly, it is also projected that the public administration would be changed and the state could conduct as a profit-driven private sector actor. "The tendency of these kinds of developments is the inner-marketization of the state, and redefinition of the role of the state as a market actor to pave the way for the appropriate operation of both the state and the private sector within the market mechanisms (Guzelsari, 2004, pp. 5-6).

In this period, in which the minimal state model and the new public management mindset were ruling, public administration policies were restructured by the stages such as organization, sphere of activity, cooperations and product/service output in the light of this mindset. And of course, it was emerged simultaneously with a mentality transformation composed of such attributives as efficient, influential, productive, profitable and quick and such concepts as liberalization, performance, specialization, flexibilization, completion, quality and transparency. According to the new public management mindset, every citizen has become already a customer, a consumer. So, the relation between the state and the citizen was transformed to the relation of seller and buyer, producer and consumer (Guzelsari, 2004, p. 5). However, on the other side, it could not be possible to actualize the theoretically predicted changes into the practical life because the state minimizing by the deregulation policies had no elbow room within the economic arena. So to speak, "government stepped back [... and t]he deregulation led to instability; with less oversight, there was more fraud and less competition" (Stiglitz, 2012, p. 179). Furthermore, global economic crises arisen at the end of 1990s demonstrates that the minimal state model could not be an appropriate and efficient model for the post-fordist paradigm. For this reason, it has been necessitated to restructure the state again. Thus, a transitional stage has begun from the minimal state model, which put the regulation attribution of the Keynesian state model into the market by the deregulation, to, which is obliged to choose the deregulation, and its governance mentality, which is the implementational aspect of the regulative state model. In other words, "this change is a transition process "from the first generation structural reforms to second generation structural reforms" or "from the Washington Consensus to the post-Washington Consensus"" (Guzelsari, 2008, p. 148).

Thereby, the truth about that the in every phase capitalism needs a state model to regulate the economic activities becomes evident. Together with the emergence of the economic crises and some critical political/social problems marking the beginning of the post-Washington Consensus process, it has been understood that minimizing the role of the state by the neoliberal policies was a mistake. This is because while the post-fordist accumulation regime, the last phase of the capitalist accumulation system, which is also always obliged to restore itself, is preserved, the requirement to amend the mode of regulation has been arisen. Hence, a transition from the minimal state model to the regulative state model and simultaneously from the new public management to the governance has been occurred. As distinct from the new public management, governance, which conveys local, regional, national and international levels; "is described as a function actualized by public-private, state-non-state, national-international actors, and as the conceptualization of the development of the new transactional relations among these actors" (Guzelsari, 2004, pp. 12-13). In fact, it is also possible to "mention the governance of corporations (corporate governance), cities (urban governance), states (good governance) and world (global governance)" as the governance models emerged under several appearances (Bayraktar, 2015, p. 74). Moreover, global capitalism needs the governance because the state should meet the required obligations for assuming the regulation, orientation and support role to contribute the internationalization process of the capital, commodity and labor. Indeed, the governance is a significant factor for the post-fordist paradigm to regulate the interconnections of the market, the state and the NGOs on local, regional, national and international bases and to govern the capital, commodity and labor internationalizing and transnationalizing as the results of the spatio-temporally globalizing capitalism throughout the world. For this reason, restructuring of the organizational, institutional, governmental and technical elements necessary for the regulative state model is suggested upon the principles of the governance. To put it in different way, as Ataay and Acar (2008) indicates:

It is possible to discuss the renewal efforts of the neoliberalism under two basic titles. While the change regarding the economy and the state is emerged by putting forward the "regulative state" model, the change regarding the democracy is arisen by improving the "governance" model. The idea that the minimal state model approach, which focuses on the free market model, deregulation, limitation of the state's intervention, is not sufficient for the efficiency of the market mechanisms and the maintenance of the free competition underlies on the basis of the change regarding the economy and the state. According to this, it is admitted that that state should make efficient provisions against cartelization and corruption and for securing the competition, providing the transparency, extending the freedom of enterprise and protecting the consumer rights to be reached the competitive market structure. It is in need of new government mechanisms to take these steps necessary for the efficient function of the market mechanism. Within this framework, a "public reform" should be realized for constituting the institutions strengthening the free market economy, developing the state's regulative functions (independent regulative institutions), and institutionalizing the regulative state model.

In addition to that, according to the WB, which is one of the main institutions providing such extensive and validated usage of this notion throughout the world, governance is "an accountable and transparent public administration establishing the appropriate circumstances for the growth principally under the guidance of the private sector", and "different from the propositions of the public management, such concepts as "accountability", "maintenance of the legitimacy", "transparency in the administration" and "participation" are among the constituent conceptions of the governance" (Guzelsari, 2004, p. 15). In fact, the innovation within the public administration by means of the governance is about the introduction of these concepts. Such expressions as accountability, competition, transparency, efficiency, decentralization, subsidiarity, democratization, liberalization, participation, pluralism, right of information act and development are started to use in the public administration *via* the governance (Williams & Young, 1994, pp. 86-88). Besides the regulation role of the state, such conceptions as "entrepreneur state", "flexible state", "market-friendly state" and/or "state-market partnership" become to be described. Furthermore, the democratization ideal, which is based on the expressions such as "pluralism", "participation" and "strong civil society" arisen from the interrelation depended on the collaboration of the civil society and the state, also becomes one of the properties of the governance recurred frequently. However, hereby, "it is endeavored that neoliberalism could obtain social legitimization not only by showing the social state implementation as the source of economic problems and creating an ideological environment in accordance with liquidation of the social state but also by identifying neoliberalism with the democracy" (Ataay, 2006, p. 23). As a result, while the social state system, which was fulfilling the responsibilities due to provide the social security and public services without charge to the citizens as a matter of their own civil rights, has been abolished, a life belonging to these citizens is tried to be constructed completely under the heels of the market and neoliberal policies *via* the discourses upon democracy and the freedoms. Thereby, according to Jessop (1998), the governance is a political paradigm shift, whereas, according to Keles (2010, p. 65), it is "a world view, which is aimed to be made sovereign among the society entirely, as a matter of fact that it is also purposed to make the capitalism sovereign under the sun not only because of being merely an economic system but also beside the all socio-cultural, political and institutional preconditions."

Nevertheless, the governance lay the sufficient ground for this transition by forming the relationships between the state, the market and the civil society on the global, national, regional and local bases fundamentally by favor of the international economic institutions as WB and IMF. Hence, governance, in other words, is management of the alliances of these three sectors established by the actors of them for securing the reign of the market, instead of the dichotomies existing up to now as the state-market the state-civil society and the market-civil society. For this reason, at the present time, various governance institutions are tried to be put forward and become operative for making the state the sufficient mechanism to provide the coordination between the production and consumption processes on the spatio-temporal basis, together with the multi-dimensional interrelation between the state/public sector, the capital/private sector and the civil society/third sector (Sorensen, 2006, p. 194; Demirci, 2013, p. 44). For as much as, the governance has also political, economic, social and cultural scopes as well as administrative feature. This is because, "[...] "the market always contains a political and social construction process", and it is possible to perceive that actually the attraction of the governance in the new age is a result of "not being successful without accomplishing any economic project with political legitimacy, social order and institutional efficiency" come out in the 1990s thoroughly" (Bayraktar, 2015, p. 73). Additionally, put it differently;

Firstly, governance basically is on the behalf of creating conditions guaranteeing international capital inflow. Secondly, today providing this liquidity and expansion is experienced in the form of programs, sanctions realized by international establishments and structures, instead of subjecting of a state to the other on the economic and administrative area. Governance, in this sense, functions as an indicator of the interventionism of the international economic institutions such as the WB, the IMF that ever-increasing and become more "directly" in the developing countries and as a notion legalizing this interventionism as well. Strengthening the political and judicial reforms, which are the substantive ingredients of the governance, together with a civil society supporting these reforms is shaped within the framework of these two aims. Especially political and judicial reforms named as "restructuring the state" is on the behalf of guaranteeing the existence of the free enterprises, capital or transnational corporations in the developing countries. While this is tried to actualize, not only the rights of the capital are endeavored to assure the juridical guarantee but also intuitions or establishments, which are dependent to the IMF and the WB directly and could not go beyond the route determined by these intuitions, are constituted (Zabci, 2002, p. 153).

Consequently, the last global crisis brings about pushing the limits of the system, as every crisis make capitalism always be obliged to go through a new phrase. The system, which reaches everywhere as far as possible on the global bases, spreads spatially in the life of the people and everyday accelerates in time more and more as a return of the technological development. Within this context, it is tried to "increase the profitability of the capital by making the public services profit-oriented activities, reducing the social spending and labor costs for the sake of the capital, and thusly both by lessening the tax burden of the capital and by providing the use of the public funds to the capital instead of the social expenses" (Ataay, 2006, p. 22). And what's more, for the capitalism, commodifying everything from the public services to the human relations, even to water, air, the nature and the human life beside the existent products and services and becoming merchantable and consumable of them also become an imperative. All these could be possible only by coming together and cooperating with each other of the three sectors. Thus, for that reason, the regulative state model and the governance have a key position within this picture, beyond being an ordinary administration notion.

NEW INSTITUTIONAL ECONOMICS

First of all, it is beneficial to understand the framework of the new institutional economics approach that it is mainly based upon well-known economist Ronald Coase's outstanding two articles, titled as "The Nature of the Firm" (1937) and "The Problem of Social Cost" (1960), besides the leading figures of the old institutional economics (OIE). Moreover, as Gandhi and Crase (2009, p. 3) describe:

New institutional economics identifies formal institutions - which have their foundation in the laws and structures of organized society, as well as informal institutions which often spontaneously develop to address specific issues and problems in the society [...]. It identifies macro level institutions: humanly devised rules or "rules of the game" that structure interactions (formal rules such as constitutions, laws and property rights, and informal rules such as traditions and codes of conduct), and micro level institutions, such as institutions of governance including markets or other modes of managing activities/ transactions and seeing activities/economic activities through.

On the other hand, the first use of the concept "governance" has been appeared in the works of NIE. First of all, O. E. Williamson, who is the first person uses the "new institutional economics" term (O. E. Williamson, 1975, p. 1) as well as one of the main theorists of the NIE, used the terms "corporate governance" and "governance structures" in his works (Insel, 2011, p. 128). According to O. E. Williamson, "[b]oth, court ordering and private ordering characterize the governance structure (or "organization") of non-standard contractual relationships. Attentive actors agree before they come to terms on a governance structure that they regard suitable. Market and hierarchy are two of the imaginable ideal types of possible governance structures. Important to see is that the choice of an efficient (better "efficacious") governance structure results not from optimizing some target function subject to a set of constraints. It may rather be understood as a form of boundedly rational or "suitable" choice from a set of governance structures in the sense of Selten's hypothesis of the casuistic structure of boundedly rational strategies" (Richter, 2005, p. 175). In short, the governance structures are mainly for minimizing the transaction costs, which is one of the foremost focus subjects of the NIE (Cetin, 2012, p. 69). In fact, the NIE has been providing a synthesis of the arguments of the OIE and the neoliberal economic theories especially by setting forth the *modus operandi* of the intertwining and working together of the state and the market instead of being confronted and paving the way for the "regulation reforms" in the 1990s as well (Guler, 2003, p. 97; Demir, 1996).

Indeed, the NIE has also put forward a solid ground for reducing the transaction costs and the costs of property rights, which was declared as the obstacles for the efficiency and the profitability of the production process against the market, by nesting the state and the market to co-operate together for the sake of the market mechanism. This is because countries, which have dynamic economics, have also strong states (Weiss & Hobson, 1999, p. 13). So, the significance of the NIE is based on the given importance to the role of the state again at the end of 1990s. Accordingly, it is clear that within the 1997 Report of the WB, which was introduced in the same year of the first conference of the the foundation of the International Society for New Institutional Economics (ISNIE) held at Washington University (Richter, 2005, p. 172), the emphasis on the state and its significant role took a place on the top issues mostly by the effect of the NIE. Furthermore, the re-increasing significance of the role of the state after the failure of the minimal state model structuring endeavors should be defined by a new kind of program different from the past ones. For this reason, the NIE gave the appropriate theoretical ground to set up a fresh agenda for the new state model and its political or administrative mechanisms in conformity with the neoliberal policies. According to this framework, for reducing the transaction costs and property rights costs to provide the market works properly, not only such policies as privatization, deregulation and competition could decrease the transaction costs but also a mutual relation and coordination of the state, the market and the NGOs should be established within the context of the term governance (Bayramoglu, 2003, p. 107). However, the result of the argumentation of the NIE has not reached very different level compared to the other economics theories in terms of the solution of the economic and social problems arisen because of the capitalism, which now expands globally from near and far, because of the reason that Bourdieu (1998) also indicates:

From the start it has been founded on a formidable abstraction. For, in the name of a narrow and strict conception of rationality as individual rationality, it brackets the economic and social conditions of rational orientations and the economic and social structures that are the condition of their application. [...] Economists may not necessarily share the economic and social interests of the true believers and may have a variety of individual psychic states regarding the economic and social effects of the utopia which they cloak with mathematical reason. Nevertheless, they have enough specific interests in the field of economic science to contribute decisively to the production and reproduction of belief in the neoliberal utopia. Separated from the realities of the economic and social world by their existence and above all by their intellectual formation, which is most frequently purely abstract, bookish, and theoretical, they are particularly inclined to confuse the things of logic with the logic of things. These economists trust models that they almost never have occasion to submit to the test of experimental verification and are led to look down upon the results of the other historical sciences, in which they do not recognise the purity and crystalline transparency of their mathematical games, whose true necessity and profound complexity they are often incapable of understanding. They participate and collaborate in a formidable economic and social change. Even if some of its consequences horrify them (they can join the socialist party and give learned counsel to its representatives in the power structure), it cannot displease them because, at the risk of a few failures, imputable to what they sometimes call "speculative bubbles", it tends to give reality to the ultra-logical utopia (ultra-logical like certain forms of insanity) to which they consecrate their lives.

CONCLUSION

Eventually, the contemporary era can be defined as Serbian writer Brana Crnčević expresses: "What a progression, what a progression! The father was a slave; the son becomes a robot" (Argin, 1992). It is important to grasp the reasons to use such concepts as progress, development and growth by adding some certain attributes for some kinds of transitions. While the capitalism is globalizing, the capital is internationalizing and the labor is transnationalizing, the vast majority of the population on the globe is becoming desperate for today and tomorrow because of ever-increasing and spreading poverty, bad living conditions, corruption, crime, wars and violence all around the earth. In addition to that, the transformation in the infrastructure causes a transition in the superstructure and establishment of new balances. In the meantime, the new role of the re-structured state mechanism originated by post-fordist accumulation regime is to solve the problems and –hegemonic– crises arisen as a result of internationalization of the labor-capital conflict, and to provide the stability of the markets operate on the international, national, regional and local bases. Furthermore, from a different point of view, the post-fordist state model is obligated to control the reflection of the production and consumption processes, which becomes flexible and simplified on the one hand, and assumes a small-scaled, fragmented and individualistic structure on the other hand, on the political, juridical, administrative, social and cultural arenas. Within this context, it has arisen a requirement of re-structuring of public administration as a main sphere of activity of the state for the last one century. Hence, it was tried to actualize the new public management relating to the minimal state model, which was the initial state model of the neoliberal agenda outlined by the Washington Consensus. Subsequently, within the period named as the post-Washington Consensus, it has been emerged that the state should undertake a certain role, position and responsibility as the result of the crises created by the neoliberal policies within economic and political areas. By this way, the governance is tried to be conceptualized, theorized and actualized as the appropriate public administration paradigm of the regulative state model today already being restructuring. Moreover, one of the conceptualizing and theorizing endeavors is rooted in the NIE theory and theorists' studies. This is because a complete and multi-dimensional web of relations, which is emerged as a current result of the global capitalism and the post-fordist accumulation regime, needs to be identified and realized according to this identification, and the mission of the regulative state model and the governance also necessitate this identification and this realization to overcome the deficiencies and the difficulties of the process, of which the capital, the commodity, the finance-capital and the labor could spread spatio-temporally throughout the world besides the inclusion of every individual into the production and consumption mechanisms. In other words, the global capitalism now needs the governance as well as the regulative state model to maintain the organization, administration, coordination and control mechanisms entirely and mutually work properly. Consequently, as Warren (1972, p. 29) also indicates; "the expansion of state functions has involved an increasingly tighter integration of state structures with the economic, political, social and cultural systems of imperialist society. Since this tighter integration takes place on the social basis of the dominance of capital, the result is bound to be increasing [...] informal authoritarianism which more and more relies on whatever legitimation it can get from such bourgeois-democratic structures as Parliament." In addition to that, to put it another way, according to Stiglitz (2012, pp. 187-188):

The powerful try to frame the discussion in a way that benefits their interests, realizing that, in a democracy, they cannot simply impose their rule on others. In one way or another, they have to "co-opt" the rest of society to advance their agenda. Here again the wealthy have an advantage. Perceptions and beliefs are malleable. [...W]ealthy have the instruments, resources, and incentives to shape beliefs in ways that serve their interests. They don't always win—but it's far from an even battle. [... It is clearly] seen how the powerful manipulate public perception by appeals to fairness and efficiency, while the real outcomes benefit only them.

REFERENCES

Akansel, I. (2016). New institutional economics (NIE): Origins of neoliberalism. *China-USA Business Review*, *15*(1), 14–32.

Akcay, U. (2013). Sermayenin Uluslararasılaşması ve Devletin Dönüşümü: Teknokratik Otoriterizmin Yükselişi. *Praksis*, *30-31*, 11–39.

Arestis, P., & Sawyer, M. (2007). Neoliberalizm ve Üçüncü Yol. In A. Saad-Filho & D. Johnston (Eds.), *Neoliberalizm: Muhalif bir Seçki* (Başlı Ş. Öncel T., Trans.). (pp. 293–302). İstanbul, Turkey: Yordam Kitap.

Argin, S. (1992). Kapitalist Toplumda İşin ve İşgücünün Kaderi: Post-Fordizm. *Birikim, 41*. Retrieved from http://www.birikimdergisi.com/birikim-yazi/4560/kapitalist-toplumda-isin-ve-isgucunun-kaderi-post-fordizm#.WVV8LIiLTIW

Ataay, F. (2006). *Neoliberalizm ve Devletin Yeniden Yapılandırılması: Türkiye'de Kamu Reformu Üzerine İncelemeler*. Ankara, Turkey: De Ki Basım Yayın.

Ataay, F. & Acar, E. (2008). Devletin Yeniden Yapılandırılması ve Yerelleşme. *İktisat Dergisi, 500*. Retrieved from http://www.yayed.org/id15-gorusler/faruk-ataay-ergul-acar-devletin-yeniden-yapilandirilmasi-ve-yerellesme.php

Bayraktar, F. (2015). 'Yönetişim' Paradigması ve Neoliberalizm: Çelişki ve Kopuş mu Uyum ve Süreklilik mi? *Ardahan Üniversitesi İktisadi ve İdari Bilimler Fakültesi Dergisi*, *2*, 71–94.

Bayramoglu, S. (2002). Küreselleşmenin Yeni Siyasal İktidar Modeli: Yönetişim. *Praksis*, *7*, 85–116.

Bayramoglu, S. (2003). Düzenleyici Devlet Düzenlenirken: OECD Türkiye Raporu Üzerine Eleştirel Bir Çözümleme. *Praksis*, *9*, 143–162.

Belek, I. (1999). *Postkapitalist Paradigmalar*. İstanbul, Turkey: Sorun Yayınları.

Bourdieu, P. (1998, December). The essence of neoliberalism. *Le Monde Diplometique*. Retrieved from http://mondediplo.com/1998/12/08bourdieu

Carroll, L. (1998). *Alice's Adventures in Wonderland and Through the Looking Glass*. London, UK: Penguin Books.

Carroll, W. K. (2007, May). *Tracking the transnational capitalist class: The view from on high*. Paper presented at the 27th International Sunbelt Social Network Conference, Corfu, Greece.

Carroll, W. K. (2012). Global, transnational, regional, national: The need for nuance in theorizing global capitalism. *Critical Sociology*, *38*(3), 365–371. doi:10.1177/0896920511434265

Cetin, T. (2012). Yeni Kurumsal İktisat. *Sosyoloji Konferansları*, *45*, 43–73.

Chhotray, V., & Stoker, G. (2009). *Governance theory and practice. A cross disciplinary approach*. London, UK: Palgrave Macmillan. doi:10.1057/9780230583344

Clarke, S. (1991). The state debate. In S. Clarke (Ed.), *The state debate* (pp. 1–69). London, UK: Macmillan. doi:10.1007/978-1-349-21464-8_1

Demir, O. (1996). *Kurumcu İktisat*. Ankara, Turkey: Vadi Yayınları.

Demirci, M. (2013). Yönetişim, Otorite ve Meşruiyet. In F. N. Genç (Ed.), *Yönetişim: Türk Kamu Yönetimine Yansımaları* (pp. 1–62). Konya, Turkey: Çizgi Kitabevi.

Dikmen, A. A. (2017). *Makine, İş, Kapitalizm ve İnsan*. İstanbul, Turkey: NotaBene.

Embong, A. R. (2000). Globalisation and transnational class relations: Some problems of conceptualization. *Third World Quarterly*, *21*(6), 989–1000. doi:10.1080/01436590020011990

Fine, B., & Harris, L. (1976). 'State expenditure in advanced capitalism': A critique. *New Left Review*, *98*, 97–112.

Firincioglu, S. (2015). Post Fordizm, Küreselleşme ve Endüstrideki Dönüşüm. *Kriz ve Kritik*, *2*, 41–44.

Foster, J. B. (2017). Küreselleşmiş Tekelci-Finans Kapitalin Yeni Emperyalizmi (E. Ekici, Trans.). *Monthy Review Türkiye*, *1*, 35–57.

Gandhi, V. P. & Crase, L. (2009, August). *New institutional economics, governance and the performance of water institutions in India*. Paper presented at the International Association of Agricultural Economists Conference, Beijing, China. Retrieved from https://ageconsearch.umn.edu/bitstream/51415/2/Contributed-Paper-626-Gandhi-Crase-Iaae2009.pdf

Guler, B. A. (2003). Yönetişim: Tüm İktidar Sermayeye. *Praksis*, *9*, 93–116.

Guzelsari, S. (2004). Kamu Yönetimi Disiplininde Yeni Kamu İşletmeciliği ve Yönetişim Yaklaşımları. *A.Ü.SBF*-GETA *Tartışma Metinleri, 66,* 1-25. Retrieved from http://www.politics.ankara.edu.tr/dergi/tartisma/2004/selime-guzelsari.pdf

Guzelsari, S. (2008). *Küresel Kapitalizm ve Devletin Dönüşümü*. İstanbul, Turkey: SAV.

Holloway, J., & Picciotto, S. (1977). Capital, crisis and the state. *Capital and Class, 1*(2), 76–101. doi:10.1177/030981687700200104

Insel, A. (2011). *Neo-Liberalizm: Hegemonyanın Yeni Dili*. İstanbul, Turkey: Birikim Yayınları.

Jessop, B. (1994). Post-Fordism and the state. In A. Amin (Ed.), *Post-Fordism: A reader* (pp. 251–279). Oxford, UK: Blackwell. doi:10.1002/9780470712726.ch8

Jessop, B. (1998). The rise of governance and the risks of failure: The case of economic development. *International Social Science Journal, 155*(155), 29–45. doi:10.1111/1468-2451.00107

Jessop, B. (2002). Globalization and the national state. In S. Aronowitz & P. Bratsis (Eds.), *Paradigm Lost: State Theory Reconsidered* (pp. 185-220). London, UK: University of Minnesota Press. Retrieved from https://bobjessop.org/2014/01/05/globalization-and-the-national-state/

Keles, R. (2010). Yönetişim Kavramına Eleştirel bir Yaklaşım. In M. A. Çukurçayır, H. T. Eroğlu, & H. Eşki-Uğuz (Eds.), *Yönetişim* (pp. 57–71). Konya, Turkey: Çizgi Kitabevi.

Majone, G. (1997). From the positive to the regulatory state: Causes and consequences of changes in the mode of governance. *Journal of Public Policy, 17*(2), 139–167. doi:10.1017/S0143814X00003524

Oguz, Ş. (2006). Sermayenin Uluslararasılaşması Sürecinde Mekânsal Farklılaşmalar ve Devletin Dönüşümü. In D. Yılmaz & ... (Eds.), *Kapitalizmi Anlamak* (pp. 147–212). Ankara, Turkey: Dipnot Yayınları.

Ongen, T. (2004). Küresel Kapitalizm ve Sermayenin Yeni Hegemonya Stratejileri. *Petrol-İş Yıllığı 2000-2003*. Retrieved from http://arsiv.petrol-is.org.tr/yayinlar/yillik/2003_yillik/01_sermaye/

Ovgun, B. (2013). *Türkiye'de Kamu Yönetiminin Dönüşümü*. Ankara, Turkey: Nika Yayınevi.

Richter, R. (2005). The new institutional economics: Its start, its meaning, its prospects. [EBOR]. *European Business Organization Law Review, 6*(2), 161–200. doi:10.1017/S1566752905001618

Robinson, W. I. (2001). Social theory and globalisation: The rise of a transnational state. *Theory and Society, 30*(2), 157–200. doi:10.1023/A:1011077330455

Robinson, W. I. (2004). *A theory of global capitalism: Production, class, and state in a transnational world*. Baltimore, MD: Johns Hopkins University Press.

Robinson, W. I. (2011, May 8). Global capitalism and 21st century fascism. *Al-Jazeera*. Retrieved from http://www.aljazeera.com/indepth/opinion/2011/04/201142612714539672.html

Robinson, W. I. (2012). Global capitalism theory and the emergence of transnational elites. *Critical Sociology, 38*(3), 349–363. doi:10.1177/0896920511411592

Sarisoy, S. (2010). Düzenleyici Devlet ve Regülasyon Uygulamalarının Etkinliği Üzerine Tartışmalar. *Maliye Dergisi, 159*, 278-298. Retrieved from https://dergiler.sgb.gov.tr/calismalar/maliye_dergisi/yayinlar/md/159/SinanSARISOY.pdf

Saylan, G. (2016). *Postmodernizm*. Ankara, Turkey: İmge Kitabevi.

Sklair, L. (2000). The transnational capitalist class and the discourse of globalization. *Cambridge Review of International Affairs, 14*(1), 67–85. doi:10.1080/09557570008400329

Sklair, L. (2001). *The Transnational Capitalist Class*. Oxford, UK: Blackwell.

Sklair, L. (2002). *Globalization: Capitalism and Its Alternatives*. New York, NY: Oxford University Press.

Sonmez, S. (2016). Bretton Woods, Fordizm ve Hegemonya. *Hacettepe Üniversitesi İktisadi ve İdari Bilimler Fakültesi Dergisi, 34*(1), 43-62. Retrieved from http://dergipark.gov.tr/download/article-file/297834

Sorensen, G. (2006). The transformation of the state. In C. Hay, M. Lister, D. Marsh (Eds.), The state: Theories and issues (pp. 190-208). Houndmills, UK: Palgrave Macmillan. doi:10.1007/978-0-230-80227-8_11

Stiglitz, J. E. (2012). *The price of inequality: How today's divided society endangers our future*. New York, NY: W. W. Norton & Company.

Warren, B. (1972). Capitalist planning and the state. *New Left Review, 72*, 3–30.

Weiss, L., & Hobson, J. M. (1999). *Devletler ve Ekonomik Kalkınma. Karşılaştırmalı bir Tarihsel Analiz* (K. Dündar, Trans.). Ankara, Turkey: Dost Kitabevi Yayınları.

Williams, D., & Young, T. (1994). Governance, the world bank and liberal theory. *Political Studies, 42*(1), 84–100. doi:10.1111/j.1467-9248.1994.tb01675.x

Williamson, J. (2000). What should the world bank think about the Washington consensus? *The World Bank Research Observer, 15*(2), 251–264. doi:10.1093/wbro/15.2.251

Williamson, O. E. (1975). *Markets and hierarchies. Analysis and antitrust implications*. New York, NY: Free Press.

Zabci, F. (2002). Dünya Bankası'nın Küresel Pazar İçin Yeni Stratejisi: Yönetişim. *SBF Dergisi, 57*(3), 151–179.

ADDITIONAL READINGS

Akansel, I. (2016). New Institutional Economics (NIE): Origins of Neoliberalism. *China-USA Business Review, 15*(1), 14–32.

Bayramoglu, S. (2002). Küreselleşmenin Yeni Siyasal İktidar Modeli: Yönetişim. *Praksis, 7*, 85–116.

Gandhi, V. P., & Crase, L. (2009, August). *New Institutional Economics, Governance and the Performance of Water Institutions in India*. Paper presented at the International Association of Agricultural Economists Conference, Beijing, China. Available from https://ageconsearch.umn.edu/bitstream/51415/2/Contributed-Paper-626-Gandhi-Crase-Iaae2009.pdf

Guler, B. A. (2003). Yönetişim: Tüm İktidar Sermayeye. *Praksis, 9*, 93–116.

Jessop, B. (1998). The Rise of Governance and the Risks of Failure: The Case of Economic Development. *International Social Science Journal, 155*(155), 29–45. doi:10.1111/1468-2451.00107

Majone, G. (1997). From the Positive to the Regulatory State: Causes and Consequences of Changes in the Mode of Governance. *Journal of Public Policy, 17*(2), 139–167. doi:10.1017/S0143814X00003524

Rhodes, R. A. W. (1997). *Understanding Governance: Policy Networks, Governance, Reflexivity and Accountability*. Philadelphia: Open University Press.

Sklair, L. (2002). *Globalization: Capitalism and Its Alternatives*. New York: Oxford University Press.

The World Bank. (1997). *World Development Report 1997: The State in a Changing World*. New York: Oxford University Press. Available from http://documents.worldbank.org/curated/en/518341468315316376/World-development-report-1997-the-state-in-a-changing-world

Williams, D., & Young, T. (1994). Governance, the World Bank and liberal theory. *Political Studies, 42*(1), 84–100. doi:10.1111/j.1467-9248.1994.tb01675.x

Chapter 15
Structural Shifts and Patterns in Turkey's Foreign Trade

Gönül Dinçer Muratoğlu
Ankara Hacı Bayram Veli University, Turkey

ABSTRACT

Foreign trade has been a principal tool of the economic policies implemented in Turkey since the foundation of the Republic in 1923. In parallel with the significant developments in the national and global economies, several structural transformations occurred in foreign trade patterns and policies of Turkey. Political approaches varied from strictly protectionist trade regimes to semi-open models and free trade regimes. Previously implemented protectionist trade policies were abandoned in the 1980s for the current open economic policy based on export-led growth model. All these facts led to drastic changes in the composition of goods subject to both Turkey's exports and imports. This chapter examines the fundamental shifts and changes in Turkey's foreign trade by reviewing historical developments, and specifies the existing structural problems in Turkey's foreign trade by analyzing detailed trade data.

INTRODUCTION

Turkey is an emerging economy with strong and dynamic links to global economy. Trade openness ratio was approximately 55% in 2017 (World Bank, 2019). However, this ratio was around 10% before 1980. This fact alone indicates a major shift in Turkish economy by means of trade policy. As noted in the related literature, the pace of economic transformation via trade is faster in developing countries than advanced economies (Krugman, 1995; Saygılı and Saygılı, 2010). When Turkey's international trade indicators are examined, various trends become obvious such as significant changes in the composition of exports and imports. Moreover, Turkey is a member of the WTO, a member of the Customs Union of the EU and signed many other free trade agreements with third countries. Such international agreements have considerably shaped the framework of international trade patterns and have narrowed the area for the design and implementation of an independent national foreign trade policy for Turkey and other developing countries.

DOI: 10.4018/978-1-7998-0333-1.ch015

Copyright © 2020, IGI Global. Copying or distributing in print or electronic forms without written permission of IGI Global is prohibited.

This study aims to review the historical development of Turkey's foreign trade policies and reveal the origins of the current problems related to trade which hinder the country's growth and development process.

In this context, firstly a chronological presentation of major national and international phenomena is going to be summarized in the first section in order to sort out the determinants of structural shifts in trade patterns.

Then in the second section, detailed trade data on sector and sub-sector level are going to be analyzed in order to comprehend the current situation of trade structures of Turkey. The data covers the time spanning from 1980 to 2017.

Lastly, major findings about the current problems of Turkey's foreign trade and an evaluation on the country's prevailing trade policy are going to be reviewed in concluding remarks.

A HISTORICAL OUTLINE OF TURKEY'S FOREIGN TRADE POLICIES

1923-1979 Period: From the Foundation of the Republic to Open Economy Era

Considering the historical course of foreign trade in Turkey, both significant trends in the global economic environment and different national policies implemented by the government has shaped various periods and determined clear distinctions among them. The first of these periods was 1923-1929, which began with the proclamation of the Republic of Turkey and ended in 1929, the year when the binding provisions of the Treaty of Lausanne over the foreign trade policy ended.

The main objective of the foreign trade policy in the first years following the establishment of the Republic of Turkey was to strengthen the national capital. On the other hand, the fact that the Lausanne Treaty had restricted the protection of customs duties in foreign trade until 1929, there was a limited area for a protectionist trade policy. Moreover, the Great Depression, which started in 1929, has been a formidable factor that prevented the formation of an independent foreign trade policy in the first years of the young Republic (Özkale and Kalaylıca, 2008).

To be more specific, customs policy was the main problem of the economy. A trade agreement signed as an addition to the Lausanne Treaty froze all customs tariffs and economic policies of Turkey, cancelled the ban of imports and exports and prevented new ones to be issued with some exceptions for five years. Furthermore, consumption taxes on the imported goods were prevented, except for the goods of state monopolies. All these provisions were decreasing Turkey's gains from customs taxes and preventing the implementation of an effective policy to protect national industry from foreign competition. As a matter of fact, the protection degree provided by the tariffs for the national economy in Lausanne remained at 12.9% (Boratav, 2013).

The mentioned trade agreement only allowed for higher prices in goods which are produced by state monopolies. In this case, a way out of Laussane's restrictive provisions on tariffs and customs duties was to obtain the state monopoly of the production or importation of some goods and services. Thus, in the first years of the republic, with the support of the sovereign approach of nurturing domestic capital accumulation, monopoly status was transferred to the local and foreign companies and thus, these companies gained high profits by benefiting from the monopoly provided by the state.

Another loophole was the fact that Laussane's and the complementary trade agreement's practices were valid for only the countries that signed them. Therefore, first steps of protectionist trade policies against other countries started to shape in 1925 (Çavdar, 2003).

Examining the composition of exports and imports in this period shows that Turkey had a proper place according to the classic form of international specialization in the world economy. Tobacco, raisins, cotton, figs, hazelnuts, wool, opium and eggs constituted for 60-72 percent of total exports, while industrial consumption goods constituted a large part of total imports (Keyder, 1982). The share of imports to GDP was 14.5% and the ratio of exports to imports was 62.6% (Bulutay, 1975).

In this period, the approach to foreign capital was in the form of attracting foreign capital within the framework of cooperation with national capital without giving any capitulation type legal privileges to them.

In this way, the rebuilding period continued until 1929 in almost open economy conditions. In 1929, new and detailed tariffs were put into practice and the protection rate of the national industry was increased to 45.7%. On the other hand, in 1929, the value of the Turkish lira came under a heavy pressure due to (i) the first installment of foreign debts taken over from the Ottoman Empire and (ii) the negative effects of excessive imports and the decrease in exports caused by the first impact of the Great Depression towards the end of the year. Therefore, a major state control over the foreign trade policy and foreign exchange regime became a necessity (Çavdar, 1982; Keyder, 1982).

Thus, after the 1923-1929 period of free-market conditions and the free exchange rate, state supported import substitution industrialization policies came into effect and protective trade policies had been implemented the over the period 1930-1945 in Turkey. The government explicitly supported import substitution industrialization by applying import quotas, customs duties and exchange control. The import quota was not applied to intermediate and capital goods in agriculture and industry; they were generally applied to consumer goods. Also, the import of some consumer goods was prohibited. Thus, the share of intermediate and capital goods in total imports increased.

As noted, during the Great Depression years, raw material prices fell much more than the prices of industrial goods, so, as a net exporter of raw materials, so it was a prerequisite for the implementation of protection measures that control imports as a natural defense response against the decrease in consumption and income levels. Behind protective walls, substitution investments started from common and previously imported consumer goods, which were the beginning of the industrialization process in Turkey, as it was in many other developing countries in the first half of the 20th century. Several measures related to foreign trade and foreign exchange controls were carried out between the years 1929-1931. Legislative control of the foreign exchange markets was gradually released to the Central Bank, which was established in 1930. The power to regulate the foreign exchange regime by law (with the Law on the Protection of the Value of Turkish Currency), was passed on to the government. Preserving the value of the national currency was one of the most important economic principles in the first decades of the Republic (Çavdar, 2003). In addition to the new customs tariff, another law was enacted in 1931 to authorize the government to issue quotas and control exports. Turkey merged foreign trade protectionism to statehood after 1932 and strived to increase the industrial accumulation.

Due to all these factors, foreign trade deficits were largely eliminated in the 1930-1939 period. With the exception of 1938, foreign trade surplus was achieved each year. In this period, foreign trade balance was mainly achieved by cutting imports almost 50%. While the share of imports in the GDP was close to 15% in 1923-29 period, this share decreased to approximately 7.5%. The period of 1930-39 refers to the growth and industrialization effort of an economy accustomed to living with chronic external deficits and external resources that cover them. The ratio of exports to imports was 110% on average (Bulutay, 1975).

On the other hand, due to the devastating effects of the Second World War and the transportation difficulties that emerged in the years 1940-1945, there have been cuts in imports of intermediate and capital goods which were needed for Turkey's exports and production (Ozkale and Kalayci, 2008). Another contractionary fact was that the majority of the active population was enlisted to the army which negatively affected national production levels. Imports were over 110 million dollars in the 1938-39 average, which declined by half in 1940-41. Exports were able to maintain the volume they had recorded in the previous period, even slightly above. In these six years, foreign trade gave a surplus of 250 million dollars (Keyder, 1982; Boratav, 2013). However, the extraordinary conditions of this period led to significant financial accumulation in the hands of a minority of businesspeople and traders who then became lobbyists for liberalization of the economy (Çavdar, 2003).

Then again, through an overall evaluation, 1930-1945 period was a time of protectionist policies both inside and outside the country.

1946-1953 on the other hand, reflects an open-economy period where a different articulation experiment with the world economy has taken place. A significant devaluation of Turkish Lira in 1946 made Turkey's foreign trade switch to a more liberal era. After 1946, import quotas have been restricted again and this was accompanied by a stagnation experienced in exports. Therefore, large scaled foreign trade deficits occurred, and one might argue that these deficits even started to become chronic beginning from this free trade era. Looking at this period in a little more detail, it is seen that the first step of the loosening of protectionism in foreign trade was the determination of the liberalization lists limiting the implementation of the quantity controls in imports after 1946 devaluation. This situation was thoroughly reinforced by the import regime which was declared in 1950 and for several years, Turkey has pursued a foreign trade policy which largely removed the protection measures except for the tariffs. External accounts also reflected this situation. Since 1930, the year 1946 was the last year in which foreign trade surpluses were continuously recorded (except 1938) (Çavdar, 2003). Exports increased by approximately 30% this year and despite 20% increase in imports, foreign trade surplus was around 100 million dollars. On the other hand, the year 1947 is the year when the economy has taken a new and totally different direction in terms of foreign relations. Foreign trade deficits in the years 1947-53 accounted for 500 million $, which were covered by US aid and foreign loans (Keyder, 1982; Boratav, 2013).

However, in 1954, the urgency of limiting foreign trade had to be recognized again in response to the increasing foreign trade deficits and the need for increased external resources caused by these gaps.

As a result, 1954-1961 was a period during which the buoyant conjuncture and liberal foreign trade policies ended, the economy was subject to relatively stagnant fluctuations, the demand for export goods fell and imports were limited because of a foreign obstruction where the external sources were not exceeding a certain level. The dependent development line that the economy was dragged after 1946, has not disappeared, but due to external circumstances, this dependent development could not be carried out by liberal foreign trade policies, but by traditional import and foreign exchange controls. In this period, import and export volumes remained at lower levels compared to the previous period. Before 1954, the share of consumer goods, which accounted for 20-25% of the total imports, dropped below 10%. This decline led to an absence of goods and led to creation of black markets on one hand, and an industrialization that substitutes imports for consumer goods on the other hand. The volume of exports contracted but remained stable. In the composition of exports, agricultural products remained largely dominant. Ratio of exports to imports was 78% on average (Kazgan, 1999).

Despite the foreign trade controls implemented in this period, foreign trade gaps had not been eliminated and resumed its chronic feature. Subsequently, due to unavoidable price increases and goods absences, an important devaluation took place in 1958, imports were facilitated again, and foreign trade controls were loosened as well (Boratav, 2013).

In the early 1960s, a period of planned development approach kick started the economy. In this period, which continued until 1980, import substitution industrialization, which was based on planning and long-term goals, was mainly supported by the government by maintaining protective foreign trade policies. These years, especially 1970s were identified with the deepening of the industrialization strategy based on import substitution and were often called the second phase of import substitution, which was the part of the evolution of the inward-looking, domestic demand–led industrialization that dated back to the 1950s (Boratav and Yeldan, 2006).

Imports was restricted via practices such as stamp duty, port tax and guaranteed deposits. In addition, import permit lists and quota lists have been issued, and importation of products other than those was prohibited. The multiple exchange rates were applied during these years. However, the excessive appreciation of the Turkish Lira had limited the rise of exports. Imports did not slow down due to the increase in the demand for intermediate and capital goods required for production. While the share of imports in GDP increased, the ratio of exports to imports showed a downward trend. This ratio was around 60% during 1970s. Exports to imports ratio decreased even more to 30% in 1970s (DİE, 1973; Kazgan, 1999).

The late 1970s witnessed an important public investment program aimed at expanding domestic production capacity in manufacturing, capital goods (such as machinery), petrochemicals, and basic intermediates. However, import substitution reached its limits in 1976 while keeping up the investment drive and financing the consequent current deficits became increasingly difficult. The foreign exchange crisis of 1977–1979 ended with an orthodox stabilization package in 1980 (Boratav and Yeldan, 2006).

During this period, the import dependency was an issue since it was necessary to import capital goods and intermediate goods in order to enhance domestic industrialization and the dependence ratio of Turkey's economy had increased noticeably. One might argue that this increased external dependence could be a consequence of insufficient import substitution policies and/ or the non-permanent structure of the protectionist policies which were abandoned in 1980s.

Another fact related to this period was the transfer of income of emigrant workers from abroad to Turkey in the 1960s which has contributed significantly to foreign exchange reserves. Workers' remittances, which amounted to 100 million dollars between 1965 and 1969, increased rapidly in 1970s and exceeded the $ 1 billion threshold and became the most important item in the compensation of foreign trade deficits. During this period, foreign aid has also been utilized to the maximum extent thus workers' remittances and foreign aids have determined the country's foreign exchange constraints since exports were too insufficient to finance imports.

In spite of these facts, the increasing public deficits led to a severe foreign debt problem in Turkey by the end of 1970s. As mentioned before, a foreign exchange crisis occurred and consequently, in the early 1980s, a structural adjustment program was prepared with the cooperation of the World Bank and IMF due to this crisis in 1977-1979.

In retrospect, when the period of 1923-1979 is evaluated in general, the following findings can be reached:

- The main purpose of the economic policies during the reconstruction period after the proclamation of the Republic was to accelerate the accumulation of national capital and to ensure national development. To this end, the state has often supported national capitalists. Although a partial accumulation of resources has been achieved in the hands of a minor group of national business people and traders, this accumulation did not become the driving force of a national development process.
- Foreign trade policies were also aimed to be formulated to support capital accumulation and development. However, during the period of 1923-1979, drastic events such as the Great Depression, the Second World War and the Oil Crisis, which had devastating effects on a global scale, took place. With the combined effect of these events and domestic political instability did not allow economic policies to be stable. Foreign trade policies too frequently changed form. They swung from liberal trade policies to protectionist policies and then again to more liberal trade policies over and over. Neither protectionist policies nor liberalizing policies have been long lasting or effective enough to reach the economic growth and development goals of the country.
- Foreign capital inflows were mostly welcomed throughout the period. The main objective was to make foreign capital act in cooperation with national capital. However, in the related years, there has been not evident progress in capital accumulation through foreign capital to boost economic development. On the other hand, foreign aids were utilized but these aids could not go beyond making the economy dependent on external politic boundaries.
- As a result of all these facts, in the second half of the 1923-1979 period, import dependency of production and exports in Turkey began to indicate chronicity. Therefore, Turkey's foreign trade deficit began to be a chronic problem of the economy.

1980-2017 Period: Open Economy Era

It was mentioned in the previous section that a severe crisis occurred in the Turkish economy by the end of 1970s and a structural adjustment program, namely January 24 Decisions was implemented in early 1980. This program has brought radical changes to Turkish economy. In accordance with this program, the deposit accounts and loan interest rates were released, and the financial system started to be liberalized in Turkey. Furthermore, with the January 24 Decisions, trade protectionist import substitution policies were abandoned permanently, and an export-oriented growth strategy has been adopted instead. In order to decrease foreign trade deficits, open economy policies were adopted, thus incentives and practices aimed at increasing exports and foreign capital inflows were emphasized more than ever. In this context, first of all, a high devaluation was carried out, and then in 1 July 1981 the exchange rate started to be adjusted on a daily basis. In addition, import tax exemptions have been imposed on imported inputs to be used in the production of export products.

The first phase of these reforms was followed by a deepening move to trade liberalization in 1984, i.e. a list of prohibited goods was prepared, and a change was made that could be considered important since the importation of all goods not explicitly mentioned in the previous period was prohibited. In other words, imports were liberalized. Exports were supported by very generous incentives. Foreign exchange controls were loosened, and banks and companies were allowed to borrow externally. According to Celasun and Rodrik, the fundamental reforms in foreign trade started in 1984 (Celasun and Rodrik, 2009).

On the other hand, January 24 of 1980 has been a turning point for Turkish economy, due to major changes in economic policies as a whole. In 1987, comprehensive customs duty reductions were made.

1989 is also another important milestone for Turkish economy since it is the year completing the transformation of 1980 in terms of financial liberalization. With the declaration of convertibility decision due to the IMF membership of Turkey has fulfilled all elements of an open economy. Short-term foreign capital inflows began right after the announcement of convertibility, which led to an inflationary process, while interest rates were raised, these conditions led to an excess of foreign exchange which then caused an appreciation in Turkish Lira. Accordingly, imports increased, and exports decreased. This situation boosted the dependence on imports and increased foreign trade deficits even more. The current account deficit and external borrowing were continuous during the period. Exports have been sustained through circumstantial exchange rate policies since there has been no increase in exports due to increasing industrial investments or technological advancements.

The liberalization of the capital account in Turkey in 1989 has pushed the economy into an unstable path since the fragility of the domestic financial system has increased substantially. The growth path of the economy has become more volatile, and the period between its boom and bust phases has shortened considerably, arbitrage-seeking and short-term capital flows constitute a rising share of total capital movements from both residents and non-residents, and this phenomenon has begun to destabilize the economy (Boratav and Yeldan, 2006).

In these circumstances, Turkey has suffered an economic crisis in 1994, where significant exchange rate increases have occurred, and foreign trade volume contracted accordingly. Therefore, a new stabilization program, referred to as April 5 Decisions, was put in order to mitigate the effects of this new crisis. This program also maintained the open economy-based growth framework as well as free trade policies. The most important events of this period in terms of foreign trade took place in the January 1, 1996, which is the introduction of the Customs Union between the European Union and Turkey. Turkey agreed to implement both the common customs tariff of the EU and the common foreign trade policy by joining the EU customs union (Ozkale and Kalayci, 2008).

In 1988-1997, the rate of increase in exports and imports remained close and the current account deficit remained at a moderate level. During these years, exchange rate movements were realized in a way to curb the foreign trade deficit. On the other hand, there were significant increases in external debt.

Since 1998, Turkey's economy re-entered a turbulent era of relatively frequent crises. Under these circumstances, a new stand-by agreement was signed with the IMF at the end of 1999. Due to this agreement, (i) inflation targeting was realized, (ii) the exchange rate targets became pre-determined, and these targets were used as nominal anchors for inflation. Appreciation of the TL process which began with high interest rates continued to rise during this period, and finally in 2001, Turkey entered into another severe economic crisis episode. Through this crisis, TL depreciated significantly again similar to 1994 crisis. Through this deep crisis, foreign trade deficit declined due to the contraction in both exports and imports. In February 2001, the determination of the value of TL against foreign currencies was left to the market (aka free-floating).

Turkey has gained a massive financial expansion and cheap credit facility resulting from favorable conditions of international markets after the 2001 crisis. The most obvious feature of Turkish economy by means of trade has been growing current account deficits since then. The growing current account deficits has been covered by short-term private financial flows and privatizations. After 2001 crisis, Turkey's external debt rose rapidly, and private sector has been the main source of new foreign debt. After 2006, Turkish economy started to operate with a considerably high rate (above 6 per cent) of current account deficit in order to achieve positive growth (Yeldan and Ünüvar, 2016).

Turkey met 2007-2008 global financial crisis with high current account deficit and high external debt. However, the new global conditions of 2008 crisis showed that the growth model of Turkey based on cheap foreign exchange and cheap imports was no longer possible (Yeldan, 2009). During the 1990s, the growth rate of national income was 3.6 per cent, while the ratio of current account deficit to gross domestic product remained below 1 per cent. Starting from 2003, annualized current deficit increased to the 3-4 per cent band, and then jumped to 6 per cent after 2006. The ratio of current account deficit to gross domestic product was over 7% in 2010-2013.

From this date on, there has been no fundamental change in terms of foreign trade policy in Turkey. Turkey continued to specialize in standard technologies and low labor cost production in line with an export-based growth strategy, within the international division of labor while on the macro-economic policy side, a significant shift towards 'speculative-led growth' have been realized (Yeldan and Ünüvar, 2016).

Turkey signed last two stand-by agreements with the IMF in 2002 and 2005, the latter one ended in 2008. These agreements contributed further to the export-oriented and open economy-based growth model which has been ongoing since 1980s.

At an international level, more specifically by terms of international trade policy, Turkey signed the General Agreement on Trade and Tariffs on December 21, 1953, which mainly aims liberalizing international trade. Throughout this process as a founding member, Turkey signed the Marrakech Agreement establishing the World Trade to be effective from the December 31, 1994. Turkey's membership of the World Trade Organization began on March 26, 1995. Being a World Trade Organization member, Turkey has also agreed to implement the Agreement on Agriculture, Agreement on the Application of Sanitary and Phytosanitary Measures, Agreement on Textiles and Clothing, Agreement on Technical Barriers to Trade, Agreement on Trade-Related Investment Measures, Agreement on Implementation of Article VI of the GATT 1994, Agreement on Implementation of Article VII of GATT 1994, Agreement on Preshipment Inspection, Agreement on Rules of Origin, Agreement on Import Licensing Procedures, Agreement on Subsidies and Countervailing Measures and the Agreement on Safeguards (WTO, 2019).

Similarly, Turkey has also adopted the Agreement on Trade-Related Aspects of Intellectual Property Rights (TRIPs), which regulates rules and measures regarding intellectual property rights in international trade, and the General Agreement on Trade in Services (GATS), which is very comprehensive and decisive in regulating the liberalization of global trade in services. All of these agreements ensure Turkey to maintain almost an entirely free trade policy in international goods and services by resetting tariffs on various industrial goods and preventing to execute new tariffs or applying additional constraints.

Furthermore, as previously noted, Turkey joined the European Union's Customs Union which came into effect in January 1, 1996 and thus has agreed to establish a more liberalized foreign trade relationship not only with EU member states, but also with EU's other trade partner countries which EU signed bilateral or multilateral free trade agreements in order to expand their export markets, increase export earnings, reduce import costs and increase competitiveness. Turkey as a member of the customs union is undertaking the obligations under these agreements unilaterally, so that other countries provide all the trade benefits provided by the EU. However, Turkey does not have the same facilities from third countries in return for not being EU member. This aspect of the customs union membership has been operating against Turkey. So, Turkey has been signing free trade agreements with most of these third countries, to ensure reciprocity and is trying to compensate for the loss of trade gains to some extent.

So far, Turkey has signed 36 free trade agreements, of which 11 Central and Eastern European countries is terminated due to EU membership of these countries. Establishing a Free Trade Area between Syria and Turkey has been suspended in 2011. Turkey-Jordan Free Trade Agreement has also been repealed in 2018 (Ministry of Trade, 2019). The remaining 19 free trade agreements (with EFTA, Israel, Macedonia, Bosnia and Herzegovina, Palestine, Tunisia, Morocco, Egypt, Albania, Georgia, Montenegro, Serbia, Chile, Mauritius, South Korea, Malaysia, Moldova, Faroe Islands and Singapore) are currently in force. the "Investment Agreement" and "Trade in Services Agreement" signed under the free trade agreement between Turkey and South Korea have entered into force as of the date of August 1, 2018 (Ministry of Trade, 2019). On the other hand, the free trade agreements of Lebanon, Kosovo, Sudan, Venezuela and Qatar will enter into force upon completion of national approval processes. In addition, negotiations with EFTA, Bosnia and Herzegovina, Serbia and Montenegro were completed to update and expand the scope of existing free trade agreements.

Turkey's membership of the WTO, the EU's customs union and other bilateral free trade agreements mentioned above, prevents Turkey to benefit from tariffs and other protective measures in foreign trade. In other words, within the current global economic structure, Turkey cannot possibly implement a purely national, independent or protectionist trade policies.

It can be stated under the explanations so far that the fundamental problems in Turkey's foreign trade have been (i) import dependency of production and exports and (ii) chronic current account deficits largely caused by foreign trade deficits, which have been ongoing at least for the last four decades. However, it is crucial to express that both these problems got highly severe after the shift of Turkey's economic policy towards short-term financial flows-dependent growth since after 2001 crisis. Most recently, with the end of low foreign exchange rate period; import-dependent and high-current account deficit based economic structure has been alarming.

AN OVERVIEW OF THE PATTERNS AND STRUCTURAL SHIFTS IN TURKISH FOREIGN TRADE

The Figure below shows the figures from 1984 (the year when detailed series of the balance sheet of the CBRT started) to 2017. It can be clearly observed that the deficit in the current account is almost negative every year since 1984 and the increase rate of this deficit has escalated from early 2000s. Current account deficits can be hard to sustain when current account deficit to GDP ratio exceeds 5% (Milesi-Ferret and Razin, 1996). In Turkey, it exceeded this red line multiple times in 1980-2017 period which might indicate a sustainability problem related to insufficient domestic savings, import dependency of domestic production and/or high private consumption expenditures especially financed with short-term loans.

The Figure also shows that the current account deficit and the foreign trade deficit are very close to each other and they are moving together. This situation emphasizes that the deficit resulting from the trade in goods is the main determinant of the current account deficit. Merchandise trade account is both negative and highly volatile and that is one of the most fundamental problems in foreign trade of Turkey. The fact that current account deficit is mainly caused by merchandise trade deficit, one might argue that current account problem of Turkey is not a short term macro political problem but it has been a fundamental and structural problem arising from inappropriate and insufficient industrialization policies of the country (Doğruel and Doğruel, 2010). The historical review presented in the previous section also confirms that Turkey has been suffering from persistent current account deficit problem for a long time due to structural insufficiencies in industrial development process.

Figure 1. Current account balance of Turkey, 1984-2017
Source: Created by the author using CBRT data

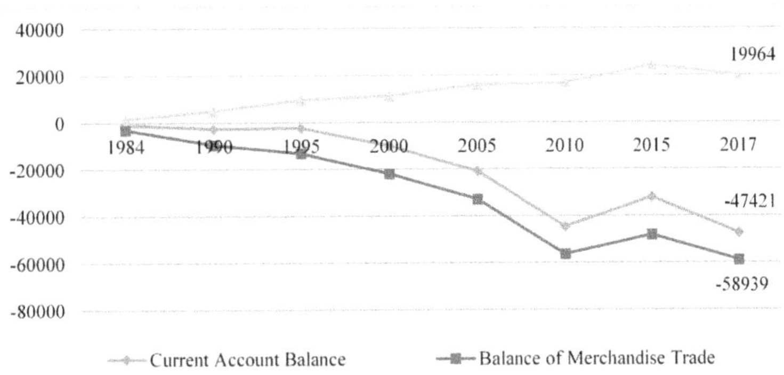

The income account, which includes the primary and secondary income balance, is negative, but relatively low, and is not volatile, as opposed to the merchandise trade series. When the service balance is examined, it is seen that this series is positive and keeps gradually increasing. On the other hand, the positive balance of trade in services is far from being sufficient to compensate for the massive current account deficit.

At this point, it must be stated that the latest data on current account and reel exchange rates indicate a weakening in the real effective exchange rate and trade balance nexus especially since 2018 (Figure 2).

One possible explanation is that this issue is stemming from low even negative total factor productivity growth in recent years which highlight the problems arising from the production side. This and rising corporate external debt rollover needs, could have pushed the rate of depreciation of the Lira-USD exchange rate above the rate of growth of the GDP deflator. Another possible reason is the increasing country risk premium in recent years, which has led to a deterioration of the income balance (Iossifov and Fei, 2019).

A more detailed examination of trade data reveals the basic structure of Turkey's foreign trade patterns and the problems related to foreign trade.

Figure 2. REER and current account (% GDP) 2003-2019
Source: Created by the author using CBRT data.

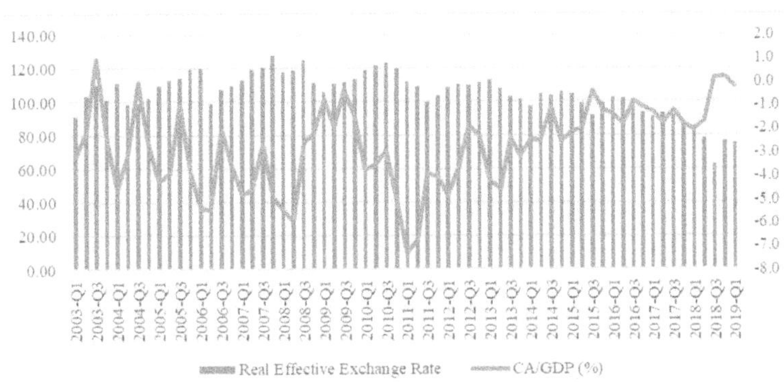

Figure 3. Merchandise trade of turkey (Billion $)
Source: Created by the author. Data are retrieved from Turkish Statistical Institute's Foreign Trade Database.

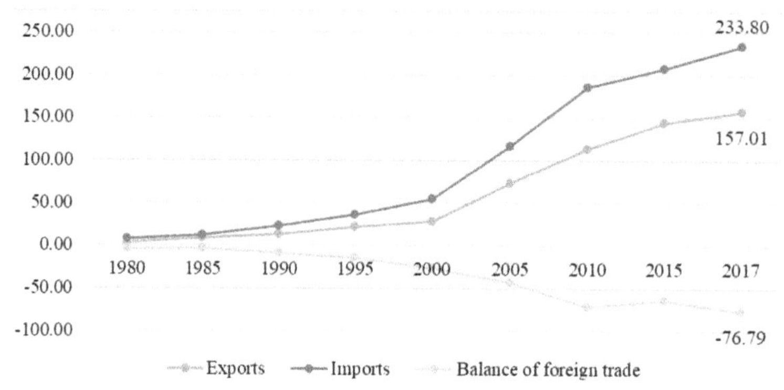

Figure 3 presents the merchandise exports and merchandise imports series over the period 1980-2017. These data reveal that the exports fell behind the imports during the period. The foreign trade balance ended in a negative balance in all years. In the period analyzed, imports increased more than exports, and in parallel with this, the foreign trade deficit increased gradually to approximately 77 billion dollars in 2017.

Exports and imports are moving together along the series. Imports are moving prior to exports. These two facts prove that Turkey's exports dependent on imports. Some recent studies indeed reveal the fact that import of intermediate goods per unit exports is higher in Turkey than many other emerging economies (Saygılı and Saygılı, 2010). It can be said that international production patterns and global value chains make exports dependent on imports in every country to some degree. However, Turkey is suffering from this dependency as a lack of national production more than being part of the international production. Therefore, the import dependency is a structural problem of Turkey's manufacturing and exports.

Exports and imports of merchandise series increased significantly after the year 2000. This increase in foreign trade volume after 2000 is a negative indicator when it is evaluated in terms of the ratio of exports to imports.

Figure 4. Proportion of imports covered by exports (%)
Source: Created by the author. Data are retrieved from Turkish Statistical Institute's Foreign Trade Database.

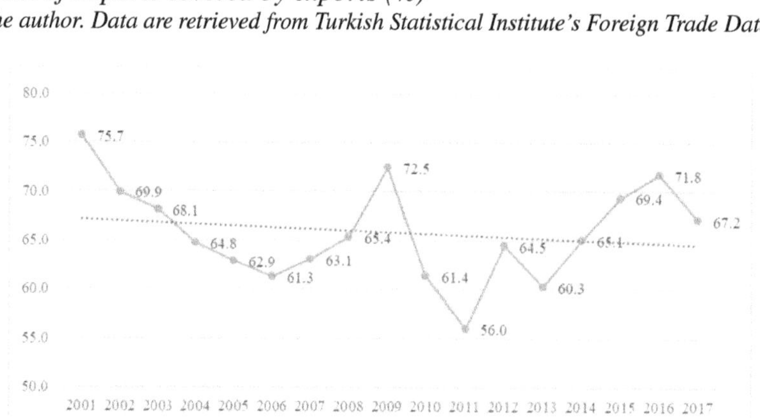

Figure 5. Shares of broad economic categories (BEC) in exports and imports, 1980-2017
Source: Created by the author using Turkstat data.

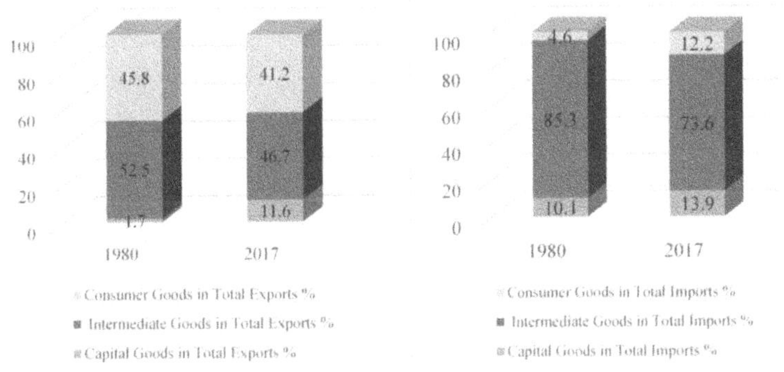

The Figure shows the proportion of imports covered by exports for the period 2001-2017. This indicator is also volatile and falls below 70 percent except for the years of crises. Besides the volatility of the series, as the trend curve shows, the proportion of imports covered by exports decreased in the period of 2001-2017. This finding indicates that Turkey's structural problems related to foreign trade have been escalating; import dependency of exports is getting severe in particular. As a matter of fact, the nominal level of import permits linked to export declarations has a high ratio over 60% since 2000s.

In the following part, the share of main sectors in the total exports and imports of Turkey are calculated using the broad economic categories classification (BEC) data for 1980-2017 period (Appendix 1A). These data indicate that the share of capital goods has been rising in Turkey's total exports. On the other hand, the shares of consumer goods and intermediate goods in total exports have been decreasing. The share of capital goods in total imports have decreased, while the share of intermediate goods and consumer goods have increased. Intermediate goods still and always constitute the largest category in Turkey's both exports and imports (Figure 5).

This finding also proves that there is a structural dependency on foreign trade in Turkey, i.e. dependency of production on raw materials and capital goods. In 2017, the share of intermediate goods in imports was close to 74%, which necessitates a more detailed examination of trade data on sub-sectoral level.

3-digit BEC classification data reveal that in 1980-2017 the shares of primary industrial supplies and unprocessed food and beverage in Turkey's total exports showed a drastic fall (Appendix 1B). In 1980, these two sub-sectors were the main items of exports, whereas in 2017, the major export sector was processed raw materials. Other sectors with a significant increase in exports were processed industrial supplies, passenger motor cars, parts of transportation vehicles, durable consumer goods, semi-durable consumer goods, non-durable consumer goods and transportation vehicles and equipment for industry. In other words, the share of unprocessed raw materials and unprocessed consumer goods decreased, while the share of processed raw materials and consumer goods increased in exports.

The most noteworthy issue in merchandise import data during the 1980-2017 period is the dramatic decline in both unprocessed and processed fuel categories (Appendix 1B). As a matter of fact, this is not a realistic data in an economy with increasing population, increasing production and increasing exports. This may be partly explained by the increase in the raw materials for industry, and partly by the introduction of confidential data application after 2000s. While there was no data hiding in the previous periods, 12.6% of total imports in 2010 and 9% of total imports in 2017 were disclosed as confidential

Figure 6. Exports and Imports (ISIC Rev. 3 Classification), 1980 and 2017
Source: Created by the author using Turkstat data.

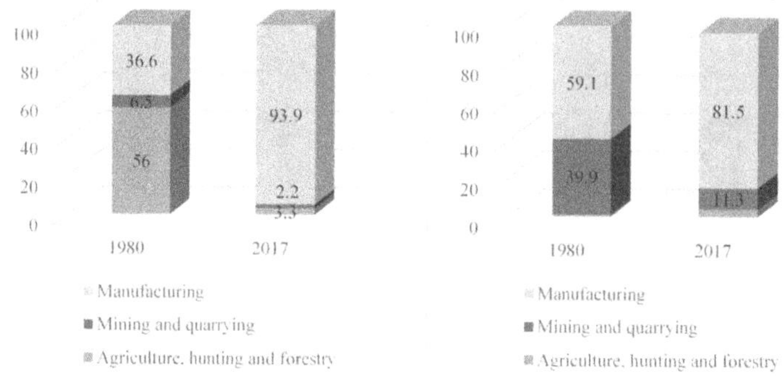

data. Thus, it is reasonable to conclude that this data consists of fuel and oil. In addition, imports of processed industrial goods, passenger motor cars and transportation vehicles have also increased during the period of review.

Another classification is ISIC Rev 3 which indicates similar changes in trade composition. Figure 6 and Appendix 1C are showing the shares of the sub-sectors in foreign trade, which were calculated by using the official detailed foreign trade data and it shows quite remarkable findings: The share of agriculture, hunting and forestry declined sharply during the 1980-2017 period, while the share of the manufacturing industry increased significantly. In other words, while being mainly a net exporter of agricultural commodities in 1980, Turkey has become an exporter of manufactured products in 2017. This fact is one of the most important structural shifts and pattern changes in Turkey's historical development of foreign trade. The share of manufacturing industry in imports has also increased significantly. Although the share of agriculture hunting and forestry in imports has increased slightly, the share of mining has decreased both in exports and imports. These findings clearly show the transformation that has been taking place in Turkey's production and export patterns from agriculture towards industry.

SITC Rev 3 trade data also support the key findings from previous data on trade in goods (Appendix 1D). To be more specific, in 1980-2017 period, Turkey's exports of live animals and food, beverages and tobacco, and crude materials except for fuel significantly decreased their share in total exports while the share of chemicals, manufactured goods, machinery and transport equipment, miscellaneous manufactured goods and non-monetary gold increased. The most significant decreases happened in the categories of crude materials except for fuel and livestock and food, while the most significant increases were realized in machinery and transportation vehicles and in miscellaneous manufactured goods categories.

According to this classification, import data show a sharp decline in imports of mineral fuels and related materials category. This, as noted earlier, is not a realistic situation, but implies the imposition of data hiding and / or a possible failure in the preparation and classification of data. Apart from this, the share of manufactured goods, machinery and transportation vehicles, miscellaneous manufactured goods and coins and non-monetary gold have increased similar to exports. Rises at the same sub-sector in both exports and imports simultaneously, in Turkey's merchandise trade reveals the increasing case for intra-industry trade as a general trend in Turkey.

When Turkey's foreign trade by country groups is analyzed, it is observed that several shifts have been happening (Appendix 1E, Appendix 1F). For example, the EU's share in Turkey's exports, since

Figure 7. Exports, share of country groups (%)
Source: Created by the author using Turkstat data.

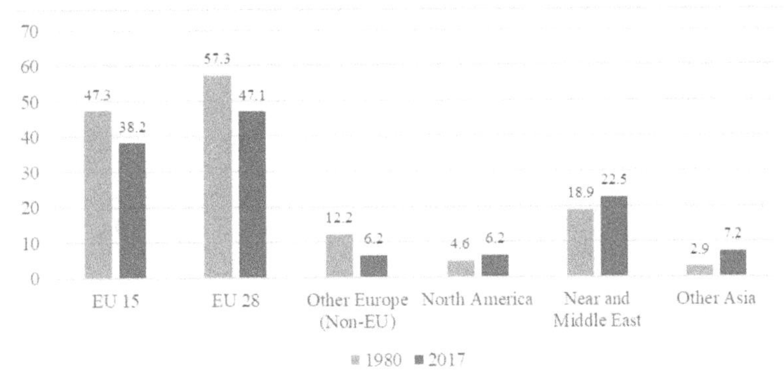

the early 2000s has showed a decreasing trend. It is also noteworthy that Near and Middle East countries and other Asian countries have increasing shares in Turkey's total exports. While the EU's share showed a significant reduction, EU still remains Turkey's most important export partner and it is obvious that Turkey retains its importance for the EU market as well (Figure 7).

Looking at the import data (Figure 8), it is observed that the share of the EU in Turkey's total imports has also declined. Despite this decline which occurred in the 2000s, the EU market remains to be the most important partner of Turkey in imports. On the other hand, the share of other European countries outside the EU is on the rise. Most striking point in the import data is the sharp falling in share of Middle Eastern countries in Turkey's total imports and an almost equal rise in the share of other Asian countries. There are some studies in the literature suggesting a negative impact of Arab Spring[1] on Turkish trade which is obvious especially in the imports of Turkey to spring countries (Sorhun, 2012). One possible explanation for this fact might be that the Arab Spring adversely impacted the economic status of the countries and the political relations between Turkey and these countries transformed (Öncel and Malik, 2015).

As for the basis of increasing in the share of other Asian countries, it should be noted that this fact is associated with China's significantly increased share in Turkey's total foreign trade. As a matter of fact, while China's share in total imports was below 1% in 1980, this share increased to 10% in 2017.

Figure 8. Imports, share of country groups (%)
Source: Created by the author using Turkstat data.

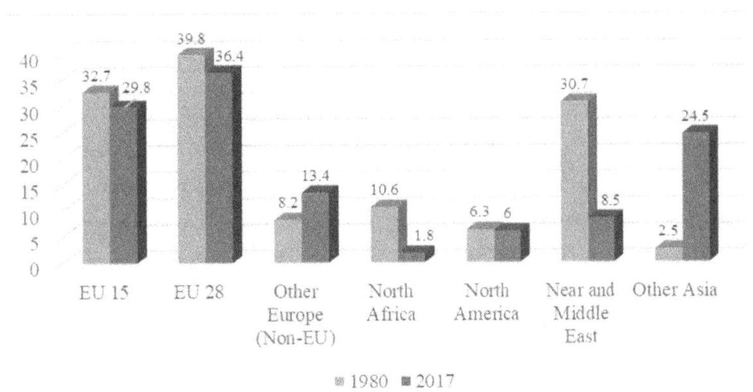

Figure 9. Balance of trade in services, 1985-2017
Source: The Figure is created by the author using CBRT data

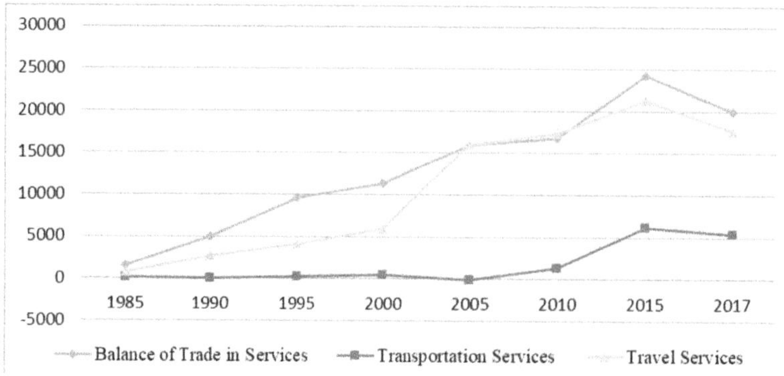

Another important topic to be examined here is international trade in services. The volume and importance of trade in services in Turkey has been gradually increasing. As mentioned earlier, the trade in services provides a positive balance in Turkey's balance of payments. Given that there is a problem of chronic trade and current account deficit in Turkey, the economic importance of services trade surplus is more clearly understood. In this respect, it is necessary to examine the trade in services in more detail.

When the trade in services is analyzed by the balance of the sub-categories (Appendix 1G); it could be seen that construction services, insurance services, financial services, official services and other services remained relatively low. Exports fell behind imports in insurance services, financial services, official services and other commercial services and these sub-sectors provide negative balance.

Figure 9 of balance of trade in services show that the increasing positive balance of the general services sector is mainly due to the transportation sector and travel sector. Exports in these two sectors exceed imports. The positive balance of the travel sector in particular is decisive in the overall services sector. On the other hand, it is observed that the balance of this sector in 2017 has decreased significantly compared to 2015. One might argue that domestic political instabilities undermined the buoyancy of tourism hence the growth of travel services in Turkey in recent years.

CONCLUSION

Throughout this study, Turkey's foreign trade is examined historically and analytically. The main findings about the major transformations, shifts and problems of Turkish foreign trade can be summarized as follows:

- Based on all these explanations and analyses so far, it can be mentioned that current account deficit linked to merchandise trade deficit consists the most fragile point for Turkish economy. The underlying cause of this problem is the underdevelopment domestic industrial production. Therefore, one might argue that this is a structural problem of Turkey rather than being a short-term macro economical problem. Turkey's merchandise trade is also quite volatile; it exhibits sharp ups and downs which are linked to the swings in real exchange rate. These facts reveal that there are both long term structural problems arising from national deficiencies and short to middle term conjectural problems arising from the global economy. However, in recent years, other pressure factors on reel effective exchange rate are becoming predominant such as large private corporate indebtedness and widening risk premium of Turkey. The insufficiency of domestic savings, fragility of private reel sector due to the high indebtedness levels and high debt rollover ratios, high current account deficits and the dependence of the economy on private capital flows (short-term flows in particular) to compensate for the foreign deficits are causing the volatility to increase and worsening the quality of production and trade indicators. The global economy is in a sluggish course since 2008 crisis as a general tendency. Therefore, without favorable conditions arising from the global economy, it is getting harder to for the Turkish economy to overcome these problems under its current structure.

- Since 1980, there has been a significant increase in exports of capital goods while imports showed an increase in the share of consumer goods. This is an important change of pattern in Turkish trade dynamics.
- On the other hand, intermediate goods keep their weight both in exports and imports. Raw materials constitute three quarters of total imports. This fact indicates the dependency of production on imported inputs as well as the dependency of exports on imports in Turkey. Import dependency of production and exports is also linked to this lack of advancement in the industrialization process of Turkey. Participation in global value chains cause import dependency of exports to some degree in almost all participant countries. Turkey has already been suffering from import dependency of production and exports. Therefore, Turkey's future participation in global value chains must be carefully assessed/designed considering this adverse precedent thoroughly.
- In the period of 1980-2017, the share of unprocessed raw materials and unprocessed goods decreased in total exports of Turkey, and the share of processed raw materials and consumer goods increased. The most significant decrease is in the categories of livestock and food and fuel; while the most significant increases were realized in machinery equipment and transportation vehicles and in miscellaneous products categories.
- These changes of composition altogether indicate a major transformation that Turkey's production and therefore exports structure has been evolving towards industry. While being mainly an exporter of agricultural commodities in 1980, Turkey has become a net exporter of manufactured products in 2017. However, this transformation is yet far from being towards technology-intense high value-added sectors.
- The weight of intra-industry trade has been increasing as a general trend in Turkey's foreign trade.
- The share of energy in imported inputs declines in the official data disclosed, indicating a problem with the data. It is recommended that foreign trade data, more specifically energy trade data to be reconstructed in order to make healthy economic analyzes and to establish scientific policy proposals based on these data.
- Increasing the production and utilization of renewable energy to reduce the dependence of imports on raw materials and fuel in Turkey is of paramount importance. This would both reduce current account deficits and save the production to some extent from exchange rate fluctuations. It would also slow down the growth rate of environmental problems.
- Trade in services has a positive balance and therefore has been contributing to mitigate the current account problems in Turkey. The surplus of trade in services is mainly caused by the surplus in transportation services and travel services. On the other hand, the balance of travel services has started to decrease in recent years.

- The positive balance of trade in services is becoming more important given the fact that chronic trade and current account deficits are highly problematic in Turkey. On the other hand, the volume of trade in services is relatively low and the positive balance of this trade is far from compensating for the deficits in merchandise trade.
- Finally, it would be fair to conclude that although Turkey is shifting towards services and industry from agriculture, there are serious problems in real sector production, hence in export and import patterns. Latest data on industrial production indicates a decline by 5.2 percent in the last quarter of 2018 and by 9.8 percent on an annual basis. This decline points out that there are serious losses in the potential growth limits of the economy. This deterioration of production is the result of the economic policies implemented in the last decades. The current account also reflects the conditions of the real sector of economy which reveal that reel sector is underdeveloped and fragile in Turkey. As the adaptation mechanisms of the real sector are relatively slower but more permanent than the financial sector, it would be convenient to highlight the urgency for solid efforts to enhance reel sector production in Turkey. This effort necessitates an altogether planned transformation that includes all the political, legal and economic measures to increase domestic savings, to boost up domestic capital accumulation, and to promote/develop tradable goods industries in order to carry the patterns of production and trade to a less vulnerable/ a stronger economic structure.

REFERENCES

Boratav, K. (2013). *Türkiye İktisat Tarihi 1908-2009.* Ankara, Turkey: İmge Kitabevi Yayınları.

Boratav, K. & Yeldan, E. (2006). Turkey, 1980–2000: Financial liberalization, macroeconomic (in) stability, and patterns of distribution. In L. Taylor (Ed.), External liberalization in Asia, post-socialist Europe, and Brazil. pp. 417-455.

Bulutay, T. (1975). *Türkiye'nin 1923-1972 Dönemindeki İktisadi Büyümesi Üzerine Düşünceler. Maliye Enstitüsü Konferansları 23. Seri.* İ. Ü. İktisat Fakültesi.

Çavdar, T. (1982). *Türkiye'de Liberalizmin Doğuşu.* İstanbul, Turkey: Uygarlık Yayınları.

Çavdar, T. (2003). *Türkiye Ekonomisinin Tarihi, 1900-1960.* Ankara, Turkey: İmge Kitabevi Yayınları.

CBRT (The Central Bank of the Republic of Turkey). (2018). *Electronic Data Delivery System.* Retrieved from https://evds2.tcmb.gov.tr/

Celasun, M. & Rodrik, D. (1989). Trade regime and an anatomy of export performance. In Developing country debt and economic performance, 3: Country studies-Indonesia, Korea, Philippines, Turkey, pp. 716-731. Chicago, IL: University of Chicago Press.

DİE. (1973). *Türkiye'de Toplumsal ve Ekonomik Gelişmenin 50 Yılı.* Ankara, Turkey: Başbakanlık İstatistik Enstitüsü Matbaası.

Doğruel, F., & Doğruel, S. (2010). *Türkiye'de Cari Açık: Temel Sorunlar ve Dinamikler. Küresel Kriz Çerçevesinde Türkiye'nin Cari Açık Sorunsalı içinde* (T. Subaşat & H. Yetkiner, Eds.). Ankara, Turkey: Efil Yayınevi.

Iossifov, P. & Fei, X. (2019). Real effective exchange rate and trade balance adjustment: The case of Turkey. *IMF Working Paper WP/19/131.*

Kazgan, G. (1999). *Tanzimat'tan 21. Yüzyıla Türkiye Ekonomisi*. İstanbul, Turkey: Altın Kitaplar Yayınevi.

Keyder, Ç. (1982). *Dünya Ekonomisi İçinde Türkiye, 1923-1929*. Ankara, Turkey: Yurt Yayınları.

Krugman, P., Cooper, R. N., & Srinivasan, T. N. (1995). Growing world trade: Causes and consequences. *Brookings Papers on Economic Activity*, *1*(1), 327–362. doi:10.2307/2534577

Milesi-Ferret, G. M., & Razin, A. (1996). Sustainability of persistent current account deficits. *International Journal of Finance & Economics*, *1*(3), 161–181. doi:10.1002/(SICI)1099-1158(199607)1:3<161::AID-IJFE19>3.0.CO;2-W

Ministry of Trade. Republic of Turkey (2019). *Free trade agreements*. Retrieved from https://www.ticaret.gov.tr/dis-iliskiler/serbest-ticaret-anlasmalari

Öncel, A., & Malik, A. (2015). The Arab spring and its impact on the foreign trade of Turkey. *Bilgi*, *31*, 17–36.

Özkale, L., & Kalaylıca, M. Ö. (2008). In G. E. Arslan (Ed.), *Dış Ticaretin Yapısal Gelişimi. Çeşitli Yönleriyle Cumhuriyetin 85. Yılında Türkiye Ekonomisi içinde* (pp. 228–363). Ankara, Turkey: Gazi Üniversitesi Yayınları.

Saygılı, M., & Saygılı, H. (2010). *Türkiye'de İhracatın Yapısal Dönüşümü. Küresel Kriz Çerçevesinde Türkiye'nin Cari Açık Sorunsalı içinde* (T. Subaşat & H. Yetkiner, Eds.). Ankara, Turkey: Efil Yayınevi.

Sorhun, E. (2012). Is the "Arab Spring" Turkey's winter? Impact of the Arab Spring on trade flows of Turkey. Retrieved from https://ecomod.net/system/files/Paper-Engin%20SORHUN.pdf

Turkish Statistical Institute. (2018). *Foreign Trade Statistics Database*. Retrieved from https://biruni.tuik.gov.tr/disticaretapp/menu_ing.zul

UN. (1986). Standard International Trade Classification (STIC) Revision 3. Department of Economic and Social Affairs Statistics Division, Statistical Papers, Series M, No: 34, Rev: 3, New York, NY.

UN. (2002). Classification by Broad Economic Categories, Defined in Terms of the Standard International Trade Classification, Revision 3 and the Harmonized Commodity Description and Coding System, Third Edition. Department of Economic and Social Affairs Statistics Division, Statistical Papers, Series M, No: 53, Rev: 4, New York, NY.

UN. (2002). International Standard Industrial Classification of All Economic Activities (ISIC) Revision 3.1. Department of Economic and Social Affairs Statistics Division, Statistical Papers, Series M, No: 4, Rev: 3.1, New York, NY.

World Bank. (2019). *World Development Report 2019: The changing nature of work*. Washington, DC: The World Bank Group.

World Trade Organization. (2019). History of the multilateral trading system. Retrieved from https://www.wto.org/english/thewto_e/history_e/history_e.htm

Yeldan, E. (2009). Kapitalizmin Yeniden Finansallaşması ve 2007/2008 Krizi: Türkiye Krizin Neresinde? *Çalışma ve Toplum*, 2009*(1)*.

Yeldan, E. (2016). An assessment of the Turkish economy in the AKP era. *Research and Policy on Turkey*, *1*(1), 11–28. doi:10.1080/23760818.2015.1099779

ENDNOTES

1 The Arab Spring refers to a series of transformative social and political events which started in Tunisia in 2010 which continued in five other countries (Libya, Egypt, Syria, Yemen and Bahrain) and also impacted most of the other countries in Middle East and North Africa to some extent.

APPENDIX

Appendix 1A

Table 1. Shares of broad economic categories (BEC) in exports and imports, 1980-2017

	The Share of Capital Goods in Total Exports %	The Share of Capital Goods in Total Imports %	The Share of Intermediate Goods in Total Exports %	The Share of Intermediate Goods in Total Imports %	The Share of Consumer Goods in Total Exports %	The Share of Consumer Goods in Total Imports %
1980	1,7	10,1	52,5	85,3	45,8	4,6
1990	2,4	18,2	46,1	72,2	51,5	9,5
2000	7,8	20,9	41,6	65,9	50,4	12,8
2010	10,3	15,5	49,5	70,9	39,8	13,3
2015	10,7	16,9	47,4	69,0	41,2	13,8
2016	11,2	18,1	46,8	67,6	41,4	14,1
2017	11,6	13,9	46,7	73,6	41,2	12,2

Source: The shares are calculated by the author using Turkish Statistical Institute's data.

Appendix 1B

Table 2. Shares of BEC (3rd Level) in exports and imports, 1980-2017

	Exports					Imports				
BEC Name	1980	1990	2000	2010	2017	1980	1990	2000	2010	2017
Industrial supplies not elsewhere specified, Primary	27,6	8,0	3,6	3,2	2,9	5,7	6,0	5,1	6,6	5,4
Industrial supplies not elsewhere specified, Processed	16,0	31,6	28,9	33,8	32,0	23,3	29,7	29,4	31,7	36,9
Fuels and lubricants, Primary	0,1	0,0	0,0	0,1	0,1	37,8	18,3	8,9	0,6	1,8
Capital goods (except transport equipment)	0,6	1,6	3,7	5,6	5,7	9,3	15,8	17,0	12,5	11,9
Capital Goods, Parts and accessories	0,3	0,6	2,1	3,0	2,9	4,9	8,6	7,2	4,9	6,7
Passenger motor cars	0,4	0,3	2,2	5,5	7,6	0,4	2,6	4,9	3,7	3,6
Transport equipment, and parts and accessories thereof	0,7	1,3	4,4	5,6	6,2	1,2	3,8	5,8	5,7	6,6
Consumer goods not elsewhere specified, Durable	3,1	3,7	7,4	7,8	8,7	0,1	0,9	2,1	1,9	1,5
Consumer goods not elsewhere specified, Semi Durable	5,1	23,6	20,7	10,3	9,6	0,4	0,8	1,7	2,9	2,2
Consumer goods not elsewhere specified, Non-Durable	0,8	7,4	10,4	6,3	5,5	1,8	2,5	2,5	3,0	2,3
Food and Beverages, Primary, Industry	6,5	1,7	0,9	0,4	0,2	0,1	2,5	0,9	1,5	1,7
Food and Beverages, Primary, Household Consumption	30,2	11,7	5,0	4,3	3,7	0,0	0,2	0,3	0,4	0,5
Food and Beverages, Processed, Industry	1,1	0,8	0,9	1,0	1,2	1,0	1,2	0,6	0,6	0,9
Food and Beverages, Processed, Household Consumption	5,2	4,6	4,2	4,0	4,7	1,8	2,0	0,6	0,7	0,8
Fuels and lubricants, Processed, Motor Spirit and Other	1,0	0,2	0,3	1,3	1,3	0,1	0,3	0,6	0,7	0,4
Fuels and lubricants, Processed	0,4	2,0	0,8	2,5	1,3	11,4	2,1	8,0	6,6	4,7
Hidden data	0,0	0,0	0,0	0,0	0,0	0,0	0,0	0,0	12,6	8,9
Transport equipment, Industrial	1,1	0,8	4,1	4,7	6,0	0,8	2,4	3,9	3,0	1,9
Transport equipment, Non-Industrial	0,0	0,0	0,1	0,2	0,1	0,0	0,2	0,1	0,1	0,9
Goods not elsewhere specified	0,0	0,0	0,2	0,4	0,4	0,0	0,1	0,4	0,3	0,3

Source: The shares are calculated by the author using Turkish Statistical Institute's data.

Appendix 1C

Table 3. Exports and imports (ISIC Rev. 3 classification), 1980-2017

	Exports					Imports				
ISIC Name	**1980**	**1990**	**2000**	**2010**	**2017**	**1980**	**1990**	**2000**	**2010**	**2017**
Agriculture, hunting and forestry	56,0	15,8	6,0	4,3	3,3	1,0	4,9	3,8	3,5	3,8
Fishing	0,9	0,3	0,1	0,1	0,3	0,0	0,0	0,0	0,0	0,0
Mining and quarrying	6,5	2,5	1,4	2,4	2,2	39,9	19,0	13,1	13,9	11,3
Manufacturing	36,6	80,9	91,8	92,6	93,9	59,1	73,6	81,1	78,4	81,5
Electricity, gas and water supply	0,0	0,0	0,1	0,2	0,0	0,0	0,0	0,2	0,0	0,0
Wholesale and retail trade	0,0	0,5	0,5	0,4	0,3	0,0	2,4	1,5	4,2	3,3
Real estate, renting and business activities	0,0	0,0	0,0	0,0	0,0	0,0	0,0	0,0	0,0	0,0
Other community, social and personal service activities	0,0	0,0	0,1	0,0	0,0	0,0	0,0	0,2	0,0	0,0

Source: The shares are calculated by the author using Turkish Statistical Institute's data.

Appendix 1D

Table 4. Exports and imports (SITC Rev. 3 Classification), 1980-2017

	Exports					Imports				
SITC Name	1980	1990	2000	2010	2017	1980	1990	2000	2010	2017
Food and live animals	42,5	17,9	10,5	9,2	9,0	1,9	5,2	2,1	2,4	3,4
Beverages and tobacco	8,2	3,5	1,9	0,8	0,8	0,0	1,6	0,7	0,2	0,3
Crude materials, inedible, except fuels	20,7	5,8	2,8	3,4	3,1	6,9	7,5	6,0	8,3	6,8
Mineral fuels, lubricants and related materials	2,0	2,3	1,2	3,9	2,8	49,4	20,8	17,6	20,7	15,9
Animal and vegetable oils, fats and waxes	0,2	1,1	0,4	0,3	0,6	1,5	1,3	0,7	0,6	0,7
Chemicals and related products, n.e.s	1,8	5,8	4,5	6,0	6,0	12,5	12,7	13,5	13,7	13,6
Manufactured goods	17,5	29,4	29,6	29,1	24,6	10,7	15,0	15,5	17,2	16,2
Machinery and transport equipment	2,8	6,6	20,7	27,9	30,6	15,6	31,7	37,7	29,0	30,4
Miscellaneous manufactured articles	4,3	27,6	28,5	17,3	17,8	1,4	4,2	6,1	6,3	5,7
Commodities and transactions, n.e.s. (Coin (other than gold coin), not being legal tender and Gold, non-monetary)	0,0	0,0	0,0	2,0	4,8	0,0	0,0	0,1	1,5	7,1

Source: The shares are calculated by the author using Turkish Statistical Institute's data.

Appendix 1E

Table 5. Exports, share of country groups (%)

Country Group Name	1980	1990	2000	2010	2017
EU 15	47,3	55,4	52,2	39,0	38,2
EU 28	57,3	57,8	56,5	46,5	47,1
Other Europe (Non-EU)	12,2	9,1	6,6	9,8	6,2
North Africa	3,6	5,0	3,9	6,2	4,8
North America	4,6	8,0	11,9	3,7	6,2
Near and Middle East	18,9	12,6	9,3	20,5	22,5
Other Asia	2,9	6,0	4,7	7,5	7,2
Free Trade Areas	0	0,0	3,2	1,8	1,3

Source: The shares are calculated by the author using Turkish Statistical Institute's data.

APPENDIX 1F

Table 6. Imports, share of country groups (%)

Country Group Name	1980	1990	2000	2010	2017
EU 15	32,7	44,4	48,8	32,3	29,8
EU 28	39,8	47,5	52,4	39,0	36,4
Other Europe (Non-EU)	8,2	9,6	11,2	16,2	13,4
North Africa	10,6	4,2	4,1	1,7	1,8
North America	6,3	11,0	7,6	7,1	6,0
Near and Middle East	30,7	12,1	6,2	7,0	8,5
Other Asia	2,5	10,6	12,7	21,7	24,5
Free Trade Areas	0,0	0,0	0,9	0,5	0,7

Source: The shares are calculated by the author using Turkish Statistical Institute's data.

APPENDIX 1G

Table 7. Trade in services, 1985-2017

	Balance of Trade in Services	Transportation	Travel	Construction Services	Insurance Services	Financial Services	Other Commercial Services	Official Services	Other
1985	1600	176	770	246	0	0	488	-80	0
1990	4966	20	2705	741	0	0	1643	-143	0
1995	9620	302	4046	1857	0	-274	3181	-239	747
2000	11277	492	5923	968	0	-303	3982	-268	483
2005	15872	-70	16087	874	0	-41	-344	-874	240
2010	16749	1340	17391	859	-541	-234	-1428	-714	76
2015	24228	6182	21248	375	-437	-1121	-1513	-1076	818
2017	19964	5397	17655	439	-743	-561	-1623	-784	441

Source: CBRT, EDDS

Chapter 16
Classes and Development

Zekeriya Eray Eser
Artvin Çoruh University, Turkey

ABSTRACT

Classes forming the social division of labor have changed with the capitalist mode of production. The inheritance from the feudal system is not suitable for the capitalist system. For this reason, the class structure which is suitable for capitalism over time has taken place in many societies. This transformation has become more difficult, especially in the late capitalist countries. This chapter examines class structures of some late-capitalist countries outside Europe and North America. Latin America, Japan, South Korea, and Turkey have historically been studied before and after periods of capitalism. While some countries have successfully completed and managed to develop their class transformations under difficult conditions, some countries have failed. Along with an unsuccessful transformation, new classes have emerged which have preventive effects on the development target. It is difficult for the countries that cannot make their class structure compatible with the capitalist system and the development target.

INTRODUCTION

Social classes and social labor are the most important elements of every economic and political organization. To understand capitalism, the pre-capitalist era and its legacy must be understood. The system before capitalism was feudalism. Therefore, this heritage comes from feudalism. The concept of feudalism is derived from the Latin word 'od Feodum' etymologically. Marc Bloch thought that the word was derived from the French word Fehu-ôd, which was the value of portable goods. It refers to movable goods used for payment from land. However, over time, this concept was used as means of payment instead of money. In short, the word evolved in the opposite way. The term tedir feudalism izm in French is defined as alan "feudalism".

Feudalism refers to a structure that has both political, economic and social dimensions as a system. It was first used by Boulainviliers in the second half of the 18th century. However, it was first used as a Feodal system by Adam Smith. In the 18th century, Montesquieu, saw this as the basis of the political system in France (Gümüş, 2010: 41).

DOI: 10.4018/978-1-7998-0333-1.ch016

Copyright © 2020, IGI Global. Copying or distributing in print or electronic forms without written permission of IGI Global is prohibited.

The need for security is one of the requirements that direct humanity to classes and the division of labor. The first city-states were established in this way. With the increase in population, the increase in organizational skills, the city-states have turned into empires. However, the empires and central states were unable to maintain their power. Feudalism has also emerged at this point. Similar to city-states, local lords and dukes dominated a region. In regions where the central state cannot be dominated, these lords have undertaken some of these duties locally. Feudal, vassal and serf classes have emerged. Classically, Feodal lords hold their land and production right. The villagers, however, have a limited right to produce. The Serfs are connected to the land and therefore the landowner. Although they have a slave-like position in European type Feudalism, they cannot be bought and sold as slaves. The feudal system has played an important role in the development of agriculture and security in the regions where the central states are weak. However, the system is specific to Europe (Ülgen, 2010: 3).

Although Feudalism was specific to Europe, many different forms were seen. Especially with the development of European national identity, the concept of "National Feodalism" has emerged and it has been applied in different ways such as British Feudalism, German Feudalism and French Feudalism (Gümüş, 2010: 42).

Although the concept of feudalism is specific to Europe, there are similar organizations around the world before Capitalism. Especially in terms of late capitalized countries, the processes of abandoning these social organization forms and transition to capitalist system have taken place in different ways.

The aim of this study is to understand the effects of social classes especially in the middle developed countries. It is tried to understand the disruption of class structure in middle developed countries and how the classes that sabotage the capitalist system emerge. The effects of the deterioration of the social classes and the abandonment of the class struggle on economic development were emphasized. Unlike the previous studies, the effect of social classes on economic development has been tried to be understood by considering many different countries.

CLASSES OF PRE-CAPITALISM PERIOD

Far Eastern culture differs greatly from European culture. This difference, of course, has been manifested in the Feudal structure which is specific to the Far East. Throughout history, two countries have emerged as political and military forces, Japan and China. Korea, Taiwan etc. the countries and regions remain between these two power centers. It is not possible to talk about a feudalism in Europe, where there was no social classes which existed in Europe, there were a different way of life, culture and social perception. In Marx's words, there was no class conflict here.

In Japan, the so-called Shogunate period is before with the period that Japan did its revolutions. Although Shogunluk system is an emperor in the country, it is based on limited powers and the country is managed by Shogun, a form of military management. However, there are also feudal lords in the country, not as strong and autonomous as in Europe. These lords have their own military units (Samurai) just as in Western Feudalism. The economy was generally based on agriculture, and there were free peasants with the feudal lord. However, there were traders, bankers. However, there was no competition, contention or conflict between these classes (Eser, 2011: 48).

In China, another central power of the Far East, historical development has been very different. China has not gone from feudalism to capitalism like Japan. First of all, it has passed to socialism. Today it still defines itself as a socialist country. But this is a very controversial statement. Before Mao's revolution in 1949, China had an economy based on agriculture. Traditionally, there was a feudalism that had been going on for hundreds of years, but it had different features than European feudalism. Due to the Chinese soil structure, there was no land ownership with large lands such as in Europe. Technological measures have been developed as there are continuous floods, but there is a need for a central authority to operate this system. Certainly, some measures have been taken to prevent social upheavals. When drought time or the other disasters happened, landowners didn't have to take the interest of the debt and to help the needy (Brunner and Gökdere, 1969: 308).

Apart from the landowners, the peasants were divided into three classes. They were wealthy, middle-income and poor peasants. The poor peasants had little or no land. Middle-income peasants were sowing their land with their own efforts. The wealthy were able to hire additional workers. The transition between these classes was relatively feasible, but the middle-income peasants were able to work hard, but it was not possible to say this for poor peasants. Moreover, it can be said that the majority in the country consists of poor peasants. This is the fact that landowners with less than 10% of the country's population have as much as 70% of the available resources. Moreover, the peasants, who were poor and had to rent land, were paying high interest to the landowners and, as a result of this, they could lose even a little land on their hands. In addition, natural disasters and political turmoil affected the peasants. Scarcity could become a normal reality, which was what happened before the Mao revolution. Moreover, the weakness of the central authority increased the discontent in the country (Brunner and Gökdere, 1969: 307-309).

Korea, like China, has moved to capitalism after many political and social events. After the country was divided into two as a country of birth, South Korea which has remained South has adopted to capitalism. Korea is a small country that has lived under the auspices of China for centuries. Due to the intense Chinese influence, political and social forms of organization were also highly influenced by China. However, Korea's pre-capitalism history was shaped by the Japanese invasion that began in 1876. As in other examples in Korea, the transition from its feudal structure to revolution or capitalist system didn't happen. With the Japanese invasion, industrial infrastructure was first established in Korea and modern production techniques entered the country but Korea's participation was at the lowest level. 80% of skilled workers are Japanese. Moreover, the investments were made to the north where the underground resources of the country are most intense and an unstable structure has occurred. This is because investments and industry are not created for Korea, but for colonial Japan. This period lasted many years. Another problem of the end of World War II led to the civil war in the country. South Korea, which chose to move to capitalism in Korea. So Korea was divided into two as a result of the civil war. But before this period, the class structures in society were already fragmented (Luther, 1984: 30-45).

Latin America experience before capitalism is so different from the rest of the world. The continent is expected to be colonial for a long time, and the system is quite similar to European feudalism. The European colonists applied this system to the continent. However, European feudalism does not have a homogeneous characteristic in itself. British feudalism, German feudalism, etc. many different applications are available. Spain and Portugal, which played an active role in the colonization of Latin America, are more likely to be close to the Spanish feudalism.

Latin America's invation and colonization has happened in very short time. However, invation and exploitation should be continued because there was a lot of precious metals continent. Spain began to establish institutions that would become permanent. Regions were divided into smaller regions and the governors were appointed to any region, which consisted of regional conquerors. Spain accepted the regions which has occupied as part of Spanish kingdom. In this country, a policy of integration and assimilation was followed. Mayan, Inca and Aztec descendants were intended to be Spanish. The Spanish monarchy, however, aimed at ensuring that the locals and the Spaniards became part of Spain as a single nation, with integration in the region. But in practice this has not been the case. The senor-serf relationship in typical feudalism is also established here. Founded for integration / assimilation, the organization called "encomiendo" has led to far beyond its purpose. The main aim of the system was to provide the Christianization of the locals by offering them to the service of the Spanish people in the region. However, this practice was quite susceptible to abuse. First, there was no periodic limitation. Therefore, this service has continued for generations. Moreover, the system has become corrupted in a short time, which means that the public should only give tax to the landowner and work. The system, which was established to teach lifestyle, religion, culture and language, became a system of slavery. Moreover, the locals were crushed under heavy taxes and handed over their land. The dream of the Spanish monarchy was to create a nation with locals and Spaniards but Spaniards has blamed locals by being ungodly, immoral etc. Because locals were different from Spaniards. So system has evolved to a congenital slavery. Although the subsequent reactions then prohibited slavery by Spain, Spain's laws were not applied in practice because of the distance (Yarar, 2013: 396-397).

In short, in contrast to the Far East, there is a very sharp classification in Latin America in the pre-capitalist period. Besides, there are racial and cultural differences, discrimination and slavery.

Before capitalism in the Ottoman Empire there were two sorts of the Muslim-non-Muslim communities have been brought together not in the class but a similar structure. Non-Muslims mostly lived in cities and engaged in non-agricultural activities. Crafts, trade and art activities which were forbidden to Turks were carried out by non-Muslims. The people who were Muslims were mostly engaged in agriculture. This caused an unbalanced wealth distribution in Ottoman society. In this context, it would not be wrong to say that the Ottoman bourgeoisie is composed of non-Muslims (Kalabak, 2014: 309). On the other hand, the ownership of the land belonged entirely to the state in the Ottoman state. However, this power had the state bureaucracy. Even though the Tımar system was subsequently collapsed, the rent and tax right of the land were given to the owner of the land. The peasants who worked the land also created another class. In summary, bureaucrat class was ruling class, craftsmen, artisans and peasants were also forming the ruled class. However, with the introduction of capitalism through the capitulations of the Ottoman state, the bourgeoisie, which consisted of non-Muslims, showed a comprador characteristic and seized the production surplus. Especially the privileges given to non-Muslims have played a big role in this. Class structure in the transition before the Republic of Turkey and the capitalist system as such.

TRANSFORMATION EXAMPLES IN THE TRANSITION TO CAPITALISM

The most striking and first example for South East Asia is the transformation in Japan. The transformation of Japan with the transition to capitalism was a first in the region but in some ways it was an example for the countries of the region. As Japan has been a closed country for many years, it has been far from the developments in the world. When it realized the developments in the world, it was late. For this reason, a series of political turmoil and the Shogunate period ended in approximately 30 years. The empire was given wide powers again after centuries. Thus, Emperor Meiji was able to realize a series of revolutions. This period is known as the Meiji Restoration. Emperor Meiji and his technocrats first decided to change the old class structure. They have understood that the classes which were the landlords, Samurai, peasants and merchants couldn't have in the capitalist system so it was required have the decision to move it to a new class structure. In this context, it was necessary to make radical decisions for the formation of bourgeois and proletarian classes. Japan is a relatively fortunate country because it is an island country and there is no religious and ethnic conflict. It did not have to end the conflict between religious, sectarian and ethnic identities. For this reason, they would first receive capital accumulation, which is *sine qua non for capitalism.* The creation of the bourgeois class is very sensitive case. The perception of inequality in society doesn't wanted and lead to hostility towards wealth. It has brought together the families of merchants who have a wealth of Samurai families with a high reputation in the community by marriage. In this way, Meiji was prevented of social reactions. The families are still who were formed during the Meiji period are among the largest shareholders of Japan and are called Zaibatsu. However, the landowners' lands were confiscated. This decision was met with little resistance and in general the landlords volunteered (Sönmez, 2003: 57).

The content of capitalism is not only an economic model but also a way of life after the industrial revolution. This means in places such as family structure and education system, where social classes should be organized according to the new system. A new format in the education system were required in this point. The education system of Germany, which has passed through Japan and has the closest culture, became a model for Japan. In this way, Japan has enabled the creation of qualified workforce. With all these transformations, Japan was equivalent to European economies during the beginning of the 20th century.

The process in Korea was very different from that in Japan. After Korea was divided into two, South Korea was in a very bad situation as a country that had left the civil war in the aftermath of many years of occupation. The meeting of the Koreans with capitalism was not a change in the direction of a decision, but Korea met with capitalism as being an occupied, colonized country. Class transformations could not be carried out in such a way that the elimination of old classes. After that, the civil war and post-division South Korea have the advantage of being a homogenous country like Japan. South Korea, which had no capital except agriculture and light industry in the hands after the division, was completely dependent on foreign aid. The fact that the United States (USA) began to reduce foreign aid has caused significant distress in South Korea in the 1950s (Luther, 1984: 46-53).

As a result of General Park's confiscation of military coup in 1961, South Korea entered into a real transformation. Although the new military administration focused on the light industry, South Korea adopted a different path after the Yushin Constitution adopted in 1972. From this point on, it has turned to heavy industry. However, unlike Japan, there is no bourgeois class that the majority of people can accept. For this reason, General Park has pardoned businessmen who have been imprisoned for corrupting for the reason of the lack of capital in the country. South Korea did not stay with it and created a system with low wages and no job security, no occupational safety, no pensions and health insurance to attract foreign capital. South Korea's transition to capitalism took place in a very different way, so the social classes were integrated into the capitalist system by hard and destructive way (Luther, 1984: 65).

Latin America has gone through a colonial phase like South Korea, but the dynamics in Latin America have been different. First of all, Latin America is too big to be considered as a whole and it is a region with different countries, cultures and geography. In general, however, the transition process in Latin America cannot be dealt with independently of the transformation of Spanish colonialism. Spain must have invaded in Latin America for a very long time and Sapians real purpose was achieved, Europeanizing Latin America. The ideal of indigenous people and Europeans to be formed as a nation, but interestingly Spain's loss of influence in the region was also a semi-European, like Simon Bolivar, and the hand of a European-educated group. After the independence of the Latin American countries, they faced a completely different problem. Particularly during the independence wars, the United Kingdom

(UK) was heavily supported, but later this support was brought to another level with the borrowing from British financial institutions. Moreover, there were different classes in the country during the Spanish colonialism. Of these, expressed as "criollo" Spanish, those who have become superior class (Ercan, 2006: 73). With the interests and suggestions of the UK financial market, the dominant classes of Latin America turned to external debts according to the idea of liberalism. In particular, Chile, Argentina, Mexico and Peru have borrowed high rates. This period is mentioned as the first globalization period and the first spread of finance capital on a global scale corresponds to this period (Yeldan, 2002: 22). Thus, with the determination of liberalism as the economic model, economies of scale, import and export freedom came to the agenda. The criollos, which were in the dominant class position, allowed the lands to be collected in their own hands. Thus, agricultural demand from Europe could be produced. However, in addition to an agriculture-based model, enterprises such as railways and mines were operated by European and North American enterprises. In addition, a trade bourgeoisie was beginning to form in the country. The peasants were landless and migrated to the cities between 1917-1927. They began to work here as craftsmen or tradesmen, but were also employed in foreign capital mines and railways. This was the complexity of the highly complex class structure with the migration. The increase in the demands of the working class with the Bolshevik revolution enabled the period to be a very complex period in terms of politics and class (Topal, 2008: 26).

The development of the period which will determine the future of Latin America is the struggle for power between the crillos. The development of the period which will determine the future of Latin America is the struggle for power between the 'criollos' and the 'caudillos' (authoritarian leaders of military origin). Economy was controlled by criollos and regional markets operated by foreign capital and traders and caudillos started a struggle to control politics and military. In the end, the caudillos, who formed large armies with mestizos (crossbreeds), ended the chaos in Argentina, Mexico, Brazil and Chile. The ruling classes as the winner of the struggle for power do not have a hegemony as criollos and caudillos alone, but together they both prevailed. However, the fate and future of the continent was mainly determined by the caudillos. The trade bourgeoisie, which was formed before 1930s, quickly became a state bourgeoisie and in parallel the administration became centralized (Topal, 2008: 27-28).

The transformation in China was different from all countries. Before the transition to the Chinese capitalist system, it went to socialism. Today he still claims to be a socialist country. However, it is a highly controversial issue, especially after consideration issues such as private enterprise and foreign capital. In 1949, after the typical agriculture-based and peculiar feudal system of China, Mao Zedong brought to life a socialist revolution in China. The turbulent political and social structure of the country until the revolution was ended and the development effort was made. However, the private sector has not been expropriated; The bourgeoisie has quickly become a state bourgeoisie by states being partner to private sector. Some of the capitalists continued their existence, even if only to a small extent by the state. Until the 1960s, the efforts to abandon the agricultural economy and industrialization continued at the expense of renouncing agriculture, but this policy was later abandoned. In the context of social classes, cooperatives have been put in place for the poor, middle-income and rich peasants. A system has been developed as small cooperatives and their large cooperatives and their communes. After 1956-57, the peasants were completely connected to the communes. In time, similar to Latin America, state-owned industries and state bureaucracy became another class, while the peasants were a different class. However, it is also a fact that class differences between the peasants decrease over time (Brunner and Gökdere, 1969: 307-330).

With the establishment of the country's transition to capitalism it took place in Turkey. The country, which was established after the national liberation war following World War I, has an appearance in all aspects. Class structure is complex, capital is scarce, skilled workforce is scarce. Inadequate industrial facilities, inherited from the past, as well as skilled labor, as a legacy from the former state of the Ottoman state has remained a huge debt. (Özçelik, Tuncer, 2007: 254-255). It is a necessity for the country to embark for urgent development. Structured revolutions establish and restructure a modern society. Further religious classes and classes were removed, with secularism and equal citizenship with the single law system, gender equality and secularism. First of all, a bourgeois class was tried to be created in order to eliminate the lack of capital. Although there were state aids, it was not allowed to evolve into the state bourgeoisie, or in other words to a bureaucratic class. As seen in Latin America, a class like Caudillos, which is a military bourgeoisie, was not formed. However, in the first years of the republic and in the period until the end of II. World War, lessons taken from the previous period were removed and the effects of foreign capital and foreigners on the economy. Measures such as cabotage law, underground resources and nationalization of mines have been taken. 46 factories were established by 1938 in an effort to drive the industry in a period when the majority of the population lived in villages. In addition, village institutes were established with the aim of increasing agricultural production and creating class consciousness of the peasant class. In summary, the transition to capitalism in Turkey in political, law, economic and class as demonstrated intense efforts for the creation of a new and modern society (Eğilmez, 2018: 135-138).

THE PERIOD AFTER CAPITALISM

After Meiji, Japan has become a country where the military have become stronger. It was the strongest country in the region with its strong economy, technological level and political domination. This process in Japan led it to World War II. However, after World War II, Japan was in the defeated side and was the first and only country hit by a nuclear bomb. After the war, the economy collapsed and the country was scattered. But Japan was longer an industrial society. Even though the system was collapsed, it had a social structure that internalized the system. However, the decisions made about Japan contained a very heavy prescription. Not only has the country lost almost half its territory, but also it has been condemned to pay compensation to the countries it has damaged, and worse, it has been decided to dismantle 1000 factories in Japan and transfer them to these countries. However, Japan was no longer a priority for USA because of the cold war period. The transfer of factories, which could cause damage to the Japanese economy, has never been experienced in this way. After theII. World War, the start of the Korean war had the opportunity to recover quickly for the Japanese economy (Hunter, 2002: 416). During this period, the needs in the region were produced by Japan and made a significant contribution to this economic recovery. In particular, the US's base in the region was Japan and producing all the needs of the United Nations forces in particular regulated Japan's foreign trade balance. In Japan, the purchasing power increased and the country's economy began to recover. More important and unexpected was the $ 22 billion aid from the United Nations in Japan in 1951-1952. In this way, the Japanese manufacturing industry in 1936 has become more production. Japan recovered its worn-out economy by using the resources and opportunities right before the 1960s. Japan made investments in strategic industries, sent observers abroad, gave support to small and medium-sized enterprises and gave export subsidies

(Eser, 2011: 59). However, Japan has never experienced any class problems. All the moves and policy principles in this made such a study.

In South Korea, capitalism began in a devastating way and continued for different reasons until the 1980s. The class structure was rigidly determined. However, after this point, the disappearance of class problems is an important result. During the period of General Park in South Korea has quickly become a Development Dictatorship. During this period, heavy industry moves were made. South Korea, which was previously dependent on foreign aid and trying to develop with an import substitution model, has become a country that has an important industrial infrastructure, technology development and more export substitution. However, this structure was built in a militarist manner with the military coup. In contrast to Japan, this infrastructure was created in a way called an internal colonial model rather than an imperialist feature. In order to attract foreign capital, the people of South Korea were obliged to bear the full cost of capital. In addition to the lack of civil and political freedoms, the working class and the labor unions, which have the right to strike, have been discipline by the state itself. In addition to this, the human capital, which was insufficient in the Park period, was met by military procedures. Up to 86% of males were recruited and trained here (Luther, 1984: 62-74). However, after the Park period, South Korea has seen the positive results of the steps taken, even under difficult conditions. A healthy class structure and democracy has developed in the country and has become one of the most important science and technology centers in the world.

In terms of Latin American history, capitalism has begun to be felt with all its existence after Spanish colonialism. In the post-independence period, many countries in Latin America have been linked to dependence on British financial institutions. In later periods, after the power and conflict of interests in the country, the military elites took over the country's administration and created another political structure. There was a politically opposite form of government with liberalism. The end of colonialism did not end exploitation, and slavery outside Cuba and Puerto Rico was not removed until the 1850s. The new structure is dominated by the despotic governments and cooperated with international capital, is a structure with large landowners (Topal, 2008: 29).

The 40-year period from the 1930s to the 1970s is the import substitution model years for Latin America. The main reason for this was the weakening of the landowners and the trade bourgeoisie of the economic crises (especially after the 1929 crisis). Therefore, central governments had to intervene in the economy. In this period, the national industrial bourgeoisie was strengthened and the new economic program was determined by the American Economic Commission (CEPAL). According to the new model, the bourgeoisie of the national industry was to be supported by the state and from time to time the state itself was set up to establish an industry. This model was immediately accepted by the industrial bourgeoisie. Therefore, this model is also called state capitalism (Bizberg, 2014: 2). However, an approach was adopted where anti-imperialist discourses were at the forefront and a national model of industry was adopted, and parallel to this, the conflict between the classes was prevented. For this purpose, the mobility and independent organization of the working class was prevented. In this period, governments established their relations with social classes through state-led mechanisms. This mechanism, which is also referred to as corporatism, is to protect the interests of industrial sector workers by means of organizations established under the guidance of the state. According to the import substitution, national interests are in the forefront. For this reason, corporatism has led to the suppression of class interests which have been reduced to common interests for the success of capitalist industrialization. In corporatism, some workers and civil officers gain a special position and gain various interests. Although import substitution policies have positive results in the period between 1930-1960, it is a fact that real wages have increased in Latin America (Topal, 2008: 30). However, the increase in real wages did not resolve the class inequalities and income imbalance, but the income imbalance increased. In this period, while the industrial bourgeoisie and the foreign capital benefited from state subsidies and the economic policies of the period were designed in accordance with the interests of these classes, inequalities between the classes did not diminish. Although Latin American countries have an import substitution model, there has been an oligarchy of industrial bourgeoisie involved in export-oriented production. The working class has been suppressed within corporatism, but in this period wages, public expenditures, social services, education, health and social insurance expenditures have also increased (Topal, 2008: 30).

Latin American countries began to pay for failures of import substitution model after 1960. This model, which has been relatively successful until this period, was influenced by the export of raw materials from Latin American countries and production due to its dependence on imported machinery and equipment. Especially the high inflation, budget deficits and high foreign debt spiral countries have started to close their international credit debts with other debts. This disappeared in the 1970s with the beginning of the oil crisis. Due to the crisis, the financial opportunities provided by North American banks have disappeared. The process resulted in a major crisis. Together with the economic crisis, the level of reconciliation between classes has weakened. Spending in areas such as social security payments, real wages, social assistance, education and health has decreased and the working class has been organized and put pressure on governments. The economic crisis turned into a crisis of representation and quickly turned into a political crisis. The rulers, the bourgeoisie and the bureaucracy were no longer able to balance, and the period of military coups in Latin America began. Brazil (1964-1989), Argentina (1966-1983), Bolivia (1971-1984) and Uruguay (1973-1985) experienced military coups. In these countries, they put too much pressure on the proletarian movement to take control. In countries such as Mexico that do not have a military coup, authoritarian governments prevented the strengthening of social opposition. Military coups and authoritarian regimes have led not only to a political transformation but also to their transformation in economic and social class relations. Latin America is now integrated into the international economic system (Ellner, 2006: 29). At this point, it has entered into a period of interest to the bourgeoisie along with the neo-liberal policies and the suppression of the working class. However, the class struggle continued under military rule. With the increase of social discomfort, the pressures on the administration in Latin American countries increased and resulted in time. However, in the Latin American countries, which entered the path of democratization in time, this bourgeois class was formed with the leading role. In Latin America, Brazil (1964-1989), Argentina (1966-1983), Bolivia (1971-1984) and Uruguay (1973-1985) passed from the military authorities to civilian administrations. However, it should be kept in mind that in this period neo-liberal policies were implemented by civil governments. Therefore, in the 1990s, the struggle of the labor unions was no longer class-based. Non-governmental organizations were taken to the center as representatives of non-class struggle. The concepts of class struggle and identity politics are mixed and class movements leave their place in the politics of identity and recognition (especially on ethnic and minority rights). The perception that the class concept limits personal freedoms has been created. One of the most important reasons why Latin American countries are still not developed countries (United Nations, World Economic Stiuation and Prospects: 141) constitutes a deteriorating class structure and perception in these periods.

The process in China was quite different after Mao. During the Mao era, the Chinese Communist Party (CCP) adopted a socialist model that was designed as the representative of the proletariat class. However, in the period after Mao, this model left China with serious problems on the road to development. These problems were mainly due to the importance of industrialization and neglect of agriculture.

Following the death of Mao Zedong in 1976, China became a social and economic stalemate, and Deng Xiaoping became the ruler (Şimşek, 2017: 103-105). Deng, who was a market economy in his mind from the beginning, expressed many times that the cultural revolution in Mao period was wrong. It has made social classes before the Mao period and foresees the need for modernization of the country in the fields of agriculture, industry, defense, science and technology (Gündal, 2015: 58). Today it is called "four modernization". Deng supported income differences as opposed to the class socialist outlook. What is meant here is not the income imbalance, but managing the administrative structure of the country as a company's departments. As China is a very difficult country to manage, large planning is necessary. During the Deng period, various administrative structures were established in the country. These structures are in competition with each other like different companies. In this sense, Deng is of the opinion that the increase in income of inequality of a village or district and the increase of income will be an example for the other region and that other regions will be motivated to increase their income. One of the most important characteristics of the Deng period and the period after it is the fight against corruption, the opening of the private enterprise and the private enterprise being secured by the state. Another feature of the state is that it is governed as a in company bir country, as a CEO at the top of all regions. For this reason, it is called ve "state capitalism" for the system formed during and after Deng. But unlike import substitution state capitalism, it is also called "new state capitalism". In this new system, it is possible to state that the classes of the bourgeoisie are more effective and even participate in the administration, although the classes do not change much compared to the Mao period.

Undoubtedly class and sociological causes of the process of Turkey's lives and the continuous rotation is important. First of all, population and migration are important in this sense. Rapidly increasing population and migration from rural to urban have caused rapid erosion of social structure and sociological structure. 20th century "New Malthusian Theory" along with population control was a time of widespread and Turkey are also affected. The reason for this birth control is the desire of families to offer their children a better future and a good education. However, it is preferred by people who are in the higher income groups in cities in Turkey birth control method. Therefore, while the population growth rate was high, the increasing population was poorer and uneducated (Eğilmez, 2018: 169-170). Housing, infrastructure and integration policies have not been provided for people who have to migrate from the village to the city due to economic problems. People who migrated from rural areas to cities had to live in slums and without security. In this process, they could not adapt to the city and moved their rural cultures to the city. As immigrants grew, there were more immigrants in the cities than in urban areas. This process was accompanied by cultural change (Akdeniz, 2005: 165-166). The rural-based people feel a part of the middle eastern culture. Citizens with minorities were more educated in western culture. While these citizens have concerns such as gender equality, freedom to drink alcohol, freedom to have fun together, and freedom of thought and expression, immigrants are only concerned about livelihood. People in different countries live in the same country. It should be noted that rural population is more prevalent in the country and that the rural-based population is prejudiced against the urban population. For this reason, the group that determines the results of the elections is more active and rural (Eğilmez, 218: 176). Another pillar of the transformation is the transformation of education in Turkey. Non-science-based approach to education and the Ottoman Empire based on religion made by Turkey in recent years is particularly. The system of education planned and implemented on the basis of a secular, science-based system (Okur, 2005: 99-100) has recently become closer to the old paradigm with the opening of imam hatip high schools after the closure of village institutes. Consequently, the culture of allegiance, which was quite functional during the Ottoman State period but which had a negative effect after Renaissance and Reform, was on the rise again. Although the culture of allegiance, which means to obey the leader and the authority, is important in achieving the military success of the Ottoman state, a society and the army, which will go to die for the leader with the emergence of new weapons and technologies, have no meaning. In the modern world, such an education system and societies that maintain this perception cannot be developed. Because the culture of allegiance requires individuals to make sacrifices for society, state and leader. This has religious, cultural references and cannot be questioned. On the other hand, individuals who produce innovation and technology and science are needed in the world after Renaissance. In summary, the culture of allegiance is an instrument of the ancient world, free thinking is the modern world. Turkish society is going backwards in this sense (Eğilmez, 2018: 189-195).

Turkey is evolving towards a modernizing society from a traditional society. Although there are reasons such as education and migration, there are also class reasons. Turkey is trying to create a bourgeois class since it was first established (Armstrong, 2008: 36). An urban industrial bourgeoisie class was formed but was insufficient. Moreover, the urban bourgeoisie is not even fully qualified as a bourgeoisie. This class is actually a generation of predominantly village and town origin merchants. In a sense the roots are trades. Therefore, a complete and appropriate bourgeoisie has not been fully formed either quantitatively or qualitatively (Duman, 2007: 45). The class awareness of the working class did not develop in the Turkish society, which caught up with the industrial revolution and was still behind. However, a different class has been formed in Turkey. This class, which can be called the "town tradesmen bourgeoisie" class, is described by Mahfi Eğilmez. On the other hand, it is stated by Mahfi Eğilmez that this class (Eğilmez, 2018: 157) does not contain the features of the bourgeois class in any way. For this reason, this study will be defined as "town tradesmen class". This class is not available in developed countries. It is a class encountered in Turkey. Although not all tradesmen are involved in this class, the reason for this statement is that tradesmen or traders do not have any contribution to the production, or are limited, in contrast to peasant, worker or bourgeois classes. While villagers contribute to agricultural production, urban workers contribute to the production of goods. The bourgeoisie and the petty-bourgeois class produce industry and services. But the town is neither a city nor a village. The town is between the two and the local merchants take the agricultural products from the peasants and sell them to the citizens in exchange for a certain profit. They are similar to the members of the organization, which are sociologically referred to as the organization of Ahi Community in the Ottoman Empire. They are traditional and mostly conservative. However, these people are generally irrelevant to science, art and cultural activities, but they are rich as the bourgeoisie (Eren and Bakan, 2017: 141-142). On the other hand, this class is based on consumption culture as it does not produce. Moreover, this consumption is the 'pretension consumption' as Veblen predicts. Migration and population growth in Turkey have been much more than this class. Together with the growing suburban culture in cities along with immigration, this new class represents a rich variety of suburban culture. Therefore, the "town tradesmen class" and suburbs class has been one of the most affecting class to class transformation in Turkey. Until 2002, the right-wing parties, which were generally ruled by the elites but still had conservative statements, came under the influence of these two classes. However, in 2002 these classes became aware of their power. Instead of the center-right elite who did not resemble them much, they had the power to choose a politician who looked exactly like them. Today, Turkey's social, class structure, establishing absolute dominance in a way classes are those classes. In this traditional, conservative structure, the allegiance culture continues to grow with strength. The reason for the recycling in the education system has been in line with the expectations and preferences of these classes which are the dominant classes (Eğilmez, 2018: 157-193).

CONCLUSION AND EVALUATION

When the most important revolutions in the history of the world are listed, the beginning of the agricultural revolution and then the industrial revolution. In addition to having a global effect rather than a regional one, which is different from the other revolutions, they are not one-dimensional but rather multi-dimensional and they have changed human life altogether. After the agricultural revolution, hunter-gathering tribes settled into life, writing, agriculture, the exchange began, and even the family structure changed and people began to live in large families in cities, towns and villages. In addition, social classes have occurred for the first time in history. The ruler, soldier, clergy and peasant classes were formed. Later, these classes evolved into different types of feudal structures. There has been a change in the same way with the industrial revolution. This time, the large family of smaller families which are formed from father, mother and children, villages and towns were passed to cities. With the industrial revolution, industrial bourgeoisie and working classes were formed, and then another white-collar class called the petty bourgeoisie was formed. However, this transformation is not occurring simultaneously in the whole world, and it is formed in different ways and at different levels as it is within it. This has led to the formation of different classes outside the classes required by capitalism, sometimes leaving class conflicts in place to compromise between classes and many different results. Without a single capitalism, there is no single class structure. However, in addition to the healthy functioning of capitalism, the development of countries with a capitalist economy depends on healthy class structures. In this study, it's been tried to explain healthy and unhealthy class structures for sustainable capitalism which would result in development of different countries and regions.

Far East Asian countries, Latin America as a single continent and Turkey were examined. Relevant examples far east countries have relatively more successful and healthy class structures. Although the cultures, histories and practices of the countries differed, the classes that emerged as a result and which had a disruptive effect on the social production relations did not occur. Although South Korea has come to this point with many unfortunate incidents and military coups, South Korea has managed to overcome these problems and has survived and its class structure remained healthy.

In Japan, which first carried out the development move from the Far Eastern countries, class transformation was much easier than many other countries. After the restoration of Meiji, the old and traditional structure was changed rapidly by the central government and no social reactions were encountered. After the Second World War, Japan, which had already settled a class structure, did not have to go to class regulation when carrying out its second development effort.

China has experienced the most diverse process in the Far East and is still continuing today. China, which has a very large and crowded population, was founded in the 20th century in the socialist revolution. While the old traditional classes have not completely disappeared, they have mostly disappeared, and the Communist Party of China has been effective in the administration of the country as the representative of the proletariat class alone. However, following the death of Mao Zedong, Deng Xiaoping headed a different model. Although China has officially defined this model as Chinese type of socialism, it has not only opened the way for the private enterprise and hence the bourgeois class, but also has a say in the administration. Today there are the class of proletariat, bourgeois class and petty bourgeois class of peasants and workers in China. Apart from this, there is a bureaucratic elite class because country administration is in the hands of one party. However, in terms of the social division of labor, this class in China has no detrimental effect on development efforts.

Since there are many countries in Latin America, the continent has been studied as a whole. Latin America is historically one of the most unfortunate regions. Beyond the class structure after many years of colonialism, ethnicity, culture, religion, language and almost all concepts have changed. As a result, many different classes emerged on the continent and a semi-European and semi-American people formed. After long years of colonialism, the people lived under poverty and oppression even after the independence of the countries in the region subjected to despotic rule and slavery. The economic crises in the region have directed the problems of foreign debt to the left organizations and the class struggle of the peoples of Latin America. Before the caudillos and then under the bourgeois class, the society could not keep up with the effort of industrialization with the import substitution model. Class struggle and class consciousness were finally overshadowed by the problems of identity and recognition within the region in the 1990s. As a result, while Latin America has a serious class of workers and peasants, it has been in the background of the bureaucratic elites, the military bourgeoisie and the industrial bourgeoisie. It is not possible to say that a healthy class structure is formed for Latin America.

Turkey's case represents the most dramatic example of classes. Although it is a country that has built both its class structure and political structure and its legal system on modern values, it has lost its dynamism over time. The failure to achieve the development goal was condemned to a skewed and unhealthy class structure as a result of political instability, military coups and social divisions. This unhealthy structure, which constitutes an obstacle to the development goal, also causes the country to suffer corruption and cultural erosion. Turkey is rapidly away from the established education system on scientific foundations. Its economy is based on unsustainable resources such as hot money, foreign debt and privatization. Turkey needs a scientific education system in order to have a productive population. However, traditional and conservative characteristics that remains is active in the suburbs and the country's "town tradesmen class" and demand in these classes and their expectations can not be opened in the opposite direction across the largest in Turkey. Turkey, then paused before due to unhealthy way of development of the class structure and identity began to go backwards. Especially the decline in socioculturalism is seen in the field of economics and education. The choices of the dominant classes of the population through elections determine the future of the country as unproductive, scientific, artistic and, most importantly, freedom of thought, the rule of law, democracy-free. It is very difficult to develop societies that do not have a healthy class structure. However, the presence and influence of unhealthy build up a healthy lack of class structure reveals quite negative consequences for Turkey. Both Turkey and Latin America will not be wrong to make that determination; it does not seem possible for them to achieve the development goal without creating a class structure suitable for capitalism. The deterioration in the class structure occurred sometimes by the state and sometimes outside the control of the state. In both cases, the lack of state and the lack of or inclusion of institutions is an important reason. In Turkey, for example, he was unable to government agencies dealing with uncontrolled immigration. On the contrary, the state has come under the control of the new classes and extractive institutions have emerged instead of inclusive institutions. This led to the departure from the goal of economic development.

REFERENCES

Akdeniz, H. (2005). Göç,Kentleşme ve Kentsel Yoksulluk Bağlamında Kap-Kaç Olgusu. Mülkiye Dergisi[Civil Service Journal], *29*(249), 161-187. Retrieved from http://dergipark.gov.tr/mulkiye/issue/249/1027

Arslan, R. (2008). Laik Türkiye Cumhuriyeti, Ordu ve Burjuva Sınıfı. Gazi Üniversitesi İktisadi ve İdari Bilimler Fakültesi Dergisi [Gazi University Administration and Economic Sciences Journal], *10*(3), 33-44. Retrieved from http://dergipark.gov.tr/gaziuiibfd/issue/28327/301017

Bakan, S. & Eren, S. S. (2017). 2000'lerde Türkiye'de Burjuvazi Sınıfının Siyasal Dönüşümü. Birey ve Toplum Sosyal Bilimler Dergisi [Individual and Society Social Sciences Journal], 7(1), 127-149. Retrieved from http://dergipark.gov.tr/birtop/issue/32816/364748

Biezberg, I. (2014). Types of capitalism in Latin America. Revue Invervention Economiques Papers in Political Economy. Retrieved from http://interventionseconomiques.revues.org/1772

Brunner, N. & Gökdere, A. Y. (1969). Çin Ekonomisi. Ankara Üniversitesi Hukuk Fakültesi Dergisi [Law Faculty Journal], 26(3). Retrieved from http://dergipark.gov.tr/auhfd/issue/42969/520225

Duman, M. (2007). Türkiye'de Burjuva Sınıfının Sosyal Profili. Sosyoekonomi, 5(5). Retrieved from http://dergipark.gov.tr/sosyoekonomi/issue/21065/226810

Eğilmez, M. (2018). *Değişim Sürecinde Türkiye*. İstanbul, Turkey: Remzi Kitabevi. [Remzi Publishing]

Ercan, F. (2006). Suskun Adamın Baladı: Latin Amerika Üzerinden Venezüella'ya Dair Düşünceler. [Praksis Journal]. *Praksis Dergisi*, *14*, 67–108.

Eser, E. Z. (2011). *Dünden Bugüne Teknoloji Transferi, Yüksek Lisans Tezi* [Master thesis]. T.C. Marmara Üniversitesi Sosyal Bilimler Enstitüsü. [Marmara University Social Sciences Institute]

Gümüş, T. T. (2010). Feodalizm: Avrupa Tarihinde Yeni Yaklaşımlar. [History Research Journal]. *Tarih Araştırmaları Dergisi*, *29*(47), 39–64.

Hunter, J. E. (2002). *Modern Japonya'nın Doğuşu*. Ankara, Turkey: İmge Kitapevi. [Imge Publishing]

Kalabak, A. Y. (2014). Osmanlı'nın Son Döneminin Sosyo Ekonomik Buhranları ve Mali Emperyalizm. [Social Economic Research Journal]. *Sosyal Ekonomik Araştırmalar Dergisi*, *14*(27), 304–326. doi:10.30976usead.302229

Luther, H. U. (1984). *Güney Kore Bir Model Olabilir mi*. İstanbul, Turkey: Belge Yayınları. [Belge Publishing]

Okur, M. (2005). Türkiye'de Milli ve Modern Bir Eğitim Sistemi Oluşturma Çabaları (1920-1928). Çağdaş Türkiye Tarihi Araştırmaları Dergisi [Modern Turkey's History Research Journal], 4(11). Retrieved from http://dergipark.gov.tr/cttad/issue/25234/266776

Özçelik, Ö., & Tuncer, G. (2007). Atatürk Dönemi Ekonomi Politikaları, Afyon Kocatepe Üniversitesi Sosyal Bilimler Dergisi [Afyon Kocatepe University Social Sciences Journal]. *Ocak*, *2007*, 253–266.

Sağ, V. (2003). Toplumsal Değişim ve Eğitim Üzerine. C.Ü. Sosyal Bilimler Dergisi [Social Sciences Journal]. *Cilt, 27*(:1), 11–25.

Sönmez, A. (2003). *Doğu Asya "Mucizesi" ve Bunalımı*. İstanbul, Turkey: İstanbul Bilgi Üniversitesi Yayınları. [Istanbul Bilgi University Publishing]

Topal, A. (2008). Türkiye'den Latin Amerika'ya Bakmak: Tarihsel Arka Plan. Latin Amerika'yı Anlamak: Neoliberalizm, Direniş ve Sol [Left Journal], 21-46. United Nations, World Economic Stiuation and Prospects. Retrieved from https://www.un.org/development/desa/dpad/wpcontent/uploads/sites/45/publication/WESP2018_Full_Web-1.pdf

Ülgen, P. (2010). Ortaçağ Avrupa'sında Feodal Sisteme Genel Bir Bakış. [Introduction Journal]. *Mukaddime Dergisi, 1*(1), 1–19.

Yarar, A. G. A. (2013). Latin Amerika'da İspanyol Sömürgeciliği ve Simon Bolivar'ın Bağımsızlık Mücadelesi. *Historical Studies (Melbourne, Vic.), 5*(1), 391–403.

Yeldan, E. (2002). Neoliberal Küreselleşlme İdeolojisinin Kalkınma Söylemi Üzerine Değerlendirmeler. [Praksis Journal]. *Praksis Dergisi, 7*, 19–34.

Compilation of References

< bok>Dahl, R. A . (1971). Polyarchy: Participation and opposition. New Haven, CT: Yale University Press .

<edb>Coleman, J. S. (1988). Conclusion: The political systems of the developing area. In G. A. Almond & J. S. Coleman (Eds.), The politics of developing areas. Princeton, NJ: Princeton University Press, 1960, 532-581.

<eref>Ollila, P. (2009). Principles of Institutional Economics. University of Helsinki WP, No: 56, 1-73. Retrieved from http://www.helsinki.fi/taloustieconomics.pdf

<eref>Samuels, W. J. (1969). On the future of institutional economics. Journal of Economic Issues, 3(3), 67-72. Retrieved from http://www.jstor.org/stable/422401

<jrn>Kenneth, A. B. (1979). Political democracy and the timing of development. American Socialical Review, 44, 572.

Abramovitz, M. (1956). Resource and output trends in the United States since 1870. *The American Economic Review*, *46*(2), 5–23.

Acaravcı, A., Artan, S., Erdoğan, S., & Bostan Göktürk, T. (2018). Türkiye'de kurumsal kalite,reel gelir ve doğrudan yabancı yatırımlar ilişkisi. *Mehmet Akif Ersoy Üniversitesi İktisadi ve İdari Bilimler Fakültesi Dergisi*, *5*(2), 132–145.

Acemoglu, D. & Robinson, J. (2008). *The Role of Institutions in Growth and Development.* Retrieved from https://siteresources.worldbank.org/EXTPREMNET/Resources/489960-1338997241035/Growth_Commission_Working_Paper_10_Role_Institutions_Growth_Development.pdf

Acemoglu, D., Johnson, S., & Robinson, J. (2004). *Institutions as the Fundamental Cause of Long-Run Growth.* Retrieved from http://economics.mit.edu/files/4469

Acemoğlu, D., Johnson, S., Robinson, J. A., & Yared, P. (2005). "Income and Democracy", *NBER Working Paper Series*, No: 11205, 5-12.

Acemoglu, D., & Johnson, S. (2005). Unbundling institutions. *Journal of Political Economy*, *113*(5), 949–995. doi:10.1086/432166

Acemoğlu, D., Johnson, S., & Robinson, J. A. (2005). Institutions as a fundamental cause of long-run growth. In P. Aghion & S. Durlauf (Eds.), *Handbook of Economic Growth* (pp. 386–469). Amsterdam, The Netherlands: Elsevier.

Acemoglu, D., & Robinson, J. (2012). *Why nations fail. The origins of power, prosperity and poverty*. New York, NY: Profile Books. Crown Publishers. doi:10.1355/ae29-2j

Acemoğlu, D., & Robinson, J. A. (2016). *Diktatörlük ve Demokrasinin Ekonomik Kökenleri, 2. Basım*. İstanbul, Turkey: Bağlam Press.

Achrol, R. S., & Gundlach, G. T. (1999). Legal and social safeguards against opportunism in exchange. *Journal of Retailing, 75*(1), 107–124. doi:10.1016/S0022-4359(99)80006-2

Açıkalın, S., & Gül, E. (2006). Sosyal Sınıflarda Tüketimin Sınıf Belirleyicilik Rolü. *Sosyal Ekonomik Araştırmalar Dergisi, 6*(12), 15–28.

Afonso, A. & Jalles, J. T. (2011). *Economic performance and government size*. ECB Working Paper Series No. 1399. ECB. Germany.

Agarwal, M. & Samantha, S. (2014). Financial crisis of 2008 and shifting economic power: Is the convergence?. *China Report, 50,* 1, pp. 45-67.

Agarwal, M. (2010). Developing countries: Impact of the crisis and the response-implications for an approach to the G20 by Russia, India and China. *China Report, 46,* 1, pp. 71-87.

Aghion, P., & Howitt, P. (1992). A model of growth through creative destruction. *Econometrica, 60*(2), 323–352. doi:10.2307/2951599

Ahmed, A. S. (1998). *Islam Today*. London, UK: Tauris Publishers, I. B.

Aho, -S. K. (2014). Finland tourism policies: From helping to build new state identities to branding a modern specific destination. In C. Costa, E. Panyik, & D. Buhalis, *European Tourism Planning and Organisation Systems The EU Member States* (pp. 44-60). Bristol, UK: Channel View Publications.

Aigner, D., Lovell, C. A. K., & Schmidt, P. (1977). Formulation and estimation of stochastic frontier production function models. *Journal of Econometrics, 6*(1), 21–37. doi:10.1016/0304-4076(77)90052-5

Akansel, I. (2016). New institutional economics (NIE): Origins of neoliberalism. *China-USA Business Review, 15*(1), 14–32.

Akbulut, Ö. (2007). Kamu Yönetiminde İşletmecilik Sorunu. *Mülkiye Journal, 254*, 73–86.

Akcay, U. (2013). Sermayenin Uluslararasılaşması ve Devletin Dönüşümü: Teknokratik Otoriterizmin Yükselişi. *Praksis, 30-31*, 11–39.

Akdemir, E. (2018). Avrupa Birliği'nin Dış İlişkileri ve Politikası: Avrupa Birliği'nin Bütünleş (eme)mesi Üzerine Bir İnceleme. *Ankara Avrupa Çalışmaları Dergisi, 17*(2), 181–218. doi:10.32450/aacd.511238

Akdemir, S. (2001). Yapısal Uyum Programları ve Uygulamalarının Değerlendirilmesi. *Ekonomik Yaklasim Association, 12*(40), 45–72. doi:10.5455/ey.10339

Akdeniz, H. (2005). Göç,Kentleşme ve Kentsel Yoksulluk Bağlamında Kap-Kaç Olgusu. Mülkiye Dergisi[Civil Service Journal], *29*(249), 161-187. Retrieved from http://dergipark.gov.tr/mulkiye/issue/249/1027

Akıncı, M. (2013). *Ekonomik Özgürlükler İle Ekonomik Büyüme Arasındaki İlişki: Gelişmiş, Gelişmekte Olan ve Azgelişmiş Ülkeler Üzerine Bir Uygulama, (Yayımlanmamış Doktora Tezi).* Erzurum, Turkey: Atatürk Üniversitesi Sosyal Bilimler Enstitüsü.

Akkerman, A. (2014). Towards a phenomenology of the winter-city: Urbanization and mind through the little ice age and its sequels. University of Saskatchewan. *Studia Phenomenological, 14*, 161–189. doi:10.5840tudphaen2014149

Aksoy, Ş. (2003). *Yeni Sağ ve Devletin Değişimi, Türkiye'de Kamu Yönetimi* (B. Aykaç, Ş. Durgun, & H. Yayman, Eds.). Ankara, Turkey: Yargı Press.

Aktan, C. C. (2006). Kurumsal İktisat, Kurallar, Kurumlar ve Ekonomik Gelisme. Sermaye Piyasası Kurulu Yayınları, Yayın no: 194, Ankara, Turkey.

Aktan, C. C. (Ed.). (2006). Kurumsal İktisat, Kurallar, Kurumlar ve Ekonomik Gelişme. Sermaye Piyasası Kurulu Yayınları, (194).

Aktan, C. C., & Vural, T. (2006). Ekonomi Politikası Yönetiminde Mali ve Parasal Kurallar. *Kurumsal İktisat Kurallar, Kurumlar ve Ekonomik Gelişme*. In C. C. Aktan (Ed.), *Sermaye Piyasası Kurulu Kurumsal Araştırmalar Serisi. No: 2. Yayın No. 194* (pp. 119–135). Ankara, Turkey: SPK.

Aktan, C. C., & Vural, T. (2006). Yeni Kurumsal İktisat. *Kurumsal İktisat Kurallar, Kurumlar ve Ekonomik Gelişme*. In C. C. Aktan (Ed.), *Sermaye Piyasası Kurulu Kurumsal Araştırmalar Serisi No: 2, Yayın No. 194* (pp. 19–43). Ankara, Turkey: SPK.

Akyüz, Y. (1977). *Sermaye bölüşüm büyüme*. Ankara, Turkey: Ankara Üniversitesi Basımevi.

Alaghehband, F. K., Rivard, S., Wu, S., & Goyette, S. (2011). An assessment of the use of transaction cost theory in information technology outsourcing. *The Journal of Strategic Information Systems*, *20*(2), 125–138. doi:10.1016/j.jsis.2011.04.003

Alan, S. (2016). *Üretim Toplumundan Tüketim Toplumuna Geçiş ve Değer Dönüşümü*. İstanbul, Turkey: Toplumsal Değişim Sempozyumu.

Alavi, H., & Khusro, A. (1971). Pakistan The burden of US Aid. In R. I. Rhodes (Ed.), *Imperialism and Underdevelopment*. New York, NY: Monthly Review Press.

Aligica, P. D. (2014). *Institutional diversity and political economy: the Ostroms and beyond*. USA: Oxford University Press.

Al-Yousif, Y. K. (2004, September). Oil economies and globalization: The case of the GCC countries. *Middle Eastern and African Economies*, *6*(2), 167–176.

Amin, S. (1977). *Accumulation on a world scale, A critique of the theory of underdevelopment*. New York, NY: Monthly Review Press.

Anderson, E. (1985). The salesperson as outside agent or employee: A transaction cost analysis. *Marketing Science*, *4*(3), 234–254. doi:10.1287/mksc.4.3.234

Anderson, E., & Weitz, B. (1992). The use of pledges to build and sustain commitment in distribution channels. *JMR, Journal of Marketing Research*, *70*(2), 18–34. doi:10.1177/002224379202900103

Angeloni, I. (2009). The Pittsburgh G20 Summit. *Inter Economics*, *44*(September/October), 262–263. doi:10.100710272-009-0304-0

Arat, Z. F. (1988). Democracy and economic development: Modernization theory revisited. *Comparative Politics*, *21*(1), 21–36. doi:10.2307/422069

Archibugil, D., & Michie, J. (1998). Technical change, growth and trade: New departures in institutional economics. *Journal of Economic Surveys*, *12*(3), 1–20.

Arestis, P., & Sawyer, M. (2007). Neoliberalizm ve Üçüncü Yol. In A. Saad-Filho & D. Johnston (Eds.), *Neoliberalizm: Muhalif bir Seçki* (BaşlıŞ.ÖncelT., Trans.). (pp. 293–302). İstanbul, Turkey: Yordam Kitap.

Argin, S. (1992). Kapitalist Toplumda İşin ve İşgücünün Kaderi: Post-Fordizm. *Birikim*, *41*. Retrieved from http://www.birikimdergisi.com/birikim-yazi/4560/kapitalist-toplumda-isin-ve-isgucunun-kaderi-post-fordizm#.WVV8LIiLTIW

Arıboğan, D. Ü. (2001). *Globalleşme Senaryosunun Aktörleri*. İstanbul, Turkey: Der Press.

Arklan, Ü., & Taşdemir, E. (2008). Bilgi Toplumu ve İletişim: Bilginin Yayılması Sürecinde Kitle İletişim Araçları ve İnternet. *Selçuk Üniversitesi İletişim Fakültesi Akademik Dergisi, 5*(3), 67–80.

Arnold, U. (2000). New dimensions of outsourcing: A combination of transaction cost economics and the core competencies concept. *European Journal of Purchasing & Supply Management, 6*(1), 23–29. doi:10.1016/S0969-7012(99)00028-3

Arrelano, M. (2004). *Panel data econometrics (Advanced tests in econometrics)*. New York, NY: Oxford University Press.

Arrow, K. J. (1962). The economic implications of learning by doing. *The Review of Economic Studies, 29*(3), 155–173. doi:10.2307/2295952

Arrow, K. J. (1994). *Methodological Individualism and Social Knowledge. The American Economic Review, 84*(2), 1–9.

Arslan, R. (2008). Laik Türkiye Cumhuriyeti, Ordu ve Burjuva Sınıfı. Gazi Üniversitesi İktisadi ve İdari Bilimler Fakültesi Dergisi [Gazi University Administration and Economic Sciences Journal], *10*(3), 33-44. Retrieved from http://dergipark.gov.tr/gaziuiibfd/issue/28327/301017

Arslan, Ü., & Ökten, N. Z. (2010). The relations between FDI and democracy: Evidence from Turkey. *International Research Journal of Finance and Economics, 56*, 111–123.

Ashley, W. J. (1894). Roscher's Programme of 1843. *The Quarterly Journal of Economics, 9*(1), 99–105. doi:10.2307/1883638

Ata, A. Y. (2009). *Kurumsal İktisat Çerçevesinde Yolsuzluğun Fırsat Ve Motivasyonları: AB Ülkeleri Üzerine Bir İnceleme*. (Unpublished doctoral dissertation), Çukurova Üniversitesi, Sosyal Bilimler Enstitüsü, Turkey.

Ataay, F. & Acar, E. (2008). Devletin Yeniden Yapılandırılması ve Yerelleşme. *İktisat Dergisi, 500*. Retrieved from http://www.yayed.org/id15-gorusler/faruk-ataay-ergul-acar-devletin-yeniden-yapilandirilmasi-ve-yerellesme.php

Ataay, F. (2006). *Neoliberalizm ve Devletin Yeniden Yapılandırılması: Türkiye'de Kamu Reformu Üzerine İncelemeler*. Ankara, Turkey: De Ki Basım Yayın.

Aubert, B. A., Patry, M., & Rivard, S. (Eds.). (2002). *Managing IT outsourcing risk: Lessons learned information systems outsourcing*. Berlin, Germany: Springer.

Aubert, B. A., Rivard, S., & Patry, M. (1996). Development of measures to assess dimensions of IS operation transactions. *Omega, 24*(6), 661–680. doi:10.1016/S0305-0483(96)00019-9

Avio, K. L. (2004). A modest proposal for institutional economics. *Journal of Economic Issues, 38*(3), 715–745. doi:10.1080/00213624.2004.11506726

Axelrod, R. (1986). An evolutionary approach to norms. *The American Political Science Review, 80*(4), 1095–1111. doi:10.1017/S0003055400185016

Aydın, T. (1997). *Bilgi Toplumu ve Demokrasi*. Trabzon, Turkey: Efor Masaüstü Yayıncılık.

Aydoğan, F. (2009). Tüketim Kültürünün Gölgesinde Kentler. *Marmara Üniversitesi İktisadi ve İdari Bilimler Dergisi, 27*(2), 203–215.

Ayres, C. E. (1977). In memoriam Clarence Ayres. *Journal of Economic Issues, 11*(3), 475–483. doi:10.1080/00213624.1977.11503458

Aysan, A. F. (2006). *Yönetisim ve Kurumlar Terimlerinin Iktisat Literaturundeki Yukselisi*. Retrieved from http://www.econ.boun.edu.tr/content/wp/ISS_EC_06_16.pdf

Aytuğ, H. K. (2011). Avrupa Birliği Ülkelerinde Tarımsal Turizm Uygulamaları ve Türkiye'de Gelişme Potansiyeli: Yeşilköy Örneği. İzmir: Dokuz Eylül Üniversitesi, Sosyal Bilimler Enstitüsü Yayımlanmamış Doktora Tezi. -Bachvarov, M. (2006). Tourism in Bulgaria. In D. Hall, M. Smith, & B. Marciszewska (Eds.), *Tourism in the new Europe The challenges and opportunities of EU enlargement* (pp. 241–255). Oxfordshire, UK: CABI.

Azman-Saini, W.N.W, Tun, Y., & Ibrahim, S. (2013). International evidence on the link between foreign direct investment and economic freedom. *Pertanika Journal of Social Sciences and Humanities, 21*(S), 157-170.

Azman-Saini, W. N. W., Baharumshah, A. Z., & Law, S. H. (2010). Foreign direct investment, economic freedom and economic growth: International evidence. *Economic Modelling, 27*(5), 1079–1089. doi:10.1016/j.econmod.2010.04.001

Badri, A. K., & Sheshgelanib, A. (2017). Economic freedom and FDI in selected developing countries. *Noble International Journal of Economics and Financial Research, 2*(5), 82–87.

Bahli, B., & Rivard, S. (2003). The information technology outsourcing risk: A transaction cost and agency theory-based perspective. *Journal of Information Technology, 18*(3), 211–221. doi:10.1080/0268396032000130214

Bain, S. J. (1971). Chamberlin's impact on microeconomic theory. In H. Townsend (Ed.), Price theory (253-287). UK: Penguin Books.

Bakan, S. & Eren, S. S. (2017). 2000'lerde Türkiye'de Burjuvazi Sınıfının Siyasal Dönüşümü. Birey ve Toplum Sosyal Bilimler Dergisi [Individual and Society Social Sciences Journal], 7(1), 127-149. Retrieved from http://dergipark.gov.tr/birtop/issue/32816/364748

Balcı, A. (2005). *Kamu Yönetiminde Çağdaş Yaklaşımlar ve Kamu Hizmet Sunumuna Etkileri.* Ankara, Turkey: Hizmet İş Union Press.

Balkız, Ö. (2007). *Sanayi Sonrası Dönüşüm: Ekonomik Analizler*, (Unpublished dissertation), Adnan Menderes University, Social Sciences Institute, Turkey.

Baltacı, C. (2004). Yeni Sağ Üzerine Bir Eleştiri. *Süleyman Demirel University Economic and Administrative Sciences Faculty Journal, 2*, 359–373.

Baltagi, B. (2001). *Econometric analysis of panel data* (2nd ed.). UK: John Wiley & Sons.

Barbash, J. (2005). John. R. Commons: Pioneer of labor economics. *University of California Working Paper,* 42-49. Retrieved from http://www.bls.gov/1989/05/art4full.pdf

Barro, R. J. (1996) "Determinants of economic growth: A cross-country empirical study", *NBER Working Paper*, Sayı: 5698, 40-41.

Barro, R. J. (1990). Government spending in a simple model of endogenous growth. *Journal of Political Economy, 98*(5), 103–125. doi:10.1086/261726

Barthelemy, J. (2003). The hard and soft sides of IT outsourcing management. *European Management Journal, 21*(5), 539–548. doi:10.1016/S0263-2373(03)00103-8

Bas, D. G. (2011). *Kapitalizmin Istikrarsızlıgı: Veblen, Keynes ve Minsky*, (Unpublished doctoral dissertation), Hacettepe Üniversitesi, Sosyal Bilimler Enstitüsü, Turkey.

Bas, D. G. (2013). Kurum İçgüdü ve Alıskanlık Kavramları Temelinde Veblen'in Kurumsal Evrim Teorisi. *Amme Dergisi, 46*(4), 45-65. Retrieved from http://www.todaie.edu.tr/resimler/ekler/

Başar, S., & Yıldız, Ş. (2009). İktisadi Büyümenin Demokratikleşme Üzerindeki Etkileri. *Balıkesir Üniversitesi Sosyal Bilimler Enstitüsü Dergisi, 12*(21), 56–75.

Baş-Dinar, G. (2014). Wesley Mitchell'ın İktisat Bilimine Katkısı Üzerine Bir Değerlendirme [An Evolution on Wesley Mitchell to Economics Science]. *İktisat ve Toplum. Economics and Society*, *46*, 59–68.

Battese, G. E., & Coelli, T. J. (1988). Prediction of firm-level technical efficiencies with a generalized frontier production function and panel data. *Journal of Econometrics*, *38*(3), 387–399. doi:10.1016/0304-4076(88)90053-X

Battese, G. E., & Coelli, T. J. (1992). Frontier production functions, technical efficiency and panel data: With application to paddy farmers in India. *Journal of Productivity Analysis*, *3*(1-2), 153–169. doi:10.1007/BF00158774

Battese, G. E., & Coelli, T. J. (1995). A model for technical inefficiency effects in a stochastic frontier production function for panel data. *Empirical Economics*, *20*(2), 325–332. doi:10.1007/BF01205442

Baumol, J. W. (1982). Contestable markets: An uprising in the theory of industry structure. *The American Economic Review*, *7*(1), 1–15.

Bausch, T., & Unseld, C. (2018). Winter tourism in Germany is much more than skiing consumer motives and implications to alpine destination marketing. *Journal of Vacation Marketing*, *24*(3), 203–217. doi:10.1177/1356766717691806

Bayraç, H. N. (2003). Yeni Ekonomi'nin Toplumsal, Ekonomik ve Teknolojik Boyutları. *Osmangazi Üniversitesi Sosyal Bilimler Dergisi*, *4*(1), 41–62.

Bayraktar, F. (2015). 'Yönetişim' Paradigması ve Neoliberalizm: Çelişki ve Kopuş mu Uyum ve Süreklilik mi? *Ardahan Üniversitesi İktisadi ve İdari Bilimler Fakültesi Dergisi*, *2*, 71–94.

Bayraktutan, Y. & Fatma Kethudaoğlu (2018). Ar-Ge ve İktisadi Büyüme İlişkisi: OECD Örneği [The relationship between R&D and economic growth: The case of OECD], *Uluslararası Sosyal Araştırmalar Dergisi*, 10(53), 679-694.

Bayraktutan, Y. & Hanife Bıdırdı (2016). Teknoloji ve Rekabetçilik: Temel Kavramlar ve Endeksler Bağlamında Bir Değerlendirme [Technology and Competitiveness: An Assessment in Terms of Main Concepts and Indexes], *Akademik Araştırmalar ve Çalışmalar Dergisi*, 8(14), 1-24.

Bayramoglu, S. (2002). Küreselleşmenin Yeni Siyasal İktidar Modeli: Yönetişim. *Praksis*, *7*, 85–116.

Bayramoglu, S. (2003). Düzenleyici Devlet Düzenlenirken: OECD Türkiye Raporu Üzerine Eleştirel Bir Çözümleme. *Praksis*, *9*, 143–162.

Beeson, M., & Bell, S. (2009). The G-20 and international economic governance: Hegemony, collectivism, or both? *Global Governance*, *15*(1), 67–86. doi:10.1163/19426720-01501005

Beheshtitabar, E. & Irgaliyev, A. (2008). *The impact of economic freedom on FDI inflows to developing countries: The case of the Middle East* (Unpublished bachelor thesis). Jönköping University, Sweden.

Belek, I. (1999). *Postkapitalist Paradigmalar*. İstanbul, Turkey: Sorun Yayınları.

Bensghir, T. K. (1996). *Bilgi Teknolojileri ve Örgütsel Değişim*. Ankara, Turkey: TODAİE.

Berggren, N. (2003). The benefits of economic freedom: A survey. *Independent Review*, *8*(2), 193–211.

Bhagwati, J. N. (2002). Democracy and development: Cruel dilemma or symbiotic relationship? *Review of Development Economics*, *6*(2), 151–162. doi:10.1111/1467-9361.00147

Biezberg, I. (2014). Types of capitalism in Latin America. Revue Invervention Economiques Papers in Political Economy. Retrieved from http://interventionseconomiques.revues.org/1772

Bilecen, H., & Kibis, E. Y. (2012). Economic growth and democracy in Turkey. *Yönetim Bilimleri Dergisi*, *10*(20), 137–155.

Bocock, R. (2009). *Tüketim, çev. Kutluk, İ.* Ankara, Turkey: Dost Yayınları.

Bocutoglu, E. (2012). *İktisadi Düşünceler Tarihi.* Trabzon, Turkey: Murathan Yayınevi.

Boratav, K. & Yeldan, E. (2006). Turkey, 1980–2000: Financial liberalization, macroeconomic (in)stability, and patterns of distribution. In L. Taylor (Ed.), External liberalization in Asia, post-socialist Europe, and Brazil. pp. 417-455.

Boratav, K. (2013). *Türkiye İktisat Tarihi 1908-2009.* Ankara, Turkey: İmge Kitabevi Yayınları.

Boschma, R. (2009). Evolutionary economic geography and its implications for regional innovation. *Journal of Policy Utrecht University, 5*(1), 55–63. Retrieved from http://econ.geo.uu.nl/peeg/peeg.html

Bourdieu, P. (1998, December). The essence of neoliberalism. *Le Monde Diplometique.* Retrieved from http://mondediplo.com/1998/12/08bourdieu

Bourdieu, P. (1982). *Distinction: A social critique of the judgment of taste.* Cambridge, MA: Harvard University Press.

Brunner, N. & Gökdere, A. Y. (1969). Çin Ekonomisi. Ankara Üniversitesi Hukuk Fakültesi Dergisi [Law Faculty Journal], 26(3). Retrieved from http://dergipark.gov.tr/auhfd/issue/42969/520225

Bulutay, T. (1975). *Türkiye'nin 1923-1972 Dönemindeki İktisadi Büyümesi Üzerine Düşünceler. Maliye Enstitüsü Konferansları 23. Seri.* İ. Ü. İktisat Fakültesi.

Bundă, N. R., Ţiţei, A. M., & Jaliu, D. D. (2012). A new institutional approach of the complex correlation between economic freedom and economic growth. *European Journal of Science and Theology, 8*, 75–84.

Burkhart, R. E. & Lewis-Beck, M. S. (1994) Comparative democracy: The economic development thesis. *American Political Science Review, 88*(4), 903–910.

Burrows, R., & Marsh, C. (1992). Consumption, class and contemporary sociology. In *Consumption and Class* (pp. 1–14). London, UK: Palgrave Macmillan. doi:10.1007/978-1-349-21725-0_1

Busse, M. (2003). Democracy and FDI. HWWA discussion paper No. 220, Hamburg Institute of International Economics, Germany.

Butkiewicz, J. L., & Yanikkaya, H. (2005). The effects of IMF and world bank lending on long-run economic growth : An empirical analysis. *World Development, 33*(3), 371–391. doi:10.1016/j.worlddev.2004.09.006

Çalık, D., & Çınar, Ö. P. (2009). *Geçmişten Günümüze Bilgi Yaklaşımları, Bilgi Toplumu ve İnternet. XIV.* İstanbul, Turkey: Türkiye'de İnternet Konferansı.

Callaghan, M. (2014). The G20, IMF and global imbalances: The policymakers' perspective. In M. Callaghan, C. Ghate, S. Pickford, & F. Rathinam (Eds.), Global cooperation among G20 countries (pp. 83–94). India: Springer India. doi:10.1007/978-81-322-1659-9_7

Callaghan, M., Ghate, C., Pickford, S., & Rathinam, F. (2014). Global cooperation among G20 countries: Responding to the crisis and restoring growth. In Global Cooperation Among G20 Countries. pp. 1-21.

Callaghan, M., Carmignani, F., Makin, A. J., & Strube, D. (2014). G20 and development. *South Asian Journal of Macroeconomics and Public Finance, 3*(2), 155–173. doi:10.1177/2277978714548627

Candan, E. (2007). Dünya Bankası Kredilerine İlişkin Genel Esaslar, Proje Kredilerinin Özellikleri, *Avantaj ve Dezavantajları. Sayıştay Dergisi, 18*(64), 41–65.

Canlıoğlu, G. (2008). *Değişen Toplum Yapılarında Bilginin Değişen Konumu (Basılmamış yüksek lisans tezi).* İstanbul, Turkey: Marmara Üniversitesi Türkiyat Araştırmaları Enstitüsü.

Cannon, J. P., Achrol, R. S., & Gundlach, G. T. (2000). Contracts, norms, and plural form governance. *Journal of the Academy of Marketing Science*, *28*(2), 180–194. doi:10.1177/0092070300282001

Canpolat, N. (2004). Merkez Bankası Yüzmekten Korkuyor mu?, *İşletme-Finans Journal,* July, 76–85.

Çapoğlu, G. (1991). *Prices, profits and financial structures.* Aldershot, UK: Edward Elgar.

Carroll, W. K. (2007, May). *Tracking the transnational capitalist class: The view from on high.* Paper presented at the 27th International Sunbelt Social Network Conference, Corfu, Greece.

Carroll, L. (1998). *Alice's Adventures in Wonderland and Through the Looking Glass.* London, UK: Penguin Books.

Carroll, W. K. (2012). Global, transnational, regional, national: The need for nuance in theorizing global capitalism. *Critical Sociology*, *38*(3), 365–371. doi:10.1177/0896920511434265

Carson, S. J., Madhok, A., & Wu, T. (2006). Uncertainty, opportunism, and governance: The effects of volatility and ambiguity on formal and relational contracting. *Academy of Management Journal*, *49*(5), 1058–1077. doi:10.5465/amj.2006.22798187

Carvalho, F. J. (2000). The changing role and strategies of the IMF and the perspectives for the emerging countries. *Brazilian Journal of Political Economy*, *20*(1), 3–17.

Case, K. E., Fair, R. C., & Oster, S. M. (2014). *Principles of Macroeconomics.* London, UK: Pearson Education Publications.

Çavdar, T. (1982). *Türkiye'de Liberalizmin Doğuşu.* İstanbul, Turkey: Uygarlık Yayınları.

Çavdar, T. (2003). *Türkiye Ekonomisinin Tarihi, 1900-1960.* Ankara, Turkey: İmge Kitabevi Yayınları.

CBRT (The Central Bank of the Republic of Turkey). (2018). *Electronic Data Delivery System.* Retrieved from https://evds2.tcmb.gov.tr/

Celasun, M. & Rodrik, D. (1989). Trade regime and an anatomy of export performance. In Developing country debt and economic performance, 3: Country studies-Indonesia, Korea, Philippines, Turkey, pp. 716-731. Chicago, IL: University of Chicago Press.

Çelik, M. Y. (2010). Küreselleşme Kalkınma İlişkisi. *Dumlupınar Üniversitesi Social Sciences Institute Journal, 26,* 183–196.

Çetin, T. (2012). *Yeni kurumsal iktisat.* Retrieved from http://dergipark.gov.tr/download/article-file/101303

Çetin, T. (2012). Yeni Kurumsal İktisat. *Sosyoloji Konferansları No: 45.* Retrieved from journals.istanbul.edu.tr/iusoskon/article/viewFile/1023018512/10230177

Cetin, T. (2012). Yeni Kurumsal İktisat. *Sosyoloji Konferansları, 45,* 43–73.

Çetin, T. (2016). Kurumsal ve Organizasyonel İktisat Üzerine [On Institutional and Organizational Economics]. *İktisat ve Toplum. Economics and Society, 64,* 10–19.

Cevizci, A. (2002). *Felsefe Sözlüğü.* İstanbul, Turkey: Paradigma Yayınları.

Chang, H. J. (2003). *Globalization, economic development and the role of the state.* London, UK: Zed Books Press.

Chang, H. J. (2011). Institutions and economic development: Theory, policy and history. *Journal of Institutional Economics, 7*(4), 473–498. doi:10.1017/S1744137410000378

Chang, H. J. (2016). *Ekonomi Rehberi* [Economy Guide]. Ankara, Turkey: Say Yayınları. [Say Publishing]

Chang, H. J., & Ve Gabriel, I. (2016). *Kalkınma Yeniden.* Ankara, Turkey: İmage Press.

Chavance, B. (2009). *Institutional economics. (F. Wells, Trans.) Routledge Press.* Taylor & Francis e-Library.

Chhotray, V., & Stoker, G. (2009). *Governance theory and practice. A cross disciplinary approach.* London, UK: Palgrave Macmillan. doi:10.1057/9780230583344

Chiu, C., Gries, P., Torelli, C., & Cheng, S. Y. Y. (2011). Toward a social psychology of globalization. *The Journal of Social Issues, 67*(4), 663–676. doi:10.1111/j.1540-4560.2011.01721.x

Chossudovsky, M. (1999). *Yoksulluğun Küreselleşmesi: IMF ve Dünya Bankası Reformlarının İçyüzü* (N. Domaniç, Trans.). İstanbul, Turkey: Çivi Yazıları Press.

City of Sapporo. (2018). Retrieved from https://www.city.sapporo.jp/somu/kokusai/wwcam/history.html

Clarke, S. (1991). The state debate. In S. Clarke (Ed.), *The state debate* (pp. 1–69). London, UK: Macmillan. doi:10.1007/978-1-349-21464-8_1

Clark, J. M. (1961). *Competition as a dynamic process.* Washington, DC: Brookings Institution.

Coase, R. H. (2005). The Institutional Structure of Production. In C. Ménard & M. M. Shirley (Eds.), Handbook of New Institutional Economics (31-40). Springer, The Netherlands. doi:10.1007/0-387-25092-1_3

Coase, R. (1984). The new institutional economics. *Journal of Institutional and Theoretical Economics, 140*(2), 229–231.

Coase, R. H. (1937). The nature of the firm. *Economica, 4*(16), 386–405. doi:10.1111/j.1468-0335.1937.tb00002.x

Coase, R. H. (1991). The institutional structure of production. *The American Economic Review, 82*(4), 713–719.

Cohen, L. (2003). *A Consumers' Republic.* New York, NY: Random House.

Colaresi, M., & Thompson, W. R. (2003). The economic development–democratization relationship. *Comparative Political Studies, 36*(4), 397–398. doi:10.1177/0010414003251174

Cole, J. H. (2003). The contribution of economic freedom to world economic growth, 1980-99. *The Cato Journal, 23*(2), 189–198.

Commons, J. R. (1931). Institutional economics. *The Journal of American Economic Review, 21*(4), 88–102. Retrieved from http://www.jstor.org/stable/495

Cooper, A. F. (2010). The G20 as an improvised crisis committee and/or a contested 'steering committee' for the world. *International Affairs, 86*(3), pp. 741-757.

Cordes, C. (2005). Veblen's 'instinct of workmanship', its cognitive foundations, and some implications for economic theory. *Journal of Economic Issues, 39*(1), 1–20. doi:10.1080/00213624.2005.11506778

Cornwell, C., Schmidt, P., & Sickles, R. C. (1990). Production frontiers with cross-sectional and time-series variation in efficiency levels. *Journal of Econometrics, 46*(1-2), 185–200. doi:10.1016/0304-4076(90)90054-W

Crawford, R. (1991). *The era of human capital.* USA: Harper Business.

Crocker, K. J., & Masten, S. E. (1988). Mitigating contractual hazards: Unilateral options and contract length. *The Rand Journal of Economics, 19*(3), 327–343. doi:10.2307/2555660

Curran, L. (2009). The impact of the financial and economic crisis on world trade and trade policy. *Inter Economics,* (September/October): 264–273.

Daraio, C., & Simar, L. (2007). *Advanced robust and nonparametric methods in efficiency analysis: Methodology and applications*. New York, NY: Springer Science & Business Media.

Davis, J. B. (2012). The 2012 Veblen-Commons award recipient, Geoffrey M. Hodgson. *Journal of Economic Issues, 46*(2), 263–264. doi:10.2753/JEI0021-3624460201

Debreu, G. (1951). The coefficient of resource utilization. *Econometrica, 19*(3), 273–292. doi:10.2307/1906814

Demir, M. A. & Bilik, M. (2018). Türkiye'nin ticaret etkinliği: Stokastik sınır çekim modeli yaklaşımı. *Ömer Halisdemir Üniversitesi İktisadi ve İdari Bilimler Fakültesi Dergisi, 11*(1), 29-48.

Demir, M. A., Bilik, M., & Aydın, Ü. (2018). Effects of political and socio-economic indicators on foreign direct investments: Stochastic frontier analysis. *İnsan ve Toplum Bilimleri Araştırmaları Dergisi, 7*(2), 1078-1096.

Demirci, M. (2013). Yönetişim, Otorite ve Meşruiyet. In F. N. Genç (Ed.), *Yönetişim: Türk Kamu Yönetimine Yansımaları* (pp. 1–62). Konya, Turkey: Çizgi Kitabevi.

Demirel, S., & Yeğen, C. (2015). Tüketim, Postmodernizm ve Kapitalizm Örgüsü. *Ankara Üniversitesi İLEF Dergisi, 2*(1), 115–138.

Demir, G. (1999). *Asya Krizi ve IMF*. İstanbul, Turkey: Der Press.

Demirkan, E., & Kaya, V. (2012). An analysis of relation between economic growth and democratization: An empiric application (a sample of Turkey). *Yönetim ve Ekonomi, 19*(2), 123–132.

Demir, Ö. (1996). *Kurumcu İktisat*. Ankara, Turkey: Vadi Yayınları.

den Aktaran Arat, Z. F. (n.d.). Democracy and development: Modernization theory revisited. Comparative Politics, 21(1), 22.</edb>

Dickson, D. (1992). Alternatif Teknoloji [Alternative Technology], (Çev. Nezih Erdoğan), İstanbul, Turkey: Ayrıntı Yayıncılık.

Dickson, P. R. (2000). Understanding the trade winds: The global evolution of production, consumption, and the internet. *The Journal of Consumer Research, 27*(1), 115–122. doi:10.1086/314313

DİE. (1973). *Türkiye'de Toplumsal ve Ekonomik Gelişmenin 50 Yılı*. Ankara, Turkey: Başbakanlık İstatistik Enstitüsü Matbaası.

Dikici, E. (2017). Tüketim Algısındaki Değişim; Kitle İletişim Araçları ve Tüketim İlişkisi. *Sosyal ve Beşeri Bilimler Dergisi, 1*(1), 58–85.

Dikmen, A. A. (2017). *Makine, İş, Kapitalizm ve İnsan*. İstanbul, Turkey: NotaBene.

Dinopoulos, E. & Şener, F. (2007). "New directions in Schumpeterian growth theory". Retrieved from https://ideas.repec.org/h/elg/eechap/2973_42.html

Doğan, A. (2005). Demokrasi ve ekonomik gelişme. *Erciyes Üniversitesi İktisadi ve İdari Bilimler Fakültesi Dergisi*, (25), 1-19.

Doğruel, F., & Doğruel, S. (2010). *Türkiye'de Cari Açık: Temel Sorunlar ve Dinamikler. Küresel Kriz Çerçevesinde Türkiye'nin Cari Açık Sorunsalı içinde* (T. Subaşat & H. Yetkiner, Eds.). Ankara, Turkey: Efil Yayınevi.

Dollar, D., & Kraay, A. (2003). Institutions, trade and growth. *Journal of Monetary Economics, 50*(1), 133–162. doi:10.1016/S0304-3932(02)00206-4

Dolls, M., Peichi, A., & Zimmermann, K. Z. (2012). *A challenge for the G20: Global debt brakes and transnational fiscal supervisory councils* (pp. 31–38). Debt Brakes-Intereconomics.

Dosi, G. (1998). Sources, procedures, and microeconomic effects of innovation. *Journal of Economic Literature, 26*, 1120–1171.

Doucouliagos, C., & Ulubaşoğlu, M. A. (2006). Economic freedom and economic growth: Does specification make a difference? *European Journal of Political Economy, 22*(1), 60–81. doi:10.1016/j.ejpoleco.2005.06.003

Dubiel, H. (1998). *Yeni Muhafazakarlık Nedir?* (E. Özbek, Trans.). İstanbul, Turkey: İletişim Press.

Dugger, W. M., & Waller, W. (1996). Radical institutionalism: From technological to democratic instrumentalism. *Review of Social Economy, 2*(2), 169–189. doi:10.1080/00346769600000035

Duman, M. (2007). Türkiye'de Burjuva Sınıfının Sosyal Profili. Sosyoekonomi, 5(5). Retrieved from http://dergipark.gov.tr/sosyoekonomi/issue/21065/226810

Dumludağ, D., & Şükrüoğlu, D. (2007). The impact of macroeconomic and institutional variables on foreign direct investment flows in emerging markets. *Marmara Üniversitesi İİBF Dergisi, 23*(2), 133–136.

Duncan, G. (2013, November). The evolution of UAE retail: From corner shops to mega malls. Retrieved from https://www.thenational.ae/business/the-evolution-of-uae-retail-from-corner-shops-to-mega-malls-1.652113

Dursun, D. (2002). *Siyaset Bilimi*. İstanbul Beta Basım Yayım Dağıtım A.Ş.

Dutt, A. K. (1987). Competition, monopoly power and the uniform rate of profits. *The Review of Radical Political Economics, 19*(4), 55–72. doi:10.1177/048661348701900405

Eatwell, J. (1982). Competition. In I. Bradley & M. Howard (Eds.), Classical and Marxian Political Economy (203-228). London, UK: Macmillan.

Egger, R., Novak, J., & Taurer, W. (2014). Austria: Where tourism has tradition. In C. Costa, E. Panyik, & D. Buhalis (Eds.), *European tourism planning and organisation systems The EU member states* (pp. 163–182). Bristol, UK: Channel View Publications.

Eğilmez, A. M. (1997). Dünya Bankası IMF ve Türkiye. İstanbul, Turkey: Creative Yayıncılık. 65.

Eğilmez, M. (2008). *Küresel Finans Krizi Piyasa Sisteminin Eleştirisi*. İstanbul, Turkey: Remzi Kitabevi.

Eğilmez, M. (2018). *Değişim Sürecinde Türkiye*. İstanbul, Turkey: Remzi Kitabevi. [Remzi Publishing]

Eichengreen, B. (2010). Lessons of the crisis for emerging markets. *International Economics and Economic Policy, 7*(1), 49–62. doi:10.100710368-010-0149-9

Elessawy, F. (2015, July). *Dubai City, A study in geography of beauty*. Conference Paper (PDF available) Conference: The Annual International Conference of Geography Dept. Alexandria University, at Alexandria

Elessawy, F. (2017). The boom: Population and urban growth of Dubai City. Retrieved from https://www.researchgate.net/publication/317564338_The_Boom_Population_and_Urban_Growth_of_Dubai_City

Embong, A. R. (2000). Globalisation and transnational class relations: Some problems of conceptualization. *Third World Quarterly, 21*(6), 989–1000. doi:10.1080/01436590020011990

Ener, M. & Demircan, S. E. (2004). *Küreselleşen Dünyada IMF Politikaları ve Türkiye*, Ankara, Turkey: Roma Press.

Epstein, P. (1999). Wesley Mitchell's grand design and its critics, the theory and measurement of business cycles. *Journal of Economic Issues, 33*(3), 525–553. doi:10.1080/00213624.1999.11506185

Ercan, F. (2006). Suskun Adamın Baladı: Latin Amerika Üzerinden Venezüella'ya Dair Düşünceler. [Praksis Journal]. *Praksis Dergisi, 14*, 67–108.

Erdogan, D. (2019). Sözleşme süresinin belirlenmesi: İşlem maliyeti teorisi bakışıyla yer hizmeti sözleşmeleri üzerine ampirik bir araştırma. *Gaziantep University Journal of Social Sciences, 18*(2), 623–637.

Erdoğdu, S. (2004). Kamu Personel Rejiminde Uyarlanma, *Kamu Yönetimi Temel Kanunu Symposium*, Ankara, Turkey: TMMOB.

Erdönmez Ataman, P., & Tulay, B. (1999). Küresel Krizlere Yeni Yaklaşımlar. *Bankacılar Journal, 31*, 64–76.

Erim, N. (2011). *İktisadi Düşünce Tarihi.* Umuttepe Yayınları, Kocaeli.

Erkan, H. & Erkan, C. (2007). Bilgi Toplumu Ve Ekonomik Kalkınma, *UNAK'07 Sayısal Dünyada Yeni Paradigmalar: Sınırsız Kütüphaneler.* Retrieved from http:/www.deu.edu.tr/husnu.erkan

Erkan, H. (2019). Bilgi Toplumu'na İlişkin. Retrieved from http:/www.deu.edu.tr/userweb/husnu.erkan/BILGI_TOPLUMUNA_ILISKIN_NOT.doc. (Unpublished Scientific Paper).

Erkan, H. (1998). *Bilgi Toplumu ve Ekonomik Gelişme.* Türkiye İş Bankası Kültür Yayınları.

Erkan, H. (2004). *Ekonomi Sosyolojisi.* İzmir, Turkey: Barış Yayınları.

Eroğlu, M.Y. (2018). Kurumsal İktisatta Açılan Yeni Bir Pencere: Douglass C. North Perspektifinden Kurumların Değerlendirilmesi. *Optimum: Journal of Economics & Management Sciences/Ekonomi ve Yönetim Bilimleri Dergisi, 5*(2), 163-178.

Eryiğit, B. H., & Sarıca, A. (2018). IMF, Dünya Bankası, OECD'nin Yönetişim Yaklaşımı ve Kü-Yerelleşme. *Marmara Üniversitesi Siyasal Bilimler Dergisi, 6*(1), 61–74.

Erzurum Anatolia's Preface. (2018). Retrieved from http://www.goerzurum.net/en/tourism-in-erzurum/winter-tourism-in-erzurum

Escaith, H. (2009). Global supply chains in times of international crisis. *Inter Economics*, (September/October): 268–273.

Eser, E. Z. (2011). *Dünden Bugüne Teknoloji Transferi, Yüksek Lisans Tezi* [Master thesis]. T.C. Marmara Üniversitesi Sosyal Bilimler Enstitüsü. [Marmara University Social Sciences Institute]

Estol, J., & Font, X. (2016). European tourism policy: Its evolution and structure. *Tourism Management, 52*, 230–241. doi:10.1016/j.tourman.2015.06.007

European Commission. (2010). *Communication from the commission to the European parliament, the council, the European economic and social committee and the committee of the regions; Europe, the world's No 1 tourist destination a new political framework for tourism in Europe.* Brussels, Belgium: European Commission.

European Commission. (2017). Overview of EU Tourism Policy. Retrieved from https://ec.europa.eu/growth/sectors/tourism/policy-overview_en

Evenett, S. J. (2009). Systemic consequences of crisis era protectionism. *Inter Economics*, (September/October): 282–286.

Fagerberg, J. (2003). Schumpeter and the revival of evolutionary economics: An appraisal of the literature. *Journal of Evolutionary Economics, 13*(2), 125–159. doi:10.100700191-003-0144-1

Farazmand, H., & Moradi, M. (2015). Determinants of FDI: Does democracy matter? *Strategic Management, 20*(1), 38–46.

Farrell, M. J. (1957). The measurement of productive efficiency. *Journal of the Royal Statistical Society. Series A (General), 120*(3), 253–290. doi:10.2307/2343100

Fındıkçı, İ. (1996). *Bilgi Toplumunda Yöneticilerde Kendini Geliştirme.* İstanbul, Turkey: Kültür Koleji Eğitim Vakfı Yayınları.

Fine, B., & Harris, L. (1976). 'State expenditure in advanced capitalism': A critique. *New Left Review, 98*, 97–112.

Fink, C., Edelman, L. F., Hatten, K. J., & James, W. L. (2006). Transaction cost economics, resource dependence theory, and customer–supplier relationships. *Industrial and Corporate Change, 15*(3), 497–529. doi:10.1093/icc/dtl008

Firincioglu, S. (2015). Post Fordizm, Küreselleşme ve Endüstrideki Dönüşüm. *Kriz ve Kritik, 2*, 41–44.

Fortman, B. G. (1966). *The theory of competition policy.* Amsterdam, The Netherlands: North Holland Publishing Company.

Foster, J. B. (2017). Küreselleşmiş Tekelci-Finans Kapitalin Yeni Emperyalizmi (E. Ekici, Trans.). *Monthy Review Türkiye, 1*, 35–57.

Frączkiewicz, M. (2013). The cultural role of the malls. *Prace Etnograficzne., 41*(4), 335–342.

Frankel, J. & Roubini, N. (2001). *The role of industrial country policies in emerging market crises.* NBER Working Paper. No: 8634.

Frederickson, G. (1971). Toward a new public administration, The Minnowbrook Perspective, Marini Frank (Ed.), San Francisco,CA: Chandler Publishing.

Freeman, C. (2002). Continental, national and sub national innovation systems-complementarity and economic growth. *Research Policy, 31*(2), 191–211. doi:10.1016/S0048-7333(01)00136-6

Fried, H. O., Lovell, C. A. K., & Schmidt, S. S. (2008). Efficiency and productivity. In H. O. Fried, C. A. K. Lovell, & S. S. Schmidt (Eds.), *The Measurement of Productive Efficiency and Productivity Change* (pp. 1–89). Oxford, UK: Oxford Scholarship. doi:10.1093/acprof:oso/9780195183528.003.0001

Friedman, M. (2002). Economic freedom behind the scenes. In J. Gwartney, R. Lawson, C. Edwards, W. Park, V. Rugy, & S. Wagh (Eds.), Economic freedom of the world: 2002 Annual Report, (pp. 17-21), The Fraser Institute, Vancouver, Canada, p. 18.

Friedman, M. (1950). Wesley C. Mitchell as an Economic Theorist. *Journal of Political Economy, 58*(6), 465–493. doi:10.1086/257011

Fujita, N. (2004). Gunnar Myrdal's Theory of cumulative causation. *Economic Research Center*, Discussion Paper 147, 72-86. Retrieved from http://www.soec.nagoya/erc/DP/paper147.pdf.

Furubotn, E. G., & Pejovich, S. (1972). Property rights and economic theory, a survey of recent literature. *Journal of Economic Literature, 10*(4), 1137–1162.

Fusfeld, D. R. (2000). A manifesto or institutional economics remarks upon receiving the Veblen-Commons award. *Journal of Economic Issues, 34*(2), 257–265. doi:10.1080/00213624.2000.11506265

Gandhi, V. P. & Crase, L. (2009, August). *New institutional economics, governance and the performance of water institutions in India.* Paper presented at the International Association of Agricultural Economists Conference, Beijing, China. Retrieved from https://ageconsearch.umn.edu/bitstream/51415/2/Contributed-Paper-626-Gandhi-Crase-Iaae2009.pdf

Garroste, P., & Saussier, S. (2008). The theories of the firm. In *E. Brousseau & J. M. Glachant* (Eds.), N. I. Economics A Guidebook (pp. 23–36). Cambridge, UK: Cambridge University Press.

Gartner, D. (2013). 21st century international institutions. *Proceedings of the Annual Meeting, (American Society of International Law),* 107. International Law in a Multipolar World. pp. 264-267. 10.5305/procannmeetasil.107.0264

Germain, R. (2009). Financial order and world politics: Crisis, change and continuity. *International Affairs, 85*(4), pp. 669-687.Gökay, B. (2009). The 2008 world economic crisis: Global shifts and fault lines. *Global Research.* Retrieved from http://www.globalresearch.ca/the-2008-world-economic-crisis-global-shifts-and-faultlines/12283

Ghai, D. (1995). *Yapısal Uyum, Küresel Bütünleşme ve Sosyal Demokrasi, Piyasa Güçleri ve Küresel Kalkınma* (R. Prendergast & F. Stewart, Eds.). İstanbul, Turkey: Yapı Kredi Press.

Ghazalian, P. L., & Amponsem, F. (2019). The effects of economic freedom on FDI inflows: An empirical analysis. *Applied Economics, 51*(11), 1111–1132. doi:10.1080/00036846.2018.1524979

Ginzbergz, E. (1997). Wesley Mitchell. *History of Political Economy, 29*(3), 371–390. doi:10.1215/00182702-29-3-371

Giray, F. (2003). Çok taraflı Yatırım Anlaşması (MAİ) ve Alternatif Öneriler Üzerine Bir Değerlendirme. *Mülkiye Journal, 240,* 135–160.

Gordon, P. A. (2017). Vision of Trump at war: How the president could stumble into conflict. *Foreign Affairs.* Retrieved from https://www.foreignaffairs.com/articles/2017-03-22/vision-trump-war

Gottschalk, P., & Solli-Sæther, H. (2006). *Managing successful IT outsourcing relationship.* Hershey, PA: IRM Press. doi:10.4018/978-1-59140-760-7

Göze, A. (1998). *Liberal, Marxist, Faşist ve Sosyal Devlet.* İstanbul, Turkey: Beta Press.

Gözlü, S. (1996). Kamu Hizmeti Veren Kuruluşlarda Toplam Kalite Yönetimi, *Kamu Yönetimi Disiplini Symposium,* Ankara, Turkey TODAIE Press.

Granovetter, M. (1995). *Getting a job: A study of contacts and careers.* Chicago, IL: Chicago University Press. doi:10.7208/chicago/9780226518404.001.0001

Green, A. (2013). Estimating the effects of democratization in African countries: A simultaneous equations approach. *Economic Systems, 37*(4), 555–571. doi:10.1016/j.ecosys.2013.02.003

Greenee, W. H. (2003). Econometric analysis (5th ed.). New York, NY: Prentice Hall.

Grossman, G. M., & Helpman, E. (1991). Quality ladders in the theory of growth. *The Review of Economic Studies, 58*(1), 43–61. doi:10.2307/2298044

Gruchy, A. G. (1977). Institutional economics: Its development and prospects. In R. Steppacher, B. Zogg-Walz, & H. Hatzfeldt (Eds.), *Economics in Institutional Perspective* (pp. 11–29). Toronto, Canada: Lexington Books.

Gujarati, D. N., & Porter, D. C. (2009). *Basic econometrics* (5th ed.). New York, NY: McGraw-Hill.

Gülalp, H. (1993). *Kapitalizm, Sınıflar ve Devlet* (O. Akınhay, Trans.). İstanbul, Turkey: Belge Press.

Gulati, R., Lawrence, P. R., & Puranam, P. (2005). Adaptation in vertical relationships: Beyond incentive conflict. *Strategic Management Journal, 26*(5), 415–440. doi:10.1002mj.458

Güleç, C. (2015). Thorstein Veblen ve Gösterişçi Tüketim Kavramı. *Erciyes Üniversitesi Sosyal Bilimler Enstitüsü Dergisi, 1*(38), 62–82.

Guler, B. A. (2003). Yönetişim: Tüm İktidar Sermayeye. *Praksis, 9*, 93–116.

Güler, E. (2012). Geçiş Ekonomileri ve Yeni Kurumsal İktisat'ın Yeniden Yükselişi. *Doğuş Üniversitesi Dergisi, 13*(1), 52–68. doi:10.31671/dogus.2018.115

Gümüş, T. T. (2010). Feodalizm: Avrupa Tarihinde Yeni Yaklaşımlar. [History Research Journal]. *Tarih Araştırmaları Dergisi, 29*(47), 39–64.

Güneş, A. (2014). Sosyolojik Olarak Din ve Toplum İlişkileri. *Fırat Üniversitesi Sosyal Bilimler Dergisi, 24*(1), 153–164.

Gürcaylılar-Yenidogan, T. (2013a). Yeni kurumsal iktisat geleneğinde işlem maliyeti teorisinin rolü ve son gelişmeler. *Business & Economics Research Journal, 4*(2), 109–134.

Gürcaylılar-Yenidogan, T. (2013b). The impact of transaction attributes and trust on ex-post opportunism. *International Journal of Management Sciences and Business Research, 2*(6), 39–44.

Gürcaylılar-Yenidogan, T. (2014). Örgütlerarası ilişkilerde sözleşme tasarımını etkileyen faktörler. *Journal of Yasar University, 9*(34), 6063–6082.

Gürer, N. (2017). The role of local governments for creating sustainable urban places in winter cities. Çağdaş Yerel Yönetimler, Cilt 26 Sayı 1 pp. 19-42.

Güvel, A. G. (2002). Piyasa Ekonomisine Biyolojik Bir Yaklaşım: Biyonomik. *Piyasa Dergisi, 1*(4), 67–73.

Guzelsari, S. (2004). Kamu Yönetimi Disiplininde Yeni Kamu İşletmeciliği ve Yönetişim Yaklaşımları. *A.Ü.SBF*-GETA *Tartışma Metinleri, 66,* 1-25. Retrieved from http://www.politics.ankara.edu.tr/dergi/tartisma/2004/selime-guzelsari.pdf

Guzelsari, S. (2008). *Küresel Kapitalizm ve Devletin Dönüşümü.* İstanbul, Turkey: SAV.

Gwartney, J. D., Lawson, R. A., & Hocombe, R. (1999). Economic freedom and the environment for economic growth. Journal of Institutional and Theoretical Economics (JITE). *Mohr Siebeck, Tübingen, 155*(4), 643–643.

Hahn, F. H., & Matthews, R. C. O. (1964). The Theory of Economic Growth: A Survey. *Economic Journal (London), 74*(296), 779–902. doi:10.2307/2228848

Halis, B. (2012). Tüketimin Değişen Yüzü: Elektronik Ticaret Uygulamaları ve Sosyal Paylaşım Ağlarının Rolü. *Tarih Kültür ve Sanat Araştırmaları Dergisi, 1*(4), 149–160.

Hall, R. E., & Jones, C. I. (1999). Why do some countries produce so much more output per worker than others? *The Quarterly Journal of Economics, 114*(1), 83–116. doi:10.1162/003355399555954

Hamilton, C. & Dennis, R. (2205). *Affluenza: When Too Much Is Never Enough.* Crows Nest; Allen & Unwin.

Hamilton, D. (1953). *Newtonian classicism and Darwinian institutionalism.* Albuquerque, NM: University of New Mexico Press.

Hansen, A. H. (1949). Wesley Mitchell, social scientist and social counselor. *The Review of Economics and Statistics, 31*(4), 245–255. doi:10.2307/1928646

Harper, D. A. (2003). *Foundations of entrepreneurship and economic development.* New York, NY: Routledge. doi:10.4324/9780203380215

Hayek, F. (1944). *The road to serfdom.* London, UK: Routledge.

Hayek, F. A. (1945). The use of knowledge in society. *The American Economic Review, 35*, 519–530.

Hayek, F. A. (1948). *Individualism and economic order.* The University of Chicago Press.

Hazar, Ç. M. (2006). *Bilgi Toplumu.* Ankara, Turkey: Turhan Kitabevi.

Heide, J. B. (2003). Plural governance in industrial purchasing. *Journal of Marketing, 67*(4), 18–29. doi:10.1509/mkg.67.4.18.18689

Heide, J. B., & John, G. (1990). Alliances in industrial purchasing: The determinants of joint action in buyer-supplier relationships. *JMR, Journal of Marketing Research, 27*(1), 24–36. doi:10.1177/002224379002700103

Helleiner, E., & Pagliari, S. (2011). The end of an era in international financial regulation? A postcrisis research agenda. *International Organization, 65*(1), 169–200. doi:10.1017/S0020818310000305

Heron, T. (2008). Globalization, neoliberalism and the exercise of human agency. *International Journal of Politics Culture and Society, 28*(1-4), 85–101. doi:10.100710767-007-9019-z

Hibou, B. (1998). *The political economy of the world bank's discourse.* CERI Working Papers. No: 39.

Hirschman, E. C., & Holbrook, M. B. (1982). Hedonic consumption: Emerging methods and propositions. *Journal of Marketing, 46*(3), 92–101. doi:10.1177/002224298204600314

Hlasny, V. (2008). Veblen's and Mitchell's profit theory of business cycles. *Ewha Journal of Social Sciences, 20*(2), 1–28.

Hodgson, G, M. (1998). The approach of institutional economics. *Journal of Economic Literature, 36*(1), 166–192. Retrieved from http://www.geoffreyhodgson.info/user/image/approachinec.pdf

Hodgson, G, M. (2000). What is the essence of institutional economics? *Journal of Economic Issues, 34*(2), 317–329. doi:10.1080/00213624.2000.11506269

Hodgson, G. M. (1998). On the evolution of Thorstein Veblen's evolutionary economics. *Cambridge Journal of Economics, 22*(4), 415–431. doi:10.1093/oxfordjournals.cje.a013726

Hodgson, G. M. (1999). *Evolution and institutions, on evolutionary economics and the evolution of economics.* UK: Edward Elgar Publishing.

Hodgson, G. M. (2006). What are institutions? *Journal of Economic Issues, 40*(1), 1–25. doi:10.1080/00213624.2006.11506879

Hodgson, G. M. (2008). How Veblen generalized Darwinism. *Journal of Economic Issues, 42*(2), 399–405. doi:10.1080/00213624.2008.11507148

Holloway, J., & Picciotto, S. (1977). Capital, crisis and the state. *Capital and Class, 1*(2), 76–101. doi:10.1177/030981687700200104

Hong, W. L., & Cun-Yan, J. (2017). A field study on climate comfortable conditions of urban public open spaces in marginal season of winter cities. *Open House International, 42*(2).

Hovland, R., & Wolburg, J. (2015). *Advertising, Society, and Consumer Culture.* London, UK: Taylor and Francis.

Hughes, H. S. (1995). *Toplum ve Bilinç. çev. Özkan, G.* İstanbul, Turkey: Metis Yayınları.

Hunter, J. E. (2002). *Modern Japonya'nın Doğuşu.* Ankara, Turkey: İmge Kitapevi. [Imge Publishing]

Huntington, S. (1991). *The third wave: Democratization in the late Twentieth Century.* University of Oklahoma Press.

Hürcan, Y. G. (1999). *Mali Disiplin Sağlanmasında Yasal Düzenlemelerin Yeri, Önemi, Dünya uygulamaları ve Türkiye Örneğinin İncelenmesi. T.C. Başbakanlık Hazine Müsteşarlığı Yayınları. Araştırma ve İnceleme Dizisi; 23.* Ankara, Turkey: T.C. Başbakanlık Hazine Müsteşarlığı.

Husic, M., & Cicic, M. (2009). Luxury consumption factors. *Journal of Fashion Marketing and Management, 13*(2), 231–245. doi:10.1108/13612020910957734

Hvidt, M. (2009, August). The Dubai model: An outline of key development-process elements in Dubai. *International Journal of Middle East Studies, 41*(3), 397–418. doi:10.1017/S0020743809091120

IMF. (2007). *International Monetary Fund handbook: Its functions, policies, and operations.* Retrieved from https://www.imf.org/external/pubs/ft/imfhb/eng/handbook.pdf

IMF. (2016). Retrieved from https://www.imf.org/external/pubs/ft/aa/pdf/aa.pdf

Indrová, J., & Petru, Z. (2014). The Czech Republic: A destination in the heart of Europe. In *C. Costa, E. Panyik, & D. Buhalis (Eds.), European tourism planning and organisation systems the EU member states* (pp. 183–197). Bristol, UK: Channel View Publications.

İnsel, A. (1997). Geçmişten Geleceğe. *Birikim Journal, 104*, 19–29.

Insel, A. (2011). *Neo-Liberalizm: Hegemonyanın Yeni Dili.* İstanbul, Turkey: Birikim Yayınları.

Iossifov, P. & Fei, X. (2019). Real effective exchange rate and trade balance adjustment: The case of Turkey. *IMF Working Paper WP/19/131.*

İpek, P. (2013, Winter). Hegemony and crisis in global political economy: The importance of legitimacy. *Perceptions, 18*(4), 29–45.

Işıklı, A. (1997). Kamu Kesimi ve Siyasal Rejimin Demokratikleşmesi. *Mülkiyeliler Birliği Journal, 200*, 75–79.

Ivanov, S., & Dimitrova, M. (2014). Managing tourism in Bulgaria: Between 'Mission Impossible' and new hope. In C. Costa, E. Panyik, & D. Buhalis (Eds.), *European tourism planning and organisation systems The EU member states* (pp. 87–125). Bristol, UK: Channel View Publications.

İyibozkurt, E. (1999). *Küreselleşme ve Türkiye.* Bursa, Turkey: Ezgi Press.

Jamala, A., Daviesa, F., Chudryb, F., & Al-Marric, M. (2006). Profiling consumers: A study of Qatari consumers shopping motivations. *Journal of Retailing and Consumer Services, 13*(1), 67–80. doi:10.1016/j.jretconser.2005.08.002

Jansson, U., Kautsky, U., & Miliander, S. (2006). Rural landscape, production and human consumption: Past, present and future. *Ambio, 35*(8), 505–513. doi:10.1579/0044-7447(2006)35[505:RLPAHC]2.0.CO;2 PMID:17334058

Jary, D. & Jary, J. (1991). Fordism and Post-Fordism, The Harpercollins Dictionary of Sociology. New York, NY: Harper Perennial Press.

Javed, O. (2015). *Essays on institutional quality, macroeconomic stabilization, and economic growth in International Monetary Fund member countries.* Retrieved from https://www.tdx.cat/bitstream/handle/10803/319439/OMER_JAVED_PhD_THESIS.pdf?sequence=1&isAllowed=y

Jessop, B. (2002). Globalization and the national state. In S. Aronowitz & P. Bratsis (Eds.), *Paradigm Lost: State Theory Reconsidered* (pp. 185-220). London, UK: University of Minnesota Press. Retrieved from https://bobjessop.org/2014/01/05/globalization-and-the-national-state/

Jessop, B. (1994). *Post Fordism and the state* (A. Amin, Trans.). London, UK: Black Well Publishers. doi:10.1002/9780470712726.ch8

Jessop, B. (1994). The transition to post-Fordism and the Schumpeterian workfare state. In R. Burrows & B. Loader (Eds.), *Towards a post-Fordist welfare state?* London, UK: Oxford Press. doi:10.4324/9780203359846_chapter_2

Jessop, B. (1998). The rise of governance and the risks of failure: The case of economic development. *International Social Science Journal, 155*(155), 29–45. doi:10.1111/1468-2451.00107

Jessop, B. (2010). The 'return' of the national state in the current crisis of the world market. *Capital and Class, 34*(1), 38–43. doi:10.1177/0309816809353480

John, F. H. (1992). Empirical linkages between democracy and economic growth, *NBER Working Paper*, No: 4066.

Jondrow, J., Knox Lovell, C. A., Materov, I. S., & Schmidt, P. (1982). On the estimation of technical inefficiency in the stochastic frontier production function model. *Journal of Econometrics, 19*(2-3), 233–238. doi:10.1016/0304-4076(82)90004-5

Jordan, P. (2006). Tourism and EU enlargement: A central European perspective. In D. Hall, M. Smith, & B. Marciszewska (Eds.), *Tourism in the New Europe The challenges and opportunities of EU enlargement* (pp. 65–80). Oxfordshire, UK: CABI. doi:10.1079/9781845931179.0065

Joskow, P. L. (2008). Introduction to New Institutional Economics, A Report Card. In E. Brousseau & J. M. Glachant (Eds.), New Institutional Economics A Guidebook (1-20). Cambridge, UK: Cambridge University Press.

Joskow, P. L. (1987). Contract duration and relationship-specific investments: Empirical evidence from coal markets. *The American Economic Review*, 168–185.

Journal of Tourism & Hospitality. (2018). Winter tourism. Retrieved from https://www.omicsonline.org/scholarly/winter-tourism-journals-articles-ppts-list.php

Justesen, M. K. (2008). The effect of economic freedom on growth revisited: New evidence on causality from a panel of countries 1970-1999. *European Journal of Political Economy, 24*(3), 642–660. doi:10.1016/j.ejpoleco.2008.06.003

Kalabak, A. Y. (2014). Osmanlı'nın Son Döneminin Sosyo Ekonomik Buhranları ve Mali Emperyalizm. [Social Economic Research Journal]. *Sosyal Ekonomik Araştırmalar Dergisi, 14*(27), 304–326. doi:10.30976usead.302229

Kaldor, N. (1960). *Essays on value and distribution.* Illinois: The Free Press of Glence.

Kaletsky, A. (2017). The role of capitalism in the rise of populism. *World Economic Forum,* Retrieved from https://www.weforum.org/agenda/2017/01/the-role-of-capitalism-in-the-rise-of-populism?utm_content=buffer569c7&utm_medium=social&utm_source=twitter.com&utm_campaign=buffer

Kalirajan, K. P., & Shand, R. T. (1999). Frontier production functions and technical efficiency measures. *Journal of Economic Surveys, 13*(2), 149–172. doi:10.1111/1467-6419.00080

Kalkandelen, A. H. (1998). Kamu Yönetiminde Yeniden Yapılanma (Süreç ve Aşamalar). *Türk İdare Journal, 420,* 97–109.

Kama, Ö. (2011). Yeni Kurumsal iktisat Okulunun Temelleri. *Gazi Üniversitesi İktisadi Ve İdari Bilimler Fakültesi Dergisi, 13*(2), 183–204.

Kama, Ö. (2011). Yeni Kurumsal İktisat Okulunun Temelleri. *Gazi Üniversitesi İktisadi Ve İdari Bilimler Fakültesi Dergisi, 13*(2), 183–204.

Kapp, W. K. (1976). The nature and significance of institutional economics. *Journal of Kyklos, 29*(2), 182-196. Retrieved from http:www.kwilliamkapp.de/documents.pdf

Kara, O. (2003). Bilgi Ekonomisinin Olası Mikro Ekonomik Etkilerinin Teorik Analizi. Pamukkale Üniversitesi ve Türkiye Ekonomi Kurumu, Ekonomi Yaz Seminerleri-2 Konferansları, Denizli

Karakaş, M. (2017). Bir Zihniyet Olarak Tüketim Kültürü ve İhtiyaçların Yabancılaşması. *International Congress On Political, Economic And Social Studies*, 19-22

Karakayalı, H., & Yanıkkaya, H. (2006). Kurumsal Faktörlerin Ekonomik Büyüme Etkileri. *Kurumsal İktisat Kurallar, Kurumlar ve Ekonomik Gelişme*. In C. C. Aktan (Ed.), *Sermaye Piyasası Kurulu Kurumsal Araştırmalar Serisi. No: 2. Yayın No. 194* (pp. 135–170). Ankara, Turkey: SPK.

Kaufmann, D., Kraay, A., & Mastruzzi, M. (2003). *Governance matters III, Governance indicators for 1996–2002.* Retrieved from http://siteresources.worldbank.org/INTWBIGOVANTCOR/Resources/govmatters3_wber.pdf

Kaya, S. & Denetçi, U. (2003). Dünya Bankası ve Dünya Bankası Kredilerinin Denetimi. *Sayıştay Dergisi*, 3-42.

Kazemi, M., & Azman-Saini, W. N. W. (2017). Foreign direct investment, economic freedom and democracy. *International Journal of Economics & Management, 11*(1), 1–15.

Kazgan, G. (1997). *Küreselleşme ve Yeni Ekonomik Düzen.* İstanbul, Turkey: Altın Kitaplar Press.

Kazgan, G. (1999). *Tanzimat'tan 21. Yüzyıla Türkiye Ekonomisi.* İstanbul, Turkey: Altın Kitaplar Yayınevi.

Kazgan, G. (2002). *Küreselleşme ve Ulus – Devlet: Yeni Ekonomik Düzen.* İstanbul, Turkey: İstanbul Bilgi University Press.

Kazgan, G. (2004). *İktisadi Düşünce veya Politik İktisadın Evrimi.* İstanbul, Turkey: Remzi Kitabevi.

Keles, R. (2010). Yönetişim Kavramına Eleştirel bir Yaklaşım. In M. A. Çukurçayır, H. T. Eroğlu, & H. Eşki-Uğuz (Eds.), *Yönetişim* (pp. 57–71). Konya, Turkey: Çizgi Kitabevi.

Kettl, D. (1997). The global revolution in public management: Driving themes, missing links. *Journal of Policy Analysis and Management, 16*(3), 446–462. doi:10.1002/(SICI)1520-6688(199722)16:3<446::AID-PAM5>3.0.CO;2-H

Keyder, Ç. (1982). *Dünya Ekonomisi İçinde Türkiye, 1923-1929.* Ankara, Turkey: Yurt Yayınları.

Khan, T. M., Clear, F., Al-Kaabi, A., & Pezeshki, V. (2010). An exploratory study of the effects of diversity dimensions and intervening variables on attitudes to diversity. *Team Performance Management, 16*(5/6), 289-308.

Killick, T., Malik, M., & Manuel, M. (1992). What can we know about the effects of IMF programmes? *World Economy, 15*(5), 575–598. doi:10.1111/j.1467-9701.1992.tb00538.x

Kilpinen, E. (2003). Clarence Ayres memorial lecture Does pragmatism imply institutionalism? *Journal of Economic Issues, 37*(2), 291–304. doi:10.1080/00213624.2003.11506576

Kım, J., & Mahoney, J. T. (2005). Property rights theory, transaction costs theory, and agency theory: An organizational economics approach to strategic management. *Journal of Managerıal and Decısıon Economıcs, 26*(4), 223–246. doi:10.1002/mde.1218

Kıraç, S., & İlhan, B. (2010). Avrupa Birliği Oluşum Süreci ve Ortak Politikalar. *Milli Eğitim Dergisi, 40*(188), 191–201.

Kirsten, J. & Kherallah, M. (2001). The new institutional economics: Applications for agricultural policy research in developing countries. *International Food Policy Research Institute*, Working Paper, No: 41, 1-38.

Kissinger, H. (2002). *Amerika'nın Dış Politikaya İhtiyacı Var mı?* (T. Evyapan, Trans.). Ankara, Turkey: METU Press.

Kızılcık, R. (2003). 21. Yüzyılda Yönetişim ve Kamu Yönetimi, Yeni Eğilimler ve Yeni Teknikler. *Türk İdare Journal, 438*, 181–193.

Kızılkaya, E. İ. (2007). Weber, Veblen ve Kapitalizmin Ruhu. Kurumsal İktisat, (Ed.) Eyüp Özveren, İmge Kitabevi Yayınları, Ankara.

Klein, P. A., & Miller, E. S. (1996). Concepts of value, efficiency, and democracy in institutional economics. *Journal of Economic Issues, 30*(1), 267–277. doi:10.1080/00213624.1996.11505776

Klicksberg, B. (1993). *Redesigning the state profile for social and economic development change*. Toluca, Mexico: Clarendon Press.

Knight, J. & Johnson, J. (2011). *The priority of democracy: Political consequences*

Kocacık, F. (2003). Bilgi Toplumu ve Türkiye. *Cumhuriyet Üniversitesi Sosyal Bilimler Dergisi, 27*(1), 1–10.

Koopmans, T. C. (1951) An analysis of production as an efficient combination of activities. In T. C. Koopmans (Ed.), Activity analysis of production and allocation (pp. 225-287), Cawles Commission for Research in Economics Monograph No: 13, New York, NY: Wiley.

Köse, S. (2003). Institutıonalism of Thorstein Veblen and the theory of business cycles. *Süleyman Demirel Üniversitesi, İİBF Dergisi, 8*(1), 283-297. Retrieved from http://sablon.sdu.edu.tr/fakulteler/iibf/dergi/files/2003-1-18.pdf

Krugman, P., Cooper, R. N., & Srinivasan, T. N. (1995). Growing world trade: Causes and consequences. *Brookings Papers on Economic Activity, 1*(1), 327–362. doi:10.2307/2534577

Kucerová, J., & Makovník, T. (2014). Tourism in Slovakia: The best-kept secret in Europe. In *C. Costa, E. Panyik, & D. Buhalis (Eds.), European tourism planning and organisation systems The EU member states* (pp. 257–278). Bristol, UK: Channel View Publications.

KUDAKA. (2012). *Kuzeydoğu Anadolu Kalkınma Ajansı*. Erzurum Konaklı Bölgesi'nde Finansal Fizibilite Raporu.

Kumbhakar, S. C. (1990). Production frontiers, panel data, and time-varying technical inefficiency. *Journal of Econometrics, 46*(1-2), 201–211. doi:10.1016/0304-4076(90)90055-X

Kuper, A. (1995). *İlkel Toplumun İcadı- Bir İllüzyonun Dönüşümleri. çev. Türkmen, İ.* İstanbul, Turkey: İnsan Yayınları.

Lacity, M. C., & Hirschheim, R. (1993). The information systems outsourcing bandwagon. *Sloan Management Review, 35*(1), 73.

Lane, J. E., & Maeland, R. (2011). Global financial crisis and international institutions: Challenges, opportunities and change. *Public Organization Review, 11*(1), 29–43. doi:10.100711115-010-0145-0

Lee, F. S. (2006). Introduction to the special issue. *The Review of Radical Political Economics, 38*(4), 497–498. doi:10.1177/0486613406293216

Lee, Y. H., & Schmidt, P. (1993). A production frontier model with flexible temporal variation in technical inefficiency. In H. Fried & K. Lovell (Eds.), *The measurement of productive efficiency: Techniques and applications* (pp. 237–255). New York, NY: Oxford University Press.

Leys, C. (1992). Azgelişmişlik ve Bağımlılık: Eleştirel Notlar, Emperyalizm, Gelişme ve Bağımlılık Üzerine, M. Ersoy (Ed.), Ankara, Turkey: Verso Press, pp. 75-92.

Limam, Y. R. & Miller, S. M. (2004). Explaining economic growth: Factor accumulation, total factor productivity, and production efficiency improvement, *University of Connecticut Department of Economics Working Paper Series*, No: 2004-20.

Lioliou, E., Zimmermann, A., Willcocks, L., & Gao, L. (2014). Formal and relational governance in IT outsourcing: Substitution, complementarity and the role of the psychological contract. *Information Systems Journal, 24*(6), 503–535. doi:10.1111/isj.12038

Lipset, S. M. (1959). Some social requisites of democracy: Economic development and political legitimacy. [</jrn>]. *The American Political Science Review, 53*, 73–74.

Li, Q., & Resnick, A. (2003). Reversal of fortunes: Democratic institutions and foreign direct investment inflows to developing countries. *International Organization, 57*(1), 175–211. doi:10.1017/S0020818303571077

Locke, J. (2002). *Uygar Yönetim Üzerine İkinci İnceleme*. Çeviren: Serdar Taşçı & Hale Akman, Metropol yayınları, İstanbul, Orijinal yazım tarihi 1690.

López-Bayón, S., & González-Díaz, M. (2010). Indefinite contract duration: Evidence from electronics subcontracting. *International Review of Law and Economics, 30*(2), 145–159. doi:10.1016/j.irle.2010.03.001

Lower, M. D. (1987). The concept of technology within the institutionalist perspective. *Journal of Economic Issues, 21*(3), 1147–1176. doi:10.1080/00213624.1987.11504699

Lucas, R. E. Jr. (1988). On the mechanics of economic development. *Journal of Monetary Economics, 22*(1), 3–42. doi:10.1016/0304-3932(88)90168-7

Lury, C. (1996). *Consumer culture*. Cambridge, UK: Polity Press.

Luther, H. U. (1984). *Güney Kore Bir Model Olabilir mi*. İstanbul, Turkey: Belge Yayınları. [Belge Publishing]

Majone, G. (1997). From the positive to the regulatory state: Causes and consequences of changes in the mode of governance. *Journal of Public Policy, 17*(2), 139–167. doi:10.1017/S0143814X00003524

Malecki, E. J. & Ewers, M. C. (2007). Labor migration to World cities: With a research agenda for the Arab Gulf. *Progress in Human Geography, 31*(4), 467-484.

Mansfield, E. (1968). *The economics of technological change*. London, UK: Longmans.

Marangos, J. (2018). The 2018 Clarence Ayres scholar An institutional riposte to the "After the Washington consensus". *Journal of Economic Issues, 52*(2), 323–335. doi:10.1080/00213624.2018.1469856

Marciniak, R.; Mohsen, M. G. (n.d.). Homogeneity in luxury fashion consumption: An exploration of Arab women. *The Business & Management Review, 5*(1), pp. 32-41.

Markham, J. W. (1950). An alternative approach to the concept of workable competition. *The American Economic Review, 40*(3), 349–361.

Marshall, G. (1998). Oxford dictionary of sociology (2nded.). Oxford, UK: Oxford University Press

Marx, K. (2003). Kapital I [Capital I], (Çev. Alaattin Bilgi), İstanbul, Turkey: Eriş Yayıncılık.

Masten, S. E. (1984). The organization of production: Evidence from the aerospace industry. *The Journal of Law & Economics, 27*(2), 403–417. doi:10.1086/467071

Masuda, Y. (1990). *Managing in the information society: Releasing synergy Japanese style*. Cambridge, MA: Basil Blackwell.

McDonald, M., Gough, B., Wearing, S., & Deville, A. (2017). Social psychology, consumer culture and neoliberal political economy. *Journal for the Theory of Social Behaviour, 47*(3), 363–379. doi:10.1111/jtsb.12135

McFarling, B. R. (2004). The Clarence Ayres memorial lecture, An institutionalist reconstruction of culture. *Journal of Economic Issues, 38*(2), 339–352. doi:10.1080/00213624.2004.11506693

Meder, M. (2001). Bilgi Toplumu ve Toplumsal Değişim. *Pamukkale Üniversitesi Eğitim Fakültesi Dergisi, 9*(9), 72–81.

Meeusen, W., & van Den Broeck, J. (1977). Efficiency estimation from Cobb-Douglas production functions with composed error. *International Economic Review, 18*(2), 435–444. doi:10.2307/2525757

Ménard, C. & Shirley, M. M. (2005). Introduction. In C. Ménard & M. M. Shirley (Eds.), Handbook of New Institutional Economics (1-20). Springer, The Netherlands.

Menard, C., & Shirley, M. M. (Eds.). (2005). *Handbook of New Institutional Economics*. The Netherlands: Springer. doi:10.1007/b106770

Menkhoff, L., & Meyer, R. (2010). *The G20 proposal on IMF governance: Has any progress been made?* (pp. 171–179). IMF Reform-Intereconomics.

Metcafe, B. D. (2008, November). Women, management and globalization in the Middle East, *Journal of Business Ethics, 83*(1), pp. 85-100.

Milesi-Ferret, G. M., & Razin, A. (1996). Sustainability of persistent current account deficits. *International Journal of Finance & Economics, 1*(3), 161–181. doi:10.1002/(SICI)1099-1158(199607)1:3<161::AID-IJFE19>3.0.CO;2-W

Miller, M. (2012). Economic development, violent leader removal and democratization. *American Journal of Political Science, 56*(4), 1002–1020. doi:10.1111/j.1540-5907.2012.00595.x

Milonakis, D. & Fine, B. (2009). *From political economy to economics method, the social and the historical in the evolution of economic theory*. London, UK: Routledge.

Ministry of Trade. Republic of Turkey (2019). *Free trade agreements.* Retrieved from https://www.ticaret.gov.tr/dis-iliskiler/serbest-ticaret-anlasmalari

Minsky, H. P. (1980). Money, financial markets, and the coherence of a market economy. *Journal of Post Keynesian Economics, 3*(1), 21–31. doi:10.1080/01603477.1980.11489192

Mitchell, W. C. (1935). Commons on institutional economics. *The American Economic Review, 25*(4), 635–652. Retrieved from http://www.jstor.org/stable/1807801

Mogdaham, V. (Ed.). (2003). *Modernizing women: Gender and social change in the Middle East. Boulder*, CO: Lyne Reiner Publications.

Moghadam, V. M. (2005). *Women's economic participation in the Middle East. Journal of Middle East Women's Studies, 1*(1), 110–146.

Molavi, A. (2007). Sudden city: A feverish dream for the future springs from the sands in Dubai. *National Geographic, 211*(1), 96–113.

Move DC. (2014). The District of Columbia's multimodal long-range transportation plan.

Nachane, D. M. (2014). Global crisis, financial institutions and reforms: An Indian perspective. In A. N. Ghosh & A. K. Karmakar (Eds.), *Analytical issues in trade, development and finance* (pp. 97–124). India: India Studies in Business and Economics Springer. doi:10.1007/978-81-322-1650-6_7

National Research Council. (2002). Community and quality of life: Data needs for informed decision making. National Academy Press, Washington, D.C. Retrieved from http://nap.edu/10262

Nelson, S. C. (2016). *Ayşe Kaya, 2015, Power and Global Economic Institutions* (pp. 523–527). Springer Review of International Organization.

North, D. (2005). Institutions and the performance of economies over time. In C. Ménard & M. M. Shirley (Eds.), Handbook of New Institutional Economics (21-30). Springer, The Netherlands. doi:10.1007/0-387-25092-1_2

North, D. (1991). Institutions. *The Journal of Economic Perspectives*, *5*(1), 97–112. doi:10.1257/jep.5.1.97

North, D. C. (1981). *Structure and change in economic history*. New York, NY: Norton.

North, D. C. (1984). Transaction costs, institutions, and economic history. *Journal of Institutional and Theoretical Economics*, *140*(1), 7–17.

North, D. C. (1990). *Institutions, institutional change, and economic performance*. Cambridge, U.K.: Cambridge University Press. doi:10.1017/CBO9780511808678

North, D. C. (2002). *Institutions, institutional change and economic performance*. Cambridge, UK: Cambridge University Press.

North, D. C. (2002). *Kurumlar, Kurumsal Değişim ve Ekonomik Performans, Çev. Gül Çağalı Güven*. İstanbul, Turkey: Sabancı Üniversitesi Yayınları.

North, D. C., & Thomas, R. P. (1973). *The rise of the western world: A new economic history*. Cambridge, UK: Cambridge University Press. doi:10.1017/CBO9780511819438

O'Brien, P. J. (1992). In M. Ersoy (Ed.), *Latin Amerikan Bağımlılık Kuramlarına Bir Eleştiri, Emperyalizm, Gelişme ve Bağımlılık Üzerine* (pp. 23–40). Ankara, Turkey: Verso Press.

O'Dennel, L. A. (1975). Rationalism, capitalism and the entrepreneur: The views of Veblen and Schumpeter. *History of Political Economy*, *5*(1), 199–214. doi:10.1215/00182702-5-1-199

O'Hara, P. A. (2002). The contemporary relevance of Thorstein Veblen's institutional-evolutionary political economy. *History of Economics Review*, *35*(1), 78–103. doi:10.1080/10370196.2002.11733370

OECD. (2003). *Developments in growth literature and their relevance for simulation models*. Paris, France: OECD Publications.

Oğuz, F. (2003). *Mülkiyet Hakları*. Ankara, Turkey: Roma Yayınları.

Oguz, Ş. (2006). Sermayenin Uluslararasılaşması Sürecinde Mekânsal Farklılaşmalar ve Devletin Dönüşümü. In D. Yılmaz & ... (Eds.), *Kapitalizmi Anlamak* (pp. 147–212). Ankara, Turkey: Dipnot Yayınları.

Okçu, M. (2007). Yönetişim Tartışmalarına Katkı: Avrupa Birliği İçin Yönetişim Ne Anlama Geliyor? *Süleyman Demirel Üniversitesi İktisadi ve İdari Bilimler Fakültesi Dergisi*, *12*(3), 299–312.

Okur, M. (2005). Türkiye'de Milli ve Modern Bir Eğitim Sistemi Oluşturma Çabaları (1920-1928). Çağdaş Türkiye Tarihi Araştırmaları Dergisi [Modern Turkey's History Research Journal], 4(11). Retrieved from http://dergipark.gov.tr/cttad/issue/25234/266776

Olk, S. (2003). The relationship between economic development and democracy in africa: a quantitative and qualitative perspective. Retrieved from https://Www.Uni-Trier.De/Fileadmin/Fb3/Pol/Studium/Ausgewaehlte_Abschlussarbeiten/Olk.Pdf

Öncel, A., & Malik, A. (2015). The Arab spring and its impact on the foreign trade of Turkey. *Bilgi, 31*, 17–36.

Önder, İ. (2002). GATS ve Kamu Hizmetleri. *Mülkiye Journal, 235*, 65–75.

Önder, İ. (2015). Thorstein Veblen, Çok Yönlü Bir İktisatçı. [Thorstein Veblen, a well-rounded economist] In A. Öncü (Ed.), *Thorstein Veblen Kullanım Kılavuzu* [User's Guide for Thorstein Veblen]. (pp. 55–80). İstanbul, Turkey: Habitus.

Ongen, T. (2004). Küresel Kapitalizm ve Sermayenin Yeni Hegemonya Stratejileri. *Petrol-İş Yıllığı 2000-2003*. Retrieved from http://arsiv.petrol-is.org.tr/yayinlar/yillik/2003_yillik/01_sermaye/

Onuf, N. (2002). Institutions, intentions and international relations. *Review of International Studies, 28*(2), 211–228. doi:10.1017/S0260210502002115

Oransay, G., & Mike, F. (2016). Doğrudan yabancı yatırımların sosyo-politik belirleyicileri üzerine bir analiz. [AKAD]. *Akademik Araştırmalar ve Çalışmalar Dergisi, 8*(14), 97–107. doi:10.20990/kilisiibfakademik.264409

Orhan, S. S. (2016). In the new institutional economics approach R. Coase and Law, D. North and social psychology context, pluralist approach opportunities in economics. *Sosyoekonomi, 24*(28), 189–208. doi:10.17233e.88088

Ovgun, B. (2013). *Türkiye'de Kamu Yönetiminin Dönüşümü.* Ankara, Turkey: Nika Yayınevi.

Özçelik, Ö., & Tuncer, G. (2007). Atatürk Dönemi Ekonomi Politikaları, Afyon Kocatepe Üniversitesi Sosyal Bilimler Dergisi [Afyon Kocatepe University Social Sciences Journal]. *Ocak, 2007*, 253–266.

Özdek, Y. (1999). Globalizmin İdeolojik Hegemonyası: Yanılsamalar. *Amme İdaresi Journal, 32*, 25–47.

Özgül, O. (2011). Sümer Sosyal Hayatında Eğitimin Yeri ve Önemi. *Erzincan Üniversitesi Sosyal Bilimler Enstitüsü Dergisi, 4*(2), 401–414.

Özkale, L., & Kalaylıca, M. Ö. (2008). In G. E. Arslan (Ed.), *Dış Ticaretin Yapısal Gelişimi. Çeşitli Yönleriyle Cumhuriyetin 85. Yılında Türkiye Ekonomisi içinde* (pp. 228–363). Ankara, Turkey: Gazi Üniversitesi Yayınları.

Özkaya, M. H. (2009). IMF'nin Değişen Rolü: Bretton Woods'tan Günümüze. *Uşak Üniversitesi Sosyal Bilimler Dergisi, 2*(2), 102–117.

Öztürk, N. (2002). IMF'nin Değişen Rolü ve Gelişmekte Olan Ülke Ekonomilerine Etkileri. *Ankara University SBF Journal, 57*(4), 95–125.

Özveren, E. (2007). Kurumsal İktisat, Aralanan Karakutu. [Institutional Economics, Spacing Blackbox] In E. Özveren (Ed.), *Kurumsal İktisat* [Institutional Economics]. (pp. 15–44). Ankara, Turkey: İmge Yayınevi. [İmage Publishing]

Özveren, E. (2007). Kurumsal İktisat: Aralanan Karakutu. In E. Özveren (Ed.), *Kurumsal İktisat* (pp. 15–45). Ankara, Turkey: İmge.

Pardo, R. P. (2012). Leadership, decision-making and governance in the European Union and East Asia: Crisis and post-crisis. *Asia Europe Journal, 9*(2-4), 73–76. doi:10.100710308-012-0316-4

Paresh, K. N., Narayan, S., & Smyth, R. (2011). Does democracy facilitate economic growth or does economic growth facilitate democracy? An empirical study of sub-Saharan Africa. *Economic Modelling, 28,* 900-910.

Patrick, S. M. (2017). Trump and world order. *Foreign Affairs*, (March/April): 52–57.

Patry, W. (2009). *Moral panics and the copyright wars.* New York, NY: Oxford University Press.

Pechlaner, H., & Fischer, E. (2006). Alpine wellness: A resource-based view. *Tourism Recreation Research, 31*(1), 67–77. doi:10.1080/02508281.2006.11081248

Peker, K. (2008). *Yeni Sağ Düşünce Ekseninde Belediye Hizmet Anlayışı* (Unpublished dissertation), Sakarya University Social Sciences İnstitute, Turkey.

Pelagidis, T., & Papasotiriou, H. (2002). Globalisation or regionalism? States, markets and the structure of international trade. *Review of International Studies, 28*(3), 519–535. doi:10.1017/S0260210502005193

Pereira, A. D., & Lopes, H. C. (2018). The market for the "old" and the "new" institutional economics. *Brazilian Journal of Political Economy, 38*(3), 450–468. doi:10.1590/0101-35172018-2774

Perelman, M. (2015). Thorstein Veblen, Bir Amerikalı İktisat Perspektifi. [Thorstein Veblen, An American Economics Perspective] In A. Öncü (Ed.), *Thorstein Veblen Kullanım Kılavuzu* [User's Guide for Thorstein Veblen]. (pp. 27–54). İstanbul, Turkey: Habitus.

Perez, F., & Esposito, L. (2010). The global addiction and human rights: Insatiable consumerism, neoliberalism, and harm reduction. *Perspectives on Global Development and Technology, 9*(1-2), 84–100. doi:10.1163/156914910X487933

Pham, C. (1976). Clarence E. Ayres on the "Market System", A Note. *Journal of Economic Issues, 10*(3), 688–694. do i:10.1080/00213624.1976.11503371

Philippe, B. (1991). *Muhafazakârlık* (C. Akalın, Trans.). İstanbul, Turkey: İletişim Press.

Piatek, D., Szarzec, K., & Pilc, M. (2013). Economic freedom, democracy and economic growth: A causal investigation in transition countries. *Post-Communist economies, 25*(3), 267–288. doi:10.1080/14631377.2013.813137

Pirgan-Matur, E. (2007). Kurumsal İktisat Açısından Firma Kuramı. [Firm theory in terms of institutional economics] In E. Özveren (Ed.), *Kurumsal İktisat* [Institutional Economics]. (pp. 283–308). Ankara, Turkey: İmge Yayınevi. [İmge Publishing]

Pitt, M. M., & Lee, L. F. (1981). The measurement and sources of technical inefficiency in the Indonesian weaving industry. *Journal of Development Economics, 9*(1), 43–64. doi:10.1016/0304-3878(81)90004-3

Polanyi, K. (1944). *The great transformation. The political and economic origins of our time.* Beacon Press Books.

Polonyi, K. (2003). *Büyük Dönüşüm: Çağımızın Siyasal ve Ekonomik Kökenleri, Çev. Ayşe Buğra.* İstanbul, Turkey: İletişim.

Poppo, L., & Zenger, T. (2002). Do formal contracts and relational governance function as substitutes or complements? *Strategic Management Journal, 23*(8), 707–725. doi:10.1002mj.249

Powell, W. W. (1990). *Neither market nor hierarchy: Network forms of organization.* Retrieved from http://www.uvm.edu/pdodds/files/papers/others/1990/powell1990a.pdf

Pressman, N. (1996). Sustainable winter cities: Future directions for planning, policy and design. *Atmospheric Environment, 30*(3), 521–529. doi:10.1016/1352-2310(95)00012-7

Prior, M. (2017). Hegemony and all that stuff. *Think (London, England), 72*, 26–29.

PSC (The Partnership for Sustainable Communities). (2012). EPA, 560-R-12-001, June.

Quinn, J. B., & Hilmer, F. G. (1994). Strategic outsourcing. *Sloan Management Review, 35*(4), 43.

Raffınot, M. (1998). *Borç Krizinden Sonra Kalkınmayı Nasıl Finanse Ederiz? Üçüncü Dünya'nın Sonu mu?* (A. İnsel, B. Gürbüz, & A. Akarçay, Trans.). İstanbul, Turkey: İletişim Press.

Rahman, J., Orzechowska-Fischer, E., & Syed, R. (2014). Reforming the international monetary system: An institutional perspective. In M. Callaghan, C. Ghate, S. Pickford, & F. Rathinam (Eds.), Global cooperation among G20 countries (pp. 161–177). India: Springer India. doi:10.1007/978-81-322-1659-9_15

Ranis, G. (2011). Technology and human development. *Yale University Economic Growth Center Discussion Paper Series*, No: 1004.

Rhodes, R. A. W. (1996). The new governance: Governing without government. *Political Studies*, *44*(4), 652–667. doi:10.1111/j.1467-9248.1996.tb01747.x

Ricardo, D. (1817). *On the principles of political economy and taxation.* Kitchener, Canada: Batoche Books.

Ricardo, D. (1955). *Principles of political economy and taxation.* London, UK: J. M. Dent and Sons Ltd.

Richter, R. (2005). The new institutional economics: Its start, its meaning, its prospects. [EBOR]. *European Business Organization Law Review*, *6*(2), 161–200. doi:10.1017/S1566752905001618

Rindfleisch, A., & Heide, J. B. (1997). Transaction cost analysis: Past, present, and future applications. *Journal of Marketing*, *61*(4), 30–54. doi:10.1177/002224299706100403

Robinson, W. I. (2011, May 8). Global capitalism and 21st century fascism. *Al-Jazeera.* Retrieved from http://www.aljazeera.com/indepth/opinion/2011/04/201142612714539672.html

Robinson, W. I. (2001). Social theory and globalisation: The rise of a transnational state. *Theory and Society*, *30*(2), 157–200. doi:10.1023/A:1011077330455

Robinson, W. I. (2004). *A theory of global capitalism: Production, class, and state in a transnational world.* Baltimore, MD: Johns Hopkins University Press.

Robinson, W. I. (2012). Global capitalism theory and the emergence of transnational elites. *Critical Sociology*, *38*(3), 349–363. doi:10.1177/0896920511411592

Rodrik, D. (2000). *Institutions for high-quality growth: What they are and how to acquire them.* Retrieved from https://www.nber.org/papers/w7540.pdf

Rodrik, D. (2006). *Goodbye Washington consensus, hello Washington confusion*? Retrieved from http://citeseerx.ist.psu.edu/viewdoc/download;jsessionid=5D6EDB435CCB6542BCDF92AE678D3747?doi=10.1.1.90.6133&rep=rep1&type=pdf

Rodrik, D., Subramanian, A., & Trebbi, F. (2002). Institutions rule: The primacy of institutions over geography and integration in economic development, *NBER Working Paper Series*, No: 9305.

Rodrik, D. (1999). Where did all the growth go? External shocks, social conflict, and growth collapses. *Journal of Economic Growth*, *4*(4), 385–412. doi:10.1023/A:1009863208706

Rodrik, D. (2000). Institutions for high-quality growth: What they are and how to acquire them. *Studies in Comparative International Development*, *35*(3), 3–31. doi:10.1007/BF02699764

Rodrik, D. (2003). Institutions, integration and geography: In search of the deep determinants of economic growth. In D. Rodrik (Ed.), *In search of prosperity: Analytic narratives on economic growth.* Princeton, NJ: Princeton University Press. doi:10.1515/9781400845897

Romer, P. M. (1986). Increasing returns and long-run growth. *Journal of Political Economy*, *94*(5), 1002–1037. doi:10.1086/261420

Romer, P. M. (1990). Endogenous technological change. *Journal of Political Economy*, *98*(5), 71–102. doi:10.1086/261725

Rutherford, M. (1998). Veblen's evolutionary programme, a promise unfulfilled. *Cambridge Journal of Economics*, *22*(4), 463–477. doi:10.1093/oxfordjournals.cje.a013729

Rutherford, M. (2000). Intuitionalism between the wars. *Journal of Economic Issues, 34*(2), 291–303. doi:10.1080/00213624.2000.11506267

Rutherford, M. (2001). Institutional economics, then and now. *The Journal of Economic Perspectives, 15*(3), 173–194. doi:10.1257/jep.15.3.173

Rutherford, M. (2001). Institutional economics: Then and now. *The Journal of Economic Perspectives, 15*(3), 173–194. Retrieved from http://pubs.aeaweb.org/pdf</eref

Ruttan, V. W. (2001). *Technology, growth and development: An induced innovation perspective*. New York, NY: Oxford University Press.

Safty, A. (2003). Democracy and governance: The global advance of democracy. İstanbul, Turkey: Bahçeşehir University Press.</bok>

Sağ, V. (2003). Toplumsal Değişim ve Eğitim Üzerine. C.Ü. Sosyal Bilimler Dergisi [Social Sciences Journal]. *Cilt, 27*(:1), 11–25.

Şahin, D. (2018). BRICS-T ülkelerinde ekonomik özgürlükler ve doğrudan yabancı sermaya yatırımları arasındaki ilişki: Bootstrap panel nedensellik testi. *Bingöl Üniversitesi Sosyal Bilimler Enstitüsü Dergisi, 8*(16), 285–294.

Sallan Gül, S. (1998). *Kamu Yönetiminde Kalite, Piyasa ve Müşteri Arayışlarının İdeolojik Temelleri*. Ankara, Turkey: TODAİE Press.

Sallan Gül, S. (2004). *Sosyal Devlet Bitti Yaşasın Piyasa*. İstanbul, Turkey: Etik Press.

Sampler, J. & Eigner, S. (2008). Sand To silicon going global. Dubai, UAE: Motivate Publishing.

Şanlısoy, S. (1999). Bilgi Toplumunda Ortaya Çıkabilecek Sorunlar. *Dokuz Eylül Üniversitesi İktisadi ve İdari Bilimler Fakültesi Dergisi, 14*(2), 169–184.

Saran, U. (2001). Küresel Değişimin Dinamikleri Kamu Yönetimi Alanındaki Etkileri. *Türk İdare Journal, 4333*, 41–49.

Sarisoy, S. (2010). Düzenleyici Devlet ve Regülasyon Uygulamalarının Etkinliği Üzerine Tartışmalar. *Maliye Dergisi, 159*, 278-298. Retrieved from https://dergiler.sgb.gov.tr/calismalar/maliye_dergisi/yayinlar/md/159/SinanSARISOY.pdf

Saussier, S. (1999). Transaction cost economics and contract duration: An empirical analysis of EDF coal contracts. *Recherches Économiques de Louvain/Louvain. Economic Review, 65*(1), 3–21.

Savas, V. F. (2000). İktisadın Tarihi. Siyasal Kitabevi, Ankara.</eref>

Saygılı, M., & Saygılı, H. (2010). *Türkiye'de İhracatın Yapısal Dönüşümü. Küresel Kriz Çerçevesinde Türkiye'nin Cari Açık Sorunsalı içinde* (T. Subaşat & H. Yetkiner, Eds.). Ankara, Turkey: Efil Yayınevi.

Şaylan, G. (2002a). *Değişim Küreselleşme ve Devletin Yeni İşlevi*. Ankara, Turkey: İmge Press.

Şaylan, G. (2002b). *Postmodernizm*. Ankara, Turkey: İmge Press.

Şaylan, G. (2003). *Kamu Yönetimi Disiplininde Bunalım ve Yeni Açılımlar Üzerine Düşünceler, Türkiye'de Kamu Yönetimi* (B. Aykaç, Ş. Durgun, & H. Yayman, Eds.). Ankara, Turkey: Yargı Press.

Sayre Wallace, S. (1997). Kamu Yönetiminin İlkeleri, Tr.: Erkan Oyal, Amme idaresi Journal, 4, 135–138.

Schalber, C., & Peters, M. (2012). Determinants of health tourism competitiveness: An Alpine case study. *Tourism Review, 60*(3), 307–323.

Schmidt, M. G. (2001). *Demokrasi Kuramlarına Giriş, (Çev.: Köktaş, M. Emin)*. Ankara, Turkey: Vadi Yayınları.

Schroer, M. (2014). Visual culture and the fight for visibility. *Journal for the Theory of Social Behaviour, 44*(2), 206–228. doi:10.1111/jtsb.12038

Schumpeter, J. A. (1934). *The Theory of Economic Development*. London, UK: Transaction Publisher.

Schumpeter, J. A. (1939). *Business cycles a theoretical, historical and statistical analysis of the capitalist process*. London, UK: McGraw Hill.

Schumpeter, J. A. (1954). *History of economic analysis*. New York, NY: Oxford University Press.

Schumpeter, J. A. (1976). *Capitalism, socialism, and democracy* (5th ed.). London, UK: Routledge.

Schumpeter, J. A. (1981). *Kapitalizm, sosyalizm ve demokrasi* (T. Akoğlu, Trans.). İstanbul, Turkey: Kurtiş Matbaası. (Original work published 1974)

SCI (Sustainable Cities Initiative). (2017). *What is Livability?* Eugene, OR: University of Oregon.

Seçilmis, E. (2016). Coase Teoremine Alternatif Bakis/An alternative view of the coase theorem. *Finans Politik & Ekonomik Yorumlar, 53*(612), 9–20.

Selvi, Ö. (2012). Bilgi Toplumu, Bilgi Yönetimi ve Halkla İlişkiler. *Gümüşhane Üniversitesi İletişim Fakültesi Elektronik Dergisi, 1*(3), 191–214.

Semmler, W. (1984). *Competition, monopoly and differential profit rates*. New York, NY: Columbia Press. doi:10.7312emm90706

Şenalp, M. G. (2003). *Yeni Kurumsal İktisat ve Küresel Yönetişim. (Yayınlanmamış Yüksek Lisans Tezi)*. Ankara, Turkey: Ankara Üniversitesi Sosyal Bilimler Enstitüsü İktisat Anabilim Dalı.

Şenalp, M. G. (2007). Dünden Bugüne Kurumsal İktisat. [Institutional Economics from yesterday till today] In E. Özveren (Ed.), *Kurumsal İktisat* [Institutional Economics]. (pp. 45–92). Ankara, Turkey: İmge Yayınevi. [İmge Publishing]

Şenel, A. (1982). *İlkel Topluluktan Uygar Topluma Geçiş Aşamasında Ekonomik Toplumsal Düşünsel Yapıların Etkileşimi*. Ankara, Turkey: Ankara Üniversitesi Siyasal Bilgiler Fakültesi Yayınları.

Şenses, F. (2004). Neoliberal Küreselleşme Kalkınma için Bir Fırsat mı, Engel mi? *ERC Working Paper in Economic.*

Şenses, F. Öniş, Z. & Bakır, C. (Eds.). (2013). Ülke Deneyimleri Işığında Küresel Kriz ve Yeni Ekonomik Düzen. İstanbul: İletişim.

Şentürk, Ü. (2008). Modern Kontrol: Tüketim. *Cumhuriyet Üniversitesi Sosyal Bilimler Dergisi, 32*(2), 221–240.

Seyidoğlu, H. (1994). *Uluslararası İktisat*. İstanbul, Turkey: Beta Press.

Shadmehri, M. T. A., Khadem, F., & Ghadimi, A. (2014). Economic schools thought: Mainstream, orthodox and heterodox economics. *Kuwait Chapter of Arabian Journal of Business and Management Review, 3*(12a), 24–30. doi:10.12816/0018843

Sheel, A. (2014). The macroeconomic policy response to the international financial and economic crisis and the G20. In M. Callaghan, C. Ghate, S. Pickford, & F. Rathinam (Eds.), Global cooperation among G20 Countries (pp. 241–280). India: Springer India. doi:10.1007/978-81-322-1659-9_21

Sherman, H. (2001). The business cycle theory of Wesley Mitchell. *Journal of Economic Issues, 35*(1), 85–97. doi:10.1080/00213624.2001.11506341

Shoufani, H. (2014). *Uncommon: Dubai.* Dubai, UAE: Uncommon Ltd.

Shukla, P., & Purani, K. (2012). Comparing the importance of luxury value perceptions in cross national contexts. *Journal of Business Research, 65*(10), 1417–1424. doi:10.1016/j.jbusres.2011.10.007

Silve, F. & Plekhanov, A. (2015). Institutions, innovation and growth: Cross-country evidence, *European Bank Working Paper Series*, No: 177.

Simmonds, A. & Gilmour, D. (2005). Governance of outsourcing from IT governance institute. Retrieved from http://www.isaca.org/Knowledge-Center/Research/Documents/Governance-of-Outsourcing_res_Eng_0105.pdf

Simon, H. A. (1957). *Models of man: Social and rational: Mathematical essays on rational human behavior in a social setting*. New York, NY: Wiley.

Sklair, L. (2000). The transnational capitalist class and the discourse of globalization. *Cambridge Review of International Affairs, 14*(1), 67–85. doi:10.1080/09557570008400329

Sklair, L. (2001). *The Transnational Capitalist Class.* Oxford, UK: Blackwell.

Sklair, L. (2002). *Globalization: Capitalism and Its Alternatives.* New York, NY: Oxford University Press.

Smith, A. (1776). An Inquiry into the Nature and Causes of the Wealth of Nations - An Electronic Classics Series Publication (Ed. Jim Manis, 2005), University Park, PA: The Pennsylvania State University.

Smith, A. (1993). An inquiry into the nature and causes of the wealth of nations. (K. Sutherland, Ed.), Oxford University Press.

Soence, M., & Zagha, R. (2011). Restoring inclusive growth in advanced economies: A conversation with economists and policy makers from the G20. *Comparative Economic Studies, 53*(3), 333–347. doi:10.1057/ces.2011.25

Solow, R. M. (1956). A contribution to the theory of economic growth. *The Quarterly Journal of Economics, 70*(1), 65–94. doi:10.2307/1884513

Sonmez, S. (2016). Bretton Woods, Fordizm ve Hegemonya. *Hacettepe Üniversitesi İktisadi ve İdari Bilimler Fakültesi Dergisi, 34*(1), 43-62. Retrieved from http://dergipark.gov.tr/download/article-file/297834

Sönmez, A. (2003). *Doğu Asya "Mucizesi" ve Bunalımı*. İstanbul, Turkey: İstanbul Bilgi Üniversitesi Yayınları. [Istanbul Bilgi University Publishing]

Sönmez, F. C. (2018). İlkel Toplumlarda Siyasi Örgütlenme ve Yaygın Ekonomik Model. *Pivolka, 8*(28), 9–13.

Sorensen, G. (2006). The transformation of the state. In C. Hay, M. Lister, D. Marsh (Eds.), The state: Theories and issues (pp. 190-208). Houndmills, UK: Palgrave Macmillan. doi:10.1007/978-0-230-80227-8_11

Sorhun, E. (2012). Is the "Arab Spring" Turkey's winter? Impact of the Arab Spring on trade flows of Turkey. Retrieved from https://ecomod.net/system/files/Paper-Engin%20SORHUN.pdf

Spithoven, A. (2019). Similarities and dissimilarities between original and institutional economic and new institutional economics. *Journal of Economic Issues, 53*(2), 440–447. doi:10.1080/00213624.2019.1594532

Sraffa, P. (1926). The laws of returns under competitive conditions. *Economic Journal (London), 36*(144), 535–550. doi:10.2307/2959866

Stark, J. (2010). Is the global economy headed for a lost decade? A European perspective. *Business Economics (Cleveland, Ohio), 45*(3), 147–151. doi:10.1057/be.2010.12

Stavrev, E. (2014). Strengthening the international monetary system. In M. Callaghan, C. Ghate, S. Pickford, & F. Rathinam (Eds.), Global cooperation among G20 countries (pp. 179–184). India: Springer India. doi:10.1007/978-81-322-1659-9_16

Stefan B. & Guimarães R. (2003). Do the poor need democracy? Tracing the debate on democracy and pro-poor development. ZEF Bonn, Zentrum für Entwicklungsforschung Center for Development Research, Universität Bonn

Stigler, G. J. (1965). *Essay in the history of economics*. The University of Chicago Press.

Stiglitz, J. E. (2012). *The price of inequality: How today's divided society endangers our future*. New York, NY: W. W. Norton & Company.

Stump, R. L., & Heide, J. B. (1996). Controlling supplier opportunism in industrial relationships. *JMR, Journal of Marketing Research*, *33*(4), 431–441. doi:10.1177/002224379603300405

Subacchi, P. (2008). New power centres and new power brokers: Are they shaping a new economic order?. *International Affairs*, 84(3), pp. 485-498.

Swedberg, R. (2007). *Principles of economic sociology*. Princeton University Press.

Tanfer, N., Çavuş, A., & Zaman, N. (2015). A new winter tourism centre in Turkey's winter tourism corridor: Konaklı. Marmara Geographical Review (Marmara Coğrafya Dergisi). No: 31, January - 2015, S.345-365. İstanbul. Retrieved from http://www.marmaracografya.com

Tang, S., Hu, Z., & Lin, Y. (2005). Knowledge as production factor: Toward a unified theory of economic growth. *Journal of Evolutionary Economics*, *2005*, 1–68.

Tanyeri, İ. (2000). Adam Smith'in rekabet analizi üzerine. *Hacettepe Üniversitesi İ.İ.B.F. Dergisi*, *18*(1), 307–320.

Tatar Peker, A. (1996). Dünya Bankası: Büyüme Söyleminden İyi Yönetme Söylemine. *Toplum ve Bilim Journal*, *69*, 5–59.

Taylor, P. J., & Colin, F. (2000). *Political geography: World-economy, nation-state and locality*. London, UK: Prentice Hall.

Tekeli, H. (1994). *Bilgi Çağı*. İstanbul, Turkey: Simav Yayınları.

Tekeli, İ. (2003). *Yönetim Kavramı Yanı sıra Yönetişim Kavramının Gelişmesinin Nedenleri Üzerine, Türkiye'de Kamu Yönetimi* (B. Aykaç, Ş. Durgun, & H. Yayman, Eds.). Ankara, Turkey: Yargı Press.

Tekman, E. (2002). *Enformatik Sistemler ve Bilgi Toplumu. Bilgi Toplumuna Geçiş, (Der., İlhan Tekeli ve Diğerleri)*. Ankara, Turkey: Türkiye Bilimler Akademisi Yayınları.

Tilman, R. (1985). The Utopian vision of Edward Bellamy and Thorstein Veblen. *Journal of Economic Issues*, *19*(4), 879–898. doi:10.1080/00213624.1985.11504441

Tilman, R. (1990). New light on John Dewey, Clarence Ayres, and the development of Evolutionary Economics. *Journal of Economic Issues*, *24*(4), 963–979. doi:10.1080/00213624.1990.11505096

Toboso, F. (2013). Methodological developments in the Old and the new institutional economics. *History of Economic Ideas*, *21*(1), 77–115.

Toffler, A. (1981). *Üçüncü Dalga. Çev. Seden, A*. İstanbul, Turkey: Altın Kitaplar Yayınları.

Topal, A. (2008). Türkiye'den Latin Amerika'ya Bakmak: Tarihsel Arka Plan. Latin Amerika'yı Anlamak: Neoliberalizm, Direniş ve Sol [Left Journal], 21-46. United Nations, World Economic Stiuation and Prospects. Retrieved from https://www.un.org/development/desa/dpad/wpcontent/uploads/sites/45/publication/WESP2018_Full_Web-1.pdf

Toy, S., Çatakçi S., EYmirli E., B., Karapinar, M., (2010). Erzurum Termal Turizm Potansiyeli, Turizm Raporları No: 3.

Tribe, K. (2003). In W. J. Samuels & J. E. Biddle (Eds.), *A companion to the history of economic thought* (pp. 215–230). Blackwell Publshing. doi:10.1002/9780470999059.ch14

Tunçsiper, B., & Bicen, Ö. F. (2014). Ekonomik Özgürlükler ve Ekonomik Büyüme Arasındaki İlişkinin Panel Regresyon Yöntemiyle İncelenmesi. *Eskişehir Osmangazi Üniversitesi İİBF Dergisi, 9*(2), 25–45.

Turkish State Meteorological Service. (2018). Retrieved from https://mgm.gov.tr/veridegerlendirme/il-ve-ilceleristatistik.aspx?k=A&m=ERZURUM&fbclid=IwAR0VScglMspCKDTIoI6FVKZJMLdc_6WbSmqJyeYoV7P9L-GxB3b4yGb5l0

Turkish Statistical Institute. (2018). *Foreign Trade Statistics Database*. Retrieved from https://biruni.tuik.gov.tr/disticaretapp/menu_ing.zul

Tutum, C. (1994). *Kamu Yönetiminde Yeniden Yapılanma*. Ankara, Turkey: TESAV Press.

Ülgen, P. (2010). Ortaçağ Avrupa'sında Feodal Sisteme Genel Bir Bakış. [Introduction Journal]. *Mukaddime Dergisi, 1*(1), 1–19.

Ülman, B. (2001). *Uzun Süreçte Küreselleşme: Bir Sihirli Kavramı Tarihteki Yerine Koyma Denemesi, Küreselleşme ve Ulus Devlet*. İstanbul, Turkey: Yıldız Technic University, Strategic Reseraches Center Press.

Ulusoy, T. (2017). Ekonofizik ve Finansal Entropi. Kastamonu Üniversitesi İİBF Dergisi, (Özel Sayı), s. 138-149. Retrieved from http://dergipark.gov.tr/iibfdkastamonu/issue/31886/350620

UN. (1986). Standard International Trade Classification (STIC) Revision 3. Department of Economic and Social Affairs Statistics Division, Statistical Papers, Series M, No: 34, Rev: 3, New York, NY.

UN. (2002). Classification by Broad Economic Categories, Defined in Terms of the Standard International Trade Classification, Revision 3 and the Harmonized Commodity Description and Coding System, Third Edition. Department of Economic and Social Affairs Statistics Division, Statistical Papers, Series M, No: 53, Rev: 4, New York, NY.

UN. (2002). International Standard Industrial Classification of All Economic Activities (ISIC) Revision 3.1. Department of Economic and Social Affairs Statistics Division, Statistical Papers, Series M, No: 4, Rev: 3.1, New York, NY.

Ünal, Y. (2009). Bilgi Toplumunu Tarihçesi. *Tarih Okulu Dergisi, 5*, 123–144.

UNWTO. (2018a). UNWTO International Conference on Tourism and Snow Culture Snow Experiences and Winter Traditions as Assets for Tourism Destinations. Retrieved from http://asiapacific.unwto.org/event/unwto-international-conference-tourism-and-snow-culture-snow-experiences-and-winter-traditions

UNWTO. (2018b). *UNWTO Tourism Highlights*. Madrid, Spain: World Tourism Organisation.

Usal, Z. (2008). Dünya Bankası ve IMF Kapsamında Uluslararası Finans Kuruluşları ve İnsan Hakları. *İ.Ü. Siyasal Bilgiler Fakültesi Dergisi,* (39), 231-246.

Uysal D., Özşahin M. C., & Özşahin Ş. (2010). Co-integration analysis of economic development and democracy: The case of Turkey. *Current Research Journal of Economic Theory*, 2/3, 102, 111.

Vanssay, X. D., & Spindler, Z. A. (1994). Freedom and growth: Do constitutions matter? *Public Choice, 78*(3-4), 359–372. doi:10.1007/BF01047764

Vaughn, K. I. (1999). Hayek's implicit economics: Rules and the problem of order. *The Review of Austrian Economics, 11*(1/2), 129–144. doi:10.1023/A:1007784225432

Veblen, T. B. (1899). The preconceptions of economic science. *The Quarterly Journal of Economics, 13*(4), 396-426. Retrieved from http://www.jstor.org/stable/1883645.

Veblen, T. (1914). *The instinct of workmanship and the state of the industrial arts*. New York, NY: The Viking Press.

Veblen, T. (1919). The place of science. In *Modern Civilization and Other Essays*. New York, NY: B. W. Huebsch.

Veblen, T. (1965). *The theory of the leisure class*. New York, NY: A. M. Kelley Bookseller.

Veblen, T. (1973). *The theory of the leisure class: An economic study of institutions*. Boston, MA: Houghton Mifflin.

Veblen, T. B. (1898). Why is economics not an evolutionary science? *The Quarterly Journal of Economics*, *12*(1), 117–182. Retrieved from http://eleganttechnology.com/resource/ECO_SCI.PDF

Veblen, T. B. (2014). *Aylak Sınıfın Teorisi. Çeviren: Enver Günsel*. İstanbul, Turkey: Tutku Yayınevi.

Venhaus, M. (2013). *Power shift to the East? American hegemony and China's ascent in times of global financial & monetary crises. Freie Universitat Berlin* (pp. 1–26). Graduate School of Global Politics.

Vergragt, P., Akenji, L., & Dewick, P. (2014). Sustainable production, consumption, and livelihoods: Global and regional research perspectives. *Journal of Cleaner Production*, *63*, 1–12. doi:10.1016/j.jclepro.2013.09.028

Vines, D. (2010). The global macroeconomic crisis and G20 macroeconomic policy coordination. *The Journal of Applied Economic Research*, *4*(2), pp. 157-175.

Vishal, C. J. (2013). Democracy and economic growth in sub-Saharan Africa: A panel data approach. *Economic Modelling*, *45*, 987–1008.

Vukotic, V. (2011). Quantum economics. *Panoeconomicus*, *58*(2), 267–276. doi:10.2298/PAN1102267V

Warde, A. (2009). Production, consumption and social change: Reservations regarding Peter Saunders' sociology of consumption. *International Journal of Urban and Regional Research*, *14*(2), 228–248. doi:10.1111/j.1468-2427.1990.tb00670.x

Warren, B. (1972). Capitalist planning and the state. *New Left Review*, *72*, 3–30.

Wathne, K. H., & Heide, J. B. (2000). Opportunism in interfirm relationships: Forms, outcomes, and solutions. *Journal of Marketing*, *64*(4), 36–51. doi:10.1509/jmkg.64.4.36.18070

Wayne, B. (1981). *Markets as networks: A multimethod study of trading networks in a securities market*. (Doctoral dissertation). Department of Sociology, Northwestern University.

Weber, M. (1927). *General economic history*. Glencoe, IL: The Free Press.

Weber, M. (1978). *Economy and society: An outline of interpretive sociology*. Berkeley, CA: University of California Press.

Weingast, B. R. (2017). *Adam Smith's Constitutional Theory*. Retrieved from https://www.researchgate.net/publication/323972866_Adam_Smith's_Constitutional_Theory

Weiss, A. M., & Anderson, E. (1992). Converting from independent to employee salesforces: The role of perceived switching costs. *JMR, Journal of Marketing Research*, *29*(1), 101–115. doi:10.1177/002224379202900109

Weiss, L., & Hobson, J. M. (1999). *Devletler ve Ekonomik Kalkınma. Karşılaştırmalı bir Tarihsel Analiz* (K. Dündar, Trans.). Ankara, Turkey: Dost Kitabevi Yayınları.

White, H. C. (1970). *Chains of opportunity: System models of mobility in organizations*. Cambridge, UK: Harvard University Press. doi:10.4159/harvard.9780674437203

Wilk, R. (2002). Consumption, human needs, and global environmental change. *Global Environmental Change*, *12*(1), 5–13. doi:10.1016/S0959-3780(01)00028-0

Williams, D., & Young, T. (1994). Governance, the world bank and liberal theory. *Political Studies*, *42*(1), 84–100. doi:10.1111/j.1467-9248.1994.tb01675.x

Williamson, O. (1993). *Transaction cost economics and organization theory.* Retrieved from file:///C:/Users/User/Downloads/Cap9_Williamson%20%20The%20Mechanisms%20of%20Governance.pdf

Williamson, O. E. (1985). The reflections of new institutional economics. *Journal of Institutional and Theoretical Economics*, 2nd Symposium pp. 187-195. Retrieved from http://www.jstor.org/stable/40750794

Williamson, O. E. (2005). Transaction cost economics. In C. Ménard & M. M. Shirley (Eds.), Handbook of New Institutional Economics (41-68). Springer, The Netherlands.

Williamson, J. (2000). What should the world bank think about the Washington consensus? *The World Bank Research Observer*, *15*(2), 251–264. doi:10.1093/wbro/15.2.251

Williamson, O. (1975). *Markets and hierarchies: Analysis and antitrust implications.* New York, NY: Free Press.

Wılliamson, O. (1990). A comparison of alternative approaches to economic organisation. *Journal of Institutional and Theoretical Economics*, *146*(1), 61–71.

Williamson, O. E. (1975). *Markets and hierarchies. Analysis and antitrust implications.* New York, NY: Free Press.

Williamson, O. E. (1979). Transaction-cost economics: The governance of contractual relations. *The Journal of Law & Economics*, *22*(2), 233–261. doi:10.1086/466942

Williamson, O. E. (1981). The economics of organization: The transaction cost approach. *American Journal of Sociology*, *87*(3), 548–577. doi:10.1086/227496

Williamson, O. E. (1985). *The economic institutions of capitalism.* New York, NY: Simon & Schuster.

Williamson, O. E. (1985). *The economic institutions of capitalism: Firms, markets, relational contracting. New York, NY: Free Press.*

Williamson, O. E. (1991). Comparative economic organization: The analysis of discrete structural alternatives. *Administrative Science Quarterly*, *36*(2), 269–296. doi:10.2307/2393356

Williamson, O. E. (1996). *The mechanism of governance.* New York, NY: Oxford University Press.

Williamson, O. E. (1998). Transaction cost economics: How it works; Where it is headed. *De Economist*, *146*(1), 23–58. doi:10.1023/A:1003263908567

Williamson, O. E. (2000). Transaction cost economics. In C. Menard & M. Shirley (Eds.), *Handbook of New Institutional Economics* (pp. 41–65). Springer.

Williams, T. G. (2002). Social class influences on purchase evaluation criteria. *Journal of Consumer Marketing*, *19*(3), 249–276. doi:10.1108/07363760210426067

Winter City Design Guidelines. (2000). *Urban System.* Fort St. John, The Energetic City.

Winter City Institute. (2018). Retrieved from https://wintercities.com/home/about

Wood, E. M. (2003). *Kapitalizmin Kökeni* (A. C. Aşkın, Trans.). Ankara, Turkey: Epos Press.

World Bank. (1980). Retrieved from http://documents.worldbank.org/curated/en/528401468739276346/pdf/multi-page.pdf

World Bank. (1994). World Development Report: Infrastructure for development. New York.

World Bank. (2016). Retrieved from http://documents.worldbank.org/curated/en/896931468189267370/pdf/99896-PUB-Box393211B-PUBLIC-PUBDATE-9-30-15-DOI-10-1596978-1-4648-0654-4-EPI-210654.pdf

World Bank. (2019). *World Development Report 2019: The changing nature of work*. Washington, DC: The World Bank Group.

World Trade Organization. (2019). History of the multilateral trading system. Retrieved from https://www.wto.org/english/thewto_e/history_e/history_e.htm

Wuthnow, J., Li, X., & Qi, L. (2012). Diverse multilateralism: Four strategies in China's multilateral diplomacy. *Journal of China Political Science.*, *17*(3), 269–290. doi:10.100711366-012-9202-6

WWCAM. (World Winter Cities Association for Mayors Pamphlet). (2016). International Relations Department, City of Sapporo. UNWTO. (2017). UNWTO World Tourism Barometer. UNWTO.

WWCAM. (World Winter City Association for Mayors). (2018). Retrieved from https://www.city.sapporo.jp/somu/kokusai/wwcam/definition.html

Yağcı, F. (2001). Dünya Ekonomisi Nasıl Yönetiliyor?, *İktisat Journal*, 416, 24–32.

Yağcı, M. (2016). A Beijing consensus in the making: The rise of Chinese initiatives in the international political economy and implications for developing countries. *Perceptions Journal of International Affairs,* Summer, 21(2). pp. 29-56.

Yalçınkaya, T. (2001). Sanayi ve Bilgi Toplumlarında Rekabet Ekonomisi. *Rekabet Bülteni Dergisi, 5*

Yalçınkaya, T. (2006). *Sosyo-ekonomik Sınıflaşma Bağlamında Tüketim Etiğine İlişkin Bir Değerlendirme: 'Tüketimci' Tüketiciler Yaratma*, II. Ulusal Uygulamalı Etik Kongresi Bildiriler Kitabı, 695-702.

Yarar, A. G. A. (2013). Latin Amerika'da İspanyol Sömürgeciliği ve Simon Bolivar'ın Bağımsızlık Mücadelesi. *Historical Studies (Melbourne, Vic.)*, *5*(1), 391–403.

Yazıcı, M. (2013). Toplumsal Değişim ve Sosyal Değerler. *Electronic Turkish Studies*, *8*(8), 1489–1501. doi:10.7827/TurkishStudies.4782

Yeldan, E. (2009). Kapitalizmin Yeniden Finansallaşması ve 2007/2008 Krizi: Türkiye Krizin Neresinde? *Çalışma ve Toplum*, 2009*(1)*.

Yeldan, E. (2002). Neoliberal Küreselleşlme İdeolojisinin Kalkınma Söylemi Üzerine Değerlendirmeler. [Praksis Journal]. *Praksis Dergisi*, *7*, 19–34.

Yeldan, E. (2016). An assessment of the Turkish economy in the AKP era. *Research and Policy on Turkey*, *1*(1), 11–28. doi:10.1080/23760818.2015.1099779

Yfantidou, G., Nikou, M., & Matsouka, O. (2018). Wınter tourısm in Greece: An approach to tourısts' behaviour and needs. *Geo Journal of Tourism and Geosites*, *21*(1), 74–87.

Yıldırım, S. (2009). *Kurumsal iktisat Bağlamında Ülkeler Arası Büyüme Farklılıklarının Analizi.* (Unpublished doctoral dissertation), Anadolu Üniversitesi, Sosyal Bilimler Enstitüsü, Eskişehir.

Yıldırım, C. (2011). Birinci ve İkinci Nesil Washington Uzlaşması: Neoliberal İktisat Politikalarının 1980'den Sonraki Evrimi. *International Journal of Economic & Social Research*, *7*(2).

Yıldız, Z., Kalağan, G., Yıldız, S., & Çetin, B. (2013). Toplumsal Dönüşüm ve İrrasyonel Tüketim. *Bartın Üniversitesi İİBF Dergisi*, *4*(8), 67–102.

Yılmaz, A. (2000). *Modern Demokrasi Gelişimi ve Sorunları*. Ankara, Turkey: Yeni Türkiye Yayınları.

Yoon, H. (2005). The changing role of the IMF: Evidence from Korea's crisis. *Asian Perspective*, *29*(2), 179–201.

Yurdakul, C., & Çağlayan, M. U. (1997). *Bilgi Teknolojileri Türkiye İçin Nasıl Bir Gelecek Hazırlamakta*. Ankara, Turkey: Türkiye İş Bankası Yayını.

Yurtseven, M. (2015). *Bilgi Toplumu Olma Yolunda Kütüphane ve Sivil Toplum Kuruluşu Etkileşimi: Türk Kütüphaneciler Derneği Örneği (Tkd) (Basılmamış yüksek lisans tezi)*. İstanbul, Turkey: Marmara Üniversitesi Türkiyat Araştırmaları Enstitüsü.

Zabci, F. (2002). Dünya Bankası'nın Küresel Pazar İçin Yeni Stratejisi: Yönetişim. *SBF Dergisi*, *57*(3), 151–179.

Zingler, E. K. (1974). Veblen vs. Commons, A comparative evaluation. *Kyklos*, *27*(2), 322–344. doi:10.1111/j.1467-6435.1974.tb01909.x

Zubritski, Y., Mitropolski, D., & Kerov, V. (2006). *İlkel Köleci ve Feodal Toplum. Çev, Belli, S.* Ankara, Turkey: Eriş Yayınları.

urija, M. (2017). *Institutions Quality and Economic Growth in Albania*. Retrieved from https://www.researchgate.net/publication/322677353_Institutions_Quality_and_Economic_Growth_in_Albania/download

About the Contributors

Ilkben Akansel gained her Assoc. Prof. Dr. title in 2017 in Economics Thought. She graduate from two different B.A., firstly in economics department; secondly in business administration, her M. Sc. was in economics too. She decided to make her Ph. D. in another field, public relations. She was appointed as Assist. Prof. Dr. in Business and Administration department in University of Artvin Faculty of Economics and Administrative Sciences. She decided to make her Assoc. Prof. Dr. proficiency exam in economics field. She was appointed as Assoc. Prof. Dr. in University of Bartin, Faculty of Economics and Administrative Sciences in Economics department. She has several international publications. She has been published many articles with some international idexes. Her areas of specialization are Institutional Economics, Political Economics, Public Relations. Her graduations are University of Gazi (Ankara, Turkey), Anadolu University of Business Administration (Eskişehir, Turkey), University of Ankara (Ankara, Turkey).

* * *

Eray Acar was born in Turkey/Antalya in 1977. He completed his primary, secondary and high school education in Antalya. Graduated from Dokuz Eylül University, Department of Public Administration, Izmir, Turkey in 2000. He works still as a lecturer at Kutahya Dumlupinar University since 2000. Special academic field is Political and social sciences. He is married and has 3 children.

Ugur Yasin Asal graduated from Department of Political Science and International Relations, Istanbul Commerce University in 2010. He received his Ph.D. with thesis on "Reformulating the Balance of Power Theory in the Modern International System: Hegemony of Hierarchy at the Example of G20" from Istanbul University in 2018. In 2018, he was appointed as Assistant Professor at Department of Political Science and International Relations, Faculty of Humanities and Social Sciences in Istanbul Commerce University. He has several scientific books and chapters such as; "Russian Foreign Policy towards Baltic States: Cooperation or Discourse?", "Basic Concepts of International Relations" and "Security Problems in Asia and its Reflections". He has also scientific articles on international relations, political systems, security and strategic studies which have been published in various journals. His research interests are foreign policy analysis, strategy, prosperity, G20 and international political economy. He is member of Council of International Relations and TOBB (The Union of Chambers and Commodity Exchanges of Turkey) Istanbul Young Entrepreneurs Assembly Research & Publications Commission.

Derya Guler Aydin received the master's degree in Economics from Hacettepe University, and the Ph.D. degree in Economics from Hacettepe University, Ankara, Turkey in 2002 and 2008, respectively. She conducted postdoctoral research at Sheffield University in 2011. She is currently working as an Associate Professor at the Department of Economics, Hacettepe University. Her research interests include History of Economic Analysis, Methodology of Science, Institutional Economics and Feminist Economics.

H. Kutay Aytuğ graduated from Dokuz Eylul University Department of Business Administration in 2004. He got his Bachelor of Science degree in European Union in 2006 and his PhD degree in European Studies at Dokuz Eylül University in 2011. He worked for Halkbank as an officer in different departments between 2010-2012. He worked as a faculty member of Political Sciences and Public Administration at Artvin Çoruh University between 2013-2017. Since 2017, he has been a faculty member of Political Sciences and International Relations department in Manisa Celal Bayar University University. Dr. Aytuğ has various international and national publications about EU tourism policy, alternative tourism and EU Turkey Relations.

Yusuf Bayraktutan was born in Erzurum. He completed his undergraduate and postgraduate education at Ankara University Faculty of Political Sciences, Gazi University and Atatürk University, Institute of Social Sciences at Wichita State University and Oklahoma State University. He worked as a research assistant at Atatürk University, Faculty of Economics and Administrative Sciences, and as an assistant professor in the Economics Department of Cumhuriyet University. He became an associate professor in 2005 and professor in 2010 at Kocaeli University, Faculty of Economics and Administrative Sciences, Department of Economics. He teaches Economic Development, Growth, Integration, EU, and International Economics, etc. He served as the chairman of the department, Dean of the Institute of Social Sciences, and some colleges, Coordinator of Educational Co-operation with the Naval Command, Economic Advisor to the Chamber of Commerce of Kocaeli and member of the publication / advisory / referee board of many national and international journals. He is the author of more than a hundred national and international publications in the form of books, book chapters, articles, papers, etc.

Zehra Doğan Çalışkan was born in 1986 in Istanbul, completed undergraduate, graduate, and doctorate education in economics, and still works as a faculty member at Abant İzzet Baysal University in Bolu.

Mehmet Yunus Çelik, was born in 1977 in Yozgat-Turkey. He completed his primary, secondary and high school education in Yozgat. He received his Bachelor's Degree in Economics from the Konya Selçuk University in 1998. In 1999 he was started the work a Research Assistant at the Faculty of Economics and Administrative Sciences, Kütahya Dumlupınar University. He received His Master of Science Degree in Economics from the Kütahya Dumlupınar University in 2002. In 2009, he received his Ph.D in Economics from the Dokuz Eylül University. He has been working as an Asistant Professor at the Department of Economics in Faculty of Economic and administrative Sciences, Kastamonu University since 2012. He works on topics such as globalization, development, new economy, social transformations, financial economics and he lectures in these topics at undergraduate and graduate levels. He has been published many articles with some international indexes.

İlke Civelekoğlu (Ph.D, University of Virginia) is an Associate Professor in the Department of Political Science and International Relations at Istanbul Commerce University. Her research interests include comparative and international political economy, politics of economic reform and institutional change in developing countries. She has published articles in journals like Turkish Studies, International Journal and Uluslararası İlişkiler Dergisi and contributed to several edited books.

Nazım Ekren graduated from Department of Economics, Bursa Academy of Economical and Commercial Sciences in 1979. He received his Ph.D. with thesis on "International Banking and the Turkish Case" from Uludağ University in 1985. In 1995, he was appointed Professor at Division of Banking, Institute of Banking and Insurance, Marmara University. In 2011, he was appointed as Professor at Department of Economics, Faculty of Commercial Sciences in Istanbul Commerce University in Istanbul. He has several books, research papers, projects, articles, presentations and speeches on his expertise. He accomplished a project on "Integration of Turkish Banks to the International Banking System" as a research fellow in Manchester Business School, International Centre for Banking and Financial Services with a scholarship awarded from the British Council, between 1989 and 1990. He was elected as a member of the Parliament in Istanbul in the 22nd and 23rd periods. (2002-2007 and 2007-2011). He served as Deputy Prime Minister and Minister of State in charge of coordination of economic affairs in the 60th Republican Government. He is a member of Turkish Academy of Sciences, American Economic Association and European Economic Association. He is the Rector of Istanbul Commerce University since 2011.

Dilek Erdogan is an Assistant Professor of at department of Aviation Management in Gaziantep Universitey, Turkey. She received her BSc., MSc and PhD all in Civil Aviation Managagement in Anadolu University, Turkey. Her phd thesis focused on the IT outsourcing relationship in Turkey and aviation industry. She published papers on reasons for IT outsourcing and selection of IT suppliers in aviation. She pursues her research in the areas of information technology management, strategic management and aviation management.

Fatma Kethudaoğlu was born in Izmit in 23.02.1984. She completed his primary, secondary and high school education in Izmit; graduated from Trakya University, Faculty of Economics and Administrative Sciences, Department of Economics in 2004. In 2005, she started her post graduate studies at Kocaeli University, Institute of Social Sciences, Economics Department, Economic Development and International Economics Program. In 2008, she completed his master's thesis titled 'Urbanization in the Context of Structural Change and the Nature of the Kocaeli Manufacturing Industry (SWOT Analysis) and in the same year she completed her doctorate education in the Economics Program of the Department of Economics, Kocaeli University. In 2018, she has got two children and has been working in the Ministry of Finance since 2009. She is working as an human resource expert at TÜBİTAK - SAGE (The Scientific and Technological Research Council of Turkey - Defense Insudtries Research and Development Institute) in Ankara / Turkey.

Mahshid Mikaeili graduated with Continuing Master's Degree in architecture with "Solar Architectural" from IAU (Islamic Azad University of Tabriz, Iran). After graduating from university in Iran she worked in her personal office and Tabriz municipality as a chief designer architect. Then she was lecture in IAU. In 2016 she got her PhD degree from Ankara University in Department of Landscape Architecture with Edge and Edgeless City Concept. Between 2016-2018 years she was a faculty member of Architectural Faculty in IAU. Since 2018, she has been a faculty member in Designing and Architectural faculty, Architecture Department of Ataturk University in Erzurum, Turkey. Dr. Mahshid Mikaeili has various international and national publications in urban open spaces, climatic design, tourism and historical site.

Gönül Muratoğlu is a PhD research assistant at Ankara Haci Bayram Veli University, Department of Economics. During her academic career, she has attended several international conferences in Europe and the USA, has been the author and co-author of many international and national articles, book reviews and book chapters. She has assisted many undergraduate and graduate level courses and participated in the organization of national and international scientific events. She currently lectures International Trade Theories course. Her MSc thesis is about the evaluation of service sector and trade in services, main theories on trade in services and the framework of GATS. Her PhD dissertation is about the Gravity Model of international trade, EU-Turkey trade and testing of EU-Turkey trade through an elaborate analysis on sub-sectoral level. Her academic interests are international economics, foreign trade, new trade theories and models, emerging market economies, sector studies of trade (manufacturing, pharmaceuticals), Turkey's history of trade and current structure & patterns of Turkey's trade, international migration, economic consequences of immigration, workers' remittances and trade links of immigration and remittances.

Itir Ozer-Imer received the master's degree in Economics from Hacettepe University, and the Ph.D. degree in Economics from Hacettepe University, Ankara, Turkey in 2001 and 2007, respectively. She has conducted postdoctoral research at George Mason University, School of Public Policy from February 2011 until February 2012. She is currently working as an Associate Professor at the Department of International Relations, Hacettepe University. Her research interests include International Political Economy, Economic Development, International Trade and Finance, Economic Integration.

Başak Özoral received her Ph.D. from the McGill University in 2011. Her research focuses on political economy, modernization in the Middle East, economy and cuture in the Middle East and globalization. She taught in Qatar University and American University in Dubai for five years. She teaches courses on Middle East, political economy, and research methods, and she regularly co-authors papers with graduate students at Istanbul Commerce University.

Havanur Ergün Tatar was born in 1986 in Kars. After completing their secondary and high school education, they graduated from Zonguldak Karaelmas University in 2007. Then, they completed their master's degree at the same university between 2007-2010. Between 2013-2017, they completed their Ph.D. in economics. They currently work as an assistant professor at Bartın University.

Emek Yıldırım was born in Ankara. As their secondary education, they graduated from the Mehmet Emin Resulzade Anatolian High School, in Ankara. They got their B.A. degree from the Department of Philosophy at the Middle East Technical University (METU), the minor degree from the Department of History at METU, M.SC. degree from the Department of Political Science and Public Administration at METU, and PhD degree from the Department of Political Science and Public Administration at Ankara University as well. Between 2008-2010, they were doing pre-PhD research at Peoples' Friendship University of Russia (РУДН/RUDN) in Moscow. Since 2012, they have been working in the Department of Political Science and Public Administration at Artvin Çoruh University. Their language skills are as English at advance level, Russian at intermediate level, and German at beginner level.

Index

A

adaptation 64, 70, 82, 102, 141-142, 201, 204, 211, 216
agricultural society 110, 113-117, 122, 124, 127
authoritarian neoliberal states 26, 28, 30-31, 33
Authoritarian state 31, 38

B

bounded rationality 13-18, 20, 24, 194-195, 204-206, 208, 211-212, 227

C

China 26, 30, 32-33, 43-47, 271, 283-284, 287, 290-291, 293
civil liberties 18, 157, 163, 165-166, 169
classes 4, 6, 8, 31, 66, 109, 115-116, 282-294
competition 3, 5, 7, 10, 15, 17-18, 26, 31, 45-47, 49, 57-67, 73, 77, 80, 118, 120-122, 137, 145, 148, 161, 173-174, 205, 222, 228, 241, 247-249, 251, 259, 283, 291
complex contract 209
consumption 4-7, 9, 12, 18, 65, 108-110, 112-115, 117, 125-128, 132, 136, 151, 175, 190, 192, 196, 226, 230, 241-244, 249, 252-253, 259-260, 266, 292
Consumption Society 110, 132
contract 13, 18, 67, 77, 143, 159, 197, 202-203, 205-211, 213, 216, 225, 227-228
contract duration 210
corruption 26, 28, 31, 77, 141, 157, 159-161, 230, 238, 248, 252, 291, 294
creative destruction 65, 82, 84
crisis 11, 29-31, 41-49, 51-52, 94, 119-120, 135, 140, 144, 147, 150-152, 191, 218-219, 224, 229, 240-242, 250, 262-266, 273, 289-290

D

democracy 26, 29-31, 51, 121, 134-138, 150, 157-164, 169, 171-179, 181-182, 223, 245, 248-249, 253, 289
deregulation 39, 141, 148-149, 156, 243, 247-248, 251
developing countries 19-20, 25-27, 29-33, 38, 43-47, 70, 75, 80, 84, 134, 138-139, 141-143, 161, 180-181, 219, 221, 225, 230, 232, 250, 258, 260

E

Economic elite 30, 38
economic freedoms 138, 157-162, 164, 172-173, 176-177, 181
economic growth 12, 15, 25-26, 28, 32, 34, 46-47, 49-50, 70-71, 73, 75-79, 83, 94, 136, 158-161, 166, 171-179, 181-182, 188, 218-219, 229-234
efficiency 17, 26-28, 33, 50-51, 74-75, 80, 84, 112, 114-115, 118, 140, 145, 148, 157, 160, 162-163, 165-166, 169, 203, 244-245, 248-249, 251, 253
Empirical Thought on Institutional Economics 200
Erzurum 88-89, 95-102
EU Tourism Policies 88-89
European Union 45, 94, 139, 157-158, 164-166, 170, 177, 217-218, 222, 230, 238, 264-265
exchange relationship 202, 205, 207-208, 210, 216

F

Fordism 136, 156
foreign direct investments 46, 75, 157, 159-164, 166, 170
foreign trade policy 258-261, 264-265
formal institutions 19, 25-28, 31-33, 52, 250
freedom 8, 30, 39, 119-120, 137-138, 145-146, 157-161, 163-166, 169, 171-179, 181, 228, 231, 248, 287, 291, 294

G

G20 41-47, 51-52, 139, 151
globalization 30, 46, 121-122, 132-133, 135, 137-138, 140-143, 149-150, 158, 218, 223, 225, 234, 241, 287
governance 13, 29-30, 32, 41-42, 45, 47, 50-52, 134, 139, 141, 144, 147-148, 152, 156, 173, 197, 201-202, 204-207, 211-212, 217, 222-226, 229, 231-234, 238-240, 246-253
governance decision 201, 212

H

hegemony 44-45, 47-49, 51-52, 287
historical school 185, 187-189, 192-195, 197, 200
history of economics 3-4, 19, 197

I

IMF 43-48, 51, 139-143, 217-224, 230-234, 238, 242, 249-250, 262, 264-265
industrial revolution 59, 73, 78, 116-120, 132, 286, 292-293
industrial society 108, 110, 116-122, 124-127, 288
inflation 12, 143, 151, 160, 174, 176-177, 218, 231, 238, 264, 290
information asymmetry 207-208, 213
information society 71, 108, 110, 120-122, 124-128, 241
innovation 63-66, 71, 73-83, 109-110, 120, 122, 125, 196, 249, 292
institution 2-4, 6-8, 12, 14-15, 19, 25-26, 28, 33, 42, 45, 49, 52, 57-58, 60-62, 66-67, 77, 140, 159, 187, 189-192, 194, 196, 200-201, 218, 220, 224-227, 238, 244
institutional change 12, 18, 27, 39, 51, 71, 76, 80-82, 109, 189-190, 196-197, 223
institutional economics 1-4, 7, 9, 11-15, 19-20, 24-26, 42, 49, 51, 74, 109, 128, 157-158, 170, 185-187, 189-197, 200, 217-218, 223-227, 229, 231-234, 239-240, 250-251
institutional theory 74, 76
institutions 1-9, 12-20, 25-28, 30-33, 39, 41-52, 58-60, 67, 70-73, 76-77, 80-84, 90, 117, 137-139, 141-143, 145, 147, 149, 151-152, 157-161, 164, 166, 170, 174, 185-197, 217-219, 223-226, 228-234, 238, 240, 242-246, 248-250, 284, 287, 289, 294
international institutions 41-42, 44-46, 52, 151, 217, 223, 230, 233

J

Japan 44, 47, 139, 229, 282-286, 288-289, 293

L

Latin America 231, 240, 243, 282, 284-290, 293-294
Liveability 89-91, 93, 106

M

market as an institution 49, 57, 60
Moral Hazard 207, 216

N

Neoclassical Economy 200
neoliberalism 19-20, 25-26, 28-31, 33-34, 39, 48, 133-134, 150-152, 238, 240, 245, 248-249
new institutional economics 1-2, 14-15, 24-26, 42, 49, 187, 192-197, 217-218, 223, 225-227, 229, 231-234, 239-240, 250-251
New Public Administration 133-134, 149-150
new public management 133, 148, 152, 156, 247-248, 252
Newtonian paradigm 108, 127, 132
North, Coase, Williamson 24

O

opportunism 18, 194, 197, 204-208, 212-213, 216
outsourcing 201-202, 204-213, 216

P

panel data 161-162, 171, 175, 177-179
paradigm shift 47, 108, 132, 247, 249
Postfordism 151, 156
primitive society 110-114, 122, 127, 132
privatization 29-30, 135, 139-143, 145, 147-152, 156, 247, 251, 294
productivity 14, 28, 31, 61-62, 71, 75-76, 78-79, 83-84, 114, 117-118, 122, 134, 144, 150-151, 162, 166, 203, 247, 267
property rights 1, 9-10, 13, 17-18, 20, 24-28, 30-33, 38, 75, 77, 84, 143, 157, 159, 163, 174, 177, 194-195, 197, 205, 209, 218, 223, 225-226, 228-233, 250-251, 265
public administration 133-135, 139, 144-145, 148-152, 239-240, 246-249, 252

Q

Quantum paradigm 108, 127-128, 132

R

Ronald Coase 2, 12, 14, 17, 202, 250
rules 2, 9-10, 13-20, 27-28, 30-33, 39, 46-47, 49-52, 64, 74, 77, 80, 84, 113, 116-117, 127, 146, 149-150, 159, 191, 194, 197, 225-226, 228, 240, 242, 250, 265
Russia 26, 30, 33, 42-44, 46

S

Schumpeter 64-65, 67, 70-71, 73, 80, 82-84
South Korea 45, 218, 229-230, 266, 282, 284, 286, 289, 293
Stagflation 218, 238
stochastic frontier analysis 157, 162-164

T

Task Complexity 211, 216
The New Right Approach 156
transaction cost 13, 201-205, 212, 216
transaction costs 10, 13-15, 17-20, 24, 26-28, 77, 150, 158, 193-197, 201-205, 209-213, 216, 218, 226-233, 251
transformation of the state 133, 239-241
transparency 45, 51, 139, 147, 152, 158, 161, 173, 230, 232-233, 244, 247-249, 252
tribe 59, 111-113, 132, 188
Turkey 30, 43-45, 88, 95, 99, 102, 157-158, 160-161, 163-166, 176, 258-273, 282, 285, 288, 291-294

U

uncertainty 10, 12, 14, 16, 26, 28, 32-33, 52, 61, 77, 122, 126-127, 196, 203-204, 206-212
United Arab Emirates 30

V

Veblen 1-13, 15, 20, 24, 27, 70-71, 73, 79-82, 84, 109, 128, 186-187, 189-190, 192, 196, 292

W

welfare state 133-134, 145, 150-151, 156, 239-241, 244-246
winter city 88-91, 93, 96-97, 101-102, 106
Winter City Movement 90, 106
winter tourism 88-91, 94-95, 97, 99, 102, 106
World Bank 46-47, 51, 139-142, 163, 171, 175, 177, 179, 181, 217-218, 220, 222, 230, 233, 238, 242, 258, 262

Purchase Print, E-Book, or Print + E-Book

IGI Global's reference books are available in three unique pricing formats:
Print Only, E-Book Only, or Print + E-Book.
Shipping fees may apply.

www.igi-global.com

Recommended Reference Books

ISBN: 978-1-5225-6201-6
© 2019; 341 pp.
List Price: $345

ISBN: 978-1-5225-7262-6
© 2019; 360 pp.
List Price: $215

ISBN: 978-1-5225-8003-4
© 2019; 216 pp.
List Price: $205

ISBN: 978-1-5225-5763-0
© 2019; 304 pp.
List Price: $205

ISBN: 978-1-5225-6980-0
© 2019; 325 pp.
List Price: $235

ISBN: 978-1-5225-7808-6
© 2019; 397 pp.
List Price: $215

Do you want to stay current on the latest research trends, product announcements, news and special offers?
Join IGI Global's mailing list today and start enjoying exclusive perks sent only to IGI Global members.
Add your name to the list at **www.igi-global.com/newsletters.**

Publisher of Peer-Reviewed, Timely, and Innovative Academic Research

IGI Global
DISSEMINATOR OF KNOWLEDGE

www.igi-global.com | Sign up at www.igi-global.com/newsletters | facebook.com/igiglobal | twitter.com/igiglobal | linkedin.com/igiglobal

Ensure Quality Research is Introduced to the Academic Community

Become an IGI Global Reviewer for Authored Book Projects

The overall success of an authored book project is dependent on quality and timely reviews.

In this competitive age of scholarly publishing, constructive and timely feedback significantly expedites the turnaround time of manuscripts from submission to acceptance, allowing the publication and discovery of forward-thinking research at a much more expeditious rate. Several IGI Global authored book projects are currently seeking highly-qualified experts in the field to fill vacancies on their respective editorial review boards:

Applications and Inquiries may be sent to:
development@igi-global.com

Applicants must have a doctorate (or an equivalent degree) as well as publishing and reviewing experience. Reviewers are asked to complete the open-ended evaluation questions with as much detail as possible in a timely, collegial, and constructive manner. All reviewers' tenures run for one-year terms on the editorial review boards and are expected to complete at least three reviews per term. Upon successful completion of this term, reviewers can be considered for an additional term.

If you have a colleague that may be interested in this opportunity, we encourage you to share this information with them.

IGI Global Proudly Partners With eContent Pro International

Receive a 25% Discount on all Editorial Services

Editorial Services

IGI Global expects all final manuscripts submitted for publication to be in their final form. This means they must be reviewed, revised, and professionally copy edited prior to their final submission. Not only does this support with accelerating the publication process, but it also ensures that the highest quality scholarly work can be disseminated.

English Language Copy Editing

Let eContent Pro International's expert copy editors perform edits on your manuscript to resolve spelling, punctuaion, grammar, syntax, flow, formatting issues and more.

Scientific and Scholarly Editing

Allow colleagues in your research area to examine the content of your manuscript and provide you with valuable feedback and suggestions before submission.

Figure, Table, Chart & Equation Conversions

Do you have poor quality figures? Do you need visual elements in your manuscript created or converted? A design expert can help!

Translation

Need your documjent translated into English? eContent Pro International's expert translators are fluent in English and more than 40 different languages.

Hear What Your Colleagues are Saying About Editorial Services Supported by IGI Global

"The service was very fast, very thorough, and very helpful in ensuring our chapter meets the criteria and requirements of the book's editors. I was quite impressed and happy with your service."

– Prof. Tom Brinthaupt,
Middle Tennessee State University, USA

"I found the work actually spectacular. The editing, formatting, and other checks were very thorough. The turnaround time was great as well. I will definitely use eContent Pro in the future."

– Nickanor Amwata, Lecturer,
University of Kurdistan Hawler, Iraq

"I was impressed that it was done timely, and wherever the content was not clear for the reader, the paper was improved with better readability for the audience."

– Prof. James Chilembwe,
Mzuzu University, Malawi

Email: customerservice@econtentpro.com **www.igi-global.com/editorial-service-partners**

IGI Global
DISSEMINATOR OF KNOWLEDGE
www.igi-global.com

Celebrating Over 30 Years of Scholarly Knowledge Creation & Dissemination

InfoSci®-Books

A Database of Over 5,300+ Reference Books Containing Over 100,000+ Chapters Focusing on Emerging Research

InfoSci®-Books Database

The **InfoSci®-Books** database is a collection of over 5,300+ IGI Global single and multi-volume reference books, handbooks of research, and encyclopedias, encompassing groundbreaking research from prominent experts worldwide that span over 350+ topics in 11 core subject areas including business, computer science, education, science and engineering, social sciences and more.

Open Access Fee Waiver (Offset Model) Initiative

For any library that invests in IGI Global's InfoSci-Journals and/ or InfoSci-Books databases, IGI Global will match the library's investment with a fund of equal value to go toward **subsidizing the OA article processing charges (APCs) for their students, faculty, and staff** at that institution when their work is submitted and accepted under OA into an IGI Global journal.*

INFOSCI® PLATFORM FEATURES

- No DRM
- No Set-Up or Maintenance Fees
- A Guarantee of No More Than a 5% Annual Increase
- Full-Text HTML and PDF Viewing Options
- Downloadable MARC Records
- Unlimited Simultaneous Access
- COUNTER 5 Compliant Reports
- Formatted Citations With Ability to Export to RefWorks and EasyBib
- No Embargo of Content (Research is Available Months in Advance of the Print Release)

**The fund will be offered on an annual basis and expire at the end of the subscription period. The fund would renew as the subscription is renewed for each year thereafter. The open access fees will be waived after the student, faculty, or staff's paper has been vetted and accepted into an IGI Global journal and the fund can only be used toward publishing OA in an IGI Global journal. Libraries in developing countries will have the match on their investment doubled.*

To Learn More or To Purchase This Database:
www.igi-global.com/infosci-books
eresources@igi-global.com • Toll Free: 1-866-342-6657 ext. 100 • Phone: 717-533-8845 x100

IGI Global
DISSEMINATOR OF KNOWLEDGE
www.igi-global.com

IGI Global
DISSEMINATOR OF KNOWLEDGE
www.igi-global.com

Publisher of Peer-Reviewed, Timely, and Innovative Academic Research Since 1988

IGI Global's Transformative Open Access (OA) Model: How to Turn Your University Library's Database Acquisitions Into a Source of OA Funding

In response to the OA movement and well in advance of Plan S, IGI Global, early last year, unveiled their OA Fee Waiver (Offset Model) Initiative.

Under this initiative, librarians who invest in IGI Global's InfoSci-Books (5,300+ reference books) and/or InfoSci-Journals (185+ scholarly journals) databases will be able to subsidize their patron's OA article processing charges (APC) when their work is submitted and accepted (after the peer review process) into an IGI Global journal.*

How Does it Work?

1. When a library subscribes or perpetually purchases IGI Global's InfoSci-Databases including InfoSci-Books (5,300+ e-books), InfoSci-Journals (185+ e-journals), and/or their discipline/subject-focused subsets, IGI Global will match the library's investment with a fund of equal value to go toward subsidizing the OA article processing charges (APCs) for their patrons.

   Researchers: Be sure to recommend the InfoSci-Books and InfoSci-Journals to take advantage of this initiative.

2. When a student, faculty, or staff member submits a paper and it is accepted (following the peer review) into one of IGI Global's 185+ scholarly journals, the author will have the option to have their paper published under a traditional publishing model or as OA.
3. When the author chooses to have their paper published under OA, IGI Global will notify them of the OA Fee Waiver (Offset Model) Initiative. If the author decides they would like to take advantage of this initiative, IGI Global will deduct the US$ 1,500 APC from the created fund.
4. This fund will be offered on an annual basis and will renew as the subscription is renewed for each year thereafter. IGI Global will manage the fund and award the APC waivers unless the librarian has a preference as to how the funds should be managed.

Hear From the Experts on This Initiative:

"I'm very happy to have been able to make one of my recent research contributions, 'Visualizing the Social Media Conversations of a National Information Technology Professional Association' featured in the *International Journal of Human Capital and Information Technology Professionals*, freely available along with having access to the valuable resources found within IGI Global's InfoSci-Journals database."

– **Prof. Stuart Palmer,**
Deakin University, Australia

For More Information, Visit: www.igi-global.com/publish/contributor-resources/open-access or contact IGI Global's Database Team at eresources@igi-global.com.

Are You Ready to **Publish Your Research?**

IGI Global
DISSEMINATOR OF KNOWLEDGE

IGI Global offers book authorship and editorship opportunities across 11 subject areas, including business, computer science, education, science and engineering, social sciences, and more!

Benefits of Publishing with IGI Global:

- Free one-on-one editorial and promotional support.
- Expedited publishing timelines that can take your book from start to finish in less than one (1) year.
- Choose from a variety of formats including: Edited and Authored References, Handbooks of Research, Encyclopedias, and Research Insights.
- Utilize IGI Global's eEditorial Discovery® submission system in support of conducting the submission and blind review process.
- IGI Global maintains a strict adherence to ethical practices due in part to our full membership with the Committee on Publication Ethics (COPE).
- Indexing potential in prestigious indices such as Scopus®, Web of Science™, PsycINFO®, and ERIC – Education Resources Information Center.
- Ability to connect your ORCID iD to your IGI Global publications.
- Earn royalties on your publication as well as receive complimentary copies and exclusive discounts.

Get Started Today by Contacting the Acquisitions Department at:

acquisition@igi-global.com

www.ingramcontent.com/pod-product-compliance
Lightning Source LLC
LaVergne TN
LVHW062136300926
849161LV00010B/2546

9781799803331